PAGODA TOEFL

80+ Reading

3rd Edition

파고다교육그룹 언어교육연구소 | 저

PAGODA Books

3rd Edition

PAGODA TOEFL 80+ Reading

초　　판 1쇄 발행 2013년 8월 28일
개정 2판 1쇄 발행 2019년 10월 7일
개정 3판 1쇄 발행 2024년 1월 5일
개정 3판 2쇄 발행 2024년 8월 22일

지 은 이 | 파고다교육그룹 언어교육연구소
펴 낸 이 | 박경실
펴 낸 곳 | **PAGODA Books** 파고다북스
출판등록 | 2005년 5월 27일 제 300-2005-90호
주　　소 | 06614 서울특별시 서초구 강남대로 419, 19층(서초동, 파고다타워)
전　　화 | (02) 6940-4070
팩　　스 | (02) 536-0660
홈페이지 | www.pagodabook.com

ISBN 978-89-6281-911-3 (13740)

파고다북스 www.pagodabook.com
파고다 어학원 www.pagoda21.com
파고다 인강 www.pagodastar.com
테스트 클리닉 www.testclinic.com

낙장 및 파본은 구매처에서 교환해 드립니다.

2023년 7월
New iBT TOEFL®의 시작!

TOEFL 주관사인 미국 ETS(Educational Testing Service)는 iBT TOEFL® 시험에서 채점되지 않는 더미 문제가 삭제되면서 시간이 개정 전 3시간에서 개정 후 2시간 이하로 단축됐으며, 새로운 라이팅 유형이 추가되었다고 발표했다. 새로 바뀐 iBT TOEFL® 시험은 2023년 7월 26일 정기 시험부터 시행된다.

- 총 시험 시간 기존 약 3시간 ···› 약 2시간으로 단축
- 시험 점수는 각 영역당 30점씩 총 120점 만점으로 기존과 변함없음

영역	2023년 7월 26일 이전	2023년 7월 26일 이후
Reading	지문 3~4개 각 지문 당 10문제 시험 시간 54~72분	지문 2개 각 지문 당 10개 시험 시간 36분
Listening	대화 2~3개, 각 5문제 강의 3~5개, 각 6문제 시험 시간 41~57분	28문제 대화 2개, 각 5문제 강의 3개, 각 6문제 시험 시간 36분
Speaking	*변함없음 4문제 독립형 과제 1개 통합형 과제 3개 시험 시간 17분	
Writing	2문제 통합형 과제 1개 독립형 과제 1개 시험 시간 50분	2문제 통합형 과제 1개 수업 토론형 과제 1개 시험 시간 30분

목차

중요 어휘 정리 무료 온라인 다운로드
www. pagodabook.com

이 책의 구성과 특징

>> New TOEFL 변경사항 및 최신 출제 유형 완벽 반영!

2023년 7월부터 변경된 새로운 토플 시험을 반영, iBT TOEFL® 80점 이상을 목표로 하는 학습지를 위해 최근 iBT TOEFL의 출제 경향을 완벽하게 반영한 문제와 주제를 골고루 다루고 있습니다.

>> 문제 유형별 Lesson 구성으로 원하는 유형 선택 학습 가능!

문제 유형별로 Lesson을 구성해, 자주 나오는 유형이나 학습자가 특히 취약한 유형을 골라 iBT TOEFL® 전문 연구원이 제시하는 문제 풀이 전략을 학습할 수 있도록 하였습니다.

>> 들고 다니며 외울 수 있는 중요 어휘 정리 PDF 파일 제공!

각 Lesson에 등장하는 지문의 중요 어휘를 정리하여 온라인 다운로드(PDF 파일)로 제공함으로써 스마트폰으로 어휘 정리를 들고 다니며 쉽고 편하게 암기할 수 있도록 구성하였습니다.

▶ 중요 어휘 정리 PDF 다운로드: www. pagodabook.com

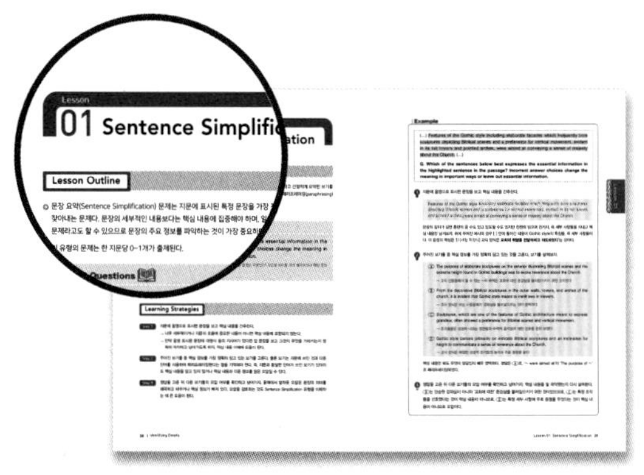

Lesson Outline & Learning Strategies

각 Lesson에 해당하는 문제 유형을 살펴보고, iBT TOEFL® 전문 연구원이 제안하는 효과적인 문제 풀이 전략과 예시 문제 학습을 통해 정답을 찾는 능력을 배양합니다.

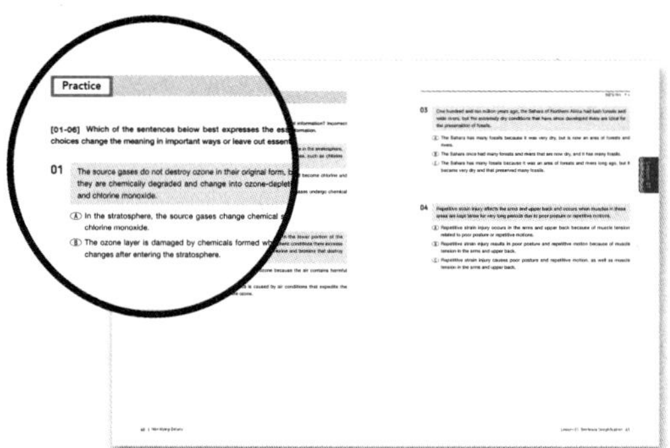

Practice

한 단락 길이의 짧은 지문부터 4~7문단에 이르는 심화된 지문까지, 점진적으로 난이도가 높아지는 연습 문제를 통해 Reading 영역 공략의 기초를 다져나갑니다.

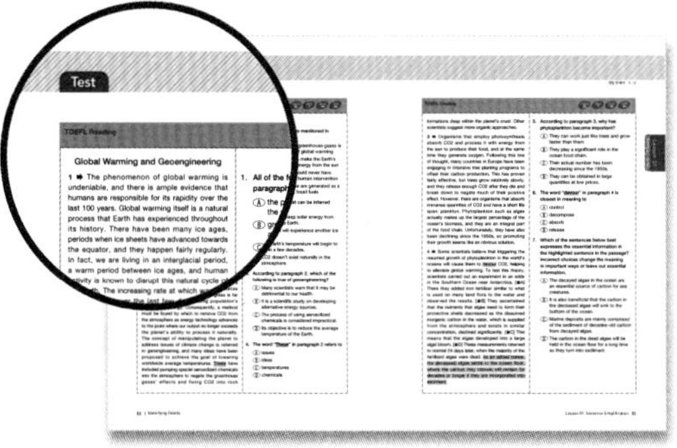

Test

실전과 유사한 유형과 난이도로 구성된 연습문제를 풀며 iBT TOEFL® 실전 감각을 익힙니다.

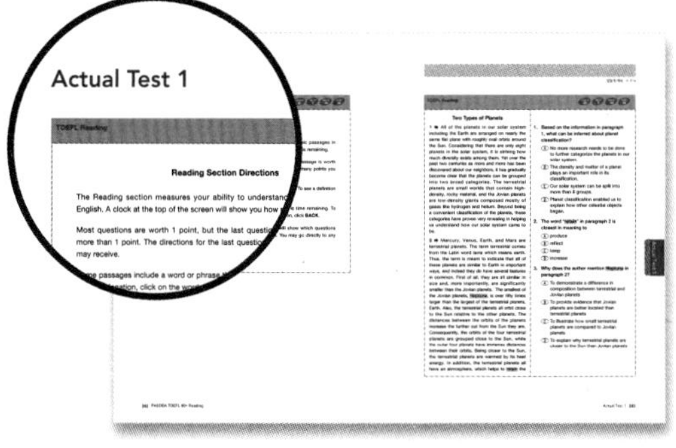

Actual Test

실제 시험과 동일하게 구성된 3회분의 Actual Test를 통해 실전에 대비합니다.

6주 완성 학습 플랜

DAY 1	DAY 2	DAY 3	DAY 4	DAY 5
Diagnostic Test	Ⅰ Identifying Details			
	Lesson 01 • Lesson Outline • Learning Strategies • Practice	Lesson 01 • Test	Lesson 02 • Lesson Outline • Learning Strategies • Practice	Lesson 02 • Test
DAY 6	**DAY 7**	**DAY 8**	**DAY 9**	**DAY 10**
Ⅰ Identifying Details				
Lesson 03 • Lesson Outline • Learning Strategies • Practice	Lesson 03 • Test	Lesson 04 • Lesson Outline • Learning Strategies • Practice	Lesson 04 • Test	Section Review • 지문 다시 읽기 • 단락 요약하기 연습
DAY 11	**DAY 12**	**DAY 13**	**DAY 14**	**DAY 15**
Ⅰ Identifying Details	Ⅱ Making Inference			
Voca Review • 단어 외우기 & 확인하기	Lesson 01 • Lesson Outline • Learning Strategies • Practice	Lesson 01 • Test	Lesson 02 • Lesson Outline • Learning Strategies • Practice	Lesson 02 • Test
DAY 16	**DAY 17**	**DAY 18**	**DAY 19**	**DAY 20**
Ⅱ Making Inference		Ⅲ Recognizing Organization		
Section Review • 지문 다시 읽기 • 단락 요약하기 연습	Voca Review • 단어 외우기 & 확인하기	Lesson 01 • Lesson Outline • Learning Strategies • Practice	Lesson 01 • Test	Lesson 02 • Lesson Outline • Learning Strategies • Practice
DAY 21	**DAY 22**	**DAY 23**	**DAY 24**	**DAY 25**
Ⅲ Recognizing Organization				
Lesson 02 • Test	Lesson 03 • Lesson Outline • Learning Strategies • Practice	Lesson 03 • Test	Section Review • 지문 다시 읽기 • 단락 요약하기 연습	Voca Review • 단어 외우기 & 확인하기
DAY 26	**DAY 27**	**DAY 28**	**DAY 29**	**DAY 30**
Actual Test				
Actual Test 1 & Review • 지문 다시 읽기 • 단락 요약하기 연습	Actual Test 2 & Review • 지문 다시 읽기 • 단락 요약하기 연습	Actual Test 3 & Review • 지문 다시 읽기 • 단락 요약하기 연습	Actual Test 1~3 Review • 지문 다시 읽기	Voca Review • 단어 외우기 & 확인하기

iBT TOEFL® 개요

1. iBT TOEFL® 이란?

TOEFL은 영어 사용 국가로 유학을 가고자 하는 외국인들의 영어 능력을 평가하기 위해 개발된 시험이다. TOEFL 시험 출제 기관인 ETS는 이러한 TOEFL 본연의 목적에 맞게 문제의 변별력을 더욱 높이고자 PBT(Paper-Based Test), CBT(Computer-Based Test)에 이어 차세대 시험인 인터넷 기반의 iBT(Internet-Based Test)를 2005년 9월부터 시행하고 있다. ETS에서 연간 30~40회 정도로 지정한 날짜에 등록함으로써 치르게 되는 이 시험은 Reading, Listening, Speaking, Writing 총 4개 영역으로 구성되며 총 시험 시간은 약 2시간이다. 각 영역별 점수는 30점으로 총점 120점을 만점으로 하며 성적은 시험 시행 약 4~8일 후에 온라인에서 확인할 수 있다.

2. iBT TOEFL®의 특징

1) 영어 사용 국가로 유학 시 필요한 언어 능력을 평가한다.

각 시험 영역은 실제 학업이나 캠퍼스 생활에 반드시 필요한 언어 능력을 측정한다. 평가되는 언어 능력에는 자신의 의견 및 선호도 전달하기, 강의 요약하기, 에세이 작성하기, 학술적인 주제의 글을 읽고 내용 이해하기 등이 포함되며, 각 영역에 걸쳐 고르게 평가된다.

2) Reading, Listening, Speaking, Writing 전 영역의 통합적인 영어 능력(Integrated Skill)을 평가한다.

시험이 4개 영역으로 분류되어 있기는 하지만 Speaking과 Writing 영역에서는 [Listening + Speaking], [Reading + Listening + Speaking], [Reading + Listening + Writing]과 같은 형태로 학습자가 둘 또는 세 개의 언어 영역을 통합해서 사용할 수 있는지를 평가한다.

3) Reading 지문 및 Listening 스크립트가 길다.

Reading 지문은 700단어 내외로 A4용지 약 1.5장 분량이며, Listening은 3~4분 가량의 대화와 6~8분 가량의 강의로 구성된다.

4) 전 영역에서 노트 필기(Note-taking)를 할 수 있다.

긴 지문을 읽거나 강의를 들으면서 핵심 사항을 간략하게 적어두었다가 문제를 풀 때 참고할 수 있다. 노트 필기한 종이는 시험 후 수거 및 폐기된다.

5) 선형적(Linear) 방식으로 평가된다.

응시자가 시험을 보는 과정에서 실력에 따라 문제의 난이도가 조정되어 출제되는 CAT(Computer Adaptive Test) 방식이 아니라, 정해진 문제가 모든 응시자에게 동일하게 제시되는 선형적인 방식으로 평가된다.

6) 시험 응시일이 제한된다.

시험은 주로 토요일과 일요일에만 시행되며, 시험에 재응시할 경우, 시험 응시일 3일 후부터 재응시 가능하다.

7) Performance Feedback이 주어진다.

온라인 및 우편으로 발송된 성적표에는 수치화된 점수뿐 아니라 각 영역별로 수험자의 과제 수행 정도를 나타내는 표도 제공된다.

3. iBT TOEFL®의 구성

시험 영역	Reading, Listening, Speaking, Writing
시험 시간	약 2시간
시험 횟수	연 30~40회(날짜는 ETS에서 지정)
총점	0~120점
영역별 점수	각 영역별 30점
성적 확인	응시일로부터 4~8일 후 온라인에서 성적 확인 가능

시험 영역	문제 구성	시간
Reading	• 독해 지문 2개, 총 20문제가 출제된다. • 각 지문 길이 700단어 내외, 지문당 10개 문제	36분
Listening	• 대화(Conversation) 2개(각 5문제씩)와 강의(Lecture) 3개(각 6문제씩)가 출제된다.	36분
Break		10분
Speaking	• 독립형 과제(Independent Task) 1개, 통합형 과제(Integrated Task) 3개 총 4개 문제가 출제된다.	17분
Writing	• 통합형 과제(Integrated Task) 1개(20분) • 수업 토론형 과제 (Writing for Academic Discussion) 1개(9분)	30분

4. iBT TOEFL®의 점수

1) 영역별 점수

Reading	0~30	Listening	0~30
Speaking	0~30	Writing	0~30

2) iBT, CBT, PBT 간 점수 비교

기존에 있던 CBT, PBT 시험은 폐지되었으며, 마지막으로 시행된 CBT, PBT 시험 이후 2년 이상이 경과되어 과거 응시자의 시험 성적 또한 유효하지 않다.

5. 시험 등록 및 응시 절차

1) 시험 등록

온라인과 전화로 시험 응시일과 각 지역의 시험장을 확인하여 신청할 수 있으며, 일반 접수는 시험 희망 응시일 7일 전까지 가능하다.

❶ 온라인 등록

ETS 토플 등록 사이트(https://www.ets.org/mytoefl)에 들어가 화면 지시에 따라 등록한다. 비용은 신용카드로 지불하게 되므로 American Express, Master Card, VISA 등 국제적으로 통용되는 신용카드를 미리 준비해 둔다. 시험을 등록하기 위해서는 회원 가입이 선행되어야 한다.

❷ 전화 등록

한국 프로메트릭 콜센터(00-7981-4203-0248)에 09:00~17:00 사이에 전화를 걸어 등록한다.

2) 추가 등록

시험 희망 응시일 3일(공휴일을 제외한 업무일 기준) 전까지 US $60의 추가 비용으로 등록 가능하다.

3) 등록 비용

2023년 현재 US $220(가격 변동이 있을 수 있음)

4) 시험 취소와 변경

ETS 토플 등록 사이트나 한국 프로메트릭(00-7981-4203-0248)으로 전화해서 시험을 취소하거나 응시 날짜를 변경할 수 있다. 등록 취소와 날짜 변경은 시험 날짜 4일 전까지 해야 한다. 날짜를 변경하려면 등록 번호와 등록 시 사용했던 성명이 필요하며 비용은 US $60이다.

5) 시험 당일 소지품

❶ 사진이 포함된 신분증(주민등록증, 운전면허증, 여권 중 하나)

❷ 시험 등록 번호(Registration Number)

6) 시험 절차

❶ 사무실에서 신분증과 등록 번호를 통해 등록을 확인한다.

❷ 기밀 서약서(Confidentiality Statement)를 작성한 후 서명한다.

❸ 소지품 검사, 사진 촬영, 음성 녹음 및 최종 신분 확인을 하고 연필과 연습장(Scratch Paper)을 제공받는다.

❹ 감독관의 지시에 따라 시험실에 입실하여 지정된 개인 부스로 이동하여 시험을 시작한다.

❺ Reading과 Listening 영역이 끝난 후 10분간의 휴식이 주어진다.

❻ 시험 진행에 문제가 있을 경우 손을 들어 감독관의 지시에 따르도록 한다.

❼ Writing 영역 답안 작성까지 모두 마치면 화면 종료 메시지를 확인한 후에 신분증을 챙겨 퇴실한다.

7) 성적 확인

응시일로부터 약 4~8일 후부터 온라인으로 점수 확인이 가능하며, 시험 전에 종이 사본 수령을 신청했을 경우 약 11-15일 후 우편으로 성적표를 받을 수 있다.

6. 실제 시험 화면 구성

TOEFL

CONTINUE

General Test Information

This test measures you ability to use English in an academic context. There are 4 sections.

In the Reading section, you will answer questions to 2 reading passages.

In the Listening section, you will answer questions about 2 conversations and 3 lectures.

In the Speaking section, you will answer 4 questions. One of the questions asks you to speak about familiar topics. Other questions ask you to speak about lectures, conversations, and reading passages.

In the Writing section, you will answer 2 questions. The first question asks you to write about the relationship between a lecture you will hear and a passage you will read. The second questions asks you to write a response to an academic discussion topic.

There will be directions for each section which explain how to answer the question in that section.

Click Continue to go on.

전체 Direction

시험 전체에 대한 구성 설명

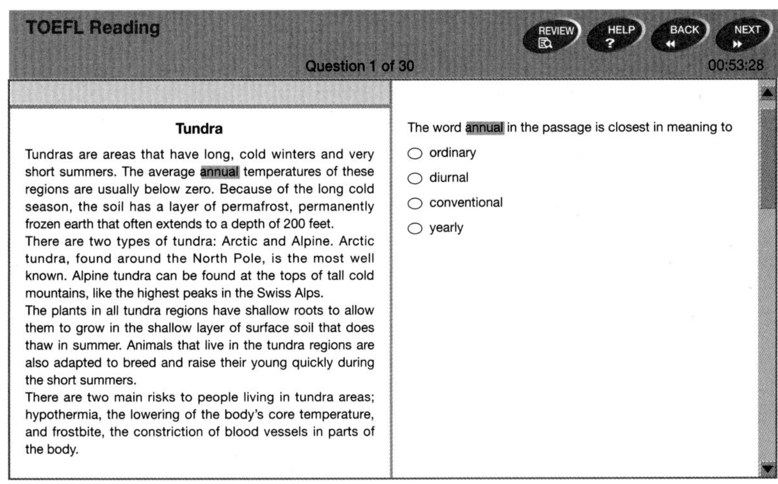

Reading 영역 화면

지문은 왼쪽에, 문제는
오른쪽에 제시

Listening 영역 화면

수험자가 대화나 강의를 듣는
동안 사진이 제시됨

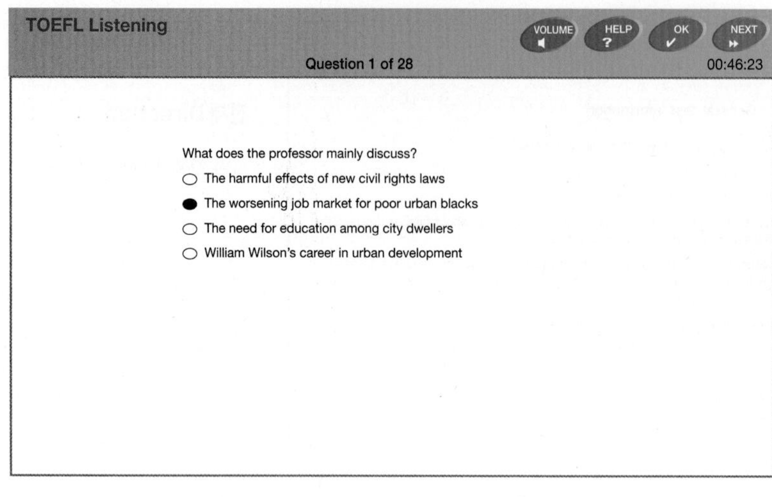

Listening 영역 화면

듣기가 끝난 후 문제 화면이 등장

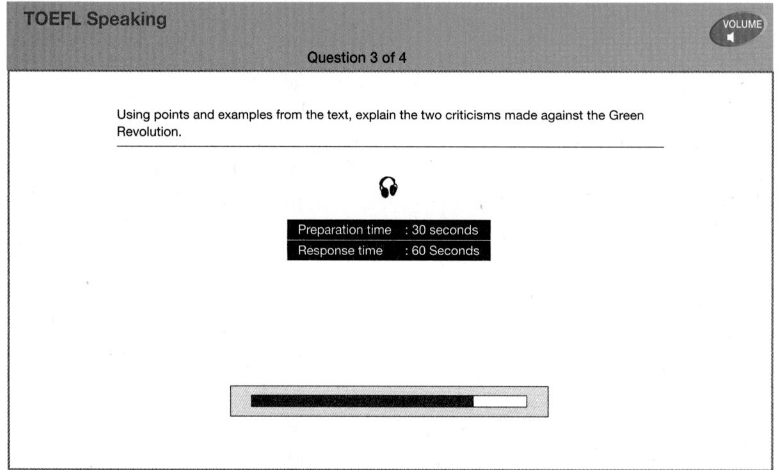

Speaking 영역 화면

문제가 주어진 후, 답변을 준비하는 시간과 말하는 시간을 알려줌

TOEFL Writing

VOLUME HELP NEXT

Question 1 of 2

In the late 14th century, an unknown poet from the Midlands composed four poems titled *Pearl*, *Sir Gawain and the Green Knight*, *Patience*, and *Cleanness*. This collection of poems is referred to as Cotton Nero A.x and the author is often referred to as the Pearl Poet. Up to this day, there have been many theories regarding the identity of this poet, and these are three of the most popular ones.

The first theory is that the author's name was Hugh, and it is based on the *Chronicle of Andrew of Wyntoun*. In the chronicle, an author called Hucheon (little Hugh) is credited with writing three poems, one of which is about the adventures of Gawain. Not only that, but all three poems are written in alliterative verse, as are all four of the poems in *Cotton Nero A.x*. Since they are written in the same style and one poem from each set concerns Gawain, some people contend that all of the *Cotton Nero A.x* poems were written by Hugh.

The second theory is that John Massey was the poet, and it is supported by another poem called *St. Erkenwald* and penmanship. Although the actual authorship of *St. Erkenwald* is unknown, John Massey was a poet who lived in the correct area and time for scholars to attribute it to him. This manuscript was written in very similar handwriting to that of the Pearl Poet, which indicates that one person is likely the author of all five of the poems.

The third theory is that the poems were actually written by different authors from the same region of England. This comes from the fact that there is little linking the poems to each other. Two are concerned with the Arthur legends, but the only link connecting the other two is that they describe the same area of the countryside. They also seem to be written in the same dialect. Taken together, these facts indicate that they were written in the same region, but they probably were not written by the same person.

Writing 영역 화면

왼쪽에 문제가 주어지고 오른쪽에 답을 직접 타이핑할 수 있는 공간이 주어짐

복사(Copy), 자르기(Cut), 붙여넣기(Paste) 버튼이 위쪽에 위치함

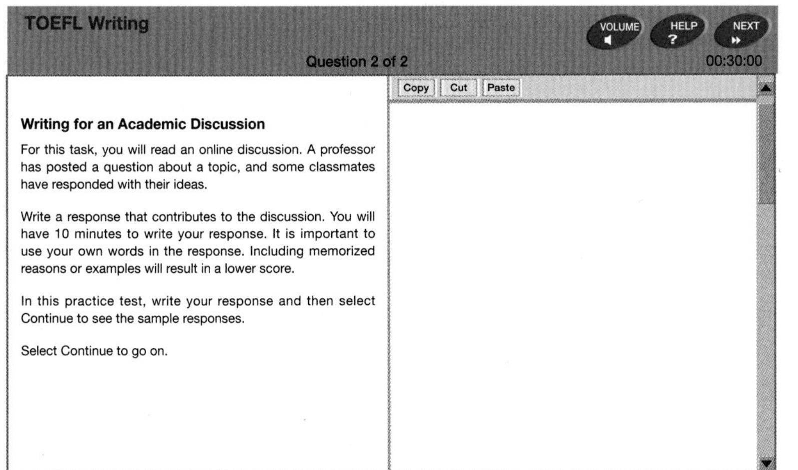

TOEFL Writing
VOLUME
HELP
NEXT
Question 2 of 2
00:30:00
Copy
Cut
Paste
Writing for an Academic Discussion
For this task, you will read an online discussion. A professor has posted a question about a topic, and some classmates have responded with their ideas.
Write a response that contributes to the discussion. You will have 10 minutes to write your response. It is important to use your own words in the response. Including memorized reasons or examples will result in a lower score.
In this practice test, write your response and then select Continue to see the sample responses.
Select Continue to go on.

Writing 영역 화면

왼쪽에 문제가 주어지고 오른쪽에 답을 직접 타이핑할 수 있는 공간이 주어짐

복사(Copy), 자르기(Cut), 붙여넣기(Paste) 버튼이 위쪽에 위치함

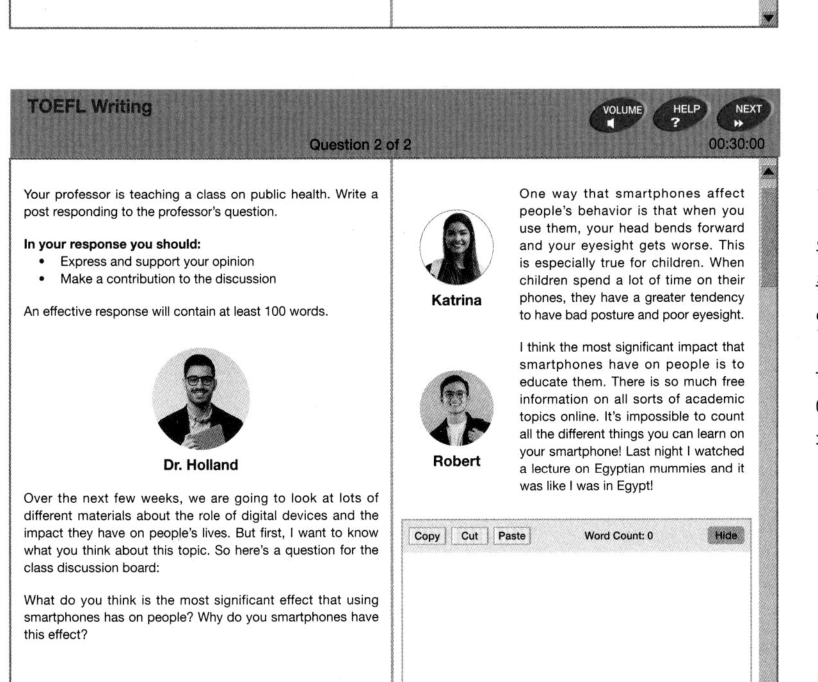

TOEFL Writing
VOLUME
HELP
NEXT
Question 2 of 2
00:30:00
Your professor is teaching a class on public health. Write a post responding to the professor's question.
In your response you should:
• Express and support your opinion
• Make a contribution to the discussion
An effective response will contain at least 100 words.
Dr. Holland
Over the next few weeks, we are going to look at lots of different materials about the role of digital devices and the impact they have on people's lives. But first, I want to know what you think about this topic. So here's a question for the class discussion board:
What do you think is the most significant effect that using smartphones has on people? Why do you smartphones have this effect?
Katrina
One way that smartphones affect people's behavior is that when you use them, your head bends forward and your eyesight gets worse. This is especially true for children. When children spend a lot of time on their phones, they have a greater tendency to have bad posture and poor eyesight.
Robert
I think the most significant impact that smartphones have on people is to educate them. There is so much free information on all sorts of academic topics online. It's impossible to count all the different things you can learn on your smartphone! Last night I watched a lecture on Egyptian mummies and it was like I was in Egypt!
Copy
Cut
Paste
Word Count: 0
Hide

Writing 영역 화면

왼쪽에 문제가 주어지고 오른쪽에 답을 직접 타이핑할 수 있는 공간이 주어짐

복사(Copy), 자르기(Cut), 붙여넣기(Paste) 버튼이 타이핑하는 곳 위쪽에 위치함

iBT TOEFL® Reading 개요

1. Reading 영역의 특징

1. 지문의 특징

Reading 영역에서는 영어권 대학의 학습 환경에서 접할 수 있는 전공별 강좌의 입문 내지 개론 수준의 지문이 다뤄지며 다양한 분야의 주제가 등장한다.

① 자연 과학: 화학, 수학, 물리학, 생물학, 의학, 공학, 천문학, 지질학 등

② 인문: 역사, 문화, 정부 정책, 문학, 그림, 조각, 건축, 연극, 춤, 특정 인물의 일대기 또는 업적 등

③ 사회 과학: 사회학, 심리학, 인류학, 경제학 등

Reading 영역에서 출제되는 글의 종류는 크게 설명(Exposition), 논증(Argumentation), 역사적인 인물 혹은 역사적인 사건의 서술(Historical / Biographical Event Narratives)로 나눌 수 있으며, 수필이나 문학 작품은 포함되지 않는다. 각 지문은 논지가 매우 분명하며 객관적인 논조로 전개되는 잘 짜인 글이다. 각 지문에는 제목이 주어지며 때로는 지문과 관련된 그림이나 사진, 도표, 그래프, 지도 등이 포함되기도 한다. 또한 용어 설명(Glossary) 기능이 있어 지문에서 밑줄 표시가 된 어휘에 마우스를 갖다 대면 그 영어 뜻이 화면 하단에 제공된다. 이러한 어휘는 일반적으로 난이도가 매우 높거나 특수한 용어다.

2. 문제의 특징

각 지문당 10개의 문제가 주어지며 크게 3가지 유형으로 나뉜다.

① 사지선다형

② 지문에 문장 삽입하기

③ 지문 전반에 걸쳐 언급된 주요 사항을 분류하여 요약표(Summary)나 범주표(Category Chart)에 넣기

※ 하나의 지문에는 Summary와 Category Chart 중 한 가지 유형의 문제만 출제되며, 이 두 문제 유형에는 부분 점수(총점 2~3점)가 있다.

2. Reading 영역의 구성

Reading 영역에서는 총 10개의 문제 유형을 통해 지문에 대한 이해도를 다각도로 평가한다. 지문 길이가 700단어 내외로 상당히 긴 편이기 때문에 자칫 어렵다고 생각할 수 있지만, 문제 풀이에 필요한 정보는 모두 지문에서 찾을 수 있다. 따라서 다양한 주제의 지문을 접하면서 실제 시험 문제 유형에 익숙해지고 나면 TOEFL의 그 어느 영역보다도 고득점에 유리한 영역이다.

TOEFL 시험의 첫 번째 영역인 Reading 지문은 기존 3~4개에서 2개로 바뀌면서 시험 시간도 36분으로 줄었다.

Part 구성	지문 수	문제 수	시험 시간
Part 1	2개	20 문제	36분

3. Reading 영역의 문제 유형

Reading 영역을 통해 평가하고자 하는 기본 능력은 다음과 같다.

- Basic Comprehension: 지문에 대한 기초적인 이해도
- Reading to Learn: 문장 / 문단 전후 관계 파악 및 전체 지문과의 연관성에 대한 이해도
- Inferencing: 지문 전체의 흐름에 대한 이해에 기반한 저자 의도 파악 능력

<Reading 영역의 10가지 문제 유형>

문제 유형	문제 설명	문제 개수
	Basic Comprehension	
어휘 (Vocabulary)	문맥 안에서 특정 어휘가 어떤 뜻으로 사용되었는지 선택지 가운데 가장 비슷한 유의어를 고르는 문제	1~2
지시어 (Reference)	문맥에서 대명사나 관계대명사 등이 지칭하는 명사를 고르는 문제	0~1
문장 요약 (Sentence Simplification)	지문에서 음영 표시된 문장을 가장 잘 간결하게 바꾸어 쓴 것을 선택지 중에서 고르는 문제	0~1
사실 정보 찾기 (Factual Information)	지문을 바탕으로 문제를 통해 특정 정보의 사실 여부를 파악하거나 육하원칙에 따라 묻는 정보를 찾는 문제	2~3
틀린 정보 찾기 (Negative Fact)	지문에서 언급되지 않았거나 지문의 정보에 비춰볼 때 잘못된 것을 가려내는 문제	1

Reading to Learn		
요약 완성 (Summary)	제시된 지문에 대한 요약의 글을 완성시키는 문제로서 선택지의 6개 문장 가운데 요약에 포함되어야 할 문장 3개를 고르는 문제	0~1
분류 (Category Chart)	지문에서 언급된 요점 혹은 그 외 중요한 정보를 분류표의 카테고리에 맞게 분류하는 문제	0~1
Inferencing		
추론 (Inference)	지문에서 명백하게 언급된 사실은 아니지만 지문의 내용을 통해 추론하는 문제	0~2
의도 파악 (Rhetorical Purpose)	글을 쓰는 방식에 대한 저자의 의도를 파악하는 문제	1~2
문장 삽입 (Insertion)	주어진 한 문장을 지문의 정해진 부분에 표시된 네 곳 중 가장 알맞은 위치에 끼워 넣는 문제	1
총 문항 수		10

4. 기존 시험과 개정 시험 간 Reading 영역 비교

	기존 iBT (~2023년 7월 전)	개정 후 iBT (2023년 7월 이후)
지문 개수	3~4개	2개
지문당 문제 수	10문제	10문제
지문당 평균 시간	18분	18분
전체 시험 시간	54~72분	36분

• 지문 길이, 난이도, 문제 난이도에는 변화가 없다.

PAGODA TOEFL 80+ Reading

Diagnostic Test

실제 TOEFL Reading 시험 구성과 유사한 진단 테스트를 풀어보면서 내 현재 실력이 얼마나 되는지, 내가 어려워하는 문제 유형이 어떤 것인지 점검해 보자.

Diagnostic Test

TOEFL Reading

Reading Section Directions

The Reading section measures your ability to understand academic passages in English. A clock at the top of the screen will show you how much time is remaining.

Most questions are worth 1 point, but the last question for each passage is worth more than 1 point. The directions for the last question indicate how many points you may receive.

Some passages include a word or phrase that is underlined in blue. To see a definition or an explanation, click on the word or phrase.

You may skip a question and return to it later, provided there is time remaining. To move on to the next question, click **NEXT**. To return to a question, click **BACK**.

Click **REVIEW** to access the review screen. The screen will show which questions have been answered and which have not been answered. You may go directly to any previous question from the review screen.

Click **CONTINUE** to proceed.

TOEFL Reading

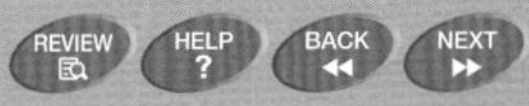

Prosperity in the Augustan Age

1 ➡ The reign of Rome's first emperor, Octavian, was a period of extensive economic development and societal change. Following the dictatorship of Julius Caesar, Rome had fallen into a period of political chaos and civil war that ended when Octavian defeated his final opponent and seized total control of the nation, taking the title of Augustus. Known for his great passion for the people and desire for honesty in politics, Augustus instituted many administrative, legal, economic, and moral reforms during his reign. These reforms brought both people and wealth flowing into the city. Shifts in agricultural production brought a huge supply of grain and other crops into Rome, and this led to the creation of the lucrative Roman markets. As Rome's population grew, much of the city was rebuilt with improved utilities and other amenities. This trend spread to other cities in the empire, and the rural population became increasingly urbanized. Although everyone did not benefit equally, he led Rome into a period of relative peace and prosperity that lasted for about two centuries.

2 ➡ After Octavian returned political order to Rome, people began to once again flock to its capital city. During the civil wars, Rome was not an attractive place to live, and many people had fled to the countryside. The majority of rural Roman people were small landowners who farmed the land, but their children were attracted to the urban life of Rome after peace returned. This was a blessing for the city because its population was rapidly diminishing due to a high death rate caused by the usual difficulties of urban life: overcrowding, poor sanitation, disease, and food shortages. Octavian supported many public works projects to alleviate these problems including the

1. Which of the following is mentioned in paragraph 1?

Ⓐ The meaning of the title Augustus
Ⓑ Octavian's contribution to Roman democracy
Ⓒ The name of a Roman ruler preceding Octavian
Ⓓ The factors that contributed to political turmoil in the Augustan age

2. According to paragraph 2, which of the following was NOT the result of Octavian's reign?

Ⓐ Political stability
Ⓑ Increase in urban population
Ⓒ Improved public amenities
Ⓓ Decline in death rate in rural areas

3. Which of the sentences below best expresses the essential information in the highlighted sentence in the passage? Incorrect choices change the meaning in important ways or leave out essential information.

Ⓐ Octavian tried to improve living conditions in Rome, but he only achieved partial success as the solution to food shortages within the city walls eluded him.
Ⓑ Except for the problem of food shortages, Octavian's efforts in solving problems like improved housing and clean water supply was met with public approval.
Ⓒ While Octavian invested heavily in improving housing and sanitation, he failed to pay attention to the lack of food in Rome.

TOEFL Reading

construction of new housing districts and public buildings, and a new aqueduct to supply the city with fresh, clean water, but no solution to the food shortages could be found within the city walls.

3 ➡ In order to satisfy its insatiable hunger, Rome had to import food from throughout the empire. This had a direct impact on agriculture in the Roman provinces, many of which were intensively agricultural areas. Before the civil wars, the pattern of landownership had begun to alter, as rich Romans bought out smaller peasant farmers around them. Many of them kept the old farmers as tenant farmers who worked but no longer owned the land, but over time slaves were increasingly used. After becoming emperor, Octavian supported the new system by paying his soldiers to retire with land. This had the dual effect of reducing the size of military while still keeping the outer provinces under Roman control through the new landowners. Since slaves are not paid, their use on these large farms throughout the empire meant that there was a massive surplus of produce, particularly of grain. Most of the grain and livestock from the farms in the Italian peninsula were sent to the capital, where markets were set up specifically for trading them.

4 ➡ The market economy also brought many benefits to the towns in the agricultural regions. As the wealth of the great landowners increased, they attempted to raise the status of their own urban centers. [■A] They financed construction projects to provide the amenities and entertainment that were enjoyed in the capital. [■B] This included public works projects like roads and bridges to facilitate trade and aqueducts to provide water to the people. [■C] They also built baths, stadiums, and theaters to bring culture and status to their people. [■D] This spread the prestige of Rome throughout its provinces as it stimulated a feeling of belonging to the empire among the recently added peoples.

Ⓓ Better housing conditions and improved sanitation were results of Octavian's public works projects, but the problem of food shortages was solved by another ruler.

4. Which of the following can be inferred from paragraph 3?

Ⓐ Octavian approved employing retired soldiers as slaves on farms.
Ⓑ The number of soldiers needed in active duty declined after Octavian became emperor.
Ⓒ It was a common practice to pay tenant farmers with grain for their labor.
Ⓓ There was no demand for markets in the outer Roman provinces.

5. The word "stimulated" in paragraph 4 is closest in meaning to

Ⓐ encouraged
Ⓑ modeled
Ⓒ required
Ⓓ maintained

6. All of the following are mentioned in paragraph 4 as changes in agricultural regions EXCEPT

Ⓐ increased sense of loyalty to the Roman empire
Ⓑ active trade between different agricultural regions
Ⓒ development of public facilities
Ⓓ introduction of various forms of entertainment found in Rome

7. The word "elaborate" in paragraph 5 is closest in meaning to

Ⓐ well-known
Ⓑ newly created
Ⓒ active
Ⓓ complex

TOEFL Reading

5 ➡ However, not all cities benefited from Rome's economic growth during the Augustan Age. If a city was in a location that gave it easy access to the empire's elaborate network of roads and waterways, it was likely to share in the new prosperity. This was particularly true for port cities like Puteoli and Ostia, which both benefited greatly from the increased trade. Puteoli was the primary port for ships bringing grain from Egypt as well as the main hub for manufactured goods from Campania to be exported throughout the empire. Ostia was Rome's original port, but it had been destroyed by pirates. During this period it was rebuilt and extensively improved. Conversely, other cities that were too far from Rome or another growing urban center often fell into decline. Many gradually disappeared or were absorbed into other cities to become their suburbs. The people from such towns moved into the new urban centers or headed for the capital. This resulted in large areas that were devoid of any sign of civilization apart from the farm houses and the quarters for their slaves.

8. Which of the following questions is answered in paragraph 5?

Ⓐ What factor determined whether a city benefited from economic progress?

Ⓑ What is an example of a port city which declined during the Augustan age?

Ⓒ What factor contributed to the decline of early Roman suburbs?

Ⓓ Why was the city of Puteoli rebuilt during this period?

TOEFL Reading

9. Look at the four squares [■] that indicate where the following sentence could be added to the passage.

Even the most remote provinces held regular Coliseum style games and races.

Where would the sentence best fit?

Click on a square [■] to add the sentence to the passage.

10. Directions: An introductory sentence for a brief summary of the passage is provided below. Complete the summary by selecting the THREE answer choices that express the most important ideas in the passage. Some sentences do not belong in the summary because they express ideas that are not presented in the passage or are minor ideas in the passage.
This question is worth 2 points.

With the end of civil war, Rome began to thrive under the rule of Octavian, who was the first Roman emperor.

-
-
-

Answer Choices

Ⓐ Unlike Puteoli which served as an active trading hub between Rome and Egypt, Ostia was destroyed by pirates.

Ⓑ However, Octavian's ambitious efforts in expanding urban areas led to a relative decline of suburbs.

Ⓒ With the development of a market economy, rural regions could also enjoy increased status as they adopted the facilities found in the capital.

Ⓓ Through Octavian's efforts, living conditions in Rome improved substantially, and people began returning to the capital.

Ⓔ As the number of slaves employed as unpaid labor increased, there was a corresponding decrease in food supply.

Ⓕ The increase in demand for food in the capital increased trade and established markets.

Drag your answer choices to the spaces where they belong.
To remove an answer choice, click on it. To review the passage, click on **View Text**.

TOEFL Reading

Factors Determining Seaweed Distribution

1 ➡ In the world's oceans, as on the land, the first stage producers in the food chain are organisms that use photosynthesis, but the areas that they can survive in are limited. The primary producers are phytoplankton, which are single-celled organisms that float near the surface of the ocean. In some areas, they are supplemented by various types of multicellular algae called seaweeds. These plants are typically divided into three groups as red algae, brown algae, and green algae, and they are extremely important to the ecosystem. In addition to providing food directly to herbivores, their decaying matter is important to food chains that depend upon detritus. They are also widely consumed by humans, who use them for food, medicine, and industrial purposes. Seaweeds also provide shelter to other organisms in the coastal community, and they often are among the first organisms to settle in previously barren areas.

2 ➡ Most species of seaweed are benthic organisms, which means that they live on the sea floor from the coastline outward along the inner continental shelf. They will anchor themselves to natural surfaces including rock, mud, coral, and organisms with shells like crustaceans, mollusks, and turtles. They can also adhere to man-made objects like cement jetties, wooden piers, and ships' hulls. Some types are very selective about what they will adhere themselves to, while others will make use of any surface that is motionless for a sufficient amount of time. Seaweeds inhabit about 2% of the seafloor, and their distribution is determined by a number of factors. These include salinity, availability of mineral nutrients, tidal exposure to air, and wave and current action, but the two most important factors are exposure to light and ambient temperature.

11. According to paragraph 1, which of the following is NOT true of seaweeds?

Ⓐ They can be a natural habitat for other living things.

Ⓑ These plants are a source of food for herbivores.

Ⓒ They play a very important part in the ecosystem.

Ⓓ These plants include phytoplankton, which are first stage producers.

12. According to paragraph 2, some types of seaweeds choose any stationary object to anchor while

Ⓐ the majority of them live on the deep ocean floor along coastlines

Ⓑ others prefer artificial structures such as cement seawalls and wrecked ships

Ⓒ the majority of them look for objects that stand still for more than a year

Ⓓ others are very picky about which surfaces they will stick themselves to

13. The word "them" in paragraph 3 refers to

Ⓐ depths

Ⓑ seaweeds

Ⓒ pigments

Ⓓ frequencies

3 ➡ As photosynthetic organisms, the distribution of seaweed is governed first and foremost by the amount of sunlight that is available. Due to this, the species that are present is dependent upon factors like depth, water conditions, and the latitude and season. Light levels diminish rapidly as the water gets deeper, and different wavelengths of light penetrate to different depths. Therefore, one popular theory held that the different types of seaweeds contain different pigments that allowed them to absorb those different frequencies, determining at what depth they would most likely be found. This concept is called chromatic adaptation, and it held that red algae should live the deepest, followed by brown algae, and then green algae. The theory of chromatic adaptation was first proposed in the 1900s and it was generally believed for about 100 years. However, this theory has been largely discounted as examples have proven that the distribution of different types of seaweed is affected far more by competition, consumption, and the ability of algae to change their growth patterns than the wavelengths of light that are available.

4 ➡ However, depth remains a significant factor, and seaweeds are still confined to the photic zone, which is up to 200 meters deep. The depth of the photic zone is largely dependent upon the clarity of the water, with very sediment-heavy waters measuring as little as a few centimeters deep. The levels of floating sediment vary with the seasons, so some species will only populate areas for short parts of the year. Moreover, the Earth's seasons are created by the relative tilt of the Earth's axis, which affects the angle at which light reaches the surface. The planet is tilted at about 23.5 degrees off of vertical, so the Northern Hemisphere receives more direct light between March and September, while the South does during the rest of the year. This has a distinct effect on seaweed growth—the closer the plants are to either pole. Areas in the tropics, which experience little seasonal change in light levels, have the most prodigious

14. What can be inferred about the theory of chromatic adaptation from paragraph 3?

Ⓐ The color of seaweeds is different depending on the quality of the water.

Ⓑ Red algae would absorb wavelengths that reach great depths in the ocean.

Ⓒ Water pressure has proven to be the main variable of photosynthesis.

Ⓓ Green algae prefer deep water since they can absorb green wavelengths.

15. Which of the sentences below best expresses the essential information in the highlighted sentence in the passage? Incorrect choices change the meaning in important ways or leave out essential information.

Ⓐ The clearness of water is proportional to the depth of the photic zone.

Ⓑ The photic zone of clear water is measured to be only a few meters deep.

Ⓒ The measurement of the photic zone determines the heaviness of water.

Ⓓ A few centimeters of the photic zone guarantees the clearness of water.

16. In paragraph 4, the author mentions the relative tilt of the Earth's axis in order to

Ⓐ emphasize the importance of having basic knowledge of science

Ⓑ suggest that seaweeds inhabit tropical areas throughout the year

Ⓒ explain why levels of sediment in water depend on the seasons

Ⓓ show the fundamental cause of seasonal variations in light levels

17. The word "prodigious" in paragraph 4 is closest in meaning to

Ⓐ balanced

Ⓑ massive

Ⓒ varied

Ⓓ healthy

seaweed growth. Seasonal variations in light levels naturally also affect the temperature of the water.

5 ➡ [■A] The ambient temperature of an area also has a profound effect upon the distribution of seaweeds. As they are exposed to much more direct sunlight year round, the tropical seas possess the largest variety of algae species. [■B] Travelling either north or south from the tropics, the variety decreases and the species also differ. [■C] The seaweeds found in higher latitudes live in colder waters, and many of them are perennial, so they live longer than two years. [■D] To survive the colder winter months, many of these marine algae die back to a tiny portion of their summer size. This remnant will lie dormant until the temperatures rise and it can resume growth. In areas where ice sheets are present during the winter, coastal areas may be scoured clean by the ice, but species will return to the shallows in the spring.

18. According to paragraph 5, which of the following is true about the effect of high temperatures on seaweeds?

Ⓐ Seaweeds in areas with large tides flourish at high temperatures.

Ⓑ High temperatures lead to increased diversity of perennial species.

Ⓒ High temperatures usually encourage seaweed growth.

Ⓓ Mediterranean temperatures are considered ideal for seaweed growth.

TOEFL Reading

19. Look at the four squares [■] that indicate where the following sentence could be added to the passage.

Although these high temperatures typically promote seaweed growth, in areas with large tides, extremes of temperature can limit seaweed distribution.

Where would the sentence best fit?

Click on a square [■] to add the sentence to the passage.

20. **Directions:** An introductory sentence for a brief summary of the passage is provided below. Complete the summary by selecting the THREE answer choices that express the most important ideas in the passage. Some sentences do not belong in the summary because they express ideas that are not presented in the passage or are minor ideas in the passage. ***This question is worth 2 points.***

The distribution of seaweeds, which are multicellular algae vital to the ecosystem, is determined by various factors.

-
-
-

Answer Choices

Ⓐ There are three kinds of seaweeds depending on their mineral content: red algae, brown algae, and green algae.

Ⓑ The amount of sunlight seaweeds can get is crucial to their distribution, which is also related to the depth of the ocean.

Ⓒ Sufficient exposure to sunlight has proven to be one of the main factors promoting growth in all living creatures.

Ⓓ The depth of the photic zone depends on the quality of the water, and it determines the survival rate and habitat of seaweeds.

Ⓔ Perennial seaweeds usually live in higher latitudes because they can survive better in warm water.

Ⓕ The temperature of the water can both promote and disturb the growth and dispersion of seaweeds.

Drag your answer choices to the spaces where they belong.
To remove an answer choice, click on it. To review the passage, click on **View Text**.

PAGODA TOEFL 80+ Reading

I
Identifying Details

Lesson

01 Sentence Simplification

Lesson Outline

◎ 문장 요약(Sentence Simplification) 문제는 지문에 표시된 특정 문장을 가장 정확하고 간결하게 요약한 보기를 찾아내는 문제다. 문장의 세부적인 내용보다는 핵심 내용에 집중해야 하며, 일종의 패러프레이징(paraphrasing) 문제라고도 할 수 있으므로 문장의 주요 정보를 파악하는 것이 가장 중요하다.

◎ 이 유형의 문제는 한 지문당 0~1개가 출제된다.

Typical Questions 

- Which of the sentences below best expresses the essential information in the highlighted sentence in the passage? Incorrect choices change the meaning in important ways or leave out essential information.

  다음 중 지문에 음영 표시된 문장의 핵심 정보를 가장 잘 표현한 문장은 무엇인가? 오답은 의미를 크게 왜곡하거나 핵심 정보를 누락하고 있다.

Learning Strategies

Step 1 지문에 음영으로 표시된 문장을 보고 핵심 내용을 간추린다.

⋯› 너무 세부적이거나 지문의 흐름에 중요한 내용이 아니면 핵심 내용에 포함되지 않는다.

⋯› 만약 음영 표시된 문장에 대명사 등의 지시어가 있다면 앞 문장을 보고 그것이 무엇을 가리키는지 정확히 파악하고 넘어가도록 하자. 핵심 내용 이해에 도움이 된다.

Step 2 주어진 보기들 중 핵심 정보를 가장 정확히 담고 있는 보기를 고른다. 물론 보기는 지문에 쓰인 것과 다른 단어를 사용하여 패러프레이징된다는 점을 기억해야 한다. 즉, 지문과 동일한 단어가 쓰인 보기가 있더라도 핵심 내용을 담고 있지 않거나 핵심 내용과 다른 정보를 담은 오답일 수 있다.

Step 3 정답을 고른 뒤 다른 보기들의 오답 여부를 확인하고 넘어가자. 문제에서 말하듯 오답은 문장의 의미를 왜곡하고 바꾸거나 핵심 정보가 빠져 있다. 오답을 검토하는 것도 Sentence Simplification 유형을 이해하는 데 큰 도움이 된다.

Example

(...) Features of the Gothic style including elaborate facades which frequently bore sculptures depicting Biblical scenes and a preference for vertical movement, evident in its tall towers and pointed arches, were aimed at conveying a sense of majesty about the Church. (...)

Q. Which of the sentences below best expresses the essential information in the highlighted sentence in the passage? Incorrect choices change the meaning in important ways or leave out essential information.

1 지문에 음영으로 표시된 문장을 보고 핵심 내용을 간추린다.

Features of the Gothic style [including elaborate facades which frequently bore sculptures depicting Biblical scenes and a preference for vertical movement, evident in its tall towers and pointed arches,] were aimed at conveying a sense of majesty about the Church.

문장의 길이가 길면 혼란이 올 수도 있고 압도될 수도 있지만 찬찬히 읽으며 잔가지, 즉 세부 사항들을 쳐내고 핵심 내용만 남겨보자. 위에 주어진 예시의 경우 [ ] 안에 들어간 내용이 Gothic style의 특징들, 즉 세부 사항들이다. 이 문장의 핵심은 '[이러한 특징의] 고딕 양식은 **교회의 위엄을 전달하려고 의도되었다**'는 것이다.

2 주어진 보기들 중 핵심 정보를 가장 정확히 담고 있는 것을 고른다. 보기를 살펴보자.

Ⓐ The purpose of elaborate sculptures on the exterior illustrating Biblical scenes and the extreme height found in Gothic buildings was to evoke reverence about the Church.
→ 고딕 건물들에서 볼 수 있는 ~의 목적은 교회에 대한 존경심을 불러일으키기 위한 것이었다

Ⓑ From the decorative Biblical sculptures in the outer walls, towers, and arches of the church, it is evident that Gothic style means to instill awe in viewers.
→ 고딕 양식은 보는 사람들에게 경외심을 불어넣으려는 것이 명백하다

Ⓒ Sculptures, which are one of the features of Gothic architecture meant to express grandeur, often showed a preference for Biblical scenes and vertical movement.
→ 조각품들은 성경에 나오는 장면들과 수직적 움직임에 대한 선호를 흔히 보였다

Ⓓ Gothic style centers primarily on intricate Biblical sculptures and an inclination for height to communicate a sense of reverence about the Church.
→ 고딕 양식은 복잡한 성경적 조각들과 높이에 주로 중점을 둔다

핵심 내용만 봐도 무엇이 정답인지 매우 명백하다. 정답은 Ⓐ로, '~ were aimed at'이 'The purpose of ~'로 패러프레이징되었다.

3 정답을 고른 뒤 다른 보기들의 오답 여부를 확인하고 넘어가자. 핵심 내용을 잘 파악했는지 다시 살펴본다. Ⓑ는 단순한 경외심이 아니라 '교회에 대한' 존경심을 불러일으키기 위한 것이었으므로, Ⓒ는 특정 조각품을 선호했다는 것이 핵심 내용이 아니므로, Ⓓ는 특정 세부 사항에 주로 중점을 두었다는 것이 핵심 내용이 아니므로 오답이다.

Practice

[01-06] **Which of the sentences below best expresses the essential information? Incorrect choices change the meaning in important ways or leave out essential information.**

01 The source gases do not destroy ozone in their original form, but once in the stratosphere, they are chemically degraded and change into ozone-depleting gases, such as chlorine and chlorine monoxide.

Ⓐ In the stratosphere, the source gases change chemical states and become chlorine and chlorine monoxide.

Ⓑ The ozone layer is damaged by chemicals formed when source gases undergo chemical changes after entering the stratosphere.

02 A significant decrease in the ozone layer, mainly found in the lower portion of the stratosphere, first appeared over Antarctica because atmospheric conditions there increase the effectiveness of reactive halogen gases containing chlorine and bromine that destroy ozone.

Ⓐ Antarctica was first found to be depleted of ozone because the air contains harmful elements such as chlorine and bromine.

Ⓑ The decrease of ozone over Antarctica is caused by air conditions that enhance the impact of the gases that harm the ozone.

03 One hundred and ten million years ago, the Sahara of Northern Africa had lush forests and wide rivers, but the extremely dry conditions that have since developed there are ideal for the preservation of fossils.

(A) The Sahara has many fossils because it was very dry, but is now an area of forests and rivers.

(B) The Sahara once had many forests and rivers that are now dry, and it has many fossils.

(C) The Sahara was an area of forests and rivers long ago, but it became very dry and that preserved many fossils.

04 Repetitive strain injury affects the arms and upper back and occurs when muscles in these areas are kept tense for very long periods due to poor posture or repetitive motions.

(A) Repetitive strain injury occurs in the arms and upper back because of muscle tension related to poor posture or repetitive motions.

(B) Repetitive strain injury results in poor posture and repetitive motion because of muscle tension in the arms and upper back.

(C) Repetitive strain injury causes poor posture and repetitive motion, as well as muscle tension in the arms and upper back.

05 In the late 15th century, after movable-type printing was introduced by Gutenberg, a German printer and publisher in Europe, an unprecedented number of people became literate and educated themselves by reading printed books, which in turn led to the people developing interests in various aspects of life.

Ⓐ People became able to read a wide range of books and learn new things, which they were not allowed to do in the past.

Ⓑ The low cost of paper made it possible to make more books for the people to read and to teach themselves new information.

Ⓒ Before the introduction of printing, people lived simpler lives as they had no need to learn things about life.

Ⓓ Printing enabled people to gain new knowledge, fulfill their curiosity, and become better informed than they had been in the past.

06 Of all the theories that describe the early development of the universe, the most popular one among researchers that is supported by a broad range of observable phenomena, such as the abundance of light elements and the cosmic microwave background, is the Big Bang theory, which proposes that all matter in the universe was once one super entity that then exploded, and the resultant debris went on to become what we see today.

Ⓐ Many scientists accept a theory that suggests the universe started out as a large entity that exploded to form smaller planets.

Ⓑ Some scientists claim that the universe started out as one entity that exploded, and the debris became the galaxies we know today.

Ⓒ Most scientists support the Big Bang theory, which says that the universe was formed by the debris from the explosion of a large entity.

Ⓓ All scientists now support the Big Bang theory that claims the universe was created in a big explosion.

07

African Culture

Africa's literary tradition, both oral and written, extends back into history for centuries. During most of Africa's history, there has existed a trend of widespread illiteracy, so the African oral tradition has always been more important in terms of the continuation of cultural tradition and knowledge of family history. In fact, it was not until the 20th century that many of the African sub-cultures began the task of putting their stories, histories, myths, and folktales in writing.

Which of the sentences below best expresses the essential information in the highlighted sentence in the passage? Incorrect choices change the meaning in important ways or leave out essential information.

Ⓐ Because many Africans haven't been able to read and write, their traditions and family histories have been transmitted verbally.

Ⓑ The African oral tradition has been considered essential in recording cultural traditions and family history in African nations.

Ⓒ The history of African families has generally been recorded by tales of family members and their experiences.

Ⓓ The African educational system has never been doubted for its ability to instruct all of its students on how to read and write.

08

Development of Cities

The expansion of population size and the formation of governments eventually led to the rise of cities that served as religious centers near temples. Some cities sprang up in areas with economic opportunity, such as locations replete with silver and gold deposits, while others rose on locations of strategic importance on major trading routes. As these cities grew, becoming larger and coming to cover more space, new services were created to meet the needs of the developing society. For example, artisans and merchants formed a small economy within the city walls which gradually led to the establishment of a steady marketplace that allowed people to buy everyday items on a regular basis.

Which of the sentences below best expresses the essential information in the highlighted sentence in the passage? Incorrect choices change the meaning in important ways or leave out essential information.

Ⓐ Cities emerged where it would be beneficial for financial growth and business means.

Ⓑ Cities expanded in many different locations, particularly on along roads with high trade volume.

Ⓒ Destinations for gold and silver traders along major trade routes grew into prosperous cities.

Ⓓ The increase in the number of cities enabled a diverse range of services to be created, and this in turn fueled further improvement in economic and trade issues.

09

Qing Dynasty

The factors that led to the rebellion and the fall of the Qing Dynasty were evident from the end of the 19th century. The reign of Emperor Qianlong is often considered to be the most impressive among the Qing Dynasty rulers, but corruption marred its final decade when the Emperor's favorite bodyguard, Heshen, abused his lord's favor and trust to amass a vast personal fortune. This, however, cannot be seen as the sole cause behind the fall of the Qing Dynasty. Qianlong's successors made several notable attempts to correct the wrongs. Jiaqing, whose reign followed immediately on after that of Qianlong, was responsible for commendable efforts to stamp out corruption and to repair the government's image. For a while, his efforts were so successful that his achievements cast doubt on the idea that the Qing Dynasty was already doomed. However, after his death, there was a relatively powerless and unstable central authority and mass civil disorder had begun and continuously grown.

Which of the sentences below best expresses the essential information in the highlighted sentence in the passage? Incorrect choices change the meaning in important ways or leave out essential information.

Ⓐ Qianlong's reign is regarded as being the greatest of the Qing Dynasty, but it gained a reputation of being corrupt by its end.

Ⓑ Heshen took advantage of the Emperor's trust to create a vast personal fortune, and destroyed his reign that was otherwise almost flawless.

Ⓒ Qianlong was a poor judge of character, which allowed him to be taken advantage of and led to the ruin of the dynasty.

Ⓓ The greatest Qing ruler, Qianlong, was taken advantage of by his favorite bodyguard, who built an enormous personal fortune.

10

Japan

In the 8th century, Japanese authorities collected land taxes from farmers that were equivalent to about three or four percent of their crop yield. This was not a heavy burden in itself, but cultivators also owed other obligations and services to the government. As part of their duties, they were required to provide one man per household equipped at their own expense as a conscript to the military, and provide labor for public projects on 60 days each year. In periods of hardship, they were eligible to receive seed rice from the authorities, but they were required to repay the government with 30 to 50 percent interest at harvest time. The poorest in fact, particularly those in the provinces closest to the capital that were subjected to stricter official supervision, were tempted during times of hardship to abandon their holdings and seek alternative livelihoods either as farmers in remote regions or as hired laborers in the capital.

Which of the sentences below best expresses the essential information in the highlighted sentence in the passage? Incorrect choices change the meaning in important ways or leave out essential information.

Ⓐ Those experiencing the most difficult situations often desired to give up their homes in search of better ways of life in other rural regions or in cities.

Ⓑ The poorest people usually lived through hard times by taking the state-provided jobs, such as working within the city as hired laborers or in isolated rural areas.

Ⓒ When those living in comfort faced economic difficulties, they often abandoned their city lives in the capital and went to rural areas in search of better opportunities to earn money.

Ⓓ Government officials tempted people to leave their livelihoods behind to work as hired laborers near the capital or as farmers in more rural areas to earn a better living.

11

Inca Sacrifices

Five centuries after Inca priests sacrificed three young children on a snow-covered peak in Argentina, archaeologists discovered them frozen in nearly perfect condition. Approximately two feet above the body of the sacrificed boy, three miniature llama figurines were found. It is presumed that the Incas may have offered the llama figurines along with the sacrifices to help ensure the fertility of the llama herds. In front of the three llama figurines were placed two male figurines, one made of gold and the other of spondylus shell, as if to suggest that they were leading the animals. These two male figurines may have been meant to represent one of two things: they could have been meant to represent the deities believed to be the natural owners of the llamas, most likely the mountain gods, or the Inca nobles who were responsible for overseeing the royal herds of animals dedicated to the gods.

Which of the sentences below best expresses the essential information in the highlighted sentence in the passage? Incorrect choices change the meaning in important ways or leave out essential information.

Ⓐ The two statuettes might be either the mountain gods, the owners of the llamas in nature, or the Inca's ruling class in charge of the royal animals which were meant to be offerings to the gods.

Ⓑ The two figures probably show the gods who took care of the mountains, or the Inca nobles who watched the llama herds that belonged to the gods.

Ⓒ One of the figures is thought to have been the owner of the llamas in nature, and the other the Inca authority who supervises the king's llama herds, which would become offerings to the gods.

Ⓓ Small male figures usually symbolize the gods who were thought to be the llamas' owners in nature, the mountain gods, or the Inca royal family who chose the offerings to the gods.

12

Type of Volcanoes

People have a stereotypical idea of what volcanoes look like, but geologists generally group volcanoes into four main types: cinder cones, composite volcanoes, shield volcanoes, and lava domes. Some of our most impressive mountains are composite volcanoes, which are also sometimes called stratovolcanoes. These volcanoes typically feature steep slopes and huge symmetrical cones built by periodic flows of lava, volcanic ash, and cinders. They can rise as high as 8,000 feet above their bases. Some famous examples of this kind of volcanic mountain include Mount Cotopaxi in Ecuador, Mount Shasta in California, Mount St. Helens in Washington, Mount Fuji in Japan, and Mount Hood in Oregon. Most composite volcanoes have craters at their summits, which can contain one central vent or a cluster of vents. As lava flows from breaks in the crater wall or cracks in the sides of the cone, they form dikes and ridges that act as gigantic ribs that help strengthen the cone. The essential feature for a volcano to be considered a composite volcano is the alternating layers of material that form a conduit system that allows magma to rise from deep within the earth's crust and spill out through cracks and fissures.

Which of the sentences below best expresses the essential information in the highlighted sentence in the passage? Incorrect choices change the meaning in important ways or leave out essential information.

Ⓐ The uniformity of the layers in a composite volcano allows it to form a conduit system for magma to rise from great depths.

Ⓑ The conduit system that allows magma to rise from great depths earns this volcano type its name.

Ⓒ This type of volcano is characterized by the different strata of material that channel magma from deep within the Earth.

Ⓓ Composite volcanoes are essentially a conduit system for the transportation of viscous magma.

13

Global Warming

Global warming is the increase in the average temperature of the Earth's near-surface air and oceans over recent decades and its projected continuation. Global average air temperatures near the Earth's surface have risen 0.74 ± 0.18 °C over the past century. [1] The Intergovernmental Panel on Climate Change (IPCC) has concluded that "most of the observed increase in globally averaged temperatures since the mid-20th century is very likely due to the observed increase in anthropogenic greenhouse gas concentrations." Natural phenomena such as solar variation combined with volcanoes probably had a small warming effect from pre-industrial times until 1950, but have had a small cooling effect since 1950. These basic conclusions have been endorsed by at least 30 scientific societies and academies of science. [2] Interestingly, despite the ample evidence collected to support global warming trends, as well as the support of these findings by the world's top scientists, there are still those who dismiss the idea of the phenomenon. However, these naysayers tend to be members of special interest groups who stand to lose money if measures are taken to curtail global warming.

1. Which of the sentences below best expresses the essential information in the highlighted sentence in the passage? Incorrect choices change the meaning in important ways or leave out essential information.

Ⓐ An organization on climate change believes that the increase in global temperature was caused by greenhouse gas emissions from industries in the late 20th century.

Ⓑ Global temperature has increased since the mid-20th century because of increased greenhouse gas emissions from human activities, according to one organization.

Ⓒ A study by an organization suggests that global warming started when the industrial revolution produced a lot of factories and machines that replaced human beings.

Ⓓ An organization has provided solid evidence that the increase in average global temperature didn't happen until the mid-20th century due to the population explosion.

2. Which of the sentences below best expresses the essential information in the highlighted sentence in the passage? Incorrect choices change the meaning in important ways or leave out essential information.

Ⓐ There are people who suspect global warming because of the evidence provided by the world's eminent scientists.

Ⓑ World-class scientists have already collected enough evidence to prove that the phenomenon called global warming exists.

Ⓒ People don't trust even world-famous scientists because they didn't provide much evidence of their theories.

Ⓓ Some people still have doubts about global warming even with a lot of supporting evidence and opinions.

14

Head Injuries

People often complain about helmet laws for those who ride motorcycles and rules that specify helmets as necessary gear for cycling, inline skating and a host of other recreational activities. [1] Though helmets may be uncomfortable, there are strong reasons for why their use is encouraged because no one knows when an accident will occur, and many injuries that occur while riding motorcycles and bicycles, or while doing other recreational activities, are injuries to the head. A severe head injury may damage cerebral blood vessels and cause bleeding into the cranial cavity. If blood is forced between the dura mater (a protective membrane) and the cranium (skull), the condition is known as an *epidural hemorrhage*. If the flow of blood goes between the lower layer of the dura mater and the brain, it is called a *subdural hemorrhage*. [2] The symptoms of these conditions vary depending on whether the damaged vessel is an artery or a vein because arterial blood pressure is higher than the blood pressure of veins, which means that artery damage can cause more rapid and severe distortion of neural tissue than vein damage. Since the nature of a head injury cannot always be immediately determined, it is important to receive medical attention quickly.

Lesson 01
Identifying Details

1. **Which of the sentences below best expresses the essential information in the highlighted sentence in the passage? Incorrect choices change the meaning in important ways or leave out essential information.**

Ⓐ Wearing helmets should be mandatory for all bike riders since many bikers injure their heads while bike-riding.

Ⓑ Well-made helmets are essential because when bikers fall, they usually get the biggest injury to their head.

Ⓒ It is urgent to produce comfortable helmets so that bikers may feel safe and have a pleasant time while riding a bike.

Ⓓ People ought to wear helmets when enjoying active recreational activities like riding a bike because accidents in such cases are likely to result in head injuries.

2. **Which of the sentences below best expresses the essential information in the highlighted sentence in the passage? Incorrect choices change the meaning in important ways or leave out essential information.**

Ⓐ Damage to an artery causes various conditions depending on whether the affected area is close to the heart.

Ⓑ If the damaged vessel is an artery, there may be a more serious condition because the blood pressure in arteries is higher than that in veins.

Ⓒ Artery damage usually leads to a fatal condition because it directly affects the neural tissues of the brain.

Ⓓ An artery is more important than a vein in terms of neural conditions, because the blood pressure in arteries is higher than that in veins.

15

Native American Dwellings

1 ➡ Of all of the tribes of Native Americans that peopled the American Southwest, the Apache, Navajo, and Pueblo are three of the best known. All three tribes have things in common such as their skills at desert survival, basket and pottery production, and a regular diet of corn, beans and squash, supplemented by meat acquired through hunting expeditions. Another common trait shared by these tribes is that they were able to create dwellings suitable for life in a hot, dry climate.

2 ➡ The Apache were a fierce, nomadic tribe which ranged over a wide area of the United States and Mexico. They were primarily hunter-gatherers, though they did practice limited farming. Their main type of dwelling was called a wickiup. [1] These shelters were built by the women of the tribe and were perfectly suited to the arid environment and constant traveling undertaken by the tribes. Wickiups were constructed of a simple wooden frame covered with brush, a type of foliage common in deserts. With such easily accessible materials, wickiups were abandoned and built anew when the tribes created a new camp.

3 ➡ The Navajo, close relatives of the Apache, were originally a nomadic tribe as well. They followed the buffalo, using dogs to pull their belongings on travois, a triangle-shaped frame used to carry heavy loads. Eventually, the Navajo followed the Pueblo example and settled down to become farmers. As nomads, they lived in simple, collapsible tents, but after becoming farmers, they built hogans. [2] These multiple-sided, wood-framed, brush-covered dwellings, built entirely of readily available desert materials, were originally built for ritualistic purposes, but they came to be used as homes once the Navajo became more sedentary.

4 ➡ Perhaps the most famous of these three peoples are the Pueblo, a term that applies to a collection of smaller tribes, including the Zuni and the Hopi. The Pueblo were established southwestern farmers who traded their harvests with other tribes such as the Navajo and Apache. As the Pueblo were full-time farmers, they needed permanent dwellings. Using bricks made of mud, the Pueblo built homes into the sides of canyons and atop mesas, flat-topped hills with steep walls common to the Southwest. The fact that Pueblo structures remain is a testament to their sturdiness.

1. **Which of the sentences below best expresses the essential information in the highlighted sentence in paragraph 2? Incorrect choices change the meaning in important ways or leave out essential information.**

Ⓐ Only women were allowed to build these shelters, which were difficult to construct under desert climatic conditions.

Ⓑ The desert environment and constant traveling of the tribe required that the women stay behind to build the shelters.

Ⓒ The women of the tribe traveled widely to gather materials in the desert in order to construct shelters.

Ⓓ Built by female tribe members, these dwellings were suited to the dry desert conditions and the tribes' frequent movements.

2. **Which of the sentences below best expresses the essential information in the highlighted sentence in paragraph 3? Incorrect choices change the meaning in important ways or leave out essential information.**

Ⓐ The tribes didn't practice any sort of rituals until they settled down and built multiple-sided dwellings of desert brush and wood.

Ⓑ Using natural materials, such as brush and wood, the tribes settled down and built shelters for performing rituals.

Ⓒ The shelters were used as homes after the tribes settled down, but these multiple-sided structures of wood and brush at first were mostly for conducting rituals.

Ⓓ Rituals were not performed by the tribes unless ready materials like wood and brush were available for building their many-sided structures.

16

Mass Production

1 ➡ Developments in industrialization quickly moved ahead in the United States following 1790. During this period, business owners and entrepreneurs worked towards increasing productivity by diversifying jobs and building more factories. [1] The resulting innovations in methods of manufacturing increased productivity as was intended, and the average person experienced a remarkable improvement in his or her standard of living. In fact, the income of the average worker increased by roughly 30 percent over the course of a generation, and products once considered luxury items became everyday fixtures even in middle-income households.

2 ➡ New methods of manufacturing were the primary factor in the increased productivity of goods. Starting in the 1760s, North American business owners opened up numerous possibilities with the outwork system, making manufacturing more efficient by distributing work to individuals or small groups of workers that were responsible for only a single step in the entire process of production. For instance, the shoe industry in the 1820s and 1830s increased the size and extent of the outwork system. Rural workers were paid in the 'piecework' method, which means they were paid according to the amount they produced.

3 ➡ This revolution in the production process definitely benefited the business owner. [2] Shoemakers, who once made shoes from start to finish, personally overseeing every step themselves, were now given designated tasks such as making only shoe soles or stitching the pieces together. While this lowered the cost of a pair of shoes, it also lowered the quality of workmanship and weakened the power of craftsmen. It not only gave business owners power over labor conditions and working speed, but also control over workers' time.

4 ➡ However, not all products were suitable for the outwork system, so entrepreneurs came up with an even more influential working environment, the modern factory. Factories made use of machines and assembly lines to produce huge amounts of high-quality products. These machines and assembly lines sped up production and lowered the cost of most products as a result. The machines became even more effective as they improved over time. They were originally powered by water or steam, but then developed into being run by electricity.

5 ➡ While these machines and assembly lines enabled an increase in the amount of goods produced and lowered their cost to consumers, there were some negative aspects. First, the demand for skilled craftsmen was reduced, giving all of the power over employment and wages to the factory owners. In addition, the countless moving parts of the machines proved hazardous to workers as they lost fingers, limbs, and even their lives in the wheels and gears of the machines.

1. **Which of the sentences below best expresses the essential information in the highlighted sentence in paragraph 1? Incorrect choices change the meaning in important ways or leave out essential information.**

Ⓐ According to the plan, average consumers were able to spend more money on products as manufacturing innovations made them available.

Ⓑ The average citizen, as business owners predicted, was willing to buy more products if they were manufactured on a larger scale.

Ⓒ Though the number of products manufactured increased, the average person did not plan on buying more goods.

Ⓓ As planned, improvements in manufacturing resulted in higher output, which greatly improved the lives of average people.

2. **Which of the sentences below best expresses the essential information in the highlighted sentence in paragraph 3? Incorrect choices change the meaning in important ways or leave out essential information.**

Ⓐ Shoemakers previously made themselves responsible for specific tasks, but were given more general duties to keep the business running smoothly.

Ⓑ In the past, shoemakers performed every step in making shoes, but now they were given specific jobs to perform.

Ⓒ Before the innovations, shoemakers took an interest in every aspect of the shoemaking process, but later they opted for performing specific tasks.

Ⓓ Once innovations were introduced, there was virtually no difference in a shoemaker's job, including the jobs of sole making and piece stitching.

17

Sparta and Athens

1 ➡ For many generations in ancient Greece, Sparta and Athens participated in a fierce rivalry. These two city-states, the largest in Ancient Greece at the time, may have shared a common language, but their cultures could not have been more dissimilar. The values of each had a significant impact on the structure of their governments and societies, and these differences eventually led to warfare.

2 ➡ Above all, Spartans valued power. Sparta's government was an oligarchy, a government run by a small, elite segment of society. Two kings oversaw an assembly of decision-making aristocrats, which meant that most of Sparta's power was in the hands of only a few wealthy families. Interested in expanding their hegemony, they set out to create a strong military to attack Greece's neighbors. Once under Spartan control, new citizens were typically enslaved and used for basic labor. Laws were strict, and these people had very little freedom. The slaves, called Helots, were responsible for all nonmilitary work, but they frequently revolted. As a result, Sparta's military was as concerned with keeping peace in its city as it was with making conquests.

3 ➡ Sparta's culture basically revolved around the acquisition and retention of power by means of its military forces. Indeed, all education focused on military strategies and war tactics, and the typical Spartan man spent most of his adult life in military service. Particularly rare for the time, women enjoyed considerable freedom and had the same rights as men. They were educated and generally physically fit, for they were expected to raise healthy, astute sons who would later become strong soldiers in the military. [1] Spartans were not allowed to participate in either trade or the production of goods, as their roles in society were strictly tied to military service. Regardless, Sparta was able to create an economy that was self-sufficient and quite successful with citizens able to enjoy a high quality of life.

4 ➡ In contrast to the overtly militaristic Sparta, Athens is thought of as the birthplace of democracy. This process of democratization began under the rule of Solon, the first known literary figure from Athens. [2] He eliminated the practice of slavery and began reforming both the harsh system of serfdom and the rigid laws put in place under the preceding ruler Draco. Solon divided citizens into four classes, based on their wealth and their ability to perform military service. The poorest class, by far the majority of the population, received political rights for the first time. They were able to vote in the Assembly, but only the upper classes could hold political office. Therefore, it should be noted that although Athens was making strides towards a more even distribution of power, it still remained controlled by a moderate, male-dominated aristocracy.

5 ➡ In addition to politics, society in Athens contrasted significantly to that of Sparta in two very distinct ways. First, although power was more evenly distributed and there were no slaves, women possessed no freedoms and were solely responsible for the care of their fathers, husbands, and children. They could not undergo formal schooling and were expected to stay indoors. Second, whereas Sparta focused on physical fitness, Athenians

were dedicated to the arts. The wealth of Athens, brought on by trade and a distributed class system, attracted many talented people from all over Greece. This created a wealthy leisure class who became patrons of the arts. With the Athenian government also sponsoring education and the arts, Athens quickly became the center of Greek literature, philosophy and art. Even in the aim to expand its influence within Greece, Athens did so not only by using its military, but also by emphasizing the development of art, architecture, and philosophy.

1. **Which of the sentences below best expresses the essential information in the highlighted sentence in paragraph 3? Incorrect choices change the meaning in important ways or leave out essential information.**

Ⓐ Spartan culture was directly influenced by its powerful military force.

Ⓑ With a society based on its military force, Spartans could neither produce nor trade goods.

Ⓒ Sparta initially allowed its citizens to trade goods, although this right was later revoked.

Ⓓ Some Spartans did trade goods with neighboring communities, but they were still soldiers.

2. **Which of the sentences below best expresses the essential information in the highlighted sentence in paragraph 4? Incorrect choices change the meaning in important ways or leave out essential information.**

Ⓐ Solon reinforced many of the laws that had been enacted by his predecessor, but he ended slavery.

Ⓑ Under Solon, slavery, serfdom, and many strict laws that had been created by Draco were removed or changed.

Ⓒ Solon thought many laws instituted by Draco were unfair, so he eliminated them.

Ⓓ Draco created many laws that divided society, so Solon passed new ones to make people more equal.

Test

TOEFL Reading

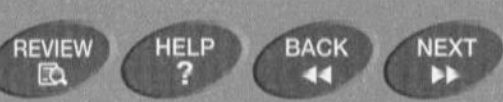

Global Warming and Geoengineering

1 ➡ The phenomenon of global warming is undeniable, and there is ample evidence that humans are responsible for its rapidity over the last 100 years. Global warming itself is a natural process that Earth has experienced throughout its history. There have been many ice ages, periods when ice sheets have advanced towards the equator, and they happen fairly regularly. In fact, we are living in an interglacial period, a warm period between ice ages, and human activity is known to disrupt this natural cycle of the Earth. The increasing rate at which warming has occurred over the last few decades is the result of human production of greenhouse gases. These gases are carbon dioxide (CO2), methane, and nitrous oxide, all of which allow solar energy to enter the atmosphere but do not allow heat to escape back into space. These gases are among the chief byproducts of the combustion of fossil fuels, with CO2 making up 72% of total emissions. Therefore, we clearly must reduce emissions of CO2.

2 ➡ Unfortunately, the majority of greenhouse gases are released through the generation of energy by burning coal. Scientists are laboring to develop alternative energy sources and alternative fuels, but their progress is far outstripped by our increasing population's demand for energy. Consequently, a method must be found by which to remove CO2 from the atmosphere as energy technology advances to the point where our output no longer exceeds the planet's ability to process it naturally. The concept of manipulating the planet to address issues of climate change is referred to geoengineering, and many ideas have been proposed to achieve the goal of lowering worldwide average temperatures. These have included pumping special aerosolized chemicals into the atmosphere to negate the greenhouse gases' effects and fixing CO2 into rock

1. All of the following are mentioned in paragraph 1 EXCEPT

Ⓐ the production of greenhouse gases is the major cause of global warming
Ⓑ greenhouse gases make the Earth's atmosphere trap energy from the sun
Ⓒ global warming would never have occurred without human intervention
Ⓓ CO2 and methane are generated as a result of burning fossil fuels

2. In paragraph 1, what can be inferred about the Earth?

Ⓐ Fossil fuels keep solar energy from entering the Earth.
Ⓑ The Earth will experience another ice age.
Ⓒ The Earth's temperature will begin to fall in a few decades.
Ⓓ CO2 doesn't exist naturally in the atmosphere.

3. According to paragraph 2, which of the following is true of geoengineering?

Ⓐ Many scientists warn that it may be detrimental to our health.
Ⓑ It is a scientific study on developing alternative energy sources.
Ⓒ The process of using aerosolized chemicals is considered impractical.
Ⓓ Its objective is to reduce the average temperature of the Earth.

4. The word "These" in paragraph 2 refers to

Ⓐ issues
Ⓑ ideas
Ⓒ temperatures
Ⓓ chemicals

TOEFL Reading

formations deep within the planet's crust. Other scientists suggest more organic approaches.

3 ➡ Organisms that employ photosynthesis absorb CO2 and process it with energy from the sun to produce their food, and at the same time they generate oxygen. Following this line of thought, many countries in Europe have been engaging in intensive tree planting programs to offset their carbon production. This has proven fairly effective, but trees grow relatively slowly, and they release enough CO2 after they die and break down to negate much of their positive effect. However, there are organisms that absorb immense quantities of CO2 and have a short life span: plankton. Phytoplankton such as algae actually makes up the largest percentage of the ocean's biomass, and they are an integral part of the food chain. Unfortunately, they have also been declining since the 1950s, so promoting their growth seems like an obvious solution.

4 ➡ Some scientists believe that triggering the resumed growth of phytoplankton in the world's oceans will cause them to devour CO2, helping to alleviate global warming. To test this theory, scientists carried out an experiment in an eddy in the Southern Ocean near Antarctica. [■A] There they added iron fertilizer similar to what is used on many land flora to the water and observed the results. [■B] They ascertained that the nutrients that algae need to form their protective shells decreased as the dissolved inorganic carbon in the water, which is supplied from the atmosphere and exists in similar concentration, declined significantly. [■C] This means that the algae developed into a large algal bloom. [■D] These measurements returned to normal 24 days later, when the majority of the fertilized algae were dead. As an added bonus, the deceased algae settle to the ocean floor, where the carbon they contain will remain for decades or longer if they are incorporated into sediment.

5. According to paragraph 3, why has phytoplankton become important?

Ⓐ They can work just like trees and grow faster than them.

Ⓑ They play a significant role in the ocean food chain.

Ⓒ Their actual number has been decreasing since the 1950s.

Ⓓ They can be obtained in large quantities at low prices.

6. The word "devour" in paragraph 4 is closest in meaning to

Ⓐ control

Ⓑ decompose

Ⓒ absorb

Ⓓ release

7. Which of the sentences below best expresses the essential information in the highlighted sentence in the passage? Incorrect choices change the meaning in important ways or leave out essential information.

Ⓐ The decayed algae in the ocean are an essential source of carbon for sea creatures.

Ⓑ It is also beneficial that the carbon in the deceased algae will sink to the bottom of the ocean.

Ⓒ Marine deposits are mainly composed of the sediment of decades-old carbon from decayed algae.

Ⓓ The carbon in the dead algae will be held in the ocean floor for a long time as they turn into sediment.

Lesson 01 Identifying Details

TOEFL Reading

5 ➡ Oceanic algal fertilization seems promising, but it has its drawbacks. In a large scale operation, there is no guarantee what type of algae will bloom, and there are other algae which produce nitrous oxide while alive and deplete oxygen after they die. These algae could create massive dead zones like those near Louisiana, where agricultural runoff of fertilizers has promoted the growth of algae to such an extent that nothing else can survive in those waters. However, another team of scientists have developed a process that circumvents these problems. They propose the construction of complexes on land where the desired algae is grown. They have demonstrated that their concept works, but it too has serious faults. The growth ponds would occupy large areas of land, and the process requires huge amounts of water. Work continues to refine this process, but it is unlikely that it will soon become a viable option.

8. In paragraph 5, the author mentions massive dead zones in order to

Ⓐ highlight how algal fertilization facilitates global warming

Ⓑ indicate a possible negative result of oceanic algal fertilization

Ⓒ give an example of air pollution caused by fertilizers

Ⓓ prove how some scientific research is threatening marine life

TOEFL Reading

9. Look at the four squares [■] that indicate where the following sentence could be added to the passage.

They used an eddy because the swirling water column kept the fertilizer from dispersing out into the ocean.

Where would the sentence best fit?

Click on a square [■] to add the sentence to the passage.

10. **Directions:** An introductory sentence for a brief summary of the passage is provided below. Complete the summary by selecting the THREE answer choices that express the most important ideas in the passage. Some sentences do not belong in the summary because they express ideas that are not presented in the passage or are minor ideas in the passage.
This question is worth 2 points.

As global warming is accelerating, scientists have become more interested in geoengineering to lower the average temperature.

-
-
-

Answer Choices

Ⓐ Greenhouse gases are byproducts of fossil fuels, and they directly cause climate change.
Ⓑ Scientists are trying to develop alternative energy sources in order to discontinue the use of fossil fuels.
Ⓒ Geoengineering includes both the artificial method of using aerosolized chemicals and the natural method of growing algae.
Ⓓ Scientists revealed that algae can effectively reduce CO2 when their growth is promoted.
Ⓔ Oceanic algal fertilization has such a bright future that its side effects and drawbacks will be solved in several years.
Ⓕ Oceanic algal fertilization has a few limitations, including the possibility of growing harmful types of algae.

Drag your answer choices to the spaces where they belong.
To remove an answer choice, click on it. To review the passage, click on **View Text**.

TOEFL Reading

Division of Lizard Species

1 ➡ Lizards comprise approximately sixty percent of all reptiles and there are around 6,000 individual species. They exhibit a wide range of attributes, including varying from just a few centimeters to about three meters in length. Despite this diversity, they are often divided into two main categories determined by their overall foraging behavior. Many lizards sit motionless and ambush their prey as it ignorantly wanders past them, whereas others actually actively seek out and hunt down their prey. These two distinct foraging methods are referred to as "sit-and-wait" and "active" foraging. This is a somewhat artificial categorization as some species actually possess a combination of attributes from both categories, but many do fall neatly into either category. Moreover, these foraging techniques have also led to significant physiological differences between the groups.

2 ➡ As the name of their category states, sit-and-wait foragers are mostly sedentary creatures. They usually perch on rocks and trees where their coloration allows them to very effectively blend in with the surface. These lizards have excellent eyesight that they use to survey their surroundings for prey. [■A] This allows them to be very selective in what they eat, which is normally insects or smaller animals that walk past them. [■B] Most species have a fleshy tongue that they use to grab their food. [■C] Therefore, they only strike when their food is unlikely to escape, and they only flee when a predator is clearly about to attack. [■D] Since they cannot travel long distances, they usually seek shelter when their lives are threatened. Chameleons embody all of the specialized attributes of the sit-and-wait foragers. They are masters of camouflage and they can change colors to blend in with their background. Their tongues are also quite long and sticky, allowing them to capture insects that are far from their

11. The word "sedentary" in paragraph 2 is closest in meaning to

Ⓐ settled
Ⓑ tolerant
Ⓒ lenient
Ⓓ indulgent

12. According to paragraph 2, which of the following is true of sit-and-wait foragers?

Ⓐ Long periods of physical activity are possible but not undertaken unless needed.
Ⓑ Their tongues are optimized for seizing the limbs of their prey.
Ⓒ They usually remain concealed in their surroundings.
Ⓓ Because they are seldom stationary for prolonged periods, their sensory faculty has to be sharp to detect prey.

13. Which of the following is NOT mentioned in paragraph 3 as a feature of active foraging lizards?

Ⓐ They are persistent in hunting down their prey.
Ⓑ They track down their prey by utilizing olfaction.
Ⓒ Their bodies are camouflaged to make it harder for predators to spot them.
Ⓓ While they have poor vision, they also have powerful jaws and sharp teeth.

perch when they rapidly extrude them.

3 ➡ The active foragers, on the other hand, are very mobile creatures. Since they move through a variety of environments, their background is constantly changing, which makes it impossible for them to effectively camouflage themselves. Instead, they typically have solid colored bodies or stripes, which serve to keep their outline obscure and confuse predators that are trying to visually track them. They tend to have long bodies with very long tails and legs. These lizards are far more opportunistic than their stationary cousins, and they locate their prey using their sense of smell. They also normally have relatively poor eyesight that allows them to see little beyond their immediate surroundings. They use their jaws to capture their prey, so they often have much more developed teeth and musculature in their mouths. Such lizards will cover large areas searching for prey, and they will run equally long distances when threatened, often changing direction and relying upon their agility to escape. Monitor lizards are exemplary members of the active forager group with their long powerful limbs and bodies and sharp, curved teeth. They readily run long distances, deliver painful wounding bites, and track their prey for long distances using their heightened sense of smell and running ability. Their tongues are slender and forked, and they regularly flick them out to sample the air for scents, much like snakes.

4 ➡ The differences between sit-and-wait and active foragers are profound, and they extend down to a cellular level. The hunting strategies that these animals employ dictate their metabolisms and their musculature. All of the cells in an organism use a chemical called Adenosine Triphosphate (ATP) to power their functions. Sit-and-wait foragers have mostly fast-twitch muscles, which create their ATP from glycogen. This process

14. Which of the sentences below best expresses the essential information in the highlighted sentence in the passage? Incorrect choices change the meaning in important ways or leave out essential information.

Ⓐ To hunt for prey and escape from predators, active foraging lizards travel long distances in a haphazard manner.

Ⓑ The amount of distance travelled by active foraging lizards to hunt for prey is equal to the amount of distance travelled by their prey to avoid predation.

Ⓒ Active foragers, which deftly travel long distances to avoid predation, also travel just as far to hunt for prey.

Ⓓ By quickly moving and shifting directions, active foragers are successful at tracking their prey which travels far when threatened.

15. Which of the following can be inferred from paragraph 4?

Ⓐ Lizards' muscles evolved to suit their respective foraging behaviors.

Ⓑ More glucose is present in sit-and-wait foragers than in active foragers.

Ⓒ Active foraging lizards need less oxygen for their metabolism than sit-and-wait foragers.

Ⓓ ATP is produced from a chemical reaction that is not easily sustained for long.

Lesson 01
Identifying Details

TOEFL Reading

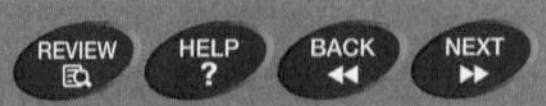

takes place without using additional oxygen, which means that they are capable of explosive surges of speed, but they tire quickly as this chemical reaction cannot be sustained. Active foragers have mostly slow-twitch muscles that process glucose using oxygen to produce ATP, which gives them their endurance. Therefore, the metabolism of sit-and-wait foragers is described as anaerobic, while that of active foragers is aerobic.

5 ➡ Despite all of these differences, both groups of lizards share many anatomical features such as their skeletal structure. Many members of both groups also employ an ability called autotomy. When they are captured by the tail, these lizards can amputate their own tail. This not only releases the lizard from the predator's grasp, but the severed member will continue to wriggle, keeping the attacker's attention. Some species take this a step further as their tails are bright blue in contrast to their brown and green bodies. This bright tail invites predators to attack it instead of the main body, increasing the lizard's chances to escape. Of course, losing the tail is detrimental to the lizard as the tail is used to store energy reserves and it aids in balancing the body while running, but they can grow a new one later.

16. What is the main purpose of paragraph 5?

Ⓐ To describe the characteristics of lizard tails

Ⓑ To prove that bright colors are not detrimental to survival

Ⓒ To introduce features that are common to both types of lizards

Ⓓ To discuss how autotomy can increase the chances of survival

17. According to paragraph 5, which of the following are functions of tails in lizards? Click on two answers.

Ⓐ They can be regenerated.

Ⓑ They help maintain equilibrium.

Ⓒ They slip out of predator's grasp.

Ⓓ They contain energy reserves.

18. According to the passage, all of the following are differences between sit-and-wait and active foragers EXCEPT

Ⓐ the way they metabolize

Ⓑ the type of food they eat

Ⓒ the method adopted in hunting

Ⓓ the level of physical activity they engage in

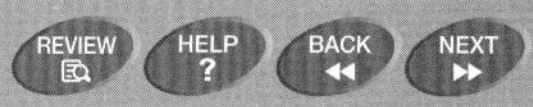

19. Look at the four squares [■] that indicate where the following sentence could be added to the passage.

They are capable of short bursts of speed that can be used to attack their prey or to flee from danger, but sustained periods of activity will quickly exhaust them.

Where would the sentence best fit?

Click on a square [■] to add the sentence to the passage.

20. Directions: An introductory sentence for a brief summary of the passage is provided below. Complete the summary by selecting the THREE answer choices that express the most important ideas in the passage. Some sentences do not belong in the summary because they express ideas that are not presented in the passage or are minor ideas in the passage.
This question is worth 2 points.

Of the numerous lizard species around the world, many can be divided into two categories according to their foraging behavior.

-
-
-

Answer Choices

Ⓐ Sit-and-wait foragers typically stay still until they are sure of successfully catching their prey or certain that a predator is about to strike.

Ⓑ Chameleons are typical sit-and-wait foragers that remain stationary and hidden by changing their body colors to blend in with their surroundings.

Ⓒ While active foragers primarily have an anaerobic metabolism, sit-and-wait foragers have an aerobic metabolism.

Ⓓ While each group has unique physiological features, they nonetheless share the same skeletal structure and self-defense mechanisms like autotomy.

Ⓔ Active foragers utilize their sense of smell to relentlessly pursue their prey, and they have slow-twitch muscles that sustain them during intense prolonged activity.

Ⓕ One of the main differences between the two groups lies in the fact that they draw on different sugars for their metabolism.

Drag your answer choices to the spaces where they belong.
To remove an answer choice, click on it. To review the passage, click on **View Text**.

Lesson

02 Fact & Negative Fact

Lesson Outline

- 사실 및 틀린 정보 찾기(Fact & Negative Fact) 문제는 지문에 제시된 세부 정보에 관해 묻는 문제이다. Fact 문제는 지문에 제시된 내용과 일치하는 보기를, Negative Fact 문제는 지문에 제시되지 않았거나 지문의 내용과 다른 보기를 고르는 문제다. 수험자가 이미 알고 있는 배경 지식과는 상관 없이 지문에 언급된 내용만으로 문제를 풀어야 한다.
- 이 유형의 문제는 한 지문당 3~4개가 출제된다.
- 질문이 출제된 단락의 번호가 문제와 함께 제시되며 해당 단락은 [➡]로 표시된다.

Typical Questions 

Fact

- Which of the following does paragraph X mention?
  다음 중 X단락에서 언급된 것은 무엇인가?
- According to paragraph X, why/how/what ~?
  X단락에 따르면, 왜/어떻게/무엇이 ~인가?
- According to paragraph X, which of the following is true of ~?
  X단락에 따르면, 다음 중 ~에 대해 사실인 것은 무엇인가?

참고 가끔 정답을 두 개 고르라는 문제도 출제된다.

Negative Fact

- According to the passage, which of the following is NOT true of ~?
  지문에 따르면, 다음 중 ~에 대해 사실이 아닌 것은 무엇인가?
- All of the following are mentioned in paragraph X EXCEPT
  다음 중 X단락에서 언급되지 않은 것은

Learning Strategies

Step 1 문제를 읽은 뒤 해당 내용이 지문의 어느 부분에서 나왔는지 확인한다. 문제에서 '단락 X'라고 직접 말해 줄 때도 있다.

⋯› Reading 영역에서는 문제 순서가 거의 지문의 흐름대로 나오는 경우가 많으므로 참고하자. 이 단락 저 단락을 넘나들며 문제가 출제되는 경우는 거의 없다.

⋯› 패러프레이징에 여전히 주의해야 한다. 지문에 쓰인 단어와 같은 단어를 쓰지만 틀린 내용을 담고 있는 보기가 있으므로 유의한다.

Step 2 패러프레이징된 보기가 있다는 점을 앞서 기억했다면, 보기를 전부 읽어보며 오답인지 정답인지 하나씩 확인해 나가자.

⋯› 먼저 질문에서 무엇을 묻고 있는지 정확히 파악한 뒤 보기를 살펴보자. 보기의 종류는 다음과 같다.

① 지문이나 질문에서 직접 언급된 단어를 포함하는 보기

② 지문·질문과 관련된 내용을 패러프레이징한 보기

③ 지문에서 아예 등장하지 않은 내용을 담고 있는 보기

⋯› 정답이 ①번 유형인 경우는 많이 없으며, 답은 보통 패러프레이징을 거치기 때문에 단어만 훑어보지 말고 보기 네 개를 전부 읽어보고 확인해야 한다.

⋯› 고난도 문제일 경우 보기 네 개가 전부 패러프레이징되어 출제될 수도 있고, 사실을 약간만 왜곡하여 수험자를 더욱 혼란스럽게 하기도 한다.

⋯› 지문에서 아예 언급되지 않은 내용을 담고 있는 보기는 오답이므로 소거하자.

Example

Q. According to paragraph 6, why did the International Style become popular?

1 문제를 읽은 뒤 해당 내용이 지문의 어느 부분에서 나왔는지 확인한다. 문제에서 '단락 X'라고 직접 말해줄 때도 있다.

···› 6단락에서 'International Style'이라는 단어를 찾는다.

6 ➡ Nonetheless, this idea, which came to be known as International Style, **served as a prototype for all modern cities which deal with the problem of accommodating high-density urban populations.** Modern design leaned towards ridding buildings of decorative elements and placing priority on function over form. By utilizing mass-produced, inexpensive building materials such as glass and reinforced concrete, large-scale urban development was made possible. Today, the construction of high-rise buildings with minimalist, repetitive structures is creating a sense of uniformity in cities throughout the world.

이 '국제 양식'은 '고밀도 도시 인구를 수용하는 문제에 대처하는 모든 현대 도시의 원형이 되었다'라고 나와 있다. 뒤에 국제 양식에 관한 설명이 더 이어진다.

2 보기를 하나씩 읽어보며 확인하도록 하자.

Ⓐ It created similar-looking cities throughout the world.

···› 지문에 언급된 내용이긴 하지만 이것 때문에 국제 양식이 인기를 끈 것은 아니다.

Ⓑ The materials it used kept the costs of large-scale urban development low.

···› '국제 양식이 사용한 자재가 대규모 도시 개발의 비용을 줄였다'고 한다.

Ⓒ It attempted to address the problem of urban sprawl in modern times.

···› '국제 양식이 현대의 도시 확산 문제를 다루려고 시도했다'고 한다. 이는 지문에 나오지 않은 내용이다. 지문에 언급된 문제는 '고밀도 도시 인구를 수용하는 것'이다.

Ⓓ It did not have any of the decorative elements from the previous era.

···› 국제 양식에 관해 부분적으로 옳지만 '전혀(any of)'라는 단어가 맞지 않는다. 장식적인 요소를 없애는 쪽으로 기울었다는 언급은 있지만 장식적 요소가 전혀 없었다고 말하고 있지는 않다.

답은 Ⓑ이다. '고밀도 도시 인구 수용을 위해 대량 생산된 값싼 건축 자재를 이용해 대규모 도시 개발이 가능해졌다(By utilizing mass-produced, inexpensive building materials such as glass and reinforced concrete, large-scale urban development was made possible.)'는 내용이 지문에 나와 있다. 보기가 항상 패러프레이징된다는 점을 기억해야 한다.

Practice

정답 및 해석 | P. 18

[01-02] **Read the following paragraphs and write T for True and F for False for questions Ⓐ-Ⓓ.**

01

Erosion is the displacement of soil and rocks by the forces of wind, water, and ice, along with the interaction of gravity and human activity. Although similar, weathering is to be distinguished from erosion in that it involves the decomposition of rocks. Erosion is caused by natural processes, but in many instances, it is helped along by increased human activity. This includes deforestation, overgrazing and road construction. In order to counteract the amount of erosion, humans have begun reforestation.

Ⓐ ______ Ice is one of the causes of erosion.

Ⓑ ______ Weathering is the same as erosion.

Ⓒ ______ Deforestation is an example of human activity that causes erosion.

Ⓓ ______ Gravity is instrumental in preventing erosion.

02

Water has many characteristics that are important for sustaining life, such as being a good solvent and having high surface tension. At four degrees Celsius, water is at its greatest density. It becomes less dense as it heats up or freezes. Because water is a stable polar molecule in the atmosphere, it plays an important role in absorbing infrared radiation, which is crucial in limiting the greenhouse effect. In addition, water has a very high specific heat capacity which helps in regulating global temperatures.

Ⓐ ______ Water is an unstable molecule.

Ⓑ ______ Water is denser at zero degrees Celsius than it is at four degrees Celsius.

Ⓒ ______ Water performs a vital role in absorbing infrared radiation.

Ⓓ ______ Water's specific heat capacity helps to control global temperatures.

03

The Tongues of Snakes

A forked tongue, a tongue which splits into two distinct parts at the tip, is a common feature of various species of reptiles such as lizards and snakes. Reptiles smell using the tip of their tongue, and a forked tongue allows them to sense the direction from which a smell is coming. Scientists believe that forked tongues might have evolved in these reptiles for various purposes. The main advantage to having a forked tongue is that more surface area is available for chemicals to contact, increasing the potential for sensing a smell. The tongue is flicked out of the mouth regularly to sample the chemical environment. This form of chemical sampling enables animals to sense non-volatile chemicals, which cannot be detected by simply using the olfactory system. This increased ability to sense chemicals allows these creatures to identify prey, recognize kinship, choose mates, and locate shelter.

According to the passage, reptiles exploit a forked tongue because

Ⓐ they perceive the odor to trace the chemical stimuli

Ⓑ they touch the body of their prey to catch it

Ⓒ they spray venom to kill their prey by flicking their tongue

Ⓓ they threaten predators like humans

04

Water on Mars

Clear evidence suggests that liquid water once existed in great quantity on the surface of Mars, including photos taken by several probes. The Viking orbiters and the Mars Global Surveyor relayed images back to Earth of surface features including channels and canyons that looked to have been formed by flowing water. Especially, runoff channels show clear signs of flowing features. The channels, which can be found in the southern areas, appear to have formed broad systems—some of which extend many hundreds of kilometers in length—of interconnecting, twisting channels that seem to merge into larger, wider channels. These channels closely resemble Earth's river systems, and geologists believe that they are remnants of long-gone rivers that once carried Mars' rainfall from the mountains down into the valleys. The flowing marks on the ground show that the atmosphere was thicker, the surface was warmer, and there was an abundance of water.

According to the passage, what does the author mention about Mars?

Ⓐ The atmosphere of Mars was once thinner than it is today.

Ⓑ The river systems of Mars were once more extensive than those of Earth.

Ⓒ There was precipitation on parts of Mars.

Ⓓ There are remains of organisms that resemble bacteria.

05

The Black Death

The Black Death, a bubonic plague that swept through Europe from 1347 to 1350, stemmed from China or central Asia and was spread by the merchants along the Silk Road. It is generally believed that the Black Plague was brought to England by people who had been infected on the European mainland. The streets were filthy as all sorts of animals and humans lived side by side, and had abundant parasites, so this communicable disease would have spread easily in such conditions. It is estimated that this pandemic killed between a third and more than half of the British population. The most immediate consequence people experienced after the Black Death struck the prosperous nation was that the decrease in population caused a shortage of labor, which led to a subsequent rise in wages. However, the landowning classes and government tried to curb this development through legislation and punitive measures, leading to deep resentment among the lower classes. Hence, of all the aftereffects of the plague, including religious and social upheavals, the Peasants' Revolt in 1381 had the most severe effects on the society.

According to the passage, what factor made the laborers become upset with government authorities?

Ⓐ Authorities did not come up with a plan for public hygiene, and the disease swiftly spread all over the country.

Ⓑ Governments forbade patients from working, and workers suffered from the hardships of life.

Ⓒ Governments suppressed the inflation of wages caused by the overall decrease of labor supply.

Ⓓ Because of the epidemic, governments prohibited trade with the European mainland.

06

Desertification in the Southwest of the United States

The Southwest of the United States has long been a hot and arid land because of climatic changes. However, this expanse has recently been rapidly devastated by desertification, which is the expansion of desert-like conditions into areas where they did not previously exist. Of all the causes that expedite the phenomenon in this area, the primary one is population growth and the problems it causes. First, the excessive number of livestock which ranchers graze there consumes much of the vegetation cover, and trample the soil at a fast pace. As a result of this, the smashed soil is easily eroded by rain or wind. The loose soil is blown completely away, leaving a stony surface, and eventually making the area more barren and arid. Another reason is the intensive firewood gathering. The lack of trees in the Southwest means there are no roots to help keep topsoil in place. In conjunction with the overcultivation, which strips fertile soil of effective nutrients, the wind and the elements sweep away the best soil, making the land infertile and more susceptible to desertification.

In the passage, all of the following are mentioned as the causes of the desertification in the southwestern U.S. EXCEPT

Ⓐ extraction of too many nutrients by overcultivation

Ⓑ excessive livestock grazing

Ⓒ logging large quantities of lumber

Ⓓ migration in search of fertile soil

07

Farming Techniques in Medieval Europe

As the population of medieval Europe gradually increased, innovative farming techniques helped yield greater amounts of food. There were several methods that contributed to increasing the agricultural output. Blacksmiths forged plows and spades that helped improve productivity by preparing the soil for planting. In addition, livestock farming produced cattle and horses of higher quality, which were used by farmers to till the land. As draft animals were able to pull heavy wooden and iron plows, the use of animals in farming led to easier breaking up of the fertile ground. This innovation enabled the farmers to till even marginal, rocky land for sowing and raising crops. Moreover, the introduction of a crop rotation system ensured that the soil in a given patch of arable land was not depleted of its nutrients, enabling long-term farming in one area. All these factors contributed to agricultural progress, allowing a more stable lifestyle to be adopted and leading to the growth of urban centers and to more civilized lives.

According to the passage, all of the following are mentioned as causes of greater crop yield EXCEPT

Ⓐ livestock ranching

Ⓑ equipment for cultivation

Ⓒ civilized lifestyle

Ⓓ enhanced agricultural expertise

08

Merce Cunningham

One of the most innovative and imaginative choreographers of the 20th century, Merce Cunningham abandoned not only conventional music forms but also commonplace patterns of development such as cause and effect and climax. He taught dancers the basic skills of dancing, but left it up to them to improvise and express themselves in whatever way they saw fit. Cunningham was not interested in telling a story or exploring psychological relationships in art, rather the subject of his dance was the dance itself. Inspired by Albert Einstein's saying, "There are no fixed points in space," Cunningham developed a creative method he termed 'Chance Operations.' This method was also influenced by Dadaism, which inspired Cunningham to create a number of dance phrases and use atypical items like dice, cards, or coins to decide on order, number of repetitions, direction, and spatial relations. He would also often invite musicians to create scores and artists to create visual environments. Cunningham would then create movements to match the results. These collaborations made it possible for Cunningham to create choreography that could never be achieved through traditional methods.

Based on the passage, which of the following is NOT true about Merce Cunningham?

Ⓐ He implemented ideas from other fields in developing his creations.

Ⓑ He encouraged his dancers to be spontaneous and expressive.

Ⓒ He often worked from what musicians and artists would present him, matching the outcome of their creations.

Ⓓ He regularly sought assistance from artists in creating scenery and musicians to enhance a performance's storyline.

09

Sand Dune

The field of physical geography defines dunes as hills that are formed by a process known as deposition, occurring when wind blows sand eroded from mountains to areas with high volumes of sand. The shape that is created when sand reaches its destination is determined not only by a dune's mass but also by the wind system in its area, both of which affect the number and positioning of slip faces, basically the steep sides of a dune. Furthermore, dunes are classified in terms of the positioning and number of slip faces they exhibit. Of all the dune types, the crescentic dune is the most prevalent dune shape on Earth, even though it comprises only a small percentage of the Earth's dune area. This fact results from the dune's relatively small mass, as the world's largest crescentic dunes are up to thirty meters in height and four kilometers in length and width. The crescentic dune displays its individual slip face on its concave side. Additionally, it is formed by a wind blowing in a single direction, and it can move, another important consideration in the study of dunes, faster and farther than any other type of dune. These are, once more, inherent traits for a small dune like the crescentic.

According to the passage, which of the following is NOT true of crescentic dunes?

Ⓐ Their movement and shape are stable for being so small.

Ⓑ They are the most frequently occurring dunes.

Ⓒ They can move more swiftly than other types.

Ⓓ They are generally smaller in scale than other dune types.

10

The Galapagos Islands

The Galapagos Islands are an archipelago of volcanic islands located 900 km west of South America. These islands are perfect for organisms' evolution because they are neither too far from nor too close to the mainland, allowing animals to travel only sporadically. Natural phenomena such as wind or ocean currents sometimes carry a few individuals of a mainland species to an island in the archipelago. If the individuals successfully reproduce on the island, their descendants may establish a population. The vast expanse of ocean that isolates the island from the mainland geographically impedes their interaction with other members of their species. Thus, over generations the island population diverges from the mainland species. Individuals of the diverging population may in turn colonize other islands in the archipelago, repeating the evolutionary process. Habitats and selection pressures that differ between the islands can foster even more divergence from the ancestral species. For example, finches living in the Galapagos Islands, also known as Darwin's finches, were most likely blown in by a storm. Over a long period of time, and hundreds of generations, these finches have evolved into 15 different species, all with varying beak size and shape. These various finches all come from the same ancestors, but they have diverged into separate species with noticeable behavioral differences from island to island.

According to the passage, the island species differ from the mainland population because

Ⓐ of the absence of enemies

Ⓑ they establish a strong social network among themselves

Ⓒ the immense ocean functions as an obstruction

Ⓓ they evolve on the island over generations

11

The Rise of Civilization

Data from diverse sources indicate that the first obvious examples of agricultural evidence date back to somewhere around 5,000 BCE in Mesopotamia, North Africa, India, or China. Clearly, in the beginning, farming was not their major way of obtaining food and served only as a supplement to their main method: hunting and gathering. The first people who tried to harvest crops had no reliable techniques or the know-how to sustain themselves purely from growing crops. However, the sudden advance in agriculture was started by people that lived near rivers and planted seeds in floodplains. This allowed people to get a stable source of water from the river instead of relying on unpredictable or seasonal rainfall. This changed the way people lived as nomadic groups of people were able to settle in one place and grow into a community. The increase in food accessibility triggered the expansion of the population, which in turn led to irrigation to bring water to the city to support the demands of the people. Because of the surplus of agricultural products, settled agriculture brought about the development of property rights and legal mechanisms to bring laws into effect. This in turn gave rise to a concept of more complex and hierarchical government organization.

According to the passage, what caused the development of an organized government?

Ⓐ Reliable hunting techniques which led to the waning dependency on farming

Ⓑ The increasing food availability that led to the need to protect their harvest from invaders

Ⓒ The source of water that was directed into the community for fishing

Ⓓ The need to enforce property laws

12

Thermoregulation

All living organisms are influenced by the external temperatures of their environment. Changes in the ambient temperature of its surroundings can cause an animal's body temperature to fluctuate. Therefore, an animal's ability to regulate its body temperature is vital to its survival in extreme environments. As such, animals indigenous to extremely cold climates have evolved various mechanisms for thermoregulation. Most land mammals and birds react to the cold by raising their fur or plumage, which reduces the flow of heat and lowers the energy cost of keeping warm. For example, an arctic fox dressed in its winter fur can sit comfortably in -50 degrees Celsius weather without any need to change its metabolic rate to warm up. Another mechanism employed by animals is shutting down circulation to peripheral systems in order to prevent further heat loss by regulating the blood flow. An Alaskan husky dog may have a core temperature of 38 degrees Celsius, but the temperature in its forelimbs may be 14 degrees and the pads of its feet 0 degrees. As a result, heat loss is reduced by lowering the temperature in the limbs to several degrees below that of the body core, where most of its vital organs are located. The polar bear has dense fur, a layer of blubber up to 11 centimeters thick and black skin for absorbing the heat from light, making it an excellent insulation machine. Some animals also possess behavioral adaptations, such as rolling up into a ball to preserve body heat.

According to the passage, all of the following are polar bears' adaptations to living in a cold area EXCEPT

Ⓐ a thick layer of fatty tissue

Ⓑ a thick coat of hair

Ⓒ the ability to mitigate the cold by varying its blood flow

Ⓓ hide pigmentation that soaks up sunlight

13

Pheromones

1 ➡ The use of pheromones as a system of communication is widespread throughout the natural world. Pheromones are specialized chemicals, that, when secreted, enable individual creatures to communicate with others of the same species. They are often referred to as 'social hormones' because they affect groups of a species. There are several differences between pheromone chemical communication and visual and auditory communication. First, visual and auditory communication is strictly limited by space, while pheromones can carry their message across great distances. Chemical signals also tell the receiver exactly who has sent the message, though with vision and hearing, the origin of the message can be perplexing.

2 ➡ Pheromones are not limited to insects, but they are found in abundance among numerous insect species. Social insects, or insects that live in organized groups, produce a wide variety of pheromones that serve particular functions depending on the situation. Dispensation of pheromones takes place through different exocrine glands on the insect's body, though their exact location on the body depends upon the species of insect. Ants and bees are two good examples of animals with advanced chemical signal abilities. However, due to the relatively undeveloped olfactory technology available to human scientists, the nature and identification of individual pheromones in these animals are extremely difficult to understand.

3 ➡ Depending on the activity, these social insects make use of different pheromones. Ants, for example, spend most of their daylight hours scouting for food to carry back to the nest. If the nest is invaded by a rival nest or another species, the defending ants can send out messages for all able-bodied members of the nest to return and help with defense. Bees, which scout for food from the air, can leave a pheromone trail that allows others of the same hive to locate a nice flowerbed full of nectar. Both ants and bees are capable of leaving a pheromone trail behind them, so if they get lost, they can smell their way back home.

1. **According to paragraph 1, chemical signals and visual and auditory signals differ in that**

Ⓐ humans have much stronger chemical signal capabilities than visual or auditory capabilities

Ⓑ pheromones can be detected over long distances by creatures that are properly equipped to receive the signals

Ⓒ the use of visual and auditory communication is much more precise than the use of chemical signal communication

Ⓓ though insects possess auditory capabilities, they only make use of them when chemical signals fail

2. **According to paragraph 3, what is NOT a function of the chemical signals used by certain social insects?**

Ⓐ As an alert to call others home when the nest or hive is in danger

Ⓑ As a way to find their way home if they get lost

Ⓒ As a method of telling others the way to a food source

Ⓓ As a means of intimidating a member of a different species

14

Communal Roosting

1 ➡ When people think of social animals, humans and their primate cousins usually come to mind. Certain insects such as ants and bees are also common examples of social creatures. However, social activity is not limited to particular mammals or insects. Some birds also exhibit social behavior, especially when resting. Though some birds live very independent lives, there are other birds that exhibit communal roosting behavior, or roosting as a group.

2 ➡ Normally, birds that forage for food as a group roost together as well. Just as foraging for sustenance provides benefits for the group, so does communal roosting. The reasons why some birds roost communally are not always clear to see, but some of them are very noticeable and logical. During frigid winters, roosting is especially beneficial. Pigeons, sparrows, and bluebirds are only a few species that huddle together for warmth in the winter. By squeezing in together, the birds reduce their own amount of body surface that is exposed to the freezing cold. In fact, just two birds huddling close can save up to a third of their body heat.

3 ➡ Another benefit believed to result from communal roosting is that the communal roost may act as a type of communication center where birds share information, either directly or indirectly. Groups of birds from the roost forage together during the day and when they return to the roost in the evening, each group can determine who is well-fed and who isn't. As a result, the well-fed birds can avoid the areas where the hungry birds foraged for the day. Through these observations, groups that didn't find as much to eat that day can follow the well-fed groups the next day back to where an abundance of food is available. This information can be invaluable for foragers, unlike solitary birds of prey that receive nourishment from a single kill made on their daily hunt.

4 ➡ Finally, as the saying goes, "There is safety in numbers." Initially, there can be added dangers from roosting and flocking together because the large groups draw the attention of predators. However, more birds mean more eyes being on the alert for danger. In addition, if or when a predator does attack, the abrupt noise and flight of the flock taking to the air can help confuse the predator to the point where it cannot focus on an individual victim. Furthermore, some species of communal birds will even work together to attack and drive away a predator, especially when there are nests full of eggs or young hatchlings.

1. **According to paragraph 2, how can birds keep warmer by huddling together in a communal roost?**

Ⓐ By huddling together, more of the body surface of each bird is exposed to cold air.

Ⓑ The birds with thicker feathers huddle towards the outside of the roost.

Ⓒ Reducing the amount of exposure to the cold reduces the loss of body heat.

Ⓓ Through roosting together, the heat from the birds can warm up the shelter.

2. **According to the passage, which of the following is NOT one of the benefits of communal roosting?**

Ⓐ Birds can work together to scare away another creature looking to harm them.

Ⓑ Birds can reduce the amount of body heat lost on cold winter nights.

Ⓒ Birds can prevent the spread of avian diseases by not roosting with other flocks.

Ⓓ Birds can distinguish the best foraging areas through the observations of roost-mates.

15

Dadaism

1 ➡ Dadaism, an innovative cultural movement, peaked in Switzerland during World War I between 1916 and 1920. This movement mainly involved the visual arts, the performing arts, and literature in nearly all forms. It focused on expressing anti-war sentiments or a total rejection of popular and classical art through cultural works known as anti-art. It is not clear why this movement was termed Dadaism, but theories range from it being chosen as a random, nonsensical term to originating from 'da, da', which means 'yes, yes' in Romanian. Whatever the origin of the term, Dadaism grew to be a powerful influence in the art world.

2 ➡ Dadaism began as an anti-war movement as a reaction to the violence of World War I. In 1916, a group of artists, including Hugo Ball, Tristan Tzara, and Emmy Hennings, gathered at the Cabaret Voltaire in Zurich, Switzerland to discuss art and put on performances. The main focus of these activities was to express their disgust with the war and its causes. According to the Dadaists, oppressive intellectualism and the interests of the rich were the inspirations for the war. Following the close of the Cabaret Voltaire, the Dada activists went on a campaign across Europe to spread their ideas through artistic expression, word of mouth, and Dada publications. With the end of World War I in 1918, the majority of the original Zurich Dadaists returned to their home countries, and some of them started extensions of the Dada movement. As Dadaism developed, it spread across the western world to cities such as Paris, Berlin, New York City, and to parts of Russia.

3 ➡ Dadaism and the traditional concept of art are very different. According to Dadaists, they created 'anti-art'; their goal was to combat the traditional ideas of art. While art was predominantly concerned with aesthetics and relaying meaning, Dadaism paid no attention to aesthetics and left interpretation up to the viewer. As art was intended to appeal to our sensibilities, Dadaist works were meant to offend us. The irony of Dadaism is that though it hoped to destroy traditional cultural aesthetics, it actually came to influence modern art in all its forms.

4 ➡ One of the strongest influences and predecessors of Dadaism was Futurism, an earlier art movement that shunned tradition and embraced speed, technology, and violence. Futurism originated among Italian artists in 1909. However, there was a major difference between Futuristic and Dadaistic dissidence; while Dadaism protested against the war, Futurism celebrated the technology of warfare and the machine age. Futuristic paintings and sculptures glorified war and promoted the growth of fascism. The main influence of Futurism on Dadaism was the diversity of materials used in the work and the idea of viewer-interpretation.

5 ➡ As Dadaism derived from other forms of art, it became the source of subsequent other forms. Most notable among the disciplines that emerged from Dadaism was Surrealism. However, it may be more accurate to say that by the 1920s Dadaism was reforming itself into Surrealism since many of the attributes of Dadaism are also prominent within Surrealism. Both movements highlighted a diversity of materials, affected a broad range of art media from painting to music, and encouraged the freedom of viewers to interpret what they saw based on their own perceptions.

6 ➡ Though Dadaism, by its very nature, opposed our cultural perceptions of what we know as art, the movement was able to gather a large following in the comparatively brief period that it was popular. The movement peaked in 1924, but it continues in some form to this very day. After the end of World War I, Dadaism became much less active due to renewed optimism in art and literature that contradicted the movement's original cynical nature.

1. According to paragraph 2, Dada activists traveled across Europe because

(A) Europe was the center of all artistic movements

(B) World War I had come to an end

(C) they wanted to take their message to others

(D) there were too many intellectuals and rich people in Switzerland

2. According to paragraph 4, which of the following is true of Futurism?

(A) Futurism didn't put a limit on the choice of art materials.

(B) Futurism helped invent various forms of weapons as artwork.

(C) Futurism fought against the rise of Fascism.

(D) Futurists believed that the viewer should not have to interpret the meaning of an artwork.

16

The Ancient Sumerian and Egyptian Civilizations

1 ➡ The invention of irrigation systems in ancient Egypt and Mesopotamia led to the development of powerful civilizations that would last for thousands of years. Both of these civilizations were able to prosper because of their ability to harness resources provided by nearby rivers. The heart of Egypt was nestled in the Nile Valley, whereas the area between the Tigris and Euphrates rivers, in what is now part of modern-day Iraq, is the region where the first civilizations of Mesopotamia developed. Mesopotamia, which comes from a Greek term meaning "between rivers," is an appropriate name since the two great rivers directly led to the rise of civilization in the region.

2 ➡ Both the ancient Egyptians and the Sumerians were extremely successful in utilizing the bounty provided by rivers. Through the development of complicated irrigation systems, they drained marshes, dug canals and cut through riverbanks to redirect water to crops planted in lower lying areas further from the rivers. The amount of cooperation necessary to sustain such systems directly led to the need for and growth of government and law. While Egypt was able to unite under a single pharaoh in a relatively isolated bountiful region between large deserts, the Sumerians had difficulty unifying the city states in the extensive area. Mesopotamia was much more susceptible to invasions from outsiders, and they constantly battled natural obstacles ranging from droughts to floods, extremes in temperature, and violent storms.

3 ➡ The basic raw materials primarily utilized to construct homes and farm structures in both areas have changed little since the first tribes settled down to build communities. These materials included mud brick and mud plaster, both made from the clay found naturally in river soil. Clay was also used in the production of pottery, sculpture, and writing tablets. Once properly mixed and sufficiently dried, the clay products were remarkably sturdy, and many have survived into the modern day. Since both areas are surrounded by desert, wood was scarce and so hardly employed, except for doors and window shutters. Stone, primarily limestone, was available in Egypt but was rare throughout most of the Mesopotamian region. Metals such as gold, silver and copper, shells, and precious stones were also used in ornamental arts.

4 ➡ Both the Egyptian and the Sumerian governments were directly linked to religious life and beliefs. The typical Mesopotamian religious and commercial structure was the ziggurat, a stepped tower, in contrast to the well-known, smooth-sided Egyptian style pyramid. However, all major towns, whether Sumerian or Egyptian, took pride in the construction of their temples. For example, the White Temple, one of the larger ziggurats, stood about 12 meters on a high platform. The purpose of the steps of a ziggurat was to put the priest or king in closer proximity to a particular god, or in reverse, to provide a platform for the deity to use in order to descend to meet the worshipers. Contrary to the ancient Egyptians, the Mesopotamians did not believe that their rulers were actual gods, but rather descendants of gods or mediators between the gods and common people. They took on lofty titles such as 'king of the universe', or more modest titles such as 'shepherd' in recognition of their role as the keeper of the people. Individual Sumerian gods were associated with specific towns and represented natural forces such as the sky, water, and wind. While they were worshipped at the ziggurats, they were also honored at smaller shrines found in the homes of individual families.

5 ➡ Another major difference between the Sumerians and the ancient Egyptians in terms of religion was the attention given to life after death. While Egyptian death rituals carefully prepared important individuals for their next life, the Sumerians gave little thought to the matter. Therefore, the majority of surviving Sumerian writing found on clay tablets deals with everyday activities such as business, city administration, law, politics, birth and death records, and economics. This is in contrast to what has been found of Egyptian records, in which the process of preparing for the afterlife and what was believed to happen after death makes up a large amount of surviving records. In addition, the Egyptian pyramids were built to house the dead, while the Mesopotamian ziggurats were used as a location in which to communicate with the gods throughout daily life.

1. According to paragraph 2, which of the following is true of the Sumerians?

Ⓐ They had one leader to whom the people gave allegiance.

Ⓑ They suffered attacks from outside and problematic weather conditions.

Ⓒ They created the first known civilization.

Ⓓ They often attacked other tribes.

2. According to paragraph 4, which of the following is NOT true of ziggurat?

Ⓐ They had stepped sides.

Ⓑ They were solely for religious purposes.

Ⓒ They were located in every major town.

Ⓓ The steps were thought to enable a priest to get closer to a god.

Test

TOEFL Reading

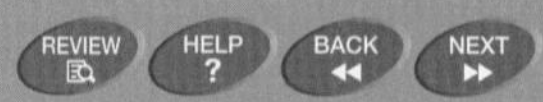

Venice's Water Supply

1 ➡ Venice is one of the most popular tourist destinations in Europe, and it is best known for its system of canals that serve in place of streets. Constructed on a collection of 117 islands which are separated by the canals and connected by bridges where feasible, it is a truly unique city. While the city's identity is defined by the waters of the lagoon it lies in, it has suffered from an ironic dilemma since its inception. These islands that have provided refuge and home to the Venetians for centuries have never been able to provide them with enough drinking water. As a French visitor of the 15th century stated, "In a city in which the inhabitants are in water up to their mouths, they often go thirsty." A variety of solutions have been used to address this lack throughout history, but none have ever been entirely satisfactory.

2 ➡ When Venice was founded in the 5th century, the location was not chosen for its abundant resources, but rather for the safety it provided. Over the centuries, the terrain of Venice allowed it to develop into a maritime power, but it also presented a problem that the people never fully overcame. There was no reliable source of potable water. Although many rivers empty into the lagoon, the massive water pressure from the Adriatic Sea prevents their fresh water from reaching the islands, so the water around the islands is far too salty for human consumption. Instead, this water was used for other domestic and industrial purposes. Each household had two separate sets of buckets: one for taking water from the canals for bathing, washing clothes, or cleaning house, and a second for collecting and storing drinking water.

3 ➡ Even with this careful division, the Venetians had to ensure that the canal water did not become polluted. In order to maintain its quality, the city council issued a pronouncement

1. Why does the author mention a French visitor of the 15th century in paragraph 1?

Ⓐ To personify the issue of water shortage in post Medieval Europe

Ⓑ To introduce an ancient proverb that points out a problem in coastal cities

Ⓒ To provide a firsthand account of a perpetual problem in Venice

Ⓓ To suggest that Venice was a popular tourist destination even in the past

2. What can be inferred from paragraph 2?

Ⓐ Venice was originally founded as a strategic military powerbase.

Ⓑ The salty water surrounding the islands originates from the Adriatic Sea.

Ⓒ Venice is a city that is lacking in natural resources.

Ⓓ The canals met the demand for water for both domestic and drinking purposes.

3. The word "pronouncement" in paragraph 3 is closest in meaning to

Ⓐ disclosure

Ⓑ reference

Ⓒ policy

Ⓓ statement

4. The word "obliged" in paragraph 4 is closest in meaning to

Ⓐ urged

Ⓑ forced

Ⓒ seized

Ⓓ mobilized

TOEFL Reading

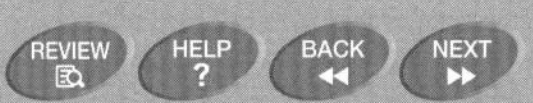

5. According to paragraph 4, how did the Venetians secure fresh water? Click on two answers.

Ⓐ Linking rain gutters to drains
Ⓑ Going ashore to obtain water
Ⓒ Exploiting underground sand deposits
Ⓓ Purifying river water

6. Which of the sentences below best expresses the essential information in the highlighted sentence in the passage? Incorrect choices change the meaning in important ways or leave out essential information.

Ⓐ The wells did not resolve the problem of water shortage altogether because of their susceptibility to weather variables, which meant that people had to seek alternate means.

Ⓑ Unfavorable weather conditions, which were responsible for flooding and dry spells, polluted the water, forcing people who were dependent on them to turn to river water.

Ⓒ The wells alone did not meet the demands of the people because they were flooded with salty water and sometimes even dried up, so they had to be connected to river water.

Ⓓ The wells were not intended to be a lasting fix at first because the water turning brackish or completely evaporating made it obvious they were dependent upon weather conditions.

in the early 14th century that forbade industries from dumping their waste into the canals. They specifically targeted the textile industry, prohibiting both the washing of cloth and dyed materials in the canals and the dumping of wastewater from the dyeing process into them. Many merchants defied the regulations, but within a century all industries that had foul-smelling byproducts had been forced to move to the seaward side of the city. Henceforth, the dyers, butchers, and others had to dump their waste into the lagoon. This early form of ecological preservation ensured that the people of Venice had moderately clean water for domestic purposes.

4 ➡ However, securing their fresh water proved to be far more challenging. Initially, the islanders were obliged to transport water from the mainland, which was difficult for many reasons. The Venetians could not control the purity of their water supply, going ashore to obtain water exposed them to attack by their hostile neighbors, and water is extremely heavy. They soon found that the islands contained sand deposits that collected rainwater, which were surrounded by thick walls of clay underground. [■A] By digging into the sand, they could use these deposits as wells, but they provided a limited supply. [■B] The Venetians created cisterns that collected rainwater and purified it. [■C] Rain gutters were connected to a central drain that emptied into an underground chamber. [■D] That water passed through limestone and sand filters that covered clay tubs. From the tubs, the water would rise up through pipes to a small fountain where people could collect it for drinking.

5 ➡ The construction of these cisterns was quite expensive, so the first of them were located on the private property of rich citizens, and only their staff and tenants had access to the water. Later, the city built other larger ones to provide water for public use, and the number

of wells dramatically increased, which rekindled immigration to the islands. The construction of these larger cisterns was halted by the Black Death, but work resumed in the 15th century. For the larger ones, they gently sloped the city squares toward central drains, which maximized the amount of water collected. Still, these wells did not provide a permanent solution as they were vulnerable during storms, which could flood the city and make the cistern water brackish, and they were also entirely dependent upon the weather, so if there was a dry spell, they would have to go ashore to collect river water. That water would either be poured into the cisterns or sold.

6 ➡ Since Venice ultimately remained dependent upon the mainland, more permanent means of transporting the water were suggested to the civic authorities. These included plans to directly channel river water to the islands and the construction of an aqueduct, but they never were realized. The immense cost of such projects prevented them from ever becoming more than ideas. Therefore, the cisterns remained the best possible answer until the 19th century when modern technology finally provided economical means to send water through pipes from the mainland.

7. **Which of the following is NOT mentioned in paragraph 5 as a problem with cisterns?**

Ⓐ They merely served as a temporary solution.

Ⓑ They would dry up during a dry spell.

Ⓒ They could be flooded with salty water.

Ⓓ They constantly needed replenishing with river water.

8. **From the passage, all of the following were utilized as methods of securing viable water EXCEPT**

Ⓐ constructing large cisterns for public use

Ⓑ segregating water-polluting industries to the coasts

Ⓒ building aqueducts that carry river water

Ⓓ traveling ashore to collect river water for sale

TOEFL Reading

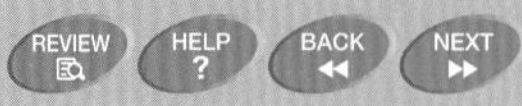

9. Look at the four squares [■] that indicate where the following sentence could be added to the passage.

   However, these led to an innovation in the 9th century.

   Where would the sentence best fit?

   Click on a square [■] to add the sentence to the passage.

10. **Directions:** An introductory sentence for a brief summary of the passage is provided below. Complete the summary by selecting the THREE answer choices that express the most important ideas in the passage. Some sentences do not belong in the summary because they express ideas that are not presented in the passage or are minor ideas in the passage. ***This question is worth 2 points.***

    Despite having an unreliable water supply, the city of Venice persisted through its people's ingenuity and determination.

    -
    -
    -

Answer Choices

Ⓐ Initially, the city imposed regulations that pushed out industries producing waste that polluted the canals to the coast and secured water for domestic purposes.

Ⓑ The rainwater collected in underground sand deposits provided an inspiration for deliberate collection of rainwater for drinking purposes.

Ⓒ The reason for Venice's lack of clean water despite being situated in a lagoon is the water pressure from the Adriatic Sea.

Ⓓ The cisterns gathered rainwater in underground chambers and purified it by passing it through limestone and sand.

Ⓔ Despite the increased number of cisterns in the city, they were not a stable solution because they were affected negatively by both too much and too little rainfall.

Ⓕ Various ideas of connecting Venice to the mainland failed to come to fruition because of high costs until water pipes were finally installed in the 19th century.

Drag your answer choices to the spaces where they belong.
To remove an answer choice, click on it. To review the passage, click on **View Text**.

TOEFL Reading 

The Brains of Birds

1 ➡ In all species of animals, brain tissue is the heaviest tissue in the body. For this reason, brains size seems to conform to a simple rule. An animal's brain is both as large as it needs and as small as it can be. For example, birds should reduce the size and weight of their heads in order to make flight easier and reduce air resistance. [■A] However, many birds actually have quite large heads and brains relative to their body size. [■B] In order to compensate for the disproportionate size of their brains, some birds are able to alter portions of their brain to minimize weight. [■C] One example of this is **song nuclei***, which are larger during the breeding season, which is usually the spring, and shrink when they are not needed. [■D]

2 ➡ Bird brains also make maximum use of minimal space through a structural property called brain lateralization. Brains are divided into right and left halves that look quite similar, but these two hemispheres are not identical. They have structural differences and specialized functions where some abilities occur in one half and not the other. On a basic level, the left half of the body is controlled by the right half of the brain, and vice versa. The distinctions become finer with specific areas of one side being largely responsible for processing certain types of information. Most animals seem to display some degree of lateralization, even ones that were thought of as having low intelligence.

3 ➡ For example, chickens have visual lateralization where their left brain is used to find food and their right brain perceives threats. Scientists conducted experiments where they used eye covers to determine what chickens used their eyes to see. They presented the birds with seeds mixed with small rocks, and while they were searching for the edible pieces, cutouts of predators were moved towards them aggressively to imitate an attack. The chickens

11. According to paragraph 1, why do the song nuclei decrease in size?

(A) To lower the amount of pressure in the head

(B) To reduce the birds' dependence on them

(C) To minimize air resistance during the breeding season

(D) To keep their brain size optimal

12. According to paragraph 2, which of the following is true about brain lateralization?

(A) It divides brain in a way that makes each section look similar to the other.

(B) It is a feature that indicates intelligence.

(C) All abilities are restricted to one half specializing in processing related data.

(D) It allows one side of the brain to control the opposite side of the body.

13. Which of the following is mentioned in paragraph 3 about the experiment with chickens?

(A) Because information received from the right eye is transferred to the left brain, chickens with their left eye covered are able to differentiate seeds from sand.

(B) The right half of the chicken's brain is superior in its ability to perceive movement than the left side, making it easier for chickens to use their right eye to track potential predators.

(C) When using both eyes, chickens show no preference in restricting processing of specific data to one half of the brain.

(D) The results of this experiment, which show how different halves of chicken brain are specialized, can be said to be true of other bird species.

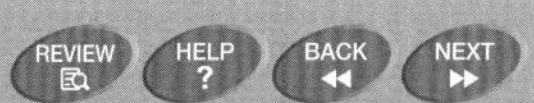

with their right eye covered had difficulty telling seeds from grains of sand, while those with their left eye covered did not notice nearby threats. Since nerve receptors on one side of the body send their information to the opposite side of the brain, this means that the left half of a chicken's brain processes visual stimuli related to small details and categorization, while stimuli related to distance and perception of movement are processed by the right half. Those with both eyes uncovered could see both things equally well. Through this lateralization, chickens are capable of feeding while still watching for predators, which is an advanced survival technique.

4 ➡ Other birds that have exhibited high levels of intelligence and lateralized behavior are the Passeriformes, often called songbirds. These birds possess the most developed song nuclei, and studies have shown that they use both sides of their brains to produce and understand songs. One such species is the zebra finch, which is known as a very loud and energetic singer. Only male zebra finches sing due to a boost of testosterone when they are an embryo. This infusion of hormones triggers the development of their song nuclei, and this hormone also triggers the nuclei's growth during their mating season. The lateralization of singing begins in the finch's brain, where the left half of the nuclei is used to understand songs that the bird hears. It uses this area to decide whether the song it is hearing is from its own or another species, and to differentiate between the songs of other finches. The right side is used in song production, and it controls the rhythm, melody, pitch, and volume of the bird's singing.

5 ➡ The lateralization of zebra finch singing extends to their vocal organs as well. The vocal organ of birds, called the syrinx, is located where their lungs connect to the airway. By changing the shape of the syrinx and vibrating parts of it when they push air out of their lungs,

14. Which of the sentences below best expresses the essential information in the highlighted sentence in the passage? Incorrect choices change the meaning in important ways or leave out essential information.

Ⓐ The chicken's brain is able to process different types of data accordingly because different receptors send varying information to the brain.

Ⓑ Because nerve receptors from the left side of the body send information to the right brain and vice versa, this means that each half of the brain is specialized.

Ⓒ Each half of the brain evidently specializes in processing different types of information as nerve receptors transmit data to different sides of the brain.

Ⓓ The nerve receptors enable the left brain to categorize data and catch minute details while at the same time allowing the right brain to track movement.

15. Why does the author mention zebra finch in paragraph 4?

Ⓐ To discuss how brain lateralization can be expanded beyond visual functioning

Ⓑ To describe how singing ability develops in songbird species

Ⓒ To suggest that songbirds have higher levels of intelligence than chickens

Ⓓ To discuss birds with highly developed song nuclei

they sing. The two halves of the syrinx can be controlled independently, and this control has been traced to the song nuclei of zebra finches. The right side of their syrinx is dominant, and it creates most of the song. The left side adds in notes that affect the rhythm and timing of the song. Since these two sides are controlled separately, the bird can produce more than one sound at a time.

6 ➡ Although dinosaurs had proportionately smaller brains than modern birds, scientists speculate that they also had lateralized brains like their descendants. Since dinosaurs only exist as fossils of mineralized bones today, it is impossible to reconstruct the interior structure of their brains. Skull structures indicate that some species may have been capable of generating sounds, but they would not have been able to sing intricate songs with those structures. Therefore, scientists doubt that they possessed special nerve tissue like song nuclei in their brains.

*__song nuclei__: a cluster of cells in bird brains that are devoted to song production

16. According to paragraph 5, all of the following are mentioned about finch vocal abilities EXCEPT

Ⓐ the left side of the syrinx plays a minor role in song production

Ⓑ the song nuclei are in charge of controlling the syrinx

Ⓒ the dominant side of the syrinx is controlled by the left side of the brain

Ⓓ due to lateralization, finches can sing multiple notes simultaneously

17. The word "speculate" in paragraph 6 is closest in meaning to

Ⓐ indicate

Ⓑ guess

Ⓒ dissent

Ⓓ contend

18. Which of the following can be inferred about bird brain development from paragraph 6?

Ⓐ Song nuclei are indicators of a more evolved brain.

Ⓑ From the size of dinosaur brains, we know they had lower intelligence than modern birds.

Ⓒ The similarity in skull structures of dinosaurs and modern birds imply that dinosaurs are ancestors to modern birds.

Ⓓ Dinosaurs, like modern birds, also used sounds to attract mates.

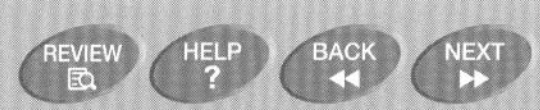

19. Look at the four squares [■] that indicate where the following sentence could be added to the passage.

In fact, their brains are much larger relative to their body size than those of their dinosaur ancestors.

Where would the sentence best fit?

Click on a square [■] to add the sentence to the passage.

20. Directions: An introductory sentence for a brief summary of the passage is provided below. Complete the summary by selecting the THREE answer choices that express the most important ideas in the passage. Some sentences do not belong in the summary because they express ideas that are not presented in the passage or are minor ideas in the passage.
This question is worth 2 points.

Bird brains display characteristics which help them optimize their brain function.

-
-
-

Answer Choices

(A) Song nuclei are parts of a bird's brain that are involved in song production and their size fluctuates according to the breeding season.

(B) Unlike modern birds, their dinosaur ancestors do not appear to have had highly developed nerve tissue like song nuclei.

(C) The reason male finches are able to sing is the production of testosterone while they were an embryo and during each breeding season.

(D) In the visual lateralization experiment with chickens, it was discovered that the left brain processes details and the right brain deals with movement.

(E) Lateralized brains help birds perform multiple tasks like identifying food and being on guard for predators at the same time.

(F) Both the song nuclei and vocal organs in zebra finches display lateralization, with left and right halves of each being responsible for different functions.

Drag your answer choices to the spaces where they belong.
To remove an answer choice, click on it. To review the passage, click on **View Text**.

Lesson

03 Vocabulary

Lesson Outline

- 어휘(Vocabulary) 문제는 지문에 음영 표시된 단어 또는 구와 의미가 같거나 맥락상 비슷한 단어를 찾는 문제다.
- 이 유형의 문제는 한 지문당 1~2개가 출제된다.

Typical Questions 

- The word "　　" in paragraph X is closest in meaning to

  X단락의 단어 '　　'와 의미상 가장 가까운 것은

- The phrase "　　" in paragraph X is closest in meaning to

  X단락의 구 '　　'와 의미상 가장 가까운 것은

Learning Strategies

Step 1 문제에 음영 표시된 단어·구를 찾아 정확한 의미를 파악한다.

→ 한 단어가 여러 가지 다른 의미를 가질 수 있다는 점을 기억해야 한다.

→ 음영 처리된 단어·구의 뜻을 모르는 경우, 앞뒤 문장과 문단의 흐름을 통해 대략적인 의미를 유추해 보도록 한다.

Step 2 주어진 보기 네 개 중 음영 표시된 단어·구와 의미상 가장 비슷한 보기를 찾는다.

Step 3 정답을 고른 뒤 다른 보기들의 오답 여부를 확인하고 넘어가자. 네 개 보기의 뜻이 각각 무엇인지, 음영 표시된 단어·구를 선택한 보기로 대체해도 의미 파악에 문제가 없는지 문맥을 다시 한 번 확인한다.

Example

Q. The word "elevated" in paragraph 5 is closest in meaning to

Ⓐ raised

Ⓑ installed

Ⓒ assembled

Ⓓ advanced

1 문제에 음영 표시된 단어·구를 찾아 어떤 의미로 쓰였는지 봐야 한다. 5단락에서 elevated라는 단어를 찾는다.

(...) These buildings were framed by large parks, and the residential areas around them were elevated on pillars. Le Corbusier's plan was shocking, and it was rejected by the Paris government. (...)

elevate라는 단어는 '올리다, 높이다'라는 뜻을 가지고 있다. 수동의 형태로 쓰였으므로 '올려진, 높여진'이라는 의미가 된다.

2 주어진 보기 네 개 중 음영 표시된 단어·구와 의미상 가장 비슷한 보기를 찾는다.

Ⓐ raised 올려진

Ⓑ installed 설치된

Ⓒ assembled 조립된

Ⓓ advanced 진보된

elevated와 가장 의미가 가까운 Ⓐ raised가 정답이다. 보기는 보통 제시된 단어보다 약간 더 쉽거나 더 흔히 쓰는 단어들로 출제되므로, 제시된 단어를 모른다 해도 해당 위치에 각각의 보기를 대신 넣어 보며 제시어를 추론하는 것이 가능할 때도 있다.

3 정답을 고른 뒤 다른 보기들의 오답 여부를 확인하고 넘어가자. Ⓓ advanced는 were ~ on pillars 사이 빈칸에 들어가기에는 의미상 어색하므로 가장 쉽게 오답임을 알 수 있다. Ⓑ installed와 Ⓒ assembled는 얼핏 보면 were ~ on pillars 사이 빈칸에 들어가기에 적절해 보이지만, 문장의 주어가 residential areas이므로 문맥상 맞지 않는다는 것을 알 수 있다.

Practice

01 The tremendous tsunami triggered by the 2004 Indian Ocean Earthquake was a catastrophe that devastated many regions of Southeast Asia, and it was recorded as one of the most destructive natural disasters in history.

The word "devastated" in the passage is closest in meaning to

Ⓐ exaggerated

Ⓑ destroyed

Ⓒ exposed

Ⓓ dominated

02 Due to the rise in global temperatures that is attributed to human activities, the Earth's glaciers and icecaps inevitably began to melt, adding to a rise in sea levels worldwide.

The word "inevitably" in the passage is closest in meaning to

Ⓐ unwillingly

Ⓑ irrationally

Ⓒ impartially

Ⓓ unavoidably

03 The bone structure of modern birds is akin to that of some dinosaurs in that both have hollow bones containing air sacs to help the functioning of their lungs.

The word "akin" in the passage closest in meaning to

Ⓐ relative

Ⓑ similar

Ⓒ distinct

Ⓓ discrete

04 Though criticized for his commercialism by Dadaists, Picasso, one of the most famous cubists, demonstrated an innate ability to depict the inner character of his subjects in an emotionally meaningful and abstract form.

The word "demonstrated" in the passage is closest in meaning to

Ⓐ ignored

Ⓑ showed

Ⓒ disguised

Ⓓ distinguished

05 The island volcano had been dormant for two centuries. However, recent measurements of natural signals such as ground deformation and volcanic temperature gradient have confirmed the possibility of an impending eruption.

The word "impending" in the passage is closest in meaning to

Ⓐ late

Ⓑ inactive

Ⓒ imminent

Ⓓ vital

06 These days, it is believed that organic foods can both help maintain health and provide better nutrition than their conventionally grown counterparts.

The word "maintain" in the passage is closest in meaning to

Ⓐ keep

Ⓑ increase

Ⓒ restore

Ⓓ supply

07

Researchers have discovered a set of genes that determine the lifespan of the common nematode. This finding sheds light on the aging process, and it may allow scientists to eventually delay the inexorable process of aging.

The phrase "sheds light on" in the passage is closest in meaning to

Ⓐ contradicts what is known about

Ⓑ emphasizes the importance of

Ⓒ provides more information about

Ⓓ calls more attention to

08

The arch was used by the early Sumerian cultures, but chiefly for underground drainage systems. It was the Romans who first developed and exploited the arch extensively for various functions.

The word "exploited" in the passage is closest in meaning to

Ⓐ utilized

Ⓑ obtained

Ⓒ improved

Ⓓ located

09

Invidious Discrimination

Invidious discrimination is the formal or informal classification of people into different groups that are subject to unequal treatment, rights, and obligations without rational justification. If there is substantive, rational justification for the unequal status, then the discrimination is not invidious. Many criteria are commonly used to justify lines of distinction, including sex, race, class, religion, age, and nationality. However, such factors often have no bearing on an individual's capacity to perform a task or be a community member. The discriminator typically holds the belief that the aggrieved group is inferior with no genuine justification. The term implies that the factors on which the discrimination is based are not essentially relevant.

1. The word "status" in the passage is closest in meaning to

Ⓐ standing

Ⓑ mechanism

Ⓒ ritual

Ⓓ strategy

2. The word "relevant" in the passage is closest in meaning to

Ⓐ consequent

Ⓑ pertinent

Ⓒ advertent

Ⓓ compulsory

10

Biodiversity

Scientists use the term biodiversity to describe the copious variety of organisms such as vegetation, animals, fungi, and micro-organisms inhabiting the Earth. While most scientists agree that there are currently at least 10 million different species, some believe that the total number of discrete species that have yet to be discovered or classified could actually be as high as 100 million. Each of these species has adapted to a specific environment ranging from high mountain peaks to the ocean floor. The term biodiversity is also used when referring to the different habitats where these species live. Each habitat is home to species that have adaptations enabling them to live in that environment, but not in others. For example, an animal cannot be moved from one of the polar regions to a tropical rain forest without the creature suffering negative effects or harming the unfamiliar environment.

1. The word "copious" in the passage is closest in meaning to

Ⓐ critical

Ⓑ plentiful

Ⓒ subsequent

Ⓓ compelling

2. The word "While" in the passage is closest in meaning to

Ⓐ Before

Ⓑ Whereas

Ⓒ Since

Ⓓ Given that

11

Suffragettes

In the years prior to World War I, British and American women fought for the right to vote. The term "suffragettes" was coined to refer to the more radical of those women, but it was often applied to all women who wanted to vote. The suffragettes had a reputation for violent protest and extreme self-sacrifice. However, the offenses they actually committed were relatively minor. Many historians argue that the so-called "constitutional suffragists," who worked within the law to achieve the desired constitutional changes, made more steady and meaningful progress towards achieving voting equality than their higher profile sisters. Some even claim that the suffragettes' shock tactics actually set the movement back by provoking criticism.

1. The phrase "prior to" in the passage is closest in meaning to

Ⓐ since

Ⓑ during

Ⓒ behind

Ⓓ preceding

2. The word "provoking" in the passage is closest in meaning to

Ⓐ prohibiting

Ⓑ stimulating

Ⓒ protecting

Ⓓ collecting

12

Tundra

Of all the biomes in the world, tundra is the coldest, and it is known for its harsh conditions. It has long, frigid winters and very short summers. There are a low variety of organisms and little human settlement because it is almost devoid of precipitation, the soil is barren and the growing season is short. In addition, tundra has an underground layer of permanently frozen soil called permafrost that extends to a depth of about 20 feet. To endure these surroundings, tundra flora and fauna have special adaptations. Tundra-dwelling plants are able to survive by growing shallow roots in the topsoil that does thaw, and animals have adapted to breeding and raising their young quickly during the short summer. There are two distinct types of tundra: Arctic tundra, which is found around the North Pole, and Alpine Tundra, which is located at the tops of tall, cold mountains such as the Himalayas or the highest peaks in the Alps.

1. The word "frigid" in the passage is closest in meaning to

Ⓐ chilly

Ⓑ dormant

Ⓒ existing

Ⓓ persistent

2. The word "dwelling" in the passage is closest in meaning to

Ⓐ supporting

Ⓑ decimating

Ⓒ inhabiting

Ⓓ verging

13

Animal Cycles

Certain critical cycles typically regulate animal behavior. One of the most obvious manifestations of these cycles is called the circadian rhythm, which refers to their behavioral pattern based on a 24-hour cycle. The circadian clock affects the basic drives of an animal, such as hunger, sleep and excretion. On top of daily cycles, animals are also affected by circannian rhythms, which operate on an annual basis. Determined primarily by seasonal changes, an animal's circannian rhythm is what drives activities like hibernation, reproduction, and migration. For instance, with the onset of winter, ground squirrels choose hibernation as the best way to cope with the frigid temperatures during the season. Before they go into dormancy, they consume more food than usual because doubling their body weight is a prerequisite for the long cold winter.

1. The word "onset" in the passage is closest in meaning to

Ⓐ integration

Ⓑ start

Ⓒ feat

Ⓓ abundance

2. The phrase "cope with" in the passage is closest in meaning to

Ⓐ consider

Ⓑ handle

Ⓒ advocate

Ⓓ retard

14

The Relationships between Organisms

Even in the absence of blossoms, many plants make and secrete nectar through extrafloral nectaries: structures that produce nectar on leaves and stems. These plants are usually found in areas where ants are abundant, such as the tropics and temperate areas. Although some types contain amino acids, nectar is mainly composed of water and dissolved sugar. These plants have developed ways to attract ants and coexist with them. Ants are persistent defenders, and they protect these plants from invaders such as flower-eating insects and other herbivores. These species of plants and the ants cannot live without each other. The highly active worker ants need much energy to support their busy lifestyle. Therefore, these plants exploit them by providing extrafloral nectar, giving the ant a profuse source of energy. In exchange for this favor, ants guard the plant from other insects which may compete with ants for the valuable resource, and they also ward off herbivores that feed on the leaves of this plant.

1. The word "persistent" in the passage is closest in meaning to

Ⓐ lasting

Ⓑ ensuing

Ⓒ firm

Ⓓ exclusive

2. The word "Therefore" in the passage is closest in meaning to

Ⓐ Hence

Ⓑ Notwithstanding

Ⓒ Furthermore

Ⓓ Meanwhile

15

Direct Carving

Traditionally, sculptures began with preliminary models made by the artist out of clay. These were then passed on to studio assistants who finalized the production in stone, plaster, or bronze. In fact, it was quite unusual for neoclassical sculptors to actually pick up mallet and chisel since the assistants were usually far more adept at carving than the original artists. In the 20th century, however, direct carving appeared as a novel way of creating sculptures without the use of intermediate clay models. Either working from memory or the subject itself, the sole artist worked on carving alone. Direct carving, as an approach to form composition, is considered a breakthrough in modern art and a revival of techniques derived from primitive art. A critical aspect of direct carving is the artist's decision to present the nature of the medium, working to reveal its appealing aesthetic and textural qualities. The subject matter and final form of direct carving often evolves from the shape, texture, or grain of the medium employed.

1. The word "adept" in the passage is closest in meaning to

Ⓐ fast

Ⓑ abrupt

Ⓒ sturdy

Ⓓ competent

2. The word "employed" in the passage is closest in meaning to

Ⓐ congregated

Ⓑ utilized

Ⓒ considered

Ⓓ hired

16

Sapa Inca

Dating back to the 12th century CE, the Inca people started off as a tribe in the Cuzco region. There they formed a small city-state which later functioned as the administrative, political and military center of the empire into which they flourished. Under the leadership and direction of Sapa Inca in 1438 CE, the people of Cuzco conquered much of modern day southern Peru. With the great wealth that the expansion generated, Sapa Inca transformed the kingdom of Cuzco, rebuilding it as a major city that served as the capital of a robust empire. Under his political rule, the central government fell under the jurisdiction of Cuzco, and there were four provincial governments controlled by leaders loyal to Sapa Inca. It is also believed that Sapa Inca was responsible for the construction of the now popular tourist destination of Machu Picchu, which may have served as his family home or a vacation spot for the nobility.

1. **The word "generated" in the passage is closest in meaning to**

Ⓐ exploited

Ⓑ superseded

Ⓒ surged

Ⓓ produced

2. **The word "robust" in the passage is closest in meaning to**

Ⓐ typical

Ⓑ strong

Ⓒ resolute

Ⓓ subsidiary

17

Urban Heat Islands

1 ➡ Anyone from a city center will notice that the temperatures there are usually higher than in the surrounding rural areas. The term "urban heat islands" was coined by researchers to describe this phenomenon. Urban heat islands have been attributed to human activity, and they often develop together with urban growth and densely populated areas. Heating and air conditioning systems, power stations, factories, and road and rail transport all generate excess heat that raises the average temperatures in urban areas. Researchers have found that the magnitude of man-made heat in metropolises is comparable to that of the Sun's radiation. Indeed, during the winter, some cities actually generate more heat than is provided by the Sun. Interestingly, the higher summer nighttime temperatures in cities are directly proportional to the heat generated by human activity. In other words, the more energy that is used to cool buildings, the more heat is generated, which heats up the atmosphere even more.

2 ➡ Another reason why urban areas are warmer is the materials people employ in the construction of cities where tall buildings, asphalt roads, and concrete sidewalks are the prevailing surfaces. Especially due to the dark hues of the buildings and roads, these materials absorb and retain more heat from solar radiation than vegetation and soil do. Although both urban and rural areas cool down after sunset, the concrete and asphalt surfaces in urban areas more gradually radiate their stored heat, which makes urban areas remain hotter.

1. The word "attributed" in paragraph 1 is closest in meaning to

Ⓐ ascribed

Ⓑ abounded

Ⓒ accommodated

Ⓓ advocated

2. The phrase "together with" in paragraph 1 is closest in meaning to

Ⓐ in terms of

Ⓑ in tandem with

Ⓒ inherent in

Ⓓ prior to

3. The word "prevailing" in paragraph 2 is closest in meaning to

Ⓐ initial

Ⓑ forceful

Ⓒ widespread

Ⓓ profound

18

American Literature

1 ➡ As the American Civil War drew to a close, an interest in rational philosophy, the scientific method, and the systematized study of history led to a transition from romanticism to realism and naturalism as the predominant literary styles. At the time, the United States was plagued by an economic depression, which only caused a more profound rejection of romanticism for a more realistic representation of American life in different contexts. Furthermore, the rapid proliferation of the immigrant population, industrialization, urbanization, and literacy rendered more readers curious about the cultural shifts America was going through. Therefore, the works that represent American realism and naturalism reflected the broad social trends of the times.

2 ➡ Because American realists were determined to reflect life as it was, their subjects were diverse. Southern life was brought under the spotlight by Joel Chandler Harris and Ellen Glasgow. Another famous writer, Hamlin Garland, depicted American life in the Great Plains. Perhaps the most famous American realist author, Samuel Clemens, who wrote under the pen name Mark Twain, made humorous and skeptical observations of life around him. He wrote about American life as he had experienced it, choosing to transcribe realistic dialects for the characters instead of using standard language in the dialogue. Indeed, it was primarily Twain who brought about the most important changes in American prose style, and created a particular American literature based on American themes and language.

3 ➡ Naturalism, an exaggerated style of realism, presented a dark world where a human's will was at the mercy of nature. Naturalist writers drew upon Charles Darwin's evolutionary theory to rationalize the concept that one's heredity and social environment were the decisive factors that shaped his or her character. Considered the foremost naturalist writer, Theodore Dreiser portrayed a dark and gloomy world in which people were powerless against forces they could not understand. He believed that, instead of fabricating romance, naturalist writers should tell the truth about human life.

1. The word "proliferation" in paragraph 1 is closest in meaning to

Ⓐ increase

Ⓑ advance

Ⓒ property

Ⓓ collision

2. The word "skeptical" in paragraph 2 is closest in meaning to

Ⓐ persistent

Ⓑ considerable

Ⓒ doubtful

Ⓓ available

3. The word "fabricating" in paragraph 3 is closest in meaning to

Ⓐ building

Ⓑ confining

Ⓒ hindering

Ⓓ contriving

19

Asexual Reproduction

1 ➡ Asexual reproduction is a method of reproduction that requires only a single organism. This type of reproduction is typically found in single-celled organisms which lack a nucleus. The majority of plants are also said to be capable of reproducing asexually. Owing to the fact that asexual reproduction does not require two genders, it not only allows rapid progress in reproduction, but also demands far less energy than sexual reproduction. Moreover, the absence of genetic recombination allows asexual reproduction to produce an intact clone of the parent organism. Asexual reproduction can be considered an inferior means of reproduction by evolutionary standards due to its considerably diminutive possibility for change. Nevertheless, it can be beneficial because it also tends to reduce the chances of mutation or other complications that can occur when combining the genes of two parents. There are three primary types of asexual reproduction: binary fission, budding, and sporulation.

2 ➡ Binary fission is used mostly by bacteria and single-celled organisms. Reproduction is achieved through a process in which a living cell divides into two equal or nearly equal segments. The process of binary fission begins with DNA replication. A variety of single-celled organisms use this method of reproduction. A good example of a bacterium that reproduces asexually through binary fission is Rickettsia, which causes diseases such as Rocky Mountain spotted fever.

3 ➡ Budding is a form of asexual reproduction in which a new organism is developed as a protrusion from another fully grown, stable organism. This type of asexual reproduction is very common in the plant world, but it can also be found in animals, such as the hydra. The hydra offspring usually stays attached to the parent organism for some time before separating from it. Since it originated from one parent, the new bud is genetically identical to its parent. In the case of sea sponges, a new sponge will start to grow from a segment of a parent sponge that falls off.

4 ➡ The third type is sporulation, or spore formation. This method involves the abundant production of reproductive cells called spores, which contain identical DNA and develop into new, independent organisms after they are dispersed. This method of reproduction can be found in many complex plant organisms such as ferns. However, it is successful only if the spores are dispersed by wind, water, or the passing of mobile organisms. The spores will fail to flourish if there is no means of dispersal.

5 ➡ For simple organisms and plants, asexual reproduction offers several advantages. For example, plants and animals that lack mobility or the ability to seek out mates often reproduce asexually. In addition, asexual reproduction allows an organism to produce numerous offspring without expending extra energy, as is the case with sexual reproduction. The production of large numbers of offspring is essential for plant life and one-celled organisms due to the high mortality rate common to such life. It is typical to find organisms that reproduce asexually in static environments that go through very few changes, like the marine environment.

1. The word "means" in paragraph 1 is closest in meaning to

(A) variety

(B) mode

(C) plan

(D) vigor

2. The word "considerably" in paragraph 1 is closest in meaning to

(A) significantly

(B) consequently

(C) initially

(D) inadvertently

3. The word "dispersed" in paragraph 4 is closest in meaning to

(A) scattered

(B) distinguished

(C) yielded

(D) thrived

4. The word "flourish" in paragraph 4 is closest in meaning to

(A) prosper

(B) predominate

(C) forage

(D) flee

5. The word "static" in paragraph 5 is closest in meaning to

(A) definite

(B) unchanging

(C) remarkable

(D) solely

20

Loie Fuller

1 ➡ Loie Fuller was an American dancer active during the late 19th and early 20th century. She achieved modest success touring the American countryside with circuses and vaudeville shows featuring other singers, dancers, and variety actors in the late 1800s, but she ultimately reached fame after crossing the Atlantic for a tour of Europe. In Paris, she was able to hone her own natural, improvisational techniques as a dancer. Her feats were not limited solely to performing, but also extended to choreography and the technical lighting aspects of stage performance.

2 ➡ Loie Fuller was born Marie Louise Fuller in Fullersburg, Illinois, a suburb of Chicago. She began her career in show business as a child actor in the United States at the age of four. Over time, she made the transition to dance and choreography and spent 25 years touring North America with variety shows, many of which spotlighted dance companies. In the early days of her dancing and choreographic career, the public did not take her seriously because she had already made a name for herself as an actress and only had minimal dance training. However, her keen observance of other performers' dancing techniques helped her develop her own styles through experimentation. She acted and danced alongside prominent performers in New York and London, who persuaded her to take the stage name Loie Fuller.

3 ➡ Loie Fuller's fame and notoriety sprang from her technical innovations in manipulating stage garments and lighting. She successfully merged the two by designing costumes that interacted with the stage lights. She employed reflective materials in designing her attire, and she used colored silks to shade stage lights and mirrors to shine the colored light onto the stage and the performers. Realizing how significant her innovations were, Fuller took out various patents on her inventions, such as using chemical compounds to produce colored gels and chemical salts for glowing, luminescent lighting and costumes. On one occasion, Fuller even strived to get her friend, the renowned scientist Marie Curie to help her make use of radium, a radioactive element, in theatrics. However, owing to the hazards related to the employment of the material, Marie Curie turned down the proposition.

4 ➡ Fuller combined these unprecedented innovations in avant-garde lighting and costumes with her free dance style and choreography. This integration of technology and dance brought her acclaim through a performance she named the *Serpentine Dance*, which premiered in February 1892 at the Uncle Celestin revue in New York City. It was after that famous performance that she toured Europe and gained popularity on the international stage. She was the first modern dancer to perform in Europe, appearing as the headliner for several shows. Her most notable European performance was *Fire Dance*, in which she performed on a glass surface that was lit from below.

5 ➡ At this time, the Art Nouveau movement was popular, and Loie Fuller was considered to be its living, dancing embodiment. Her choreography and technical innovations took her beyond the world of dance into other artistic fields including painting and sculpture. Her fame and influence in the world of art led to her being painted by Henri de Toulouse-

Lautrec and sculpted by Auguste Rodin. Although she died in 1928, there is still much interest in her work. Especially, the field of choreography has been strongly influenced by Fuller's creativity.

1. The word "**feats**" in paragraph 1 is closest in meaning to

Ⓐ doctrines
Ⓑ accounts
Ⓒ dynamics
Ⓓ achievements

2. The word "**merged**" in paragraph 3 is closest in meaning to

Ⓐ converted
Ⓑ deterred
Ⓒ blended
Ⓓ depleted

3. The word "**unprecedented**" in paragraph 4 is closest in meaning to

Ⓐ unparalleled
Ⓑ dim
Ⓒ elegant
Ⓓ coincident

4. The word "**notable**" in paragraph 4 is closest in meaning to

Ⓐ persuasive
Ⓑ outstanding
Ⓒ bountiful
Ⓓ potent

5. The word "**embodiment**" in paragraph 5 is closest in meaning to

Ⓐ concrete example
Ⓑ evolvement
Ⓒ antithesis
Ⓓ physical expansion

Test

TOEFL Reading

Origins of Writing

1 ➡ A codified writing system is considered to be the key characteristic of civilization. The development of writing shows that a culture has reached a point of stability at which its people are able to devote time to recording their past. They have moved beyond considerations of simple survival to create a sedentary community with a social identity. When and where this first occurred is difficult to ascertain with absolute certainty, but most historians agree that the oldest written language is that of the Sumerian people of Mesopotamia. While it is possible that other written languages preceded Sumerian, and many examples like Egyptian have been suggested, there is little evidence to support such claims.

2 ➡ The writing system of the Sumerians is called cuneiform, which means "wedge-shaped" in Latin, and it was made by using a blunt reed to press shapes into clay tablets. Like other ancient writing systems, cuneiform began as a pictographic language, which means that the symbols directly represented the things that they named. Around 9,000 years ago, the first evidence of proto-writing emerged in Mesopotamia in the form of counting tokens. The tokens were made from clay and incised with different markings to denote different items and amounts. Over time, these developed into hundreds of characters, which meant that only a select few were completely literate, and they were typically scribes, whose occupation was making written documents. Over the centuries, these shapes gradually became more abstract in both form and meaning until they came to directly represent phonetic speech instead of ideas.

3 ➡ Their preferred material had many virtues as well. The oldest samples of many languages were made in stone, bone, and wood. Unlike stone, clay is easy to write on, and it is far more

1. The word "key" in paragraph 1 is closest in meaning to

Ⓐ elementary
Ⓑ essential
Ⓒ underlying
Ⓓ substantial

2. Based on paragraph 1, how do we know Sumerian is the oldest written language?

Ⓐ Most historians claim it to be so.
Ⓑ No evidence of other writing systems older than Sumerian exists.
Ⓒ There is little possibility that other written languages preceded Sumerian.
Ⓓ Mesopotamia is where the oldest culture was discovered.

3. Which of the following can be inferred about cuneiform from paragraph 2?

Ⓐ It had different symbols for objects and numbers.
Ⓑ Pictographic languages similar to Sumerian developed around the same time it did.
Ⓒ The transition from representing ideas to sounds made more people literate.
Ⓓ The development of proto-writing took place over a very long period of time.

4. According to paragraph 3, what is an advantage of clay tablets over other materials? Click on two answers.

Ⓐ They can be mass-produced.
Ⓑ They allow recording of everyday events.
Ⓒ They could easily be stacked into caches.
Ⓓ They are not damaged by either water or fire.

TOEFL Reading

durable than wood or bone. Both can be destroyed in fire, but clay is baked, which actually makes it more durable by turning it into ceramic. This meant that writing could easily be used for daily activities instead of just memorials. [■A] The Egyptians also developed their own phonetic script, but they wrote it upon scrolls made from papyrus reeds, which were easy to produce, but could easily be damaged by water and obliterated by fire. [■B] Since clay tablets could be produced in massive quantities and are very durable, archaeologists often find them in caches containing thousands. [■C] Archaeologists refer to these caches as archives, and they seem to have been begun as libraries intended to keep information for future generations. [■D]

4 ➡ By analyzing the contents of cuneiform archives, it is possible to trace the growth of writing in Mesopotamia. The earliest use of the language was for bookkeeping, specifically to facilitate tax collection. Later, this expanded to include documenting storage inventories and business records and various legal papers like those for weddings and divorces. This factual information grew to include histories, myths and religious texts, and ultimately poetry and literature. The development of fiction is particularly important, as it signifies that a culture has begun to imagine its own future as well as record its past. As the use of writing proliferated, its transition from a symbolic to a phonetic language continued to progress. The number of characters decreased from over 1,000 to 600, further simplifying the writing system, and allowing the number of literate people to increase.

5 ➡ After the region was conquered by the Akkadian Empire, the local culture and language gradually disappeared, but their writing system survived. The Akkadians adopted cuneiform script and attached new sounds and words

5. The word "documenting" in paragraph 4 is closest in meaning to

Ⓐ recording
Ⓑ arranging
Ⓒ initiating
Ⓓ composing

6. Which of the following is mentioned in paragraph 5?

Ⓐ The period in which Sumerian cuneiform was overtaken by Aramaic
Ⓑ The difference between Sumerian and Old Persian cuneiform
Ⓒ The conquerors who continued to utilize Sumerian cuneiform
Ⓓ The role Darius the Great played in spreading Sumerian cuneiform

7. According to paragraph 6, all of the following are common of both Sumerian and Latin EXCEPT

Ⓐ their traces can still be found in modern languages
Ⓑ the cultures which initially developed them no longer exist
Ⓒ the writing systems lasted longer than the spoken forms
Ⓓ no current cultural groups have adopted them as their mother tongues

TOEFL Reading

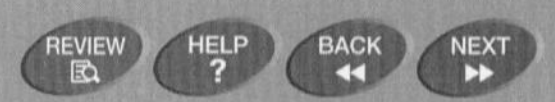

to its characters for their own language. This pattern continued over the centuries as the Babylonians and other subsequent kingdoms now and then claimed control of the region, and cuneiform continued to be used and refined. The literature of the Sumerians also was kept and read by these cultures whose scribes needed it in order to correctly translate Sumerian into their own languages. Eventually, cuneiform was superseded by Aramaic, but not before it inspired the Old Persian cuneiform developed by Darius the Great of Persia. It continued in literary and scientific use in the Parthian Empire until they were subjugated by the Roman Empire.

6 ➡ Today, Sumerian is considered to be a dead language since it is not spoken as the native tongue of any cultural group. However, the resilience of its writing system places it into a special category along with other dead languages like Latin. Although these two languages expanded in different ways—cuneiform was adopted from the defeated Sumerians while the Latin alphabet was spread by the conquering Romans—they share many similarities in that both were used throughout large portions of the world and by various cultures, and their alphabets far outlived their spoken usage. They also both continued to be used for literary, scientific, and religious purposes long after their originators had faded into history. However, there are only a few qualified experts today that can decipher cuneiform, whereas most of the languages of Europe still use the Roman alphabet.

8. Which of the sentences below best expresses the essential information in the highlighted sentence in the passage? Incorrect choices change the meaning in important ways or leave out essential information.

Ⓐ Cuneiform and the Latin alphabet are similar in the sense that they are used in many parts of the world even today, but they differ in that the former comes from Sumerians and the latter is from the Romans.

Ⓑ Cuneiform is different from Latin because it is the language of the conquered, but that did not prevent it from persisting long in other cultures even after it was no longer a spoken language.

Ⓒ While they originate from different cultures, both Sumerian and Latin spread to many cultures with their writing systems and are still in use even though they are no longer spoken languages.

Ⓓ Sumerian cuneiform and the Latin alphabet spread differently, but they are alike in that their written form existed long after they were no longer spoken, and they were widely used outside their cultures.

TOEFL Reading

9. Look at the four squares [■] that indicate where the following sentence could be added to the passage.

Many of the tablets in such archives were turned into ceramic when the buildings that held them were destroyed.

Where would the sentence best fit?

Click on a square [■] to add the sentence to the passage.

10. **Directions:** An introductory sentence for a brief summary of the passage is provided below. Complete the summary by selecting the THREE answer choices that express the most important ideas in the passage. Some sentences do not belong in the summary because they express ideas that are not presented in the passage or are minor ideas in the passage. ***This question is worth 2 points.***

The oldest writing system known to us is the Sumerian cuneiform.

-
-
-

Answer Choices

Ⓐ The reason why cuneiform survived over the centuries is because the scribes of other cultures needed it to translate Sumerian into their native tongue.

Ⓑ What began initially as a means of keeping business records and legal documents eventually allowed a flourishing of poetry, fiction, and religious texts.

Ⓒ While the characters originally represented certain objects or ideas, their numbers dropped as cuneiform developed to directly represent sound rather than ideas.

Ⓓ Sumerian, like Latin, is a language whose writing system still survives today even though it is no longer spoken as a mother tongue by any cultural group.

Ⓔ Because clay tablets do not perish in fire, Sumerian scribes preferred them over other materials like wood, bone, and papyrus scrolls.

Ⓕ Even long after the Sumerian culture had disappeared, surrounding kingdoms continued using cuneiform, adopting and refining it for their own use.

Drag your answer choices to the spaces where they belong.
To remove an answer choice, click on it. To review the passage, click on **View Text**.

TOEFL Reading

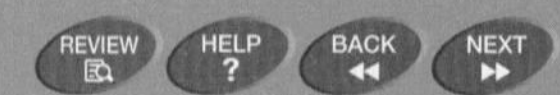

Thermal Stratification

1 ➡ In an aquatic environment, the distribution of organisms is determined by many factors, including temperature, light, salinity, and pressure, but the most important one is temperature and the phenomena of thermal stratification. When sunlight strikes the surface of a body of water, a small amount is reflected, but most of the solar radiation penetrates the water and gradually weakens until it is ultimately absorbed. Although water is colorless and transparent, it is far denser than air and absorbs solar energy quickly. [■A] Up to 99 percent of sunlight has been absorbed by 100 meters under the surface in extremely clear water. [■B] When any sediment or organisms are present in the water, the depth that light can reach decreases. [■C] Visible light contains different wavelengths and the longest ones, like infrared, are absorbed first, while the shorter ones, like ultraviolet, reach farther into the water, which makes deep water appear blue. [■D]

2 ➡ The rate at which water absorbs solar radiation has two important repercussions. Firstly, it means that photosynthesis is limited to up to 30 meters below the surface because the amount of light necessary for this process to occur does not exceed that depth. Therefore, virtually all of the primary producers in oceans and lakes exist in that area. In shallow bodies of water and along shorelines, some plant species like kelp are able to thrive anchored to the bottom, where they can grow large, forming underwater forests that support a variety of organisms by providing both food and shelter. However, these cannot live in the open water, so at the base of the food chain there are microscopic, often single-celled organisms that live suspended near the surface called phytoplankton. These are fed upon by organisms called zooplankton, which are miniscule crustaceans and invertebrates that roam the surface waters at night and retreat

11. The word "ultimately" in paragraph 1 is closest in meaning to

Ⓐ thoroughly
Ⓑ eventually
Ⓒ effectively
Ⓓ readily

12. According to paragraph 1, which of the following is true about absorption of light?

Ⓐ A dense body of water absorbs light faster than one of lower density.
Ⓑ High levels of sediment in water reflect most of the solar energy.
Ⓒ Most of the light is absorbed near the surface.
Ⓓ Longer wavelengths go deeper into the water.

13. According to paragraph 2, all of the following are true about kelp EXCEPT

Ⓐ it grows to an enormous size
Ⓑ it produces organic carbon compounds
Ⓒ it grows in shallow water
Ⓓ it becomes food for other organisms

14. Which of the sentences below best expresses the essential information in the highlighted sentence in the passage? Incorrect choices change the meaning in important ways or leave out essential information.

Ⓐ Zooplankton travel up to surface waters during the night to feed on phytoplankton and stay in deep water during the day to hide from predators.
Ⓑ Phytoplankton survives by hiding from predators during the day and migrating vertically at night to feed on zooplankton, which are microscopic organisms.

down into the depths during the day to avoid small fish that detect their prey visually, forming a vertical cycle of daily migration.

3 ➡ The second important result of the rate at which water absorbs solar radiation is that only the first few meters of water are heated. This means that deep water is cold even in tropical seas, and for any warmth to reach deeper, it must be exchanged by currents that circulate water vertically. Water is densest at four degrees Centigrade, and its density falls whether its temperature increases or decreases from there. Since the surface water is warmer, it is also less dense, which means that it remains on the surface and is heated even more, ensuring that it does not mix with deeper, cooler, denser water. So, deep bodies of water in tropical areas or in temperate areas during the summer usually have a distinct layer of warmer water near the surface with much colder water beneath it. This division of water into layers caused by temperature differences is called a thermocline, and its depth varies according to the amount of wave action present at the surface.

4 ➡ In lakes in the tropics, the surface water remains warm all year long, so the thermocline is a permanent feature that forms a significant division of physical properties. The water near the surface is well lit, warm, and has a large amount of oxygen in suspension, whereas the depths are dark, frigid, and almost thoroughly lacking oxygen. Since the photosynthetic organisms that generate oxygen are limited to the area above the thermocline, and the stark stratification does not allow the water to exchange, oxygen cannot be replenished in the depths. The extreme conditions of the deep water are hostile to most organisms, but the corpses of dead organisms and feces from living ones settle to the bottom. This means that while conditions in the top layer are friendly, the lack of exchange with the deeper water means that few nutrients are available to the organisms that

Ⓒ Zooplankton are microscopic organisms that live in both surface and deep waters, which helps them feed phytoplankton through a vertical migration cycle.

Ⓓ Zooplankton primarily feed on phytoplankton, which are microorganisms that migrate daily to avoid predators during the day and to feed at night.

15. According to paragraph 3, which of the following is the definition of a thermocline?

Ⓐ The depth at which the effect of wave action is felt the most

Ⓑ Multiple layers of water differentiated by density

Ⓒ The point at which the temperature of water changes

Ⓓ The change in density of water due to seasonal changes

16. The word "replenished" in paragraph 4 is closest in meaning to

Ⓐ supplied

Ⓑ restored

Ⓒ obtained

Ⓓ reproduced

17. According to paragraph 5, which of the following is true about overturn?

Ⓐ It allows temperate waters to be more productive than tropical waters.

Ⓑ It removes stratification through wave action which causes water circulation.

Ⓒ It sends nutrients downwards and oxygenated water to the surface.

Ⓓ It results in the entire lake attaining the same temperature and density.

live up there.

5 ➡ In bodies of water in temperate and polar regions, the situation is rather different as they endure dramatic shifts as the seasons change. In the summer they also develop a thermocline as the surface water is warmed, but they also freeze at the surface when air temperatures drop below zero for long periods in the winter. The transition between these extremes in the spring and fall means that the entire lake reaches the same temperature and density twice a year. When the thermal stratification is removed, winds at the surface can create wave action that causes water to circulate throughout the lake. This overturn allows oxygenated water from above to exchange with water rich in nutrients like phosphorus from below. Because of this process, temperate lakes tend to be much more productive than tropical ones, and even polar ones are more uniform.

18. According to paragraph 5, which of the following is carried downward each spring and fall in temperate waters?

Ⓐ Phytoplankton
Ⓑ Oxygen
Ⓒ Phosphorus
Ⓓ Warm surface water

19. Look at the four squares [■] that indicate where the following sentence could be added to the passage.

In very cloudy water, solar radiation may only be able to penetrate a few centimeters.

Where would the sentence best fit?

Click on a square [■] to add the sentence to the passage.

20. Directions: An introductory sentence for a brief summary of the passage is provided below. Complete the summary by selecting the THREE answer choices that express the most important ideas in the passage. Some sentences do not belong in the summary because they express ideas that are not presented in the passage or are minor ideas in the passage. ***This question is worth 2 points.***

Thermal stratification plays an important role in determining the distribution of aquatic organisms.

-
-
-

Answer Choices

Ⓐ Thermocline layers are more pronounced in tropical waters where the surface water is constantly heated while the depths are not.

Ⓑ The rate of solar radiation absorption results in photosynthesis limited to surface water and the creation of thermoclines.

Ⓒ Because light is limited to the top layer of water, primary producers like plankton can only survive in surface water.

Ⓓ That water reaches maximum density at four degrees Centigrade is evident from the depth at which thermoclines form.

Ⓔ In temperate and polar waters, a semiannual mixing of water allows an exchange of nutrients and oxygen.

Ⓕ The depth to which solar radiation penetrates water is highly dependent upon the clarity of water.

Drag your answer choices to the spaces where they belong.
To remove an answer choice, click on it. To review the passage, click on **View Text**.

Lesson

04 Reference

Lesson Outline

- 지시어(Reference) 문제는 지문에 음영 표시된 단어 또는 구가 무엇을 가리키는지 찾는 문제다. 여기서 해당 단어나 구는 대명사인 경우가 많다. 영어는 앞에 나온 단어를 다시 반복하지 않기 위해 대명사를 쓰기 때문에 해당 대명사가 의미하는 원래 단어가 무엇인지 묻는 것이다. It, They, Its, Their, That 등의 대명사가 자주 등장한다.
- 이 유형의 문제는 한 지문당 1개 정도 출제되며, 아예 출제되지 않을 때도 있다.

Typical Questions 

- The word "　　" in the passage / in paragraph X refers to

  지문/X단락의 단어 '　　'가 가리키는 것은

- The phrase "　　" in paragraph X refers to

  X단락의 구 '　　'가 가리키는 것은

Learning Strategies

Step 1 문제에 음영 표시된 단어·구를 지문에서 찾는다. 보통 문제에서 '단락 X'에 있다고 말해준다.

Step 2 음영 표시된 단어·구를 찾은 뒤 이 단어나 구가 해당 문장 안에서 무엇을 가리키는지 파악한다. 단어·구가 들어 있는 문장을 읽어보면 보통 답이 눈에 들어오지만, 난이도가 높을 경우에는 그 앞의 문장까지 살펴봐야 할 수도 있으므로 찬찬히 읽어보고 의미를 파악하자.

보통 음영 표시된 단어·구가 가리키는 대상은 앞에서 먼저 제시되지만, 간혹 뒤에 나오는 경우도 있으므로 주의한다.

Step 3 정답을 고른 뒤 다른 보기들의 오답 여부를 확인하고 넘어가자. 일단 정답을 음영 표시된 부분에 넣어보고 의미가 여전히 맞는지 읽어본 뒤, 오답들을 훑어보며 비슷한 것은 없는지 확인한다.

Example

The boundary between the Cretaceous and Paleogene periods is clearly defined throughout the world. In areas where the boundary is exposed, the rocks above and below the border have often quite distinct colors. Moreover, there is always a thin band of clay separating the two. When Luis Alvarez and his son were studying geologic formations in Italy in the 1970s, his son pointed out the clay layer to his father. Although scientists knew at the time that it marked the end of the age of reptiles, no one really knew why it had formed and what its true significance was.

Q. The word "it" in paragraph 5 refers to

Ⓐ world
Ⓑ layer
Ⓒ Italy
Ⓓ age

1 문제에 음영 표시된 단어·구를 지문에서 찾는다.

Although scientists knew at the time that it marked the end of the age of reptiles, no one really knew why it had formed and what its true significance was.

2 음영 표시된 단어·구를 찾은 뒤 이 단어나 구가 해당 문장에서 어떤 것을 가리키는지 파악한다. '그것'이 파충류 시대의 종말을 표시한다고 했으므로 앞에 있는 문장을 살펴보자.

When Luis Alvarez and his son were studying geologic formations in Italy in the 1970s, his son pointed out the clay layer to his father.

알바레즈와 아들이 지형을 연구하고 있을 때 아들이 점토층을 가리켰다는 내용이다. 이 문장 바로 뒤에 it이 있는 문장이 따라나오면서 '그것은 파충류 시대의 종말을 나타냈다'고 했으므로 점토층이 답이라는 것을 알 수 있다. 따라서 Ⓑ가 정답이다.

3 정답을 고른 뒤 다른 보기들의 오답 여부를 확인하고 넘어가자. 의미상 it으로 대체될 수 있으면서 marked의 주어가 되기에 맥락상 자연스러운 단어는 layer 밖에 없다는 것을 확인할 수 있다.

Practice

01 Our brain has two halves: the left hemisphere and the right hemisphere. The former relates to language skills, while the latter affects our perception and dreams.

The phrase "The former" in the passage refers to

Ⓐ our brain

Ⓑ two halves

Ⓒ the right hemisphere

Ⓓ the left hemisphere

02 Created in 1439, Gutenberg's printing press developed into a fast-selling technology though its prototype was invented in Asia. It ultimately supplanted other types of printing presses; however, it was in turn replaced by a more sophisticated printing press.

The word "It" in the passage refers to

Ⓐ Gutenberg's printing press

Ⓑ its prototype

Ⓒ other types of printing press

Ⓓ more sophisticated printing press

03 Though the majority of scientists accept Darwin's theory of evolution, which indicates that all species descended from common ancestors over time through the process called natural selection, some are insistent that the universe, the Earth, and humans were created by a supernatural being or God.

The word "some" in the passage refers to

Ⓐ scientists

Ⓑ ancestors

Ⓒ species

Ⓓ humans

04 While cave paintings, believed to have been drawn in the Paleolithic era, are found worldwide, the ancient cave paintings spotted in Indonesia are peculiar in that they depict outlines of human hands, created by placing one hand against the wall and applying paint with the other.

The phrase "the other" in the passage refers to

Ⓐ outline

Ⓑ human

Ⓒ paint

Ⓓ hand

05 The first half of the 20th century gave rise to Dadaism and Surrealism, which were influenced by the Realism movement of the 19th century. The former began in Zurich, Switzerland, during World War I, while the latter developed shortly afterward through the Dada activities in Paris in the early 1920s.

The phrase "the latter" in the passage refers to

Ⓐ the 20th century

Ⓑ Dadaism

Ⓒ Surrealism

Ⓓ Realism

06 Earth's internal heat is harnessed as an energy source in the form of geothermal energy, and the environmental impact of geothermal energy may not be as extensive as that of other sources of energy. At present, a great deal of the earth's population is able to use electricity from steam in subterranean geothermal wells at a cost comparable to that of other sources, such as fossil or nuclear fuels.

The word "that" in the passage refers to

Ⓐ heat

Ⓑ energy

Ⓒ source

Ⓓ impact

07

During respiration, animals take in oxygen to burn their consumed food, and carbon dioxide (CO2) is produced as a byproduct. In the past, early fishes dwelling in the sea may have developed the skills to breathe in the air. This is because it is much more efficient and beneficial for these creatures to extract oxygen from air than water, as it is hundreds of times denser and more viscous and contains less oxygen.

The word "it" in the passage refers to

Ⓐ respiration

Ⓑ sea

Ⓒ air

Ⓓ water

08

Animal Domestication

Evidence that the domestication of wild animals by Neolithic people was achieved through manipulation of biological processes in certain species has been uncovered by archaeologists from sites across the world. The evidence supportive of this hypothesis includes animal bones found at a number of Neolithic sites. Among them, the bones of goats are the most common, with the remains of the species outnumbering the bones of other species. This could be indicative of selective breeding for the purpose of food production, or at least of intentional exploitation of an animal species through manipulation of its breeding cycle.

The word "them" in the passage refers to

Ⓐ archaeologists

Ⓑ sites

Ⓒ bones

Ⓓ species

09

Pinyon Jay and Pinyon Pine

One good example of coevolution is the relationship between the Pinyon Jay, a medium-sized bird in the crow family, and the Pinyon Pine, which yields Pinyon nuts in the Southwestern U.S. and Mexico. The seed of the Pinyon Pine is the staple food for the Pinyon Jay, so the birds tend to nest in the pine trees. Also, the Pinyon Jay plays a crucial role in regenerating Pinyon trees, as it preserves vast numbers of seeds in the ground for future consumption, and the excess seeds are in an ideal position to germinate and mature into new trees.

The word "it" in the passage refers to

Ⓐ Pinyon Jay

Ⓑ seed

Ⓒ Pinyon Pine

Ⓓ staple food

10

Chimpanzees vs. Humans

Researched by a renowned anthropologist Jane Goodall, the study of a chimpanzee known as David Greybeard revealed many astonishing discoveries about chimpanzees. Today we know that the genetic information of chimpanzees differs from that of humans by a mere one percent. In addition, the blood composition and immune system of a chimpanzee are also surprisingly similar to those of humans. The brains and central nervous systems of the two are also almost identical. Above everything else, much like people, chimpanzees have also demonstrated the ability to reason, cooperate with others, make decisions, and even use tools. Through her observation of David, she discovered chimpanzees utilize hunting tools for termites, premeditate their circumstances, and impart knowledge to the next generation.

The word "that" in the passage refers to

Ⓐ chimpanzee

Ⓑ genetic information

Ⓒ blood composition

Ⓓ human

11

Silent Era

In the early part of the 20th century, as the name "Silent Era" suggests, the film industry had strong technological restrictions on recording and playing back motion pictures with sound. The advent of Edison's kinetoscope allowed people to see moving images, but it did not project film onto a screen. The kinetoscope introduced a rudimentary approach which created the illusion of movement by spinning a strip of film bearing sequential images, but without dialogue. Therefore, actors were required to hone their skills to convey ideas without words through miming or gestures. In addition, movie exhibitors utilized title cards, or inter-titles, to narrate story points, present key dialogue, and often to comment on the action for the audience. The role of the title writer became essential within the film industry, and was often separated from the original scenario writer.

1. The word "it" in the passage refers to

Ⓐ kinetoscope

Ⓑ recording

Ⓒ film

Ⓓ screen

2. The word "their" in the passage refers to

Ⓐ actors

Ⓑ skills

Ⓒ words

Ⓓ gestures

12

Extinction of Animals

Numerous predominately larger animal species became extinct at the end of Pleistocene epoch. Of the many hypothesized causes, the most prominent ones are glaciations caused by natural climate change and human migration. In the latter instance, the spread of human hunting and gathering societies over North and South America began about 12,000 years ago at the end of the last glacial period. This coincided with the decline of many animal species, and by about 10,000 years ago most of the large mammalian species such as mammoths, mastodons, and many other creatures had disappeared. Although extinction is also a part of natural evolutionary processes, the number of animal species that became extinct in these places, and their apparently rapid rate of extinction after humans arrived, have led some scientists to conclude that human hunters forced many mammalian creatures into extinction.

1. The phrase "the latter instance" in the passage refers to

Ⓐ Pleistocene epoch

Ⓑ glaciations

Ⓒ climate change

Ⓓ human migration

2. The word "their" in the passage refers to

Ⓐ animals species

Ⓑ places

Ⓒ scientists

Ⓓ hunters

13

Eye Makeup

It was common to find ancient Egyptians, both men and women, wearing eye makeup, which was one of the most notable features of Egyptians of high status. Unlike present day makeup, which is simply used to make the wearer more attractive, ancient Egyptian makeup had other specific purposes, ranging from beauty to protection. Egyptians employed the ancient eye cosmetic 'kohl,' a mixture made from a variety of ingredients, to darken their eyelids. It was originally used to prevent the occurrence of eye ailments, and there was also a belief that darkening the surfaces near the eyes would safeguard them against the harsh rays of the Sun. Moreover, mothers would apply kohl to their infants' eyes soon after birth. Some did this because they thought it would strengthen the child's eyes. Others believed it could prevent the child from being cursed by the 'evil eye', which was believed by many ancient cultures to cause injury or bad luck to those targeted by an envious person.

1. The word "It" in the passage refers to

Ⓐ status

Ⓑ makeup

Ⓒ protection

Ⓓ kohl

2. The word "Some" in the passage refers to

Ⓐ surfaces

Ⓑ eyes

Ⓒ mothers

Ⓓ children

14

Quilting

Quilting is the process of sewing together two or more layers of cloth, often with a layer of padding between them. It was initially used to make clothing to shield the wearer from frigid weather, and for a while it was put to use as armor padding. However, as firearms appeared, it could no longer function as a cushion against impact. Therefore, it has been used mainly as an insulating cover against cold air since then. In the 18th and 19th centuries, quilting was often a communal activity, involving women and girls within a family, or in a larger community. 'Quilting bees' in which teams spent time working together on one quilt were essential social events in many communities, and were typically held in the agricultural off-season, between periods of high demand for farm labor. Quilts were frequently made to commemorate major life events, mostly wedding ceremonies. During this period, women employed quilts to articulate their concerns about social issues and to fortify the bonds among them.

1. **The word "it" in the passage refers to**

Ⓐ quilt
Ⓑ clothing
Ⓒ wearer
Ⓓ weather

2. **The word "their" in the passage refers to**

Ⓐ events
Ⓑ communities
Ⓒ ceremonies
Ⓓ women

15

Echolocation

1 ➡ Most animals rely on their sense of sight to find their way around and perform important daily tasks. However, some animals live in dimly lit or dark environments which render their vision almost useless, while others have such poor vision that they have to rely on other senses to avoid obstacles and find food. Many of these animals, like whales, dolphins, bats, and shrews, rely on a technique called echolocation.

2 ➡ Animals that use this technique emit short, extremely high-pitched sounds and then listen for the echoes to bounce back to them. They then carefully interpret the echoes to determine an object's size, direction of movement, and distance from them. The time interval between the emission of the sound and the return of the echo indicates the distance to the object. The longer the interval is, the further away it is. The volume of the echo tells the animal the size and texture of the object. In fact, echolocation is so effective that researchers have observed bats using it to locate and avoid thin wires while flying at great speeds.

1. The word "others" in paragraph 1 refers to

Ⓐ tasks

Ⓑ animals

Ⓒ environments

Ⓓ senses

2. The word "it" in paragraph 2 refers to

Ⓐ technique

Ⓑ direction

Ⓒ distance

Ⓓ object

16

Volcanoes

1 ➡ Because volcanoes channel magma—super-heated molten rock—out from beneath the Earth's crust onto the surface, some regard them as the Earth's plumbing system. Volcanic eruptions generally take place near the boundaries of the continental or tectonic plates, although some known as hot spot volcanoes are located over extremely active points beneath the surface of continental plates. On land, volcanoes, which generally do not last long, either form broad, flat cones as a result of the build-up of the material from previous eruptions, or cinder cones, which are much like a chimney. Underwater volcanoes sometimes form steep pillars which eventually break the surface of the ocean, forming new islands.

2 ➡ Active volcanoes are those that are currently releasing steam, different types of lava, and gases like carbon dioxide at present. These often also produce pyroclastic flows, which are fast moving rivers of fluidized hot gas, ash, and rock. They may also become lahars, mixtures of rock, mud, and water with the consistency of concrete that flow from the volcano down through river valleys at high speeds. Areas with active volcanoes are often popular tourist spots because they have nature's miracles like hot springs, geysers, and mud pots. But by bad fortune, they also often have earthquakes.

3 ➡ It can be hard to say whether volcanoes are in an active state. Some volcanoes that have shown no activity for a certain amount of time are classified as dormant, but they have the potential to erupt again without warning. Others that are deemed to have permanently ceased are classified as extinct. People are so confident that extinct volcanoes will never erupt again that resorts have been built in the craters of some of these volcanoes.

1. **The word "which" in paragraph 1 refers to**

Ⓐ cinder cones

Ⓑ volcanoes

Ⓒ pillars

Ⓓ islands

2. **The word "they" in paragraph 2 refers to**

Ⓐ river valleys

Ⓑ areas with active volcanoes

Ⓒ tourist spots

Ⓓ earthquakes

17

Mantle

1 ➡ The first stage of terrestrial planetary evolution is *differentiation*, which is the separation of material based on its density. In this stage, heavier materials steadily sink to the center of the bodies to form a solid, metallic core, which in turn is surrounded by a relatively thin surface crust. At present, the Earth is composed of three main layers; the hard yet thin layer where we currently dwell, generally known as the crust; a central ball of molten iron, which is the core; and the mantle, the area between the two, which actually represents two thirds of the Earth's matter. Unlike the hard crust, the nature of the mantle is quite flexible and it resembles a thick liquid.

2 ➡ The mantle is not uniform but has three distinct structural areas. At the point where the crust and the mantle meet, both of them are a random mixture of different types of rock. Deeper into the mantle, the rock gradually becomes malleable, thus creating a soft zone. It is this zone that enables the tectonic plates of the crust to move about. Below the soft zone is the transition zone, where softer minerals become crystals, and it is the place through which slabs of surface rocks descend and slag from the core rises into the mantle. This area is in constant motion, so there are formations of thick and thin spots where heat energy can rise from the core, sometimes reaching the surface.

3 ➡ Not much is known about the rest of the mantle because it cannot be studied directly. Rather it is studied through seismic measurements of earthquakes that occur as far below the Earth's surface as the transition zone, but no deeper.

1. **The phrase "the two" in paragraph 1 refers to**

Ⓐ planetary evolution and differentiation

Ⓑ material and density

Ⓒ the crust and the core

Ⓓ the core and the mantle

2. **The phrase "this zone" in paragraph 2 refers to**

Ⓐ the crust

Ⓑ the mantle

Ⓒ the soft zone

Ⓓ the transition zone

18

Methods of Diffusion

1 ➡ Diffusion is a process that occurs when cultural elements of a society are adopted by another, which often causes them to extend to other distant regions. Complementing independent discovery and innovation, diffusion is considered the primary process of cultural exchange throughout history by some anthropologists. Diffusion occurs in three discrete patterns: direct contact, intermediate contact, and stimulus diffusion.

2 ➡ When a cultural item is borrowed by a society in close geographical proximity to the society of origin, the cultural item often continues to spread to other cultures. This phenomenon is referred to as direct contact diffusion, and the spread of paper provides an example of this. The Chinese military began employing paper in 8 BCE. However, when it later spread to other East Asian cultures, they were not able to figure out how to produce it. The Chinese finally sent instructors to Korea, the first country to receive this technology, in 604 AD, long after paper had been invented in China. A few years later, paper and papermaking techniques were introduced to Japan by a Buddhist priest and, even later, to the Middle East. Paper would not make its way to Europe until the 11th century through the Islamic part of Spain. Allowing the extensive diffusion of ideas, paper prompted major advances in cultures after its arrival, with China experiencing the Han Dynasty, the spread of Islam through the Middle East, and Europe going through the Renaissance.

3 ➡ When third parties introduce cultural items to a new society, it is known as intermediate contact diffusion. Historically, traders not only brought new goods to different regions, but also introduced new ideas to the people there as well. An example of this process can be seen in the introduction of horses to the native tribes of North America. In fact, they were introduced to horses by explorers from Spain. Soon, the cultures of the plains tribes were revolutionized as horses became a vital component of them.

4 ➡ Stimulus diffusion appears when a popular feature of one culture is not initially adopted by another culture, but some stimulus diffused into the receiving culture spawns the invention or development of a unique local trait through experimentation. For instance, the Industrial Revolution began in late 18th-century England, but it was not immediately adopted by other countries. However, after it stimulated experiments at mechanizing local manufacturing, the Industrial Revolution eventually took hold in the rest of Europe and in the United States by the 19th century.

1. The word "it" in paragraph 2 refers to

Ⓐ phenomenon

Ⓑ direct contact diffusion

Ⓒ Chinese military

Ⓓ paper

2. The word "they" in paragraph 3 refers to

Ⓐ third parties

Ⓑ traders

Ⓒ horses

Ⓓ native tribes

3. The word "it" in paragraph 4 refers to

Ⓐ stimulus diffusion

Ⓑ experimentation

Ⓒ Industrial Revolution

Ⓓ England

19

Symbiotic Relationships

1 ➡ Symbiosis, or the close, interdependent relationships between two or more organisms of different species, can be found naturally in all ecological systems. The benefits from these relationships diverge, so symbiotic relationships are categorized in three ways: parasitism, commensalism, and mutualism. Among them, parasitism and mutualism in particular show how a symbiotic relationship can benefit a species.

2 ➡ Parasitism is a symbiotic relationship in which one species prospers as another species is harmed. However, as shown in Darwin's theory of evolution, the tables can turn over generations. Through the process of natural selection, the harmed species can recover by taking the defensive. A good example of this can be found in the parasitic relationship between the rabbits of Australia and the myxoma virus. Rabbits were introduced to Australia via the European colonization of the continent. The rabbits soon multiplied to the point where they had become serious pests. The virus was introduced by scientists to curb the rabbit population. This was a successful trial at first glance, and the rabbit population was reduced. Then, the rabbit's immune system went on the defensive. Within three years, rabbits were being born with immunity to it. This demonstrates both parasitic symbiosis, as the virus prospered at the expense of the rabbit population, and the ability of organisms like the rabbits to adjust in order to survive.

3 ➡ Commensalism, a symbiotic relationship in which one species prospers while the other is unaffected, is much more difficult to find in nature. This is because, according to biologists, close interaction between two organisms is unlikely to result in neutral effects for either party. Commensalism usually occurs in situations where one species is either vulnerable to predators or has an inefficient means of locomotion. For example, mice may take advantage of a prairie dog burrow for protection from the sharp of eyes of hawks hunting from the sky. The prairie dogs' labor has benefited the mice, while the prairie dogs get nothing from the relationship. In marine habitats, some smaller creatures benefit by affixing themselves to larger creatures, allowing them to travel further distances to find food or new territory, but giving nothing back in return.

4 ➡ The third form of symbiosis is mutualism. Each species involved in this type of symbiotic relationship receives benefits. These can be lifelong relationships and can even span generations of both species. Acacia trees and various species of ants found in Mexico, Central America and South America provide a good example of this type of symbiosis. The acacia trees grow large thorns to fend off grazing herbivores, but there is a second line of defense. The thorns are hollow and house colonies of stinging ants. The ant colonies act as guardians of the acacia trees by discouraging mammals from grazing on the trees as well as preventing invasions by other insects that could harm the trees. In return, the acacia trees produce a special sap (containing protein-lipid bodies) on the tips of leaflets that supplies the ants with sustenance.

5 ➡ It is important to remember that these different types of symbiosis are not unchangeable. In fact, a relationship that begins as commensalism can develop into

mutualism or parasitism. For example, for a long time the relationship between the oxpecker birds and the large herd mammals of Africa was thought to be the perfect example of mutualism. The oxpeckers foraged for insects on the backs of buffalo, elephants and other herd mammals. The oxpeckers were supplied with food and the mammals received relief from parasitic insects. However, it was later found that they also tend to keep wounds open on the backs of their hosts, and even feed on the blood that seeps out, making them more parasitic. Thus, the type of symbiotic interaction can change during the lifetime of the organisms due to developmental changes as well as changes to the environment in which the relationship takes place.

1. The word "it" in paragraph 2 refers to

Ⓐ virus

Ⓑ rabbit

Ⓒ immune system

Ⓓ ability

2. The word "themselves" in paragraph 3 refers to

Ⓐ larger creatures

Ⓑ smaller creatures

Ⓒ mice

Ⓓ hawks

3. The word "they" in paragraph 5 refers to

Ⓐ oxpeckers

Ⓑ mammals

Ⓒ insects

Ⓓ hosts

20 The Stages of Cognitive Development

1 ➡ The most influential theory in the history of developmental psychology is Piaget's theory of cognitive development, which is concerned with one's ability to think and understand. Jean Piaget, a Swiss psychologist, centered his theory on the development of intelligence. His theory is concerned with the emergence and acquisition of schemata, methods of how a person views the world. According to Piaget, children pass through distinct stages as they acquire new ways of mentally representing information. He conceived of four stages of childhood development and described the level of awareness of the external world children exhibit at each stage.

2 ➡ The Sensorimotor stage is the first of the four stages described by Piaget and lasts from birth to approximately two years of age. According to his theory, this is the time when children build up a general understanding of their surroundings. First, the child develops basic reflexes, which slowly become voluntary actions over the first six weeks, and then develops habits through the repetition of actions. At this time, infants will intentionally try to grab objects. Also, from twelve to eighteen months, children conduct simple experiments to find new ways of overcoming challenges.

3 ➡ The Preoperational stage is the second of Piaget's four stages of cognitive development and lasts from approximately age two to age seven. By observing children at play, Piaget was able to identify several events in which new thought processes occur. During this stage, children display symbolic functioning, characterized by their use of symbols, words, or pictures to represent something that is not physically present. Piaget found that children lack perception of conservation of mass, volume, and number if the original form changes at this stage. Furthermore, a child can only focus on a singular aspect of a stimulus or situation. For example, if you pour a tall glass of milk into a shallow bowl, the child will think that the amount of milk has decreased because it is lower. It is possible for children to think intuitively, that is, they have the ability to have quick insights, to believe something without understanding the reasons why.

4 ➡ The Concrete Operational stage, from age seven to age eleven, is the third stage of Piaget's theory. It is characterized by using logic aptly and involves several distinct processes. First, children take several aspects into account when solving problems. Second, they are aware that objects can be changed and then returned to their original form depending on situations or surroundings. Finally, it is in this stage when egocentrism disappears, and children are capable of understanding something from another point of view.

5 ➡ The final stage in Piaget's theory is the Formal Operational stage. It initiates between the ages of eleven and fifteen and continues into adulthood. This stage is characterized by the ability to think abstractly and to draw conclusions from available information. As a result of thinking more abstractly, adolescents are able to imagine their ideal selves and situations. They contemplate their future and their goals. In addition, problem-solving is more systematic, and they can hypothesize outcomes. Deductive reasoning complements their greater problem-solving abilities.

1. The word "it" in paragraph 3 refers to

Ⓐ glass
Ⓑ bowl
Ⓒ child
Ⓓ milk

2. The word "their" in paragraph 4 refers to

Ⓐ processes
Ⓑ children
Ⓒ aspects
Ⓓ objects

3. The word "They" in paragraph 5 refers to

Ⓐ conclusions
Ⓑ adolescents
Ⓒ situations
Ⓓ outcomes

Test

TOEFL Reading

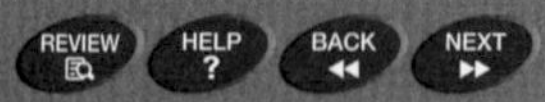

Bird Colonies

1 ➡ Many species of birds gather together into large groups to nest or roost in a particular location. These congregations are called bird colonies, and if their purpose for gathering is to reproduce and then rear their young, their group is referred to as a breeding colony. The majority of colonial nesting birds are seabird species like albatrosses and auks, but many wetland species like herons and perching birds like swallows also form colonies. Roosting birds have not gathered together for mating purposes, but rather for migration, so they do not build nests as they will only remain for a short time. Flocks of roosting birds typically stay overnight in trees or in fields and move on the following day. In either case, bird colonies can contain thousands or even hundreds of thousands of individuals. Nesting colonies and communal roosting provide many advantages for the birds that engage in these practices, but they can also have some serious disadvantages.

2 ➡ The main advantage of colonial nesting is the safety it can provide. Colonial nesting is practiced by around 13 percent of all bird species, and close to 95 percent of seabirds nest colonially on sea cliffs and islands. Nesting colonially provides better chances for survival in many ways. Many birds will nest in areas that are free from their natural predators, like rocky islands in the ocean. The vast numbers that they typically nest in also provides added security as there are more birds capable of mounting a defense against predators. In addition, many birds that nest colonially practice synchronized breeding, which means that they mate and their offspring hatch together. This means that there will be many more young than predators could ever consume, and once they are satiated, they will leave the rest alone. Other birds use much more sophisticated tactics to protect their young from predation.

1. According to paragraph 1, which of the following is true of bird colonies?

Ⓐ Nesting birds mostly gather together for migration to warmer countries.

Ⓑ Types of colonies are different in terms of the purpose of gathering.

Ⓒ Roosting birds often borrow other birds' nests to stay overnight.

Ⓓ There are many bird colonies which contain only a few dozen individuals.

2. Which of the sentences below best expresses the essential information in the highlighted sentence in the passage? Incorrect choices change the meaning in important ways or leave out essential information.

Ⓐ The number of young birds is so large that no realistic number of predators could eat them all, so some will survive.

Ⓑ When predators are completely satisfied, they will release other young birds and fly away.

Ⓒ The majority of young birds could survive even after violent attacks from their predators.

Ⓓ Nesting birds raise their young together to increase the chance of survival in many ways.

TOEFL Reading

3 ➡ One species that goes to great lengths to protect its young is the Yellow-rumped Caciques that live in northern South America. These insectivorous birds are highly social, and they mount a multi-tiered defense to ensure their survival in the canopy. When possible, they nest in trees on islands to reduce the amount of terrestrial predators like snakes, effectively creating a moat. This does not deter primates who can negotiate the canopy, so Caciques usually build their nests in trees that contain active wasp nests. They must maintain a careful distance since the wasps will attack them as well if they feel threatened, but the wasps have been observed chasing away monkeys that were intent on raiding the birds' nests. They also mingle their new nests with older unused ones to provide decoy nests that waste predators' time and increase the chance of early detection. When other bird species invade their territory, the male Caciques will attack them en masse to chase them away. This technique is referred to as mobbing, and the males have even been observed protecting other birds that use old Cacique nests. The nesting colonies that most effectively integrate these tactics tend to suffer from predators the least.

4 ➡ For other species, the allocation of an adequate food source is a more immediate concern than safety. Cliff swallows, as their name implies, build their mud nests on the faces of cliffs and other vertical surfaces, including bridges and buildings, which makes them inaccessible to most predators. Although they may nest solitarily, cliff swallows tend to form colonies which sometimes number in the thousands. Since their nests are so well protected, their colonies are formed for feeding. Cliff swallows are aerial hunters, and they take advantage of air currents that cause dense swarms of insects, which their large groups can effectively consume. However, when food is scarce, those who have had trouble finding prey

3. All of the following are mentioned in paragraph 3 about the Yellow-rumped Caciques EXCEPT

Ⓐ they are from northern South America
Ⓑ they employ mobbing as a defense mechanism
Ⓒ they form a mutually beneficial relationship with wasps
Ⓓ they protect their nests from snakes and primates

4. According to paragraph 3, Caciques build their nests around abandoned ones because

Ⓐ it is an effective way of enlisting the help of wasps
Ⓑ they want to avoid terrestrial predators
Ⓒ they try to lure their predators to empty nests
Ⓓ it allows the male Caciques to protect other birds that use the abandoned ones

5. According to paragraph 4, which of the following is NOT true of cliff swallows?

Ⓐ They hunt swarms of insects riding air currents.
Ⓑ Their nests are mostly not exposed to their predators.
Ⓒ Their nests are usually located near food sources.
Ⓓ They capture their prey more effectively in groups.

TOEFL Reading

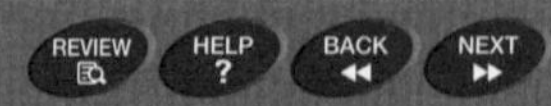

will watch their neighbors. When they see one return with food, they will follow it back out to the source. In addition, individuals who find prey during unfavorable weather conditions will also utter a cry that signals the colony to follow them. By increasing the size of its hunting party, the bird that found a swarm can use the other birds to help it track the swarm's movement.

5 ➡ However, forming colonies can also have detrimental effects, particularly when it comes to safety. Nesting colonies appear to provide increased protection against terrestrial predators, but they often attract larger predatory birds. Great horned owls have been observed repeatedly attacking the center of tern colonies at night, encountering little to no resistance. [■A] Albatross will also raid penguin colonies in small hunting groups, stealing young away from their hapless parents who lack offensive ability. [■B] Many species of island dwelling and seabirds were discovered by sailors who exploited them for food, and some like the Great Auk were completely annihilated. [■C] In addition, humans inadvertently and knowingly introduce invasive species like rats and foxes that can wreak destruction. [■D] Roosting colonies have also fallen victim to humans as with the Passenger Pigeon. These birds once traveled in flocks of over a million birds, but humans quite deliberately hunted them to extinction using nets.

6. In paragraph 4, how does the author explain colonial nesting?

- (A) By highlighting food shortages which put cliff swallows in danger
- (B) By comparing cliff swallows with other birds focused more on nesting
- (C) By illustrating the habits of cliff swallows such as nesting and hunting
- (D) By refuting a statement that all seabirds gather to protect their young

7. The word "them" in paragraph 4 refers to

- (A) individuals
- (B) prey
- (C) conditions
- (D) other birds

8. It can be inferred from paragraph 5 that

- (A) albatrosses are the most dangerous threat to seabirds
- (B) terns are primary prey of great horned owls
- (C) forming colonies turned out to be safer than living alone
- (D) humans make deliberate attempts at controlling bird populations

TOEFL Reading

9. Look at the four squares [■] that indicate where the following sentence could be added to the passage.

But, the greatest disadvantage of nesting colonies comes from the influence of humans.

Where would the sentence best fit?

Click on a square [■] to add the sentence to the passage.

10. **Directions:** An introductory sentence for a brief summary of the passage is provided below. Complete the summary by selecting the THREE answer choices that express the most important ideas in the passage. Some sentences do not belong in the summary because they express ideas that are not presented in the passage or are minor ideas in the passage. ***This question is worth 2 points.***

There are pros and cons of nesting and roosting together for bird colonies.

•
•
•

Answer Choices

(A) The major advantage of bird colonies is safety because they can protect their nests from predators more effectively.
(B) Some species intentionally build their nests around active wasp nests to chase away monkeys that threaten young birds.
(C) Some bird colonies that nest in safe places such as cliff swallows focus more on the allocation of a food source.
(D) Colonial nesting sometimes can be dangerous because large groups are more noticeable to predatory birds and humans.
(E) Most bird species are observed practicing colonial nesting, and the majority of them are seabird species.
(F) The introduction of invasive species has led to the extinction of many island dwelling seabird species and a decrease in colonial nesting practices.

Drag your answer choices to the spaces where they belong.
To remove an answer choice, click on it. To review the passage, click on **View Text**.

TOEFL Reading

How to Avert Another Dust Bowl

1 ➡ During the 1930s, a series of catastrophic dust storms ravaged the North American plains, severely damaging the local ecology and crippling the agricultural industry. This disaster, called the Dust Bowl, was a culmination of events that had begun many decades before, and it could have been avoided. Prior to the 1850s, much of the high prairie was referred to by settlers as the Great American Desert due to its lack of surface water and trees, and they accordingly avoided settling there. This name was actually fairly accurate since the plains receive only about 25 centimeters of rain in an average year, which technically makes them arid, if not actual desert. However, settlement was encouraged from the next decade onward, and the techniques used for farming there became increasingly detrimental to the land.

2 ➡ The plains were covered in native, deep-rooted grasses that held the topsoil in place regardless of weather conditions. Initially, people began raising cattle there to take advantage of those grasses by allowing the animals to graze on them. However, the harsh winters, a drought, and general overgrazing soon took their toll, and farming replaced ranching. Over the following decades, increasingly larger plots of land were granted or sold to farmers who raised cash crops like grains and cotton. Encouraged by a wetter period, agriculture continued to expand and became more mechanized. Deep plowing disturbed the thin topsoil, and farmers increasingly left their fields barren in the winter months. When an extreme drought and strong windstorms occurred, there was nothing to hold the soil in place, and clouds of black dust swept across the continent.

3 ➡ Following the disaster, many areas had lost 17 to 28% of their fertile topsoil, which reduced the land's value. This forced many farmers into bankruptcy, and those who remained turned

11. According to paragraph 2, which of the following did NOT influence the creation of the Dust Bowl?

Ⓐ Grasses and shrubs
Ⓑ Weather conditions
Ⓒ Overgrazing
Ⓓ Droughts

12. The word "viable" in paragraph 3 is closest in meaning to

Ⓐ advisable
Ⓑ valuable
Ⓒ disposable
Ⓓ usable

13. According to paragraph 3, farmers turned to crop rotation because

Ⓐ it allows indigenous plants to grow faster and drives out harmful plants
Ⓑ it prevents insects from thriving in the environment and eradicates them
Ⓒ it protects the soil from environmental threats and keeps it moist
Ⓓ it decreases the amount of erosion and naturally fertilizes the soil

14. All of the following are mentioned in paragraph 4 as factors that contributed to droughts and pollution EXCEPT

Ⓐ frequent use of chemical fertilizers
Ⓑ increased profitability of the land
Ⓒ lack of concern for the environment
Ⓓ fewer windbreaks planted around fields

TOEFL Reading

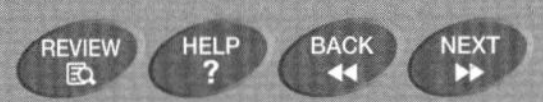

increasingly to chemical fertilizers to keep their land viable. However, many farmers in areas that were less affected began to adopt preventative measures to protect their farms. Interestingly, the techniques that have been most effective are not recent inventions. To keep their land productive, many farmers have resumed crop rotation. They allow some of their fields to grow wildly for a year or two, which reduces erosion by encouraging native plants to grow, and fertilizes the soil naturally. Others divide up their fields into different crops and plant them in rotation, which allows the plants to fertilize each other in turn.

4 ➡ In order to combat the constant wind that affects the area, farmers have taken to planting windbreaks. These are rows of trees and shrubs planted around fields to disrupt the airflow and deflect it upwards. This not only protects the soil from wind and water erosion, but it also keeps the crops warmer, allowing the plants to grow taller and be healthier. This can also increase the land's profitability by planting trees that produce fruit or are used for timber. However, both of these practices have fallen increasingly out of favor as large corporations have gradually been taking over the agricultural industry. Due to their high profit margins, these companies prefer to use chemical fertilizers and have little regard for erosion. As a result, recent droughts have become more damaging, and pollution has increased.

5 ➡ Due to the continued growth of cities and their suburbs, the spread of industrialized agriculture is difficult to restrain. To feed increasing populations, more food must be available, which means more land must be used. However, the cities themselves may provide an answer. In Japan, a surprisingly large amount of urban land is used for small scale farming. These farms are located mostly in residential areas and they typically grow vegetables and other

15. It can be inferred from paragraph 5 that urban farms

Ⓐ not only provide economic benefits, but also improve living conditions

Ⓑ make a relaxed city atmosphere by providing increased average temperatures

Ⓒ help people lead sustainable lifestyles by growing their own fruits and vegetables

Ⓓ prevent soil erosion and rain runoff in the city, lessening the damage to the land

16. The word "they" in paragraph 5 refers to

Ⓐ cities

Ⓑ farms

Ⓒ areas

Ⓓ vegetables

17. According to paragraph 6, what method can be used to prevent another disaster similar to the Dust Bowl?

Ⓐ Crop rotation

Ⓑ Rural farming

Ⓒ Grazing

Ⓓ Eliminating shrubs

TOEFL Reading

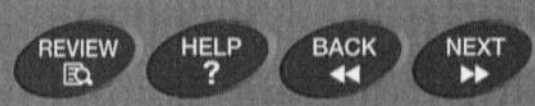

produce. The city environment protects them from the wind and provides them with an ample supply of water from rain runoff. The economic benefits of such farming are clearly evident, as around one-third of the entire country's agricultural output comes from urban farms, and they account for 25% of farming households. These farms have many other benefits as well. They create green space in the city, which reduces average temperatures, boosts oxygen levels, and provides people with a more relaxed atmosphere.

6 ➡ If nothing is done to reverse the trend of large-scale farming in the United States, it may lead to another disaster similar to the Dust Bowl. [■A] For instance, in the last few years, serious droughts have reduced the agricultural output of the plains so severely that there was a shortage of animal feed both domestically and in other nations that rely on American exports. [■B] If company farms adopt the techniques that farmers did after the 1930s, much of the damage can be reversed. [■C] As Japan's statistics prove, urban farming can also serve to reduce the burden those farms are forced to bear. [■D] But, while urban gardening has become a trend in some U.S. cities, it is still very limited.

18. Which of the sentences below best expresses the essential information in the highlighted sentence in the passage? Incorrect choices change the meaning in important ways or leave out essential information.

Ⓐ A decrease in U.S. agricultural output caused by droughts affected many countries.

Ⓑ A shortage of animal feed led to a significant reduction in agricultural output.

Ⓒ Many nations have been relying on American exports over the last few years due to droughts.

Ⓓ Intense droughts destroyed the plains, which led to a shortage of cattle that many nations depend on.

19. Look at the four squares [■] that indicate where the following sentence could be added to the passage.

However, we need not suffer through such hardship again.

Where would the sentence best fit?

Click on a square [■] to add the sentence to the passage.

20. Directions: An introductory sentence for a brief summary of the passage is provided below. Complete the summary by selecting the THREE answer choices that express the most important ideas in the passage. Some sentences do not belong in the summary because they express ideas that are not presented in the passage or are minor ideas in the passage.
This question is worth 2 points.

The Dust Bowl, a series of catastrophic dust storms, severely damaged the North American plains in the 1930s.

-
-
-

Answer Choices

Ⓐ Overgrazing, deep plowing, serious droughts, and windstorms all contributed to the creation of the Dust Bowl.

Ⓑ After the disaster, farmers went back to crop rotation and planting windbreaks to prevent another disaster from happening.

Ⓒ Crop rotation was proven to be successful in some parts of the United States, while planting trees and shrubs was more effective in others.

Ⓓ Large corporations started damaging the land again by using chemical fertilizers and other harmful methods.

Ⓔ Urban farming, a fairly recent method, is gaining popularity for the benefits it provides to the city and its environment.

Ⓕ Like in Japan, urban gardening is gradually becoming a trend in other East Asian countries as well.

Drag your answer choices to the spaces where they belong.
To remove an answer choice, click on it. To review the passage, click on **View Text**.

II

Making Inference

Lesson 01 Rhetorical Purpose

Lesson 02 Inference

Lesson

01 Rhetorical Purpose

Lesson Outline

- 의도 파악(Rhetorical Purpose) 문제는 지문에 음영 표시된 단어·구·절의 역할을 묻거나 지문에서 해당 단어·구·절, 크게는 문단이 왜, 어떤 목적을 위해 언급되었는지 찾는 문제다. 'Rhetorical'은 '수사적인'이라는 의미로, 이 수사적 표현에는 직유, 은유와 반복 등 다양한 방법이 있다. 음영 표시된 내용을 통해 지문이 말하고자 하는 것이 무엇인지 그 의미를 정확히 파악해야 한다.
- 이 유형의 문제는 한 지문당 1~2개가 출제된다.

Typical Questions 

- The author mentions ▒▒▒ in order to 글쓴이가 ▒▒▒를 언급하는 이유는
- Why does the author mention ▒▒▒ in paragraph X/in the passage?
  X단락에서/지문에서 글쓴이가 ▒▒▒를 언급하는 이유는 무엇인가?
- In paragraph X, the author mentions ▒▒▒ to
  X단락에서 글쓴이가 ▒▒▒를 언급하는 이유는
- What is the purpose of paragraph X as it relates to paragraph Y?
  Y단락과 관련하여 X단락의 목적은 무엇인가?

Learning Strategies

Step 1 문제에 음영 표시된 단어·구·절을 지문에서 찾자.

···› Vocabulary 문제나 Reference 문제와 달리 더 깊은 의미를 파악해야 하는 문제이므로 해당 문장뿐 아니라 앞과 뒤의 문장까지 함께 고려해야 한다는 점에 유의하자.

···› 음영 표시된 내용은 앞뒤 문장의 내용에 반박하거나, 비교·대조하거나, 예시를 들기 위한 장치인 경우가 많다.

Step 2 보기들을 하나씩 읽으며 정답을 찾는다. 해당 단어·구·절이 어떤 식으로 앞뒤 문장과 관계를 맺고 있는지, 논리적 관계와 논리 전개 방식에 초점을 맞춘다.

Step 3 앞서 배운 대로 다른 보기들의 오답 여부를 확인하는 것을 잊지 말자. 저자의 의도 및 설명 방식 면에서는 맞는 것처럼 보이지만, 지문의 세부 정보와 다른 내용이 담긴 오답도 있을 수 있다.

Example

Griffith was working with two different strains of the pneumonia bacteria. A strain of bacteria is a population of bacterial cells that all descend from one parent cell, with one or more inherited characteristics that make it different from other strains. One of the strains Griffith used had a protective covering that made its surface smooth, while the other's surface was rough. Therefore, they were designated as type S and type R. The covering made it difficult for an organism's immune system to detect the bacteria, so it was virulent. That means it was capable of surviving and reproducing long enough to cause disease symptoms and be transmitted to other organisms. The R strain lacked this covering.

Q. In paragraph 2, the author mentions that The R strain lacked this covering to

Ⓐ emphasize that it was rarely transmitted to other organisms

Ⓑ explain the role of the protective covering that bacterial strains have

Ⓒ indicate that it was non-virulent

Ⓓ show how Griffith distinguished it from type S

1 문제에 나온 단어·구·절을 지문에서 찾자. 해당 내용은 제시된 문단의 맨 마지막 문장으로 등장하고 있다.

2 보기들을 하나씩 읽으며 정답을 찾는다.

Ⓐ emphasize that it was rarely transmitted to other organisms

⋯▸ R형 균주가 다른 생물에 옮겨지는 경우가 거의 없다는 점을 강조하기 위해서

Ⓑ explain the role of the protective covering that bacterial strains have

⋯▸ 박테리아성 균주가 가진 보호막의 역할을 설명하기 위해서

Ⓒ indicate that it was non-virulent

⋯▸ R형 균주가 치명적이지 않다는 점을 가리키기 위해서

Ⓓ show how Griffith distinguished it from type S

⋯▸ 그리피스가 R형 균주를 S형 균주와 구분한 방법을 보여주기 위해서

R형 균주에 보호막이 없다는 점이 명시되기 전에 나온 내용을 살펴보자. 보호막 때문에 면역 체계가 박테리아를 잘 감지하지 못해서 박테리아가 치명적이었다고 나와 있다. 그리고 R형 균주에는 이 보호막이 없었다는 내용이 나오므로 박테리아가 가진 보호막의 역할, 즉 면역 체계에 잘 감지되지 않게 해주는 역할을 설명하고 있음을 알 수 있다. 따라서 Ⓑ가 정답이다.

3 다른 보기들의 오답 여부를 확인하는 것을 잊지 말자. S형 균주가 다른 생물체에 전파 가능하며 치명적이라는 언급은 있으나, R형 균주가 그렇지 않다는 말은 지문에 없으므로 Ⓐ와 Ⓒ는 오답이다. 또한 지문에는 그리피스가 서로 다른 두 개의 균주로 작업했다는 언급은 있지만 둘을 어떻게 구분했는지 그 방법에 대해서는 언급된 바가 없으므로 Ⓓ도 오답이다.

Practice

01 One of the best examples of adapting to desert conditions is small mammals, such as kangaroo rats, that have the ability to burrow underground to avoid the extreme heat.

Why does the author mention kangaroo rats?

Ⓐ To make an otherwise difficult concept easier for the reader to understand

Ⓑ To introduce the most important adaptation of the animal

Ⓒ To mention an adaptation ability that all desert mammals have

Ⓓ To provide an example of an organism that is well adapted to desert climates

02 There are many animal behaviorists that support the idea that animals can recall past events, anticipate the future, and make choices and plans. However, there is still no explanation for how honeybees, with brains weighing four ten-thousandths of an ounce, can find relocated sources of food.

Why does the author mention with brains weighing four ten-thousandths of an ounce?

Ⓐ To illustrate the cleverness of honeybees

Ⓑ To describe the small size of the brain

Ⓒ To emphasize the mysteriousness of honeybees' mental abilities

Ⓓ To disagree with the honeybees' mental abilities

03 Some scientists had assumed that the honeybee's ability to communicate with body movements showed no special intelligence. However, an interesting test of the honeybee's abilities was recently conducted. Researchers in one study moved the location of the food they should find 25 percent further away each successive time. The honeybees looking for food started to anticipate the next location of the food source. The researchers would find the bees circling the location and waiting for the food when they arrived.

Why does the author mention an interesting test of the honeybee's abilities?

Ⓐ To compare the abilities of different scientists

Ⓑ To argue that what some scientists have assumed might be wrong

Ⓒ To demonstrate the complexity of honeybee communication

Ⓓ To list the different kinds of honeybee communication

04

One behavior that indicates animal cognition is choice. In one experiment, chimpanzees compared two pairs of containers that had chocolate chips in them. One pair might hold, for instance, four chips and two chips, the other three chips and one chip. When allowed to choose which they wanted, the chimpanzees nearly always chose the pair with the most chips.

Why does the author mention chimpanzees?

Ⓐ To clarify why chimpanzees have cognitive ability

Ⓑ To classify the behaviors of humans and chimpanzees

Ⓒ To illustrate how chimpanzees are trained

Ⓓ To provide evidence of an animal making a conscious choice

05

Native Americans of the North American Southwest had to adapt to the desert region. The Hopi and Zuni Indians used irrigation ditches to transport water to their fields since water is scarce in the arid Southwest. Water was so important to them that rain was a major theme in the rituals of their religion. Other smaller tribes, like the Ute and the Shoshone, roamed the dry and mountainous regions between the Rocky Mountains and the Pacific Ocean. Their nomadic lifestyles were simpler and more strongly influenced by nature. For sustenance, they gathered seeds and hunted small creatures like rabbits and snakes.

Why does the author mention the Ute and the Shoshone?

Ⓐ To illustrate why Native Americans were nomadic

Ⓑ To compare the lifestyles of different tribes in the Southwest

Ⓒ To provide evidence of the settlements of Southwestern tribes

Ⓓ To disagree about how Native Americans subsisted in the desert

06

The Manufacturing Belt

The Manufacturing Belt is an area in the northeastern and north-central United States where the economy was formerly based on heavy industries and manufacturing. Unfortunately, the expansion of international free trade agreements in the 1960s made it much cheaper to produce heavy industrial goods like steel in third world countries and import them into the United States than to produce them there. This led to factory closures all over the Manufacturing Belt, decimating the area's economy. During each successive recession, starting with one in 1969, manufacturing jobs disappeared and were replaced by lower-paying service industry jobs. The area's new name, the Rust Belt, is a reference to the rusting machinery left over from the industrial days and a figurative reference to the general decline of the region.

Why does the author mention third world countries in the discussion of the Manufacturing Belt?

Ⓐ To indicate that the economy of the area was fragile

Ⓑ To show that the area would recover from the effects

Ⓒ To explain how the region's economy was set back

Ⓓ To indicate the severity of the impact on the economy

07

Archaeopteryx

Archaeopteryx is the oldest-known animal fossil that is generally accepted as a bird because its feathers were very similar in structure and design to modern-day bird plumage. In fact, the first-known fossils of Archaeopteryx discovered clearly show traces of the feathers that the animal had. Other scientists, however, believe Archaeopteryx was closer to a dinosaur because it had many dinosaur characteristics that birds lack. Unlike modern birds, Archaeopteryx had small teeth as well as a long bony tail. Its three fingers bore claws and moved independently, unlike the fused fingers of living birds. Also, skeletal structures related to flight seem to be incompletely developed, which suggests that Archaeopteryx may not have been able to sustain flight for great distances. These structures, therefore, cannot be said to have evolved for the purpose of flight, because they were already present in dinosaurs before either birds or flight evolved.

Why does the author mention small teeth as well as a long bony tail in the passage?

Ⓐ To explain why Archaeopteryx are intriguing to scientists

Ⓑ To give examples of features that are more like dinosaurs

Ⓒ To confirm the fact that Archaeopteryx was a bird

Ⓓ To show the way in which Archaeopteryx hunted its prey

08

Fuel in Europe

Britain faced serious energy shortage problems during the 18th century. Prior to that time, wood was the primary source of fuel and an essential building material. However, due to the population increase in large cities consumption of wood rose, resulting in rapid deforestation throughout the European continent as well as Britain. The supply was limited as the result of deforestation, while demand was continuously rising to the point where there was not enough lumber for essential housing and industries. Moreover, other alternative fuels, such as coal, were not available at the time due to certain limits in infrastructure and known methods of production. Therefore, Britain's iron industry, which called for lumber to burn to melt iron ore in blast furnaces to produce raw iron, languished due to the limited supply of wood in the 1790s. At that time, the vast forests of Austria made it possible for it to become the world's largest iron producer for a few decades until it too reached the same barrier Britain had already experienced.

The author mentions Austria in the passage in order to

Ⓐ show how a pattern repeated itself in Europe

Ⓑ show that wood is not the best material to be used for energy

Ⓒ show how much more advanced Britain was at the time

Ⓓ show why the iron industry was so vital in that time period

09

Fossils

Fossils are marks or remains left by a myriad of flora and fauna that inhabited the Earth thousands to millions of years ago. Some fossils are the hard parts of organisms such as seashells or bones that were preserved after a plant or animal died, while others are the tracks or trails of animals moving about. The majority of fossils are found in sedimentary rocks. Such fossils are formed from plant or animal remains that were quickly buried under mud or sand that collected on the bottoms of rivers, lakes, swamps, and oceans. After thousands of years, pressure turned the sediment into rock. At the same time, minerals seeped into the remains and replaced the organic material. This eventually created a stone replica of the organism. Other fossils are entire plants or animals that have been preserved in ice, tar, or solidified sap. For example, small bugs or invertebrates got trapped in tree sap, and as the sap turned into amber over time, they became fossilized. Places where there are few scavengers such as bacteria or fungi, which would decompose the organism, are ideal for fossilization.

In the passage, the author mention seashells or bones in order to

Ⓐ emphasize the importance of the presence of decomposers

Ⓑ contrast fossils of organisms' hard parts to those of tracks or trails

Ⓒ illustrate which parts of organisms are likely to become fossils

Ⓓ give an example of fossils which are found in solidified sap

10

Decrease of Pollinators

In order to reproduce, plants must be pollinated. This usually occurs through cross-pollination, the process by which pollen is transferred from one plant to another by the help of pollinators such as butterflies, bees, or moths. Unfortunately, a number of factors caused the number of beneficial pollinators to shrink in many ecosystems worldwide during the end of the 20th century. Since plants are the primary food source for animals, the reduction of one of the primary pollination agents, or even their possible disappearance, has raised concern. So, the conservation of pollinators has become a part of biodiversity conservation efforts. Of all the threats to the main pollinator, wild bees, increased international trade in modern times has introduced some serious biological ones to new areas of the world. Diseases such as American foulbrood and chalkbrood and parasites such as varroa mites if untreated generally cause the death of the colony in the areas where they do not have much resistance to these pests. In addition, the small African hive beetle is causing much loss of bees, and exotic fire ants have decimated ground-nesting bees in wide areas of the southern US.

Why does the author mention American foulbrood and chalkbrood in the passage?

Ⓐ To describe diseases carried by migrating organisms

Ⓑ To exemplify the primary parasites which can harm butterflies

Ⓒ To give an example of a cross-species disease

Ⓓ To indicate diseases that can travel through worldwide exchange

11

Urbanization in America

1 ➡ Urbanization in America was provoked by the country's rapid industrialization, which attracted many immigrants to work in America's mines and factories. However, in the late 19th and early 20th century, systematic urban planning in the United States had not yet been utilized. Builders arbitrarily constructed urban areas, so people tended to live together in haphazard cities marked by overcrowding and little differentiation between business and residential areas. Moreover, roads and buildings were created as the need arose, with a number of negative effects both for the cities themselves and for the people who inhabited them.

2 ➡ For example, the lack of proper planning in New York City led to severe health problems for its rapidly growing population. The problem stemmed from the fact that no one had planned for the massive immigration that took place in New York City and most buildings were simply constructed when an individual or business had a personal reason to do so. Therefore, the city had developed in such a way that there was no proper place to dispose of the massive amounts of waste people generated. This created the ideal location for the spread of infectious diseases such as malaria and cholera, so in the early decades of the 20th century, thousands of people died.

3 ➡ Furthermore, in Chicago, since much of the city consisted of densely packed wooden structures, the conflagration known as Great Fire of Chicago entirely destroyed more than three square miles of the city. Almost 100,000 people were left homeless, and about 300 lost their lives. At that time, the individual builders did not recognize the dangers in constructing many wooden buildings so close together.

1. **Why does the author mention malaria and cholera in paragraph 2?**

Ⓐ To name the diseases that killed the most people in early New York City
Ⓑ To provide examples of diseases that are spread by poor sanitation
Ⓒ To indicate diseases that often affect people in urban areas
Ⓓ To describe epidemics that struck poorly organized cities

2. **Why does the author discuss Chicago in paragraph 3?**

Ⓐ To demonstrate the reason why port cities developed in the early United States
Ⓑ To argue that early cities in the United States had a sanitation problem
Ⓒ To exemplify the cities that suffered because of unsystematic city planning
Ⓓ To explain how urbanization should properly be conducted

3. **Which of the following best describes the organization of the passage?**

Ⓐ Differences between two American cities are outlined.
Ⓑ Two examples of the repercussions of poor urban planning are described.
Ⓒ The development of urban planning in the United States is detailed.
Ⓓ The results of urbanization are illustrated by contrasting two cities.

12

Orchestras

1 ➡ The history of the modern orchestra that we are familiar with today goes all the way back to ancient Egypt. The first orchestras were made up of small groups of musicians that gathered for festivals, holidays or funerals. During the time of the Roman Empire, the government suppressed non-governmental musicians and informal ensembles were banned, but they reappeared after the Empire fell. It wasn't until the 11th century that families of instruments started to appear with differences in tones and octaves.

2 ➡ True modern orchestras started in the late 16th century when composers started writing music for instrumental groups, though the instruments used then are not the ones seen today. The 17th century showed a rise in stringed instruments such as violins, cellos and violas, and they evolved into the heart of the modern orchestra. At this time, innovations occurred in instrument construction, music composition, and performance techniques.

3 ➡ The next major development in orchestras came about due to Richard Wagner's need for music to accompany his musical dramas in the 18th century. His stage work called for unprecedented complexity and range of instrumentation, and most of these instruments, from the oboe to the clarinet, are still used today. In addition, he devised a larger role for the conductor in the direction of the musicians. Wagner's musical theories took a fresh look at the importance of tempo, dynamics, the bowing of stringed instruments, and the role of principals in the orchestra. These innovations brought about a revolution in orchestral composition, which set the orchestral performance style for the following eighty years.

4 ➡ Orchestras today hold central positions of importance in most large cities and in cultural life. Modern orchestras have reached the point to which they can make use of a wide choice of instrumentation, and improvements are made as the opportunity comes along. By examining how orchestras evolved, we can gain a valuable insight into the development of music over the ages.

1. In paragraph 1, the author mentions the Roman Empire in order to

Ⓐ demonstrate the influence of the Roman Empire on music

Ⓑ provide an example of obstacles faced by musical development

Ⓒ identify a major era of orchestral development

Ⓓ assert the importance of music in the western world

2. In paragraph 3, the author mentions from the oboe to the clarinet in order to

Ⓐ indicate that orchestral instruments are wind instruments

Ⓑ name some of the instruments that are still in use today

Ⓒ provide examples of orchestral instruments applied by Wagner

Ⓓ give examples of the only instruments that could play Wagner's complex pieces

3. What's the purpose of paragraph 4 in the overall discussion of orchestras?

Ⓐ It shows the factors behind the evolution outlined in the preceding paragraphs.

Ⓑ It questions the evolution of music throughout the ages.

Ⓒ It highlights how orchestras go about making their performances better.

Ⓓ It indicates the state of orchestras in the modern world.

13

The Harlem Renaissance

1 ➡ Harlem, an African-American neighborhood in New York City, attained national and worldwide fame in the 1920s and 1930s with the occurrence of the Harlem Renaissance. It was a cultural movement that wasn't really a renaissance or revival that the name implies. Instead, it brought African-American culture into the spotlight, causing many to consider it the birth of African-American art. In fact, this was the first time in which mainstream publishers and critics gave African-Americans serious notice, while African-American literature and arts attracted the attention of the nation.

2 ➡ Though it was mostly a literary movement, it also had a direct influence on developments in other areas of African-American arts and politics. A variety of factors provided the base for this movement. By the turn of the century, a black middle class had developed with the assistance of more opportunities for education and jobs. Thousands of African-Americans moved from the South to the cities of the North in pursuit of employment. This Great Migration as it was called was due to the jobs supplied by World War I. As more African-Americans made Harlem their home, it turned into the cultural and political center of African-Americans. A new political agenda calling for equal rights began here. This newfound racial pride led to a steady development in literature, arts, and music. The fiction of James Weldon Johnson and the poetry of Claude McKay received recognition by the end of World War I, and these works inspired a great deal of the literature that would soon follow, such as McKay's collection of poetry, *Harlem Shadows*, and Jean Toomer's *Cane*.

3 ➡ The Harlem Renaissance came at a time when African Americans started to see themselves in a new light. This revelation generated emphasis on realism and ethnic consciousness with nationalistic tendencies. After infusing their art with these new and profound values, especially in literary areas, African-Americans were also perceived in a different way by the mainstream American public.

4 ➡ The Harlem Renaissance was not defined by one single literary style or political ideology. What united participants was their sense of being part of a common goal and their determination to express the African-American experience artistically. There were common themes showcasing the roots of the African-American experience: a sense of racial pride and the desire for equality. The strongest aspect of the movement was the diversity of its expression. No fewer than sixteen black writers published more than 50 volumes of poetry and fiction between the mid-1920s and the mid-1930s.

1. **In paragraph 2, why does the author mention the Great Migration?**

Ⓐ To detail one of the most famous migrations in American history

Ⓑ To emphasize the number of African-Americans that migrated to northern cities

Ⓒ To prove that World War I could not have been fought without support from minorities

Ⓓ To name the movement of African-Americans to New York

2. **In paragraph 2, why does the author mention World War I?**

Ⓐ To give a timeline for when African-American writers were most productive

Ⓑ To explain why African-Americans began campaigning for equal rights

Ⓒ To highlight what created employment opportunities for African-Americans

Ⓓ To show a relationship between war and the African-American community

3. **What is the purpose of the passage?**

Ⓐ To provide specific examples for the causes of an artistic movement

Ⓑ To relate the Harlem Renaissance to other renowned American styles

Ⓒ To show the process by which the Harlem Renaissance developed

Ⓓ To present the various themes associated with the Harlem Renaissance

14

The Attribution of Behavior

1 ➡ When people observe the world and its events, most do not see them as a series of arbitrary occurrences. On the contrary, they tend to perceive and evaluate those events by giving them meaning. This tendency to make conclusions that are usually based on one's individual motives, generally results in accurate interpretations; however, it can also be affected by personal, biased factors. Sometimes, a limited amount of information is available to give the individual clear insight into another's behavior. At other times, individuals might have hidden motives or goals that distort their views, or they might lack precise cognitive perception due to a failure to use all of their resources. This is the concern of the social psychology theory known as attribution theory, which seeks to explain the manner in which people judge the behaviors of others as well as their own.

2 ➡ Attribution is the process of gathering input from our experiences of the world and giving this information meaning. Meaning comes in the form of a reason for the occurrence, and it consistently serves to explain an individual's perceptional tendencies and, in turn, their world view. Furthermore, as perception is relative among individuals, any given event or person's behavior is bound to be interpreted differently. Considering a man's behavior when he is late for a flight provides a good example. He is rushing through a terminal, running with his bags, and bumping into other travelers because he is so worried he will miss his flight. How would you interpret his behavior? Is he being selfish and aggressive, or is he justified in doing so because he's late for his flight? Certainly, there could be different claims about his actions, and this would not only affect the meaning assigned to this situation but also characterize the observer's belief system and personality.

3 ➡ When it comes to assigning meaning to human behavior, we must choose whether the behavior is due to personality, an internal causative factor, or whether others would behave the same way if faced with the same situation, an external causative factor. A fundamental contributor to attribution theory, social psychologist Harold Kelley, assumed the way people interpret behavior is generally logical and correct. With this presupposition, he identified a few simple questions that he believed allowed people to explain behavior. First, does this person always react this way when faced with this situation? Also, would others have the same reaction if they were in the same situation? And last, does this person exhibit the same behavior in other situations? These questions allow an individual to determine if a behavior is internal or dependent upon situational factors; by answering these questions, the observer can assess the acting individual and, in theory, accurately determine his personality.

4 ➡ However, the observer's bias usually plays a considerable role in attribution. When one considers that behaviors do not generally come with explanations for why the individuals performed those particular actions, there is limited information for observers to use for attributing behaviors. Because observers do not always have all the resources necessary for making completely accurate judgments, they look to their biases for reasoning. One type of bias is known as Fundamental Attribution Bias, and it occurs when the observer credits a behavior to an individual's personality rather than an external causative factor. A person using this type of bias might, for example, observe a woman stammer through a public speech. He might deduce that she didn't practice for her speech or that she just doesn't have the natural talent for the task. But the observer doesn't know this fact: the woman is simply preoccupied because her mother was just admitted into a hospital with a life-threatening illness. In another case, the observer may start with Fundamental Attribution Bias to explain someone's simple mistake, but then would cite external, self-serving causes had he been the one committing the same error.

5 ➡ Over time, attributions shape a person's cognitive perception, bolstering their biases and influencing their beliefs and aspirations. Clearly, since individuals tend to make self-serving judgments and almost never have all the details to perfectly understand behavior, extreme care should be taken when judging others.

1. In paragraph 2, the author mentions a man's behavior when he is late for a flight to

Ⓐ provide the reader with a common example of a theory in practice

Ⓑ examine the effect that air travel can have on people's behavior

Ⓒ cite the inspiration for a popular psychological theory

Ⓓ illustrate how research on a theory was carried out

2. Why does the author mention personality in paragraph 3?

Ⓐ To show how factors other than personality are important, as everybody reacts similarly in specific situations

Ⓑ To contrast externally and internally driven behavior such as when people act differently in the same situation

Ⓒ To show how people generally understand others' behavior incorrectly based on their own biased personalities

Ⓓ To show how we can consciously change our personalities over time and in turn, our manner of attribution

3. Which of the following best describes the relationship of paragraph 5 to the rest of the passage?

Ⓐ It proposes a new theory based on recent psychological research.

Ⓑ It introduces some controversial ideas about a prevailing theory.

Ⓒ It provides a critique of a psychological theory that has been disproven.

Ⓓ It issues a warning about the behavior detailed in the passage.

15

The Inca Empire

1 ➡ The Inca Empire existed from the 13th to the 16th century in the highlands of Peru. Prior to the arrival of Europeans on the South American continent, it had been the largest state to exist among the many civilizations that had previously appeared in North and South America. Geographically, the Inca Empire covered a vast amount of territory, existing in parts of what is now Ecuador, Bolivia, Chile, Argentina, and of course Peru. The capital, in Cuzco, merged the numerous independent and multi-ethnic societies under one rule using methods ranging from peaceful annexation to forceful control.

2 ➡ The Inca are famous for their architectural and engineering skills, both of which were derived not so much from technological advances, but from massive amounts of labor. Without the use of mortar, the Inca were able to produce massive structures with precisely cut stones. In fact, it has been said that one could not fit a knife blade in the joints of these carefully carved stones, which were fitted together by repeatedly lowering a rock on another and carving away any excess stone until there was no space between them. Despite its impressiveness, the Inca reputation for stonework is somewhat misleading. In fact, the construction techniques the Inca are known for were saved only for their most renowned structures, which were generally government buildings. Other structures were certainly not given the same amount of careful development, and so didn't have the same longevity. It is an exception to find smaller structures developed for housing common Inca.

3 ➡ In addition to their ability to create imposing buildings, even by modern standards, the Inca were able to produce a large network of well-maintained roads. This was made possible by their philosophy of pouring huge amounts of labor into development efforts. As a result, they were able to create 14,000 miles of roads, permitting a relatively rapid flow of people, goods and information, even without the use of the wheel. Indeed, all goods and materials were transported by hand. Utilizing this network, the Inca had runners, known as chasqui, who swiftly transmitted information and royal goods throughout the empire for the Inca elite. For their heavy loads, the Inca used their most prized animal, the llama, an animal similar to a camel in both its looks and its endurance. However, perhaps most significantly, this comprehensive transportation network facilitated the movements of the Inca army, aiding the spread of Inca culture and power to even more distant regions.

4 ➡ Although the Inca Empire certainly had no contact with the earlier Roman Empire, it had a few similarities that enabled it to generate huge amounts of power and influence over vast areas. First of all, the highly developed Inca travel network, the first of its kind in the Americas, encompassed large amounts of territory, much like the Roman system. In addition, the Inca Empire was organized in a similar manner to the Roman Empire, with a king and advisors to provide council. Because this group could conduct an organized consolidation of Inca power, the Inca were able to flourish with the efficient allocation of their resources. One more notable similarity between these empires can be seen in the use of their armies. Both empires thought it necessary to use the smallest possible force in any battle. This not only motivated soldiers to fight and overcome their enemies, but it also

kept military expenses to a minimum.

5 ➡ As they placed a high value on both natural and human resources, the Inca undertook methods other than conquest to integrate other cultures into theirs. One method was to remove the local chief from his people and take him to the Inca capital in Cuzco. There, he and his family would be bathed in riches and informed of Inca ways. He would then be returned to his people along with numerous gifts for everyone. This, without a doubt, was an extremely effective way to integrate more cultures into the enormous Inca Empire, and it saved them from having to fund the large armies necessary to control others by force. This efficient means of integration assisted the Inca in putting their energy into producing the monumental stone architecture we can still see today.

1. **Why does the author mention knife blade in paragraph 2?**

Ⓐ To demonstrate the quality of Inca steel

Ⓑ To show the precise craftwork of the Inca

Ⓒ To illustrate a common Inca carving technique

Ⓓ To explain how Inca builders were able to build such large structures

2. **Why does the author mention Roman Empire in paragraph 4?**

Ⓐ To illustrate how successful the Inca military was

Ⓑ To compare the Inca Empire to a more familiar example

Ⓒ To explain why the Inca Empire was so short-lived

Ⓓ To describe how the Inca built their road network

3. **What is the purpose of paragraph 5 in the overall discussion of the Inca Empire?**

Ⓐ It introduces another method that the Inca used to expand their empire.

Ⓑ It examines the factors that caused the ultimate end of the Inca Empire.

Ⓒ It proposes a new theory based on new discoveries in the region.

Ⓓ It points out a common misconception about the Inca culture.

Test

TOEFL Reading

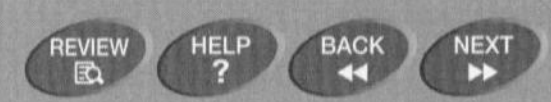

The High Middle Ages

1 ➡ The High Middle Ages is a period of European history that spans from the late 11th century to the early 14th century. It was a period of transition and expansion that has been attributed to political, psychological, and agricultural changes that preceded the era. Prior to this period, Europe had fragmented into a patchwork of minor kingdoms and principalities that often warred with one another, which was only worsened by frequent invasions from all sides. Various barbarian tribes from the steppes of Asia harassed them from the East, Vikings came raiding from the North, and the Muslim conquests had overtaken much of the Mediterranean to the South. However, strong leaders eventually emerged who dealt crushing defeats to some invaders and made peace with others, allowing the borders of Europe to solidify into strong kingdoms and a sense of cultural identity to develop. Psychologically, the people of Europe thought that the world would end around the year 1000 due to prophecies, and the pervasive war and strife made it seem like the end really was near, but the apocalypse did not come, and they emerged into an era of optimism and increased freedom. Economically, agriculture boomed as farmers converted from a two-field to a three-field system. Together, these factors led to a massive population increase, the development of trade guilds and international commerce, and a reorganization of the social order.

2 ➡ During the High Middle Ages, the population of Europe dramatically increased. This was due in part to the halting of incursions from foreign invaders that had formerly plagued the region, but not only because fewer people were being killed. Removal of that threat also allowed people to expand into areas that had been lost and left to revert to nature as well as areas that had never been settled. These areas included Eastern Europe from the Baltic Sea in

1. **Why does the author list the different invaders in paragraph 1?**
   - Ⓐ To identify which invaders made peace with and integrated into European society
   - Ⓑ To point out what led to political instability in medieval Europe
   - Ⓒ To exemplify the diversity of the invaders who expanded their territory to Europe
   - Ⓓ To imply that disintegration within Europe was the result of invasions

2. **Which of the following can be inferred about the changes that Europe underwent in paragraph 1?**
   - Ⓐ Some of the minor kingdoms in Europe were merged into bigger states.
   - Ⓑ The three-field farming system was more effective.
   - Ⓒ Social turmoil ended with the beginning of the 11th century.
   - Ⓓ People no longer believed in prophecies after the apocalypse did not come.

3. **The word "reflected" in paragraph 2 is closest in meaning to**
   - Ⓐ guaranteed
   - Ⓑ encouraged
   - Ⓒ shown
   - Ⓓ enabled

4. **According to paragraph 2, what led to the increase in population? Click on two answers.**
   - Ⓐ Waves of foreign immigration
   - Ⓑ Restoration of the Balkan region
   - Ⓒ Pioneering of unsettled land
   - Ⓓ Less deaths from war and strife

TOEFL Reading 

the north to the Balkan region in the south and parts of Spain and Italy. They converted this land from a wilderness of forests and swamps into productive farmland in what is referred to as the "great clearances." Increased arable land naturally provided a surplus of food, which was reflected by population growth. No accurate figures exist, but the population of Europe is estimated to have reached somewhere between 100 and 120 million people, and many regions held more people than they would again until the 19th century.

3 ➡ As agriculture and the population flourished, trade also received a massive boost. As various industries expanded, their supply outgrew the local demand, and they began exporting their products to other parts of the continent. To protect their collective interests and maintain strict standards for their products, these skilled tradesmen and merchants formed societies known as guilds. [■A] These associations became very wealthy, and they came to dominate not only trade, but also local politics. [■B] This was particularly true in Italy, due to its central location and many port cities, where one state actually became a separate political entity. [■C] The Republic of Florence originated in 1115 when the people revolted against their duke and formed a commune that was ruled by a council chosen by a leader elected by the guild members of Florence. [■D] It was comprised of cloth finishers and textile merchants who imported cloth from Flanders, in what is now northern Belgium. The weavers in Flanders in turn imported the wool they made into cloth from England. Members of this guild also became bankers, and they served as go-betweens for the Papacy and King Henry III of England, which shows just how far their influence reached.

4 ➡ As the merchant class emerged, the foundation of society also underwent a dramatic shift. Prior to the High Middle Ages, Europe was

5. Which of the sentences below best expresses the essential information in the highlighted sentence in the passage? Incorrect choices change the meaning in important ways or leave out essential information.

Ⓐ There were an estimated 100 to 120 million people in Europe, and there were even more people living in other regions until the 19th century.

Ⓑ While there is no historical record stating 100 to 120 million people lived in Europe, we know that this figure does not exceed that of 19th century Europe.

Ⓒ Due to the lack of definite records, we can only estimate that about 100 to 120 million people lived in Europe, and this figure was unrivaled until the 19th century.

Ⓓ Roughly 100 to 120 million people are estimated to have lived in Europe, and many other regions would not reach that figure until the 19th century.

6. According to paragraph 3, which of the following indicates how successful the guilds came to be?

Ⓐ They formed a commune which ruled the Republic of Florence.

Ⓑ They expanded their trade to other continents.

Ⓒ They acted as liaisons for heads of state.

Ⓓ They imposed rigorous guidelines about the products they imported.

Lesson 01
Making Inference

TOEFL Reading

supported by system called feudalism, wherein peasants served as tenant farmers for their lords, who managed the land for their King. Each peasant family was allotted a portion of land to farm or raise livestock on. When harvest time came, their produce was given to the lord, who gave some to the church and the peasants and kept the rest for himself. In return for their labor, the lord provided the peasants with protection. The peasants were not slaves to the lord, but they were tied to the land and could not leave it without the lord's permission. However, this relationship began to change as the lords came to own the land outright. Some lords actually purchased their land from the King, whereas most came from families that had controlled it for many generations, and the King simply allowed them to keep it in return for taxes. To raise money for these taxes, they initially sold some of their share of the harvest. Later, they began charging the farmers rent for the land they worked. This meant that the peasants could keep most of their harvest, but they had to sell it at markets to be able to pay their rent. The peasants enjoyed greater autonomy, but they were no longer guaranteed land to work or a home to live in, so they had to compete with each other.

7. According to paragraph 4, all of the following are true about the feudal system EXCEPT

Ⓐ part of the peasants' harvest was given to the peasants

Ⓑ peasants could choose to either grow crops or raise livestock

Ⓒ many lords managed the same piece of land for many generations

Ⓓ the kings owned all of the land

8. Which of the following is mentioned in paragraph 4?

Ⓐ Changes in the relationship between peasants and lords

Ⓑ Methods by which taxes were collected

Ⓒ Reasons for changes in ownership of land

Ⓓ The length of time for which the feudal system was maintained

TOEFL Reading

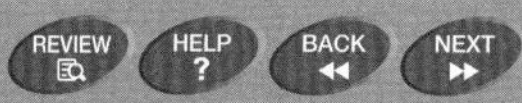

9. Look at the four squares [■] that indicate where the following sentence could be added to the passage.

One of the most powerful of these guilds was the Arte di Calimala.

Where would the sentence best fit?

Click on a square [■] to add the sentence to the passage.

10. **Directions:** An introductory sentence for a brief summary of the passage is provided below. Complete the summary by selecting the THREE answer choices that express the most important ideas in the passage. Some sentences do not belong in the summary because they express ideas that are not presented in the passage or are minor ideas in the passage. ***This question is worth 2 points.***

The High Middle Ages of Western Europe was a period of optimism and expansion.

-
-
-

Answer Choices

Ⓐ Transitioning away from the feudal system meant farmers could keep their harvest in return for paying rent to their lords.

Ⓑ Reclaimed land led to increased food production, which in turn allowed the population of Europe to grow.

Ⓒ Prior to the High Middle Ages, the people of Europe lived in constant turmoil and anxiety about the future.

Ⓓ The influence of guilds in politics can be seen from one's role as intermediary between the Papacy and King Henry III.

Ⓔ The settlement of uncharted land spanned the entire Balkan region and extended to southern Europe.

Ⓕ Guilds were societies formed as merchants looked for ways to trade more effectively while protecting their interests.

Drag your answer choices to the spaces where they belong.
To remove an answer choice, click on it. To review the passage, click on **View Text**.

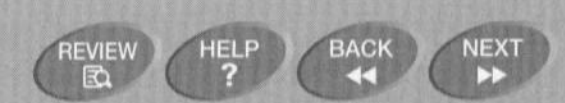

Soil Fertilization

1 ➡ In order to maintain a high level of production, farmers must apply materials to the soil to make it more fertile. These fertilizers may be spread upon the surface or worked into the soil, and they provide nutrients that the plants require to grow properly such as nitrogen, phosphorus, and potassium. Modern farmers have a variety of fertilizers to choose from that can be organic, like animal manure, green manure, and compost, or inorganic chemical compounds.

2 ➡ The first intentional use of fertilizer involved manure, which is a mixture of animal excreta and some plant matter such as straw from their bedding. As people began to raise livestock alongside their crops, they soon noticed that the animal's waste improved plant growth. So, they began to collect their animals' feces from their pens and the fields that they graze in to spread it over the soil. As horses, donkeys, and oxen became the chief means of transportation, the roads were covered in their indiscriminate leavings, which were collected and transported to farms. This ample supply of fertilizer allowed farmers to focus their farms increasingly on select products, and animal rearing became separated from raising crops. After the invention of automobiles removed animals from transportation, manure became much more difficult to obtain and transport as the ranches that continued to generate it were typically located far from the farms that relied upon it for fertilizer.

3 ➡ Natural fertilizers can also be made almost entirely from plant matter, as is the case with green manure and compost. These two fertilizers primarily consist of dead plant matter that is used to enrich the soil, but they differ in important ways. Green manure is plants that are allowed to grow in a field until they are mature, but are then tilled directly into the soil. These

11. All of the following are mentioned in paragraph 1 EXCEPT

Ⓐ the purpose of applying fertilizers
Ⓑ the advantages of opting for fertilizers
Ⓒ the types of fertilizers available
Ⓓ the method by which fertilizers are utilized

12. The word "relied" in paragraph 2 is closest in meaning to

Ⓐ reaped
Ⓑ seized
Ⓒ adhered
Ⓓ depended

13. What is the purpose of paragraph 3 as it relates to paragraph 2?

Ⓐ To explain an event that may have caused the decline in supply of animal manure as explained in paragraph 2
Ⓑ To provide an explanation of how the distinction between animal and green manure came into existence
Ⓒ To continue the explanation of various types of organic fertilizers that began in paragraph 2
Ⓓ To further expand on how the change in farming to producing select products impacted the supply of compost

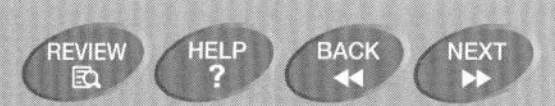

plants are typically ones that are good at fixing nitrogen into the soil like beans and clovers. They may or may not be allowed to flower and produce food for harvest, but they are still mixed into the ground while the plants are green. Compost, on the other hand, is made from plants that have been removed from the ground and gathered together in a different location. There, they are allowed to decompose above ground until they break down into nutrient rich humus. This material is then transported to fields where it is also worked into the soil.

4 ➡ Other natural means of fertilization rely upon the application of living organisms. Studies have shown that 95% or so of all plant species have symbiotic relationships with a variety of fungi. [■A] These fungi grow in and around a plant's root system, increasing the roots' surface area and helping them to absorb nutrients, particularly phosphorous. [■B] Farmers can boost their crop production by adding fungi to soil that lacks them. [■C] Many kinds produce edible parts such as truffles that they can harvest. [■D]

5 ➡ Farmers can also replenish their soil by growing different crops sequentially over years or seasons through a system called crop rotation. Farmers quickly realized that continually raising the same crop on the same plot of land inevitably depletes the soil of the nutrients that those plants require. In response they began dividing their land into halves: leaving one half to grow its natural flora while the other half was planted, and switching them the following year. The unplanted field was called fallow, and the natural growth improved the soil quality. Later, people noticed that certain plants had more beneficial effects than others, and many of them also provided food as well, which led them to plant certain crops in succession. This ensured that their land was not only replenished, but also always productive.

14. According to paragraph 3, what is the main difference between green manure and compost?

Ⓐ The time needed for decomposition to take place

Ⓑ The way they are utilized in farming

Ⓒ The types of matter from which they form

Ⓓ The method by which they are produced

15. In paragraph 4, the author states that

Ⓐ adding fungi to soil provides other benefits besides helping plants absorb nutrients

Ⓑ fungi generally foster a mutually beneficial relationship between plants and nutrients

Ⓒ plants could not have absorbed nutrients like phosphorus without the help of fungi

Ⓓ in regions where fungi are absent, it is hard to experience much crop growth

16. According to paragraph 5, what is the benefit of crop rotation?

Ⓐ Regular harvesting of the same crop

Ⓑ Continuous renewal of nutrients

Ⓒ Encouraging the growth of native flora

Ⓓ Planting of crops more useful than others

TOEFL Reading

REVIEW HELP BACK NEXT

6 ➡ All of these natural methods of fertilization mostly fell out of use in large scale agriculture after the invention of inorganic fertilizers. After scientists ascertained exactly which nutrients were most beneficial to crops, they devised methods to produce them as chemical compounds that could be applied to the soil directly. These dramatically increase plant growth, and their usage has grown rapidly worldwide, particularly since the 1950s. It is believed that modern food production would only be one third of the current amount without them.

7 ➡ Despite their obvious benefits, the usage of inorganic fertilizers has begun to decline since the 1990s due to their many side effects. Firstly, using too much fertilizer can damage the plants it is meant to help. Secondly, excess fertilizer unavoidably enters the water supply where these pollutants can harm organisms directly when they drink the water. They also promote the growth of some kinds of bacteria, which then grow exponentially in fresh or salt water. When these blooms of bacteria die off, they devour the oxygen in the water, leaving zones where nothing can survive. Other types of bacteria that fertilizers promote release chemicals into the water that make it toxic. Fertilizers can also damage the soil itself by various means. Nitrogen fertilizers can raise the soil's acidity, which damages fungi and increases aluminum availability, making the soil infertile. Phosphorous compounds also often contain heavy metals like cadmium, which builds up in the soil and can be harmful to livestock and people that consume the crops grown in it.

17. Why does the author state that modern food production would only be one third of the current amount without them in paragraph 6?

Ⓐ To highlight how much food production has increased in modern times

Ⓑ To emphasize the role organic fertilizers play in increasing the world's food supply

Ⓒ To suggest that inorganic fertilizers are more effective than organic fertilizers

Ⓓ To imply that future food production relies on a consistent supply of fertilizers

18. Which of the following is NOT mentioned in paragraph 7 as negative side effect of inorganic fertilizers?

Ⓐ Promoting the growth of infectious bacteria

Ⓑ Turning the soil acidic and infertile

Ⓒ Contaminating water for crops and livestock

Ⓓ Accumulating heavy metals in soil

TOEFL Reading

19. Look at the four squares [■] that indicate where the following sentence could be added to the passage.

In return, the fungi receive sugar that the plant generates through photosynthesis.

Where would the sentence best fit?

Click on a square [■] to add the sentence to the passage.

20. Directions: An introductory sentence for a brief summary of the passage is provided below. Complete the summary by selecting the THREE answer choices that express the most important ideas in the passage. Some sentences do not belong in the summary because they express ideas that are not presented in the passage or are minor ideas in the passage. ***This question is worth 2 points.***

Soil fertilization, the purpose of which is to promote the growth of crops, can be achieved through different types of fertilizers.

-
-
-

Answer Choices

Ⓐ Unlike animal manure, which was primarily composed of animal leavings, green manure and compost came mostly from dead plant matter.

Ⓑ For the crop rotation method, people discovered that some plants were more beneficial than others and those were the ones used in sequential rotation.

Ⓒ Chemical fertilizers created by scientists in the 1950s dramatically increased food production and enjoyed wide popularity.

Ⓓ As ranching and agriculture diverged paths, it became harder for farms to secure enough animal manure.

Ⓔ Despite their contribution to world food production, inorganic fertilizers were not without side effects, leading to their decline in the 1990s.

Ⓕ Natural methods of fertilization such as crop rotation do not directly supply nutrients, but they foster an environment where more nutrients are accessible to plants.

Drag your answer choices to the spaces where they belong.
To remove an answer choice, click on it. To review the passage, click on **View Text**.

Lesson

02 Inference

Lesson Outline

- 추론(Inference) 문제는 지문에서 명시되지는 않았지만 지문의 내용을 바탕으로 추론·유추할 수 있는 것을 찾는 문제다. 지문 내용에 관한 전문적인 지식을 요구하는 것이 아니므로, 지문 내용만 이해하면 수월하게 추론할 수 있다.
- 이 유형의 문제는 한 지문당 1~2개 정도 출제되지만, 아예 출제되지 않는 경우도 가끔 있다.

Typical Questions 

- In paragraph X, what does the author imply about ~?
  X단락에서 글쓴이가 ~에 대해 암시하는 것은 무엇인가?
- According to paragraph X, what can be inferred about ~?
  X단락에 따르면, ~에 대해 추론 가능한 것은 무엇인가?
- It can be inferred from paragraph X that　X단락에서 추론할 수 있는 것은
- Which of the following can be inferred from paragraph X?
  다음 중 X단락에서 추론 가능한 것은 무엇인가?

참고 문제에 infer, imply라는 단어가 들어가면 Inference 유형이다.

Learning Strategies

Step 1 문제에서는 항상 특정 단어·절을 제시하며 그것에 관해 무엇을 추론할 수 있는지 묻는다. 따라서 그 단어·절이 지문의 어느 부분에 위치했는지 먼저 확인해야 한다.

⋯→ 추론 문제이기 때문에 해당 문장뿐만 아니라 앞뒤의 문장도 파악해야 한다.

Step 2 이제 보기를 확인하며 지문에서 언급된 내용을 바탕으로 추론 가능한 것들인지 확인하자. 언제나 그렇듯 패러프레이징의 중요성을 잊지 말자. 지문에서 쓰인 단어가 그대로 들어갔다고 해서 항상 정답이 되지는 않는다. 어떤 Inference 문제는 해당 단어·절이 들어간 문장 전체의 패러프레이징이라고 해도 될 정도로 표현만 다르게 쓰인 비슷한 내용이 정답인 경우가 있다.

⋯→ 보통 한두 문장을 연결해서 추론하는 문제가 많으며, 때로는 한 단락의 내용을 바탕으로 추론하는 문제가 출제되기도 한다.

Step 3 정답을 고른 뒤 다른 보기들의 오답 여부를 확인하고 넘어가자. 지문에서 아예 언급하지 않은 내용을 이야기하지는 않는지, 아니면 지문에 나온 내용을 어떤 식으로 틀리게 유추했는지 살펴본다.

Example

Q. Which of the following can be inferred about 19th century Europe from paragraph 4?

1. 문제에서 제시된 단어나 절이 지문의 어디에 위치했는지 파악하자. 4단락에서 19th century Europe을 찾는다.

During the following Age of Enlightenment, many rulers undertook ambitious plans to redesign their capitals as symbols of their regime's status and wealth. One city that typifies this process is Paris, France. **By the 19th century**, Paris was massively overcrowded, and poverty, pollution, and disease wracked much of the city. When Emperor Napoleon III came to power in 1852, he commissioned Georges-Eugene Haussmann to oversee a comprehensive public works project, which he did from 1853 until his dismissal in 1870. As Napoleon III had been inspired by Hyde Park in London, Haussmann built new large parks and replanted some of the older existing ones in the city to provide the citizens with more green space.

2. 이제 보기를 확인하며 지문의 내용에서 추론 가능한 내용인지 확인하자.

Ⓐ London went through a wide-scale renovation similar to that of Paris.

⋯› 런던이 지문에서 언급되기는 했지만, 런던의 대규모 개선 작업에 관한 내용은 유추할 수 없다.

Ⓑ There was much social turbulence in 19th century Paris.

⋯› 역시 지문에서 언급되지 않았으므로 유추할 수 없다.

Ⓒ Haussmann was one of the most influential architects of the day.

⋯› 오스만이 지문에서 언급된 것은 사실이지만, 이 사람이 당시 가장 영향력 있는 건축가 중 한 사람이었다는 내용 역시 지문에서 유추하기 어렵다.

Ⓓ Napoleon III was not the only ruler who sought to renovate his capital.

⋯› '나폴레옹 3세가 수도를 개선하려고 한 유일한 통치자가 아니었다'고 한다. 단락 맨 앞에 '많은 통치자들이 수도를 다시 설계하려고 했다'는 내용이 있으므로 19세기 유럽에서 수도를 개선하려고 한 통치자는 나폴레옹 3세 한 사람만이 아니었다는 것을 유추할 수 있다.

위와 같은 이유로 정답은 Ⓓ가 된다.

Practice

01 Evolution had produced little more than simple bacteria and algae for most of Earth's 4.5 billion years of existence. However, 542 million years ago, the Cambrian period began the Paleozoic Era with the lineages of numerous fauna materializing. The Cambrian period's name comes from Cambria, the classical name for Wales, where the first fossilized remains from the period were discovered.

Based on the passage, which of the following can be inferred about the name Cambria?

Ⓐ It is no longer widely used to refer to Wales.

Ⓑ It is common for scientists to refer to this region by its original name.

Ⓒ It is used to refer to several types of animals found in Wales.

Ⓓ It is a term unlikely to be found in reference to fossils from Wales.

02 Insomnia is a sleep disorder which results in people having difficulty falling asleep, waking up often during the night and having difficulty getting back to sleep, waking up too early in the morning, or waking up feeling just as tired as they did the night before. Insomnia sufferers also have problems like sleepiness, fatigue, inability to concentrate, and irritability during the day. Contrary to popular perception, insomnia is unrelated to the number of hours of sleep a person gets. Some people just need more or less sleep than others.

Which of the following can be inferred from the passage about insomnia?

Ⓐ People with insomnia sleep fewer hours than those without insomnia.

Ⓑ Insomnia negatively impacts its sufferers during the day.

Ⓒ Daytime symptoms of insomnia can have more adverse effects on a person's life than those that occur at night.

Ⓓ All people with insomnia suffer from psychological problems.

03

Musicals are stage, television, or film productions using popular-style songs that have had a long and varied history. Musicals were performed as early as the 5th century BCE when the ancient Greeks included music and dance in their dramas. The songs were usually used to allow the chorus to comment on the actions of the main characters. The Romans copied and expanded on the Greek use of music in theatre, adding metal chips to the soles of dancers' shoes. This was the first form of tap dancing. During the Middle Ages, traveling minstrels and nomadic musical troupes performed popular songs and slapstick comedy for entertainment. Eventually, this was formalized into operas and other forms of musical theater.

According to the passage, what can be inferred about musicals?

Ⓐ They typically include traditional music.

Ⓑ They were introduced to the Romans by traveling minstrels.

Ⓒ They have existed for over 2000 years.

Ⓓ They were used in puppetry displays.

04

In 900 AD, Islamic books containing calligraphy and decorative drawings became the primary method through which artists conveyed their artistic expression. There were two developments which rendered the production of books feasible at that time. One of the strides in that direction was the advent of paper. Before then, they used parchment, which is the skin of animals such as sheep and goats prepared for use as writing material. Unlike parchment, paper was neither expensive nor difficult to produce, and it could be done on a large scale. Another contribution was the invention of a simpler form of writing known as rounded script. This alphabet effectively replaced angular script, which was difficult and required great expertise to write due to the characters' uneven heights and the irregularities in its writing patterns.

Based on the reading, it can be inferred that

Ⓐ in 900 AD, it was not easy to produce parchment

Ⓑ in 900 AD, Islamic people exclusively exploited angular script

Ⓒ prior to 900 AD, Islamic people could not purchase parchment

Ⓓ prior to 900 AD, historians strived to develop a simple method of writing

05 In studying chemistry, or any other scientific discipline, it is of the utmost importance to keep in mind that scientific theories are merely logical interpretations of the results of many experiments. These theories do not come out of thin air or by accident. Rather, they are arrived at by trial and error, especially by the hard work put forth by thousands of people over the course of many years. It is not uncommon for theories to be modified over time or replaced by better theories if further experiments uncover results that previously accepted theories were unable to explain. Basically, what are viewed as established theories at this very moment in time are not set in stone, but only represent what scientists have come up with thus far.

According to the passage, what can be inferred about theories?

Ⓐ Once a sound theory has been established, it should never be questioned.

Ⓑ Good theories never need to be replaced or modified with further experiments.

Ⓒ Updated methods of conducting experiments have contributed to producing better theories.

Ⓓ Chemistry is a unique scientific discipline because so many theories are made for it.

06

Women in the Olympics

According to Greek mythology, the Olympic Games always included a women's festival called the Heraia. It took place every four years just before the men's and may well have been open to girls from all the Greek states. There were three footraces, one for each of the three age divisions. These divisions are not cited exactly in the ancient sources, but scholars guess that they ranged from ages six to eighteen. The winners of the Heraia, just like the victors in the men's games, received an olive wreath crown and a share of the single ox slaughtered for the patron deity on behalf of all the game's participants. The Heraia victors attached painted portraits of themselves to Hera's temple in the Olympic sanctuary. Though the paintings are long gone, the niches on the temple columns into which they were set are still evident.

Which of the following can be inferred from the passage about the winners of the Heraia?

Ⓐ Some of them later married the winners of the Olympics.

Ⓑ Some of them later became members of religious orders.

Ⓒ They became mythical goddesses to future generations of girls.

Ⓓ They were held in high esteem for their accomplishments.

07

Vikings

The Vikings have long been portrayed as strong barbarians who attacked and raided many parts of Europe. However, that is only one aspect of Viking culture. They were ferocious warriors, successfully defending their borders against the Roman army, which earned them the label 'barbarians'—which is what the Romans called all groups they could not defeat. However, the Vikings were also accomplished sailors, traders, farmers, craftsmen, and explorers, with a rich tradition of human rights which are still in evidence in modern Scandinavia. During the three-hundred-year-long Viking era, they traded furs, iron objects, and slaves for silk, spices, and silver. Viking society was divided into three classes: earls, freemen, and slaves. Although birth was the main factor in determining one's class, it was possible for individuals to change their status either up or down the hierarchy.

Which of the following can be inferred from the passage about the Vikings?

Ⓐ The Vikings were feared by their neighboring countries.

Ⓑ The Vikings regarded a person's class as fixed at birth.

Ⓒ Viking society was a predominantly agricultural society.

Ⓓ The Vikings aimed to have their own empire to rival that of Rome.

08

Gorillas

Primatologists continue to study the relationships between various gorilla populations in order to determine just how many species there are. Until recently, it was mostly agreed that there are three gorilla species: the Mountain Gorilla, the Western Lowland Gorilla, and the Eastern Lowland Gorilla. However, the present agreement is that there are only two species of gorilla, and that each of these has two subspecies. The first of these two species is the Western Gorilla, with its two subspecies, the Western Lowland Gorilla and the Cross River Gorilla. The second of these two species is the Eastern Gorilla, with its two subspecies, the Mountain Gorilla and the Eastern Lowland Gorilla. Another subspecies, sometimes called the Bwindi Gorilla, has been proposed as an additional third subspecies for the Eastern Gorilla, though this proposal has not been entirely accepted among primatologists.

According to the passage, which of the following can be inferred about animal species?

Ⓐ There are always two subspecies under one species.

Ⓑ The scientific classification of gorilla species has never changed.

Ⓒ The standards scientists use to classify animal species can change over time.

Ⓓ Primatologists have recently finalized the classification of gorilla species.

09

The First Civilization

No one has been able to accurately determine when or where small groups of nomadic hunter-gatherers first embarked on creating civilization. Despite the absence of solid evidence, there is a general belief that civilization began approximately 10,000 years ago, when people may have inadvertently planted seeds in the ground as a way of preserving them. It would have surprised the initial farmers to see a sapling break through the surface of the soil where they had previously buried seeds. This was the initial momentum for the development of farming methods, and it eventually made it possible to produce enough food to support a large scale population in a small area. This fact can easily be seen in historical records, which clearly show that farming and the first large scale civilizations developed more or less contemporaneously.

What can be inferred about the first farmers according to the passage?

Ⓐ They had knowledge about the way to choose proper soil for planting seeds.

Ⓑ They were able to preserve all of their seeds in the ground.

Ⓒ It is most likely that the first people discovered farming practices by chance.

Ⓓ It is definitively known when the first farmers started to preserve seeds.

10

Meerkats

Meerkats are small mammalian creatures that inhabit southwestern Angola and South Africa in groups which number from 20 to 50. Recently, scientists have become aware that meerkats display complex social behavior. For example, research has revealed that meerkats have a fairly strict social hierarchy and that the creatures often compete for power within the group. In addition, contrary to many other animals, meerkats display many altruistic behaviors within their colonies. For example, one or more meerkats stand sentry while others are foraging or playing to warn them of approaching danger. When a predator is spotted, the meerkat performing as sentry gives a warning bark, and other members of the group will run and hide in one of their burrow's many tunnels. Meerkats also babysit the young in the group. Meerkat babysitters protect the young from threats, often endangering their own lives.

According to the passage, what can be inferred about animal species other than meerkats?

Ⓐ They make individuals participate in group work.

Ⓑ They do not need to babysit their young.

Ⓒ They typically flee and hide when approached by predators.

Ⓓ They are not likely to sacrifice themselves for others.

11

Moths

Moths vary greatly in size, ranging in wingspan from about 4 millimeters to nearly 300 millimeters. Highly diversified, they live in all but polar habitats. They are insects closely related to butterflies. Like butterflies, the wings, bodies, and legs of moths are covered with dust-like scales that come off if the insect is handled. There are, however, several differences between butterflies and moths. Although some moth species are active during the day, moths generally tend to be nocturnal. Compared to butterflies, they have stouter bodies and proportionately smaller wings. Whereas butterflies are known for their bright-colored wings, moths are usually dull colors like black, gray, brown and white with zigzag patterns that help them stay hidden. Another difference is their antennae. Unlike butterflies which have thin antennae in the shape of a golf club, moths have distinctive feathery antennae. Additionally, when at rest, they fold their wings, wrap them around their body, or hold them extended at their sides.

It can be inferred from the passage that moths

Ⓐ usually have an extraordinarily huge wingspan

Ⓑ have more delicate bodies than other insects

Ⓒ can exist in a wide array of habitats

Ⓓ are usually diurnal like butterflies

12

Glacier Decline

1 ➡ Glacier National Park in Montana, USA, is dominated by mountains which were carved into their present shapes by huge glaciers during the last ice age, but most of the glaciers in this region have largely disappeared over the last 12,000 years. When the area of Glacier National Park was first examined by climatologists in the mid-1800s, it contained over 150 glaciers. However, in the present day, only about 25 active glaciers remain in the park, mostly with just a small portion of their initial reported volume. It is believed that global warming is the main cause of this great retreat, and if current warming trends continue, there will be no mountain glaciers by 2030.

2 ➡ The impact of glacier retreat on the park's environment is a lack of habitat for flora and fauna dependent on snow-melt water. The loss of glaciers will also have an unfavorable influence on agriculture. Most summer water comes from the melting of the ice that remains in the mountains as well as systems tapping the aquifer by the Rocky Mountains. This was the primary source of water for over half of the area's inhabitants, and it was responsible for making the initial settlement of the region possible, but its volume has decreased dramatically.

1. It can be inferred about Glacier National Park from paragraph 1 that

Ⓐ it is inevitable that there will be no glaciers left in the park

Ⓑ the mountains looked very different before the ice age

Ⓒ Glacier National Park was established in the mid-1800s

Ⓓ the park only contains about 150 glaciers today

2. Which of the following is likely to happen as temperatures continue to rise?

Ⓐ There will not be enough water to irrigate arable land.

Ⓑ The glaciers will become larger within the anticipated future.

Ⓒ The supply of drinking water will increase due to the ice melting at a faster rate.

Ⓓ Animals will migrate to other states in search of sufficient water.

13

Biological Membranes

1 ➡ Biological membranes are thin, sheet-like structures that encase all cells, as well as each organelle inside eukaryotic cells. These membranes not only divide biochemical processes into separate compartments, but also actively participate in many of those reactions. For instance, cell membranes have specific transport systems that carry nutrients into cells and toxic waste out of cells, and chloroplast membranes convert sunlight into necessary chemical energy. Furthermore, cellular membranes provide a hydrophobic environment for biochemical reactions that involve water-insoluble molecules.

2 ➡ In spite of their specialized physiological functions, all cellular membranes consist mainly of two kinds of chemical components, lipids and proteins. Proteins are chains of amino acids, while lipids are bio-molecules that are soluble in organic solvents but poorly soluble in water. This definition for lipids differs from those for proteins, carbohydrates, and nucleic acids because it is based on solubility and not structure. The population of lipid molecules within a cell, like the population of water-soluble molecules, is structurally and functionally varied. Each type of biological membrane has a characteristic protein content that is specifically suited to its particular biological function.

1. **What can be inferred from paragraph 1 about biochemical processes in cells?**

Ⓐ Every process requires a unique environment created by an organelle within eukaryotic cells.

Ⓑ Conversion of sunlight to chemical energy is an exclusive process of the chloroplast membrane.

Ⓒ Some biochemical reactions may not require the participation of a biological membrane.

Ⓓ Waste disposal and nutrient intake can be done through the same transport system simultaneously.

2. **It can be inferred from the passage that**

Ⓐ the major function of membranes is almost identical regardless of their types

Ⓑ carbohydrates are fat-soluble components which can be dissolved in lipids

Ⓒ all membranes have only one function respectively according to their characteristics

Ⓓ the definition of proteins is based not on solubility but on structure

14

DDT

1 ➡ DDT, the first modern pesticide, is a colorless solid that is insoluble in water but shows good solubility in organic solvents, fats, and oils. After its invention in the early stages of World War II, it was used effectively against mosquitoes and other disease-spreading insects. It actually eradicated malaria from Europe and North America. The Swiss chemist who developed it was awarded the Nobel Prize for Physiology or Medicine in 1948.

2 ➡ However, in the 1960s, an American activist created a stir by publishing a book in which she claimed that DDT caused cancer and harmed bird reproduction by thinning eggshells. The outcry eventually led to a ban on the use of the pesticide. DDT has been shown to be highly toxic to aquatic animals like crayfish, shrimp, and many species of fish. In addition, many environmentalists have blamed DDT for the near extinction of the bald eagle in the United States. DDT is a persistent organic pollutant, which means that apex predators, like the bald eagle, will have a higher concentration of the chemicals in their systems than other animals in the same area.

3 ➡ There is an ongoing controversy over the harmful effects of DDT as there have been no proven cases of DDT harming humans or causing cancer. Thus, many countries fighting problems with malaria and other insect-borne diseases continue to use DDT as the benefits to their societies outweigh the potential risks.

1. Which of the following can be inferred about the effects of DDT?

Ⓐ DDT can cause long term genetic modifications.

Ⓑ DDT probably thinned the shells of bald eagle eggs, almost wiping out the species.

Ⓒ DDT played a crucial role in the increase of the mosquito population.

Ⓓ DDT is safer for humans than other pesticides.

2. What can be inferred from the fact that DDT is a persistent organic pollutant?

Ⓐ DDT can cause cancer in humans.

Ⓑ DDT can linger in animals' blood and bodily tissues.

Ⓒ DDT can eradicate insect-borne diseases in the world.

Ⓓ DDT can kill bald eagles and aquatic animals.

15

Insect Navigation

1 ➡ Throughout the year many species migrate seasonally, but they do not just aimlessly roam looking for a suitable location. Rather they have a particular destination they must find and advanced orientation and navigation skills are required to successfully complete this task. To effectively migrate and make shorter journeys, these species have evolved several different systems. Such navigational skills are often transferred genetically instead of learned through experience or instruction. Insects in particular have developed remarkable inherent systems that allow them to find their way.

2 ➡ When an insect needs to find food, it must leave its nest to search for nutrition to bring back. Clearly, insects must possess a system that allows them to return home, so they typically have a number of different mechanisms comprising their navigational systems. Walking insects, for example, use chemical cues to not only locate food, but also plot their journeys back to their nests. For example, ants extensively use pheromones—hormones that affect others' behavior—to coordinate the nest's tasks, one of which is marking trails and food sources. By using pheromones to create trails, ants can orient themselves and provide directions to food sites or other locations.

3 ➡ Instead of using chemical signals as a means to navigate, some insects use the Sun for navigation. Thus, upon leaving their nests, they use it as a point of reference to analyze their position and plot their course. The Sahara Desert ant provides an example of an insect that has evolved to use the Sun for navigation. When it leaves its nest, searching for food, it periodically takes calculations from the Sun to identify its position relative to home. Therefore, it can quickly find its way back to the nest, which is visibly undetectable in the sand. Its hidden nest enhances the Sahara Desert ant's survivability because predators cannot locate large numbers of the species.

4 ➡ But how do these insects navigate when the Sun itself is hidden? Sometimes the Sun is not visible as when it is blocked by something, like a hill or vegetation, so most of these insects have evolved a system connected to their circadian rhythm, a biologically-based daily activity cycle that allows them to estimate where the sun will be based on time. This might seem like a discouraging procedure when one considers that the Earth's relation to the Sun changes throughout the year. However, insects can accommodate these changes by adjusting their circadian rhythms to synchronize their biological processes with the Sun's constant deviations.

5 ➡ Harsh weather conditions can also obscure the Sun. In some rainy areas, the Sun might not be visible for weeks at a time due to the cloudy conditions that prevail. Under these conditions, estimating the Sun's location is not a possibility. To handle this challenge, insects use more direct methods for navigation. Landmarks can be used to develop the homing information necessary for successful journeys. Such visual confirmations can assist with other kinds of navigation. In addition, insects can make distance computations, which basically are made by counting the number of footsteps and any turns they take after venturing from their starting point. By integrating these two behaviors into a process known as path integration, many insects are able to precisely compute their location. Indeed, if an animal cannot determine where it is in relation to its original starting point, it will be lost and exposed to predators and other environmental hazards. Survival is obviously dependent on the ability to navigate. Therefore, by evolving these various methods, insects can overcome environmental challenges and ensure the survival of their species.

1. **What can be inferred from the passage about ant behavior?**

Ⓐ They use pheromones to defend their nest from predators.

Ⓑ Individual species may have multiple means for navigation.

Ⓒ Pheromones are useless in a desert environment.

Ⓓ Ants have poor eyesight, so they must rely on their other senses.

2. **Which of the following can be inferred from paragraph 5 about animal navigation?**

Ⓐ Animal's social behavior is crucial for the development of new navigational methods.

Ⓑ New methods of navigation will evolve depending on environmental conditions.

Ⓒ Genetic studies of animals will assist with human navigation.

Ⓓ Animals owe their navigational success exclusively to advanced computation abilities.

16

The Energy Transition in Europe

1 ➡ Throughout history, shifts in development were often marked by the utilization of a new, more efficient energy resource. Preceding the advent of the Industrial Revolution, England, in addition to other European countries, switched their energy source from wood to coal, which became its predominant fuel resource. There were several interrelated factors leading up to this influential change. First, there was massive deforestation in Europe. This created a problem in and of itself, which was then magnified when crops were planted to replace the trees. This increase in food supply corresponded with a rapid rise in population. Overpopulation only worsened the environment and led to even more demand for lumber as an energy source. To remedy this problem, governments took action and sought out ways to limit the use of wood and replace it as the primary energy source.

2 ➡ Prior to the beginning of the Industrial Revolution, the cost of lumber in England dramatically escalated due to depleted domestic quantities. The forests in England were all but destroyed to provide enough wood to fuel small towns and overcrowded cities, which relied on wood for energy to heat homes and fuel industries. In reaction to the economic and environmental impacts of long time clear-cutting within its borders, the English government took steps to protect its forests. As early as the 14th century, the King of England sought to protect areas like the Forest of Dean from widespread logging; however, he still allowed just enough logging for his personal use. To make up for the lack of supply, England had to import timber from Scandinavia and Eastern Europe, an expensive option, or seek out alternative energy resources.

3 ➡ Coal, which had been used since medieval times, was initially used only by blacksmiths to heat their furnaces. Although an abundant energy source, it had several disadvantages. The main issue with coal was its copious emission of sulfur impurities and carbon dioxide during combustion. When used as a household heating source, coal would soil clothes, give food a foul taste, and make a house unbearably smoky. Even in industrial conditions, coal was unsuitable for most processes. Breweries attempted to use coal in the process of making their beers, but they discovered that the sulfur emitted from coal altered the taste of their brews, making them undrinkable. In addition, when used for smelting in the archaic furnaces of the time, coal left high amounts of sulfur impurities infused in metals, making them useless.

4 ➡ On the other hand, there were still many reasons to pursue coal as an alternative energy source. Coal supplied more energy than wood with the same amount of production input. Moreover, coal was both more bountiful and cheaper to supply than wood. With the start of the Industrial Revolution, a plentiful energy source was needed to produce the iron necessary for industry. In response to this growing demand, scientists began placing more attention on making it a feasible resource and worked to develop new inventions to improve coal's use. In 1709, Abraham Darby, an Englishman, invented the coking process, a way to purify coal to eliminate its smoke-producing substances. Another advantage of this technological breakthrough was that it made the coal itself more resistant to being crushed by its own weight. This not only allowed coal to become a possible resource for heating stoves and furnaces but also spurred the development of larger and more effective furnaces, thus opening up the use of coal as a universal heating source in homes and industry.

5 ➡ Although new technologies needed to be invented and implemented before coal could be a viable fuel replacement, with England leading the way, the world soon saw it emerge as the principal energy resource. Once considered an inferior source of energy, coal became one of the world's leading energy resources. In fact, this is true even today, as the United States relies on coal for 90% of its energy for electricity. It is still the fastest growing energy source used in the world, with a 25% increase in use between 2001 and 2004. In addition, with coal burning technologies still improving, it will soon be possible to harness upwards of 85% of coal's potential energy, 40% more than what can be utilized today. Indeed, the problems that pre-industrial England faced led to the acceptance of coal as an energy source both at home and for the rest of the world until now.

1. According to paragraph 2, it can be inferred that

Ⓐ England was forced to rely on expensive wood imports for many centuries

Ⓑ deforestation was a major problem in England even before the Industrial Revolution

Ⓒ the King of England reserved some forests to personally engage in logging

Ⓓ England suffered from a lack of resources due to the Industrial Revolution

2. Which of the following can be inferred about coal from paragraph 4?

Ⓐ It was not a universal heating source before the Industrial Revolution.

Ⓑ Prior to the Industrial Revolution, scientists had failed to improve coal's usefulness.

Ⓒ Abraham Darby wanted to make coal a stronger and cleaner source of fuel.

Ⓓ It was more difficult to purchase coal due to the availability and price.

Test

TOEFL Reading

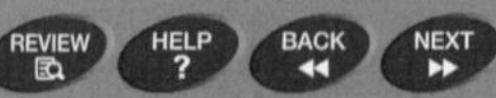

Arts and Crafts of the Aztecs

1 ➡ Although it is unknown where they actually originated, the Aztecs had become the dominant culture in the Valley of Mexico by the middle of the 15th century. [■A] Many aspects of their culture appear to have been borrowed from their neighboring tribes, which makes defining them as an individual society rather difficult. [■B] Their writing system, language, building techniques, and arts and crafts all bear similarities to other Native American groups living in their vicinity, but under them many of these reached their peak of expression. [■C] The artists of Aztec society were divided into two groups: utilitarian and luxury. [■D] The utilitarian artists created objects for everyday use like basic clothing and sandals, woven baskets, and kitchen tools. The luxury artists used precious metals, gemstones, and feathers to create items for aristocrats and priests, who occupied the highest levels of society.

2 ➡ Both groups of artists were specialists who required years of training in the proper techniques for their art form. The main differences were where they lived and how devoted they were to their craft. The utilitarians lived in rural areas outside of the major cities, and they produced their goods from their homes. They typically only worked as artists part-time, and spent the rest of their time engaged in agriculture. The ratio shifted according to the seasonal demands for field labor and utilitarian products. One of the chief products they produced was cotton cloth that was used to make clothing, but was also used as a form of currency. They also manufactured kitchen goods like wooden utensils, ceramic pottery, and knives. Their blades were made from the volcanic glass obsidian, which required a difficult and sophisticated method to work. These blades had the sharpest edge known in history, and they were used for many different

1. What can be inferred about the Aztecs in paragraph 1?

Ⓐ There is no record of when the Aztecs settled down in the Valley of Mexico.

Ⓑ The Aztecs forced their belief system on other tribes in the Valley of Mexico.

Ⓒ Aztec artists were considered to hold the highest status in society.

Ⓓ Various forms of Native American art that remain today originated from Aztec society.

2. Based on paragraph 2, what can be inferred about the utilitarians?

Ⓐ They were not efficient at making goods for society.

Ⓑ Agriculture was another source of income for them.

Ⓒ They were primarily weapon manufacturers.

Ⓓ The competition with luxury artists prevented them from being farmers full-time.

3. According to paragraphs 2 and 3, all are differences between the two groups of artists EXCEPT

Ⓐ the types of products they made

Ⓑ the places they lived in

Ⓒ the time they devoted to their crafts

Ⓓ the amount of training they received

TOEFL Reading

domestic and production tasks, including weapons.

3 ➡ Conversely, the luxury artists lived within the cities, and much of their artwork was done on commission. This is because the materials they worked with were extremely valuable, and their clients were the upper classes. The luxury artists worked on their art full time, and they had no other responsibilities. They produced jewelry and sculptures that represented gods and important historical figures from metals like gold, silver, and copper and gemstones. They also used natural materials like shells, wood, and feathers. Much of the brilliantly colored feathers they used to make headdresses, cloaks, and even to adorn armor were imported from South America, which shows how widely they traded for the materials they needed. The stones they worked with were precious and semi-precious and they included rubies, jade, amethyst, opal, turquoise, and moonstone. To polish these stones to a high gleam, they used grit of varying fineness, much as modern artists use sandpaper.

4 ➡ The upper class citizens who purchased the luxury items made up only about ten percent of Aztec society, but their appetite for new jewelry and clothing seemed limitless. In fact, legend says that the Aztec ruler would never wear the same outfit more than once. It was also customary for nobles to buy jewelry to give it to other nobles to establish and reinforce social and political connections. The priests also wore lavish robes and jewelry, and many of the temples and palaces were decorated with precious metal and stones. The walls of some rooms were covered with gold from floor to ceiling, which would light up brilliantly at the correct time of day. This ostentatious display of wealth may ultimately have led to the Aztecs' downfall.

5 ➡ When the Spanish conquistadores arrived

4. Which of the sentences below best expresses the essential information in the highlighted sentence in the passage? Incorrect choices change the meaning in important ways or leave out essential information.

Ⓐ One example of how far they traded for materials is the brilliant colored feathers that they imported from South America for garments.

Ⓑ The headdresses made from the brilliantly colored feathers were widely traded.

Ⓒ The headdresses, cloaks, and armor that they made were exported to South America, which shows how widely popular they were.

Ⓓ Trading as far as South America to obtain the brilliant colored feathers needed for headdresses and cloaks made these items pricey.

5. The word "reinforce" in paragraph 4 is closest in meaning to

Ⓐ exaggerate

Ⓑ strengthen

Ⓒ undermine

Ⓓ converge

6. According to paragraph 4, how were the items produced by luxury artists used?

Ⓐ For trading with other artists

Ⓑ For paying tax to the Aztec rulers

Ⓒ In decorating the temples

Ⓓ In religious ceremonies conducted by priests

TOEFL Reading

in Central America, they were eager to gain land and servants for the Crown of Spain, souls for the Church, and gold for everyone, including them. As they encountered smaller tribes near the coasts, many of whom were enemies of the Aztecs, they learned about the fabulous wealth that the residents of the Valley of Mexico had. When Hernando Cortes and his soldiers reached the capital city of Tenochtitlan, what they found exceeded even their inflated expectations. Due to omens that had preceded the Spaniards' arrival, and Cortes proclaiming himself the envoy of a powerful king, the Spanish were well received. They were given luxurious gifts, as was the Aztec custom, which whetted their desire for more riches. Eventually, they turned on their hosts, and after battles and an epidemic of smallpox ravaged the Aztecs, their empire fell.

7. In paragraph 5, why does the author mention Spanish conquistadores?

Ⓐ To provide an example of how famous the Aztecs' jewelry was

Ⓑ To explain how the utilitarian and luxury artists came to be distinguished

Ⓒ To signal the beginning of the Aztecs' downfall

Ⓓ To identify the people that introduced new technology to the Aztecs

8. According to paragraph 5, why were the Spanish well received by the Aztecs?

Ⓐ The Spanish gave the Aztecs luxurious gifts.

Ⓑ The Aztecs had received a positive omen about newcomers.

Ⓒ The Spanish claimed to be sent by a powerful king.

Ⓓ The Spanish had come to gain souls for the Church.

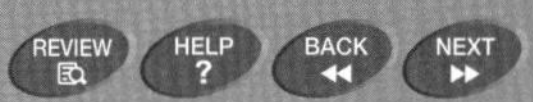

9. Look at the four squares [■] that indicate where the following sentence could be added to the passage.

This was particularly true for their art which reached its highest levels of sophistication and beauty.

Where would the sentence best fit?

Click on a square [■] to add the sentence to the passage.

10. **Directions:** An introductory sentence for a brief summary of the passage is provided below. Complete the summary by selecting the THREE answer choices that express the most important ideas in the passage. Some sentences do not belong in the summary because they express ideas that are not presented in the passage or are minor ideas in the passage. ***This question is worth 2 points.***

The artists of Aztec society were divided into two groups: utilitarian and luxury.

-
-
-

Answer Choices

(A) The utilitarian artists created everyday objects and divided their time between their craftwork and agriculture.

(B) With the arrival of the Spanish, most of the Aztec artists and their amazing artworks were shipped to Europe.

(C) Some of the temple walls were lined with gold from floor to ceiling, which lit up when sunlight hit them at the right angle.

(D) Obsidian, the volcanic glass from which Aztec blades were made, was a common resource in the Valley of Mexico.

(E) The luxury artists used many rare resources to make products for the upper class, with some precious goods being imported from South America.

(F) The Aztecs' vast wealth and exquisite artworks played a role in their downfall.

Drag your answer choices to the spaces where they belong.
To remove an answer choice, click on it. To review the passage, click on **View Text.**

TOEFL Reading

Evolution of Human Hunting

1 ➡ Before the advent of agriculture, humans relied upon a hunter-gatherer lifestyle to survive. This meant that some members of the group would spend their time searching for fruits, vegetables, and nuts and seeds. The other members of the group, typically the males, would spend their time hunting whatever game was available. This meant that they had a fairly varied omnivorous diet in the warmer months, but they depended heavily upon meat in the winter, and for most of the year during the ice age. However, the majority of primates past and present have been herbivores that prefer to eat fruit, leaves, roots and the occasional insect. That primates of the genus *Homo* have depended upon hunting for millennia is indisputable, but their motivations for doing so have remained obscure. One of the prevailing theories regarding this shift in diet focuses on a combination of climatic change, evolution, and expansion to explain why humans came to eat meat and how it benefited them.

2 ➡ Primates originally evolved in tropical and subtropical parts of Africa as herbivores, and had differentiated into many species of apes by about 15 million years ago. The equatorial forest they inhabited provided them with a bounty of flora that were fit for consumption, so they had no need to resort to other food sources. However, as the Rift Valley was created, the tectonic forces behind it caused the climate to become much drier. The forests dwindled as grassland took over the landscape. Around 6 million years ago, the last ancestor of humans not in the genus *Homo*, *Australopithecus*, evolved to cope with the changing ecology. It was capable of walking on two legs, and it had an erect posture and increased brain volume. These adaptations made it possible for the species to exploit the resources of its environment more effectively. Standing upright allowed it to see farther while on the

11. It can be inferred from paragraph 1 that

Ⓐ humans have been much healthier since they started eating meat

Ⓑ it was quite difficult to gather enough wild plants to eat during the winter

Ⓒ humans started hunting because the soil was too infertile for farming

Ⓓ it was important to keep a balance between a vegetarian and a meat diet

12. According to paragraph 2, which of the following is NOT true of *Australopithecus*?

Ⓐ They effectively adapted to environmental changes.

Ⓑ They could walk erect, which helped them see farther.

Ⓒ Their brain capacity was larger than their antecedents'.

Ⓓ They were the first ancestors classified as human beings.

13. The word "dwindled" in paragraph 2 is closest in meaning to

Ⓐ extended

Ⓑ declined

Ⓒ mingled

Ⓓ prospered

14. According to paragraph 3, which of the following is true of *Homo ergaster*?

Ⓐ Their teeth evolved to be more suitable for their new diet.

Ⓑ They first made stone tools to split fruits, nuts and logs.

Ⓒ Their brain volume was only half that of modern humans.

Ⓓ They had to travel long distances to look for warmer areas.

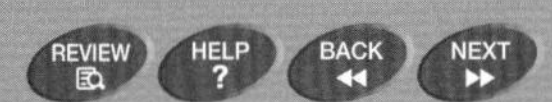

ground, moving between clusters of trees in the savannah. These adaptations also helped it survive a cooling trend during which humans diverged from the apes.

3 ➡ Many scientists classify *Homo habilis* as the first member of the genus *Homo* even though it closely resembles the *Australopithecines*. However, it had a larger brain capacity, about half that of modern humans, and as its name suggests, it made tools. These tools consisted of shaped stones that could be used to crush or cleave open other weaker objects. The next representative on the evolutionary stage, however, shows clear signs of human lineage. *Homo ergaster*, whose name means traveler, was the first species to successfully infiltrate the Eurasian continent. [■A] It had a long torso and limbs along with narrow hips, which are adaptations for traveling long distances. [■B] *Ergaster* also had further increased brain size and smaller teeth, which means that its diet had shifted. [■C] Collections of stone tools and animal bones accompanied by the remains of *Homo habilis*, *Homo ergaster*, and its descendant *Homo erectus*, point to that new form of nutrition: bone marrow. [■D]

4 ➡ The majority of the bones found at these sites were the lower legs of antelopes, which contained little meat and would have been discarded by larger predators. The humans collected these bones, which they smashed open with their stone tools to expose the protein-rich marrow within. This provided them with a supplement that not only sustained them as vegetation disappeared, but also provided them with the nutrition needed to support their rapid cerebral development. All mammals consume their mother's milk as infants, allowing them to develop rapidly both physically and mentally. Consuming animal protein appears to have had a similar effect on humans. Once they developed a taste for meat, they would have found ways to more readily procure it.

15. According to paragraph 4, humans obtained bone marrow at first by

Ⓐ hunting weaker animals which were easy to capture

Ⓑ gathering carcasses and cleaving their bones with stone tools

Ⓒ waiting for weary animals chased by predators to come close

Ⓓ approaching their prey and attacking it with hunting weapons

16. Which of the sentences below best expresses the essential information in the highlighted sentence in the passage? Incorrect choices change the meaning in important ways or leave out essential information.

Ⓐ They created sharpened sticks and stone axes to hunt for large animals, but these weapons were actually not practical.

Ⓑ Their hunting sticks and axes could only be used for catching prey at close range since they were not sophisticated.

Ⓒ They were trying to make ideal hunting weapons such as long-handled axes to capture animals at a long distance.

Ⓓ Their weapons were so outdated that they ran into danger whenever attacking their prey with these sticks and axes.

TOEFL Reading

This undoubtedly led to their first attempts at hunting. Their weapons at the time, sharpened sticks and shaped stone axes, were not ideal hunting tools, as they would have required them to get quite close to their prey to attack it. Their prey was often much better equipped to fight, so they had to rely upon their other abilities. The one that served them best was their ability to travel long distances.

5 ➡ Most experts agree that the first form of hunting was most likely what is referred to as persistence hunting. This form of hunting works for humans because they can walk upright and they have superior thermoregulation. When hunters located an animal, they would chase it until they lost sight of it. Since they could walk upright, they could easily track their prey visually and surprise it again when it stopped to rest. This process would repeat until the animal, unable to sweat as efficiently as humans, and covered in a coat of fur that they lacked, would collapse from heat exhaustion. The humans could then kill the animal with little to no risk. This hunting technique enabled humans to expand throughout Eurasia, and provided them with a key for surviving the coming ice age. *Homo neanderthalensis* and *Homo sapiens* developed more sophisticated tools and hunting strategies and are regarded as true hunter-gatherers, but they owe a debt to their ancestors who first scavenged and hunted.

17. In paragraph 5, the author explains persistence hunting by

Ⓐ refuting a statement that hunting was quite perilous

Ⓑ describing the process of tracking an animal

Ⓒ comparing it with hunting strategies of *Homo sapiens*

Ⓓ outlining the merits of thick fur during an ice age

18. According to paragraph 5, which of the following is true of thermoregulation?

Ⓐ Human bodies perspire effectively to shed excess heat.

Ⓑ Animals can keep their body temperature stable due to their lack of thick fur.

Ⓒ Humans and animals regulate their body heat in a similar way.

Ⓓ Animals gasp for breath and sweat heavily to cool off.

TOEFL Reading 

19. Look at the four squares [■] that indicate where the following sentence could be added to the passage.

Its teeth were no longer well suited to consuming rough vegetables, so it must have found a new food source.

Where would the sentence best fit?

Click on a square [■] to add the sentence to the passage.

20. **Directions:** An introductory sentence for a brief summary of the passage is provided below. Complete the summary by selecting the THREE answer choices that express the most important ideas in the passage. Some sentences do not belong in the summary because they express ideas that are not presented in the passage or are minor ideas in the passage.
This question is worth 2 points.

The ancestors of people, who had relied solely on a vegetarian diet, started hunting due to environmental change and human evolution.

-
-
-

Answer Choices

(A) While female primates focused on gathering edible plants, males spent most of their time hunting for wild animals.

(B) Early humans underwent changes in their physical form and made tools, which allowed them to successfully procure new food sources.

(C) Humans evolved in tropical areas about 15 million years ago, so they didn't worry about their food sources.

(D) Primates have diverged into various *Homo* species, such as *Homo habilis*, *Homo erectus* and modern human beings, *Homo sapiens*.

(E) As the climate got drier and the vast forests gradually shrank, human ancestors evolved to adjust to these changes.

(F) Humans' ability to walk erect and control their body temperature led to persistence hunting, a primitive form of hunting.

Drag your answer choices to the spaces where they belong.
To remove an answer choice, click on it. To review the passage, click on **View Text**.

III
Recognizing Organization

Lesson 01 Insertion

Lesson 02 Summary

Lesson 03 Category Chart

Lesson

01 Insertion

Lesson Outline

- 문장 삽입(Insertion) 문제는 삽입이라는 단어가 의미하는 것처럼 문제에서 제시하는 하나의 문장을 지문에 표시된 네 개의 [■] 중 어느 위치에 넣을지 찾는 문제다. 해당 문장을 어디에 넣었을 때 앞뒤 문장의 의미가 가장 자연스럽게 연결되는지 알아보는 게 중요하다.
- 이 유형의 문제는 한 지문당 1개가 출제되며, 보통 9번 문제로 나온다.

Typical Questions 

- Look at the four squares [■] that indicate where the following sentence could be added to the passage.
  지문에 다음 문장이 들어갈 수 있는 위치를 나타내는 네 개의 사각형[■]을 확인하시오.

  〈삽입 문장〉

  Where would the sentence best fit? 이 문장이 들어가기에 가장 적합한 곳은?

Learning Strategies

Step 1 문제에서 제시되는 문장을 읽어보고 의미를 이해한다.

···› 제시된 삽입 문장은 두 문장을 이어주는 역할을 하기 때문에 어떤 뜻인지 정확히 파악하고 있어야 한다.

Step 2 이제 네 개의 사각형[■]이 어디에 위치했는지 확인해 본다. 보통 해당 단락에서 한 문장씩 건너 표시되어 있다. [■] 앞뒤의 문장을 읽어보며 삽입 문장이 어떤 문장들과 가장 잘 어울리고, 가장 잘 연결되는지 찾아본다.

···› 해당 단락 전체를 읽어보고 의미를 파악하면 내용 흐름이 더 명확히 눈에 들어오기 때문에 답 찾기가 더 수월해진다.

Example

Q. Look at the four squares [■] that indicate where the following sentence could be added to the passage.

Roman construction methods developed from the Greek model.

Where would the sentence best fit?

1 지문에서 제시하는 문장을 읽어보고 의미를 이해한다.

= 로마의 건축 방식은 그리스 모델에서 발달했다.

2 이제 네 개의 사각형[■]이 어디에 위치했는지 확인해 본다. 보통 해당 단락에서 한 문장씩 건너 표시되어 있다. [■] 앞뒤의 문장을 읽어보며 삽입 문장이 어떤 문장들과 가장 잘 어울리고, 가장 잘 연결되는지 찾아 본다.

> One of the hallmarks of organized development throughout the history of Europe has been grid pattern streets that run in cardinal directions. [■A] [1] Many treatises cite the cities of the Greeks and Romans as the inspiration for European construction. [■B] [2] Towns in Ancient Greece were laid out on a grid system with a public square or marketplace in the center. [■C] [3] The Romans, in tandem with their far-reaching conquests, built hundreds of cities across their empire according to a plan that provided both security and easy movement. [■D]

[■A] 뒤에 오는 문장[1]은 '많은 논문이 그리스와 로마 도시들을 유럽 건축에 영감을 준 것으로 꼽는다'고 설명한다.
[■B] 뒤에 오는 문장[2]은 '고대 그리스의 마을들은 중앙에 광장이나 시장을 둔 격자형 체계로 설계됐다'고 설명한다.
[■C] 뒤에 오는 문장[3]은 '로마인들은 그들의 광범위한 정복과 동시에 안보와 쉬운 이동을 제공하려는 계획에 따라 제국 각지에 수백 개의 도시를 지었다'고 설명한다.
[■D] 뒤에는 아무 내용이 없으므로 제시된 문장이 맨 뒤에 들어가는 것이 가장 적합한지 본다.

'로마의 건축 방식은 그리스 모델에서 발달했다'는 내용을 생각했을 때, 문장 2에서 고대 그리스의 건축 시스템이 나온 뒤 문장 3에서 로마인들의 건축 계획이 언급되었으므로 제시된 문장이 이 두 문장 사이에 들어갈 때 연결이 가장 매끄럽다. 따라서 [■C]가 정답이다.

Practice

[01-05] Read the following sentences and put them in correct order.

01 Ⓐ Having such a simple and central use, the form that columns take has changed very little over the millennia. Ⓑ They are used primarily to support beams or arches that hold the upper parts of walls or ceilings. Ⓒ In architecture and structural engineering, a vertical architectural support that transmits the weight of the structure downward is called a column.

02 Ⓐ In ancient times, people baked clay sculptures in the sun after forming them. Ⓑ Historically, terracotta was used to make sculptures and pottery, as well as bricks and roof tiles. Ⓒ The resulting products were similar to the pottery of today. Ⓓ Later, potters put terracotta sculptures in the ashes of open hearths to harden.

03 Ⓐ However, some insist that prehistory started when the first tools were invented, about 2.5 million years ago. Ⓑ Although there is still much debate about when prehistory started and ended, it is generally agreed that it began about 100,000 to 200,000 years ago when the first modern Homo sapiens appeared. Ⓒ Others would say it began around 40,000 BCE with the appearance of Cro-Magnons. Ⓓ Prehistory is the period of human history before written records.

04 Ⓐ This disease, if untreated, can eventually result in damage to the brain and liver. Ⓑ Therefore, copper, although necessary, should be considered toxic to the human body in large quantities. Ⓒ Wilson's disease is a hereditary disease that causes copper to accumulate in the body. Ⓓ Similarly, research shows that people with some mental illnesses, such as schizophrenia, had high concentrations of copper in their systems.

05 Ⓐ The word renaissance literally means 'rebirth', and refers to the widespread intellectual and cultural changes brought about after European culture emerged from the Dark Ages. Ⓑ The Italian Renaissance began in the 14th century during the initial phase of the Renaissance movement in Europe. Ⓒ While these changes were significant for the Italian elite, life remained almost unchanged during the Middle Ages for the majority of the population. Ⓓ However, the ideas of the Italian Renaissance influenced the rest of Europe, thus embellishing the Northern Renaissance and English Renaissance.

06

Monarch Butterflies

[■A] Although there have been monumental strides in science, many natural phenomena still remain unexplained. [■B] Each year, Monarch butterflies make two massive migrations from the United States and Canada, covering thousands of miles. [■C] Although this seemingly instinctive behavior is common among other animals, particularly birds, there are still many questions as to why Monarchs have evolved such a behavior and how they can complete such an impressive task. [■D]

Look at the four squares [■] that indicate where the following sentence could be added to the passage.

One of the most puzzling of these is the life of the exquisite Monarch butterflies.

Where would the sentence best fit?

07

Alaska

In 1867, the Russian government decided to sell all of its Alaskan territories. The United States Congress approved the purchase of Alaska in 1867 and officially took control of the region later that year. [■A] The U.S. War Department governed Alaska until 1877. Congress established Alaska as a judicial land district in 1884 and built federal courts, government offices, and schools. [■B] The government realized the region's greater value when large deposits of gold and copper were discovered. [■C] Beginning in the early twentieth century, the government encouraged the development of mines, railroads, farms, and other enterprises that would assist economic growth in the region. [■D] The discovery of oil and natural gas was accompanied by further growth of Alaska's population, and Alaska became an official state in 1959.

Look at the four squares [■] that indicate where the following sentence could be added to the passage.

Prior to this discovery, most Americans believed that Alaska was entirely worthless.

Where would the sentence best fit?

08

Food Production in the Aztec Empire

What has now become Mexico was once occupied by the Aztec Empire, one of the most civilized cultures that existed in what is today's Central America. [■A] The pre-conquest Aztec society had some of the least conducive conditions for agriculture: a harsh climate and barren soil. [■B] These predicaments, however, were effectively dealt with through the remarkable farming and irrigation systems the Aztec people developed. [■C] Of the various crops grown by the Aztecs, their staple crop was maize cultivated in the highland terraces and valley farms across the entire empire. [■D] Grinding tools were an essential for Aztec women to pulverize maize for fixing coarse meal such as for tortillas. Other assorted crops that the Aztecs relied upon were avocados, beans, squashes, sweet potatoes, tomatoes, and chilies.

Look at the four squares [■] that indicate where the following sentence could be added to the passage.

The Aztec people could have a higher crop yield by utilizing these methods.

Where would the sentence best fit?

09

Silk Production

According to the historical record, the Zhou dynasty had a systematic process for the production of silk. The text elaborates on silk production by categorizing the various professions citing the existence of a silk master, dyers, and weavers. [■A] The laborious silk production in China was conceived on a very large scale from the very beginning. [■B] For example, mulberry-leaf pickers provided food for the silkworms, some people were trained in reeling the cocoons, and others would learn to weave the cloth. [■C] The workers were mainly women and resided in the women's section of the palace. By the 18th and 19th century, fascinated by the process, westerners sought to procure reference material showing the various stages of production. [■D]

Look at the four squares [■] that indicate where the following sentence could be added to the passage.

An enormous number of workers were divided into groups and trained to do one specific task in the silk creation process.

Where would the sentence best fit?

10

The Conquest of Mexico

Up until the 16th century, the tale of the conquest of Mexico was told in terms of the military prowess of Spain. [■A] It was thought that the better equipped soldiers and advanced tactics alone accounted for the Spaniards' dominance of the region. [■B] The indigenous populations were strangers to these new diseases, which led to catastrophic epidemics. [■C] This caused a decrease in the total number of members in the population able to defend their villages, giving the more advanced Spanish military little challenge in their invasion. [■D] Another factor was that the local ecology underwent drastic changes as new foreign organisms replaced local plants and animals. It is believed that though disease played a major role in the success of the European campaigns, it was this ecological change that allowed for the consolidation of military successes and the enduring pattern of conquest that took over so many people and so much land.

Look at the four squares [■] that indicate where the following sentence could be added to the passage.

However, it later turned out that an enormous factor in their success was the diseases brought by the Europeans and their African slaves.

Where would the sentence best fit?

11

Farming Methods

To this day, many countries utilize a number of methods to increase food production or improve farming conditions, including mechanical techniques and synthetic chemicals. However, there are other places in the world in which using irrigation and fertilizer is not reasonable. [■A] Instead, locally adapted farming techniques in these regions have shown some very positive results in increasing productivity. [■B] African farmers began to see increases in productivity by simultaneously planting wheat together with leguminous trees. [■C] The tree begins to grow slowly, sheltering the wheat and giving it enough time to mature and be harvested. [■D] Afterwards, the tree shoots up several feet. The leaves eventually fall to the ground, fertilizing it and providing the ground with much needed organic material. The trees are later cut down and the lumber is used as fuel. Through this technique, African farmers will continue to see annually increasing productivity in crop output as the land they cultivate becomes more nutrient rich.

Look at the four squares [■] that indicate where the following sentence could be added to the passage.

Africa, with its hot, arid climate, is one such place where the cost of irrigating the land and transporting fertilizer is too high.

Where would the sentence best fit?

12

Railway Construction in the U.S.

By 1855, the Illinois Central Railroad, with its primary routes connecting Chicago, Illinois with New Orleans, Louisiana and Alabama, had laid down more track than any other single railroad company in the country. The railroad company began to understand its strength in the industry and sought additional streams of revenue. [■A] Railroads not only made money from the traffic of their trains as people used railroads ever more increasingly to travel all over the country, but also from real estate speculation. [■B] For example, railroads began buying cheap land in places where they planned to create stops. [■C] A good instance of this is Manteno, Illinois, which served as one of Illinois Central's stops. [■D] In 1854, Illinois Central purchased the full rights to the land when the area was nothing more than a barren crossroads without even a single house. By 1860, this desolate expanse had grown into a bustling town replete with hotels, lumberyards, and warehouses.

Look at the four squares [■] that indicate where the following sentence could be added to the passage.

It was possible to raise the market value by developing the areas in proximity to the stops, and the property could be resold at a sizeable profit.

Where would the sentence best fit?

13

Erosion Agents in the Desert

In the adverse climate and barren soil of the desert, there are still agents for geologic change. [■A] It openly changes the desert by erosion in river valleys and lakes, but more importantly, it secretly affects the environment during the tremendous temperature changes between day and night. [■B] The dew or mist that settles on rocks during the night is absorbed by the minerals and salts in the stone. [■C] When the day approaches it is evaporated into the air, and this small hydrologic cycle repeats. [■D] As the rocks absorb the water, they slightly expand, and during the day they shrink again, causing small but important damage to them. Although this may seem insignificant, these subtle changes lead to dramatic changes in the appearance of rocks over a long period of time. Cracks or scars on the relics of ancient times demonstrate this type of erosion, and in some extreme cases, it can even burst large boulders.

Look at the four squares [■] that indicate where the following sentence could be added to the passage.

Water is one of the major elements that cause dramatic changes in such areas.

Where would the sentence best fit?

14

Colonial Gardens

Since garden plantings and designs have varied considerably depending on the time period, wealth, and their purpose, the house garden in the colonial period in the United States is not readily defined. However, because of the overwhelmingly strong British influence in colonial America, the "colonial garden" generally refers to the most common type of garden found in the 13 British colonies. Colonial gardens tended to be small and close to the house. [■A] A straight walkway generally extended on a line from the entrance of the house through the center of the garden. [■B] The paths in the gardens were generally made of flat, hard materials such as brick, gravel, or stone. [■C] Plantings in colonial gardens were generally not separated by botanical species. [■D] Such plants were often grown closer to the house, while vegetables that needed space to grow (such as corn or pumpkins) would often be grown further away from the house.

Look at the four squares [■] that indicate where the following sentence could be added to the passage.

Fruits, herbs, ornamental flowers, and vegetables were usually mixed together in the same planting bed.

Where would the sentence best fit?

15

Steam Engines

Floods in the coal mines were the most devastating hazard confronted by English miners in the 18th century. It was James Watt's steam engine that eventually addressed this predicament. Watt's early steam engines allowed water to be effectively pumped out of deep mines. [■A] His first steam engine was installed in 1776, and it caused a paradigm shift in the production lines of factories worldwide. [■B] First of all, the advent of factory steam engines facilitated better outcome and shorter time for production. [■C] Moreover, there was no longer a need for water power as a factory power source, so places for factory construction became less restricted, allowing them to be built anywhere. [■D] Finally, because factories with steam engine power called for manual laborers in large numbers, there was mass population movement from the countryside to the ever-expanding urban centers. The influence of mass movement transformed England from a cottage industry and agrarian society into a factory-based, urban-dwelling industrial powerhouse within fifty years.

Look at the four squares [■] that indicate where the following sentence could be added to the passage.

Watt, however, was interested in developing steam engines for use in factories.

Where would the sentence best fit?

16

The Orion Nebula

When we look at the Orion Nebula with all of its young stars and collection of dust and gases, what we are seeing amidst the chaos is a star factory and what our own solar system may have looked like in its infancy. [■A] The ages of the stars that make up the nebula are between roughly 300,000 and 2 million years old, which is very young for stars. In comparison, our own Sun is 4.5 billion years old. [■B] The smallest of these young stars are usually reddish in color and low in mass. In addition to these smaller stars, there are four gigantic hot stars that form the Trapezium. The Trapezium can be considered the heart of the nebular star factory. The largest of these four stars, Theta 1 Orionis C, is around 20 times as large as our Sun and about 100,000 times as bright. In fact, it is so bright that it can light up the entire nebula on its own. [■C] The immediate area around the Trapezium is crowded with hundreds of lesser stars because of the abundance of basic nebular materials. [■D] All of this raw material for forming stars makes this area one of the most densely congested clusters of stars anywhere in the known regions of our galaxy.

Look at the four squares [■] that indicate where the following sentence could be added to the passage.

The stars of the Trapezium emit ultraviolet radiation that causes the dust and gases of the nebula near them to shine brightly.

Where would the sentence best fit?

17

The Purpose and Study of Chemistry

1 ➡ Life has changed more in the past two centuries than in all of the previously recorded history of mankind. The population of the earth has increased greater than fivefold since 1800, and human life expectancy has nearly doubled due to our ability to control the spread of diseases, synthesize medicines, and increase the yields of food crops. Our modes of transportation have changed from horseback to automobiles and airplanes because of our ability to harness the energy available in petroleum. Many goods that we now manufacture are made of ceramics and polymers, rather than wood and metal, because of our ability to create materials with properties unlike any found in the natural world.

2 ➡ In one way or another, directly or indirectly, each of these life-changing developments involves chemistry, or the study of the composition, properties, and transformations of matter. [■A] Likewise, chemistry is in a great many ways responsible for the profound social changes that have taken place over the past two hundred years. [■B] Furthermore, chemistry is at the core of the current revolution in molecular biology that is exploring the ins and outs of how life is genetically controlled. [■C] In fact, no educated person today can truly understand the world around us without at least a basic knowledge of chemistry. [■D]

Look at the four squares [■] that indicate where the following sentence could be added to the passage.

Chemistry is responsible for the changes that take place in the natural world.

Where would the sentence best fit?

18

American Revolutionists and Their System of Government

1 ➡ As with any influential document, the underlying purposes of the Constitution of the United States can only be revealed through the study of the conditions and events which led to its composition and subsequent adoption by the people. Firstly, it must be remembered that there were two great factions at the time of the adoption of the U.S. Constitution. One party emphasized strength and efficiency in government and the other its popular aspects.

2 ➡ Naturally, the men who led in stirring up the revolt against the dominating presence of Great Britain and in keeping the fighting temper of the Revolutionists at a high level were the boldest and most radical of thinkers—men like Thomas Jefferson, Samuel Adams, Thomas Paine, and Patrick Henry. [■A] Generally, these men neither held large property nor possessed much practical business experience. But, in an era of disorder, they consistently put more stress upon personal liberty than on social control. [■B] These men pushed to the extreme the doctrine of human rights which had evolved in England during the trials and tribulations of the small land holders and commercial classes against the power of the aristocracy. [■C] These conditions corresponded to the prevailing economic conditions in America at the close of the 18th century. [■D] A number of these radicals viewed all government, especially of a highly centralized nature, as a spawn of evil. Government was tolerated only because it is necessary to maintain some kind of order, but at the same time, it must be kept to a minimum through constant vigilance.

Look at the four squares [■] that indicate where the following sentence could be added to the passage.

As they associated strong government with monarchy, they came to believe that the best government was one which governed least.

Where would the sentence best fit?

19

Elements

1 ➡ Everything we can see around us is formed from one or more of the 118 presently known elements. [■A] Elements are fundamental substances that cannot be changed chemically or broken down into a simpler form. [■B] For example, silver is an element. [■C] Other elements can be added to silver to make a new substance, but silver itself cannot be broken down any further. [■D] The remaining elements are ones that have been produced artificially by nuclear chemists using high-energy particle accelerators.

2 ➡ [■A] For instance, the element hydrogen accounts for approximately 75% of the mass in the universe, and the elements oxygen and silicon account for approximately 77% of the Earth's crust. [■B] Likewise, the elements oxygen, carbon, and hydrogen make up more than 90% of the human body. [■C] In contrast, it is estimated that there is probably less than a total of 20 grams of the radioactive and unstable element francium scattered across the entire planet Earth at any given time. [■D]

1. Look at the four squares [■] that indicate where the following sentence could be added to paragraph 1.

Ninety-four of the 118 known elements occur naturally.

Where would the sentence best fit?

2. Look at the four squares [■] that indicate where the following sentence could be added to paragraph 2.

The 94 known naturally occurring elements exist in widely different amounts.

Where would the sentence best fit?

20

Eclipses

1 ➡ [■A] Eclipses occur when a celestial object moves into the shadow of another object and becomes obscured. [■B] Solar eclipses, which take place when the Moon blocks the Sun from Earth's surface, and lunar eclipses, appearing when the Moon is obscured by Earth's shadow, are not the only eclipses occurring in space. [■C] Even outside of our solar system, it's possible for an eclipse to take place anytime a planet or a moon moves into the shadow of another moon or planet. [■D]

2 ➡ Earth's umbra, or shadow, forms a lunar eclipse when Earth sits between the Sun and the Moon. This phenomenon occurs at least twice a year and lasts approximately two hours. [■A] Furthermore, when the Moon passes through Earth's umbra, it isn't in complete darkness. [■B] It still receives refracted sunlight from Earth's atmosphere, giving a yellow, red, or even blue hue depending on the amount of clouds or dust present within the atmosphere at that time. [■C] However, because lunar eclipses are more prevalent and perhaps less striking than solar eclipses, they are considered less noteworthy. [■D]

1. Look at the four squares [■] that indicate where the following sentence could be added to paragraph 1.

However, from our perspective on Earth, lunar and solar eclipses can be dramatic events to witness.

Where would the sentence best fit?

2. Look at the four squares [■] that indicate where the following sentence could be added to paragraph 2.

Due to this colorful display, observing a lunar eclipse can be an unforgettable experience.

Where would the sentence best fit?

21

Weightlessness and the Human Body

1 ➡ [■A] Millions of years of evolution have prepared the human body for living on Earth, not traveling in space. [■B] To journey into space, astronauts must be inside a spacecraft traveling with thrust powerful enough to push it out of Earth's atmosphere and into orbit. [■C] Traveling in orbit creates a largely weightless living environment for their bodies. [■D]

2 ➡ The human body requires physical exertion, or having loads placed on its muscles and bones. However, during space travel, these loads, which are normally present in the form of gravity on Earth, do not exist. [■A] Because there is no pressure on the skeleton, bones break down and weaken. [■B] Likewise, since muscles aren't causing any kind of force, they decrease in size and strength, losing their ability to forcefully contract. [■C] Blood vessels in the lower extremities constrict, forcing more body fluids into the thoracic cavity and head; this lowers red blood cell levels. [■D] As a result, the body adapts to the higher fluid levels in the upper parts of the body by lowering the amount of circulating blood. This, along with the musculoskeletal atrophy the body is experiencing, can result in devastating problems.

1. Look at the four squares [■] that indicate where the following sentence could be added to paragraph 1.

They can therefore experience significant atrophy and deterioration in a short amount of time.

Where would the sentence best fit?

2. Look at the four squares [■] that indicate where the following sentence could be added to paragraph 2.

There are also circulatory system reactions that further complicate matters.

Where would the sentence best fit?

22

The Effects of Pesticides

1 ➡ Before the use of pesticides, farmers used other methods such as rotating crops, planting mixtures of crops, and using trap crops to protect their plants from pests. In the 20th century, however, advances in science led to the development of synthetic pesticides, which replaced biological agents in the form of natural enemies to manage target pest populations. While the development of these synthetic pesticides may seem to be a huge benefit for agricultural industries, there are often ecological complications resulting from their use.

2 ➡ Pesticides are extremely effective at killing pest populations. [■A] However, they tend to kill not only a target insect population but also its competitors and natural enemies even though it is not intentional. However, as the target species dies off, its natural enemies have no source of food and begin to die off as well. [■B] As a result, the target pest population resurges, returning in even greater numbers than before. [■C] This is possible because as the effects of the pesticide fade, any natural enemies must wait for their food supply to return. [■D] Known as target pest resurgence, the natural enemies are put at an extreme disadvantage as their populations fail to repopulate.

3 ➡ Another ecological reaction to pesticide use is known as secondary pest outbreak. When a key pest species is continually targeted using a pest management tactic, another species that had previously occupied the area as a minority replaces the key pest. Since there is now no enemy to keep the secondary pest population in control, the population of this species increases, becoming the new key pest. As a result, the overall pest population is not actually reduced in the area; it is simply replaced with another species of insect. In fact, the European spruce sawfly had been successfully targeted with biological controls for the twenty years following 1940 in New Brunswick, Canada. However, from 1960 to 1962, an effective synthetic pesticide was used against another arthropod in the area, the spruce budworm. Indeed, the populations of both insects declined drastically. Then, in 1964, there was an outbreak of the spruce sawfly that overwhelmed the entire insect population of the area. This indicates yet another side effect of pesticide use, which is related to genetic resistance.

4 ➡ Natural selection is a process that ensures the survival of species, and it induces the development of pesticide resistance in targeted insect species. [■A] When pesticides are used, even if they are effective, there are a few individuals that are resistant to their effects, transmitting the resistance to subsequent and even more robust generations. [■B] Therefore, in this case, the only 'progress' made with the continual use of pesticides is in creating a species of insect immune to the effects of pesticides. [■C] In addition, it doesn't take much time for a resistant species to come about. [■D] In 1946, after only 7 years of the widespread use of DDT, an effective synthetic insecticide, pesticide resistance was observed in houseflies. By 1990, astonishingly, over 500 species of arthropods were found to be resistant to pesticides. Of course, growers tried to solve this by using higher amounts or other forms of pesticide. Even with these measures, however, those insects that were resistant to one pesticide were also resistant to others.

5 ➡ The dilemmas associated with pesticide use have been coined the "pesticide treadmill." Although it might seem like a losing battle with so many things that can go wrong from pesticide use, there are some alternatives for reducing pest damage to crops. Biological control agents in the form of predators and natural enemies are effective at regulating pests without any effort from humans. Beyond question, these agents are important for keeping plant-feeding insects from becoming economic nuisances. If pesticides are to be used, selectivity, the use of pesticides without affecting natural enemies needs to be achieved.

1. Look at the four squares [■] that indicate where the following sentence could be added to paragraph 2.

This situation inevitably results in the fact that there is no enemy to suppress the target pest population.

Where would the sentence best fit?

2. Look at the four squares [■] that indicate where the following sentence could be added to paragraph 4.

The genetic inheritance of such trait causes a large increase in the numbers of pests that are immune to the pesticide.

Where would the sentence best fit?

Test

TOEFL Reading

Change in 8th Century Japan

1 ➡ During the 8th century, Japan experienced a period of dramatic change that affected all aspects and levels of Japanese society. This era is referred to as the Nara period because the capital of Japan was relocated to Nara, which then remained the seat of power for many generations. Previously, the emperor and his entire entourage would often relocate and have a new palace complex built. The use of a palace by a new ruler after the last one had died had been taboo and strictly avoided. The changes that occurred during this period included urbanization, political restructuring, religious conversion, and a shift in architectural style. The main reasons behind these comprehensive changes were that a new Japanese government had been established that controlled a large empire and the fostering of Buddhism. The changes were facilitated by intentional importation of religion and culture from China.

2 ➡ The Nara period began in 710, when Empress Gemmei established the first permanent capital city of Japan in Nara. Japanese rulers had used palaces to conduct their governments since the late 6th century, but as power became increasingly centralized, the rights and privileges of the royal family grew apace. This necessitated the building of a capital city on an impressive scale to support the government. The new royal city cost far more than a palace to construct, so it prohibited the government from relocating, and it caused the people to become more sedentary. Nara and the imperial palace were closely modeled on the city of Chang'an, the capital city of Tang dynasty China. The site for the city was chosen using Chinese principles of geographic harmony, and its streets were laid out in the same strict grid pattern that the Chinese used. Its population quickly swelled to 200,000 people, which was roughly 7 percent of the total population of the country.

1. The word "fostering" in paragraph 1 is closest in meaning to

Ⓐ encouraging
Ⓑ suppressing
Ⓒ maintaining
Ⓓ adapting

2. According to paragraph 1, all of the following took place during the 8th century Japan EXCEPT

Ⓐ city growth
Ⓑ governmental changes
Ⓒ religious changes
Ⓓ economic recession

3. According to paragraph 2, which of the following can be inferred about the city of Nara?

Ⓐ Empress Gemmei established it to show off her power.
Ⓑ It was built on grand scale to prevent its government from moving to different places.
Ⓒ Its construction was primarily motivated by the influx of Tang culture.
Ⓓ The grand scale and stability of the city contributed to the growth of its population.

TOEFL Reading

3 ➡ After Nara became the permanent capital, the government began to exert more control over economic and administrative activities. Roads were built to connect Nara with the provincial capitals, which allowed trade to flourish. Coins were minted as official currency, although they were not widely used for regular commerce. The tax system was also restructured, making tax collection more routine and efficient. The most significant emperor from this period was Emperor Shomu, a devout Buddhist who reigned from 724 to 749. He had to deal with political unrest and epidemics of diseases like smallpox, and he viewed the Buddhist religion as the means to overcome them. However, many other factions were opposed to his promotion of Buddhism, and rebelled against his rule. Eventually, Emperor Shomu won an important victory over his Shinto opponents, and he began a program of temple building throughout the nation to sponsor the religion and unify the people, although he stopped short of making it an official state religion.

4 ➡ One of the most important cultural developments of the Nara period was the permanent establishment of Buddhism in Japan. Buddhism was introduced to Japan through Korea in the 6th century, but it faced stiff resistance from traditionalists that advocated the indigenous Shinto faith. Shinto is a mixture of shamanism and mountain worship. The religion had no definitive composition, and its practice varied with location, so it was called Shinto to distinguish it from Buddhism. Emperor Shomu declared that he was the "Servant of the Three Treasures" of Buddhism: the Buddha, the teachings and laws of Buddhism, and the Buddhist community. Then, he ordered the construction of a huge temple in Nara with a giant bronze Buddha. [■A] He sent out monks to convert the people to Buddhism, but they also advised the people on secular matters. [■B] Japan gradually began to develop its own form

4. According to paragraph 3, all of the following changes were caused by the establishment of a permanent capital EXCEPT

Ⓐ the control of the government over the people became more intense

Ⓑ advances in transportation encouraged domestic trade to thrive

Ⓒ the emergence of official currency revolutionized the market economy

Ⓓ the tax system was revised so that taxes could be gathered in an efficient manner

5. Which of the sentences below best expresses the essential information in the highlighted sentence in the passage? Incorrect choices change the meaning in important ways or leave out essential information.

Ⓐ His opponents blamed Emperor Shomu for his attempt to make Buddhism an official state religion, so he brought his temple building program to an end.

Ⓑ In the face of opposition, Emperor Shomu successfully established Buddhism as an official state religion.

Ⓒ Emperor Shomu managed to win over his opponents but failed to make Buddhism an official state religion.

Ⓓ Although his attempt to make Buddhism an official state religion ended in failure, Emperor Shomu spread the religion and integrated society through temple building.

TOEFL Reading

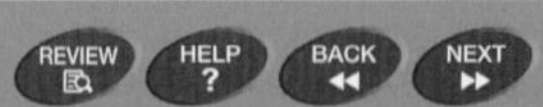

of Buddhism that incorporated many aspects of Shinto, like festivals and rituals. [■C] This helped the religion to convert new members and ensured its lasting popularity. [■D]

5 ➡ As Buddhism spread, it came to influence architecture as well. The designs of temples shifted to match those in China, and this eventually affected all public buildings. These new permanent buildings had stone foundations, massive vertical and horizontal support structures, and huge, tiled roofs. The interiors were made of paper screens which could be rearranged depending upon the situation. However, the continental style was intended for a much different climate than that found in Japan, and certain elements were adapted fairly early on. The roofs of buildings were much wider, and they gently curved to their eaves to deal with the much heavier rainfall. The heavy exterior walls of Chinese buildings were not feasible in the climate. Since the walls did not have to support the building's weight, they were replaced with thin panels of wood and paper. This synthesis of style and materials mimicked that of Buddhism and Shinto temples, as many Buddhist temples were constructed in old Shinto ones, and Shinto shrines were often attached to Buddhist temples.

6. According to paragraph 4, which of the following is the most distinguishing characteristic of Shinto?

Ⓐ It was loosely organized and integrated various religious practices from diverse regional and local traditions.

Ⓑ It placed more emphasis on pragmatic aspects of religion than on the preaching of scripture.

Ⓒ It was based on reverence for the spirits of nature and animals.

Ⓓ It was open to foreign religions and its development was influenced by Korean and Chinese practices.

7. Which of the following is mentioned in paragraph 5 as a Japanese adjustment made to the Chinese style of architecture?

Ⓐ colossal stone structures with ornamental carvings

Ⓑ wider roofs with curved eaves

Ⓒ durable interior walls made of synthetic materials

Ⓓ heavy exterior walls to support the building's weight

8. The word "feasible" in paragraph 5 is closest in meaning to

Ⓐ affordable

Ⓑ internal

Ⓒ practical

Ⓓ connected

TOEFL Reading

9. Look at the four squares [■] that indicate where the following sentence could be added to the passage.

They taught people how to survive famines, build reservoirs, repair roads and rice fields, build houses, and practice medicine.

Where would the sentence best fit?

Click on a square [■] to add the sentence to the passage.

10. **Directions:** An introductory sentence for a brief summary of the passage is provided below. Complete the summary by selecting the THREE answer choices that express the most important ideas in the passage. Some sentences do not belong in the summary because they express ideas that are not presented in the passage or are minor ideas in the passage. ***This question is worth 2 points.***

The Japanese Nara period is a remarkable era when Buddhism had a strong influence on Japan's politics, culture, and architecture.

-
-
-

Answer Choices

Ⓐ At the beginning of the 8th century, when Empress Gemmei ascended to the throne, she had to build a new royal city after frequent epidemic outbreaks.

Ⓑ The establishment of a permanent capital city made it easier for the imperial government to impose nationwide control.

Ⓒ The establishment of Nara, modeled on a Chinese capital, brought about the dramatic alienation of Japanese aristocracy from the ordinary people.

Ⓓ Buddhism was introduced in the 6th century, but it had been only partially accepted until the Nara period, when it was embraced by Emperor Shomu.

Ⓔ Shinto, which worshipped natural and ancestral spirits, developed into the indigenous faith of Japan due to Shomu's continuous efforts.

Ⓕ As a result of the increasing power of Buddhism in Japan, the traditional Japanese style of architecture was swayed by the influence of Buddhist temple architecture.

Drag your answer choices to the spaces where they belong.
To remove an answer choice, click on it. To review the passage, click on **View Text**.

The Origin of the Solar System

1 ➡ Once it had become firmly established that the Earth was not the center of the universe and that the known planets revolved around the Sun, scientists began theorizing how the Solar System could have formed. The most widely accepted theory that explains this process is called the nebular hypothesis, and it contends that the Solar System formed from a nebula that collapsed inward due to gravity. As the material condensed, its rotation caused it to form into a disk with most of its matter in the center. After the center became a young star, the remainder of the disk formed into planets. Planets orbiting other stars and stars with disks around them that have been detected and confirmed provide some of the strongest support for this theory.

2 ➡ Our solar system began to form about 4.6 billion years ago from a nebula created when a massive star reached the end of its existence and exploded, creating an extensive cloud composed almost entirely of hydrogen and helium. The gaseous material in the nebular cloud started to collapse inward due to gravitational attraction. [■A] As these hydrogen molecules **coalesced***, they formed into an increasingly dense central core. [■B] The force of gravity is equal in all directions, so the matter formed into a sphere, which is a perfectly uniform shape. [■C] Energy cannot be destroyed, so as the molecules collided and the core became denser, the energy of their movement was kept but redirected into rotation around the center of the core. [■D] This phenomenon is called the conservation of angular momentum, and it made the core spin as it contracted. Much like an ice skater will spin faster when they pull their arms in, the denser the core became the faster it spun. This rotation caused the remaining matter in the cloud to also rotate and flatten out at the equator and spread into a disk surrounding the core.

11. Which of the following is true regarding the nebular hypothesis mentioned in paragraph 1?

Ⓐ It allowed scientists to predict accurately that planets orbit stars with disks around them.

Ⓑ It allowed scientists to turn away from the dominant belief that the Earth was the center of the universe.

Ⓒ It represents our current understanding of how our solar system came to be.

Ⓓ It was proven to be untrue by the evidence of planets orbiting other celestial bodies.

12. According to paragraph 2, how did nebular matter form into a core and a surrounding disk?

Ⓐ The force of attraction between hydrogen molecules being equal in all directions, it formed matter into a sphere and a disk.

Ⓑ The extra energy compelled the hydrogen molecules to collide with each other.

Ⓒ Angular momentum made the dense core spin faster, causing the outside layer of the sphere to break away to form a disk.

Ⓓ Gravity caused matter to form into a spinning core, and that movement caused the remaining material to form a disk.

3 ➡ The kinetic energy of the molecules was also converted into heat as they collided, and as the pressure on the center of the core increased, the temperature rose and it began to glow brightly. This dense, hot core in a nebular cloud is called a protostar. The pressure and heat continued to increase until the atoms of hydrogen in the center began to fuse together, which created an internal source of energy that eventually became strong enough to counteract gravitational contraction, and the young star reached a state of equilibrium. By the time our Sun had become a stable young star, its nebula had mostly disappeared, and the disk of gas and dust that was left over began to accrete into the other celestial bodies of the system.

4 ➡ Today there are many objects that orbit around the Sun, including eight planets, many dwarf planets, asteroids, and comets. The planets began as dust grains contained in the disk around the protostar that grew larger through accretion. The dust grains collided with other grains and stuck together, repeating the process until they became the seeds of planets called protoplanets, which are about 10 km in diameter. There were thousands of these protoplanets, and they increased in size by impacting each other until they reached their current sizes. The inner four planets, Mercury, Venus, Earth, and Mars, formed so close to the Sun that their matter is composed mostly of elements that had high melting points like metals such as iron, nickel, and aluminum, and silicon based rocky material. These elements only represented a small fraction of the nebular material, which accounts for why the rocky planets are not very big.

5 ➡ The frigid outer planets may have formed around rocky and metallic material like the inner planets, but most of their material is gaseous. The area where they formed is so far from the Sun that gases are often frozen into ices. This

13. According to paragraph 3, why did the temperature in the center of the core rise?

Ⓐ The collision of molecules increased the pressure on the center of the core.

Ⓑ There was a conversion of kinetic energy to heat energy.

Ⓒ The fusion of hydrogen atoms created more energy.

Ⓓ The kinetic energy of the molecules caused the core's center to glow.

14. Which of the sentences below best expresses the essential information in the highlighted sentence in the passage? Incorrect choices change the meaning in important ways or leave out essential information.

Ⓐ Energy generated from the fusion of hydrogen atoms was sufficient to offset contracting forces and allow the star to reach equilibrium.

Ⓑ The force of gravitational contraction ultimately became strong enough to force the hydrogen atoms to fuse together to help the star reach equilibrium.

Ⓒ The force of gravitational contraction was strong, but it was not strong enough to subject the core to enough pressure and heat for hydrogen atoms to fuse together to reach a state of equilibrium.

Ⓓ The increasing pressure and heat caused the fusion of hydrogen atoms in the core's center, and this led to the star finally overcoming gravity.

material was much more plentiful than the material that the inner planets formed from, so Jupiter, Saturn, Uranus, and Neptune all began as massive cores of ice. Jupiter formed a few million years before Saturn, but they both collected huge amounts of hydrogen and other gases around their cores. Uranus and Neptune are believed to have begun forming between the two giants, and were later flung outward to their current orbits. Their development appears to have halted at the ice core stage because Jupiter and Saturn had already absorbed most of the available hydrogen.

6 ➡ The internal and external temperatures of the planets are determined by three main factors: their distance from the Sun, their size, and their density. The surfaces of the inner planets range from hot to warm, depending on how close they are to the Sun and how thick their atmospheres are. Since they are composed of dense material, their core temperatures are incredibly high. On the other hand, the outer planets are all extremely cold on their surfaces because they are far from the Sun. However, although their material is not dense, their cores are hot because they are under extreme pressure due to the planets' immense size.

*__coalesce__: to come together and form a larger group

15. Which of the following can be inferred from paragraph 4 about the formation of planets?

Ⓐ The protoplanets formed after the protostar had transformed into a stable star.

Ⓑ The asteroids and comets in our solar system do not derive their composing material from the dust grains.

Ⓒ All of the protoplanets eventually merged to form the eight planets that orbit the Sun today.

Ⓓ The proximity of inner planets to the Sun prevented gaseous materials from becoming major constituents of the planets.

16. The phrase "accounts for" in paragraph 4 is closest in meaning to

Ⓐ dominates

Ⓑ explains

Ⓒ compensates

Ⓓ restores

17. According to paragraph 5, which of the following is true about the outer planets?

Ⓐ They grew in size partially through collision with other protoplanets.

Ⓑ Their cores were primarily created from metallic elements.

Ⓒ Saturn took a longer time to form than Jupiter.

Ⓓ They are composed of mostly gases.

18. According to paragraph 6, all of the following are differences between the inner planets and outer planets EXCEPT

Ⓐ the elements which constitute them

Ⓑ the temperatures of their cores

Ⓒ their distances from the Sun

Ⓓ their surface temperatures

TOEFL Reading

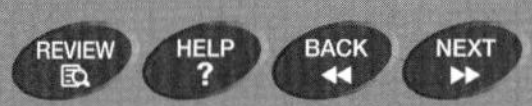

19. Look at the four squares [■] that indicate where the following sentence could be added to the passage.

Even tiny molecules of gas have mass, and that mass is attracted to other mass due to the force of gravity.

Where would the sentence best fit?

Click on a square [■] to add the sentence to the passage.

20. Directions: An introductory sentence for a brief summary of the passage is provided below. Complete the summary by selecting the THREE answer choices that express the most important ideas in the passage. Some sentences do not belong in the summary because they express ideas that are not presented in the passage or are minor ideas in the passage.
This question is worth 2 points.

Our solar system formed approximately 4.6 billion years ago.

-
-
-

Answer Choices

(A) The outer planets were formed with materials remaining after the inner planets were formed, which was mostly hydrogen.

(B) As hydrogen molecules fused together to form a dense core and their energy made the core spin and form a disk, a protostar came into existence.

(C) The nebulous disk surrounding the young Sun contained gas and dust which coalesced to eventually form protoplanets.

(D) The reason why the inner planets are smaller than the outer planets is that gases in frozen form were much more common than metals.

(E) New celestial bodies form when nebular material across the universe contracts inwards due to the pull of gravity.

(F) The conversion of kinetic to heat energy during the fusion of hydrogen atoms allowed the protostar to burn brightly.

Drag your answer choices to the spaces where they belong.
To remove an answer choice, click on it. To review the passage, click on **View Text**.

Lesson

02 Summary

Lesson Outline

- 요약(Summary) 문제는 말 그대로 지문을 네 문장으로 요약하는 문제다. 다만 맨 처음에 올 문장, 즉 '도입 문장(Introductory Sentence)'은 문제에서 제시되며 수험자는 뒤에 올 3개 문장을 보기에서 골라야 한다.
- 이 유형의 문제는 한 지문당 1개가 출제되며, 아예 출제되지 않을 때도 있다. 다만 출제되지 않을 경우 Category Chart 유형의 문제가 대신 나온다. 지문을 '요약하는' 문제이므로 맨 마지막 문제로 출제된다.

Typical Questions 

Directions: An introductory sentence for a brief summary of the passage is provided below. Complete the summary by selecting the THREE answer choices that express the most important ideas in the passage. Some sentences do not belong in the summary because they express ideas that are not presented in the passage or are minor ideas in the passage. ***This question is worth 2 points.***

지시문: 지문을 간략하게 요약한 글의 첫 문장이 아래 제시되어 있다. 지문의 가장 중요한 내용을 표현하는 세 개의 선택지를 골라 요약문을 완성하시오. 일부 문장들은 지문에 제시되지 않았거나 지문의 지엽적인 내용을 나타내기 때문에 요약문에 포함되지 않는다. ***이 문제의 배점은 2점이다.***

〈도입 문장〉

-
-
-

Answer Choices

참고 보기는 보통 6개가 주어진다.

Ⓐ --------------------- Ⓓ ---------------------

Ⓑ --------------------- Ⓔ ---------------------

Ⓒ --------------------- Ⓕ ---------------------

Drag your answer choices to the spaces where they belong.
To remove an answer choice, click on it. To review the passage, click on **View Text**.

선택한 답안을 맞는 곳에 끌어다 넣으시오.
선택한 답안을 삭제하려면, 답안에 대고 클릭하시오. 지문을 다시 보려면 지문 보기를 클릭하시오.

Learning Strategies

Step 1 도입 문장(Introductory Sentence)은 해당 지문을 관통하는 중심 문장이다. 이 문장을 중심으로 뒤에 오게 될 나머지 세 문장이 결정되므로 잘 읽어보자.

···› 문제에서 말하듯 '가장 중요한' 개념을 찾아야 한다. 문제에서는 '어떤 문장은 지문에 나오지 않았거나 중요한 내용이 아니기 때문에 답이 될 수 없다'고 명확히 밝히고 있다.

Step 2 각 단락을 한 문장으로 요약한다면 어떻게 요약할지 생각해 보자. 보통 각 단락을 요약한 문장이나 그 단락에서 가장 중요한 내용을 담은 문장이 답이다. 다시 한 번 기억해야 할 점은 지나치게 세부적인 내용은 답이 될 수 없다는 것이다.

Step 3 정답을 고른 뒤 오답 보기를 확인해 보자. 사소한 점을 언급했는지, 지문에 나오지 않은 내용이나 틀린 내용을 제시하고 있는지 짚고 넘어간다.

Example

1 ➡ The cities of Europe are known for their unique blend of classical and modern architecture, which reflects a long and complex history involving a series of transformations. One of the hallmarks of organized development throughout the history of Europe has been grid pattern streets that run in cardinal directions.

2 ➡ Many treatises cite the cities of the Greeks and Romans as the inspiration for European construction. Towns in Ancient Greece were laid out on a grid system with a public square or marketplace in the center. Roman construction methods developed from the Greek model. The Romans, in tandem with their far-reaching conquests, built hundreds of cities across their empire according to a plan that provided both security and easy movement. Strict geometrical order was imposed, with the city center holding a square for conducting business and city services surrounded by a compact grid of wide, linear roads inside a rectangular defensive wall.

3 ➡ Even though different architectural styles came into vogue, it did not create discord in the cityscape because these styles synthesized with features from previous ones. Therefore, even though parts of the cities were rebuilt throughout different eras, they blended in harmoniously.

4 ➡ Nonetheless, this idea, which came to be known as International Style, served as a prototype for all modern cities which deal with the problem of accommodating high-density urban populations. Modern design leaned towards ridding buildings of decorative elements and placing priority on function over form.

Directions: An introductory sentence for a brief summary of the passage is provided below. Complete the summary by selecting the THREE answer choices that express the most important ideas in the passage. Some sentences do not belong in the summary because they express ideas that are not presented in the passage or are minor ideas in the passage. ***This question is worth 2 points.***

The cities of Europe underwent centuries of change in architectural style to reach their current appearance.

-
-
-

Answer Choices

Ⓐ With the advent of modernism, urban design concepts steered away from ornate elements and stayed true to functional aesthetics.

Ⓑ The emphasis on a grid system to provide efficient transportation and security began with the Ancient Greeks and Romans and persisted in European cities.

Ⓒ Many European leaders wanted to display the majesty of their nations by reintroducing Greek and Roman architectural styles.

Ⓓ The decorative elements in modern buildings were round and symmetrical while those from classical buildings were pointed.

Ⓔ The renovation of cities cleared up overcrowding and laid down the foundations for public health facilities.

Ⓕ While many styles influenced European cities over the centuries, they were essentially based on previous styles that blended to create the current cityscape.

Drag your answer choices to the spaces where they belong.
To remove an answer choice, click on it. To review the passage, click on **View Text**.

1 도입 문장을 중심으로 뒤에 오게 될 나머지 세 문장이 결정되므로 잘 읽어보자.

⋯› '유럽의 도시들은 현재의 모습에 이르기까지 건축 양식에 있어 수백 년간의 변화를 거쳤다'가 중심 내용이라는 점을 기억한다.

2 각 단락을 한 문장으로 요약한다면 어떻게 요약할지 생각해 보자.

단락 1: 제시된 도입부 문장으로 요약 가능하다.
단락 2: 격자형 체계를 강조하며 고대 그리스 및 로마인들의 영향을 받았다고 한다. ⋯› Ⓑ
단락 3: 다양한 건축 양식이 유행했지만 과거 양식들의 특징과 합쳐졌다고 한다. ⋯› Ⓕ
단락 4: 오늘날의 디자인은 장식적인 요소보다 기능에 더 우선 순위를 둔다고 한다. ⋯› Ⓐ

3 정답을 고른 뒤 오답 보기를 확인해 보자. 오답은 지문에 나온 내용이 아니거나, 지문에 나왔지만 지나치게 세부적이라 중요 핵심 문장이라고 하기 어려운 것들이다.

Practice

정답 및 해석 | P. 89

[01-04] Choose the best summary of each passage.

01

The Printing Industry

When the printing industry began making use of steam power in the early 19th century, it led to widespread social changes. Newspaper and popular book publishing expanded rapidly, supporting rising literacy rates. This, in turn, caused more widespread political participation among the public, as people were able to read about the issues of the day and the candidates who were representing them. Political parties started to adapt to mass participation in elections. When universal white male suffrage was adopted in the United States, it resulted in the election of General Andrew Jackson in 1828—the first American president elected by a popular vote.

Ⓐ Literacy rates rose quickly after newspaper and book publishing expanded.
Ⓑ The increase in newspaper production allowed people to be more knowledgeable about political candidates.
Ⓒ The printing industry began using steam power in the early 19th century.
Ⓓ The introduction of the steam-powered printing press had profound effects on society.

02

The Canary Islands

1 ➡ The Canary Islands, a Spanish archipelago made up of 7 islands and 6 islets, lie off the west coast of Africa. The archipelago is divided into two provinces: Las Palmas de Gran Canaria, which includes Gran Canaria, Fuerteventura, Lanzarote, and all six islets, and Santa Cruz de Tenerife, which is made up of Tenerife, La Palma, La Gomera, and El Hierro. Since the islands belong to Spain, they are part of the European Union and are considered to have some of Europe's best beaches and the most dramatic landscapes. This has made them extremely popular tourist destinations.

2 ➡ The islands are actually the tips of a submerged volcanic mountain range, and they have the highest point in the Spanish territories, which is also the third highest volcano in the world. The varied altitudes of the Canary Islands has created many microclimates spawning varied landscapes ranging from volcanic plateaus, cloud forests, and storm-battered cliffs to green fields and agricultural areas where grapes and olives are grown. The Canary Islands also boast many national parks to protect their natural vegetation and indigenous wildlife. Of course, there are canaries on the islands that bear the songbirds' name, but unlike the yellow domesticated varieties, the canaries indigenous to the islands are a dull brown.

Ⓐ The islands were formed through volcanic activity.
Ⓑ The islands have varied landscapes because of the high altitudes of the islands.
Ⓒ The islands are full of bright yellow songbirds that share their name.
Ⓓ The islands' unique geographical features have made them popular tourist spots.

03

Fossil Dating

1 ➡ Nineteenth-century geologists could only create a relative geologic timescale when dating fossils. A relative dating technique measures geologic time by observing the various rock strata, or layers. When fossils are put in order, from those found near the surface to those found embedded in deeper rock layers, there is a general order to the findings. The upper layers are from more recent periods in time, while the deeper layers predate them. Furthermore, fossils get more complex as time passes, presenting the developmental steps of various species over time. Therefore, upon discovering fossils embedded in rock strata, geologists can determine the relative ages of their findings by comparing them to the layers surrounding them.

2 ➡ However, since there was no completely accurate way to date rocks, these dating techniques could only use fossil content to determine which layers were older or younger. Therefore, these techniques put rocks only in their chronological order without indicating the actual date when an event took place.

3 ➡ Since such relative dating techniques are likely to result in erroneous estimates of fossil dates, absolute dating methods like radiometric dating techniques were developed in the late 1940s. Radiometric dating, which involves analyzing series of isotopes of elements such as uranium and lead, works by identifying the relative proportions of any two compounds. These elements all have very long lives, lasting from 1 to 50 million years, and they allow scientists to approximate the age of a fossil that can't be dated using relative dating techniques. Both absolute and relative dating techniques are used today, supplementing each other for higher accuracy.

Ⓐ Fossils show that organisms evolve and become more complex over time, providing support for evolutionary theory.

Ⓑ Fossil dating has traditionally been done by making relative estimations, and in modern times, it has been supplemented by absolute dating methods.

Ⓒ Rock strata are layers of rock that contain fossils from the earliest periods of the Earth, and they can be analyzed for their content.

Ⓓ By analyzing naturally-occurring elements, 19th-century scientists devised an absolute way of determining the age of a fossil.

04

Landscape Architecture

1 ➡ When people think of architecture, they rarely envision plants, parks, or gardens, but an architectural specialty known as landscape gardening or landscape architecture has little to do with building construction. Rather, landscape architects arrange both natural and cultivated land elements, including hills, valleys, rivers, ponds, trees, grass, and flowers.

2 ➡ Various forms of landscape architecture have existed since 3000 BCE or even earlier. The ancient Egyptians planted gardens inside courtyards and walled enclosures, and over time they gradually became formal gardens designed to emphasize such features as artificial ponds and orchards. Other important civilizations, including the Babylonians, Assyrians, Persians, and Greeks, planned and constructed formal gardens with the help of landscape planners.

3 ➡ In Europe, landscape architecture began to emerge as a true art form during the 15th and 16th centuries. As kings and nobles built large palaces for themselves and their families, they often employed professional architects to design immense formal gardens. During this period, many of the gardens were symmetrical and organized. Shrubbery and ornamental trees were carefully trimmed and planted in straight rows, and flowerbeds, ponds, and sculptures all fit into regimented plans. Formal gardens became even more elaborate and complex during the 17th century.

4 ➡ During the 20th century, landscape architecture underwent additional changes. Prominent architects in the first half of the century believed that structures should blend in with their surroundings. During the second half of the century, the focus of landscape architecture shifted primarily to large-scale public projects and away from private gardens. Many landscape architects now work with city, state, or national governments to design green areas inside cities. In the United States, the growth of urban areas has given landscape architects new opportunities to practice their art, as they shape the environments in which growing numbers of people live, work, and relax.

Ⓐ From the 15th through 17th centuries, the European nobility fostered more sophisticated landscape architecture.

Ⓑ Contemporary landscape architects provide city dwellers with beautiful buildings in which to live, work, and relax.

Ⓒ Landscape architecture is a long-running tradition of manipulating the natural and cultivated elements of human environments.

Ⓓ Most ancient civilizations applied landscape architecture to create courtyard gardens.

05

Animal Communication

1 ➡ Due to the fact that animals either possess only basic auditory communication skills or lack them altogether, many animals rely on visual communication methods. Insects and birds, especially, possess very sophisticated visual systems of communication. These visual systems primarily belong to two different categories—passive signals and active signals—and may be used separately or in a combination of the two.

2 ➡ Passive signals require no energy expenditure on the part of the animal. This is due to the fact that passive signals are part of their physical appearance. For instance, butterflies come in a variety of colors and in a multitude of designs. With brightly colored eyespots, stripes and solid colors, butterflies are able to communicate their gender, age and species. These passive signals also inform creatures of other species that they are inedible or poisonous. Likewise, many species of birds display different patterns of colors for much the same reason as butterflies, especially to differentiate gender and to initiate reproduction.

3 ➡ The use of active signals is much more physical and requires energy from the creatures using them. Courtship and mating rituals are one area in which active signals are displayed with vigor. Some insects will perform intricate airborne dances to attract mates. At night, fireflies produce certain flashes that communicate that they are ready to reproduce or that they have already done so. Certain bird species also perform mating dances. A male prairie chicken may spend hours strutting and hopping in circles around a female trying to convince her to mate with him. Birds also make use of active signals to warn their flock of danger such as the approach of a predator by beating their wings or rapidly taking flight. These visual warnings quickly spread throughout the flock and are copied in turn by other members.

Directions: An introductory sentence for a brief summary of the passage is provided below. Complete the summary by selecting the THREE answer choices that express the most important ideas in the passage. Some sentences do not belong in the summary because they express ideas that are not presented in the passage or are minor ideas in the passage. ***This question is worth 2 points.***

Birds and insects have implemented visual measures to communicate.

-
-
-

Answer Choices

(A) Visual forms of communication are extremely obvious.

(B) Active signals can show willingness and ability to mate as well as warn others of danger.

(C) Birds use elaborate decoration to send out passive signals about their species.

(D) Fireflies use flashes of light in a sequence that represents language.

(E) Passive signals are sent by the communicator's physical features.

(F) There are two types of visual systems in animal communication.

06

Animal Cognition

1 ➡ In the first part of the 20th century, animal psychology was full of experiments that sought to uncover basic thought processes that could then be used to explain the advanced intellect of humans. Derived from the psychology movement known as behaviorism, these experiments were intended to classify specific behaviors through identifying a relationship between a stimulus and a response. The data from these experiments would then be used to explain the behavior scientifically, disregarding the influences of mental or emotional states, which, it was presupposed, animals didn't experience.

2 ➡ Then, in the late 1950s, developments in cognitive psychology made it the predominant form for explaining the behavior of both humans and animals. It addressed behavior from the opposite direction of behaviorism as it was concerned with internal states and their effects on outcomes rather than stimulus and response. In addition, animal behavior was analyzed by comparing it to what was known of human mental processes. Previously, the common animals used in behaviorist experiments were birds, dogs, and rats. However, cognitive psychologists chose to direct their research towards primates like monkeys and apes since they share a developed limbic system with and are genetically similar to humans. This shared neurological trait, which is involved in emotion, motivation, and the connection of emotions to memory, could hypothetically give researchers more reasonable grounds for applying their theories to human behavior.

3 ➡ Since cognitive psychology became the standard for analyzing animal cognition, it has found many parallels between human and animal behavior. Research on animal cognition has been centered in the areas of language, memory, and problem-solving. It has been found that monkeys possess a similar short-term memory phenomenon to humans, but the most progress has been made in researching spatial memory. Animals are particularly talented at remembering where objects are spatially. A prime example of this occurs in squirrels, which store their food supplies in hiding places covering broad areas. Despite radical changes in the environment, they can proficiently remember their storage locations by using spatial memory.

Directions: An introductory sentence for a brief summary of the passage is provided below. Complete the summary by selecting the THREE answer choices that express the most important ideas in the passage. Some sentences do not belong in the summary because they express ideas that are not presented in the passage or are minor ideas in the passage. ***This question is worth 2 points.***

Discoveries in animals' thought processes have given scientific insight into human beings' cognitive operations.

-
-
-

Answer Choices

Ⓐ Early attempts at understanding human thought processes were carried out by analyzing the way animals behave.

Ⓑ With all of the advances in behavioral sciences and research techniques, it is still impossible to fully explain all behaviors.

Ⓒ Cognitive psychology reversed the way psychologists observed and explained behavior, causing them to even change the animals used in experiments.

Ⓓ Monkeys and apes share most of the same genetic material and behavioral patterns as human beings.

Ⓔ Cognitive psychology is the preferred method for analyzing animals' behavior, with attention placed on memory, problem-solving, and language.

Ⓕ Profound changes in a landscape might confuse and disorient animals that don't have a refined spatial memory.

07

The Columbian Exchange

1 ➡ Following the arrival of Christopher Columbus's expedition in the Caribbean, waves of conquerors and colonists came to the Americas. When these Europeans interacted with the Native Americans, they exchanged many things either intentionally or by chance. Much of this exchange took place in the form of actual trade. Whether positive or negative, these exchanges had dramatic effects on both the New World and the Old World.

2 ➡ Columbus brought back many souvenirs to his Spanish sponsors from the Caribbean. His original mission had been to open a new trade route to the spices and other riches of Asia. Having essentially failed that mission, the king and queen of Spain took interest in what he did find. These included new crops like maize, tomatoes, potatoes, pumpkins and chocolate, some of which later became staples in the European diet. What interested the Spanish the most about the Americas, though, was gold because of its monetary value and rarity. The Spanish conquerors sent small armies of soldiers to explore the land they had claimed and bring back all of the gold. On the other hand, the Europeans introduced many crops to the Americas as well, the most important being sugar cane and coffee. They also brought many animals including chickens, pigs and cows, but the animal that became the most important to the Native Americans was the horse.

3 ➡ However, this exchange also had its downside. The Europeans brought warfare and oppression, but unknown to them at the time, they also brought something far worse than swords and guns: new diseases. Europe had suffered for centuries through many plagues that sometimes destroyed whole villages. Over time, the survivors of these plagues built up immunities to the epidemics. Diseases like smallpox, influenza, cholera, typhus, and the Pest were still serious in Europe, but they spread to the new land, and devastated the Native Americans. It is impossible to accurately estimate the mortality rate, but it is estimated that within 130 years, foreign diseases had killed 80 to 90 percent of Native Americans from Canada to Argentina. These diseases were spread through conquest, colonization and even brief trade meetings. When the English came later to colonize North America, only a small fraction of the local inhabitants remained.

Directions: An introductory sentence for a brief summary of the passage is provided below. Complete the summary by selecting the THREE answer choices that express the most important ideas in the passage. Some sentences do not belong in the summary because they express ideas that are not presented in the passage or are minor ideas in the passage. ***This question is worth 2 points.***

When Christopher Columbus discovered the New World, he opened the way for trade between Europe and the Americas.

-
-
-

Answer Choices

Ⓐ The main goal of the expedition was a military takeover of valuable trading ports in Asia, but they failed to reach that continent.

Ⓑ The most significant exchanges at the time involved gold from the Americas and livestock from Europe.

Ⓒ The Spanish sent armies throughout Central and South America to find gold and they conquered many tribes.

Ⓓ These exchanges had lasting effects for both continents in both positive and negative ways.

Ⓔ Despite their intent, the Europeans brought diseases that nearly wiped out most of the native population.

Ⓕ Foreign crops, livestock, technology and riches all changed hands with the Native Americans.

08

Inca Roads

1 ➡ The Inca people first established their civilization in the highlands of Peru in the 13th century. The Inca Empire was the largest empire in South America before the Spanish conquered the region. In order to connect and more easily rule this vast empire, the Inca created a network of roads which made up the most extensive transportation system in the Americas at the time. From their capital in Cusco, the Inca incorporated many neighboring cultures; some joined peacefully, while others were convinced by military force. The Inca imposed their own culture throughout their empire much like Alexander the Great did in his own. They required the people to speak their language, Quechan, and they had to worship the Incan sun god, Inti, above all others. Likewise, they believed the systematic network of roads helped to maintain and spread their unique culture.

2 ➡ The Inca road system consisted of two main north-south running roads that were linked to each other and outlying areas by many smaller connecting roads. The western road ran mostly along the coastal plain, but it curved in closer to the foothills of the Andes near desert areas. The eastern one, which was paved with stone usually one to three meters wide, ran through the high mountain valleys and grasslands of the Andes Mountains. Along the roads there were rest stops called tambos which were spaced about one day's walk apart, with larger ones every five to six days apart. Travelers could rest in the stone buildings and replenish their supplies from food stocked up there.

3 ➡ The Incas never developed wheels, and horses were introduced later by the Spanish, so the traffic on these roads consisted of people and llamas. As a result, when the roads crossed steep slopes, they would often have long flights of stairs to make walking easier. In sandy areas they built low walls to keep the sand from blowing onto the road. Furthermore, where the roads went through steep areas, they would build taller walls to keep people from falling. At their height, the roads stretched for a total of 40,000 kilometers. However, after the Spanish invaded in 1533, the roads were no longer maintained. The Spanish tore up some sections, and others deteriorated under the metal shoes of their horses. Most of the system was eventually reclaimed by nature, but there are efforts today to restore as much of it as possible.

Directions: An introductory sentence for a brief summary of the passage is provided below. Complete the summary by selecting the THREE answer choices that express the most important ideas in the passage. Some sentences do not belong in the summary because they express ideas that are not presented in the passage or are minor ideas in the passage. ***This question is worth 2 points.***

The Incas built an extensive network of roads to connect the largest empire in the Americas.

-
-
-

Answer Choices

Ⓐ The road system included two main roads that stretched across the empire from north to south.

Ⓑ The Inca modeled their conquest of neighboring tribes on Alexander the Great's campaign.

Ⓒ With the extensive road system, the Inca wanted to integrate the empire by spreading their language and religion.

Ⓓ The roads had special rest stops where travelers could restock their foodstuffs and sleep at night.

Ⓔ Although the Inca took the great care in making their roads, they were not maintained later.

Ⓕ There continues to be conservation efforts underway today to restore the roads to their former state.

09

History of Museums

1 ➡ The word 'museum', first used in English in the 17th century, evolved from the Greek term 'mouseion', or 'seat of the Muses.' The establishment of museums came about for several reasons, such as the wish to preserve culture, build social, political, and economic status, and for the pursuit of knowledge. Though museums are dominantly Western in origin, the idea of museums is not absent from other regions of the world such as Africa and Asia.

2 ➡ The first museums were not like we know them today but were more like libraries or centers of scholarly endeavors. They were originally established to serve as sources of inspiration and intellectual enlightenment. In Egypt, Pharaoh Akhenaton had a huge library constructed to house the tributes and gifts given by his allies and the various subjects that lived under his rule. King Ptolemy, another ruler of Egypt, first used the term mouseion in the 3rd century BCE. Ptolemy founded the Museum of Alexandria in order to encourage studies in the sciences. Scholars from all around the world congregated in Alexandria to further the learning of science, philosophy, and literature, just to name a few disciplines.

3 ➡ The famous museums of Europe that we are familiar with today are able to trace their establishment back to the private collections of rich merchants, nobility, and church dignitaries. It became a type of competition as the royalty of England, France, and Spain strived to build grander collections than each other. These collections eventually grew to such a size that they required entire multi-winged buildings to house them. In fact, even entire palaces, such as the French Louvre, were given over completely to the storage of museum collections. In the 17th century, as world trade was becoming established and objects from abroad became a subject of interest, the wealthy took to forming private museums that showcased objects of human achievement and the natural world on a broader scale.

4 ➡ It was not until the 18th century that the collections of the rich from the Renaissance and the 17th century moved into the public arena. The first public museum opened in Europe with the rise of a wealthier middle class spurred on by the Industrial Revolution. This promoted an interest in the wonders of science and an interest in the arts in the general public. In the New World, Americans desired to keep up with Europe and began establishing museums as early as 1750. It was not until 1814, however, that the first building constructed specifically to serve as a museum, the Peale Museum, opened in Baltimore. Its collection of art, natural specimens, and various curiosities inspired the modern museums that we are familiar with today.

Directions: An introductory sentence for a brief summary of the passage is provided below. Complete the summary by selecting the THREE answer choices that express the most important ideas in the passage. Some sentences do not belong in the summary because they express ideas that are not presented in the passage or are minor ideas in the passage. ***This question is worth 2 points.***

Since ancient times, museums have represented economic, social, and intellectual developments.

-
-
-

Answer Choices

Ⓐ The first museums were founded in Asia, with the concept spreading west.

Ⓑ In early times, building a museum could give one economic status.

Ⓒ The earliest museums were quite different from present-day museums because of their function as academic research centers.

Ⓓ The European elites displayed private collections.

Ⓔ The Renaissance caused most museums to transition from private to public.

Ⓕ Many private collections eventually became part of public museums.

10

Supernovas

1 ➡ Supernovas are massive explosions that occur throughout the galaxies of the universe after a star depletes its supply of fuel and collapses under its own weight. The resulting shock waves from these explosions spread out from the center of the explosion carrying along with them the material from the star's atmosphere. This material is rich in chemical elements produced during the star's lifetime, and as the debris travels through space it becomes the base material for new stars and planets. Although supernovas are rare, some can be seen even in the daytime and may glow for long periods.

2 ➡ A star's mass determines whether or not it will result in a supernova explosion. All stars go through the process of converting hydrogen to helium in the form of thermonuclear fusion reactions at their cores. These reactions take place as the intense heat and a star's gravitational force pull hydrogen atoms together, fusing them into helium atoms and releasing great amounts of energy. Once their hydrogen is depleted, stars enter a carbon-building phase, where the helium is turned into carbon. When the helium is gone, most stars will slowly cool to the point where they no longer emit radiation. However, when a star is particularly massive, the burning cycle is not complete with the exhaustion of helium. In the larger stars, weight causes the carbon core to shrink, raising the temperatures high enough to change carbon to oxygen, neon, silicon, sulfur, and ultimately, iron. Iron is one of the most stable elements found in stars and the atoms cannot fuse further. When the star reaches this point, the pressure produced by core reactions cannot balance the gravitational attraction between atoms, which results in the core collapsing, or imploding. This implosion leads to a build-up in kinetic energy that sends the star exploding outward as a supernova.

3 ➡ There are two main types of supernovas called Type I and Type II. The means of classification is related to a supernova's absorption of elements in its spectrum of light. Simply, Type II supernovas contain a line of hydrogen in their atmosphere, whereas Type I supernovas do not. Within each type, there are variations. Generally, Type I supernovas originate from older stars, while Type II supernovas come from younger ones. Type IIs contain plentiful amounts of hydrogen in their atmospheres, though it is diminished at their cores.

4 ➡ Supernovas are constantly being sought after because they provide key information in the study of the final evolutionary stage of huge stars. Additionally, scientists are searching for clues to the origins of chemical elements, which constitute the makeup of everything in the universe, from stars to organic life. Furthermore, these phenomena help measure distances between points in the universe through the examination and measurement of radiation produced by the star's atmospheric shell.

Directions: An introductory sentence for a brief summary of the passage is provided below. Complete the summary by selecting the THREE answer choices that express the most important ideas in the passage. Some sentences do not belong in the summary because they express ideas that are not presented in the passage or are minor ideas in the passage. ***This question is worth 2 points.***

Stars can sometimes explode and form supernovas, which spread materials for creating new planets across the universe.

-
-
-

Answer Choices

(A) Supernovas can occur if a star contains the necessary elements.

(B) Supernovas contain nutritious chemical elements that fertilize plant life.

(C) Stars remain stationary for long periods upon exploding and changing into supernovas.

(D) The two kinds of supernovas can be classified by the amount of hydrogen they possess.

(E) All chemical elements originate from stars and supernova explosions.

(F) Supernovas can give insight into the origins of the universe and the development of stars.

11

Earthquake Engineering

1 ➡ A structure that has been properly engineered to withstand earthquakes of greater than average magnitude does not necessarily have to be extremely strong or expensive. In the past, people assumed that buildings had to be sturdier in order to withstand strong earthquakes, especially in areas where they frequently occurred, which meant a greater expense for materials. However, those who work in earthquake engineering offer a very different opinion. As a distinct subset of both structural and civil engineering, earthquake engineering is the study of building and structural behavior once they are subjected to seismic loading.

2 ➡ Earthquake engineers essentially have two main objectives when designing buildings and other structures. First, they attempt to predict the potential consequences that strong earthquakes would pose in urban areas by trying to understand the interaction between the civil infrastructure (buildings, bridges, etc.) and the ground. Secondly, based upon their understanding and their predictions, they design, construct, and maintain structures that will withstand significant seismic activity and still remain able to be used by people, vehicles, etc.

3 ➡ Seismic loading is the application of agitation earthquakes generate to a structure. This agitation occurs at contact surfaces of the structure with the ground, adjacent structures, or gravity waves from a tsunami. In other words, if the agitation affects where a structure sits, and if it is connected to a neighboring structure somehow, that neighboring structure will also be affected by the agitation. The severity of seismic loading from any one event depends on several factors: the anticipated earthquake's parameters at the site of the agitation, the geotechnical parameters of the site, and the parameters of the building. Analysis of these factors has allowed architects and engineers to construct much safer and taller buildings.

4 ➡ Ancient builders had a fatalistic view of earthquakes. For instance, the Greeks believed that earthquakes were a direct result of the wrath of gods, such as Poseidon, the god of the sea and the Greek pantheon's most notorious 'Earth-Shaker.' Thus, these ancient people didn't think the effects of earthquakes could be resisted by humans. Nowadays, however, attitudes toward earthquakes have changed dramatically. It is now known that by compensating for seismic loading, structures can be built with the ability to resist earthquakes to varying extents.

5 ➡ Most structures in major cities are now built with earthquake or seismic performance in mind. Earthquake or seismic performance is a structure's ability to maintain its safety and serviceability during or following an event of seismic activity. The structure is normally considered 'safe' if it does not endanger the lives and well-being of those in or around it by collapsing, either partially or completely. A structure is considered 'serviceable' after a seismic event if it is still able to fulfill the operational functions for which it was designed. For instance, if a bridge can still support the traffic it was built for after an earthquake, it would be considered serviceable. The basic concepts in modern earthquake engineering, which are implemented in the major building codes around the world, assume that a properly engineered structure will now survive 'the Big One.' This term refers to the likelihood of a major earthquake in a particularly vulnerable location, like California's Bay Area which lies close to the San Andreas Fault.

6 ➡ In order to best build structures that would survive major seismic events, engineers need to know the quantified level of an actual or anticipated seismic event in association with the direct damage to an individual structure subject to such an event. The best way to go about doing this is to put a detailed model of the structure in question on a shake-table. Shake-tables are exactly what the name implies. They are tables, platforms, or stages that are capable of simulating seismic agitation, which allows engineers to observe and gauge the possibilities of a real-life event. This method has been in use for more than a century, and it has greatly helped with the construction of safer buildings.

7 ➡ The use of the shake-table is just a small part of what is known as seismic performance analysis, or just seismic analysis. Seismic analysis is an important intellectual tool of earthquake engineering. It breaks complex topics down into smaller more-manageable parts in order to gain a better understanding of the seismic performance of structures. Seismic analysis as a formal engineering concept is still a relatively recent development in the discipline. Generally, seismic analysis is based on the methods of structural dynamics—the behavior of structures exposed to seismic loading.

Directions: An introductory sentence for a brief summary of the passage is provided below. Complete the summary by selecting the THREE answer choices that express the most important ideas in the passage. Some sentences do not belong in the summary because they express ideas that are not presented in the passage or are minor ideas in the passage. *This question is worth 2 points.*

Earthquake engineering is the study of the behavior of structures that are subject to seismic loading.

-
-
-

Answer Choices

Ⓐ Seismic loading is the effect of an earthquake on a structure determined by various factors.

Ⓑ Agitations from earthquakes occur at the surfaces that connect a structure and the ground.

Ⓒ Seismic performance is how well buildings can continue their safety and serviceability after an earthquake.

Ⓓ Ancient people thought that earthquakes were deadly punishment from brutal gods such as Poseidon.

Ⓔ Engineers use virtual reality to analyze the dynamics of structures subject to earthquakes.

Ⓕ Engineers use shake-tables to predict the possible consequences of a real earthquake.

12

The Relationship between Climate Change and Agriculture

1 ➡ Climate change and mankind's agricultural activities are two tightly interrelated processes that are virtually impossible to separate and take place on a global scale. This close relationship has many people alarmed because global warming is currently projected to have a significant impact on the conditions that affect agriculture. These conditions include temperatures, glacial runoff, precipitation, carbon dioxide levels, and the known and unknown interactions between these various factors. All of these conditions are important because they determine the capacity of the planet to produce enough food for humankind, as well as for all domesticated animals. The overall effect of climate change on agricultural activities will depend greatly upon the balance of these effects. Thus, an assessment of climate change's effects on agricultural activities might help to properly anticipate and adapt farming techniques to maximize agricultural production.

2 ➡ Simultaneously, agricultural activities have been shown to produce significant effects on climate change. This primarily occurs through the production and release of carbon dioxide and other greenhouse gases, like nitrous oxide and methane. Additionally, agriculture alters the planet's land cover. This can change the planet's ability to absorb or reflect heat and light from the sun. Changes in cover, such as desertification and deforestation, coupled with the use of fossil fuels like coal, petroleum, and natural gas, are major contributors to carbon dioxide levels. And agricultural activities like raising livestock and rice cultivation also increase levels of nitrous oxide and methane in the planet's atmosphere.

3 ➡ In spite of technological developments like genetically modified organisms, irrigation systems, and improved varieties of crops, the weather is still a major player in agricultural production along with the properties of the soil in which food is grown. The effects of climatic conditions on agriculture are more directly related to variables in local climates than to global climate patterns. The average surface temperature of the Earth has increased by one degree Fahrenheit over the last century. Though this does not sound like a significant increase, its effects are sizeable and are being felt. As a consequence, agronomists—scientists specializing in the utilization of plants for human use—consider the necessity of any assessment to be individually considered for a given local region.

4 ➡ Despite the threat of climate change, on the other hand, agricultural trade has actually increased in recent years. Trade now provides significant amounts of food, not only on a national level, but for export to other nations. The international aspects of trade and security as they apply to food imply the need to also consider the effects of climate change on agriculture on a global scale.

5 ➡ According to a study published in *Science*, southern Africa could lose more than 30% of its main crop, maize, by 2030, and South Asia's losses of regional staples, like rice, millet, and maize, could be over 10%, all due to climate change. The impact of these major events will affect millions. The 2001 Intergovernmental Panel on Climate Change Third Assessment Report stated that the poorest nations would be the hardest hit by the effects of climate change. They conclude that the reductions in crop yield in most tropical and subtropical regions will be due to decreased water availability and new or changed incidences of pest species. Presently, many of the rain-fed crops of Africa and Latin America are near their maximum temperature tolerances, so their yields are likely to decrease sharply in the event of even small climate changes. Projections for the loss of productivity are placed in the neighborhood of 30% over the course of the 21st century. This loss will undoubtedly be felt by every nation on the planet.

6 ➡ Over the long term, climatic changes affect agricultural activities in numerous ways. Obviously, climatic changes can mean a drop in productivity, in terms of both quantity and quality. Changes in climate could also influence agricultural methods, especially in the use of water for irrigation and of herbicides, insecticides, and fertilizers. The environmental effects will be very obvious, such as the frequency and intensity of soil drainage, soil erosion, and a reduction in the diversity of crops. Other changes that are expected are adaptations in other organisms as they become more or less competitive with humans. What is more, humans may find it urgent to develop more competitive organisms, such as flood-resistant rice or salt-resistant wheat.

Directions: An introductory sentence for a brief summary of the passage is provided below. Complete the summary by selecting the THREE answer choices that express the most important ideas in the passage. Some sentences do not belong in the summary because they express ideas that are not presented in the passage or are minor ideas in the passage. ***This question is worth 2 points.***

Concerns over the effects of global warming on agriculture have led to the realization that climate change and human agricultural activities are two closely interconnected processes.

-
-
-

Answer Choices

Ⓐ Deforestation has a greater negative effect on climate change than desertification since trees are capable of reducing carbon dioxide levels in addition to lowering temperatures.

Ⓑ Agriculture affects the climate through changes in land cover and the production and release of greenhouse gases, such as carbon dioxide, nitrous oxide, and methane.

Ⓒ It is predicted that global warming will greatly impact agriculture with changes in and interactions among temperature, precipitation, and carbon dioxide levels.

Ⓓ Climate change is projected to cause southern Africa to lose more than 30% of its main crop by 2030 and South Asia to lose 10% of its regional staples.

Ⓔ The poorest nations would be most affected by the climate change according to the 2001 Intergovernmental Panel on Climate Change Third Assessment Report.

Ⓕ Reduced quality and quantity of agricultural productivity, changes in agricultural methods, and other environmental effects will be due to climate change over the long term.

Test

TOEFL Reading 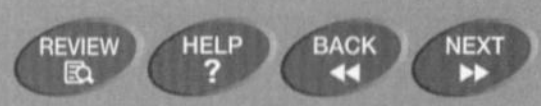

The Establishment of Dynastic Egypt

1 ➡ The Nile River Valley has provided shelter to the core of Egyptian society since time immemorial. However, its surroundings have not always looked as desolate as they do today. The area was much less arid, and a large portion of it was tree-dotted grassland instead of rolling sand dunes. The first inhabitants of the region were hunter-gatherers who roamed the region around 120,000 years ago. But the climate shifted, and the relentless heat and lack of rainfall forced the early Egyptians to cluster along the banks of the river. As these groups became more sedentary, they formed the first cultures along the river and began to rely upon agriculture for their survival. The most important of these early societies were the Badari who most likely originated in the desert on the western bank of the Nile. They were skilled at producing ceramics, stone tools, and using copper.

2 ➡ Following the Badari came the Naqada culture, which grew into the first civilization to wield control over the entire valley including its people and resources. Their first capital was built at Hierakonpolis, and they extended their control northwards up the river. This brought them into contact with other societies developing in the Middle East. They also encountered the Nubians and the Ethiopians to the south, with whom they later traded extensively. Over a thousand years, they developed into a society that manufactured a wide variety of goods that reflected their increasing power and elite classes. They also began developing the logographic writing system that would evolve into hieroglyphics and established the white crown and falcon as symbols of royal power.

3 ➡ The first dynasty of Egypt was founded by the pharaoh Narmer around 3,150 BCE by uniting Upper and Lower Egypt. He made his capital at Memphis, which allowed him to control both the agricultural work force of the

1. According to paragraph 1, which of the following is NOT true of the Nile River Valley?

Ⓐ The woodlands near the valley have changed to desolate areas.

Ⓑ Inhabitants were forced to leave the area due to climate change.

Ⓒ Agriculture evolved as people were gathered along the riverside.

Ⓓ The earliest settlers of the area lived by hunting and gathering.

2. According to paragraph 2, which of the following is true of the Naqada culture?

Ⓐ They settled in an isolated area enclosed by woods.

Ⓑ Their royal emblem was a white crown and falcon.

Ⓒ They transferred the capital back to Hierakonpolis.

Ⓓ Their language was borrowed from the Middle East.

3. The word "encountered" in paragraph 2 is closest in meaning to

Ⓐ controlled

Ⓑ dominated

Ⓒ met

Ⓓ enlightened

4. In paragraph 3, what can be inferred about the first dynasty of Egypt?

Ⓐ It ended with the regional conflict between Upper and Lower Egypt.

Ⓑ Its people developed architectural techniques during this era.

Ⓒ Trading with the Middle East was its largest source of revenue.

Ⓓ Narmer was the final pharaoh of this dynasty.

TOEFL Reading

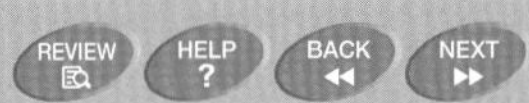

Nile Delta and the valuable trade routes to the Middle East. The growing wealth and power of the subsequent rulers can be seen in the structures erected to memorialize the pharaohs after their deaths. These included the large stepped pyramids known as mastaba tombs that were constructed at Abydos. The ability to devote so much time, resources, and labor to mortuary arrangements shows how stable their society had become, but they were not the most remarkable achievements of the Egyptians. The most colossal structures ever built by the Egyptians appeared during the next era.

4 ➡ During the Old Kingdom, there were significant advances in technology, architecture, and art, which were made possible by the ever increasing agricultural production and the equally growing population. The Pyramids at Giza and the Sphinx were built at this time, and they expressed the glory of the god-king and the centralization of power. Under the direction of the pharaoh's spokesperson, the vizier, a justice system was established to secure law and order, taxes were collected to finance the state, irrigation projects were undertaken to improve farming, and peasants were mobilized to work on various projects. Education also flourished at this time, and a new class of scribes and officials grew up to serve the pharaoh.

5 ➡ The pharaohs granted increasing amounts of land to these upper classes and to their own cults and burial sites to ensure their worship even after death. [■A] Such largess deteriorated the economy, and after many centuries the central powerbase was eroded to the point that other local leaders began to defy their monarchs. [■B] Combined with a series of severe droughts beginning in 2200 BCE, this destabilized the kingdom and it plummeted into a period of conflict and famine that lasted for 140 years referred to as the Intermediate Period. [■C] In addition, there was such total lack of respect for central authority that the majority

5. The word "These" in paragraph 3 refers to

Ⓐ rulers
Ⓑ structures
Ⓒ deaths
Ⓓ pyramids

6. According to paragraph 4, which of the following is true of the Old Kingdom?

Ⓐ Irrigation facilities were built or expanded to develop farming.
Ⓑ The rate of deforestation accelerated to expand farmland.
Ⓒ The pharaohs devolved their power to regional governments.
Ⓓ Peasants paid tribute to their lord in exchange for protection.

7. Which of the sentences below best expresses the essential information in the highlighted sentence in the passage? Incorrect choices change the meaning in important ways or leave out essential information.

Ⓐ After the kingdom was destabilized by internal conflicts and severe droughts, a new era called the Intermediate Period began around 2200 BCE.
Ⓑ The Intermediate Period tried to resolve serious droughts because the Old Kingdom went out of existence around 2200 BCE due to poverty and hunger.
Ⓒ Although natural disasters such as droughts devastated the kingdom around 2200 BCE, the Intermediate Period lasted for 140 years thereafter.
Ⓓ Regional rulers' disobedience to the pharaoh, in addition to serious droughts around 2,200 BCE, resulted in the collapse of the kingdom, leading to the Intermediate Period of discord and hunger.

TOEFL Reading

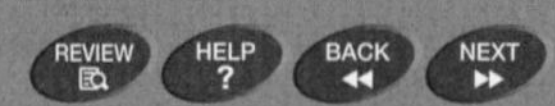

of the tomb complexes and the pyramids were looted at this time. [■D]

6 ➡ Eventually the fragments were recombined under the rule of Mentuhotep II, forming the Middle Kingdom. He and his successors regained lost territory in Nubia, attacked Palestine, and subdued Libya, securing Egypt's borders. This period also saw cultural development including writing to produce literature for entertainment, instead of just the practical and religious uses of the Old Kingdom, and a new style of statues. Since many of the latter were commissioned for women, this shows that a certain level of gender equality was achieved, as well as private wealth. However, the population began to outstrip agricultural production, and famine and outside pressures led to the downfall of the kingdom. This established a pattern for Egypt of collapsing and recovering that would repeat until the last dynasty was finally conquered by the Romans.

8. All of the following are mentioned in paragraph 6 EXCEPT

Ⓐ the fragmented kingdoms were reunified into one by Mentuhotep II

Ⓑ the Middle Kingdom focused on strengthening its national defense

Ⓒ the last dynasty of Egypt was toppled by repeated civil wars

Ⓓ gender equality was achieved during the Middle Kingdom

TOEFL Reading

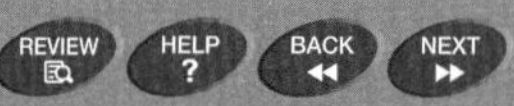

9. Look at the four squares [■] that indicate where the following sentence could be added to the passage.

The empire fragmented during this period, allowing local leaders and their individual kingdoms to thrive.

Where would the sentence best fit?

Click on a square [■] to add the sentence to the passage.

10. **Directions:** An introductory sentence for a brief summary of the passage is provided below. Complete the summary by selecting the THREE answer choices that express the most important ideas in the passage. Some sentences do not belong in the summary because they express ideas that are not presented in the passage or are minor ideas in the passage. ***This question is worth 2 points.***

The ancient civilization of Egypt flourished in the region of the Nile River Valley until the last dynasty perished.

-
-
-

Answer Choices

Ⓐ The first dynasty uniting Upper and Lower Egypt was established by Narmer, who controlled agriculture and trading.

Ⓑ The Pyramids at Giza were built as royal tombs for the Egyptian Pharaohs because the ancient people believed strongly in the afterlife.

Ⓒ The Old Kingdom achieved remarkable developments in technology, architecture, and art based upon centralized royal power.

Ⓓ The destabilized fragments were unified into the Middle Kingdom, but the final dynasty eventually ended under Roman occupation.

Ⓔ The Badarian culture evolved on the western side of the Nile, and it is known for its ceramics and stone tools.

Ⓕ Mentuhotep II achieved great military strength to restore his royal power and establish a highly centralized government.

Drag your answer choices to the spaces where they belong.
To remove an answer choice, click on it. To review the passage, click on **View Text**.

TOEFL Reading

Adaptations to Living in the Deep Ocean

1 ➡ When discussing the open ocean, it is useful to imagine a section of the water as a vertical column extending from the surface to the sediments at the bottom. This "water column" makes it easier to divide the water into layers as determined by chemical, physical, or biological definitions; the water column of the deep ocean is typically divided into five basic layers with the upper two determined by how far sunlight penetrates into the water when it is clear of pollution or sediment. The top layer is called the epipelagic zone, and it stretches down to a depth of 200 meters. There is enough light there to support plant life, and it is rich in oxygen. The second layer is called the mesopelagic zone, and it extends to a depth of 1000 meters. It is referred to as the twilight zone because there is light available, but it is dim and fades with increasing depth until none is visible. The amount of oxygen that is present is also much lower than in the layer above.

2 ➡ The species that live in the mesopelagic zone are divided into three categories based upon their feeding behavior. There are species classified as detritivores that feed upon organic debris that drift down from the epipelagic zone like corpses, feces, shed skin, and exoskeletons. Other species are herbivores that hide in the relative safety of the mesopelagic zone during the day and migrate upwards at night to feed closer to the surface. There are also carnivorous species that feed on the other two types that spend all of their time in the mesopelagic zone, or migrate up at night. These include bristlemouth, squid, cuttlefish, wolf eels, swordfish, and other semi-deep sea organisms.

3 ➡ Life in the mesopelagic zone is difficult, and the organisms that inhabit this zone have been forced to adapt to their environment. Most of these adaptations are related to catching

11. Which of the sentences below best expresses the essential information in the highlighted sentence in the passage? Incorrect choices change the meaning in important ways or leave out essential information.

Ⓐ The depths of different water layers depend on the clarity or murkiness of the water, which determines how deeply light can penetrate.

Ⓑ The term 'water column' was coined to describe the vertical division of the ocean according to the physical properties that each layer exhibits.

Ⓒ A water column usually contains five layers, the upper two of which are determined by the depth that sunlight reaches into the water.

Ⓓ Water layers are arranged differently according to chemical, physical or biological qualities, and the ocean is typically divided into five layers.

12. Which of the following can be inferred from paragraph 2?

Ⓐ Most of the species living in the mesopelagic zone migrate vertically to feed upon organic debris.

Ⓑ The mesopelagic zone is not richer in food sources, but it is safer to reside in than the epipelagic zone above it.

Ⓒ There are no plants living in the mesopelagic zone due to the limited amount of light.

Ⓓ Much of the food made in the epipelagic zone makes its way down to the mesopelagic.

TOEFL Reading

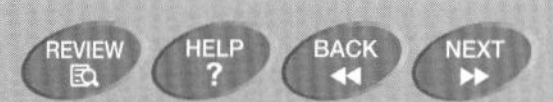

their prey or avoiding becoming prey for other organisms. Common physical adaptations include very large, sensitive eyes, camouflage, and bioluminescence. Large, sensitive eyes collect what little light is available to allow the creatures to perceive and avoid threats and locate prey. The camouflage techniques that organisms in the mesopelagic zone use vary among three main types. Some animals have uniformly dark bodies that allow them to blend in with the dark water around them. Other species lack coloration altogether and have translucent bodies instead. This means that they are invisible except for their internal organs, which in turn means that predators have difficulty identifying what they are. The final type of camouflage is having a mottled appearance that breaks up the organism's outline.

4 ➡ One adaptation that is common to all categories of organisms that live in the mesopelagic zone is bioluminescence, or the creation of light from within their bodies. The light can be generated from special organs called photophores, which contain bacteria that produce light through chemical reactions when stimulated. Other animals have their own light-producing cells called photocytes within the organs. In both cases, the light is created without generating heat, making it a kind of cold light. Deep sea fish typically use bioluminescence to attract food or confuse predators that are trying to eat them. Lantern fish use theirs both for seeking prey and for defensive purposes. The fish use the photophores to break up their outlines by making light that matches the brightness of the light above them. This makes it difficult for predators below them to make out their outlines. Some types of squid also use their sophisticated photophores to make complicated light shows, presumably as a means of communication.

5 ➡ In any part of the ocean, the organisms that

13. All of the following are mentioned in paragraph 3 as the advantages of having large, sensitive eyes to the mesopelagic animals EXCEPT

Ⓐ they are beneficial to the animals in protecting themselves from danger and spotting prey

Ⓑ they are evolved to gather ambient light in the mesopelagic zone

Ⓒ they enable the animals to distinguish prey from predators

Ⓓ they point upward to detect the silhouette of prey above

14. The word "perceive" in paragraph 3 is closest in meaning to

Ⓐ follow

Ⓑ see

Ⓒ evaluate

Ⓓ react to

15. According to paragraph 4, what is NOT true of bioluminescence?

Ⓐ It is the production and emission of light by a living organism.

Ⓑ Its main functions are to evade predators and to lure and catch prey.

Ⓒ Some species use it to attract mates by signaling other individuals.

Ⓓ Photophores and photocytes are special organs that are responsible for it.

live there deplete the oxygen supply that the water contains when they are active. Since the mesopelagic zone has significantly less oxygen than the epipelagic zone, organisms that stay in that layer tend to be much less active. [■A] Instead of hunting for their prey, these animals will simply float along, scattered throughout the zone, waiting for their preferred food to pass by them. [■B] The animals appear to be sluggish, but when their food gets near enough to attack, or when they are threatened by another predator, these creatures are capable of great bursts of speed. [■C] After successfully eating or avoiding attack, they will return to their inactive states. [■D] Bony fish are able to float like this due to an organ filled with gas called a swim bladder. The swim bladder is located in the top half of an organism's body, below its center of mass. This helps the fish to remain stable and to stay at a particular depth without using energy to swim.

16. Why does the author mention lantern fish in paragraph 4?

Ⓐ To give an example of a species that breaks up its outline as a means of camouflage

Ⓑ To explain the role of photophores in catching its prey

Ⓒ To show its unique way of creating light within its body

Ⓓ To compare it to other species that have more common camouflage techniques

17. According to paragraph 5, which of the following are actions that organisms living in the mesopelagic zone take in order to make up for the insufficient supply of oxygen?

Ⓐ They do not chase their prey, but simply wait for the prey to come to them.

Ⓑ They use a special organ called a swim bladder to withstand the high pressure of the water.

Ⓒ They migrate up near the surface to breathe in more oxygen at night.

Ⓓ They have well-developed gills that allow them to absorb as much oxygen as possible.

18. The word "scattered" in paragraph 5 is closest in meaning to

Ⓐ outer

Ⓑ specialized

Ⓒ spread apart

Ⓓ tiny

19. Look at the four squares [■] that indicate where the following sentence could be added to the passage.

Many of them actually use their bioluminescence to attract their food to them.

Where would the sentence best fit?

Click on a square [■] to add the sentence to the passage.

20. Directions: An introductory sentence for a brief summary of the passage is provided below. Complete the summary by selecting the THREE answer choices that express the most important ideas in the passage. Some sentences do not belong in the summary because they express ideas that are not presented in the passage or are minor ideas in the passage.
This question is worth 2 points.

Marine animals living in the deep ocean have adapted to an environment where light and oxygen become scarce as depth increases.

-
-
-

Answer Choices

(A) A water column is a conceptual column of water that describes the stratification of the water layers in the ocean where different types of species live.

(B) There are three kinds of species living in the epipelagic zone based on what they feed on: detritivores, herbivores, and carnivores.

(C) Most mesopelagic organisms undertake a vertical migration, moving to the epipelagic zone to feed at night.

(D) Animals living in the mesopelagic zone have adapted to the harsh environment and have developed their own ways to survive such as large, sensitive eyes, camouflage, and bioluminescence.

(E) Some deep sea animals have the ability to create light by a chemical reaction in their light-emitting organs using bacteria.

(F) Organisms living in the oxygen-deficient layer choose to be sluggish rather than hunting prey in order to conserve oxygen.

Drag your answer choices to the spaces where they belong.
To remove an answer choice, click on it. To review the passage, click on **View Text.**

Lesson

03 Category Chart

Lesson Outline

- 분류(Category Chart) 문제는 지문에서 제시된 정보를 각각 알맞은 범주(category)에 분류해서 넣는 문제다. 문제에서 제시된 5~7개의 보기 중 주어진 범주에 맞는 보기를 클릭해서 순서에 상관 없이 표의 [•] 옆에 끌어다 놓으면 된다.
- 이 유형의 문제는 한 지문당 1개가 출제되거나, 아예 출제되지 않을 때도 있다. 요약(Summary) 문제와 함께 출제되는 경우는 거의 없다.

Typical Questions 

Directions: Complete the table by matching the sentences below. Select the appropriate sentences from the answer choices and match them to the category to which they relate. TWO of the answer choices will NOT be used. ***This question is worth 3 points.***

지시문: 아래 문장들을 알맞게 넣어 다음 표를 완성하시오. 선택지 중 적절한 문장들을 골라 관계된 개념과 연결하시오. 선택지 두 개는 정답이 될 수 없다. ***이 문제의 배점은 3점이다.***

Answer Choices	Category A
Ⓐ ---------------------	•
Ⓑ ---------------------	•
Ⓒ ---------------------	•
Ⓓ ---------------------	Category B
Ⓔ ---------------------	•
Ⓕ ---------------------	•
Ⓖ ---------------------	

참고 질문 내용은 지문에 따라 조금씩 다르지만, 거의 항상 'Select the appropriate choices/sentences ~ (적절한 보기/문장들을 선택하시오)'와 같이 제시된다.

각 범주에 표시된 [•]를 통해 해당 범주에 몇 개의 정답이 들어갈지 알 수 있다. 선택지는 보통 5~7개가 주어지며 이 중에서 2~3개 선택지는 정답이 될 수 없다는 점에 주의하자.

Learning Strategies

Step 1 먼저 문제에서 어떤 범주에 대해 묻는지 본다. 비교·대조 문제가 가장 일반적이고 자주 등장한다.

···› 보통 두 가지 범주에 대해 물으므로 각 범주가 지문의 어디에서 언급되었는지 찾아본다.

···› 범주가 언급된 부분을 찾으면, 그 부분을 자세히 읽어보며 비교·대조되는 부분을 찾는다.

Step 2 주어진 선택지는 많지만 이중에서 몇 개는 정답이 될 수 없다는 점에 유의하면서, 이제 각 선택지를 하나씩 읽어보고 어떤 선택지가 지문에서 언급되었는지 파악한다. 그리고 이 선택지가 들어갈 범주를 다시 확인한다.

Step 3 오답 확인의 중요성은 아무리 강조해도 지나치지 않다. 걸러낸 오답을 보며 이 오답이 지문에서 언급되지 않은 내용인지, 아니면 지문과 아예 다른 내용인지 확인해 보도록 한다.

Example

Nocturnal vs. Diurnal

1 ➡ There are two basic sleep cycles in the animal kingdom—diurnal and nocturnal. Animals that are active during the day and sleep at night are diurnal. Those who are active at night and sleep during the day are nocturnal.

2 ➡ Nocturnal animals usually have highly developed senses of hearing and smell to compensate for the absence of light. Some have specially adapted eyesight. This usually involves the animals having enlarged pupils, the black part of the eye, or sometimes even larger-than-usual eyes. It is the pupils that allow light to enter the eyes, so by having larger pupils, nocturnal animals' eyes allow more light to enter the eye, enabling the animals to see more clearly at night. Some other nocturnal animals have special adaptations to help them find their way around in the dark. Many bats use a type of natural sonar. They emit a high-pitched sound and listen to the echoes of that sound to find nearby objects or prey.

3 ➡ Diurnal animals, on the other hand, are active during the daylight hours. Their senses are equally balanced. Their eyes generally have small pupils to prevent too much light from entering the eye. On the other hand, many have a large number of cone cells, allowing them to see in color. Once the sun sets, diurnal animals have difficulty moving around as they cannot see well in low light. Animals are not the only diurnal organisms; some flowering plants, like Namaqualand daisies, only open their flowers in daylight, closing them again when it is cloudy or dark. However, with the advent of electric lighting, many diurnal animals, including pets and city-dwelling birds, are remaining active long into the night.

Directions: Complete the table by matching the sentences below. Select the appropriate sentences from the answer choices and match them to the category to which they relate. TWO of the answer choices will NOT be used. ***This question is worth 3 points.***

Answer Choices	Nocturnal	Diurnal
Ⓐ These animals are often blind.	•	•
Ⓑ These flowering plants only open their flowers in daylight.	•	•
Ⓒ These animals have stronger senses of smell and hearing.	•	
Ⓓ These animals have small pupils to allow as much light as possible to enter their eyes.		
Ⓔ Some of these animals have large eyes to facilitate better sight.		
Ⓕ Electric light has lengthened the active period of these animals.		
Ⓖ These animals sleep during the day.		

1 먼저 문제에서 어떤 범주에 대해 묻는지 본다. 문제를 보면 Nocturnal/Diurnal로 범주가 나뉘어져 있으므로 이 두 생물을 분류하는 특징에 관해 묻는다는 것을 알 수 있다. 이제 Nocturnal/Diurnal 동물들의 특징이 지문의 어디에서 언급되었는지 찾아본다. 해당 부분을 읽어보며 각 범주의 특징을 파악한다.

2 주어진 선택지는 많지만 이중에서 몇 개는 정답이 될 수 없다는 점에 유의하며 각 선택지를 하나씩 읽어본다.

Ⓐ These animals are often blind.

⋯▸ 지문에서 언급되지 않은 내용이다. 따라서 범주에 넣지 않는다.

Ⓑ These flowering plants only open their flowers in daylight.

⋯▸ 주행성(diurnal)이 동물뿐 아니라 식물에도 있다고 하며 예로 든 Namaqualand daisies의 특징이다. 따라서 Diurnal 범주에 들어간다.

Ⓒ These animals have stronger senses of smell and hearing.

⋯▸ 야행성(nocturnal) 동물의 특징 중 맨 첫 번째로 언급되는 내용이다. 따라서 Nocturnal 범주에 들어간다.

Ⓓ These animals have small pupils to allow as much light as possible to enter their eyes.

⋯▸ 작은 동공은 주행성 동물의 특징이며 이는 햇빛을 적게 받아들이기 위한 것이므로 틀린 설명이다. 따라서 범주에 넣지 않는다.

Ⓔ Some of these animals have large eyes to facilitate better sight.

⋯→ 어둠 속에서 더 잘 보기 위해 더 큰 눈을 가지는 경우가 있다고 지문에서 언급되었다. 따라서 Nocturnal 범주에 들어간다.

Ⓕ Electric light has lengthened the active period of these animals.

⋯→ 전기 불빛 때문에 이 동물들의 활동 시간이 길어졌다고 주행성 동물의 특징에 나와 있다. 따라서 Diurnal 범주에 들어간다.

Ⓖ These animals sleep during the day.

⋯→ 낮 시간에 잠을 잔다는 내용이므로 Nocturnal 범주에 들어간다.

따라서 정답은 Nocturnal: Ⓒ, Ⓔ, Ⓖ / Diurnal: Ⓑ, Ⓕ가 된다.

❸ 오답 확인의 중요성은 아무리 강조해도 지나치지 않다. 범주에 넣지 않은 Ⓐ와 Ⓓ를 다시 읽어보고 확인한다.

Practice

01

The American Civil War

Even 150 years after the last shots of the American Civil War were fired, Northerners and Southerners still debate the actual cause for the conflict. The cause that usually comes to mind is the issue of owning human beings in the form of slaves. The people in the northern states that would become the Union had never owned slaves in truly significant numbers, and their economy had already outgrown dependence upon slavery. The North had shifted over to a mostly industrialized economy that had huge numbers of immigrants from Europe as its workforce. However, the South continued to rely upon slave labor on farms and plantations, and the Southerners felt that the abolitionist, or anti-slavery, activities of the North threatened their life and livelihood in the South. But it would be a mistake to imagine that all Southerners had slaves and fought to protect the right to own them. The majority of Southerners were actually poor white farmers who resented the plantation owners. They fought not to protect the rights of these elites, but to preserve their sovereignty from what they saw as an overbearing government.

Directions: Complete the table by matching the sentences below. Select the appropriate sentences from the answer choices and match them to the category to which they relate. TWO of the answer choices will NOT be used. ***This question is worth 3 points.***

Answer Choices	The North	The South
Ⓐ It had a large population of slaves due to the onrush of industrialization. Ⓑ It depended upon workforce that mostly consisted of immigrant laborers in factories. Ⓒ It needed to rely on slaves because of its agricultural economy. Ⓓ The people thought they would face a critical situation if the slavery system ended. Ⓔ It has some states that still maintain the slavery system. Ⓕ The people were mostly impoverished peasants who fought to protect their own rights. Ⓖ It was composed of people who disapproved of slavery and tried to abolish it.	• Ⓑ •	• Ⓒ • •

02

Tornadoes and Hurricanes

The North American continent suffers from two distinct forms of violent weather during the summer months: hurricanes and tornadoes. Hurricanes and tornadoes both rotate in a circular motion, and they both rotate in the same direction in which the Earth is also rotating. Both occur in areas of low atmospheric pressure and at the center of these low pressure systems is a part of the storm known as the eye of the storm. The eye is an area of almost complete calm created by the cyclonic vortex around it. Hurricanes, though, are spawned over the open ocean, while tornadoes almost always form over land. Both phenomena are characterized by extremely high winds, but the winds in tornadoes are far stronger. Tornadoes occur far more often than hurricanes, and they can form in mere minutes, whereas a hurricane takes weeks to form. This is because a tornado forms from a pre-existing thunderstorm, while a hurricane is a storm itself. However, hurricanes pose more of a risk to human life and property because they are accompanied by a wave called a storm surge. These waves act much like a tsunami, pushing inland as the storm strikes the coastline.

Directions: Complete the table by matching the phrases below. Select the appropriate phrases from the answer choices and match them to the category to which they relate. TWO of the answer choices will NOT be used. ***This question is worth 3 points.***

Answer Choices	Tornadoes	Hurricanes
Ⓐ originate over the land	• Ⓐ	• Ⓓ
Ⓑ revolve in the reverse direction of the Earth's rotation	•	•
Ⓒ have a higher frequency and a shorter formative period	•	•
Ⓓ accompanied by dangerous waves that threaten human beings		•
Ⓔ first develop over water and possibly move inland		
Ⓕ result from continental high atmospheric pressure		
Ⓖ take a relatively longer time to occur		
Ⓗ generate more powerful winds than the other		
Ⓘ occur autonomously without other source		

Lesson 03 Recognizing Organization

03

Fungi vs. Plants

1 ➡ Living things are organized for study into large, basic groups called kingdoms. Fungi were listed in the Plant Kingdom for many years. Then scientists learned that fungi show a closer relation to animals, but are unique and separate life forms. Now, fungi are placed in their own kingdom. The principal reason for this is that none of them possess chlorophyll, so, unlike plants, they cannot synthesize their own carbohydrates. They obtain their supplies either from the breakdown of dead organic matter or from other living organisms.

2 ➡ Furthermore, the walls of fungal cells are not made of cellulose, as those of plants are, but of another complex sugar-like polymer called chitin, the material from which the hard outer skeletons of shrimps, spiders, and insects are made. The difference between the chemical composition of the cell walls of fungi and those of plants is of enormous importance because it enables the tips of the growing hyphae, the threadlike cells of the fungus, to secrete enzymes that break down the walls of plant cells without having any effect on those of the fungus itself.

Directions: Complete the table by matching the sentences below. Select the appropriate phrases from the answer choices and match them to the category to which they relate. TWO of the answer choices will NOT be used. ***This question is worth 3 points.***

Answer Choices	Fungi	Plants
Ⓐ They have no chlorophyll. Ⓑ They synthesize their own carbohydrates. Ⓒ They acquire carbohydrates exclusively from dead organic matter. Ⓓ Their cell walls contain the same kind of material as shrimp and insect shells. Ⓔ They cannot synthesize carbohydrates. Ⓕ They use chlorophyll to produce their own food. Ⓖ They possess hyphae which secrete enzymes that have no effect on plant cells.	• Ⓐ • •	• Ⓑ •

04

Left and Right Brain Hemispheres

1 ➡ The human brain, while being one organ, is divided into two halves, or hemispheres. Each hemisphere has different functions and processes information in different ways. Depending on the task being performed, one hemisphere or the other is more dominant.

2 ➡ The left hemisphere focuses on details. It is better at logical and analytical thought. When performing structured tasks that involve following various steps or when concentration on a particular part of our environment is required, the left side of the brain is used. The left side of the brain, one specialty of which is symbolic thought, enables people to decode language to find the literal or superficial meaning. However, the detail-oriented left hemisphere is not good at spatial perception, that is, the ability to discern the relationship between objects in view. That requires less attention to detail.

3 ➡ In contrast, the right hemisphere processes information on a more general level. It is the part of the brain that provides an overall view of places, things, and situations. Since the right hemisphere is the center of human imagination, people rely on this hemisphere when performing open-ended tasks requiring a creative approach. When processing language, it is the right hemisphere that enables people to understand humor, emotion, and metaphors, thereby providing connotative or contextual meanings. Furthermore, the right hemisphere is the source of our spatial awareness, enabling us to analyze our environment three dimensionally and judge distances.

Directions: Complete the table by matching the phrases below. Select the appropriate phrases from the answer choices and match them to the category to which they relate. TWO of the answer choices will NOT be used. ***This question is worth 3 points.***

Answer Choices	Left	Right
Ⓐ enables us to notice details in our environment	•	•
Ⓑ enables us to judge distances	• Ⓖ	•
Ⓒ enables us to dream		• Ⓔ
Ⓓ enables us to solve problems creatively		
Ⓔ enables us to put things in context		
Ⓕ enables us to structure problems that need to be solved		
Ⓖ enables us to understand language literally		

05

Education and Schooling

1 ➡ In the United States, the common belief is that schools are where people must go for an education. However, some people believe that going to school interrupts a child's education. The difference between schooling and education suggested by this statement is important.

2 ➡ Education is much more broad and all-inclusive than schooling. There are no limits in education. Education includes both formal schooling and a whole world of informal learning. The agents of education can be a respected grandparent, people debating on a radio talk show, another child, or a famous scholar. While schooling is predictable in some ways, education is often spontaneous. For instance, a casual conversation with a stranger may introduce a person to a new subject they previously knew little about. People begin their educations in infancy and never stop. It is a lifelong process that starts long before a person starts school, and should continue to be an integral part of a person's entire life.

3 ➡ Schooling, on the other hand, is a more formalized and specific process. The general pattern of schooling varies little from one setting to another. Children usually arrive at school at the same time, sit in assigned seats, are taught by adults, do homework, take exams, etc. The segments of reality that are being taught, whether they are the alphabet or simple calculating, usually have been limited by the boundaries of the subject being taught. For instance, high school students are aware that they are not likely to learn the truth concerning political problems in their communities or what new techniques filmmakers are exploring. Definite boundaries exist in the course of formalized schooling.

Directions: Complete the table by matching the sentences below. Select the appropriate sentences from the answer choices and match them to the category to which they relate. TWO of the answer choices will NOT be used. ***This question is worth 3 points.***

Answer Choices	Education	Schooling
Ⓐ People are involved in it from birth to death.	•	•
Ⓑ Its context is usually the same everywhere.	•	•
Ⓒ What it may produce is largely predictable.	•	
Ⓓ There are no limits to it.		
Ⓔ It interferes with the continuity of study.		
Ⓕ It is often unexpected and unplanned.		
Ⓖ It should be totally disregarded as being useful in human development.		

06

Hardwoods vs. Softwoods

1 ➡ In woodworking and construction, the types of wood that are used are usually divided into two groups: hardwood and softwood. The reasoning behind these groupings would seem to be fairly obvious. As a rule, hardwoods tend to be harder than softwoods. However, this is not always the case. Hardwoods are indeed denser than softwoods, but not all of them are harder. For example, balsa wood is one of the softest types of wood on the planet, but it is actually designated as a hardwood. Therefore, the genuine distinction between these two types of wood is more elaborate.

2 ➡ The true discrepancy between hardwoods and softwoods has to do with the type of tree that they come from. Hardwoods are deciduous trees, which are broad-leafed trees that lose their leaves every autumn and typically produce hard shelled seeds. These include trees like maple, oak, cherry, and mahogany. Softwoods are usually evergreens, which means that they do not drop their leaves seasonally, and their foliage is thin and needle-like. Their seeds are usually contained in a cone (which is why they are often called conifers) and they do not have a hard, protective shell. This group includes pine, fir, spruce, and cedar, among others.

3 ➡ These differences between the two groups are all observable from the outside, but the most important difference lies within. At a microscopic level, the structure of the trees is dissimilar. Softwoods have long, vertically growing cells that provide strength and carry water and nutrients up through the tree. They transfer materials through their cells' walls, which means that they can retain water within them. This is how they can stay green all year. Hardwoods have a system of vessels that transport those materials much like blood vessels in animals. The vessels look like pores in the wood, and their walls are made of strong cells called vessel elements. Their walls afford added strength to the tree, and the other cells that surround them are packed tightly together, making the wood denser. However, they do not function as well in the winter, which is why these trees lose their leaves every year.

Directions: Complete the table by matching the phrases below. Select the appropriate phrases from the answer choices and match them to the category to which they relate. TWO of the answer choices will NOT be used. ***This question is worth 3 points.***

Answer Choices	Hardwoods	Softwoods
Ⓐ contain tube-like structures to carry water and nutrients	•	•
Ⓑ usually grow at higher altitudes in dense forests	•	•
Ⓒ are non-deciduous trees which have evergreen leaves	•	
Ⓓ typically have harder cells of higher density		
Ⓔ shed their foliage on an annual basis		
Ⓕ produce seeds with hard shells contained in a cone		
Ⓖ are able to store moisture in their cellular structure		

07

The U.S. Census

1 ➡ The U.S. Constitution mandates that a census be conducted every decade. In its early years, the U.S. government faced many problems in fairly charging taxes and allocating resources. The census solved many of these difficulties by providing accurate records of the population in each state or territory. Legislators in Congress were able to use this information to determine the amount of taxes to collect from each state. In addition to taxation, the census also dictated the number of elected officials that represented each region in Congress.

2 ➡ The first official U.S. census was taken in 1790. Thomas Jefferson, then the Secretary of State, directed the census. He appointed assistant U.S. marshals to travel across the country and determine the number of residents in every American household. However, this system of gathering information created several challenges for the assistant marshals. The United States was a relatively new nation, so there were very few accurate maps of the whole country, especially of remote regions. In addition, many citizens did not trust the assistant marshals and were reluctant to answer their questions. Despite these difficulties, the first census was completed in 18 months and determined the population of the United States to be 3.9 million.

3 ➡ The census of 1790 was very different from the census conducted today. Although the current census still determines legislative representation, modern computers now allow the U.S. Census Bureau, the organization now in charge of collecting and compiling census data, to sort and catalog information much more quickly than in 1790. Beginning in 1940, the Census Bureau began employing statistical sampling techniques that allowed it to collect data from a small portion of the population. This data was then used to estimate information for the entire country. The use of statistical sampling greatly reduced the amount of time needed to conduct the census. During the 1960s, the Census Bureau developed computerized address files, and in 1970 it conducted the census almost entirely by mail. In fact, more than 90 percent of Americans now receive a census form in the mail. Only a small number of households respond in person to the questions of a census enumerator.

Directions: Complete the table by matching the phrases below. Select the appropriate phrases from the answer choices and match them to the category to which they relate. TWO of the answer choices will NOT be used. ***This question is worth 3 points.***

Answer Choices	Census of 1790	Modern Census
Ⓐ completed every two years	•	•
Ⓑ census officials sometimes regarded with suspicion	•	•
Ⓒ conducted completely by the counting officials	•	
Ⓓ travel to every remote region not required		
Ⓔ conducted without any field personnel		
Ⓕ devised partly to determine congressional representation		
Ⓖ U.S. postal carriers included in the process		

08

Diabetes

1 ➡ Diabetes, in essence, is the body's inability to produce or use insulin. Through digestion, food is turned into glucose, a type of sugar, which in turn is used by our cells for energy. Insulin is a hormone, naturally produced in healthy bodies, which helps the cells of the body process glucose. If insulin is not present, cells cannot take in glucose. People with type 1 diabetes do not produce enough insulin for their cells to take advantage of the food that they eat. Although type 1 diabetes is known as juvenile diabetes, people of any age can contract type 1 diabetes. Type 2 diabetes occurs when the body's cells cannot use insulin even though the body produces enough of it. Type 2 diabetes, sometimes called adult-onset diabetes, usually occurs in people above the age of 40. Although these are in fact two rather distinct disorders, they both involve insulin and are both known as diabetes.

2 ➡ People contract diabetes in different ways, not all of which are completely known. This much is known: diabetes is not contagious. You cannot get the disease by touching someone or drinking from the same glass. People can inherit diabetes, however. Because type 2 diabetes runs in the family, people with affected ancestors are more likely to contract it. Some people think that overeating and obesity are causes of diabetes, and doctors do recommend a balanced diet and daily exercise to reduce the risk of diabetes even if it runs in the family. Blacks and Hispanics contract the disease about twice as frequently as whites do, but it is not entirely clear how much heredity and lifestyles contribute to this phenomenon. It is difficult to know exactly how type 1 diabetes is contracted. Unlike type 2 diabetes, type 1 diabetes does not appear to run in the family, so there is probably no genetic link. Researchers are investigating the role of viruses in the disease, but the fact is that the experts simply do not know how type 1 diabetes is contracted. They do know, however, that a number of factors contribute to the onset of diabetes and that a healthy lifestyle will help prevent the disease.

Directions: Complete the table by matching the phrases below. Select the appropriate phrases from the answer choices and match them to the category to which they relate. TWO of the answer choices will NOT be used. ***This question is worth 3 points.***

Answer Choices	Type 1	Type 2
Ⓐ suspected viral implications	•	•
Ⓑ demonstrates a hereditary pattern of incidence	•	•
Ⓒ known for afflicting young people	•	•
Ⓓ involves the inability to use insulin to process glucose	•	
Ⓔ has undetermined causes		
Ⓕ can be transmitted by direct contact		
Ⓖ probably does not have a genetic link		
Ⓗ occurs with insulin in adequate supply		
Ⓘ results from a dysfunction related to glucose production		

09

Paleolithic and Neolithic Cultures

1 ➡ Beginning around two million years ago, the Stone Age is marked by two distinct epochs: the Paleolithic and Neolithic. The defining characteristics of these two epochs were the chief means of food production. Hunting was practiced in the Paleolithic period, and farming was practiced in the Neolithic period. Indeed, the technological innovations of stone tools leading to the development of primitive hunting weapons in the Paleolithic age and agricultural techniques stimulating the rise of agricultural societies in the Neolithic period resulted in the development and divergence of these two periods. As a result, there were significant cultural and lifestyle distinctions between the two.

2 ➡ Hunting both defined the Paleolithic period and necessitated a nomadic lifestyle as proto-human hunters had to follow their food sources. Since Paleolithic people moved too often to create permanent dwellings, they found cover in caves or built makeshift shelters from wooden branches for temporary accommodations. Interestingly, cave paintings give perhaps the most valuable insight into Paleolithic lifestyles. The works presented abstract images of the hunting lifestyle in the first part of the Stone Age. In addition, they served as learning manuals to assure prosperous hunting, indicating that although Paleolithic groups were independent, they were also sympathetic to the plight of their fellow man. Paleolithic people ate their catch and consumed grains and fruits. Later, a method to farm these goods and further ensure a steady supply of foodstuffs would emerge.

3 ➡ The development of agriculture led to a major transition in the way humans lived. Ten thousand years ago, our species, Homo sapiens, entered the Neolithic Age by discovering techniques for domesticating animals and a limited number of plants. Most importantly, as hunting was less necessary, Neolithic people were sedentary. This meant that they could not only build and inhabit permanent dwellings, but they could also form settlements. Along with this settled lifestyle came the development of pottery as both a practical container and a predominant form of art. In Paleolithic times, carrying such an object was impractical; however, it would now be used to preserve food surpluses and record images representing life in Neolithic times. Of interest was the introduction of purely ornamental art forms, suggesting prototypical attempts at revealing a spiritual world.

Directions: Complete the table by matching the phrases below. Select the appropriate phrases from the answer choices and match them to the category to which they relate. TWO of the answer choices will NOT be used. ***This question is worth 3 points.***

Answer Choices	Paleolithic People	Neolithic People
Ⓐ decorated their shelters with art that recorded their lifestyle	•	•
Ⓑ adapted to hunting by taking on a nomadic lifestyle	•	•
Ⓒ created the first agricultural techniques for food production	•	•
Ⓓ chose short-term shelter instead of permanent dwellings	•	
Ⓔ emerged out of the arrival of stone tools		
Ⓕ developed governments for their settlements		
Ⓖ hinted at a spiritual world with cave art		
Ⓗ built permanent dwellings in close proximity to others		
Ⓘ developed transportable art in the form of pottery		

10

Behavioral and Cognitive Psychology

1 ➡ It has been more than five centuries since the introduction of the scientific study of human behavior, or psychology. In that time, many theories and schools of thought have been developed to evaluate and manage human behavior, including mental illnesses and issues affecting everyday life. In the 20th century, two notable scientific approaches were developed in order to explain and treat behavior. Both behavioral psychology and cognitive psychology aim to achieve the same results, but their philosophies oppose each other.

2 ➡ Behavioral psychology works from the viewpoint that any behavior can be studied and explained scientifically without the effects of mental and emotional states. Occurring parallel to the development of psychoanalysis, behaviorism developed with discoveries in behavioral conditioning by B. F. Skinner, who performed research on subject conditioning, and Ivan Pavlov, who developed the stimulus-response theory and asserted it with his famous experiments using dogs. Behavioral psychology developed from theories based on empirical data. Since the basic premise of behavioral psychology is that all behavior can be explained, experiments focused on outcome rather than any kind of internal processes the subjects were experiencing while participating in them.

3 ➡ Cognitive psychology aims at explaining human activity by looking at the interplay of internal mental processes. Its views are based on evaluating processes like memory, problem-solving, language processing, and perception, with an emphasis on how they interact between a stimulus and a response. In cognitive psychology, it is considered possible to analyze an individual's behavior based on his or her needs, ambitions, and impulses rather than sensory input and individual experiences. This is perhaps the most significant difference between cognitive and behavioral psychology.

4 ➡ Applying these two contrasting schools of psychology to an educational setting provides the best illustration of their differing viewpoints. Behavioral psychology's principles are prevalent in a teacher-dominated classroom. Since stimulus and response are considered critical factors, the teacher presents knowledge to students, who, it is assumed, are motivated to learn it due to external consequences. In practice, this knowledge comes in the form of facts students passively memorize. On the other hand, because cognitive psychology postulates that one's internal state is of primary importance, it describes learners as active processors of data. Therefore, cognitive psychology is significant in the modern, learner-centered classroom, where students discover and construct knowledge on their own and consequently develop learning strategies that maximize their academic experiences.

Directions: Complete the table by matching the phrases below. Select the appropriate phrases from the answer choices and match them to the category to which they relate. TWO of the answer choices will NOT be used. ***This question is worth 3 points.***

Answer Choices	Behavioral Psychology	Cognitive Psychology
(A) supposes students only learn without an instructor	•	•
(B) believes behavior is independent of a person's mood	•	•
(C) considers an individual's ability to process information	•	
(D) prevails in classes where students work actively		
(E) regards all behavior as explainable		
(F) developed theories based on experiment stimuli		
(G) presumes consequences influence students to work		

11

Development of the State

1 ➡ Anthropologists do not concur on how human societies develop. The competing theories focus on the transformation of civilization from simple to complex organizational forms. One of the most compelling assumptions is that this hierarchical pattern of transformation does, in fact, exist. This chronological pattern of evolution is categorized by bands, tribes, chiefdoms, and state societies, respectively. Although there are an almost infinite number of situations which could affect the transition from one political structure to the next, each system appears out of necessity.

2 ➡ Hunter-gatherer bands are considered to be the most rudimentary form of human society. They are often based on kinship, or family relationships; and they are usually not larger than an extended family, numbering less than 100 members. As an informal organizational system, a band has no written regulations, and therefore no records to refer to for guidance. So, it is governed by its elder family members, who are looked up to for advice and direction. Because there is minimal leadership, decisions and power are shared equally among band members. Generally, itinerant bands do not generate a surplus, which leads to a subsistence mentality. Finally, these bands have no graded status levels; therefore, tribal members are not separated into classes, castes, or social strata.

3 ➡ A tribe is markedly larger since it consists of many families and communities associated together. Hence, it differs from a state inasmuch as familial ties are crucial to a tribe member's social standing. Tribal systems form during times when resources, achieved by plant and animal domestication, are plentiful but unpredictable, and its effectiveness and flexibility allow tribe members not only freedom during surplus periods but also food reserves during hard times. However, due to the large amount of mingling among members both within and outside of tribes, there are often conflicts within the tribes regarding ideological differences. Because a number of different languages may also be spoken, there may be identity and ideology crises and cultural fragmentation. Having these challenges, tribes often join together with one common leader, transitioning into the next-to-last stage of state development.

4 ➡ Consisting of possibly thousands of people, a chiefdom is considerably larger than a tribe. A chiefdom also differs from tribes and bands in that there are social levels, and it is centralized. Often, a chiefdom is temporarily formed by several tribes uniting, only to collapse and fragment until they reunite into another chiefdom. A chiefdom is characterized by having a chief who exercises control over several communities. A simple chiefdom is formed by a central community surrounded by several worker-class, auxiliary communities that provide support with goods and services. Chiefdoms follow a system of taxation and tribute, in which the commoner supplies the elite with resources such as food and labor. Therefore, widespread inequality usually exists between these two chiefdom classes. Class status is inherited although sometimes individuals may improve their status by accomplishing something important, marrying a person of higher social status, or being related to someone who has improved their own ranking. The chief is entitled to a number

of privileges simply because he was born to powerful parents, and these entitlements are often supported by a series of myths that assert his power. To further bolster their significance, these myths are often created with a religious tone in order to assure their popular acceptance. When dissatisfaction threatens a chiefdom, the chief and the elite exert their force to suppress upheaval. This may temporarily insure that the elite remain in power, but it also creates a constant source of conflict between the two classes. Ultimately, chiefdoms are unstable because they create a society in which individuals of the lower class are oppressed with few opportunities to improve their situation.

5 ➡ Of all the human organizational structures, the most stable stage of development is the state, which resembles a chiefdom in its social class system and centralization. However, the stratification model of a state is pyramid-shaped, with a multitude of social levels between its hypothetical base and peak. Furthermore, with their much larger size and progressive development, states can create sovereignty over vast amounts of territory. This is made possible with institutions such as armed forces, civil services, courts, and police, all of which are available due to a state's high level of production. Moreover, having an association between rulers and citizens that is not based on kin, states are a major departure from the preceding stages of development. Since state-organized societies are self-governing political units, they are more adaptable to crises affecting the population. If conflict turns popular opinion against the state, the state will more likely change to popularly-accepted governing agents than fragment.

Directions: Complete the table by matching the sentences below. Select the appropriate phrases from the answer choices and match them to the category to which they relate. TWO of the answer choices will NOT be used. ***This question is worth 3 points.***

Answer Choices	Tribes	Chiefdoms
Ⓐ They may have multiple languages.	•	•
Ⓑ They are characterized by being oppressive.	•	•
Ⓒ They tend to be family-based.	•	
Ⓓ They are generally led by a respected elder of the family.		
Ⓔ There is a distinct class system.		
Ⓕ There are self-governing units.		
Ⓖ The members easily socialize with those within and outside their group.		

12

Ancient Greek Sculptures

1 ➡ There is evidence that the ancient Greeks produced numerous forms of art, but only a few of them have survived through ages, and most of those are sculptures. Even though we have a limited number of relics, it is evident that the ancient Greeks were able to create sculptures of astonishing beauty with very simple technology. In fact, the sculpture of the ancient Greeks has had a profound influence on the development of Western concepts of art and beauty. Ancient Greek art provided the foundation for Roman art. Centuries later, ancient Greek sculpture inspired the artists of the Italian Renaissance and influenced Western art up until the 19th century, leading to the advent of modernism. The subtlety and expressiveness of influential ancient Greek sculpture developed between the 8th and the 1st century BCE in three distinct periods.

2 ➡ The earliest ancient Greek sculptures still in existence are from the 8th century BCE. This date represents the onset of the Archaic Period, during which sculptures were being produced to ornament the graves of affluent aristocrats, such as the most famous example found on the grave of an Athenian soldier named Kroisos. Known as kouroi, these sculptures were carved in stone, usually marble, using rudimentary iron tools. This simple technology put limitations on the poses artists could depict; therefore, a kouros has a very rigid and unnatural pose, standing straight upright with feet together. Every kouros face wears the same blank expression. Also, they invariably depict healthy young men, even when commissioned for graves of older men like Kroisos. This attests to the fact that these statues were not meant to be portraits of particular individuals, but were instead symbolic of ideals such as beauty, piety, honor, and sacrifice. The only significant variation between the statues is their size as individuals of higher social standing had larger kouroi marking their graves.

3 ➡ Socio-political changes in Greece in the early 5th century BCE brought an end to the supremacy of the aristocracy, and thus kouroi, which only they had been able to afford, fell out of fashion. This led to changes in style and function of Greek sculpture that mark the beginning of the Classical Period. This period differs for a few significant reasons. Sculptors had learned how to reinforce stone with metal and were also starting to learn how to cast sculptures in metals such as bronze. As technical proficiency increased, artists were able to depict a wider range of poses and expressions, so their sculptures became more natural and realistic. The *Discus Thrower*, a sculpture by Myron, exemplifies these trends of the Classical Period by showing a discus thrower in the middle of a throw; the dynamically-styled pose captures vigorous and convincing movement with flexed muscles and a concentrated expression. Sculptures continued to be used to decorate graves and began to depict actual people with a wider range of expressive poses. During the Classical Period, sculpture also started to be used for other purposes as well, including the decoration of temples like the Parthenon in Athens.

4 ➡ During the late 4th century, as the military conquests of Alexander the Great spread across Eurasia, Greek art spread with them, reaching as far east as Pakistan. Equally, there was an abrupt influx of cultural influences that were absorbed by Greek artists. At this time, referred to by art historians as the Hellenistic Period, the style of ancient Greek sculpture changed radically once again. Classical tendencies towards naturalism, dynamic poses, and movement continued to gain sophistication, but artists also introduced drapery and textures into their sculptures. These elements were used to accentuate the dynamism and movement of a pose. In the *Nike of Samothrace*, one of the most prominent of all ancient Greek sculptures, drapery is used to enhance the pose with extraordinary effects. Although its head and arms have now been lost, we can still imagine the beautiful winged goddess, robes billowing in the wind, with wings outspread, ready to take flight. In addition, during this period, the subject matter of sculpture became more realistic. Domestic scenes became acceptable, and artists no longer felt obligated to depict ideals of beauty or physical perfection, so more realistic portraits of men and women of all ages began to emerge.

Directions: Complete the table by matching the sentences below. Select the appropriate sentences from the answer choices and match them to the category to which they relate. TWO of the answer choices will NOT be used. ***This question is worth 3 points.***

Answer Choices	Archaic Period	Hellenistic Period
Ⓐ Sculptures were usually commissioned by wealthy patrons.	•	•
Ⓑ It was brought about due to influences from other cultures.	•	•
Ⓒ Sculptures began to have various decorative purposes.	•	
Ⓓ Subjects were depicted with a fresh realism instead of idealistic fantasy.		
Ⓔ Sculptures were rigid but very natural.		
Ⓕ Sculptures had one primary decorative purpose.		
Ⓖ Sculptures symbolized societal status.		

Test

TOEFL Reading

The Introduction of the U.S. Electrical System

1 ➡ In modern American society, electricity has become so commonplace that many people take it utterly for granted. Much like the air that we breathe, people do not recognize the importance of electricity until they are deprived of it. Despite the monthly bills we receive for the lifeblood of our homes and offices, we simply expect it to be there, until the lights inexplicably will not turn on during a power outage. This complacent attitude towards such a vital resource is actually a fairly recent development. Although scientists already knew the properties of electricity, they were unable to harness it for practical use until the late 19th century. Once they had achieved that feat, development progressed rapidly, and it has had a massive influence upon both American society and the world in general.

2 ➡ It is difficult to say with certainty when the first operational electrical system was created. However, the earliest ones operated on direct current, which is an electric charge that only flows in one direction. When electricity distribution was introduced to the United States, it was based on the DC system, which was championed by Thomas Edison. DC current was well suited to the main uses of electricity of the day: incandescent light bulbs and motors. It could also be used to charge storage batteries, which allowed for valuable load moderation and provided an emergency supply when generator output was interrupted. The generators could also easily be chained in sequence, which allowed power plants to easily lower their output during low demand periods and provide a more reliable power supply. Edison also invented a meter that made accurate billing of customers according to actual usage possible, which like many of his inventions only worked with DC.

3 ➡ Due to the many patents that Edison held, he had a vested interest in DC remaining the

1. In paragraph 1, why does the author mention lifeblood?

Ⓐ To compare the significance of electricity and exercise

Ⓑ To show that modern people pay expensive medical bills

Ⓒ To emphasize the importance of electricity in our lives

Ⓓ To give an example of what we easily take for granted

2. All of the following are mentioned in paragraph 2 EXCEPT

Ⓐ DC is an electric current that flows in one direction only

Ⓑ Thomas Edison invented and popularized direct current

Ⓒ it is uncertain when the first electrical system was set up

Ⓓ artificial light was one of the first uses of electricity

3. In paragraph 2, what can be inferred about electricity?

Ⓐ Power plants tried to increase output to meet soaring demand.

Ⓑ The invention of the meter allowing accurate billing was not welcomed.

Ⓒ Most of Edison's inventions were sold to U.S. electric companies.

Ⓓ The amount of electricity used varied with the time of day.

4. The word "which" in paragraph 2 refers to

Ⓐ meter

Ⓑ billing

Ⓒ usage

Ⓓ DC

TOEFL Reading

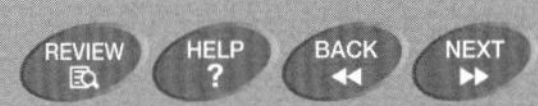

standard, but the Westinghouse Electric & Manufacturing Company provided competition in the form of alternating current. Alternating current was developed in Europe, where it gained a reputation for reliability after the Ganz Works electrified the city of Rome in 1886. With alternating current, the direction of the electric charge periodically reverses to move in the opposite direction. Unlike direct current, which had to generate power at the same voltage level as the devices that would use it, alternating current could be modulated using an invention called a transformer. This meant that power could be generated and emitted from the factory at very high voltage through fewer, relatively thinner wires, and then reduced by the transformer to usable levels for the customers. Therefore, alternating current power stations could be much larger and located farther from their recipients.

4 ➡ In light of these benefits, George Westinghouse decided to license Nicola Tesla's patents for AC technology. This led to a conflict between Edison and Westinghouse referred to as the "War of Currents," which involved many American and European companies who invested heavily in one of the two current systems, hoping that their choice would become predominant. [■A] Edison seized upon the fact that alternating current had a greater potential to be lethal at lower voltages, which was what most consumers would use. [■B] The alternating nature of AC current can cause the heart to lose its coordination, instigating a rhythm that will quickly become fatal if not corrected. [■C] He actively lobbied against AC use in state legislatures, spread disinformation, publicly executed animals using AC current, and even funded the inventor of the electric chair in spite of his own opposition to capital punishment. [■D]

5 ➡ Despite Edison's efforts, alternating current eventually became the industry standard. The

5. Which of the sentences below best expresses the essential information in the highlighted sentence in the passage? Incorrect choices change the meaning in important ways or leave out essential information.

Ⓐ AC could be transformed to usable levels, while DC power had to be produced at the required voltage for appliances.

Ⓑ AC power could be modulated to high voltage levels using a transformer, as opposed to DC which maintained the same voltage level.

Ⓒ DC electricity had been widely used for electric devices before a transformer was invented to generate AC at very high voltage.

Ⓓ AC power should be produced at the standard voltage for appliances in contrast with DC which could be transformed to any voltage.

6. According to paragraph 4, which of the following is NOT mentioned as one of Edison's efforts to prevent AC systems from being adopted?

Ⓐ He spread fictitious rumors about AC systems.

Ⓑ He showed animals killed by electric shock.

Ⓒ He proposed the abolition of the death penalty.

Ⓓ He invested in the business of electric chairs.

7. The word "predominant" in paragraph 4 is closest in meaning to

Ⓐ lucrative

Ⓑ superior

Ⓒ essential

Ⓓ preceding

TOEFL Reading

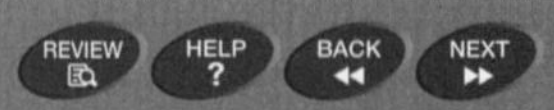

first successful transmission of DC electricity over a long distance in the U.S. occurred in 1889 at the Willamette Falls Station in Oregon City, Oregon. Unfortunately, that power plant was destroyed the following year in a flood. When the Willamette Falls Power Company rebuilt their facility, they chose to incorporate experimental AC generators produced by Westinghouse. During that same year, it was decided to harness the power of Niagara Falls to generate electricity, and a special commission of experts was assembled to decide which type of current to use. They eventually awarded the contract for the generators for the Niagara Falls project to Westinghouse, but they gave Edison's General Electric Company the contract to construct the transmission lines to Buffalo, New York in conciliation. Afterward, General Electric overruled Edison and proceeded to rapidly and thoroughly invest in AC power. Today, DC has endured for only a few specific purposes like third-rail electric railways.

8. According to paragraph 5, which of the following is true of the Willamette Falls Station?

Ⓐ It decided to adopt the AC system when it was rebuilt.

Ⓑ Its generators were damaged by an earthquake in 1890.

Ⓒ It first succeeded in transmitting AC current in the U.S.

Ⓓ Its original facility was designed to be suitable for AC electricity.

TOEFL Reading

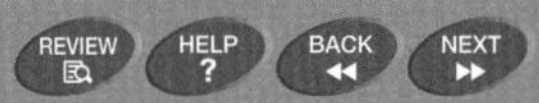

9. Look at the four squares [■] that indicate where the following sentence could be added to the passage.

Focusing upon this flaw, Edison launched a publicity campaign designed to discourage the adoption of AC systems.

Where would the sentence best fit?

Click on a square [■] to add the sentence to the passage.

10. **Directions:** Complete the table by matching the sentences below. Select the appropriate sentences from the answer choices and match them to the category to which they relate. TWO of the answer choices will NOT be used. ***This question is worth 3 points.***

Answer Choices	Direct Current	Alternating Current
(A) It was usually used for third-rail electric railways in the past because of its high voltage. (B) It was created in Europe and became popular after it was used for the electrical system in Rome. (C) It was first transmitted over a long distance from the Willamette Falls Station in the U.S. (D) It was criticized by its opponents for its potential risk of threatening life at lower voltages. (E) It became the final winner of the "War of Currents" with the cooperation of Edison. (F) It was selected as the final choice to carry out the Niagara Falls project. (G) Its supporters conducted a campaign to keep the other system from being widely used.	• •	• • •

Drag your answer choices to the spaces where they belong.
To remove an answer choice, click on it. To review the passage, click on **View Text**.

TOEFL Reading

Historical Records and Language Translation

1 ➡ The recorded history of a culture is a narrative based upon written accounts and various other documented forms of communication. For many cultures, their written history extends back to the Bronze Age, but others only acquired a writing system fairly recently, so their recorded history is accordingly short. The term prehistory refers to the time before recorded history, so it ends with the creation of a culture's writing system. Of course, writing systems do not spring into existence fully formed, so there is a transition period between prehistory and history that is referred to as protohistory. During this time, literacy grows and there are documents that can be used to create a historical record, but people within the culture have not yet begun to record their own history.

2 ➡ The earliest examples of written histories came from the Middle East and Egypt alongside the earliest comprehensible writing systems. These were the archaic cuneiform script of the Sumerians and the Egyptian hieroglyphs, and they are vastly different writing systems that were created independently around 3500 BCE. Sumerian writing emerged as a way to keep track of business transactions and payment of taxes to the government, and it was written upon clay tablets. The earliest Egyptian writings were chronologies that recorded the succession of the Pharaohs and the important events of their reigns. Their descendants had long since forgotten how to read their texts, so modern archaeologists had to decipher them. Many of these historical records were lost for centuries until archaeologists discovered keys to them in ancient ruins. The inscriptions that they found were not intended to be used as ciphers, but because they were written in three different scripts they served that purpose well.

3 ➡ Sumerian was translated due to the discovery of the Behistun Inscription in

11. It can be inferred from paragraph 1 that

Ⓐ most people were literate or highly educated in protohistory

Ⓑ the process of developing a written language is often a gradual one

Ⓒ all the earliest forms of inscriptions were more like drawings

Ⓓ the earliest recorded history dates back to the Neolithic Age

12. According to paragraph 2, which of the following is true of Egyptian hieroglyphs?

Ⓐ Most Egyptian descendants understood their ancient language.

Ⓑ These letters were engraved on cave walls at a historical site.

Ⓒ All documents were encoded to keep their military secrets.

Ⓓ They were used to record historic events related to Pharaohs.

13. The word "they" in paragraph 2 refers to

Ⓐ archaeologists

Ⓑ inscriptions

Ⓒ ciphers

Ⓓ scripts

14. All of the following are mentioned in paragraph 3 EXCEPT

Ⓐ the Behistun Inscription helped to decipher ancient Sumerian writings

Ⓑ Modern Persian uses the same alphabetic structure as that of the old one

Ⓒ the Behistun Inscription is about the life story of the Persian King Darius

Ⓓ Darius became king after he assassinated the preceding king, Cyrus

northwestern Iran. The inscription relates a short biography of the Persian King Darius the Great and tells about the many military victories that brought him to the throne in the upheaval following the death of Cyrus the Great. Commissioned sometime during his reign, the inscription was written in three different cuneiform script languages: Old Persian, Elamite, and Babylonian. These were the languages that were spoken in his realm and the regions he had conquered, allowing all of his subjects and future generations to know of his glory. The Old Persian was translated with the help of middle and modern Persian, with which it shares an alphabetic structure, and thereafter the other scripts were gradually deciphered.

4 ➡ Egyptian hieroglyphics were translated with the help of an artifact called the Rosetta Stone. Like the Behistun Inscription, this stone is believed to have originally been displayed in a public building like a temple, but it was recycled and used in the construction of a fort near Rashid (Rosetta) in the Nile Delta, where it was later discovered by a French soldier. From top to bottom, the inscription is written in Ancient Egyptian hieroglyphs, Demotic script; an ancient Egyptian script used for document writing, and Ancient Greek. The text of the stone is a decree from King Ptolemy V that established him as the new divine ruler of Egypt. Though the upper portion was clearly incomplete, in combination they provided an essential translation key. Other similar inscriptions have since been found, but an essential clue that reveals new knowledge is often referred to as Rosetta Stone due to its influence.

5 ➡ In most cases, the deciphering of ancient texts is a lengthy and difficult process that involves the work of many linguists over multiple generations. One language that has been successfully parsed out through sheer determination is that of the ancient Maya. [■A] Mayan hieroglyphs have been found throughout

15. Which of the sentences below best expresses the essential information in the highlighted sentence in the passage? Incorrect choices change the meaning in important ways or leave out essential information.

Ⓐ The languages could convey his honor to his people and posterity since these were the ones used in his territories.

Ⓑ His people could read his honorable story because it was written in the languages they could all understand.

Ⓒ These languages were widely spoken in his kingdom, so his subjects and descendants had no difficulty in reading them.

Ⓓ His subjects and posterity were familiar with his glorious stories because they were handed down by word of mouth.

16. In paragraph 4, why does the author mention Rosetta Stone?

Ⓐ To give an example of the historic landmark near the Nile Delta

Ⓑ To introduce a well-known inscription that helped to decode old Egyptian

Ⓒ To demonstrate that it is the oldest stone artifact in existence

Ⓓ To emphasize its importance as an edict issued by King Ptolemy V

17. According to paragraph 5, which of the following is true of Mayan hieroglyphs?

Ⓐ They are known as the most complicated language in the world.

Ⓑ Mayan people provided essential clues to translate these letters.

Ⓒ The decoding project made rapid progress in the 1950s and 70s.

Ⓓ Scientists revealed that the number system also represented sounds.

TOEFL Reading

Central America dating back to around 300 BCE, making it the oldest language of its complexity and completeness found anywhere in the Americas. [■B] By 1900, little had been translated except for their number system, but scientists gradually came to understand that some images represented not only actual words, but also groups of sounds that formed syllables. [■C] Following breakthroughs in the 1950s and 70s, translation rapidly progressed. [■D] Today, researchers can read most of the available texts, and the Mayan people have begun to relearn their old writing system.

6 ➡ Unfortunately, some languages like Etruscan, a proto-language from the society that preceded the Romans, still defy attempts at translation. The Etruscan alphabet was derived from the Greek alphabet, and the oldest inscriptions in it date back to around 500 BCE. Thousands of inscriptions have been found on monuments, statues, vases, tombstones, and even personal items like jewelry, and linguists can read the words phonetically. However, they are only confident about the meanings of a few hundred words, including some that were borrowed by Latin and subsequently English.

18. According to paragraph 6, which of the following is NOT true of Etruscan?

Ⓐ Linguists can understand most of the available texts.

Ⓑ Latin and English borrowed some words from it.

Ⓒ The Greek alphabet was the source of the Etruscan one.

Ⓓ Its oldest inscriptions are from around 500 BCE.

TOEFL Reading

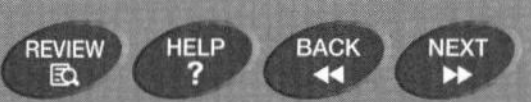

19. Look at the four squares [■] that indicate where the following sentence could be added to the passage.

It was originally thought to be entirely pictographic, with images directly representing objects or events.

Where would the sentence best fit?

Click on a square [■] to add the sentence to the passage.

20. Directions: Complete the table by matching the sentences below. Select the appropriate sentences from the answer choices and match them to the category to which they relate. TWO of the answer choices will NOT be used. ***This question is worth 3 points.***

Answer Choices	Sumerian cuneiform	Mayan hieroglyphs
Ⓐ The inscription that helped to decode them was written in three different languages. Ⓑ Linguists are still not convinced about the meaning of most of the words. Ⓒ They are well known for their complexity and completeness. Ⓓ They were first developed to submit reports on business and taxes to the government. Ⓔ It was revealed that some of their images represent both sounds and words. Ⓕ Its essential translation key was located near Rashid in the Nile Delta. Ⓖ They were found throughout Central America, dating back to around 300 BCE.	• •	• • •

Drag your answer choices to the spaces where they belong.
To remove an answer choice, click on it. To review the passage, click on **View Text**.

Actual Test

Actual Test 1

Actual Test 2

Actual Test 3

Actual Test 1

TOEFL Reading

Reading Section Directions

The Reading section measures your ability to understand academic passages in English. A clock at the top of the screen will show you how much time is remaining.

Most questions are worth 1 point, but the last question for each passage is worth more than 1 point. The directions for the last question indicate how many points you may receive.

Some passages include a word or phrase that is underlined in blue. To see a definition or an explanation, click on the word or phrase.

You may skip a question and return to it later, provided there is time remaining. To move on to the next question, click **NEXT**. To return to a question, click **BACK.**

Click **REVIEW** to access the review screen. The screen will show which questions have been answered and which have not been answered. You may go directly to any previous question from the review screen.

Click **CONTINUE** to proceed.

TOEFL Reading

Two Types of Planets

1 ➡ All of the planets in our solar system including the Earth are arranged on nearly the same flat plane with roughly oval orbits around the Sun. Considering that there are only eight planets in the solar system, it is striking how much diversity exists among them. Yet over the past two centuries as more and more has been discovered about our neighbors, it has gradually become clear that the planets can be grouped into two broad categories. The terrestrial planets are small worlds that contain high-density, rocky material, and the Jovian planets are low-density giants composed mostly of gases like hydrogen and helium. Beyond being a convenient classification of the planets, these categories have proven very revealing in helping us understand how our solar system came to be.

2 ➡ Mercury, Venus, Earth, and Mars are terrestrial planets. The term terrestrial comes from the Latin word *terra* which means earth. Thus, the term is meant to indicate that all of these planets are similar to Earth in important ways, and indeed they do have several features in common. First of all, they are all similar in size and, more importantly, are significantly smaller than the Jovian planets. The smallest of the Jovian planets, Neptune, is over fifty times larger than the largest of the terrestrial planets, Earth. Also, the terrestrial planets all orbit close to the Sun relative to the other planets. The distances between the orbits of the planets increase the further out from the Sun they are. Consequently, the orbits of the four terrestrial planets are grouped close to the Sun, while the outer four planets have immense distances between their orbits. Being closer to the Sun, the terrestrial planets are warmed by its heat energy. In addition, the terrestrial planets all have an atmosphere, which helps to retain the

1. Based on the information in paragraph 1, what can be inferred about planet classification?

Ⓐ No more research needs to be done to further categorize the planets in our solar system.

Ⓑ The density and matter of a planet plays an important role in its classification.

Ⓒ Our solar system can be split into more than 8 groups.

Ⓓ Planet classification enabled us to explain how other celestial objects began.

2. The word "retain" in paragraph 2 is closest in meaning to

Ⓐ produce

Ⓑ reflect

Ⓒ keep

Ⓓ increase

3. Why does the author mention Neptune in paragraph 2?

Ⓐ To demonstrate a difference in composition between terrestrial and Jovian planets

Ⓑ To provide evidence that Jovian planets are better located than terrestrial planets

Ⓒ To illustrate how small terrestrial planets are compared to Jovian planets

Ⓓ To explain why terrestrial planets are closer to the Sun than Jovian planets

TOEFL Reading

Sun's heat and accounts for the much higher average temperatures of the terrestrial planets as compared to their more distant cousins. However, the most significant distinguishing feature of the terrestrial planets is their dense composition. Their surfaces are composed primarily of silicate rocks and they have recorded their violent histories, accounting for the dramatic landscapes of these planets, which are marked by comet impact craters, canyons, mountains, and volcanoes.

3 ➡ Jupiter, Saturn, Uranus, and Neptune are called Jovian planets. The term is derived from the name of the Roman god Jove, also called Jupiter, and hence designates their similarity to the planet Jupiter. The four Jovian planets are the true giants in our solar system, dwarfing the terrestrial planets. Also, with orbits that take them so far away from the Sun's warmth, they are the most frigid of all the planets, with the outermost planets reaching below -200 degrees Celsius. Another conspicuous feature of the Jovian planets is their surfaces. Despite their seemingly solid appearance, these planets are composed primarily of gases; therefore, unlike the rocky terrestrial planets, they do not have a well-defined surface. [■A] Instead, their atmospheres, which are mostly hydrogen and helium, become more and more dense closer to the core, blending into a liquid interior under very intense pressures. [■B] Also prominent are the spectacular systems of rings and moons that encircle all four of these gaseous giants. [■C] In marked contrast to the terrestrial planets, which have at most two moons, Jupiter has 63 moons. [■D] When one considers the dramatic differences between them, it is clear that terrestrial planets have radically different characteristics from Jovian planets.

4 ➡ The phenomenal differences between the Jovian and terrestrial planets are explained by the different ways they formed at the birth of our solar system. The current theory holds that the solar system was originally a huge rotating

4. Which of the sentences below best expresses the essential information in the highlighted sentence in the passage? Incorrect answer choices change the meaning or leave out essential information.

Ⓐ Craters, canyons, mountains and volcanoes account for the dramatic landscape of the terrestrial planets with rocky surfaces.

Ⓑ Because they have had violent histories, these planets have craters.

Ⓒ Therefore, their surfaces, covered with craters, canyons, mountains and volcanoes are mostly silicate rock.

Ⓓ Terrestrial planets, due to their rocky, silicate surfaces, show signs of historic trauma evidenced by various geographical features.

5. The word they in paragraph 3 refers to

Ⓐ Jovian planets

Ⓑ terrestrial planets

Ⓒ orbits

Ⓓ surfaces

6. According to paragraph 3, what is distinctive about Jovian planets in comparison to terrestrial planets?

Ⓐ They were formed before the development of terrestrial planets.

Ⓑ They consist primarily of gases.

Ⓒ Their atmospheres are made primarily of hydrogen.

Ⓓ Their cores are relatively solid.

cloud known as a solar nebula. This cloud was made up primarily of gases like helium and hydrogen, along with much smaller amounts of denser material. As this cloud spun, it gradually flattened to become a disk with a denser area at the center. Our solar system was formed out of this cloud as the gases condensed and coalesced. Gases condense in conditions of low temperature and high pressure. However, the conditions near the center of the nebula were too intense for this to happen. So the planets that formed there were composed mostly of compounds with high melting points such as silicates and metals, and thus were smaller since these compounds were less plentiful. These became the terrestrial planets. Farther out in the nebula, where conditions were more favorable, the gases could condense and be drawn together by gravity to form the Jovian planets. This explains the differences in composition, size, and density between the two kinds of planets in our solar system.

7. According to paragraph 4, which of the following is true about our solar system?

Ⓐ It was created by compacting gases.

Ⓑ Gases compact then condense before they coalesce.

Ⓒ Gases contract when temperatures fall and pressure increases.

Ⓓ Gravity played a role only in the formation of the Jovian planets.

8. The word "coalesced" in paragraph 4 is closest in meaning to

Ⓐ combined

Ⓑ arranged

Ⓒ disseminated

Ⓓ expanded

TOEFL Reading 

9. Look at the four squares [■] that indicate where the following sentence could be added to the passage.

Thus, there is no precise distinction between the exterior atmosphere and the interior surface.

Where would the sentence best fit?

Click on a square [■] to add the sentence to the passage.

10. **Directions:** Complete the table by matching the sentences below. Select the appropriate sentences from the answer choices and match them to the category to which they relate. TWO of the answer choices will NOT be used. ***This question is worth 3 points.***

Answer Choices	Terrestrial Planets	Jovian Planets
Ⓐ In terms of size, they dwarf the other category of planets. Ⓑ They are compact compared to the other category of planets. Ⓒ They warm up by shuffling closer to the Sun's heat energy. Ⓓ Planets in this group are comparable in size to one another. Ⓔ They have a rocky exterior. Ⓕ They are characterized as having many moons. Ⓖ There is an inadequate supply of gas on these planets.	• • •	• •

Drag your answer choices to the spaces where they belong.
To remove an answer choice, click on it. To review the passage, click on **View Text**.

TOEFL Reading

Gutenberg and Metal Type Printing

1 ➠ [■A] Movable type is a system of printing and typography that uses movable cast-metal pieces to represent individual symbols and characters. [■B] The development of movable type began with woodblock printing in ancient Egypt. [■C] Later building on these developments, 15th century German printer and goldsmith, Johannes Gutenberg, gained fame by implementing a novel printing system using movable metal type as one of its components. [■D] Before printing technology arrived in Europe, books had to be meticulously copied by hand by monks. Woodblock printing was quickly adopted when it reached Europe because it was easier and more dependable than copying by hand, but it wasn't much faster.

2 ➠ Before metal type, printing was accomplished through a relatively slow method—woodblock printing. This arduous process necessitated the carving out of text and illustrations from the surface of wooden blocks, using one block for each printed page. Then in late 13th century China, it was replaced by movable wooden type. This allowed printers to use individual pieces that could be fitted together to form words and eliminated the need to carve out a completely new image any time a new page was to be printed. Production times profoundly decreased, but there were still limitations to using wood as a printing instrument. Wood is a durable material; however, when faced with the stresses of repeated printing, it wears down, needing fairly regular replacement. Furthermore, because of wood's natural grain and veining, characters had to be carefully chiseled out, affecting the clarity of the letters and requiring more time to produce.

3 ➠ To overcome these limitations, attempts at using metal to form type were made. For this, carved wooden pieces were pressed into sand to form a negative of each character or

11. What is the function of paragraph 1 as it relates to the rest of the passage?

Ⓐ It introduces some historical background about the subject and a person who influenced its development.

Ⓑ It provides the background of a person who revolutionized the field of paper printing.

Ⓒ It illustrates a major technological change in printing and the methods used to create movable type.

Ⓓ It identifies the subject and the consequences of an invention that revolutionized the way paper was printed.

12. According to paragraph 2, which of the following is NOT a limitation of wood used for printing?

Ⓐ It deteriorates relatively quickly.

Ⓑ It takes a long time to carve.

Ⓒ It has a texture that affects the readability of the letters.

Ⓓ It is not readily available in some locations.

13. According to paragraph 3, which of the following is NOT true of Gutenberg's printing?

Ⓐ Prints from his press were clearer and more uniform than those of other printing techniques.

Ⓑ Gutenberg developed an ink used exclusively for printing.

Ⓒ Gutenberg used his machines for olive oil and wine production.

Ⓓ It was a dependable process for creating printed pages.

Actual Test 1

TOEFL Reading

symbol. Molten metals such as bronze, copper, iron, and tin were then poured into matrices, or molds, to cast type. Metal movable type like this had been evolving for several centuries in Asia before Johannes Gutenberg was able to create a practical and efficient printing system. Unlike the inventors who placed their attention on the individual mechanical parts used in printing, Gutenberg addressed the process by considering all of the parts involved in printing as a whole. He was able to create a process for producing metal movable type, which differed from earlier attempts as he used copper matrices to produce sharper images than had previously been made. Furthermore, Gutenberg developed new oil-based inks designed especially for printing. These inks were made using turpentine, soot, and walnut oil, and they had an oily consistency that made them excellent for application using a printing press. Lastly, he created a technique for printing that used a wooden printing press structurally similar to the screw-type machines used for olive oil and wine production, which allowed uniform pressure to be applied to all parts of the printed page. The effect was a consistent print that had ink evenly distributed throughout the image.

4 ➡ Gutenberg's most famous book printing is the *Gutenberg Bible*, of which he produced 180 copies. While this book was not the first one printed with his movable type process, it is the one that serves not only as an icon of Gutenberg, but also as the beginning of the age of the printed book. With his invention, Gutenberg ushered in a printing era lasting several centuries, and the processes for creating movable metal type remained unchanged for almost as long, resulting in profound effects on most societies around the world. This was mainly due to metal type's high durability. It allowed printing to become an economical choice for recording information, facilitating a proliferation of printed materials. In fact, metal type's effectiveness would influence societies by making printed materials available to not

14. The word "it" in paragraph 4 refers to

Ⓐ printing
Ⓑ *Gutenberg Bible*
Ⓒ movable type process
Ⓓ icon

15. Which of the following sentences below best expresses the essential information in the highlighted sentence in the passage? Incorrect answer choices change the meaning in important ways or leave out essential information.

Ⓐ It is known that movable metal type influenced many societies around the world.
Ⓑ Gutenberg's printing methods endured for hundreds of years, influencing cultures worldwide.
Ⓒ Gutenberg redesigned his invention numerous times, allowing the durable equipment to be used for several centuries.
Ⓓ Societies around the world provided input for Gutenberg when he was developing movable metal type.

16. According to paragraph 4, which of the following sentences about the *Gutenberg Bible* is true?

Ⓐ It was Gutenberg's first printing using his newly created printing process.
Ⓑ It was the first book ever created using a printing machine.
Ⓒ It was printed with movable metal type and oil-based inks.
Ⓓ It was the result of profound changes in most European societies.

only the educated elite but also to the masses. Indeed, in metal type's early years, this was seen as a threat to the upper classes, and in some societies, state governments would make laws limiting metal type printing to only their use.

5 ➡ It is believed that Gutenberg helped establish the Renaissance by producing a reliable and efficient way to reproduce writings and images in mass quantities. Metal-type printing enabled the mass production of books for the first time, with news and information spreading across Europe faster than ever before. It also made books much cheaper, which caused a rapid increase in literacy. People were exposed to new ideas and subjects that they would not have been able to study in the past. Indeed, the exchange of ideas rapidly accelerated, sparking the beginning of the scientific revolution.

17. According to paragraph 4, early metal type was seen as a threat to the upper classes because

Ⓐ printing was more efficient than it had been in the past

Ⓑ books could now be accessed by the lower classes of society

Ⓒ they would now have to create laws limiting who could produce books

Ⓓ the masses were now printing books using movable metal type

18. The word "reliable" in paragraph 5 is closest in meaning to

Ⓐ reputable

Ⓑ decent

Ⓒ complex

Ⓓ dependable

TOEFL Reading

19. Look at the four squares [■] that indicate where the following sentence could be added to the passage.

By the 8th century A.D., the Chinese were using this technique to print whole books filled with text and illustrations.

Where would the sentence best fit?

Click on a square [■] to add the sentence to the passage.

20. **Directions:** An introductory sentence for a brief summary of the passage is provided below. Complete the summary by selecting the THREE answer choices that express the most important ideas in the passage. Some sentences do not belong in the summary because they express ideas that are not presented in the passage or are minor ideas in the passage. ***This question is worth 2 points.***

Movable type is a printing process of great historical importance.

-
-
-

Answer Choices

Ⓐ Paper prints have existed since the 1400s, the period in which Gutenberg began developing his well-known printing system.

Ⓑ Wooden type required great care on the part of craftsmen as it had to be chiseled out and took a long time.

Ⓒ Printing was originally accomplished by using an entire block of carved wood, but this was later replaced with movable wood type.

Ⓓ Because metal is a very durable material, it is quite useful for forming the types used in the printing process.

Ⓔ Gutenberg revolutionized printing by creating a printing system that used movable metal type as one of its components.

Ⓕ Gutenberg's accomplishments increased the rate at which information was exchanged, sparking new influential movements.

Drag your answer choices to the spaces where they belong.
To remove an answer choice, click on it. To review the passage, click on **View Text**.

Actual Test 2

TOEFL Reading

Reading Section Directions

The Reading section measures your ability to understand academic passages in English. A clock at the top of the screen will show you how much time is remaining.

Most questions are worth 1 point, but the last question for each passage is worth more than 1 point. The directions for the last question indicate how many points you may receive.

Some passages include a word or phrase that is underlined in blue. To see a definition or an explanation, click on the word or phrase.

You may skip a question and return to it later, provided there is time remaining. To move on to the next question, click **NEXT**. To return to a question, click **BACK**.

Click **REVIEW** to access the review screen. The screen will show which questions have been answered and which have not been answered. You may go directly to any previous question from the review screen.

Click **CONTINUE** to proceed.

TOEFL Reading

Earthquake Prediction

1 ➡ Earthquakes are among the most devastating natural disasters that affect the planet, and their unpredictable nature makes them even more serious. The accurate prediction of seismic events has long been a goal of scientists that could help to prevent the massive loss of lives that often accompanies such widespread destruction. Unfortunately, no reliable way of predicting earthquakes has been identified, but scientists continue to research many promising methods of earthquake prediction that fall into two broad categories: long-term prediction and short-term prediction.

2 ➡ The long-term prediction of earthquakes is done by studying the historical record of seismic activity along a particular segment of a fault zone. By plotting out a timeline of when past earthquakes occurred and the magnitude of each quake, scientists can create a pattern of activity that allows them to determine the average interval between events of a particular size. By studying these gaps in seismic activity, they can determine the average length of time that passes between events of a significant magnitude. Based upon when the last quake of a particular size occurred, they can make an educated guess as to when the next one may strike. Since this method deals with average amounts, it can only be used to predict when an earthquake has the potential to occur. This means that they cannot be more accurate than a specified time interval of a few years to a few decades.

3 ➡ Short-term prediction is focused on being able to determine when the next earthquake will occur accurately enough to evacuate people from the surrounding area before it hits. In order to do so, scientists devote their time to studying events that occurred shortly before previous earthquakes called precursors. Throughout history, a variety of physical and

1. Which of the following best expresses the essential information in the highlighted sentence? Incorrect answer choices change the meaning in important ways or leave out essential information.

Ⓐ Thankfully, scientists have developed reliable methods to predict when earthquakes will occur, and these fall into two basic categories.

Ⓑ Unfortunately, scientists may never discover any way to accurately predict earthquakes in the long term, but short term methods show promise.

Ⓒ Scientists have not discovered any fool-proof way to predict earthquakes, but they are researching many potential methods that fit into long and short-term prediction.

Ⓓ Scientists have developed many ways to predict earthquakes, however they are only useful for broad, long-term predictions.

2. According to paragraph 2, how is long-term prediction of earthquakes done?

Ⓐ By comparing quakes of similar size on a fault segment with those of nearby faults

Ⓑ By analyzing seismic gaps identified in earthquake activity patterns

Ⓒ By comparing historical timelines of quakes on various segments of a fault

Ⓓ By calculating the average time interval between every earthquake

3. The word "specified" in paragraph 2 is closest in meaning to

Ⓐ stated

Ⓑ observed

Ⓒ typical

Ⓓ definite

chemical phenomena have been observed both by survivors and by scientists who were in the area prior to the events. Easily observed phenomena include deformation of land features and changes in water chemistry and the water level in wells and lakes. Others that require sophisticated devices to detect are more directly related to altered seismic activity. Fault zones are never completely stable, so there are frequent small tremors and seismic waves, but as an earthquake becomes imminent, the speed of seismic waves, the frequency of stronger tremors, which are called foreshocks, and the electrical resistance of rocks can all be altered.

4 ➡ One theory that explains many of these precursors is referred to as the dilatancy model. As the rocks that are under pressure along a fault line approach their breaking point, they can increase in volume significantly. [■A] This swelling, or dilation as it is called, is the result of microcracks forming between the crystalline layers of the rock. [■B] This alters the density of the rock, which changes how it transmits seismic energy, and the water also alters its electrical conductivity. [■C] When dilation occurs throughout large rock formations, it can dramatically alter the shape of the land as the inevitable quake rupture approaches. [■D] One such area of uplift that has scientists concerned has developed near Los Angeles along the San Andreas Fault. Since long-term prediction shows that a high magnitude quake in this area is likely to happen soon, scientists are monitoring this feature, which is called the Palmdale Bulge, very closely for further precursors. Dilatancy can also affect groundwater movement and water quality in wells or lakes. As water fills the rock fissures, the volume of water in wells and lakes may drop. The chemistry of the water can also be altered as gases and minerals are released from the rocks as they split apart. In particular, levels of radon gas have been shown to increase in water as tension increases along fault zones. The frequency and intensity of tremors also tend to increase, and then abruptly decline immediately before a major quake begins. This

4. According to paragraph 3, all of the following are precursors of earthquakes EXCEPT

Ⓐ changes in geological features
Ⓑ resistivity of rocks
Ⓒ instability of fault zones
Ⓓ increased seismic activity

5. The word "imminent" in paragraph 3 is closest in meaning to

Ⓐ of much significance
Ⓑ great in intensity
Ⓒ occurring in short intervals
Ⓓ about to happen

6. Why does the author mention the San Andreas Fault in paragraph 4?

Ⓐ To provide an example of a precursor event that changes land formation
Ⓑ To explain why this area is called the Palmdale Bulge
Ⓒ To introduce a region which is a counter-example of the dilatancy model
Ⓓ To highlight the effectiveness of long-term prediction in identifying a high-risk area

7. According to paragraph 4, which of the following is true about precursor events involving water?

Ⓐ The concentration of radon in water filling the rock fissures decreases.
Ⓑ Changes in groundwater levels increase the frequency of foreshocks.
Ⓒ Minerals released from rocks cause a change in water chemistry.
Ⓓ Bodies of water experience a volume increase.

Actual Test 2

calm before the storm is believed to be caused by a momentary increase in rock strength before the water impregnates them.

5 ➡ The phenomena in the dilatancy model can be organized into a typical sequence of events. In Stage I, stress builds up in an area of the fault zone. In Stages II and III, the effects of dilatancy are felt as the rocks expand and water fills in the micro-fissures. Stage IV is the large magnitude quake, and Stage V is the aftermath of the event, which often includes further strong tremors called aftershocks. Unfortunately, these stages are not uniform in length in every earthquake, nor do the precursors guarantee that a large quake will even occur. Every seismic event is unique, which makes it extremely difficult to use precursor events to accurately predict when a quake will happen. For example, when the Loma Prieta earthquake struck in 1989, two magnitude 5 foreshocks preceded the earthquake by 15 and 2 months, and in each case scientists predicted that a stronger earthquake would strike within a few days. However, no quake occurred, and people were unprepared when the magnitude 6.9 earthquake finally came. With further research and analysis, many scientists believe refinement of the dilatancy model is possible, or that a new, better method may be developed.

8. How is paragraph 5 organized?

Ⓐ It outlines the dilatancy model and then provides reasons why a new method of quake prediction needs to be developed.

Ⓑ It explains how the dilatancy model is divided into five stages and its limitations in real-life application.

Ⓒ It shows the progression of a major earthquake and the reason why prediction of earthquakes is difficult.

Ⓓ It groups precursor events into five distinct categories and provides real-life examples of how they manifest.

TOEFL Reading

9. Look at the four squares [■] that indicate where the following sentence could be added to the passage.

The weaker grains in the rock separate and groundwater flows into the openings, forcing them to stay apart.

Where would the sentence best fit?

Click on a square [■] to add the sentence to the passage.

10. **Directions:** An introductory sentence for a brief summary of the passage is provided below. Complete the summary by selecting the THREE answer choices that express the most important ideas in the passage. Some sentences do not belong in the summary because they express ideas that are not presented in the passage or are minor ideas in the passage. ***This question is worth 2 points.***

While accurate prediction of earthquakes has been a scientific goal for many years, no completely reliable method has been found yet.

-
-
-

Answer Choices

Ⓐ While a sequence of stages of major quakes is known, the duration of each stage is not identical, making prediction hard.

Ⓑ An example of land deformation is the Palmdale Bulge along the San Andreas Fault where a high-magnitude quake is likely to take place soon.

Ⓒ Stages I through III of the dilatancy model are precursor events that precede the major quake and aftershocks that are labeled Stages IV and V respectively.

Ⓓ Events like land swelling, increasing foreshocks, and changes in water levels are indicators of an impending earthquake.

Ⓔ By creating a timeline of seismic activity, scientists identify a pattern that helps them predict when the next quake of a similar size may occur.

Ⓕ Prediction of the Loma Prieta quake failed because scientists failed to accurately predict how long after the preceding foreshocks the quake would take place.

Drag your answer choices to the spaces where they belong.
To remove an answer choice, click on it. To review the passage, click on **View Text**.

TOEFL Reading

The Development of Motion Pictures

1 ➡ The development of motion pictures began in the mid-19th century with the invention of the zoetrope. Artists would create a series of drawings that showed various stages of movement, for example of a couple dancing. These drawings were placed within a cylinder that had an opening for a person to look through. When the cylinder was rotated at an appropriate speed, it would appear to the viewer that the dancers were actually moving instead of the cylinder. This optical illusion is called the phi phenomenon, and it occurs because as humans view a series of images in rapid succession, our eyes perceive continuous movement. The images of the dancers do not change, but our mind processes the information in such a way that it appears to be one image that moves. By the 1870s, camera technology had advanced far enough that artist Eadweard Muybridge was able to use a series of cameras to replicate this phenomenon.

2 ➡ Eadweard Muybridge was a professional photographer who was famous for his images of natural landscapes and studies of the western United States. In 1872 he was approached by Leland Stanford to help him settle a question about the movement of horses. Many people believed that when a horse moves at a trot or a gallop, it keeps at least one foot on the ground for balance. [■A] The shutter speeds of cameras had become fast enough that Muybridge was able to line up 24 in a row to capture the movement of the horse. [■B] As a jockey rode the horse past the cameras at 36 miles per hour, it triggered trip wires that activated the cameras. [■C] Some of the resulting photographs showed that the horse did indeed have all of its feet in the air at times. [■D] Muybridge converted the images into silhouettes and placed them together into a device of his own design to project them onto a screen for an audience

11. Why does the author mention phi phenomenon in paragraph 1?

   Ⓐ To introduce the concept which makes motion pictures viable
   Ⓑ To emphasize the versatility of our visual abilities
   Ⓒ To explain why zoetropes came in a cylindrical form
   Ⓓ To suggest that artists who produced zoetropes were clearly scientists

12. The word "converted" in paragraph 2 is closest in meaning to

   Ⓐ reproduced
   Ⓑ transferred
   Ⓒ changed
   Ⓓ applied

13. What can be inferred about Muybridge's work in paragraph 2?

   Ⓐ He specifically requested the jockey to ride the horse at a certain speed.
   Ⓑ Cameras were not advanced enough to take multiple shots with a single lens.
   Ⓒ It was the first time he ever worked with a moving animal.
   Ⓓ He inadvertently provided a breakthrough in the field of zoology.

14. The word "flexible" in paragraph 3 is closest in meaning to

   Ⓐ fragile
   Ⓑ bendable
   Ⓒ adaptable
   Ⓓ stiff

to view, thus creating the first motion picture exhibition.

3 ➡ The next great innovation in motion pictures came in the late 1880s with the creation of celluloid photographic film and cameras that could take photographs in sequence through a single lens. The flexible celluloid allowed strips of film to be rolled onto reels that fed the camera, which allowed a few minutes instead of a few seconds of action to be filmed. After meeting Muybridge, Thomas Edison decided to develop his own motion picture camera and an exhibition apparatus. The final result was the Kinetoscope, which passed the film strip between a lamp and a viewing lens. Unfortunately, only one person at a time could use a Kinetoscope, so when the first commercial motion picture house opened in New York City in 1894, the owner had to purchase ten machines. Despite the considerable investment this required, Kinetoscope parlors were launched in major cities across the country, and Edison's company reaped great profits.

4 ➡ Due to the amount of revenue that Kinetoscopes were generating, Edison did not feel compelled to develop a projection system. However, his counterparts in other companies recognized that films shown to larger audiences would be far more profitable because of the machine to viewer ratio. Much of the innovation took place at other companies, but Edison was eventually approached to mass produce the end result, the Vitascope. This machine used a high-intensity light bulb to project the film onto a wall or sheet, and the technology remained essentially the same for decades. The earliest films that were produced seem simple by today's standards, but they had a profound effect on the viewing public. They were filmed from one perspective and depicted an action or event with no alteration. They showed dancing, athletic events, scenes from nature, and famously, a train arriving at a station. The angle the train movie was shot from made it appear as though the train was coming at the viewers, and

15. Which of the following is NOT mentioned in paragraph 3 about the Kinetoscope?

Ⓐ It made use of celluloid film.
Ⓑ It projected film strips a few minutes long through a viewing lens.
Ⓒ It allowed only one viewer at a time.
Ⓓ It required significant financial investment for its use.

16. According to paragraph 4, why was Edison late in joining the move toward a projection system?

Ⓐ His Kinetoscope business would suffer with an increased machine to viewer ratio.
Ⓑ He believed there could be no further innovation beyond his Kinetoscope.
Ⓒ He did not have the foresight to realize that larger audiences would be more profitable.
Ⓓ His company was the last to be approached about mass producing a projection system.

17. Which of the following best expresses the essential information in the highlighted sentence? Incorrect answer choices change the meaning in important ways or leave out essential information.

Ⓐ The film of a train was shot in such a way that it made the audience think that the train would crash into them, so they ran away.
Ⓑ The film of a train showed it approaching the station at a bad angle and hitting people, which terrified the audience.
Ⓒ The train in one film was shown approaching the camera at great speed, which made some of the audience afraid.
Ⓓ The film of a train was very popular because the angle of the camera made it look like the train was going to strike the viewers.

TOEFL Reading 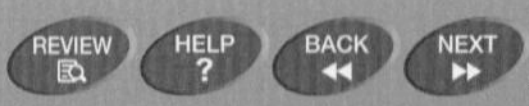

some people close to the screen fled their seats in panic.

5 ➡ The second phase of films began to tell stories, and they also incorporated different scenes and shots from multiple distances and angles. These films were only 5 to 10 minutes long, because film reels could only hold that much film. Sound did not become available until the late 1920s when the technology became commercially viable. So, any dialogue between characters or explanation of the story had to be achieved via using a blank screen with writing called a title card. For this reason, movies from this era of cinema are referred to as "silent films," but theater owners would often employ a pianist or organist to play music to accompany the scenes. The films were often distributed with prepared sheet music to ensure that the music played was appropriate, and some films had complete scores for large theaters employing orchestras. When sound technology became adequate to include a soundtrack with speech, music, and sound effects, film studios transitioned to making "talking pictures" seemingly overnight.

18. All of the following are mentioned in paragraph 5 EXCEPT

Ⓐ how films emerged as a medium for storytelling
Ⓑ the progress of relatively sophisticated filmmaking techniques in early films
Ⓒ the time period in which the transition to "talking pictures" took place
Ⓓ the reason why theater owners prepared sheet music for orchestras

TOEFL Reading

19. Look at the four squares [■] that indicate where the following sentence could be added to the passage.

Others maintained that the horse had all four feet off of the ground at certain points.

Where would the sentence best fit?

Click on a square [■] to add the sentence to the passage.

20. Directions: An introductory sentence for a brief summary of the passage is provided below. Complete the summary by selecting the THREE answer choices that express the most important ideas in the passage. Some sentences do not belong in the summary because they express ideas that are not presented in the passage or are minor ideas in the passage. ***This question is worth 2 points.***

Motion pictures rapidly developed from a scientific novelty to a form of mainstream entertainment in the late 19th and early 20th century.

-
-
-

Answer Choices

Ⓐ Muybridge's clever set up of cameras allowed him to provide the verdict that horses did indeed have all four feet off the ground when galloping.

Ⓑ Edison's Kinetoscope was an innovation on its own, but it also was the first to allow the public to consume short films as a form of entertainment.

Ⓒ Sensing great profitability with larger audiences, many jumped into developing a projection system, resulting in the Vitascope.

Ⓓ Early "silent films" made up for the lack of sound by including title cards and live music accompaniment until the transition to "talking pictures" took place.

Ⓔ Even though early Kinetoscope parlors had to make a heavy investment upfront, the high demand for them offset that cost.

Ⓕ The phi phenomenon, which allows us to perceive a sequence of still images as moving, is the scientific breakthrough that drove the film industry.

Drag your answer choices to the spaces where they belong.
To remove an answer choice, click on it. To review the passage, click on **View Text**.

Actual Test 3

TOEFL Reading

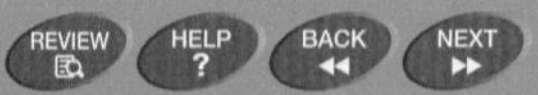

Reading Section Directions

The Reading section measures your ability to understand academic passages in English. A clock at the top of the screen will show you how much time is remaining.

Most questions are worth 1 point, but the last question for each passage is worth more than 1 point. The directions for the last question indicate how many points you may receive.

Some passages include a word or phrase that is underlined in blue. To see a definition or an explanation, click on the word or phrase.

You may skip a question and return to it later, provided there is time remaining. To move on to the next question, click **NEXT**. To return to a question, click **BACK**.

Click **REVIEW** to access the review screen. The screen will show which questions have been answered and which have not been answered. You may go directly to any previous question from the review screen.

Click **CONTINUE** to proceed.

TOEFL Reading

Tyrannosaurus Rex

1 ➡ Quite possibly the most recognizable of all dinosaurs is the *Tyrannosaurus rex*, or as it is commonly abbreviated, *T. rex*. The incredibly fierce appearance and superior hunting skills of this well-known theropod earned it its befitting name, which means "tyrant lizard king" in Greek. The *T. rex* lived throughout what is now western North America and had a far wider hunting range than other predatory dinosaurs of the time. Based on fossil records of *T. rex* found in various rock formations in North America, this feared hunter was active during the final three million years of the Cretaceous Period, which was approximately 65 million years ago. The time frame in which they lived makes the *T. rex* one of the last dinosaurs to roam the planet before the cataclysmic event that led to their subsequent extinction, whatever that event may have been.

2 ➡ *Tyrannosaurus rex* was an imposing creature without a doubt. The largest complete fossilized specimen to be discovered is specimen FMNH PR2081, affectionately referred to as 'Sue'. Sue was discovered by amateur paleontologist Sue Hendrickson in the Hell Creek Formation near Faith, South Dakota. The fossil gave scientists a good idea about the probable size of *T. rex*. Sue measured approximately 42 feet long and measured about 13 feet tall at the hips. With fossils having no remaining soft tissue to weigh, it is impossible to determine Sue's accurate weight. As a result, only estimates have been made and they have varied. However, the most modern estimates range between 6 and 7.5 tons. Despite the fact that *T. rex* was obviously huge, it was still a bit smaller than *Spinosaurus* and *Giganotosaurus*, two other bi-pedal (walking on two legs) Cretaceous carnivores.

3 ➡ An important feature of *T. rex* was its neck. The neck of *T. rex* formed a natural S-shaped curve, similar to other theropods, but the neck

1. According to paragraph 1, where did the name of *T. rex* come from?

Ⓐ They were carnivorous dinosaurs.
Ⓑ They ruled other species of dinosaurs.
Ⓒ They were good at hunting prey.
Ⓓ They were distributed over a large area.

2. What can be inferred about dinosaurs from paragraph 1?

Ⓐ There are no more fossils left to study to find out the cause of their extinction.
Ⓑ The exact cause of their demise is still unclear.
Ⓒ The Cretaceous Period had an extreme climate that made them extinct.
Ⓓ The names of the dinosaurs are related to their habitat.

3. What is NOT true about *Tyrannosaurus rex* in paragraph 2 and 3?

Ⓐ From the fossilized skeleton we can estimate a rough weight.
Ⓑ Most of them have two fingers, but sometimes three.
Ⓒ At least two other similar species were greater in size than *T. rex*.
Ⓓ 'Sue' is the only complete fossilized specimen.

4. The word "imposing" in paragraph 2 is closest in meaning to

Ⓐ heroic
Ⓑ superior
Ⓒ ordinary
Ⓓ impressive

of the *T. rex* was short and muscular in order to support the weight of its massive head. The forearms of *T. rex* were long thought to have only two digits, but at least one specimen shows evidence of a third digit. In comparison, the sturdy hind legs of *T. rex* were among the longest in proportion to body size of any other theropod. The tails of all *T. rex* species were long and heavy, and could contain over forty vertebrae. The massive size of their tails was an absolute necessity since it was required to help balance their huge heads and torsos. Moreover, to help compensate for their bulk, many of the bones in a *T. rex* skeleton were hollow. These hollow bones helped reduce their weight without any real loss of strength.

4 ➡ The largest discovered *T. rex* skulls measure up to 5 feet in length. As with other theropods, their skulls have large openings known as fenestrae, which, like the hollow bones, helped reduce the predator's overall weight. In addition, the fenestrae also provided areas for muscle attachment. Other than the fenestrae, *T. rex* skulls were very different from those of other large theropods that existed at that time. [■A] The rear of the skull was extremely wide, but the front of the skull had a narrow snout, which allowed for unusually good binocular vision. [■B] However, many of the bones were pneumatized, which simply means that they contained tiny air spaces similar in appearance to a honeycomb. [■C] This honeycomb pattern may have made the bones lighter and more flexible despite their extraordinarily massive size. [■D] These and other important skull-strengthening features are how the *T. rex* developed its legendary powerful bite, which was greater than any other predator of its time. The tip of the upper jaw was U-shaped, while most other carnivores had V-shaped upper jaws. This U-shape enabled an increase in the amount of tissue and bone a *T. rex* could rip out of its prey with one bite. However, it also increased the amount of stress that was placed on the front teeth.

5. According to paragraph 3, what is true about the *T. rex*'s body?

Ⓐ Its tail was disproportionately long compared to its body.

Ⓑ Similar to other theropods, its neck was short and muscular.

Ⓒ Most of its power came from its hollow bone formation.

Ⓓ Its huge head and heavy tail kept its body in balance.

6. Why does the author mention V-shaped upper jaws in paragraph 4?

Ⓐ To point out some characteristics *T. rex* shares with other carnivores

Ⓑ To explain why most carnivores have a particular jaw shape

Ⓒ To show that U-shaped upper jaws are more effective than V-shaped ones

Ⓓ To illustrate the process of evolution of the carnivores' body parts

7. All of the following characteristics about *T. rex* are mentioned in paragraph 4 EXCEPT

Ⓐ their skulls had big holes where muscles were attached

Ⓑ the fronts of their skulls were very wide

Ⓒ their narrow snouts gave them clear vision

Ⓓ the interior of their bones looked like a honeycomb

TOEFL Reading

5 ➡ One of the most famous features of *T. rex* was their teeth, which displayed obvious heterodonty. The term heterodonty refers to differences in the shapes of the teeth. The premaxillary teeth located at the front of the upper jaw were packed closely together with D-shaped cross sections. They curved backwards with ridges on the rear surface and chisel-like blades on the tips. These dental features of the premaxillary teeth all worked to reduce the risk that the teeth would snap off when the *T. rex* bit into and pulled at its prey. The rest of the teeth in a *T. rex* skull were large and thick, more like deadly banana-shaped points than daggers.

8. Which of the sentences below best expresses the essential information in the highlighted sentence in the passage? Incorrect answer choices change the meaning in important ways or leave out essential information.

Ⓐ The characteristics of the premaxillary teeth helped to prevent *T. rex* from breaking its teeth while hunting prey.

Ⓑ The premaxillary teeth have a high chance to be broken when they are used as a hook to pull dead prey.

Ⓒ The special shape of premaxillary teeth allowed *T. rex* to quickly grow another tooth to replace a lost one.

Ⓓ *T. rex* was able to keep its premaxillary teeth longer than other species because of its unique characteristics.

TOEFL Reading

9. Look at the four squares [■] that indicate where the following sentence could be added to the passage.

   The bones of the skull were very large, and some of the smaller bones, such as the nasal bones, were fused together, making the skull more solid.

   Where would the sentence best fit?

   Click on a square [■] to add the sentence to the passage.

10. **Directions:** An introductory sentence for a brief summary of the passage is provided below. Complete the summary by selecting the THREE answer choices that express the most important ideas in the passage. Some sentences do not belong in the summary because they express ideas that are not presented in the passage or are minor ideas in the passage. ***This question is worth 2 points.***

    The *Tyrannosaurus rex* was a dinosaur species that lived during part of the Cretaceous Period.

    •
    •
    •

Answer Choices

Ⓐ From the fossilized specimen called Sue, the average weight of the *T. rex* is estimated at between 6 to 7.5 tons.

Ⓑ Most of the *T. rex* were thought to have two fingers with a small rate of mutation cases of three fingers.

Ⓒ The large openings on their skulls and other hollow bones helped reduce the overall weight.

Ⓓ The only characteristic that *T. rex* shared with other theropods was the large holes on the skull called fenestrae.

Ⓔ Much of the data about the size of the species came from the most complete example ever discovered called Sue.

Ⓕ The different shapes of its teeth allowed *T. rex* to bite and pull its prey with less chance of them breaking off.

Drag your answer choices to the spaces where they belong.
To remove an answer choice, click on it. To review the passage, click on **View Text**.

TOEFL Reading

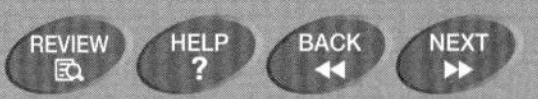

Live Performance

1 ➡ When actors that have achieved success both on stage and on screen are asked which medium they prefer to work in, they overwhelmingly choose the former. Despite the fact that film contracts often come with a much higher paycheck attached, they find acting in plays to be more rewarding. The reason for this is that the theater is a live event, where the performers and the audience occupy the same time and space and can interact with each other. The distinction between live and recorded performance is extremely important, as the theater provides three things that films cannot. The performers have an active relationship with the audience, the members of the audience become a single entity, and every performance is unique.

2 ➡ Live performances appeal to actors because as they perform a play they develop a kind of rapport with the audience. They are occupying the same space at the same time, breathing the same air, and involved in the world of the play's narrative. On a film set, the only people who can watch the performance are the crew, who are supposed to distance themselves from the action in order to record it, and the director, who provides instruction and criticism between takes. With a live performance, the audience is just as involved as the actors, and their reactions to the events they witness can affect the actors. Of course, their intentional communication through applause, cheering, and silence has an effect on the actors. But their unconscious reactions, barely stifled laughter at an intentionally comedic moment, a collective gasp of surprise at a shocking twist, or murmuring of dread in a suspenseful scene, can influence an actor, triggering her to give an unparalleled performance.

3 ➡ While they are watching a play, the audience also enters into a kind of collective

11. Which of the following questions is answered by paragraph 1?

Ⓐ What standard is used to determine an actor's success on stage and screen?

Ⓑ What are features characteristic of recorded performances?

Ⓒ What contributes to actors being paid better for film contracts than other media?

Ⓓ What are the reasons behind actors finding acting in plays rewarding?

12. According to paragraph 2, which of the following is true about live performances?

Ⓐ Live performances are reciprocal communication between actors and their audience.

Ⓑ Unconscious reactions of an audience are more powerful than intentional communication.

Ⓒ For successful live performances, the actors must respond to the audience's reactions.

Ⓓ Actors prefer live performances because they can perform without interference from directors.

13. Which of the following can be inferred about film production from paragraph 2?

Ⓐ Unlike plays, acting in a detached space is a technique that is effective on film sets.

Ⓑ During the shooting of the film, the movie director is the only person allowed to provide feedback to actors.

Ⓒ Actors performing in films keep their distance from identifying with the film narrative and their roles.

Ⓓ It is harder for actors performing for films to become motivated to outdo their previous work.

consciousness that responds to the cues the actors give. They enter the theater as individuals with their own personalities and preconceived notions, but they rapidly transform into a single entity as they share the experience. They empathize with the characters, laugh at the same jokes, and are awed by the same revelations. This all occurs despite the fact that, apart from the few friends they may have arrived with, they are in a room full of complete strangers. [■A] This kind of response cannot be found in a cinema, where the viewers remain individuals who are focused solely on the characters on the screen. [■B] The environment keeps them largely isolated with its pitch darkness and booming sound system, and they rarely react collectively. [■C] Television programs also fail to engage their audience so completely due to the frequent interruptions caused by commercial breaks. [■D] The audience members can mingle during intermissions and chat about the previous acts, and they can also communicate during the play as their laughter and applause become contagious, increasing in intensity as they recognize that others share their impressions about the play. When an audience is particularly impressed, they often stand to applaud enthusiastically. Called a standing ovation, the audience members are not only congratulating the performers, but also themselves and each other for appreciating the excellence of the performance they have shared. One play that elicited an extreme example of this group mentality was 1935's *Waiting for Lefty*. This play had an explicitly political message, and it was staged in such a way that the audience played the role of a group of union members. The audience was so moved by the play that they were shouting in unison, showing their support for the false political rally.

4 ➡ The final aspect of live performances that appeals so strongly to actors is that every performance is unique from the others. Even though the performers should adhere to the script of the play as much as possible, there are subtle differences between each performance

14. According to paragraph 3, how is theatrical performance different from other media?

Ⓐ The performance is given in a very dim environment.

Ⓑ Most of the audience barely knows each other.

Ⓒ The performance is interrupted by breaks.

Ⓓ The audience may give a standing ovation at the end of the performance.

15. Why does the author mention *Waiting for Lefty* in paragraph 3?

Ⓐ To provide an example of how plays can unite the audience into a single entity

Ⓑ To point out the dangers of incorporating political themes in performing arts

Ⓒ To show that a standing ovation is not the only way an audience can show its appreciation for a performance

Ⓓ To provide background knowledge of the social atmosphere of the 1930s

16. Which of the following best expresses the essential information in the highlighted sentence? Incorrect answer choices change the meaning in important ways or leave out essential information.

Ⓐ While actors do their best at keeping each performance consistent, both experts and the audience can tell the difference between each performance.

Ⓑ While the differences between each performance are usually minor enough that only experts can detect them, everyone knows that each performance is unique.

that only an expert would be capable of perceiving, although on some level everyone involved, including the cast and the audience, is aware of this fact. Unlike a movie that remains unchanged unless it is edited into a new version, every time a play is performed it is happening in the present, and that means that anything can happen. This knowledge gives the theater an air of vitality because a mistake could be made, accidents could happen, conflict could arise, and there may even be a hint of stage fright. On the other hand, instances of sheer brilliance may occur as the actors endeavor to make each performance surpass those that came before. This brings about the ultimate thrill of live performances, that they possess the same uncertainty as real life. The actors and the audience live the story as it unfolds, and while they have a notion of where it may be heading, it is no more predictable than the future is in reality. One of the essential purposes of drama is to depict the uncertainty of the human condition, and live performances portray that uncertainty in the most immediate way possible.

Ⓒ It is a given that professional actors should keep discrepancies between each performance to a minimum so they are obvious only to experts, but the audience can perceive them sometimes.

Ⓓ While actors try to keep their performance consistent across all performances, the performers and the audience realize that experts can notice variations between each performance.

17. The word "vitality" in paragraph 4 is closest in meaning to

Ⓐ fatality

Ⓑ tension

Ⓒ energy

Ⓓ intensity

18. According to paragraph 4, how are live performances similar to real life?

Ⓐ Actors know what the ultimate goal of the play is.

Ⓑ Actors are creating the play in the present as they are performing it.

Ⓒ Actors perform on stage according to the script of the play.

Ⓓ Actors ceaselessly attempt to outdo their previous performances.

TOEFL Reading 

19. Look at the four squares [■] that indicate where the following sentence could be added to the passage.

Conversely, the theater creates an environment that is very conducive to socializing.

Where would the sentence best fit?

Click on a square [■] to add the sentence to the passage.

20. **Directions:** An introductory sentence for a brief summary of the passage is provided below. Complete the summary by selecting the THREE answer choices that express the most important ideas in the passage. Some sentences do not belong in the summary because they express ideas that are not presented in the passage or are minor ideas in the passage.
This question is worth 2 points.

Live performances hold an attraction that cannot be compared to other media.

-
-
-

Answer Choices

Ⓐ Plays possess a certain tension because mistakes committed live before an audience cannot be withdrawn.

Ⓑ *Waiting for Lefty* demonstrated the power of plays in evoking a violent political response from the viewers.

Ⓒ The audience members find themselves immersed in the play together as one body sharing a common experience.

Ⓓ Live performances are never truly the same each time and they embody the uncertainties of life.

Ⓔ Unlike commercial breaks between TV dramas, intermissions during plays allow those present to socialize with others.

Ⓕ Actors enjoy performing live because they become inspired by the reactions of the audience.

Drag your answer choices to the spaces where they belong.
To remove an answer choice, click on it. To review the passage, click on **View Text**.

PAGODA TOEFL

80+ Reading

3rd Edition

파고다교육그룹 언어교육연구소 | 저

해설서

PAGODA Books

PAGODA TOEFL

80+ Reading

3rd Edition

파고다교육그룹 언어교육연구소 | 저

해설서

PAGODA Books

Diagnostic Test

1. C	2. D	3. A	4. B	5. A	6. B	7. D	8. A	9. D	10. C, D, F
11. D	12. D	13. B	14. B	15. A	16. D	17. B	18. C	19. B	20. B, D, F

본서 | P. 23

아우구스투스 시대의 번영

1 ➡ 로마의 초대 황제였던 옥타비아누스의 통치 기간은 폭넓은 경제 발전과 사회적 변화의 시기였다. 율리우스 카이사르의 독재 후에, 로마는 정치적 혼란과 내전의 시기에 빠졌으나, 옥타비아누스가 그의 마지막 적수를 물리치고 국가에 대한 완전한 통치권을 움켜쥐어 아우구스투스의 칭호를 얻으면서 그러한 시기는 막을 내렸다. 백성에 대한 그의 대단한 열정과 정치적 공명함을 열망한 것으로 유명했던 아우구스투스는 자신의 통치 기간 동안 많은 행정적, 법적, 경제적, 도덕적 개혁을 했다. 이러한 개혁들로 인해 사람들과 부가 도시로 유입되었다. 농업 생산의 변화는 로마에 막대한 양의 곡물과 기타 작물들이 공급되게 만들었으며, 이로 인해 수익성 높은 로마의 시장들이 생겨났다. 로마의 인구가 늘어남에 따라, 도시의 많은 부분이 개선된 시설물과 다른 생활 편의 시설을 갖춰 재건되었다. 이러한 추세가 제국의 다른 도시들로 퍼졌고, 시골의 인구가 점차 도시로 이주하였다. 비록 모든 사람들이 동일하게 혜택을 누린 것은 아니었지만, 그는 로마를 상대적인 평화와 번영의 시대로 이끌었으며 이는 약 두 세기 동안 지속되었다.

2 ➡ 옥타비아누스가 로마에 정치 질서를 되찾아온 후, 사람들이 다시 수도로 모여들기 시작했다. 내전 기간 동안 로마는 살기에 그다지 매력적인 장소가 아니었고 많은 백성들이 시골 지역으로 피신했다. 대다수의 로마 시골 사람들은 농지를 경작하는 소지주(小地主)였지만, 평화를 되찾은 후 그들의 자녀들은 로마의 도시 생활에 매혹되었다. 이것은 도시에게는 축복이었는데, 과밀 거주, 열악한 위생, 질병, 식량 부족 등 도시 생활에서 흔히 나타나는 어려움들에 의해 야기된 높은 사망률로 인해 도시의 인구가 급속하게 감소하고 있었기 때문이었다. 옥타비아누스는 이러한 문제들을 완화하기 위해 새로운 주거 지역과 공공 건물, 그리고 도시에 신선하고 깨끗한 물을 공급해줄 새로운 송수로의 건설을 포함한 많은 공익 사업을 지원하였으나, 식량 부족에 대한 해결책은 도시 내에서 찾을 수 없었다.

3 ➡ 채워지지 않는 배고픔을 충족시키기 위해서, 로마는 제국 전역으로부터 음식을 수입해야 했다. 이는 농업 집약적 지역이 많은 로마 지방의 농업에 직접적인 영향을 주었다. 내전이 있기 이전에, 부유한 로마인들이 주변의 소농민들을 매수하면서 토지 소유 유형이 변화하기 시작했다. 그 부유한 로마인들 중 상당수는 이전의 농부들을 노동은 하지만 더 이상 토지를 소유하지 않는 소작농의 형태로 두었지만, 시간이 지나면서 노예가 점점 더 널리 쓰였다. 황제가 된 후 옥타비아누스는 자신의 군사들에게 토지를 지급하여 퇴직하게 함으로써 새로운 시스템을 지지했다. 이것은 군대의 크기를 줄이면서 외곽 지방

1. 다음 중 1단락에서 언급된 것은 무엇인가?
- Ⓐ 아우구스투스라는 칭호의 의미
- Ⓑ 옥타비아누스가 로마의 민주주의에 기여한 것
- Ⓒ 옥타비아누스 이전 로마 통치자의 이름
- Ⓓ 아우구스투스 시대의 정치적 혼란의 원인이 된 요소들

2. 2단락에 따르면, 다음 중 옥타비아누스의 통치의 결과가 아닌 것은?
- Ⓐ 정치적 안정
- Ⓑ 도시 인구의 증가
- Ⓒ 더 나아진 공공 편의 시설
- Ⓓ 시골 지역 사망률의 감소

3. 다음 중 지문에 음영 표시된 문장의 핵심 정보를 가장 잘 표현한 문장은 무엇인가? 오답은 의미를 크게 왜곡하거나 핵심 정보를 누락하고 있다.
- Ⓐ 옥타비아누스는 로마의 생활 여건을 개선하기 위해 애썼으나, 도시 내 식량 부족에 대한 해결을 이루지 못한 채 부분적인 성공만을 거두었다.
- Ⓑ 식량 부족 문제 외에, 개선된 주거 환경과 깨끗한 식수 공급 같은 문제 해결을 위한 옥타비아누스의 노력은 대중들의 호평을 받았다.
- Ⓒ 옥타비아누스는 주거 환경과 위생 개선을 위해 막대한 투자를 하였으나, 로마의 식량 부족에는 주의를 기울이지 못했다.
- Ⓓ 나아진 주거 환경과 개선된 위생 조건은 옥타비아누스의 공익 사업의 결과였지만, 식량 부족 문제는 다른 통치자에 의해 해결되었다.

4. 다음 중 3단락에서 추론 가능한 것은 무엇인가?
- Ⓐ 옥타비아누스는 은퇴한 군인들을 농장의 노예로 고용하는 것을 승인했다.
- Ⓑ 옥타비아누스가 황제가 된 후 현역에 필요한 군인의 수가 감소했다.
- Ⓒ 소작농들에게 노동의 대가로 곡물을 지급하는 것이 관행이었다.
- Ⓓ 로마 외곽 지방에서는 시장에 대한 수요가 없었다.

에 새로운 지주를 둠으로써 로마의 통제를 유지할 수 있다는 점에서 이중적 효과를 가져다 주었다. 노예들은 보수를 지급받지 않았기 때문에, 전 제국적으로 이러한 대규모 농장에 노예들을 사용하였다는 것은 농산품, 특히 곡물이 엄청나게 과잉되었다는 것을 의미했다. 이 탈리아 반도의 농장에서 생산된 곡물과 가축의 대부분은 수도로 보내졌으며, 특별히 그것들을 교역하기 위한 시장이 그곳에 세워졌다.

4 ➡ 시장 경제는 농업 지역의 도시에도 많은 이익을 가져다 주었다. 대지주의 재산이 늘어남에 따라, 그들은 자신들이 사는 지역 도심지의 지위를 향상시키고자 하였다. [■A] 그들은 수도에서 누리던 생활 편의 시설과 오락을 (지역 도심지에) 제공하기 위한 건설 사업에 자금을 댔다. [■B] 여기에는 무역을 용이하게 할 도로와 다리, 그리고 백성들에게 물을 공급할 수로와 같은 공익 사업이 포함되었다. [■C] 그들은 또한 백성들에게 문화와 지위를 가져다 줄 대중목욕탕, 경기장, 극장을 지었다. [■D] 심지어 가장 먼 곳에 위치한 지방에서도 대경기장 스타일의 게임과 경기들이 정기적으로 개최되었다. 이는 새로 추가된 백성들 사이에 제국에 대한 소속감을 북돋우며, 제국 전역에 로마의 명성을 퍼뜨렸다.

5 ➡ 하지만 모든 도시가 아우구스투스 시대에 로마의 경제적 성장으로 이익을 본 것은 아니었다. 만약 어떤 도시가 제국의 정교한 도로망과 수로망에 접근하기 쉬운 곳에 위치해 있다면, 그 도시는 새로운 번영을 함께 누릴 가능성이 있었다. 여기에는 특히 증가한 무역으로부터 엄청난 혜택을 누렸던 푸테올리와 오스티아 같은 항구 도시가 해당되었다. 푸테올리는 이집트산 곡물을 실어오는 배를 위한 주요 항구였을 뿐 아니라 캄파니아산 제조 물자를 제국에 수출하기 위한 주요 중심지였다. 오스티아는 본래 로마의 항구였지만, 해적에 의해 파괴되었었다. 이 시기에 그곳은 재건되고 광범위하게 개선되었다. 반대로 로마나 여타 성장 중에 있는 도시 중심지와 너무 멀리 떨어져 있는 다른 도시들은 종종 쇠퇴에 이르렀다. 많은 도시들이 점차적으로 사라지거나, 다른 도시에 흡수되어 그들의 교외 지역이 되어버렸다. 그러한 지역 출신 사람들은 새로운 도시 중심지로 이동하거나 수도로 향했다. 이로 인해 농가와 노예를 위한 거주지를 제외하고는 그 어떤 문명의 흔적도 찾아 볼 수 없는 커다란 지역들이 생겨났다.

5. **4단락의 단어 'stimulated(북돋았다)'와 의미상 가장 가까운 것은**

Ⓐ 장려했다
Ⓑ 모범적 역할을 했다
Ⓒ 요구했다
Ⓓ 유지했다

6. **다음 중 4단락에서 농업 지역의 변화로 언급되지 않은 것은**

Ⓐ 로마 제국에 대한 충성도 증가
Ⓑ 서로 다른 농업 지역간의 활발한 무역
Ⓒ 공공 편의 시설 개발
Ⓓ 로마에서 찾아볼 수 있는 다양한 형태의 오락 유입

7. **5단락의 단어 'elaborate(정교한)'와 의미상 가장 가까운 것은**

Ⓐ 잘 알려진
Ⓑ 새로 만들어진
Ⓒ 능동적인
Ⓓ 복잡한

8. **다음 중 5단락에서 답을 찾을 수 있는 질문은 무엇인가?**

Ⓐ 도시가 경제 발전으로부터 이익을 얻게 되었는지 아닌지를 결정한 요소는 무엇인가?
Ⓑ 아우구스투스 시대에 쇠퇴한 항구 도시의 예는 무엇인가?
Ⓒ 초기 로마 교외 지역 쇠퇴의 원인이 된 요인은 무엇인가?
Ⓓ 푸테올리시가 이 시기에 재건된 이유는 무엇인가?

9. 지문에 다음 문장이 들어갈 수 있는 위치를 나타내는 네 개의 사각형[■]을 확인하시오.

심지어 가장 먼 곳에 위치한 지방에서도 대경기장 스타일의 게임과 경기들이 정기적으로 개최되었다.

이 문장이 들어가기에 가장 적합한 곳은? [■D]

10. **지시문:** 지문을 간략하게 요약한 글의 첫 문장이 아래 제시되어 있다. 지문의 가장 중요한 내용을 표현하는 세 개의 선택지를 골라 요약문을 완성하시오. 일부 문장들은 지문에 제시되지 않았거나 지문의 지엽적인 내용을 나타내기 때문에 요약문에 포함되지 않는다. ***이 문제의 배점은 2점이다.***

내전 종료와 함께, 로마는 초대 황제였던 옥타비아누스의 통치 하에 번영하기 시작했다.

Ⓒ 시장 경제의 발전과 함께, 시골 지역 또한 수도에서 찾아볼 수 있는 편의 시설을 채택하면서 높아진 지위를 누릴 수 있었다.
Ⓓ 옥타비아누스의 노력으로 로마의 생활 요건이 상당히 향상되었고, 사람들이 수도로 돌아오기 시작했다.
Ⓕ 수도의 식량 수요가 늘어남에 따라 교역이 증가하고 시장이 형성되었다.

Ⓐ 로마와 이집트 사이의 활발한 무역 중추 역할을 했던 푸테올리와는 달리 오스티아는 해적에 의해 파괴되었다.
Ⓑ 하지만 도시 지역을 확대하고자 했던 옥타비아누스의 야심찬 노력은 교외 지역의 상대적 쇠퇴로 이어졌다.
Ⓔ 무보수 노동자로 고용됐던 노예의 수가 증가하면서 식량 공급이 그에 상응하여 감소하였다.

어휘 reign n 통치 기간 | extensive adj 폭넓은, 광범위한 | dictatorship n 독재 | defeat v 패배시키다 | seize v 장악하다, 점령하다 | institute v (제도, 정책 등을) 도입하다 | utility n (수도, 전기, 가스 같은) 공익사업 | amenities n 생활 편의 시설 | prosperity n 번영, 번성 | flock v 모이다, 떼 지어 가다/오다 | flee v 달아나다, 도망치다 | landowner n 토지 소유자, 지주 | diminish v 줄어들다, 약해지다 | sanitation n 위생 시설 | shortage n 부족 | alleviate v 완화하다 | aqueduct n 송수로, 도수관 | insatiable adj 채울 수 없는, 만족할 줄 모르는 | intensively adv 강하게, 집약적으로 | landownership n 토지 소유 | peasant farmer (보통 가난하고 지위가 낮은) 소농민 | tenant farmer 소작농(토지를 빌려서 자기의 가축, 농구, 경영자본을 사용하여 농업을 영위하는 자) | massive adj 거대한 | livestock n 가축 | peninsula n 반도 | finance v 자금을 대다 | facilitate v 용이하게 하다 | prestige n 위신, 명망 | stimulate v 자극하다, 격려하다 | a feeling of belonging 소속 의식, 일체감 | primary adj 주된, 주요한 | hub n 중심지, 중추 | manufactured adj 제작된 | pirate n 해적 | conversely adv 정반대로, 역으로 | absorb v 흡수하다 | head for ~로 향하다 | be devoid of ~이 없다 | quarter n (도시 내의) 구역, 지구

본서 | P. 27

해조의 분포를 결정하는 요소들

1 ➡ 육지에서와 같이 전 세계 대양에서 먹이 사슬의 제1차 생산자들은 광합성을 사용하는 생물체들이지만 그들이 생존할 수 있는 지역은 제한되어 있다. 제1차 생산자들은 해수면 근처에 떠다니는 단세포 생물인 식물성 플랑크톤이다. 몇몇 지역에서는 해조라 불리는 다양한 종류의 다세포 조류들이 이를 보완한다. 이런 식물들은 흔히 홍조, 갈조, 녹조라는 3개의 집단으로 나뉘며 생태계에 매우 중요하다. 초식동물들에게 직접적으로 먹이를 제공할 뿐만 아니라 그것들의 부패물은 유기 분해물에 의존하는 먹이 사슬에 중요하다. 그것들은 인간에게도 널리 쓰이는데, 음식, 약, 산업 목적으로 이용된다. 해조는 또한 해안 지역의 다른 생물들에게 안식처를 제공하며, 종종 이전에 황량했던 지역들에 먼저 정착하는 생물체들 중 하나다.

2 ➡ 해조류 종들 대부분은 저서생물들인데, 이것은 그것들이 해안선부터 시작해 바깥쪽으로 내대륙붕을 따라서 바다 밑바닥에 서식한다는 것을 뜻한다. 그것들은 바위, 진흙, 산호를 포함한 자연물 표면과 갑각류, 연체동물과 바다거북처럼 껍데기가 있는 생물에 들러붙는다. 또한 시멘트로 만든 둑, 나무로 만든 부두와 배의 선체 같은 인공 구조물 표면에도 들러붙을 수 있다. 어떤 종류들은 들러붙을 표면을 고르는 데에 매우 까다로운 반면, 다른 종류들은 충분한 시간 동안 가만히 멈춰 있는 모든 표면을 활용한다. 해조는 해저의 약 2퍼센트에 서식하며, 그것들의 분포는 여러 요소에 의해 결정된다. 여기에는 염도, 무기 영양소의 유무, 조석 간만에 따른 공기에의 노출, 파도와 해류가 포함되지만 가장 중요한 두 가지 요소는 빛에의 노출과 주변 온도다.

3 ➡ 광합성 생물로써 해조의 분포는 다른 무엇보다도 받을 수 있는 햇빛의 양에 의해 결정된다. 이로 인해 존재하는 종들은 수심, 물의 상태, 위도와 계절 같은 요소들에 좌우된다. 물이 깊어질수록 조도는 급격하게 감소하고 각각 다른 빛의 파장들은 다른 깊이까지 투과한다. 그래서 한 인기 있는 이론은 이 다양한 종류의 해조들은 그들로 하여금 서로 다른 파장들을 흡수할 수 있게 해 주는 서로 다른 색소

11. 1단락에 따르면, 다음 중 해조에 대해 사실이 아닌 것은 무엇인가?
Ⓐ 다른 생물체들의 자연 서식지가 될 수 있다.
Ⓑ 이 식물들은 초식동물들의 먹이 공급원이다.
Ⓒ 생태계에서 매우 중요한 역할을 한다.
Ⓓ 이 식물들에는 제1차 생산자들인 식물성 플랑크톤이 포함된다.

12. 2단락에 따르면, 해조의 몇몇 종류들은 몸을 고정하는 데 정지되어 있는 아무 물체나 선택하는 반면에
Ⓐ 대다수의 해조들은 해안선을 따라 깊은 대양저에 서식한다
Ⓑ 다른 해조들은 시멘트 방파제와 난파선과 같은 인공 구조물을 선호한다
Ⓒ 대다수의 해조들은 1년 넘게 가만히 있는 물체들을 찾는다
Ⓓ 다른 해조들은 어느 표면에 들러붙을지에 대해서 매우 까다롭게 군다

13. 3단락의 단어 'them(그들)'이 가리키는 것은
Ⓐ 깊이
Ⓑ 해조
Ⓒ 색소
Ⓓ 파장

14. 3단락에서 색소 적응 이론에 대해 추론 가능한 것은 무엇인가?
Ⓐ 해조의 색상은 수질에 따라서 다르다.
Ⓑ 홍조는 대양의 깊은 곳까지 투과하는 파장들을 흡수할 것이다.
Ⓒ 수압은 광합성의 주요 변수인 것으로 입증되었다.
Ⓓ 녹조는 녹색 파장들을 흡수할 수 있기 때문에 심해를 선호한다.

들을 보유하고 있으며, 이것은 그들이 어느 정도 깊이에서 발견될 가능성이 가장 많은지를 결정한다고 주장했다. 이 개념은 색소 적응이라고 불리는데, 이 이론은 홍조가 가장 깊은 곳에 서식하고, 그 다음으로 갈조, 그리고 녹조가 서식할 거라고 주장했다. 색소 적응 이론은 1900년대에 처음 제안되었고 약 100년 동안 널리 믿어졌다. 하지만 이 이론은 다양한 종류의 해조의 분포가 흡수 가능한 빛의 파장들보다는 경쟁, 섭취, 조류가 스스로의 성장 양상을 바꿀 수 있는 능력에 훨씬 더 크게 영향을 받는다는 것을 증명하는 사례들로 인해 대대적으로 외면을 받게 되었다.

4 ➡ 하지만 수심은 중요한 요소로 남아 있으며 해조의 서식은 여전히 200미터 깊이에 달하는 투광대에 제한되어 있다. 투광대의 깊이는 물의 투명도에 크게 좌우되며 침전물이 매우 많은 물에서는 몇 센티미터 밖에 미치지 못한다. 물에 떠다니는 침전물 양의 정도는 계절에 따라 다르기 때문에 몇몇 종들은 1년 중 짧은 기간 동안만 그 지역에 서식한다. 게다가 지구의 계절들은 지축의 상대적 기울기에 의해 생성되는데 이는 빛이 표면에 닿는 각도에 영향을 끼친다. 지구는 수직으로부터 23.5도 기울어져 있는데, 이로 인해 북반구는 3월과 9월 사이에 더 많은 양의 직사광선을 받는 반면 남반구는 1년 중 그 나머지 부분에 그렇게 된다. 이는 해조 성장에 뚜렷한 영향을 끼치는데, 식물들이 각각의 극에 더 가까울수록 더 그렇다. 조도에 큰 계절적 변화가 없는 열대 지방이 가장 엄청난 해조 성장을 보인다. 조도의 계절적 변화는 또한 자연적으로 수온에도 영향을 끼친다.

5 ➡ [■A] 한 지역의 주변 온도는 해조의 분포에도 엄청난 영향을 끼친다. 일년 내내 더 많은 양의 직사광선에 노출되기 때문에 열대 바다는 가장 다양한 종류의 해조 종들을 보유하고 있다. [■B] 이런 고온은 보통 해조 성장을 촉진하지만 조차가 큰 지역에서는 극단적인 온도가 해조 분포를 제한할 수 있다. 열대 지방에서 북쪽 또는 남쪽으로 이동하면 다양성이 감소하고 종들도 달라진다. [■C] 고위도에서 발견되는 해조는 더 차가운 물에 서식하며 그 중 많은 것들은 다년생이기 때문에 2년 넘게 산다. [■D] 추운 겨울에 살아남기 위해서 많은 해조류는 그들의 여름 크기의 작은 부분에 불과한 크기로 시들어 줄어든다. 이 남은 부분은 온도가 올라갈 때까지 동면하다가 성장을 재개할 수 있다. 겨울에 판빙이 존재하는 지역들에서 해안 지역은 얼음으로 씻겨져 깨끗해지지만 해조 종들은 봄이 되면 얕은 곳으로 돌아올 것이다.

15. 다음 중 지문에 음영 표시된 문장의 핵심 정보를 가장 잘 표현한 문장은 무엇인가? 오답은 의미를 크게 왜곡하거나 핵심 정보를 누락하고 있다.

Ⓐ 물의 투명도는 투광대의 깊이에 비례한다.
Ⓑ 맑은 물의 투광대는 고작 몇 미터 깊이인 것으로 측정된다.
Ⓒ 투광대의 측정은 물의 무게를 결정한다.
Ⓓ 투광대의 몇 센티미터가 물의 투명도를 보장한다.

16. 4단락에서 글쓴이가 '지축의 상대적 기울기'를 언급하는 이유는

Ⓐ 기본적인 과학 지식을 갖는 것의 중요성을 강조하기 위해
Ⓑ 해조가 일년 내내 열대 지방에 서식한다는 것을 암시하기 위해
Ⓒ 물 속 침전물 양의 정도가 왜 계절에 좌우되는지 설명하기 위해
Ⓓ 계절에 따른 조도 차이의 근본적인 원인을 보여주기 위해

17. 4단락의 단어 'prodigious(엄청난)'와 의미상 가장 가까운 것은

Ⓐ 균형 잡힌
Ⓑ 엄청난
Ⓒ 다양한
Ⓓ 건강한

18. 5단락에 따르면, 다음 중 고온이 해조에 미치는 영향에 대해 사실인 것은 무엇인가?

Ⓐ 조차가 큰 지역에 사는 해조는 고온에서 번성한다.
Ⓑ 고온은 다년생 종들의 다양성 증가를 초래한다.
Ⓒ 고온은 보통 해조 성장을 촉진한다.
Ⓓ 지중해의 온도는 해조 성장에 이상적인 것으로 여겨진다.

19. 지문에 다음 문장이 들어갈 수 있는 위치를 나타내는 네 개의 사각형 [■]을 확인하시오.

이런 고온은 보통 해조 성장을 촉진하지만 조차가 큰 지역에서는 극단적인 온도가 해조 분포를 제한할 수 있다.

이 문장이 들어가기에 가장 적합한 곳은? [■B]

20. 지시문: 지문을 간략하게 요약한 글의 첫 문장이 아래 제시되어 있다. 지문의 가장 중요한 내용을 표현하는 세 개의 선택지를 골라 요약문을 완성하시오. 일부 문장들은 지문에 제시되지 않았거나 지문의 지엽적인 내용을 나타내기 때문에 요약문에 포함되지 않는다. ***이 문제의 배점은 2점이다.***

생태계에 필수적인 다세포 조류인 해조의 분포는 다양한 요소들에 의해 결정된다.

Ⓑ 해조가 받을 수 있는 햇빛의 양은 그들의 분포에 필수적이며, 이것은 대양의 깊이와도 관련이 있다. Ⓓ 투광대의 깊이는 수질에 좌우되며, 이것은 해조의 생존율과 서식지를 결정한다. Ⓕ 수온은 해조의 성장과 확산을 촉진하기도 하며 방해하기도 한다.

Ⓐ 무기질 함량에 따라서 3가지 종류의 해조, 즉 홍조, 갈조, 녹조가 존재한다.
Ⓒ 햇빛에 충분히 노출되는 것은 모든 생물체의 성장을 촉진하는 주요 요소 중 하나인 것으로 증명되었다.
Ⓔ 다년생 해조들은 따뜻한 물에서 더 잘 생존하기 때문에 흔히 고위도에 서식한다.

어휘 single-celled 단세포의 | supplement v 보충하다 | multicellular adj 다세포의 | food chain 먹이 사슬 | detritus n 유기 분해물, 쓰레기 | barren adj 황량한, 척박한 | benthic adj 해저의, 물밑에 사는 | continental shelf 대륙붕 | crustacean n 갑각류 동물 | jetty n 둑, 방파제 | pier n 부두 | hull n (배의) 선체 | selective adj 까다로운, 선택적인 | adhere v 들러붙다, 부착되다 | salinity n 염도 | current n 해류 | ambient adj 주위의 | latitude n 위도 | wavelength n 파장 | penetrate v 침투하다, 투과하다 | pigment n 색소 | discount v 무시하다, (무가치한 것으로) 치부하다 | confine v 국한시키다 | photic adj 빛의 | sediment n 침전물 | turbidity n 탁도 | populate v 거주하다, (어떤 장소를) 차지하다 | tilt n 경사 | axis n 축 | tropics n 열대 지방 | seasonal adj 계절적인, 계절에 따라 다른 | prodigious adj 굉장한, 놀랄 만한 | variation n 변화, 차이 | profound adj 엄청난, 심오한 | promote v 촉진하다, 장려하다 | extreme n 극단, 극도 | perennial adj 다년생의 | remnant n 남은 부분, 나머지 | dormant adj 휴면기의 | scour v 문질러 닦다, 씻어 없애다 | shallows n (강·바다의) 얕은 곳

I. Identifying Details

Lesson 01 Sentence Simplification

본서 | P. 34

Practice

01 B	02 B	03 C	04 A	05 D	06 C	07 A	08 A	09 B	10 A
11 A	12 C	13 1. B 2. D		14 1. D 2. B		15 1. D 2. C		16 1. D 2. B	
17 1. B 2. C									

Test

1. C	2. B	3. D	4. B	5. A	6. C	7. D	8. B	9. B	10. C, D, F
11. A	12. C	13. C	14. C	15. A	16. C	17. B, D	18. B	19. C	20. A, D, E

Practice

본서 | P. 36

[01-06] 다음 문장 중 핵심 정보를 가장 잘 표현한 것은 무엇인가? 오답은 의미를 크게 왜곡하거나 핵심 정보를 누락하고 있다.

01 원천 가스들은 원래 상태에서는 오존을 파괴하지 않지만, 일단 성층권에 다다르게 되면 화학적으로 분해되면서 염소와 일산화염소 같이 오존을 고갈시키는 형태의 가스로 변한다.

Ⓐ 성층권에서 원천 가스들은 화학적 상태를 바꾸고 염소와 일산화염소가 된다.
Ⓑ 오존층은 원천 가스들이 성층권에 진입한 후 화학적 변화를 겪으면서 형성된 화학 물질로 인해 손상을 입는다.

어휘 source n 원천, 근원 | degrade v (화학적으로) 분해하다/되다 | deplete v 대폭 감소시키다 | chlorine n 염소 | monoxide n 일산화물

02 주로 성층권의 낮은 부분에서 찾을 수 있는 오존층의 현저한 감소는 남극에서 처음으로 나타났는데, 이는 그곳의 대기 상태가 오존을 파괴하는 염소와 브롬이 포함된 할로겐 가스의 반응 효과를 증가시켰기 때문이다.

Ⓐ 남극은 최초로 오존이 고갈된 것으로 확인된 지역인데, 이는 공기가 염소와 브롬 같은 해로운 원소를 포함하고 있기 때문이다.
Ⓑ 남극 상공의 오존 감소는 오존을 해치는 가스의 영향을 강화하는 대기 조건 때문에 발생한다.

어휘 significant adj 상당한 | stratosphere n 성층권 | Antarctica n 남극 대륙 | reactive adj 반응하는 | halogen gas 할로겐 가스 | chlorine n 염소 | bromine n 브롬

---

03 일억 일천만 년 전 북아프리카의 사하라 사막에는 무성한 산림과 넓은 강이 있었지만, 이후 그곳에서 발달한 지극히 건조한 기후는 화석 보존에 이상적이다.

Ⓐ 사하라 사막은 아주 건조했기 때문에 수많은 화석들이 있지만, 현재 그곳은 산림과 강이 있는 지역이다.
Ⓑ 사하라 사막은 현재는 메말라버린 많은 산림과 강을 한때 갖고 있었으며, 많은 화석도 보유하고 있다.
Ⓒ 사하라 사막은 오래전 산림과 강이 있는 지역이었으나, 현재는 매우 건조하고 그로 인해 많은 화석이 보존되었다.

어휘 conditions n 날씨, 환경 | preservation n 보존, 보호, 유지 | fossil n 화석

---

04 반복성 긴장 장애는 팔과 등덜미에 영향을 미치며, 나쁜 자세나 반복적인 동작으로 인해 이들 부위의 근육이 장기간 긴장했을 때 발생한다.

Ⓐ 반복성 긴장 장애는 팔과 등덜미에 발생하는데 나쁜 자세나 반복적인 동작으로 인한 근육의 긴장이 원인이다.
Ⓑ 반복성 긴장 장애는 팔과 등덜미 근육의 긴장 때문이며 나쁜 자세와 반복적인 동작을 초래한다.
Ⓒ 반복성 긴장 장애는 팔과 등덜미 근육의 긴장은 물론 나쁜 자세와 반복적인 동작을 야기한다.

어휘 repetitive adj 반복적인, 되풀이되는 | strain n 긴장, 염좌, 좌상 | posture n 자세

---

05 15세기 후반 활자 인쇄술이 독일 인쇄업자이자 출판업자인 구텐베르크에 의해 유럽에 도입된 이후, 전례 없는 수의 사람들이 글을 읽고 쓸 수 있게 되었으며 인쇄된 책을 읽음으로써 스스로를 교육했고, 그 결과 사람들이 삶의 다양한 측면에 관심을 갖게 되었다.

Ⓐ 사람들은 다양한 범위의 책들을 읽고 새로운 것들을 배울 수 있게 되었는데, 이는 과거에는 허용되지 않았던 일이었다.
Ⓑ 종이의 저렴한 가격으로 인해 더 많은 책이 만들어져서 사람들이 책을 읽고 새로운 정보를 스스로에게 가르칠 수 있게 되었다.
Ⓒ 인쇄술이 도입되기 전 사람들은 삶에 관해 배울 필요가 없었기 때문에 더 단순한 삶을 살았다.
Ⓓ 인쇄술은 사람들이 새로운 지식을 습득하고 호기심을 채우며 과거보다 더 많은 것을 알 수 있도록 해주었다.

어휘 printing n 인쇄(술) | unprecedented adj 전례 없는 | literate adj 글을 읽고 쓸 줄 아는 | aspect n 측면, 양상 | in turn 결국, 차례차례

---

06 우주의 초기 발달 과정을 설명하는 모든 이론들 중 연구자들 사이에서 가장 인기 있고, 풍부한 경원소와 우주 배경 극초단파 같은 관찰 가능한 광범위한 현상들로 뒷받침되는 이론은 빅뱅 이론이다. 이 이론은 우주의 모든 물질이 한때 하나의 거대한 독립체였고, 그것이 폭발하여 그 남은 잔해가 우리가 오늘날 보는 것들이 되었다고 주장한다.

Ⓐ 많은 과학자들은 우주가 하나의 큰 독립체로 시작해서 그것이 폭발해 작은 행성들을 생성했다고 하는 이론을 받아들인다.
Ⓑ 일부 과학자들은 우주가 하나의 독립체가 폭발하면서 시작되었으며 그 잔해가 오늘날 우리가 아는 은하계가 되었다고 주장한다.
Ⓒ 대부분의 과학자들은 빅뱅 이론을 지지하는데, 이것은 우주가 거대한 독립체의 폭발에서 나온 잔해로 구성되었다는 내용이다.
Ⓓ 오늘날 모든 과학자들이 우주가 큰 폭발로 인해 생겼다고 주장하는 빅뱅 이론을 지지한다.

어휘 universe n 우주, 은하계 | phenomenon n 현상 | element n 원소, 성분 | cosmic adj 우주의, 장대한 | microwave n 극초단파 | propose v 제안하다 | matter n 물질 | resultant adj 그 결과로 생긴 | debris n 잔해, 파편

07

아프리카 문화

말로 전해지는 문학과 글로 쓰인 문학을 통틀어 아프리카 문학의 전통은 몇 세기 전 역사로 확장된다. 아프리카 역사 전반에 걸쳐 문맹은 널리 퍼진 추세였고, 이로 인해 문화적 전통과 족보에 대한 지식을 이어나가는 데 아프리카의 구전은 항상 더 중요하게 생각되었다. 사실 20세기가 되어서야 아프리카의 많은 하위 문화들은 그들의 이야기, 역사, 신화, 그리고 민담을 글로 기록하기 시작했다.

다음 중 지문에 음영 표시된 문장의 핵심 정보를 가장 잘 표현한 문장은? 오답은 문장의 의미를 크게 왜곡하거나 핵심 정보를 누락하고 있다.

Ⓐ 많은 아프리카인들이 읽고 쓰지 못했기 때문에 그들의 전통과 가족사는 말로 전해져 왔다.
Ⓑ 아프리카의 구전은 아프리카 나라들에서는 문화적 전통과 가족사를 기록하는 데 중요하게 여겨졌다.
Ⓒ 아프리카 가족의 역사는 일반적으로 가족 구성원들과 그들의 경험에 대한 이야기로 기록되었다.
Ⓓ 아프리카의 교육 체계는 모든 학생들에게 어떻게 글을 읽고 쓰는지 교육하는 능력 면에서 의심받은 적이 없다.

어휘 literary adj 문학의, 문학적인 I oral adj 구두의, 입의 I continuation n 연속, 지속 I sub-culture n 소문화, 하위 문화

08 **도시의 발달**

인구 증가와 정부 수립은 신전 근처에서 종교적인 중심지 기능을 하는 도시들의 발달을 낳았다. 어떤 도시들은 은과 금 매장량이 충분한 곳처럼 경제적인 기회가 있는 지역에 생겨났는가 하면, 다른 도시들은 주요 무역로 상의 전략적 거점에 생겨났다. 이런 도시들이 성장해서 점점 더 방대해지고 더 많은 공간을 차지하면서, 발달하는 사회의 여러 요구를 충족시키기 위해 새로운 서비스가 생겨났다. 예를 들면, 공예가와 상인들은 성곽 내에 작은 규모의 경제를 조성했고, 이는 점차 사람들이 정기적으로 일상용품을 구매할 수 있는 안정된 시장 설립으로 이어졌다.

다음 중 지문에 음영 표시된 문장의 핵심 정보를 가장 잘 표현한 문장은? 오답은 문장의 의미를 크게 왜곡하거나 핵심 정보를 누락하고 있다.

Ⓐ 도시들은 경제적 성장과 사업 수단에 유리할 만한 곳에 생겨났다.
Ⓑ 도시들은 서로 다른 다양한 위치에서, 특히 무역량이 많은 길을 따라 확장되었다.
Ⓒ 주요 무역로를 따라 금과 은 상인들이 목적지로 삼은 곳들은 번창하는 도시로 성장해 나갔다.
Ⓓ 도시 수의 증가는 다양한 서비스가 생기게 했으며 이는 경제와 무역에서 더 큰 성장을 부추겼다.

어휘 expansion n 확장, 팽창 I temple n 신전, 사원 I spring up 갑자기 생겨나다 I replete adj 가득한 I deposit n 매장층 I strategic adj 전략상 중요한 I artisan n 장인, 공예가 I marketplace n 시장, 장터 I gradually adv 점차, 점진적으로 I on a regular basis 정기적으로

09 **청 왕조**

청 왕조에 반란과 몰락을 가져다 준 요소들은 19세기 말부터 명백히 드러났다. 건륭제의 통치는 청 왕조의 황제들 중 가장 훌륭했던 것으로 여겨지지만, 황제가 가장 아꼈던 화신이라는 이름의 호위 무사가 황제의 호의와 믿음을 악용해 막대한 개인 재산을 축적하면서 부정부패가 마지막 10년을 훼손했다. 그러나 이것이 청 왕조 몰락의 유일한 이유라고 보기는 어렵다. 건륭제의 계승자들은 잘못된 것들을 바로잡기 위해 여러 가지 주목할 만한 시도를 했다. 건륭제의 바로 뒤를 이은 가경제는 부정부패를 근절하고 정부의 위상을 바로 잡기 위해 인정받을 만한 노력을 한 주역이다. 한동안 그의 노력은 매우 성공적이어서 그의 업적들이 청 왕조가 이미 명을 다했다는 생각에 의구심을 제기했다. 그러나 그가 죽고 난 후 중앙 권력은 상대적으로 힘이 없고 불안정했으며 많은 시민 소요가 시작되었고 점차 증가해갔다.

다음 중 지문에 음영 표시된 문장의 핵심 정보를 가장 잘 표현한 문장은? 오답은 문장의 의미를 크게 왜곡하거나 핵심 정보를 누락하고 있다.

Ⓐ 건륭제의 통치는 청 왕조에서 가장 위대했던 것으로 여겨지지만 기간 말에는 부패했다는 평가를 들었다.
Ⓑ 화신은 막대한 개인 재산을 모으는데 황제의 신뢰를 이용했고, 그런 일이 없었더라면 거의 나무랄 데가 없던 황제의 통치를 훼손했다.
Ⓒ 건륭제는 사람을 제대로 판단하지 못해 이용당하고 말았으며 이는 왕조의 몰락으로 이어졌다.
Ⓓ 가장 위대했던 청의 군주 건륭제는 그가 가장 아끼던 호위무사가 막대한 개인 재산을 쌓는 데 이용당했다.

어휘 rebellion n 반란, 모반 I evident adj 분명한, 확실한 I reign n 통치, 통치 기간 I mar v 손상시키다 I abuse v 남용하다, 오용하다 I amass v 모으다, 축적하다 I sole adj 유일한, 혼자의 I fall n 몰락 I successor n 계승자 I commendable adj 칭찬 받을 만한 I cast doubt on ~을 의심하다 I wrong n 잘못된 것 I stamp out ~을 근절하다 I doom v 불행한 운명(결말)을 맞게 하다

10 **일본**

8세기에 일본 당국은 농부들에게서 곡물 수확량의 3~4퍼센트에 상응하는 토지세를 거뒀다. 그 자체로는 그다지 큰 부담이 아니었지만 경작자들은 그밖에도 정부에 바쳐야 할 다른 의무와 봉사가 있었다. 의무의 일환으로 그들은 한 가계당 한 명의 남자를 자비로 장비를 갖추어 징집병으로 군대에 제공하고, 매년 60일 동안 공공사업에 노동력을 제공할 것을 요구받았다. 어려움이 닥쳤을 때 그들은 당국으로부터 볍씨를 받을 수 있었지만 수확기에 30에서 50퍼센트의 이자를 더해 정부에 갚아야 했다. 실제로 가장 가난한 자들, 특히 수도에서 인접한 지역에 살면서 엄격한 공무의 감독하에 있었던 사람들은 어려운 시기에는 자신의 소작지를 포기하고 먼 지역의 농부 또는 수도의 고용 노동자로 대안적인 생계 수단을 찾고자 하는 유혹을 느꼈다.

다음 중 지문에 음영 표시된 문장의 핵심 정보를 가장 잘 표현한 문장은? 오답은 문장의 의미를 크게 왜곡하거나 핵심 정보를 누락하고 있다.

Ⓐ 가장 어려운 상황을 겪고 있던 사람들은 집을 포기하고 다른 시골 지역이나 도시에서 더 나은 삶을 찾고자 했다.

Ⓑ 가장 가난한 사람들은 주로 나라에서 공급하는 일, 이를 테면 고용 노동자로 도시 안이나 고립된 시골 지역에서 일을 함으로써 어려운 시기를 견뎠다.

Ⓒ 편하게 살던 사람들은 경제적 어려움과 조우했을 때 때때로 수도에서의 도시 생활을 포기하고 더 많은 돈을 벌 수 있는 기회를 찾아 시골로 떠났다.

Ⓓ 정부 관리들은 사람들이 더 나은 생계를 위해 터전을 떠나 수도 주변에서 고용 노동자로 일하거나 시골에서 농부로 살도록 부추겼다.

어휘 authority n 지휘권, 권한, 권위자 | equivalent adj 동등한 | yield n 수확량 | owe v 빚을 지다 | at one's own expense 사비로 | eligible adj ~을 할 수 있는 | province n (행정 단위) 주, 지방 | tempt v 유혹하다, 유도하다 | conscript v 징집하다 n 징집병

11 **잉카의 제물**

잉카의 성직자들이 아르헨티나의 눈 덮인 산 정상에서 세 명의 어린 아이들을 제물로 바친 지 5세기가 흐른 뒤, 고고학자들은 그들이 거의 완벽한 상태로 얼어 있는 것을 발견했다. 제물이 된 소년의 사체의 약 2피트 위쪽에서 세 개의 작은 라마 조각상이 발견되었다. 잉카인들이 라마 무리의 다산을 보장받고자 하는 의미에서 제물과 함께 라마 조각상을 바쳤으리라고 추측된다. 세 개의 라마 조각상 앞에는 두 개의 남자 조각상이 있었는데, 하나는 금으로, 다른 하나는 국화조개 껍데기로 만들어져 마치 동물들을 이끄는 것을 시사하는 것 같았다. 이 두 개의 남성 조각상은 둘 중 하나를 나타내기 위해서였을 것이다. 자연에서 라마의 주인이라고 믿는 신들, 아마도 산신을 나타내거나, 또는 신에게 바치는 왕족의 동물 무리 관리를 맡은 잉카의 귀족들을 나타내기 위한 것이었을 것이다.

다음 중 지문에 음영 표시된 문장의 핵심 정보를 가장 잘 표현한 문장은? 오답은 문장의 의미를 크게 왜곡하거나 핵심 정보를 누락하고 있다.

Ⓐ 두 개의 작은 조각상은 자연에서 라마의 주인이었던 산신들이나 신들에게 바치는 제물이 될 왕실 동물을 돌보던 잉카의 통치 계급을 상징하는 것으로 생각된다.

Ⓑ 두 조각상은 아마 산을 관장했던 신이나 신에게 속해 있는 라마 무리를 지켰던 잉카 귀족을 보여주는 듯하다.

Ⓒ 조각상 중 하나는 자연에서 라마의 주인이고, 다른 하나는 신에게 바치는 제물이 될 국왕 소유의 라마 무리를 감독하는 잉카의 관리였던 것으로 생각된다.

Ⓓ 작은 남성 조각상들은 보통 자연에서 라마의 주인으로 생각되는 신, 즉 산신이나 혹은 신에게 바치는 제물을 선택했던 잉카의 왕족을 상징한다.

어휘 priest n 성직자, 사제 | miniature n 축소 모형, 미니어처 | figurine n 작은 조각상 | fertility n 생식력, 비옥함 | herd n (짐승) 떼 | deity n 신, 하느님 | oversee v 감독하다 | dedicated adj 전념하는, 헌신적인

12 **화산의 종류**

사람들은 화산의 생김새에 관해 정형화된 생각을 가지고 있지만 지질학자들은 일반적으로 화산을 네 가지 주요 형태인 분석구, 복식화산, 방패화산, 용암돔으로 분류한다. 가장 인상적인 산 중 일부는 복식화산들인데, 이들은 때때로 성층화산이라고도 불린다. 이들 화산은 일반적으로 주기적인 용암의 흐름과 화산재 및 분석으로 형성된 가파른 경사와 거대한 대칭 원뿔이 특징이다. 그들은 기저 위로 8천 피트 높이만큼 솟을 수 있다. 이런 형태의 화산 중 유명한 예시로 에콰도르의 코토팍시산, 캘리포니아주의 샤스타산, 워싱턴주의 세인트헬렌스산, 일본의 후지산, 오리건주의 후드산이 있다. 대부분의 복식화산들은 정상에 분화구가 있는데, 분화구에는 하나의 중심 열수구나 열수구 군집이 있을 수 있다. 분화구 벽의 틈이나 원뿔의 경사면에 난 틈에서 용암이 흘러나오면서 용암은 그 원뿔을 더 견고하게 만들어주는 거대 늑골의 역할을 하는 암맥과 융기를 형성한다. 화산이 복식화산이라고 간주되기 위한 필수 특징은 구성 물질이 번갈아 층을 이룸으로써 마그마를 지각 내부 깊은 곳으로부터 솟아오르게 하여 갈라진 금과 균열이 생긴 틈을 통해 쏟아져 나오게 하는 관로 체계를 형성하는 것이다.

다음 중 지문에 음영 표시된 문장의 핵심 정보를 가장 잘 표현한 문장은? 오답은 문장의 의미를 크게 왜곡하거나 핵심 정보를 누락하고 있다.

Ⓐ 복식화산의 층 균일성은 마그마를 깊은 곳으로부터 솟아오르게 하는 관로 체계를 형성하게 해준다.

Ⓑ 마그마를 깊은 곳으로부터 솟아오를 수 있게 해주는 관로 체계는 이런 화산 형태에 그 이름을 부여해 준다.

Ⓒ 이런 형태의 화산은 지구 내 깊은 곳으로부터 마그마를 운반하는 여러 다른 물질 층으로 특징지어진다.

Ⓓ 복식화산은 본질적으로 점성이 있는 마그마의 운반을 위한 관로 체계이다.

어휘 stereotypical adj 정형화된, 진부한 | cinder n 분석, 재, 잉걸불 | cinder cone 분석구 | composite adj 합성의 | composite volcano 복식화산 | stratovolcano n 성층화산 | symmetrical adj 대칭적인 | vent n 통풍구, 환기구 | ridge n 산등성이, 산마루 | conduit system 관로 체계, 관로식 | cluster n 무리, 송이 | spill out 넘쳐흐르다, 쏟아져 나오다 | fissure n 길게 갈라진 틈

13 지구 온난화

지구 온난화는 최근 수십 년에 걸쳐 일어났고 계속 일어날 것이라고 예측되는 지표면 근처의 대기와 대양의 평균 온도 상승을 말한다. 지표면 근처의 평균 대기 온도는 지난 세기에 0.74 ± 0.18 ℃ 상승했다. [1] 기후 변화에 관한 정부간 패널(IPCC)은 "20세기 중반 이래 관측된 세계 평균 기온 상승의 대부분은 인간이 발생시킨 온실 가스의 농도 증가 때문일 가능성이 높다"고 결론을 내렸다. 태양의 변화 같은 자연 현상이 화산과 함께 산업화 이전 시대부터 1950년까지 미미한 온난화 효과를 가져왔을지 모르지만, 1950년부터는 소소한 냉각 효과를 가져오고 있다. 이런 기초적 결론은 최소 30여 개의 과학 협회와 과학원으로부터 지지를 받았다. [2] 흥미롭게도 연구 결과에 대한 세계 일류 과학자들의 지지뿐만 아니라 지구 온난화 동향을 뒷받침하는 풍부한 수집 증거에도 불구하고 여전히 이 현상에 관한 견해를 일축하는 사람들이 있다. 그러나 이런 반대자들은 지구 온난화를 줄이기 위한 조치를 취하는 경우 돈을 잃게 되는 특정 이익 집단에 속한 경우가 많다.

1. **다음 중 지문에 음영 표시된 문장의 핵심 정보를 가장 잘 표현한 문장은? 오답은 문장의 의미를 크게 왜곡하거나 핵심 정보를 누락하고 있다.**

   Ⓐ 한 기후 변화 단체는 20세기 후반에 산업으로부터 배출된 온실 가스가 전 세계 온도 상승을 야기했다고 믿는다.
   Ⓑ 한 단체에 따르면, 인간 활동으로 인해 늘어나는 온실 가스 배출량 때문에 20세기 중반부터 전 세계 온도가 상승하고 있다.
   Ⓒ 한 단체가 실시한 연구는 지구 온난화가 많은 공장과 기계가 생산되어 사람을 대체하게 된 산업 혁명 때부터 시작되었다고 시사한다.
   Ⓓ 한 단체는 20세기 중반의 폭발적 인구 증가 전까지 평균 세계 온도 상승이 일어나지 않았다는 확실한 증거를 제공했다.

2. **다음 중 지문에 음영 표시된 문장의 핵심 정보를 가장 잘 표현한 문장은? 오답은 문장의 의미를 크게 왜곡하거나 핵심 정보를 누락하고 있다.**

   Ⓐ 세계적으로 저명한 과학자들에 의해 제공된 증거 때문에 지구 온난화를 의심하는 사람들이 있다.
   Ⓑ 세계적인 과학자들은 지구 온난화라고 불리는 현상이 존재한다는 것을 증명할 증거를 이미 충분히 수집했다.
   Ⓒ 사람들은 심지어 세계적으로 유명한 과학자조차 믿지 않는데 그 이유는 그들이 자신들의 이론에 관한 충분한 증거를 제공하지 못했기 때문이다.
   Ⓓ 몇몇 사람들은 많은 뒷받침 증거와 의견들에도 불구하고 지구 온난화에 관해 여전히 의심을 품고 있다.

어휘 intergovernmental adj 정부간의 I anthropogenic adj 인위적인 I endorse v 지지하다 I trend n 동향, 추세 I ample adj 충분한 I dismiss v 묵살하다, 떨쳐 버리다 I naysayer n 반대론자 I curtail v 축소하다, 삭감하다

---

14 머리 부상

사람들은 때때로 오토바이를 타는 사람들을 위한 헬멧 관련법과 자전거, 인라인 스케이트, 그리고 다른 많은 여가 활동에 헬멧을 필수 장비로 명시한 규정에 대해 불평한다. [1] 헬멧이 불편할 수는 있어도 헬멧의 사용이 장려되는 확실한 이유가 있는데, 아무도 사고가 언제 일어날지 모르고 오토바이와 자전거를 타는 중에 혹은 여가 활동 중에 일어나는 많은 부상이 머리 부상이라는 점 때문이다. 심각한 머리 부상은 뇌 혈관을 손상시켜 두개강에 출혈을 일으킬 수 있다. 혈액이 경뇌막(보호막)과 두개골(머리뼈) 사이에 스며들면 '경막외 출혈'이라는 질환이 생긴다. 혈류가 아래쪽인 경뇌막과 경막하강으로 흘러들면 '경막하 출혈'이라고 한다. [2] 이런 질환의 증상들은 손상된 혈관이 동맥이냐 정맥이냐에 따라 달라지는데, 이유는 동맥의 혈압이 정맥의 혈압보다 높아서 동맥 손상이 정맥 손상보다 더 급격하고 심각한 신경 조직의 뒤틀림을 유발할 수 있기 때문이다. 머리 부상의 특성은 항상 바로 규명할 수 있는 것이 아니기 때문에 빠른 의료 조치를 받는 것이 중요하다.

1. **다음 중 지문에 음영 표시된 문장의 핵심 정보를 가장 잘 표현한 문장은? 오답은 문장의 의미를 크게 왜곡하거나 핵심 정보를 누락하고 있다.**

   Ⓐ 헬멧을 쓰는 것은 이륜차를 타는 모든 사람들에게 의무사항이어야 하는데 이는 많은 이륜차 운전자가 이륜차를 타다가 머리에 부상을 입기 때문이다.
   Ⓑ 이륜차를 타다 넘어지면 주로 머리에 가장 큰 부상을 입기 때문에 잘 만들어진 헬멧이 필수적이다.
   Ⓒ 이륜차 운전자들이 이륜차를 탈 때 안전하게 느끼고 즐거운 시간을 가질 수 있도록 편안한 헬멧을 만드는 것이 시급하다.
   Ⓓ 자전거 타기와 같은 적극적인 레크리에이션 활동을 할 때는 사고가 날 경우 머리 부상으로 이어질 가능성이 높기 때문에 헬멧을 착용해야 한다.

2. **다음 중 지문에 음영 표시된 문장의 핵심 정보를 가장 잘 표현한 문장은? 오답은 문장의 의미를 크게 왜곡하거나 핵심 정보를 누락하고 있다.**

   Ⓐ 동맥 손상은 손상된 부위가 심장에 가까운지 여부에 따라 여러 증상을 일으킨다.
   Ⓑ 손상된 혈관이 동맥인 경우 동맥의 혈압이 정맥의 혈압보다 높기 때문에 더 심각한 증상이 발생할 수도 있다.
   Ⓒ 동맥 손상은 뇌의 신경 조직에 직접적으로 영향을 미치기 때문에 보통 치명적인 증상으로 이어진다.

Ⓓ 신경 질환에서 동맥은 정맥보다 더 중요한데, 그 이유는 동맥의 혈압이 정맥의 혈압보다 높기 때문이다.

어휘 specify **v** 명시하다 | gear **n** 기어, 장비 | a host of 다수의 | cerebral **adj** 뇌의 | cranial cavity 두개강 | dura mater 경뇌막 | cranium **n** 두개골 | epidural hemorrhage 경막외 출혈 | subdural hemorrhage 경막하 출혈 | vein **n** 정맥 | artery **n** 동맥 | distortion **n** 뒤틀림, 염좌

15

미국 원주민의 주거지

1 ➡ 미국 남서부에 거주했던 모든 미국 원주민 부족 가운데 아파치족, 나바호족, 푸에블로족이 가장 유명한 세 부족이다. 이 세 부족은 공통적인 특징을 갖고 있는데 예를 들면 사막에서 살아남는 기술 및 바구니와 도자기 제작 기술, 사냥을 통해 얻은 고기와 함께 옥수수, 콩, 호박을 먹는 일상 식습관이 있다. 이 부족들이 공유하는 또 다른 공통적 특징은 뜨겁고 건조한 기후 속에서 살아가기 적합한 주거지를 만들 수 있었다는 것이다.

2 ➡ 아파치족은 호전적인 유목민이었으며 미국과 멕시코의 방대한 지역에 걸쳐 거주했다. 그들은 본래 수렵 채집인들이었지만 농사도 조금씩 지었다. 주거지의 주요 형태는 위키업이라고 불렸다. [1] 이 거처는 부족의 여자들이 지었으며 건조한 환경과 부족의 지속적인 이주에 아주 적합했다. 위키업은 사막에서 흔히 볼 수 있는 잎 형태인 수풀로 간단한 나무 골조를 덮어 지었다. 쉽게 구할 수 있는 재료로 만들기 때문에 부족들이 새로운 야영지를 세울 때면 위키업은 버려지고 새로 지어졌다.

3 ➡ 아파치족의 가까운 친척인 나바호족 역시 원래 유목민이었다. 무거운 짐을 운반하는 데 쓰이는 삼각형 모양의 틀인 트러브아에 물건을 싣고, 개를 이용해 이 운반 용구를 끌면서 들소들을 따라다녔다. 결국 나바호족은 푸에블로족의 선례를 따라 농경 민족이 되기 위해 정착했다. 그들은 유목민으로서 간단한 조립식 텐트에 살았지만 농경 민족이 된 후에는 호간을 지었다. [2] 여러 면으로 이뤄졌으며 나무 골조에 수풀을 덮었고 사막에서 쉽게 구할 수 있는 재료로 지어진 이러한 주거지는 본래 제의적인 목적으로 지어졌으나 나바호족이 점차 정착 생활을 하면서 주거용 집으로 사용되었다.

4 ➡ 아마도 이들 중 가장 유명한 부족은 주니족과 호피족을 포함한 작은 부족 집단을 일컫는 푸에블로족일 것이다. 푸에블로족은 나바호족, 아파치족과 같은 다른 부족들과 수확한 것을 교역했던 남서쪽의 정착된 농경 민족들이었다. 푸에블로족은 농사에 주력하는 사람들이었기 때문에 영구적인 주거지가 필요했다. 푸에블로족은 진흙으로 만든 벽돌을 사용해 남서쪽 지방에서 흔히 볼 수 있는 꼭대기가 평평하고 주위가 가파른 언덕인 메사 위와 협곡 옆에 집을 지었다. 푸에블로족의 건축물이 아직 남아 있는 것은 견고하다는 증거이다.

1. 다음 중 2단락에 음영 표시된 문장의 핵심 정보를 가장 잘 표현한 문장은? 오답은 문장의 의미를 크게 왜곡하거나 핵심 정보를 누락하고 있다.

Ⓐ 오직 여성들만 이러한 주거지들을 짓도록 허락되었는데, 사막 기후 환경에서는 건설하기가 힘들었다.
Ⓑ 사막 환경과 부족의 끊임없는 이동 때문에 여성들은 뒤에 남아 주거지를 지을 필요가 있었다.
Ⓒ 부족의 여성들은 사막에서 재료를 모아 주거지를 건설하기 위해 넓은 지역을 돌아다녔다.
Ⓓ 여성 부족원들이 지은 이러한 주거지들은 건조한 사막 환경과 부족의 잦은 이동에 적합했다.

2. 다음 중 3단락에 음영 표시된 문장의 핵심 정보를 가장 잘 표현한 문장은? 오답은 문장의 의미를 크게 왜곡하거나 핵심 정보를 누락하고 있다.

Ⓐ 부족들은 정착해서 사막의 수풀과 나무로 만들어진 여러 면으로 된 집을 짓기 전까지는 어떤 종류의 의식도 행하지 않았다.
Ⓑ 부족들은 정착해서 수풀이나 나무 같은 자연적 재료들을 사용해 의식을 행할 수 있는 주거지를 지었다.
Ⓒ 주거지는 부족들이 정착한 후에는 집으로 사용되었지만, 이 나무와 수풀로 만들어진 여러 면으로 된 구조물은 처음에는 주로 의식을 행하는 데 쓰였다.
Ⓓ 의식은 부족들이 여러 면으로 된 구조물을 지을 수 있을 만큼의 나무와 수풀 같은 재료가 즉시 공급될 수 있게 준비되지 않는 한 행해지지 않았다.

어휘 people **v** ~에 살다, 거주하다 | pottery **n** 도자기 | squash **n** 호박 | supplement **v** 보충하다 | expedition **n** 탐험, 원정 | fierce **adj** 사나운, 험악한 | nomadic **adj** 유목의, 방랑의 | range over 돌아다니다, ~까지 미치다 | undertake **v** 착수하다 | travois **n** (북미 평원 지방 인디언의) 두 개의 장대를 줄에 매어 개나 말이 끌게 하는 운반 용구 | foliage **n** 나뭇잎 | sedentary **adj** 한 곳에 머물러 사는 | testament **n** 증거

16

대량 생산

1 ➡ 공업화의 발전은 1790년 이후 미국에서 빠르게 진행되었다. 이 시기에 사업주와 기업가들은 직업을 다양화하고 더 많은 공장을 세우면서 생산량 증대를 목표로 일했다. [1] 제조 방식의 혁신 결과, 의도했던 대로 생산량이 증대되었고, 일반인들은 생활 수준이 현저하게 높아지는 것을 실제로 느꼈다. 실제로 평균 노동자의 수입은 한 세대에 걸쳐 대략 30퍼센트 증가했고, 한때 사치품으로 여겨졌던 물건이 중산층 가정에서조차 일상용품으로 여겨지게 되었다.

2 ➡ 새로운 제조 방식은 상품 생산성 향상의 주된 요인이었다. 1760년대를 시작으로, 북미의 사업주들은 전체 생산 과정의 한 단계만 담당하는 개인이나 소규모 노동자에게 일을 분배함으로써 생산의 효율성을 높이는 분업 체계의 무한한 가능성을 열었다. 예를 들어 1820년대와 1830년대의 제화 산업은 분업 체계의 규모와 범위를 넓혔다. 시골의 노동자들은 '성과급' 방식으로 돈을 받았는데 이는 그들이 생산한 만큼 돈을 받았다는 뜻이다.

3 ➡ 생산 과정에서의 이와 같은 대대적 변화는 사업주에게는 분명 이득이 되었다. [2] 한때 제조 과정 각 단계를 직접 감독하면서 처음부터 끝까지 신발을 만들었던 제화공들은 이제 구두창을 만들거나 조각들을 꿰매는 것과 같은 지정된 업무만 하게 되었다. 이는 신발 한 켤레의 가격을 낮춘 반면 기술의 질도 낮아졌으며 장인의 권력은 약화되었다. 이는 사업가들에게 노동 조건과 업무 속도뿐만 아니라 노동자들의 시간을 조정할 수 있는 권력을 주었다.

4 ➡ 그러나 모든 제품이 이 분업 체계에 적합한 것은 아니었기 때문에 기업가들은 더욱 영향력이 강한 근무 환경인 현대식 공장을 고안했다. 공장은 질 높은 제품들을 대량 생산하기 위해 기계와 조립 라인을 이용했다. 이 기계와 조립 라인은 생산 속도를 높였고 결과적으로 대부분의 제품 비용을 낮추었다. 기계는 시간이 지남에 따라 개선되면서 더욱 효과적으로 변했다. 원래 물이나 증기로 가동되던 것들이었으나 이후 전기로 가동되는 단계까지 발전했다.

5 ➡ 이 기계와 조립 라인이 생산량의 증가를 가져와서 소비자 가격을 낮췄지만 몇 가지 부정적인 면도 있었다. 첫째로, 채용 및 임금에 관한 권력이 공장 소유주에게 넘어가게 되면서 실력 있는 장인들에 대한 수요가 줄어들었다. 게다가 노동자들이 기계의 바퀴와 전동 장치에 손가락, 팔다리, 심지어 생명까지 잃으면서 작동 중인 수많은 기계 부품들이 노동자들에게 위험하다는 사실이 입증되었다.

1. 다음 중 1단락에 음영 표시된 문장의 핵심 정보를 가장 잘 표현한 문장은? 오답은 문장의 의미를 크게 왜곡하거나 핵심 정보를 누락하고 있다.

Ⓐ 계획에 의하면, 제조업 혁신이 제품들을 구매 가능하게 만들면서 일반 소비자는 제품에 돈을 더 쓸 수 있었다.
Ⓑ 기업가들이 예상했던 대로, 일반 시민들은 제품들이 대규모로 생산된다면 더 많은 제품들을 기꺼이 구매하려 했다.
Ⓒ 제조되는 제품의 수는 증가했지만 일반인들은 더 많은 물건을 사는 것을 계획하지는 않았다.
Ⓓ 계획대로 제조업의 진보는 더 많은 생산이라는 결과를 낳았고 일반인들의 삶의 질을 크게 향상시켰다.

2. 다음 중 3단락에 음영 표시된 문장의 핵심 정보를 가장 잘 표현한 문장은? 오답은 문장의 의미를 크게 왜곡하거나 핵심 정보를 누락하고 있다.

Ⓐ 제화공은 기존에 특정 업무만을 했지만 작업이 원활히 진행되도록 더 포괄적인 직무도 떠맡게 되었다.
Ⓑ 과거에는 제화공이 제조 과정에서 모든 일을 다 했지만 이제는 주어진 특정 업무만을 수행하게 되었다.
Ⓒ 혁신 이전에 제화공은 제조 과정의 모든 단계에 관심이 있었지만 이후 특정한 업무를 하는 것을 택했다.
Ⓓ 혁신이 도입된 이후 밑창을 만들고 꿰매는 일을 포함해 제화공의 일에 실질적으로 달라진 점은 없었다.

어휘 industrialization n 산업화 | entrepreneur n 기업가 | manufacture v 제조하다 | roughly adv 대략 | distribute v 분배하다 | sole n 밑창, 발바닥 | gear n 기어, 장비 | innovation n 혁신 | improvement n 향상 | efficient adj 효율적인 | designate v 지정하다 | stitch v 바느질하다

---

17 **스파르타와 아테네**

1 ➡ 고대 그리스에서 여러 세대 동안 스파르타와 아테네는 치열한 경쟁 관계였다. 당시 고대 그리스에서 가장 컸던 이 두 도시 국가는 같은 언어를 사용했지만 문화는 이보다 더 다를 수가 없었다. 각 도시 국가의 가치관은 그 정부와 사회 구조에 큰 영향을 끼쳤고 이러한 차이점은 결국 전쟁으로 이어졌다.

2 ➡ 무엇보다 스파르타인들은 힘을 가치 있게 여겼다. 스파르타 정부는 소수의 엘리트 사회 구성원들이 지배하는 과두 정치 체제였다. 두 명의 왕이 의사 결정 기관인 귀족 회의를 감독했는데 이는 스파르타의 권력 대부분이 소수 부유한 집안의 손에 달려 있다는 의미였다. 자신들의 패권을 확장하는 데 관심이 있던 그들은 그리스의 이웃 국가들을 공격하기 위해 강력한 군대를 양성하기 시작했다. 일단 스파르타의 통치하에 놓이면 새로운 시민들은 대개 노예가 되어 단순 노동에 동원되었다. 법률은 엄격했고 그들에게는 자유가 거의 주어지지 않았다. 헬로트라고 불리는 노예들은 모든 비군사적 작업을 담당했지만 자주 폭동을 일으켰다. 그 결과 스파르타 군대는 대외 정복 활동 못지 않게 그 도시 내의 평화를 유지하는 일에도 관여했다.

3 ➡ 스파르타의 문화는 기본적으로 군사력을 통한 권력의 획득 및 유지가 중심이었다. 실제로 모든 교육은 군사 전략과 전쟁 전술에 초점이 맞춰졌으며 전형적인 스파르타 남자는 성인의 삶 대부분을 군복무를 하며 보냈다. 당시로서는 아주 드물게도 여성들 또한 상당한 자유를 누렸으며 남성과 똑같은 권리를 가졌다. 그들은 교육을 받았고 대체로 신체가 건강했는데, 이는 훗날 군대에서 강인한 군인이 될 건강하고 영리한 아들들을 길러야 한다는 기대 때문이었다. [1] 스파르타인들의 사회적 역할은 군 복무에 엄격하게 한정되어 있었기 때문에 상업이나 물자의 생산에 참여하는 것은 허용되지 않았다. 그럼에도 스파르타는 상당히 성공적인 자급자족 경제를 창출할 수 있었으며 시민들도 꽤 높은 삶의 질을

누릴 수 있었다.

4 ➡ 명백히 군국주의적인 스파르타와는 달리, 아테네는 민주주의의 탄생지로 여겨진다. 민주화 과정은 첫 아테네 출신의 문학가로 알려진 솔론의 통치 아래 시작되었다. 2 그는 노예 제도를 폐지하고 전임 통치자 드라코 아래 정착되었던 가혹한 농노제와 엄격한 법을 개혁하기 시작했다. 솔론은 시민들을 부와 군복무 수행 능력에 따라 네 계급으로 나누었다. 인구의 대부분인 가장 빈곤한 계급은 처음으로 정치적 권리를 부여받았다. 그들은 의회에서 투표를 할 수 있었으나 공직에 오를 수 있는 것은 상위 계급뿐이었다. 따라서 아테네는 좀 더 고른 권력의 분배 쪽으로 이동하고 있긴 했지만 여전히 온건한 남성 주도적 귀족 정치 상태를 유지했다는 점을 주목해야 한다.

5 ➡ 정치 외에도 아테네 사회는 두 가지 측면에서 스파르타와 크게 대조되었다. 첫째, 권력이 보다 고르게 분포되어 있고 노예가 없었음에도 불구하고 여성들에게는 자유가 없었으며, 아버지, 남편, 자녀의 뒷바라지를 여성들이 전담해야 했다. 여성들은 공식적인 학교 교육을 받을 수 없었고 집 안에만 머물러 있어야 했다. 둘째, 스파르타는 체육에 초점을 맞춘 반면 아테네인들은 예술에 헌신적이었다. 상업과 분할된 계급 제도에 의해 축적된 아테네의 부는 그리스 전역의 재능 있는 많은 사람들을 끌어들였다. 이로써 예술 활동의 후원자가 된 부유한 유한 계급이 생겨났다. 아테네 정부 또한 교육과 예술을 후원했기 때문에 아테네는 빠르게 그리스 문학, 철학과 예술의 중심지가 되었다. 아테네는 군대를 이용해서뿐만 아니라 예술, 건축, 철학의 발달에 중점을 둠으로써 그리스 내에서 그 영향력을 확대하고자 했다.

1. 다음 중 3단락에 음영 표시된 문장의 핵심 정보를 가장 잘 표현한 문장은? 오답은 문장의 의미를 크게 왜곡하거나 핵심 정보를 누락하고 있다.

Ⓐ 스파르타 문화는 강력한 군사력에 직접적으로 영향을 받았다.
Ⓑ 군사력을 바탕으로 하는 사회에서 스파르타인들은 물자 생산은 물론 상업도 할 수 없었다.
Ⓒ 비록 나중에 폐지되었지만, 처음에는 스파르타도 시민들에게 상업을 허락했다.
Ⓓ 일부 스파르타인들은 근접한 이웃 사회와 교역을 하기도 했지만 그들은 여전히 군인이었다.

2. 다음 중 4단락에 음영 표시된 문장의 핵심 정보를 가장 잘 표현한 문장은? 오답은 문장의 의미를 크게 왜곡하거나 핵심 정보를 누락하고 있다.

Ⓐ 솔론은 전임자가 제정했던 법률의 다수를 강화했지만 노예 제도는 없앴다.
Ⓑ 솔론 치하에서 드라코가 만든 노예제도, 농노제, 그리고 많은 엄격한 법들이 삭제되거나 변경되었다.
Ⓒ 솔론은 드라코가 제정한 많은 법들이 불공평하다고 생각해서 그것들을 제거했다.
Ⓓ 드라코가 사회를 분열한 많은 법률을 만들었기에 솔론은 사람들을 더 평등하게 하기 위해 새로운 법들을 통과시켰다.

어휘 participate v 참여하다 | rivalry n 경쟁 관계 | oligarchy n 과두 정치 | assembly n 의회 | hegemony n 패권, 주도권 | revolt v 반란을 일으키다, 반역하다 | tactic n 전술 | fit adj 건강한 | self-sufficient adj 자급자족의 | militaristic adj 군국주의적인 | eliminate v 제거하다 | serfdom n 농노제 | distribution n 분배 | undergo v 겪다 | patron n 후원자 | seek v 추구하다 | fierce adj 치열한 | impact n 영향 | oversee v 감독하다 | aristocrat n 귀족 | enslave v 노예로 만들다 | retention n 유지 | considerable adj 상당한 | astute adj 영리한 | overtly adv 명백히 | democratization n 민주화 | reform v 개혁하다 | preceding adj 앞서는, 전임의 | evenly adv 균등하게 | dedicate v 헌신하다, 바치다 | territory n 영토, 영역

Test

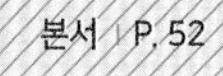
본서 P. 52

지구 온난화와 지구공학

1 ➡ 지구 온난화 현상은 부인할 수 없고 지난 100년간 그것이 급속해진 데에는 인간의 책임이 있다는 충분한 증거가 있다. 지구 온난화 자체는 지구가 역사상 계속 겪어온 자연스러운 과정이다. 판빙이 적도 쪽까지 나아갔던 기간인 빙하기가 많이 있었고 그 시기는 꽤 정기적으로 발생한다. 실제로 우리는 빙하기 사이의 따뜻한 기간인 간빙기를 살아가고 있으며 인간 활동은 지구의 이런 자연 순환을 방해한다고 알려졌다. 지난 수십 년 동안 온난화의 증가 속도는 인간의 온실가스 배출의 결과다. 이 가스는 이산화탄소(CO2), 메탄, 아산화질소인데 이들 모두 태양 에너지는 대기에 들어오도록 하면서 열이 우주로 빠져나가는 것을 막는다. 이 가스들은 화석 연료 연소의 주요 부산물에 속하며 CO2가 총 배출량의 72퍼센트를 차지한다. 그러므로 우리는 확실히 CO2 배출량을 줄여야 한다.

1. 다음 중 1단락에서 언급되지 않은 것은

Ⓐ 온실가스 생산은 지구 온난화의 주요 원인이다
Ⓑ 온실가스는 지구의 대기가 태양으로부터 온 에너지를 가두게끔 만든다
Ⓒ 지구 온난화는 인간의 개입 없이는 절대 발생하지 않았을 것이다
Ⓓ CO2와 메탄은 화석 연료 연소의 결과로 생산된다

2. 1단락에서 지구에 관해 추론 가능한 것은 무엇인가?

Ⓐ 화석 연료는 태양 에너지가 지구에 들어오는 것을 막는다.
Ⓑ 지구는 또 다른 빙하기를 겪을 것이다.
Ⓒ 지구의 기온은 몇 십 년 안에 떨어지기 시작할 것이다.
Ⓓ CO2는 자연적으로 대기에 존재하지 않는다.

2 ➡ 불행하게도 대다수의 온실가스는 석탄 연소에 의한 에너지 생성을 통해 배출된다. 과학자들은 대체 에너지원과 대체 원료를 개발하기 위해 노력 중이지만 그들의 진척은 증가하는 인구의 에너지 수요에 추월되었다. 따라서 우리의 배출량이 지구가 자연적으로 처리할 수 있는 용량을 더 이상 초과하지 않는 지점까지 에너지 기술이 진보할 동안 대기에서 CO2를 제거하는 방법을 찾아야만 한다. 지구를 통제해 기후 변화의 문제들에 대처한다는 개념은 지구공학이라 불리며, 지구 평균 기온을 낮추려는 목적을 달성하기 위해 많은 방안들이 제시되었다. 이것들에는 온실가스의 효과를 무효화하기 위해 에어로졸화된 특별한 화학물질을 대기에 주입하는 것과 CO2를 지각 내 깊이 위치한 암석 층에 가두는 것이 포함되었다. 다른 과학자들은 더 유기적인 접근을 제안한다.

3 ➡ 광합성을 활용하는 생물체들은 CO2를 흡수하고 태양으로부터의 에너지로 그것을 처리해 식량을 생산하는 동시에 산소를 생성한다. 이런 논리를 따라 유럽의 많은 나라들은 집중적인 나무 심기 프로그램을 도입해 탄소 배출량을 상쇄하려고 해왔다. 이는 꽤 효과적인 것으로 드러났지만 나무는 상대적으로 천천히 자라며 죽은 후에 분해되면서 상당한 양의 CO2를 배출하는 것으로 그들의 긍정적인 효과를 거의 무효화한다. 하지만 엄청난 양의 CO2를 흡수하고 짧은 수명을 지닌 플랑크톤이란 생물체가 있다. 조류와 같은 식물성 플랑크톤은 실제로 대양 생물량의 가장 큰 비중을 차지하며 먹이 사슬의 필수적인 부분을 차지한다. 불행히도 그들은 1950년대 이후 계속 감소 중인데, 그러므로 그들의 성장을 촉진시키는 것은 명백한 해결책으로 보인다.

4 ➡ 몇몇 과학자들은 대양에서 식물성 플랑크톤의 성장 재개를 촉발하는 것은 그들로 하여금 CO2를 삼켜버려 지구 온난화를 완화하게 만드는 데 도움이 될 것이라 믿는다. 이 이론을 시험하기 위해 과학자들은 남극대륙 근처 남빙양의 소용돌이에서 실험을 진행했다. [■A] 그들은 그곳의 물에 육지의 많은 식물군에게 사용되는 것과 비슷한 철 비료를 넣고 결과를 관찰했다. [■B] 그들이 소용돌이를 활용한 것은 빙빙 도는 물기둥이 비료가 대양으로 흩어지는 것을 막아줬기 때문이다. 그들은 조류가 그들의 보호막을 형성하는 데 필요로 하는 영양분이 감소하면서, 물 속에 녹아 있는, 대기에서 공급되며 동일한 농도로 존재하는 무기 탄소도 상당히 줄어들었다는 것을 확인했다. [■C] 이것은 조류가 커다란 조류 대증식 상태로 발달했다는 것을 뜻한다. [■D] 이런 수치는 24일 후 비료를 준 조류 대다수가 죽자 정상으로 돌아왔다. 여기에 추가적인 혜택으로, 죽은 조류는 해저에 가라앉는데, 조류에 함유된 탄소는 퇴적물에 섞여들 경우 수십 년 또는 그 이상의 기간 동안 해저에 묻히게 된다.

5 ➡ 대양 조류 비옥화는 가능성이 있어 보이지만 그것은 단점도 있다. 대규모 실행 시 어느 종류의 조류가 증식할지 보장이 없고, 살아있는 동안 아산화질소를 생산하고 죽은 후에 산소를 고갈시키는 다른 조류들도 있다. 이런 조류들은 비료 농업 유출수가 그 무엇도 그 해역에 살아남을 수 없을 정도까지 조류 성장을 촉진시킨 루이지애나 지역 근처의 경우와 비슷한 거대한 죽음의 해역을 만들 수 있다. 하지만 또 다른 과학자 팀은 이런 문제점을 피해 갈 수 있는 과정을 개발했다. 그들은 육지에 원하는 조류를 양식하는 시설의 건축을 제안한다. 그들은 이 개념이 효과적이라는 것을 보여주었지만 이 또한

3. 2단락에 따르면, 다음 중 지구공학에 관해 사실인 것은 무엇인가?

Ⓐ 많은 과학자들은 그것이 우리 건강에 해로울 수 있다고 경고한다.
Ⓑ 그것은 대체 에너지원의 개발에 관한 과학적 연구다.
Ⓒ 에어로졸화된 화학물질을 사용하는 과정은 실용적이지 않다고 간주된다.
Ⓓ 그것의 목적은 지구의 평균 기온을 감소시키는 데 있다.

4. 2단락의 단어 'These(이것들)'가 가리키는 것은

Ⓐ 문제
Ⓑ 방안
Ⓒ 기온
Ⓓ 화학물질

5. 3단락에 따르면, 식물성 플랑크톤이 중요해진 이유는 무엇인가?

Ⓐ 나무처럼 작용하며 나무보다 빠르게 성장한다.
Ⓑ 대양의 먹이 사슬에 중요한 역할을 한다.
Ⓒ 실제 숫자가 1950년대 이후로 감소 중이다.
Ⓓ 저렴한 값에 대량으로 획득할 수 있다.

6. 4단락의 단어 'devour(삼키다)'와 의미상 가장 가까운 것은?

Ⓐ 통제하다
Ⓑ 분해하다
Ⓒ 흡수하다
Ⓓ 풀어 주다

7. 다음 중 지문에 음영 표시된 문장의 핵심 정보를 가장 잘 표현한 문장은 무엇인가? 오답은 의미를 크게 왜곡하거나 핵심 정보를 누락하고 있다.

Ⓐ 대양의 부패한 조류는 해양 생물체에게 필수적인 탄소 원천이다.
Ⓑ 죽은 조류의 탄소가 해저로 가라앉는다는 것도 유익하다.
Ⓒ 해양 침전물은 대체적으로 죽은 조류로부터 생긴 수십 년 된 탄소 침전물로 구성되어 있다.
Ⓓ 죽은 조류의 탄소는 침전물로 바뀌면서 해저에 오랫동안 갇혀 있게 된다.

8. 5단락에서 글쓴이가 '거대한 죽음의 해역'을 언급하는 이유는

Ⓐ 조류 비옥화가 어떻게 지구 온난화를 촉진시키는지 강조하기 위해
Ⓑ 대양 조류 비옥화에서 발생할 수 있는 부정적인 결과를 보여주기 위해
Ⓒ 비료가 야기하는 공기 오염의 사례를 언급하기 위해
Ⓓ 어떤 과학 연구들이 어떻게 해양 생물을 위협하는지 증명하기 위해

심각한 결점을 지녔다. 그 양식 연못들은 넓은 지역을 차지하게 될 것이고 그 과정은 많은 양의 물을 필요로 한다. 이 과정을 개선하기 위한 작업은 지속되고 있지만 이것이 머지 않아 실행 가능한 선택사항이 될 가능성은 적어 보인다.

9. 지문에 다음 문장이 들어갈 수 있는 위치를 나타내는 네 개의 사각형 [■]을 확인하시오.

그들이 소용돌이를 활용한 것은 빙빙 도는 물기둥이 비료가 대양으로 흩어지는 것을 막아줬기 때문이다.

이 문장이 들어가기에 가장 적합한 곳은? [■B]

10. 지시문: 지문을 간략하게 요약한 글의 첫 문장이 아래 제시되어 있다. 지문의 가장 중요한 내용을 표현하는 세 개의 선택지를 골라 요약문을 완성하시오. 일부 문장들은 지문에 제시되지 않았거나 지문의 지엽적인 내용을 나타내기 때문에 요약문에 포함되지 않는다. ***이 문제의 배점은 2점이다.***

지구 온난화가 가속화되면서 과학자들은 평균 기온을 낮추기 위해 지구공학에 더 관심을 갖게 되었다.

Ⓒ 지구공학은 에어로졸화된 화학물질을 사용하는 인공적인 방법과 조류를 키우는 자연적인 방법 둘 다 포함한다.
Ⓓ 과학자들은 조류의 성장이 촉진되면 그들이 효과적으로 CO2를 감소시킬 수 있다는 것을 밝혀냈다.
Ⓕ 대양 조류 비옥화는 해로운 종류의 조류를 길러낼 수 있는 가능성을 포함해 여러 단점이 있다.

Ⓐ 온실가스는 화석 연료의 부산물이고 직접적으로 기후 변화를 야기한다.
Ⓑ 과학자들은 화석 연료 사용을 중지하기 위해 대체 에너지원을 개발하려고 노력 중이다.
Ⓔ 대양 조류 비옥화의 미래는 매우 밝기 때문에 그것의 부작용과 결점은 몇 년 안에 해결될 것이다.

어휘 phenomenon n 현상 I global warming 지구 온난화 I undeniable adj 부인할 수 없는 I ample adj 충분한 I rapidity n 급속, 신속 I equator n 적도 I interglacial period 간빙기 I byproduct n 부산물 I combustion n 연소 I fossil fuel 화석 연료 I emission n 배출 I generation n 발생, 생성 I labor v 힘쓰다, 노력하다 I alternative adj 대체 가능한, 대안이 되는 I outstrip v 앞지르다, 능가하다 I output n 생산량, 산출량 I exceed v 넘다, 초과하다 I manipulate v 조종하다, 조작하다 I geoengineering n 지구공학 I negate v 무효화하다 I crust n 지각 I organic adj 유기적인 I line of thought 사고방식 I intensive adj 집중적인, 치열한 I offset v 상쇄하다 I life span 수명 I biomass n (특정 지역 내의) 생물량 I integral adj 필수적인 I trigger v 촉발시키다 I devour v 먹어 치우다, 삼켜버리다 I alleviate v 완화하다 I eddy n 회오리, 소용돌이 I fertilizer n 비료 I disperse v 흩어지다, 해산하다 I ascertain v 알아내다, 확인하다 I dissolved adj 용해된, 녹은 I inorganic adj 무기물의 I algal bloom 조류 대증식 I deceased adj 죽은 I sediment n 침전물 I fertilization n 비옥화 I drawback n 결점 I guarantee n 보장 I deplete v 고갈시키다 I dead zone 죽음의 해역(물속에서 산소가 충분하지 않아 생물이 살 수 없는 지역) I agricultural runoff 농업 유출수 I circumvent v 면하다, 피해 가다 I refine v 개선하다 I viable adj 실행 가능한

도마뱀 종 구분

1 ➡ 도마뱀들은 전체 파충류의 약 60퍼센트를 구성하며 약 6천 가지의 개별적인 종들이 있다. 그들은 단지 몇 센티미터부터 약 3미터까지 다양한 길이의 차이를 포함해 광범위한 특징을 보여준다. 이런 다양성에도 불구하고 그들은 보통 전반적인 채집 행동에 따라서 두 개의 주요 범주로 나뉜다. 많은 도마뱀들은 움직이지 않고 앉아서 그들의 먹이가 아무 것도 모르고 그들을 지나쳐 걸어갈 때 습격하는 반면, 또 다른 도마뱀들은 그들의 먹이를 실제로 활동적으로 찾아내서 사냥한다. 이런 두 가지 다른 채집 방식은 '앉아서 기다리는' 채집과 '활동적인' 채집으로 불린다. 몇몇 종들은 사실 두 가지 범주의 특징들의 조합을 소유하고 있기 때문에 이것은 꽤 인위적인 범주화이지만 많은 종들은 한쪽 범주에 명확하게 포함된다. 게다가 이런 채집 기법들은 집단 간의 상당한 생리적 차이를 야기했다.

11. 2단락의 단어 'sedentary(앉아 있는)'와 의미상 가장 가까운 것은

Ⓐ 정착한
Ⓑ 잘 견디는
Ⓒ 관대한
Ⓓ 너그러운

12. 2단락에 따르면, 다음 중 앉아서 기다리는 채집자들에 대해 사실인 것은 무엇인가?

Ⓐ 긴 시간 동안의 신체적 활동은 가능하지만 필요하지 않은 이상 시작되지 않는다.
Ⓑ 그들의 혀는 먹이의 사지를 사로잡는 데 최적화됐다.

2 ➡ 범주의 이름이 명시하는 것처럼 앉아서 기다리는 채집자들은 대부분 앉아 있는 동물들이다. 그들은 보통 바위나 나무에 올라앉는데 그들의 색깔이 이런 표면에 매우 효과적으로 섞여들게 해 준다. 이런 도마뱀들은 먹이를 찾아 주변을 살펴보는 데 사용하는 뛰어난 시력을 갖고 있다. [■A] 이것은 그들이 먹이를 매우 까다롭게 고르도록 만드는데, 그들이 먹는 것은 보통 그들을 지나치는 곤충이나 작은 동물들이다. [■B] 대부분의 종들은 먹이를 잡아챌 수 있는 두툼한 혀를 갖고 있다. [■C] 그들은 먹이를 공격하거나 위험에서 도망칠 수 있도록 짧은 시간 동안 폭발적인 속력으로 움직일 수 있지만, 지속적인 활동은 그들을 빨리 지치게 한다. 그러므로 그들은 먹이가 도망칠 확률이 없을 때에만 공격하며, 포식자가 확실히 공격하려고 할 때에만 도망친다. [■D] 장거리 이동을 못 하기 때문에 그들은 보통 생명의 위협을 느끼면 피신처를 찾는다. 카멜레온은 앉아서 기다리는 채집자의 모든 특수화된 특징들을 갖고 있다. 그들은 위장의 대가이며 주변 환경에 섞여들기 위해 색깔을 바꿀 수 있다. 그들의 혀 또한 꽤 길고 끈적여서 재빠르게 혀를 내밀면 걸터앉은 곳에서부터 먼 곳에 있는 곤충들을 잡을 수 있다.

3 ➡ 반면에 활동적인 채집자들은 매우 잘 움직이는 동물들이다. 다양한 환경 속을 이동하기 때문에 그들의 주위 환경은 끊임없이 바뀌는데, 이것은 그들이 효과적으로 위장하는 것을 불가능하게 한다. 대신 그들은 보통 단색의 몸이나 줄무늬를 갖고 있는데, 이는 윤곽을 모호하게 만들어 그들을 시각적으로 추적하는 포식자들을 헷갈리게 만드는 역할을 한다. 그들은 긴 몸통과 매우 긴 꼬리와 다리를 갖고 있는 경향이 있다. 이런 도마뱀들은 움직이지 않는 종들보다 훨씬 더 기회주의적이며 후각을 사용하여 먹이의 위치를 알아낸다. 또한 그들은 바로 근처 환경 외에는 잘 보지 못하는 상대적으로 좋지 않은 시력을 갖고 있다. 그들은 턱을 사용해 먹이를 잡기 때문에 대개 훨씬 더 발달된 치아와 입 근육계를 갖고 있다. 이런 도마뱀들은 먹이를 찾아 넓은 구역을 돌아다니는데, 위협을 받을 경우에는 보통 방향을 바꾸고 민첩함에 의존해 도망치며 마찬가지로 먼 거리를 달리게 된다. 왕도마뱀들은 길고 힘이 센 사지 및 몸통과 날카롭고 휘어진 이빨을 지닌 활동적인 채집자 집단의 전형적인 일원이다. 그들은 쉽게 장거리를 달리고, 물어서 고통스러운 상처를 입힐 수 있으며, 향상된 후각과 달리기 능력을 사용해 장거리에 걸쳐 먹이를 추격한다. 그들의 혀는 얇고 끝이 갈라져 있으며 뱀들이 하는 것처럼 정기적으로 혀를 밖으로 날름거리며 공기 냄새를 맡는다.

4 ➡ 앉아서 기다리는 채집자와 활동적인 채집자의 차이는 매우 크며 이는 세포 단위까지 이어진다. 이 동물들이 활용하는 사냥 전략은 그들의 신진대사와 근육계를 결정짓는다. 생물의 모든 세포는 아데노신삼인산(ATP)이라는 화학물질을 사용해 기능에 동력을 공급한다. 앉아서 기다리는 채집자들은 대부분 글리코겐에서 ATP를 만들어 내는 속근을 갖고 있다. 이 과정은 추가적인 산소 사용 없이 일어나며, 이는 폭발적으로 속력을 올릴 수는 있지만 이 화학 작용이 지속될 수 없기 때문에 빠르게 지친다는 것을 의미한다. 활동적인 채집자들은 대부분 ATP 생산을 위해 산소를 사용해 포도당을 처리하는 지근을 갖고 있는데, 이것은 그들에게 지구력을 준다. 그러므로 앉아서 기다리는 채집자들의 신진대사는 무산소라고 하며 활동적인 채집자들의 것은 유산소이다.

Ⓒ 그들은 보통 주변 환경 속에 숨은 채로 있다.
Ⓓ 오랜 시간 동안 가만히 있는 경우가 흔치 않기 때문에 그들의 감각은 먹이를 감지하기 위해 예민해야 한다.

13. 다음 중 3단락에서 활동적인 채집 도마뱀들의 특징으로 언급되지 않은 것은 무엇인가?

Ⓐ 먹이를 추격하는 데 끈질기다.
Ⓑ 후각을 활용해 먹이를 추적한다.
Ⓒ 그들의 몸통은 포식자들이 발견하기 더 힘들도록 위장되어 있다.
Ⓓ 좋지 않은 시력을 갖고 있지만, 강력한 턱과 날카로운 이빨 또한 갖고 있다.

14. 다음 중 지문에 음영 표시된 문장의 핵심 정보를 가장 잘 표현한 문장은 무엇인가? 오답은 의미를 크게 왜곡하거나 핵심 정보를 누락하고 있다.

Ⓐ 먹이를 사냥하고 포식자들에게서 도망치기 위해 활동적인 채집 도마뱀들은 마구잡이로 장거리를 이동한다.
Ⓑ 활동적인 채집 도마뱀들이 먹이를 사냥하는 데 이동하는 거리는 그들의 먹이가 포식을 피하기 위해 이동하는 거리와 동일하다.
Ⓒ 포식을 피해 민첩하게 장거리를 이동하는 활동적인 채집자들은 먹이를 사냥하기 위해서도 그만큼 멀리 이동한다.
Ⓓ 빠르게 움직이며 방향을 바꿈으로써, 활동적인 채집자들은 위협을 받으면 멀리 이동하는 그들의 먹이를 성공적으로 추적한다.

15. 다음 중 4단락에서 추론 가능한 것은 무엇인가?

Ⓐ 도마뱀 근육은 그들 각각의 채집 행동에 적합하게 진화했다.
Ⓑ 활동적인 채집자보다 앉아서 기다리는 채집자에게 더 많은 양의 포도당이 존재한다.
Ⓒ 활동적인 채집자는 앉아서 기다리는 채집자보다 신진대사에 더 적은 양의 산소를 필요로 한다.
Ⓓ ATP는 오랜 기간 지속이 쉽지 않은 화학 반응을 통해 생산된다.

16. 5단락의 주요 목적은 무엇인가?

Ⓐ 도마뱀 꼬리의 특징을 묘사하기 위해
Ⓑ 밝은 색은 생존에 해가 되지 않는다는 것을 증명하기 위해
Ⓒ 양쪽 종류의 도마뱀에게 공통적인 특징들을 소개하기 위해
Ⓓ 자절이 생존의 가능성을 어떻게 높이는지 논의하기 위해

17. 5단락에 따르면, 다음 중 도마뱀 꼬리의 기능은 무엇인가? 두 개를 고르시오.

Ⓐ 재생될 수 있다.
Ⓑ 균형 유지를 돕는다.
Ⓒ 포식자의 손아귀에서 빠져나온다.
Ⓓ 에너지 비축분을 담고 있다.

5 ➡ 이런 차이점들에도 불구하고 양쪽 도마뱀 집단들은 골격 구조와 같은 많은 해부학적 특징들을 공유한다. 양쪽 집단의 많은 일원들은 또한 자절(自切)이라는 능력을 활용한다. 꼬리가 붙잡혔을 때, 이 도마뱀들은 자신의 꼬리를 절단할 수 있다. 이것은 도마뱀을 포식자의 손아귀에서 풀어줄 뿐만 아니라 절단된 부위는 계속 꿈틀거려서 공격자의 관심을 계속 사로잡는다. 더 나아가 몇몇 종들의 꼬리는 갈색과 녹색 몸통과는 대조적으로 밝은 파란색을 띤다. 밝은 색의 꼬리는 포식자들이 주된 몸통 대신 꼬리를 공격하게 유인하여 도마뱀이 도망갈 수 있는 가능성을 높여준다. 물론 꼬리는 에너지 비축분을 저장하는 데 사용되며 달릴 때 몸의 균형을 잡는 데 도움을 주기 때문에 꼬리를 잃는 것은 도마뱀에게 해롭지만, 나중에 새로운 꼬리가 자라나게 할 수 있다.

18. **지문에 따르면, 다음 중 앉아서 기다리는 채집자와 활동적인 채집자의 차이점이 아닌 것은**

Ⓐ 신진대사 방식
Ⓑ 먹이의 종류
Ⓒ 사냥에 채택된 방식
Ⓓ 신체적 활동량

19. 지문에 다음 문장이 들어갈 수 있는 위치를 나타내는 네 개의 사각형 [■]을 확인하시오.

그들은 먹이를 공격하거나 위험에서 도망칠 수 있도록 짧은 시간 동안 폭발적인 속력으로 움직일 수 있지만, 지속적인 활동은 그들을 빨리 지치게 한다.

이 문장이 들어가기에 가장 적합한 곳은? [■C]

20. **지시문:** 지문을 간략하게 요약한 글의 첫 문장이 아래 제시되어 있다. 지문의 가장 중요한 내용을 표현하는 세 개의 선택지를 골라 요약문을 완성하시오. 일부 문장들은 지문에 제시되지 않았거나 지문의 지엽적인 내용을 나타내기 때문에 요약문에 포함되지 않는다. ***이 문제의 배점은 2점이다.***

전 세계의 무수히 많은 도마뱀 종들 중 많은 것들은 채집 행동에 따라 두 개의 범주로 나뉠 수 있다.

Ⓐ 앉아서 기다리는 채집자들은 보통 먹이를 성공적으로 포획할 수 있거나 포식자가 공격하려는 것이 확실해질 때까지 가만히 있는다.
Ⓓ 각 집단이 고유한 생리적인 특징들을 갖고 있기는 하지만, 그럼에도 불구하고 그들은 동일한 골격 구조와 자절과 같은 자기방어 기제를 공유한다.
Ⓔ 활동적인 채집자들은 후각을 활용해 먹이를 끈질기게 추격하며, 격렬하고 지속된 활동을 지속시키는 지근을 소유하고 있다.

Ⓑ 카멜레온은 움직이지 않고 주변 환경과 섞이게 몸통 색깔을 바꿈으로써 숨은 채로 있는 전형적인 앉아서 기다리는 채집자다.
Ⓒ 활동적인 채집자는 주로 무산소 신진대사를 하는 반면, 앉아서 기다리는 채집자는 유산소 신진대사를 한다.
Ⓕ 두 집단 간의 주된 차이점 중 하나는 그들이 신진대사를 위해 서로 다른 당분에 의존한다는 사실이다.

어휘 comprise v ~으로 구성되다 | attribute n 자질, 속성 | forage v 먹이를 찾다 | motionless adj 움직이지 않는 | ambush v 매복했다가 습격하다 | ignorantly adv 무식/무지하게 | artificial adj 인위적인 | physiological adj 생리학의 | sedentary adj 주로 앉아서 지내는 | perch v 걸터앉다 | coloration n (생물의) 천연색 | fleshy adj 살집이 있는 | sustained adj 지속된 | embody v 상징하다 | extrude v 밀어내다 | stripe n 줄무늬 | obscure adj 모호한, 잘 알려져 있지 않은 | opportunistic adj 기회주의적인 | musculature n 근육계 | agility n 민첩 | exemplary adj 모범적인 | readily adv 손쉽게 | heightened adj 고조된 | forked adj 한쪽 끝이 두 갈래인 | profound adj 엄청난, 심오한 | cellular adj 세포의 | dictate v ~을 좌우하다 | surge n 급증, 급등, 솟아오름 | endurance n 인내, 참을성 | anaerobic adj 무산소성의 | aerobic adj 유산소의 | anatomical adj 해부상의 | skeletal adj 뼈대의 | autotomy n 자기 절단 | amputate v 절단하다 | grasp n 단단히 붙잡기, 지배, 점유 | severed adj 절단된 | detrimental adj 해로운 | reserve n 비축물

Lesson 02 Fact & Negative Fact

본서 I P. 60

Practice

01 T, F, T, F　02 F, F, T, T　03 A　04 C　05 C　06 D　07 C　08 D
09 A　10 C　11 D　12 C　13 1. B 2. D　14 1. C 2. C　15 1. C 2. A
16 1. B 2. B

Test

1. C	2. B	3. D	4. B	5. B, C	6. A	7. D	8. C	9. B	10. A, E, F
11. D	12. D	13. A	14. C	15. D	16. C	17. B	18. A	19. B	20. A, E, F

Practice

본서 I P. 63

[01-02] 지문을 읽고 문제 Ⓐ~Ⓓ에 옳을 경우 T, 틀릴 경우 F라고 쓰시오.

01 침식은 중력과 인간 활동과의 상호 작용과 함께 바람, 물, 얼음 등의 물리적인 힘에 의해 토양이나 암석이 변위되는 것이다. 침식과 유사하기는 하지만 풍화는 암석의 분해를 수반한다는 점에서 침식과 구별되어야 한다. 침식은 자연적인 변화 과정에 의해 야기되지만 많은 경우 인간의 활동으로 촉진된다. 산림 벌채, 지나친 방목과 도로 건설 등이 이러한 인간 활동에 포함된다. 침식 작용을 줄이기 위해 인류는 다시 나무를 심기 시작했다.

Ⓐ T 얼음은 침식의 원인 중 하나이다.　Ⓑ F 풍화는 침식과 같다.
Ⓒ T 산림 벌채는 침식을 초래하는 인간 활동의 한 예시다.　Ⓓ F 중력은 침식을 방지하는 데 도움이 된다.

어휘 erosion n 침식 I displacement n 이동, (물리) 변위 I interaction n 상호 작용 I gravity n 중력 I weathering n 풍화 I distinguish v 구별하다 I decomposition n 분해, 부패 I deforestation n 산림 벌채 I overgraze v 지나치게 풀을 많이 뜯다 I construction n 공사, 건설 I counteract v 대응하다 I reforestation n 숲 다시 가꾸기

02 물은 훌륭한 용매이면서 높은 표면 장력을 가지고 있는 등 생명체를 지탱하는 데 중요한 성질을 지니고 있다. 물은 섭씨 4도에서 밀도가 가장 높다. 물은 가열되거나 얼수록 밀도가 낮아진다. 대기 중에서 물은 안정된 극성 분자이기 때문에 적외선을 흡수하는 데 중요한 역할을 하는데, 이는 온실 효과를 제한하는 데 필수적이다. 또한 물은 지구의 기후를 조절하는 일에 도움을 주는 아주 높은 특정 열용량을 지니고 있다.

Ⓐ F 물은 불안정한 분자다.　Ⓑ F 물은 섭씨 4도에서보다 섭씨 0도에서 밀도가 더 높다.
Ⓒ T 물은 적외선을 흡수하는 데 중요한 역할을 한다.　Ⓓ T 물의 특정 열용량은 지구의 온도 조절을 돕는다.

어휘 solvent n 용매 I Celsius adj 섭씨의 I molecule n 분자 I infrared adj 적외선의 I radiation n 광선, 복사, 방사선

03

뱀의 혀

갈라진 혀, 즉 혀끝이 두 부분으로 나뉜 혀는 도마뱀과 뱀 같은 여러 파충류의 흔한 특징이다. 파충류는 혀끝을 사용하여 냄새를 맡고, 갈라진 혀는 냄새가 오는 방향을 감지할 수 있게 한다. 과학자들은 이러한 파충류에서 갈라진 혀가 여러 다양한 목적을 위해 진화했다고 여긴다. 갈라진 혀를 갖는 것의 주된 이점은 더 많은 표면적이 화학 물질과 접촉하게 만들고, 냄새를 감지하는 잠재력을 증가시킨다는 것이다. 혀는 화학적 환경을 조사하기 위해 입 밖으로 규칙적으로 움직인다. 이러한 형태의 화학적 표본 추출법은 동물들이 비휘발성 화학 물질을 감지할 수 있게 하는데, 이는 단순히 후각 체계를 사용하는 것으로는 감지되지 않는다. 화학 물질을 감지하는 이러한 증가된 능력은 먹이를 찾아내고, 동족을 알아보고, 짝을 선택하고, 집을 찾는 일을 가능하게 한다.

지문에 의하면, 파충류가 갈라진 혀를 사용하는 이유는

Ⓐ 화학적 자극을 추적하기 위해 냄새를 감지한다　Ⓑ 먹이를 잡기 위해 건드린다
Ⓒ 혀를 날름거려서 먹이를 죽이기 위한 독을 분사한다　Ⓓ 인간과 같은 포식자를 위협한다

어휘 reptile n 파충류 I lizard n 도마뱀 I flick v 혀를 날름거리다 I olfactory adj 후각의 I volatile adj 휘발성의 I kinship n 친족, 동류의식

04

화성의 물

명백한 증거들이 한때 화성 표면에 상당량의 물이 존재했다는 것을 시사하고 있는데, 그 중에는 몇몇 무인 우주 탐사선에 의해 찍힌 사진도 포함되어 있다. 바이킹 궤도 선회 우주선과 화성 전역 조사선이 흐르는 물에 의해 형성된 것으로 보이는 해협과 협곡 같은 표면의 모습을 찍은 사진을 지구로 전송했다. 특히 강우에 의한 수로는 물이 흐른 흔적을 명백하게 보여준다. 남쪽 지대에서 발견된 이 수로는 방대한 체계를 형성한 것으로 보이는데, 이들 중 일부는 길이가 수백 킬로미터에 달하는 것도 있으며, 서로 교차하고 얽혀 더 커다랗고 넓은 수로로 합쳐지는 것으로 보인다. 이러한 수로들은 지구의 하천계와 비슷해서 지질학자들은 수로들을 산에서 계곡으로 화성의 빗물을 운반했던 오래 전 없어진 강의 흔적으로 여긴다. 지면 위에 물이 흐른 흔적은 대기의 밀도가 더 높고, 표면은 더 따뜻했으며 풍부한 물이 있었음을 보여준다.

지문에 의하면, 글쓴이는 화성에 관해 무엇을 언급하는가?

Ⓐ 화성의 대기는 한때 오늘날보다 더 희박했다.
Ⓑ 화성의 하천계는 한때 지구의 것보다 더 방대했다.
Ⓒ 화성의 일부 지역들에 강수가 있었다.
Ⓓ 세균과 비슷한 생물체의 유해가 있다.

어휘 probe **n** 무인 우주 탐사선 I channel **n** 수로, 해협 I runoff **n** 땅 위를 흐르는 빗물 I twist **v** 구불구불하게 나다 I merge **v** 합치다, 합병하다

05

흑사병

1347년부터 1350년까지 유럽 전역을 휩쓸었던 임파선종 전염병인 흑사병은 중국이나 중앙 아시아에서 시작하여 실크로드를 따라 상인들에 의해 확산되었다. 흑사병은 유럽 본토에서 감염된 사람들에 의해 영국으로 들어왔을 것이라고 널리 믿어진다. 모든 종류의 동물과 사람이 함께 살았기 때문에 거리는 더러웠고, 많은 기생충이 있었기 때문에 이 전염병은 그런 상황에서 더 빠르게 확산되었을 것이다. 이 전염병은 영국 인구의 1/3에서 절반 이상을 죽음으로 몰아넣었다고 추산된다. 흑사병이 이 번영하던 나라를 강타한 후 사람들이 경험한 즉각적 결과는 인구 감소로 노동력이 부족해졌다는 것이었으며, 이는 임금 상승을 초래했다. 그러나 지주 계급과 정부는 법이나 처벌 조치를 통해 이러한 상황을 규제하려고 노력했으며 이로 인해 하층 계급 사이에 분노가 깊어지는 결과가 초래되었다. 그래서 종교적, 사회적 폭동을 포함한 전염병의 모든 여파들 중에서 1381년의 농민 봉기가 사회에 가장 심각한 영향을 끼쳤다.

지문에 의하면, 노동자들이 정부 당국에 분개하게 만든 요인은 무엇인가?

Ⓐ 당국은 공중 위생 대책을 마련하지 않았고 질병은 빠른 속도로 나라 전역에 퍼지게 되었다.
Ⓑ 정부는 환자들이 일하는 것을 금지했고 노동자들은 생활고에 시달렸다.
Ⓒ 정부는 노동력 공급의 전반적 저하로 야기된 임금 상승을 억제했다.
Ⓓ 전염병 때문에 정부는 유럽 본토와의 교역을 금지했다.

어휘 plague **n** 전염병 I sweep **v** 급속히 퍼지다 I stem **v** ~에서 기원하다, 시작하다 I infect **v** 감염시키다 I filthy **adj** 더러운 I parasite **n** 기생충 I communicable **adj** 전염성의 I strike **v** 덮치다, 발생하다 I curb **v** 억제하다 I resentment **n** 분개, 억울함 I pandemic **n** 세계적인 유행병 I wage **n** 임금 I punitive **adj** 처벌을 위한, 가혹한 I upheaval **n** 격변, 대변동

06

미국 남서부의 사막화

미국의 남서부 지역은 기후 변화 때문에 오랜 기간 동안 덥고 건조한 지역이었다. 그러나 이 넓은 지역은 최근 사막화로 급속히 황폐화되었는데, 이는 사막과 유사한 환경이 이전까지 그렇지 않았던 지역으로 확산되는 현상이다. 이 지역에 이러한 현상을 가속화하는 모든 원인들 중 가장 주된 원인은 인구 증가와 그로 인해 야기되는 문제들이다. 우선 목장 주인들이 방목한 엄청난 수의 가축이 지면을 덮고 있는 초목의 많은 부분을 먹어치우고, 빠른 속도로 흙을 밟아 뭉갠다. 이 결과로, 밟힌 흙은 바람이나 비에 쉽게 침식된다. 푸석푸석한 흙은 완전히 날아가고, 돌 같은 표면만 남아 궁극적으로 그 지역은 더 척박하고 건조해진다. 또 다른 이유는 과도한 장작 모으기이다. 남서부 지역의 수목 부족은 표토를 제자리에 붙잡아둘 뿌리가 없음을 의미한다. 비옥한 토양에서 효과적인 영양소를 빼앗는 과다한 경작과 더불어, 바람과 비바람은 가장 양질의 토양을 쓸어가서 땅을 더 척박하고 사막화에 더 취약하게 만든다.

지문에서 미국 남서부 지역 사막화의 원인으로 언급되지 않은 것은

Ⓐ 과도한 경작으로 너무 많은 영양분을 뽑아냄
Ⓑ 지나친 가축 방목
Ⓒ 많은 양의 벌목
Ⓓ 비옥한 토양을 찾아 이동함

어휘 arid **adj** 매우 건조한 I devastate **v** 완전히 파괴하다 I expedite **v** 촉진하다 I rancher **n** 목장 주인 I graze **v** 방목하다, 풀을 뜯다 I smash **v** 박살내다 I overcultivation **n** 과도한 경작 I trample **v** 짓밟다, 밟아 뭉개다 I barren **adj** 척박한, 황량한 I in conjunction with ~와 함께 I strip **v** ~을 빼앗다, 박탈하다 I susceptible **adj** 취약한

07

중세 유럽의 농업 기술

중세 유럽의 인구가 점차 증가하면서, 혁신적 농업 기술이 더 많은 양의 식량 산출을 도왔다. 농업 산출량을 증가시키는 데 기여한 몇 가지 방법들이 있었다. 대장장이는 토양에 씨를 뿌리기 위한 준비를 함으로써 생산성을 향상하는 데 도움을 주는 쟁기와 삽을 만들었다. 게다가 목축은 더욱 질 좋은 소와 말을 산출했고, 이 가축들은 농부들이 땅을 경작하는 데 이용되었다. 짐 끄는 짐승들이 무거운 나무 쟁기와 철 쟁기를 끌 수 있었기 때문에 농업에 동물들을 이용하는 것은 비옥한 토양을 갈아엎는 것을 용이하게 했다. 이러한 혁신은 농부들이 수익성이 별로 없는 암석투성이 땅마저 작물 경작에 활용할 수 있게 해주었다. 게다가 곡식 돌려짓기(윤작)의 도입은 농사 짓는 땅의 토양에 영양분이 고갈되지 않게 했으며 오랜 기간 한 지역에서 농사를 지을 수 있게 했다. 이러한 모든 요인은 농업 발전에 기여해, 더 안정된 생활 양식의 도입을 가능하게 했고 도시의 성장과 더 문명화된 삶으로 이어졌다.

지문에 따르면, 더 많은 양의 곡식 수확을 얻게 된 요인으로 언급되지 않은 것은

Ⓐ 목축업　Ⓑ 경작을 위한 장비　Ⓒ 문명화된 생활 양식　Ⓓ 진보된 농업 기술력

어휘 forge v (금속을) 만들다 I plow n 쟁기 I spade n 삽 I livestock farming 목축업 I deplete v 고갈시키다 I till v (논, 밭을) 갈다, 경작하다 I draft animal 짐수레 끄는 동물, 역축 I ensure v 보장하다 I arable adj 곡식을 경작하는 I patch n 작은 땅

08

머스 커닝햄

20세기 가장 혁신적이고 창의적인 안무가 중 한 명인 머스 커닝햄은 전통적인 음악 형식뿐 아니라 원인과 결과, 클라이막스 등 일반적인 전개 패턴까지 버렸다. 그는 무용수들에게 무용의 기본적인 스킬을 가르치되 각자 적합하다고 생각하는 방식대로 즉석에서 연기하고 표현하게 내버려 두었다. 커닝햄은 예술에서 이야기를 전달하거나 심리학적 관계를 탐색하는 데는 관심이 없었고, 오히려 그의 무용의 주제는 무용 그 자체였다. "우주에는 고정된 지점이 없다"는 알버트 아인슈타인의 말에서 영감을 받아, 커닝햄은 '챈스 오퍼레이션'이라 이름 붙인 창의적인 방법을 개발했다. 이 방법은 다다이즘의 영향을 받은 것이기도 한데, 커닝햄은 여기서 영감을 얻어 다양한 춤의 흐름(phrase: 무용에서 작은 동작들이 모여 하나의 흐름을 만들어 내는 것을 일컫는 단위)을 만들고 주사위, 카드, 동전 등의 특이한 물건들을 이용해 순서, 반복 횟수, 방향, 공간적 관계를 결정하기도 했다. 그는 종종 음악가들을 초청해 작곡을 하게 했고 예술가들을 불러 시각적 환경을 만들게 했다. 커닝햄은 그런 다음 그 결과에 어울리는 동작을 창작하곤 했다. 이러한 협력을 통해 커닝햄은 전통적인 방법을 통해서는 절대 얻을 수 없는 안무를 창조할 수 있었다.

지문에 의하면, 다음 중 머스 커닝햄에 관한 내용으로 사실이 아닌 것은 무엇인가?

Ⓐ 작품을 만들어내는 일에 다른 영역의 아이디어를 도입했다.
Ⓑ 무용수들에게 즉흥적이고 표현력 있게 춤을 추라고 장려했다.
Ⓒ 종종 음악가와 예술가가 그에게 제시하는 것들을 가지고 그들의 창작의 결과물들을 서로 연결시켜가며 작업했다.
Ⓓ 장면을 만드는 일에 예술가들의 도움을, 공연의 이야기를 강화하기 위해 음악가들의 도움을 정기적으로 구했다.

어휘 innovative adj 혁신적인 I choreographer n 안무가 I abandon v 버리다 I conventional adj 관습적인, 전통적인 I commonplace adj 아주 흔한 I development n 발전, 전개 I improvise v 즉흥적으로 하다 I express v 표현하다 I explore v 탐구하다 I psychological adj 심리적인 I inspire v 영감을 주다 I fixed adj 고정된 I space n 공간 I atypical adj 이례적인 I dice n 주사위 I order n 순서 I repetition n 반복 I spatial adj 공간의 I traditional adj 전통적인

09

사구

자연 지리학에서 사구는 퇴적이라는 과정으로 형성된 언덕으로 정의하며, 산에서 침식된 모래를 바람이 모래가 많은 지역으로 나를 때 발생한다. 모래가 목적지에 도착할 때 생기는 모양은 사구의 크기뿐 아니라 그 지역의 풍계에 따라 결정되며, 이 두 가지는 기본적으로 사구의 경사진 측면, 즉 사구활주사면의 수와 위치에 영향을 준다. 뿐만 아니라 사구는 그 활주사면의 위치와 수를 기준으로 분류된다. 모든 사구 종류 중에서 신월사구는 비록 지구의 사구 지역에서 적은 비율만을 차지하지만 지구상에 나타나는 사구 모양 중에서는 가장 일반적이다. 이것은 사구의 크기가 상대적으로 작기 때문인데, 세계 최대의 신월사구는 높이가 최대 30m, 길이와 폭이 4km 정도이다. 신월사구는 오목한 측면에 하나의 활주사면이 나타난다. 또한 한 방향에서 불어오는 바람으로 형성되고, 다른 유형의 사구보다 더 빠르고 멀리 이동할 수 있다는 점도 사구에 관한 연구에서 또 한 가지 중요한 사항이다. 다시 언급하지만 이는 신월사구처럼 작은 사구의 고유한 특성이다.

지문에 의하면, 다음 중 신월사구에 관한 내용으로 사실이 아닌 것은 무엇인가?

Ⓐ 아주 작아서 움직임과 모양이 안정적이다.　Ⓑ 가장 자주 발생하는 사구이다.
Ⓒ 다른 종류보다 더 빠르게 이동할 수 있다.　Ⓓ 다른 사구 종류보다 일반적으로 규모가 더 작다.

어휘 physical geography 지학, 자연 지리학 I define v 정의하다 I dune n 사구 I deposition n 퇴적, 퇴적물 I occur v 발생하다 I erode v 침식되다 I destination n 목적지 I slip face 사구활주사면 I steep adj 가파른 I classify v 분류하다 I prevalent adj 일반적인, 널리 퍼져 있는 I comprise v 구성하다, 차지하다 | relatively adv 상대적으로, 비교적 | display v 보이다 | concave adj 오목한 | consideration n 생각, 고려 | inherent adj 내재하는, 고유의 | trait n 특성

10

갈라파고스 제도

갈라파고스 제도는 남아메리카에서 서쪽으로 900km 거리에 위치한 화산섬 제도이다. 이 섬들은 생물체의 진화에 안성맞춤인데 그 이유는 본토에서 너무 멀지도 가깝지도 않은 위치에 있으면서 동물들이 산발적으로만 이동하게 하기 때문이다. 바람과 해류 같은 자연 현상들은 때때로 제도에 있는 섬에 본토 생물들의 일부 개체를 이동시킨다. 만약 이 개체들이 성공적으로 섬 안에서 번식한다면, 이들의 후손은 거기 자리를 잡을 것이다. 섬을 본토와 고립시키는 거대한 바다는 지역적으로 동종의 다른 개체와의 교류를 방해한다. 그러한 이유로 수 세대가 지나면 이 섬의 동물군은 본토의 종과 달라진다. 달라진 동물군의 개체는 차례로 제도에 있는 다른 섬들에 대량 서식하고, 진화 과정을 반복한다. 섬들 사이의 서로 다른 서식지와 도태압(바람직하지 못한 유전형이나 표현형을 제거하는 정도)은 조상이 되는 종들과 더 많은 차이를 낳는다. 예를 들어 갈라파고스 제도에 사는 일명 다윈의 핀치로 알려져 있는 핀치는 폭풍우에 의해 날아온 것으로 여겨졌다. 오랜 시간이 흐르고 수백 세대가 지나고 난 이후 이 핀치들은 15개의 서로 다른 종들로 진화했고, 모두 부리의 크기와 모양이 다르다. 이런 다양한 핀치들은 동일한 조상에서 왔으나 섬마다 눈에 띄게 다른 행동적 특성을 가지고 있는 다른 종들로 분리되었다.

지문에 의하면, 섬에 사는 종들이 본토의 동물군과 다른 이유는

Ⓐ 적이 없어서
Ⓑ 서로간에 강한 사회적 관계를 수립해서
Ⓒ 광대한 바다가 장애물 역할을 해서
Ⓓ 수 세대에 걸쳐 섬에서 진화해서

어휘 sporadically adv 산발적으로 | expanse n 지역, 영역 | impede v 지연시키다, 방해하다 | diverge v 갈라지다, 나뉘다 | colonize v 대량 서식하다, 식민지로 만들다 | foster v 조성하다 | finch n 되새류(부리가 짧은 작은 새) | beak n 부리

11

문명의 발생

여러 출처에서 나온 자료들이 농업의 증거에 관한 명확한 최초의 사례들이 기원전 5천년 경 메소포타미아, 북아프리카, 인도, 중국의 어딘가로 거슬러 올라간다는 것을 보여준다. 분명히 초반에 농업은 식량을 얻는 주된 방법이 아니었고 주로 식량을 얻는 방법이었던 수렵과 채집을 보완하는 역할만 했을 뿐이었다. 곡식 기르기를 시도한 최초의 사람들은 전적으로 곡식 경작만을 통해 스스로 살아갈 만큼 믿을 수 있는 기술이나 지식을 가지고 있지 않았다. 그러나 농업의 획기적인 발전은 강 유역 거주자들이 범람원에 씨앗을 심었을 때 시작되었다. 이것은 사람들이 불규칙적이고 계절적인 비에 의존하기보다 강에서 안정적인 물 공급을 얻게 해 주었다. 이를 통해 유목 생활을 하던 사람들의 무리가 한 곳에 정착하여 사회를 형성할 수 있게 되면서 사람들이 살아가는 방식이 바뀌었다. 식량 유용성의 증가는 인구 확산의 계기가 되었고, 결과적으로 사람들의 요구를 충족시키기 위해 도시 내로 물을 끌어오는 관개를 낳았다. 잉여 농작물로 인해, 정착 농업은 재산권 및 법을 시행할 법률 구조의 발달을 불러왔다. 이것은 또한 더 복잡하고 위계질서가 있는 정부 기관에 대한 개념을 발전시켰다.

지문에 의하면, 조직화된 정부의 발전을 야기한 것은 무엇인가?

Ⓐ 농업에 덜 의존하도록 만든 믿을 만한 사냥 기술
Ⓑ 침입자로부터 수확물을 보호할 필요로 이어진 식량 유용성의 증가
Ⓒ 낚시를 위해 공동체 안으로 끌어들인 수원
Ⓓ 재산권법을 시행할 필요성

어휘 supplement n 보충(물), 추가 | sustain v 살아가게 하다, 지속하게 하다 | nomadic adj 유목의, 방랑의 | trigger v 촉발시키다 | expansion n 확대, 확장 | irrigation n 관개 | surplus n 과잉 | give rise to ~이 생기게 하다 | hierarchical adj 계급에 따른

12

체온 조절

모든 생물체들은 주변 환경에 따른 외부 온도에 영향을 받는다. 주변 환경 온도의 변화는 동물의 체온을 변하게 한다. 그래서 체온을 조절하는 동물의 능력은 극단적 환경에서의 생존에 필수적이다. 그러한 이유로 극도로 추운 기후의 토착 동물들은 체온 조절을 위한 다양한 방법을 발달시켰다. 대다수의 육상 포유류와 새는 두꺼운 털이나 깃털을 길러 열의 흐름을 줄이고 따뜻함을 유지하는 데 필요한 에너지 비용을 낮춘다. 예를 들어, 겨울 털을 갖춘 북극 여우는 따뜻함을 유지하기 위해 신진 대사율을 변화시키지 않고도 영하 50도의 날씨에서도 편하게 앉아있을 수 있다. 동물이 사용하는 또 다른 방법은 혈액의 흐름을 통제하여 열 손실을 막기 위해 말단부 순환을 차단하는 것이다. 알래스카 허스키 개는 38도로 심부 체온을 유지하면서도 사지의 온도는 14도로 유지하고 발바닥은 0도로 유지한다. 그 결과 대부분의 중요한 기관이 있는 몸 중심부의 온도보다 팔다리의 온도를 몇 도 낮춰 열의 손실을 막을 수 있다. 북극곰의 경우 두꺼운 털과 11센티미터에 달하는 지방층, 빛에서 열을 흡수하는 어두운 피부색이 북극곰을 뛰어난 단열 기계로 만든다. 일부 동물은 몸의 열을 보존하기 위해 공 모양으로 몸을 둥글게 하는 등의 행동 적응 방식을 갖고 있다.

지문에 의하면, 추운 지역에서의 삶을 위한 북극곰의 적응 방법으로 언급되지 않은 것은

Ⓐ 두꺼운 지방 조직
Ⓑ 두꺼운 털층
Ⓒ 혈류에 변화를 줘서 추위를 누그러뜨리는 능력
Ⓓ 태양을 흡수하는 피부색

어휘 thermoregulation **n** 체온 조절 I ambient **adj** 환경의, 주변의 I fluctuate **v** 계속 변화하다, 변동을 거듭하다 I extreme **adj** 극도의, 극심한 I indigenous **adj** 원산의, 토착의 I plumage **n** 깃털 I metabolic **adj** 신진대사의 I forelimb **n** 앞다리 I dense **adj** 빽빽한, 조밀한 I peripheral **adj** 주변의, 지엽적인 I limb **n** 팔, 날개 I possess **v** 소유하다

13 페로몬

1 ➡ 의사 소통 체계로서의 페로몬 사용은 자연 세계 전반에 널리 퍼져 있다. 페로몬은 분비될 경우 한 개체가 같은 종의 다른 개체와 의사 소통할 수 있게 하는 특화된 화학 물질이다. 종종 '사회적인 호르몬'으로 불리는데 이는 한 종의 무리들에 영향을 미치기 때문이다. 페로몬 화학 물질 의사 소통은 시각적 혹은 청각적 의사 소통 방식과 여러 가지 차이가 있다. 우선 페로몬은 메시지를 먼 곳까지도 전달할 수 있는 반면 시각적, 청각적 의사 소통은 공간에 따라 엄격히 제한된다. 또한 시각과 청각은 메시지의 근원이 헷갈리기도 하지만 화학적 신호는 수신자에게 누가 그 메시지를 보냈는지 정확히 알려준다.

2 ➡ 페로몬은 곤충에만 국한된 것은 아니지만 수많은 곤충 종에서 발견된다. 사회적인 곤충들 즉 조직화된 무리에서 살아가는 곤충들은 상황에 따라 특정한 기능을 하는 다양한 페로몬을 만들어낸다. 비록 외분비선의 위치는 곤충 종마다 다르지만 페로몬 분비는 곤충 몸에 있는 여러 외분비선들을 통해 일어난다. 개미와 벌은 발달한 화학 신호 능력을 갖고 있는 좋은 예시다. 그러나 사람인 과학자들은 상대적으로 후각 기능이 덜 발달했기 때문에 이런 동물들의 개별 페로몬의 특징과 동일성을 이해하기 매우 어렵다.

3 ➡ 활동에 따라, 이 사회적인 곤충들은 별개의 페로몬을 사용한다. 예를 들어, 개미는 식량을 찾아 돌아다니다 식량을 지고 다시 보금자리로 돌아오는 일에 낮 시간의 대부분을 쓴다. 만약 보금자리가 경쟁 서식지나 다른 종에게 침입을 받았을 경우, 방어를 하는 개미는 모든 활동 가능한 보금자리 구성원들에게 돌아와서 방어하는 것을 도우라는 메시지를 보낼 수 있다. 공중에서 식량을 찾는 벌은 페로몬 흔적을 남길 수 있으며 이는 같은 벌집의 다른 벌들이 꿀로 가득 찬 좋은 화단을 찾아가도록 한다. 개미와 벌 모두 뒤에 페로몬 흔적을 남길 수 있어서 만일 길을 잃더라도 서식지로 다시 냄새를 맡고 돌아갈 수 있다.

1. 1단락에 따르면, 화학적 신호와 시청각 신호가 다른 점은

Ⓐ 인간은 시청각 능력보다 훨씬 더 강한 화학 신호 능력을 갖고 있다
Ⓑ 페로몬은 신호를 받는 데 적절한 능력을 갖춘 생물에 의해 먼 거리에서도 감지될 수 있다
Ⓒ 시청각적 의사 소통 사용은 화학 신호 의사 소통을 사용하는 것보다 훨씬 더 정확하다
Ⓓ 곤충은 청각 능력을 소유하고 있지만 화학 신호가 실패했을 때에만 청각 능력을 사용한다

2. 3단락에 따르면, 특정 사회적 곤충들이 사용하는 화학적 신호의 기능이 아닌 것은 무엇인가?

Ⓐ 보금자리나 집이 위험에 처했을 때 다른 이들을 집으로 부르기 위한 경보
Ⓑ 길을 잃었을 때 집을 찾는 방법
Ⓒ 먹이 공급원으로 가는 길을 다른 이들에게 알리는 방법
Ⓓ 다른 종의 일원을 위협하는 수단

어휘 communication **n** 의사소통 I specialized **adj** 특화된, 전문화된 I chemical **n** 화학 물질 I secrete **v** 분비하다 I visual **adj** 시각의 I auditory **adj** 청각의 I strictly **adv** 엄격하게 I limit **v** 제한하다 I distance **n** 거리 I exactly **adv** 정확히 I perplexing **adj** 당혹스러운 I insect **n** 곤충 I abundance **n** 풍부함, 많음 I organized **adj** 조직화된 I particular **adj** 특정한 I function **n** 기능 I dispensation **n** 분비 I exocrine gland 외분비선 I exact **adj** 정확한 I advanced **adj** 발달한 I relatively **adv** 상대적으로 I olfactory **adj** 후각의 I identification **n** 식별, 인지 I extremely **adv** 극도로, 극히 I scout **v** (찾아서) 돌아다니다, 정찰하다 I invade **v** 침략하다 I defense **n** 방어 I locate **v** 찾아내다 I flowerbed **n** 화단

14 집단 서식

1 ➡ 사회적인 동물을 생각할 때, 인간과 인간의 사촌인 영장류가 보통 떠오른다. 개미와 벌과 같은 곤충들 역시 사회적인 생명체의 일반적인 예이다. 그러나 사회적 활동은 특정 포유류나 곤충에 국한된 것이 아니다. 일부 새들 역시, 특히 쉴 때 사회적인 행동을 보여준다. 비록 어떤 새들은 매우 독립적인 생활을 하지만, 단체로 모여 지내는 집단 서식 행동을 보여주거나 무리를 지어 서식하는 새들이 있다.

2 ➡ 보통 무리를 지어 먹거리를 찾는 새들은 서식도 함께한다. 함께 먹이를 찾는 것이 집단에게 이득을 가져다 주듯, 집단 서식 또한 이점이 있다. 일부 새들이 집단적으로 서식하는 이유는 항상 분명히 드러나지는 않지만, 그 이유들 중 몇 가지는 매우 알아차리기 쉬우며 이치에 맞는다. 집단 서식은 아주 추운 겨울에 특히 이점이 있다. 비둘기, 참새, 그리고 파랑새는 겨울에 보온을 위해 함께 웅크려 지내는 일부 종들이다. 새

들은 함께 꼭 붙어 있으면서 추운 날씨에 노출되는 몸 표면적을 줄인다. 실제로 새 두 마리만 가까이 웅크려도 체열의 1/3까지 절약할 수 있다.

3 ➡ 집단 서식에서 얻는 또 다른 이점으로 생각되는 것은 새들이 정보를 직접 혹은 간접적으로 나누는 의사 교환 중심지 형태로 집단 서식지가 기능할 수 있다는 점이다. 무리를 지은 새들은 낮에 함께 먹이를 찾으며, 저녁에 다시 돌아왔을 때 각 무리는 누가 잘 먹었고 못 먹었는지 판단할 수 있다. 결과적으로, 잘 먹은 새들은 배고픈 새들이 그날 먹이를 찾으러 간 장소를 피할 수 있다. 이러한 관찰을 통해, 그날 먹이를 충분히 찾지 못한 무리는 먹이를 잘 섭취한 그룹을 따라 다음날 먹이가 풍부한 곳으로 갈 수 있다. 매일의 사냥에서 잡은 하나의 먹이에서 영양분을 섭취하는 혼자 사는 맹금류와 달리 이 정보는 먹이를 찾는 새들에게 매우 소중한 정보가 될 수 있다.

4 ➡ 마지막으로, 속담에서 말하듯 '뭉치면 산다.' 처음에는 큰 집단이 포식자의 주의를 끌기 때문에 집단으로 함께 떼를 짓는 것이 위험을 높일 수 있다. 그러나 새가 더 많다는 것은 위험 경고를 감지하는 눈이 더 많다는 것을 의미한다. 게다가 포식자가 공격해 왔을 때 그 갑작스런 소음과 떼 지은 비행은 포식자가 어떤 개체에 초점을 두어야 할지 헷갈리게 할 수 있다. 더구나 집단 서식하는 새들 중 어떤 종은 특히 둥지가 알이나 갓 부화한 새끼들로 가득 차 있을 때 포식자를 쫓기 위해 함께 공격하기도 한다.

1. 2단락에 따르면, 새들은 어떻게 집단 서식에서 함께 모여 따뜻함을 유지할 수 있는가?

Ⓐ 함께 모임으로써 각 새의 몸 표면이 차가운 공기에 더 많이 노출된다.
Ⓑ 더 두꺼운 깃털을 가진 새들이 집단 바깥쪽으로 모인다.
Ⓒ 추위에 노출된 정도를 줄이는 것이 체온 손실을 줄인다.
Ⓓ 함께 모임으로써 새들의 열기가 서식지를 따뜻하게 한다.

2. 지문에 따르면, 다음 중 집단 서식의 이점이 아닌 것은 무엇인가?

Ⓐ 새들은 자신을 공격하려고 하는 다른 생물을 함께 힘을 모아 쫓아버릴 수 있다.
Ⓑ 새들은 추운 겨울 밤에 체온 손실 정도를 줄일 수 있다.
Ⓒ 새들은 다른 무리와 함께 서식하지 않음으로써 조류 관련 질병의 확산을 막을 수 있다.
Ⓓ 새들은 함께 서식하는 새들을 관찰하여 가장 먹이를 찾기 좋은 곳을 구별할 수 있다.

어휘 communal roosting 집단 서식 | forage v 식량을 찾아다니다 | sustenance n 음식물, 먹이 | frigid adj 몹시 추운 | huddle v 떼지어 모이다 | solitary adj 군거하지 않는, 혼자인 | invaluable adj 매우 귀중한 | abrupt adj 갑작스런 | drive v 만들다, 몰아가다 | hatchling n 갓 부화한 새

---

15 **다다이즘**

1 ➡ 혁신적인 문화 운동의 하나인 다다이즘은 제1차 세계대전 중이던 1916년부터 1920년 사이 스위스에서 절정에 달했다. 이 운동은 주로 시각 예술, 공연 예술 및 거의 모든 형태의 문학을 포함했다. 이는 반예술이라 알려진 문화적 활동을 통해 반전 정신 또는 대중 예술과 전통 예술에 대한 총체적인 거부에 초점을 맞추었다. 이러한 운동에 왜 다다이즘이라는 이름이 붙었는지는 명확하지 않지만 아무 의미 없는 임의의 단어라는 설에서부터 루마니아어로 'yes, yes'라는 의미의 'da, da'에서 유래했다는 설까지 다양하다. 그 용어의 기원이 무엇이든 다다이즘은 예술계에 큰 영향을 주게 되었다.

2 ➡ 다다이즘은 제1차 세계대전의 폭력성에 대한 반발로서 반전 운동의 일환으로 시작되었다. 1916년 휴고 볼, 트리스탄 차라, 에미 헤닝스를 비롯한 한 무리의 예술가들이 스위스 취리히의 카바레 볼테르에 모여 예술에 대해 토론하고 공연을 상연했다. 이러한 활동의 주된 초점은 전쟁과 그 대의에 관한 혐오감을 표현하는 것이었다. 다다이스트들은 억압적 지성주의와 부유층의 이해 관계를 전쟁의 원인으로 보았다. 카바레 볼테르가 폐쇄된 뒤 다다 운동가들은 유럽 전역에서 캠페인을 벌여 예술적 표현, 입소문, 다다 간행물을 통해 자신들의 사상을 확산시켰다. 1918년 제1차 세계대전이 끝나면서 취리히의 초창기 다다이스트들 대부분은 자국으로 돌아갔고, 일부는 다다 운동을 확장하기 시작했다. 다다이즘은 파리, 베를린, 뉴욕시, 러시아 일부 지역 등 서구 세계의 도시로 퍼지면서 발전했다.

3 ➡ 다다이즘과 전통적인 예술의 개념은 매우 다르다. 다다이스트들에 따르면 그들은 '반예술'을 창조했는데, 목적은 전통적인 예술 개념에 대항하기 위함이었다. 예술은 주로 미학 및 의미 전달에 관한 것인 반면, 다다이즘은 미학에 아무런 관심도 기울이지 않고 관람하는 이에게 해석을 맡겼다. 예술은 감수성에 호소하려 하지만 다다이스트의 작품은 불쾌하게 하려는 의도를 갖고 있었다. 다다이즘의 아이러니는 그것이 기존의 문화적 미학을 파괴하고자 했음에도 실제로는 모든 형태의 현대 예술에 영향을 주게 되었다는 점이다.

4 ➡ 다다이즘에 가장 큰 영향을 준 이전 사조들 중 하나로 미래주의가 있는데, 이는 전통을 멀리하고 속도, 기술과 폭력을 포용하는 예술 동향이다. 미래주의는 1909년 이탈리아 예술가들 사이에서 유래했다. 그러나 미래주의와 다다이즘의 반체제 사이에는 커다란 차이점이 있다. 다다이즘은 전쟁에 반대했지만 미래주의는 전쟁의 기술과 기계 시대를 찬양했다는 점이다. 미래주의의 그림과 조각은 전쟁을 미화하고 파시즘의 성장을 옹호했다. 미래주의가 다다이즘에 끼친 주된 영향은 작품에 사용된 소재의 다양성과 관람하는 이의 해석이라는 아이디어였다.

5 ➡ 다다이즘은 다른 형태의 예술에 뿌리를 두고 있지만 이후 나타난 다른 형식의 뿌리가 되기도 했다. 다다이즘으로부터 나타난 사조 중 가장 눈에 띄는 건 초현실주의였다. 그러나 다다이즘의 많은 특징이 초현실주의에도 두드러지게 나타났기 때문에 1920년대에 이르러 다다이즘이

초현실주의로 변형되었다고 말하는 편이 보다 정확할 것이다. 두 가지 운동 모두 소재의 다양성을 강조했고, 그림부터 음악까지 폭넓은 예술 매체에 영향을 주었으며 관람하는 이가 각자의 인식을 바탕으로 보이는 것을 해석하는 자유를 장려했다.

6 ➡ 다다이즘은 그 속성상 우리가 알고 있는 예술에 대한 문화적 인식에 반대했지만 유행했던 기간이 상대적으로 짧았음에도 커다란 여파를 몰고 올 수 있었다. 이런 운동이 절정에 다다른 것은 1924년이었으나 어떤 형태로든 오늘날까지 계속되고 있다. 제1차 세계대전이 끝난 후 다다이즘이 원래 지니고 있던 냉소적인 속성과 반대로 예술과 문학에 낙관주의가 새로이 샘솟으면서 다다이즘은 활기를 잃게 되었다.

1. 2단락에 따르면, 다다 운동가들이 유럽 전역을 여행한 이유는

Ⓐ 유럽은 모든 예술 운동의 중심이었다
Ⓑ 제1차 세계대전이 종전을 맞았다
Ⓒ 다른 이들에게 메시지를 전달하고 싶어했다
Ⓓ 스위스에는 지성인과 부유한 사람들이 너무 많았다

2. 4단락에 따르면, 다음 중 미래주의에 관한 내용으로 사실인 것은?

Ⓐ 미래주의는 미술 재료의 선택에 제한을 두지 않았다.
Ⓑ 미래주의는 예술 작품으로서 다양한 무기의 형태를 발명하는 데 도움을 주었다.
Ⓒ 미래주의는 파시즘의 발현에 맞서 싸웠다.
Ⓓ 미래주의자들은 보는 사람이 예술 작품의 의미를 해석할 필요가 없어야 한다고 믿었다.

어휘 peak v 정점에 달하다 I visual art 시각 예술 I sentiment n 감정, 정서 I rejection n 거부 I random adj 임의의 I oppressive adj 억압적인 I intellectualism n 지성주의 I extension n 확장 I disseminate v 전파하다 I combat v 싸우다 I predominantly adv 주로 I aesthetics n 미학 I appeal v 호소하다 I predecessor n 전신 I embrace v 포용하다 I protest v 항의하다 I promote v 장려하다 I reform v 변형하다 I prominent adj 두드러진 I stab v 찌르다 I relay v 전달하다 I sensibility n 감성 I shun v 피하다 I dissidence n 반체제, 불일치 I glorify v 찬양하다 I surrealism n 초현실주의 I perception n 인식 I comparatively adv 상대적으로 I attribute n 속성 I cynical adj 냉소적인

---

16 **고대 수메르와 이집트 문명**

1 ➡ 고대 이집트와 메소포타미아에서 이루어진 관개 시스템의 발명은 수천 년 동안 지속된 강력한 문명의 발전으로 이어졌다. 두 문명 모두 가까운 강에서 제공되는 자원을 이용하는 능력 덕분에 번영할 수 있었다. 이집트의 중심은 나일 계곡에 자리 잡았던 반면 현재 이라크의 일부인 티그리스와 유프라테스강 사이의 지역은 메소포타미아 문명이 처음 발달한 지역이다. 두 개의 큰 강이 이 지역의 문명 발달과 직접 관련되었으므로 그리스어로 '강 사이'라는 뜻을 지닌 메소포타미아는 아주 적절한 이름이라 할 수 있다.

2 ➡ 고대 이집트인과 수메르인 모두 강이 제공하는 혜택을 활용하는 데 매우 능수능란했다. 복잡한 관개 시스템 개발을 통해 이들은 습지대에서 물을 빼고 운하를 팠으며 강둑을 터서 강에서 멀리 떨어진 낮은 지역에 심은 작물들에게까지 물을 대었다. 그런 시스템의 유지에는 대규모의 협력이 필수적이었고 이는 곧 정부와 법의 필요성과 성장을 가져왔다. 넓은 사막 사이에 상대적으로 비옥한 지역이 격리되어 있는 형태의 이집트는 한 파라오 아래 잘 뭉칠 수 있었던 반면, 수메르인은 방대한 지역에 있는 도시국가들을 통합하는 데 어려움을 겪었다. 메소포타미아는 외부의 침략에 훨씬 더 취약했고 가뭄부터 홍수, 극한 기온과 험한 폭풍우까지 자연적인 장애물과 끊임없이 싸워야 했다.

3 ➡ 두 지역에서 집을 짓고 농장을 만들기 위해 사용된 기본적인 재료는 최초의 부족들이 정착해 공동체를 형성했을 때 이후로 거의 변함이 없었다. 이러한 재료로는 진흙 벽돌과 진흙 반죽이 있었는데 두 가지 모두 강의 토양에서 자연적으로 발견되는 점토로 만들어진 것이었다. 점토는 도자기, 조각, 서판을 만드는 데도 사용되었다. 적절히 반죽하고 충분한 건조 과정을 거친 점토 제품은 놀랄 만큼 튼튼했으며 현재까지 많이 남아 있다. 두 지역 모두 사막에 둘러싸여 있었기 때문에 나무는 귀해서 문이나 덧창문 이외에는 거의 사용되지 않았다. 이집트에서는 석회암을 비롯한 돌을 구할 수 있었지만 메소포타미아 전역에서는 돌이 귀했다. 금, 은, 구리와 같은 금속, 조개껍데기, 보석도 장식에 사용되었다.

4 ➡ 이집트와 수메르 정부는 종교 생활 및 신앙과 직접적으로 관련되어 있었다. 전형적인 메소포타미아 종교 및 상업 시설의 구조는 지구라트로, 즉 그 유명한 매끈한 옆면의 이집트 스타일 피라미드와 달리 계단으로 된 성탑 형태였다. 그러나 수메르든 이집트든 모든 큰 마을들은 신전 건축에 자부심을 가졌다. 예를 들어, 규모가 큰 지구라트 중 하나인 백색 신전은 높이가 약 12미터에 달하는 토대 위에 세워져 있었다. 지구라트에 딸린 계단의 목적은 사제나 왕을 특정 신에게 좀 더 가까이 두기 위한 것이거나 반대로 예배자들을 만나기 위해 신이 내려오도록 플랫폼을 제공하기 위한 것이기도 했다. 고대 이집트인과 달리 메소포타미아인들은 통치자가 진짜 신이 아니라 신의 자손이거나 신들과 평범한 인간 사이의 중개자라고 믿었다. 그들은 '우주의 왕' 같은 고상한 호칭을 쓰기도 했고 백성들의 수호자로서의 역할을 인식해 '목자' 같은 좀 더 겸손한 호칭을 택하기도 했다. 각 수메르 신들은 특정한 마을과 결부되었고 하늘, 물, 바람 같은 자연의 힘을 대표했다. 사람들은 지구라트에서 신들을 숭배하기도 했지만 각 가정에 마련된 작은 사당에서 예배를 드리기도 했다.

5 ➡ 수메르와 고대 이집트 종교에서 발견되는 또 하나의 큰 차이점은 죽음 뒤의 삶에 대한 관심이었다. 이집트의 장례 절차에서는 중요 인물

들의 다음 생을 위해 세심한 준비가 이루어졌지만 수메르인들은 이 문제에 대해 그리 깊이 생각하지 않았다. 따라서 현재까지 남아 있는 점토판에서 발견되는 수메르인들의 글 대부분은 일과 도시 행정, 법, 정치, 출생 및 사망 신고, 경제 등의 일상적인 활동을 다루고 있다. 이는 사후 세계를 준비하는 절차와 죽음 뒤에 일어난다고 믿었던 일들이 남아 있는 기록의 상당 부분을 차지했던 이집트와 대조적이다. 또한 이집트의 피라미드는 죽은 사람을 수용하기 위해 만들어졌던 반면, 메소포타미아의 지구라트는 일상 생활에서 신들과의 소통을 위한 장소로 활용되었다.

1. 2단락에 따르면, 다음 중 수메르인들에 관해 옳은 것은 무엇인가?

Ⓐ 사람들이 충성하는 한 명의 지도자가 있었다.
Ⓑ 외부의 공격과 해결하기 어려운 기상 상황에 시달렸다.
Ⓒ 최초로 알려진 문명을 세웠다.
Ⓓ 다른 부족을 자주 공격했다.

2. 4단락에 따르면, 다음 중 지구라트에 관해 사실이 아닌 것은 무엇인가?

Ⓐ 옆면이 계단으로 되어 있었다.
Ⓑ 오직 종교적 목적만을 위한 것이었다.
Ⓒ 모든 주요 마을에 있었다.
Ⓓ 계단은 사제가 신에게 더 가까이 갈 수 있게 해주는 것으로 인식되었다.

어휘 civilization n 문명 | irrigation n 관개 | prosper v 번영하다 | nestle v 자리잡다 | harness v 이용하다 | drain v 물을 빼내다 | dig v 파다 | riverbank n 강둑 | redirect v 방향을 바꾸다 | cooperation n 협력 | isolated adj 격리된, 떨어진 | unify v 통합하다 | invasion n 침입 | bountiful adj 풍부한 | susceptible adj 취약한 | obstacle n 장애물 | drought n 가뭄 | decorative adj 장식적인 | be associated with ~과 연관되다 | afterlife n 내세 | brick n 벽돌 | plaster n 회반죽 | clay n 점토 | pottery n 도자기 | sturdy adj 튼튼한 | scarce adj 부족한, 드문 | primarily adv 주로 | rare adj 희귀한 | precious adj 소중한 | proximity n 근접 | descend v 하강하다 | intermediator n 중개자 | lofty adj 아주 높은, 우뚝 솟은 | shrine n 사당

Test

본서 | P. 80

베니스의 상수도

1 ➡ 베니스는 유럽에서 가장 인기 있는 관광지 중 하나이며 길거리 대신 활용되는 수로 체계로 가장 잘 알려져 있다. 수로로 분리되고 가능한 곳엔 다리로 연결된 117개의 섬 위에 지어진 이곳은 진정으로 유일무이한 도시다. 도시의 정체성은 그것이 위치한 석호의 물로 정의되지만 도시는 시작부터 역설적인 딜레마로 어려움을 겪었다. 베니스 사람들에게 수 세기 동안 도피처와 거주지를 제공한 이 섬들은 그들에게 결코 충분한 식수를 제공할 수 없었다. 15세기의 한 프랑스 방문객이 말한 것처럼 "물이 거주민들의 입까지 차오른 도시에서 그들은 자주 목말라했다." 역사를 통틀어 이 결핍을 해결하기 위해 다양한 방법들이 사용되었지만 그 어떠한 것도 완벽하게 만족스럽지 못했다.

2 ➡ 베니스가 5세기에 세워졌을 때 그 위치는 풍성한 자원이 아니라 그곳이 제공하는 안전성 때문에 선택되었다. 수 세기에 걸쳐 베니스의 지형은 이 도시가 해상 세력으로 발달하게 해 주었지만, 또한 사람들이 절대로 완전하게 극복하지 못한 문제를 제시했다. 믿을 만한 식수 원천이 없었던 것이다. 비록 많은 강들이 그 석호로 물을 흘려 보냈지만 아드리아해의 강력한 수압이 담수가 섬들로 흘러가는 것을 막았기 때문에 섬들 주변의 물은 사람들이 마실 물로 쓰기에는 너무 짰다. 대신 그 물은 다른 가정 및 산업 용도로 사용되었다. 각 가정은 서로 다른 두 가지 종류의 양동이를 갖고 있었는데 한 종류는 목욕, 빨래와 집 청소를 위해 수로에서 물을 긷는 용도로, 또 다른 종류는 식수를 모으고 보관하는 용도로 사용되었다.

1. 1단락에서 글쓴이가 '15세기의 한 프랑스 방문객'을 언급하는 이유는 무엇인가?

Ⓐ 중세시대 이후 유럽의 물 부족 문제를 전형적으로 보여주기 위해
Ⓑ 해안 도시의 문제점을 가리키는 고대 속담을 소개하기 위해
Ⓒ 베니스의 끊임없이 계속되는 문제를 직접 경험한 이야기를 제공하기 위해
Ⓓ 베니스가 과거에도 인기 있는 관광지였다는 것을 시사하기 위해

2. 2단락에서 추론 가능한 것은 무엇인가?

Ⓐ 베니스는 원래 전략적인 군사 기지로 세워졌었다.
Ⓑ 섬들을 둘러싼 짠물은 아드리아해에서 유래된다.
Ⓒ 베니스는 천연 자원이 부족한 도시다.
Ⓓ 수로는 가정용과 식수용을 위한 물의 수요를 둘 다 충족시켰다.

3. 3단락의 단어 'pronouncement(공표)'와 의미상 가장 가까운 것은

Ⓐ 폭로
Ⓑ 언급
Ⓒ 정책
Ⓓ 성명

3 ➡ 이런 세심한 구분에도 불구하고 베니스 사람들은 수로의 물이 오염되지 않도록 주의해야 했다. 수질을 유지하기 위해 시의회는 14세기 초반에 산업체들이 수로에 폐기물을 버리는 것을 금하는 공표를 내렸다. 그들은 특별히 직물업계를 겨냥했고, 직물과 염색된 물질을 수로에서 세탁하는 것과 염색 과정에서 나온 폐수를 수로에 버리는 것을 둘 다 금했다. 많은 상인들은 그 규칙들을 거역했지만 한 세기 내로 악취가 나는 부산물을 배출하는 모든 산업은 도시의 바닷가 쪽으로 강제로 이동하게 되었다. 그 이후로 염색업자, 도살업자와 다른 사람들은 그들의 폐기물을 석호에 버려야 했다. 이런 생태 보존의 초기 형태는 베니스 사람들이 가정용으로 적당히 깨끗한 물을 사용할 수 있게끔 했다.

4 ➡ 하지만 담수를 확보하는 것은 훨씬 더 어려운 일로 드러났다. 초기에 섬사람들은 본토에서 물을 운반할 수밖에 없었는데 이것은 많은 이유에서 어려웠다. 베니스 사람들은 물 공급의 순도를 관리할 수 없었고, 물을 얻기 위해 육지로 나가는 것은 그들을 적대적인 이웃들의 공격에 노출시켰으며, 물은 매우 무거웠다. 그들은 곧 섬 지하에 두꺼운 점토 벽으로 둘러싸인 빗물을 모은 모래 광상이 있다는 것을 발견했다. [■A] 그들은 모래를 파서 이런 광상들을 우물로 사용할 수 있었지만 공급은 제한적이었다. [■B] 하지만 이것들은 9세기의 혁신으로 이어졌다. 베니스 사람들은 빗물을 모으고 정화하는 수조들을 만들었다. [■C] 낙수받이는 지하실로 흐르는 중앙 배수관으로 연결되었다. [■D] 그 물은 점토 통을 덮은 석회석과 모래 여과층을 통과했다. 그 통에서 물이 파이프를 통해 작은 분수로 올라왔고 사람들은 그것을 모아서 식수로 쓸 수 있었다.

5 ➡ 이런 수조들의 건설은 꽤 비쌌기 때문에 초반의 수조들은 부유한 시민들의 개인 땅에 위치했고 오직 그들의 직원과 세입자들만 물을 이용할 수 있었다. 나중에 도시는 공용으로 물을 제공하기 위해 다른 큰 수조들을 지었고 우물의 개수는 급격히 증가했으며 이것은 섬들로의 이주를 다시 불러일으켰다. 이런 큰 수조들의 건설은 흑사병으로 중단되었지만 작업은 15세기에 재개되었다. 더 큰 수조들을 위해 그들은 도시 광장을 중앙 배수관을 향해 완만하게 경사지게 만들어서 모아지는 물의 양을 극대화했다. 그럼에도 불구하고 이런 우물들은 영구적인 해결책을 제공하지는 못했는데, 이것은 우물들이 도시를 침수시켜 수조 물을 짜게 만드는 폭풍우에 취약했고, 또한 날씨에 전적으로 의존했기 때문에 건기가 닥치기라도 하면 육지로 가서 강물을 길어와야 했기 때문이다. 그 물은 수조에 부어지거나 판매되었다.

6 ➡ 베니스가 궁극적으로 본토에 의존한 채로 남았기 때문에 물을 운반하는 보다 영구적인 방법들이 도시 당국에 제안되었다. 여기에는 강물을 섬들에 직접적으로 운송하는 것과 송수로를 건설하는 것이 포함되었지만 이것들은 전혀 실현되지 않았다. 이런 작업에 들어가는 어마어마한 비용이 그 생각들이 단순히 생각 이상으로 발전되는 것을 막았다. 따라서 수조는 19세기에 현대 기술이 드디어 본토에서 파이프를 통해 물을 보낼 수 있는 경제적인 방법을 제공하기 전까지 가장 최선의 방법으로 남아 있었다.

4. **4단락의 단어 'obliged(~할 수밖에 없었다)'와 의미상 가장 가까운 것은**

Ⓐ 설득했다
Ⓑ (강제로) ~하게 만들었다
Ⓒ 붙잡았다
Ⓓ 동원했다

5. **4단락에 따르면, 베니스 사람들은 담수를 어떻게 확보했는가? 두 개를 고르시오.**

Ⓐ 낙수받이를 배수관으로 연결함
Ⓑ 육지로 나가 물을 확보함
Ⓒ 지하 모래 광상을 활용함
Ⓓ 강물을 정화함

6. **다음 중 지문에 음영 표시된 문장의 핵심 정보를 가장 잘 표현한 문장은 무엇인가? 오답은 의미를 크게 왜곡하거나 핵심 정보를 누락하고 있다.**

Ⓐ 그 우물들은 날씨 변수에 대한 민감성 때문에 물 부족 문제를 완전히 해결하지 못했고 이것은 사람들이 대안 수단을 찾아야 했다는 것을 뜻한다.
Ⓑ 홍수와 건기의 원인이 되는 불리한 기후 조건은 물을 오염시켰고 그것에 의존하던 사람들이 강물로 돌아서게끔 했다.
Ⓒ 그 우물들 자체로는 사람들의 수요를 충족시킬 수 없었는데 이것은 그것들이 짠 물로 범람되고 종종 말라버리기까지 해서 강물에 연결되어야 했기 때문이다.
Ⓓ 그 우물들은 처음에는 영구적인 해결책으로 의도된 것이 아니었는데 이것은 물에 염분이 섞이거나 완전히 증발하는 것이 그 우물들이 기후 조건에 의존한다는 것을 명백하게 했기 때문이다.

7. **다음 중 5단락에서 수조들의 문제점으로 언급되지 않은 것은 무엇인가?**

Ⓐ 그저 일시적인 해결책 역할을 했다.
Ⓑ 건기에 말라버렸다.
Ⓒ 짠물로 범람될 수 있었다.
Ⓓ 강물로 계속 보충할 필요가 있었다.

8. **다음 중 지문에서 사용 가능한 물을 확보하는 방법으로 활용되지 않은 것은**

Ⓐ 공용으로 큰 수조들을 건축하는 것
Ⓑ 물을 오염시키는 산업을 해안가로 분리하는 것
Ⓒ 강물을 운반하는 송수로를 건설하는 것
Ⓓ 육지로 나가 판매용으로 강물을 길어오는 것

9. 지문에 다음 문장이 들어갈 수 있는 위치를 나타내는 네 개의 사각형 [■]을 확인하시오.

하지만 이것들은 9세기의 혁신으로 이어졌다.

이 문장이 들어가기에 가장 적합한 곳은? [■B]

10. **지시문:** 지문을 간략하게 요약한 글의 첫 문장이 아래 제시되어 있다. 지문의 가장 중요한 내용을 표현하는 세 개의 선택지를 골라 요약문을 완성하시오. 일부 문장들은 지문에 제시되지 않았거나 지문의 지엽적인 내용을 나타내기 때문에 요약문에 포함되지 않는다. ***이 문제의 배점은 2점이다.***

미덥지 못한 물 공급에도 불구하고 베니스는 시민들의 독창성과 투지를 통해 살아 남았다.

Ⓐ 초반에 도시는 수로를 오염시키는 폐기물을 배출하는 산업체들을 해안가로 밀어내는 규정을 시행하고 가정용 물을 확보했다.
Ⓔ 도시 내 수조의 개수 증가에도 불구하고 그것들은 너무 많은 강수량과 너무 적은 강수량 둘 다에 부정적으로 영향을 받았기 때문에 안정적인 해결책이 아니었다.
Ⓕ 베니스를 본토와 연결하는 다양한 방법들은 높은 비용 때문에 결실을 맺지 못했다가 19세기에 드디어 수도관이 설치되었다.

Ⓑ 지하 모래 광상에 모아진 빗물은 식수용으로 빗물을 의도적으로 모으는 것에 대한 영감을 제공했다.
Ⓒ 석호에 위치해 있음에도 불구하고 베니스가 깨끗한 물이 부족한 이유는 아드리아해의 수압 때문이다.
Ⓓ 수조들은 지하실에 빗물을 모아 석회석과 모래를 통과시켜 그것을 정화했다.

어휘 tourist destination 관광지 | canal n 운하, 수로 | feasible adj 실현 가능한 | lagoon n 석호 | ironic adj 역설적인 | inception n 시작, 개시 | inhabitant n 주민 | lack n 부족, 결핍 | found v 설립하다 | terrain n 지형 | maritime adj 바다의, 해양의 | potable water 음료수, 식수 | water pressure 수압 | consumption n 소비, 소모 | pronouncement n 공표, 선언 | forbid v 금하다 | waste n 폐기물 | textile n 직물, 옷감 | prohibit v 금하다 | wastewater n 폐수 | dyeing n 염색, 염직 | byproduct n 부산물 | henceforth adv ~이후로 | ecological adj 생태계의 | preservation n 보존 | fresh water 담수, 민물 | oblige v 의무적으로 ~하게 하다 | mainland n 본토 | go ashore 상륙하다, 뭍에 오르다 | hostile adj 적대적인 | clay n 점토 | cistern n 수조 | rain gutter 낙수받이 | drain n 배수관 | limestone n 석회석 | tub n 통 | tenant n 세입자 | rekindle v 다시 불러일으키다 | immigration n 이주, 이민 | resume v 재개하다 | slope v 경사지다, 기울어지다 | vulnerable adj 취약한 | brackish adj 염분이 섞인 | dry spell 건조기 | civic adj 도시의 | aqueduct n 송수로 | realize v 실현하다 | economical adj 경제적인 | means n 수단

조류의 뇌

1 ➡ 모든 동물 종에게 뇌 조직은 몸에서 가장 무거운 조직이다. 이런 이유로 인하여 뇌 크기는 간단한 규칙을 따르는 듯하다. 동물의 뇌는 필요한 만큼 크고 가능한 만큼 작다. 예를 들면 조류는 비행을 쉽게 하고 공기 저항을 감소시키기 위해 머리의 크기와 무게를 줄여야 한다. [■A] 하지만 많은 조류는 사실 몸 크기에 비해 꽤 큰 머리와 뇌를 가지고 있다. [■B] 실제로 그들의 뇌는 그들의 조상인 공룡들의 것보다 몸 크기에 비해 훨씬 더 크다. 뇌의 불균형한 크기를 보완하기 위해 몇몇 조류는 무게를 줄이기 위해 뇌의 일부분을 변형할 수 있다. [■C] 이것의 한 예는 흔히 번식기인 봄에는 더 커졌다가 더 필요하지 않을 때는 줄어드는 소리핵*이다. [■D]

2 ➡ 또한 조류의 뇌는 뇌 편재화라고 불리는 구조적인 특성을 통해 최소의 공간을 최대한 활용한다. 뇌는 꽤 비슷해 보이는 우뇌와 좌뇌로 나뉘지만 이 둘은 동일하지 않다. 그들은 구조적 차이와 특화된 기능을 가지고 있는데 어떤 능력들은 한쪽에서 발생하지만 그 반대 편에서는 발생하지 않는다. 기본적으로 몸의 왼편은 우뇌의 통제를 받고 그 반대로도 그렇다. 한쪽의 특정 구역이 특정 종류의 정보를 처리하는 주된 임무를 맡게 된다는 점에서 차이점이 더 세부적으로

11. 1단락에 따르면, 소리핵의 크기가 감소하는 이유는 무엇인가?
Ⓐ 머리 속의 압력을 낮추기 위해
Ⓑ 그것에 대한 조류의 의존도를 감소시키기 위해
Ⓒ 번식기 중 공기 저항을 최소화시키기 위해
Ⓓ 뇌 크기를 최적화된 상태로 유지시키기 위해

12. 2단락에 따르면, 뇌 편재화에 대해 사실인 것은 무엇인가?
Ⓐ 그것은 각 부분이 서로 비슷하게 보이는 모습으로 뇌를 나눈다.
Ⓑ 그것은 지능을 나타내는 특성이다.
Ⓒ 모든 능력은 관련된 데이터를 처리하는 데 특화된 한쪽으로 제한되어 있다.
Ⓓ 그것은 뇌의 한쪽이 몸 반대쪽을 제어할 수 있게 한다.

13. 다음 중 3단락에서 닭에 대한 실험에 대해 언급된 것은 무엇인가?
Ⓐ 오른쪽 눈에서 받은 정보가 좌뇌로 이동되기 때문에 왼쪽 눈이 덮인 닭은 모래에서 씨앗을 구분해 낼 수 있다.

드러나게 된다. 낮은 지능을 소유한 것으로 간주되던 동물들도 포함해 동물 대부분은 어느 정도의 편재화를 나타낸다.

3 ➡ 예를 들어서 닭은 좌뇌를 사용하여 음식을 찾고 우뇌로 위협을 감지하는 시각 편재화를 보인다. 과학자들은 눈 덮개를 사용해 닭이 눈을 어떻게 사용하는지 알아내기 위한 실험을 진행했다. 그들은 닭에게 작은 돌멩이와 섞여 있는 씨앗을 주었고 닭이 먹을 수 있는 것들을 골라내는 동안 포식자 모형이 습격을 흉내내며 공격적으로 다가오게 했다. 오른쪽 눈이 덮인 닭은 모래와 씨앗을 구분하는 데 어려움을 겪은 반면에 왼쪽 눈이 덮인 닭은 주변의 위협을 눈치채지 못했다. 몸 한 편의 수용체가 반대쪽 뇌로 정보를 보내기 때문에 이것은 닭의 좌뇌가 작은 세부 사항과 범주화와 관련된 시각 자극을 처리하는 반면에 거리와 운동 지각과 관련된 자극은 우뇌가 처리한다는 것을 뜻한다. 양쪽 눈이 덮이지 않은 닭은 두 가지를 전부 잘 볼 수 있었다. 이런 편재화를 통해 닭은 포식자를 경계하며 먹이를 먹을 수 있는데, 이것은 고급 생존 기법이다.

4 ➡ 높은 지능과 편재화된 행동을 나타내는 조류는 흔히 명금이라고 불리는 참새목 조류들이다. 이 새들은 가장 발달된 소리핵을 보유하고 있는데 연구들은 이들이 뇌 양쪽을 사용해 노래를 부르고 이해한다는 것을 보여주었다. 이런 종 중 하나가 금화조인데 매우 소리가 크고 활동적인 명금으로 알려져 있다. 배아일 때 분비되는 테스토스테론 때문에 오직 수컷 금화조만 노래한다. 이런 호르몬의 투입은 소리핵의 발달을 촉발시키고 이 호르몬은 또한 짝짓기 시기 중 핵의 성장을 촉발시킨다. 노래 부르기의 편재화는 금화조 뇌에서 시작되는데, 핵의 좌편은 새가 듣는 노래를 이해하는 데 사용된다. 자신이 듣는 노래가 동종의 것인지 타종의 것인지 결정하고 다른 금화조들의 노래를 구분하는 데 이 영역을 사용한다. 오른쪽은 노래 생산에 사용되고 새 노래의 리듬, 멜로디, 음의 높이와 크기를 통제한다.

5 ➡ 금화조의 노래 부르기의 편재화는 그들의 발성 기관으로 확장된다. 울대라고 불리는 조류의 발성 기관은 폐가 기도로 연결되는 부분에 위치한다. 울대의 모양을 변형시키고 폐에서 공기를 밀어내면서 울대의 부분들을 진동시킴으로써 노래한다. 울대 양쪽은 각각 별개로 제어될 수 있는데 이 제어권은 금화조의 소리핵에게 있다는 것이 밝혀졌다. 울대 오른편이 우세한 쪽으로 노래 대부분을 만들어낸다. 왼편은 노래의 리듬과 타이밍에 영향을 주는 음을 추가한다. 양쪽이 각각 따로 제어될 수 있기 때문에 새들은 한 번에 한 음 이상을 낼 수 있다.

6 ➡ 비록 공룡들은 현대 조류들보다 비교적 작은 뇌를 소유했지만 과학자들은 그들이 후손들처럼 편재화된 뇌를 지녔을 거라 추측한다. 공룡들은 오늘날 광물화된 뼈 화석으로만 존재하기 때문에 뇌의 내부 구조를 복원하는 것은 불가능하다. 두개골 구조는 몇몇 종이 소리를 내는 것은 가능했지만 그런 구조로 정교한 노래를 부를 수는 없었을 거라는 것을 보여준다. 그러므로 과학자들은 그들이 뇌에 소리핵과 같은 특별한 신경 조직을 보유했을 거라고는 확신하지 않는다.

***소리핵**: 조류 두뇌에서 노래를 만들어 내는 역할을 전담하는 세포괴

Ⓑ 닭의 우뇌는 왼편보다 움직임을 지각하는 능력이 뛰어나서 닭이 오른쪽 눈을 사용하여 잠재적인 포식자를 추적하기 쉽게 만든다.
Ⓒ 양쪽 눈을 사용할 때 닭은 특정 데이터를 처리하는 것을 뇌 한쪽으로 제한시키는 성향을 보여주지 않는다.
Ⓓ 닭 뇌의 각 반구가 어떻게 특화되었는지 보여주는 이 실험의 결과는 다른 조류 종에게도 적용된다고 볼 수 있다.

14. **다음 중 지문에 음영 표시된 문장의 핵심 정보를 가장 잘 표현한 문장은 무엇인가? 오답은 의미를 크게 왜곡하거나 핵심 정보를 누락하고 있다.**
Ⓐ 서로 다른 수용체들이 뇌에 다른 정보를 전달하기 때문에 닭의 뇌는 서로 다른 종류의 데이터를 그에 맞춰 처리할 수 있다.
Ⓑ 몸 왼편에 있는 수용체가 우뇌에 정보를 보내고 그 반대로도 그렇기 때문에 이것은 뇌의 각 반구가 특화되었다는 것을 뜻한다.
Ⓒ 수용체가 데이터를 뇌의 다른 편으로 전달하기 때문에 뇌의 각 반구는 분명히 서로 다른 종류의 정보를 처리하는 것으로 특화되어 있다.
Ⓓ 수용체는 좌뇌가 데이터를 분류하고 사소한 세부 사항을 감지할 수 있게 하는 동시에 우뇌가 움직임을 추적할 수 있게 한다.

15. **글쓴이가 4단락에서 금화조를 언급하는 이유는 무엇인가?**
Ⓐ 뇌 편재화가 어떻게 시각 기능을 넘어서서 확장될 수 있는지를 논의하기 위해
Ⓑ 노래 부르는 능력이 명금 조류들 안에서 어떻게 발달하는지 묘사하기 위해
Ⓒ 명금들은 닭보다 높은 수준의 지능을 갖고 있다는 것을 제안하기 위해
Ⓓ 잘 발달된 소리핵을 지닌 조류들에 대해 논의하기 위해

16. **5단락에 따르면, 다음 중 금화조의 발성 능력에 대해 언급되지 않은 것은**
Ⓐ 울대의 왼편은 노래 생산에 작은 역할을 한다
Ⓑ 소리핵은 울대의 제어를 맡고 있다
Ⓒ 울대의 우세한 편은 뇌의 왼편에 의해 제어된다
Ⓓ 편재화에 의해 금화조는 동시에 여러 음을 낼 수 있다

17. **6단락의 단어 'speculate(추측하다)'와 의미상 가장 가까운 것은**
Ⓐ 나타내다
Ⓑ 짐작하다
Ⓒ 반대하다
Ⓓ 주장하다

18. **다음 중 6단락에서 조류 뇌 발달에 대해서 추론 가능한 것은 무엇인가?**

Ⓐ 소리핵은 보다 진화된 뇌의 지표다.
Ⓑ 공룡의 뇌 크기를 통해서 우리는 그들이 현대 조류보다 낮은 지능을 소유했다는 것을 알 수 있다.
Ⓒ 공룡과 현대 조류의 두개골 구조의 유사점은 공룡이 현대 조류의 조상이라는 것을 암시한다.
Ⓓ 현대 조류처럼 공룡도 짝을 끌어들이기 위해 소리를 사용했다.

19. 지문에 다음 문장이 들어갈 수 있는 위치를 나타내는 네 개의 사각형 [■]을 확인하시오.

실제로 그들의 뇌는 그들의 조상인 공룡들의 것보다 몸 크기에 비해 훨씬 더 크다.

이 문장이 들어가기에 가장 적합한 곳은? [■B]

20. **지시문:** 지문을 간략하게 요약한 글의 첫 문장이 아래 제시되어 있다. 지문의 가장 중요한 내용을 표현하는 세 개의 선택지를 골라 요약문을 완성하시오. 일부 문장들은 지문에 제시되지 않았거나 지문의 지엽적인 내용을 나타내기 때문에 요약문에 포함되지 않는다. ***이 문제의 배점은 2점이다.***

조류의 뇌는 뇌 기능을 최적화할 수 있게 도와주는 특성을 나타낸다.

Ⓐ 소리핵은 노래 생산에 관련된 조류 뇌의 부분이며 그 크기는 번식기에 따라 변동한다.
Ⓔ 편재화된 뇌는 새들로 하여금 먹이를 구별하고 포식자를 경계하는 것과 같은 여러 활동을 동시에 수행할 수 있게 돕는다.
Ⓕ 금화조의 소리핵과 발성 기관은 모두 편재화를 나타내며 각각의 좌편과 우편은 다른 기능을 맡고 있다.

Ⓑ 현대 조류와 달리 그들의 조상인 공룡은 소리핵처럼 매우 발달된 신경 조직을 지닌 것처럼 보이지 않는다.
Ⓒ 수컷 금화조가 노래할 수 있는 이유는 배아였을 때와 번식기 때마다 테스토스테론이 생산되기 때문이다.
Ⓓ 닭을 대상으로 한 시각 편재화 실험에서 좌뇌는 세부 사항을 처리하고 우뇌는 움직임을 다룬다는 것이 발견됐다.

어휘 tissue n 조직 | conform v 따르다 | flight n 비행 | air resistance 공기 저항 | ancestor n 조상, 선조 | compensate v 보상하다, 보완하다 | disproportionate adj 균형이 안 맞는, 불균형의 | alter v 변형하다 | song nuclei 소리핵 | breeding season 번식기 | shrink v 줄어들다 | structural adj 구조상의, 구조적인 | lateralization n 편재화 | hemisphere n 반구 | specialized adj 특화된 | distinction n 차이 | intelligence n 지능 | perceive v 감지하다 | edible adj 먹을 수 있는 | cutout n 오려내기 | predator n 포식자 | aggressively adv 공격적으로 | imitate v 모방하다, 흉내 내다 | nerve receptor 수용체 | stimulus n 자극, 자극제 | categorization n 범주화 | perception n 지각, 자각 | songbird n 명금 | infusion n 투입, 주입 | trigger v 촉발시키다 | mating season 짝짓기 시기 | differentiate v 구별하다, 구분 짓다 | pitch n (음의) 높이 | extend v 확장하다 | syrinx n (새의) 울대 | airway n 기도 | vibrate v 떨다, 진동하다 | independently adv 자주적으로 | dominant adj 우세한, 지배적인 | descendant n 자손, 후손 | mineralized adj 광물화된 | intricate adj 복잡한, 정교한

Lesson 03 Vocabulary

본서 | P. 88

Practice

01 B　02 D　03 B　04 B　05 C　06 A　07 C　08 A　09 1. A 2. B
10 1. B 2. B　11 1. D 2. B　12 1. A 2. C　13 1. B 2. B　14 1. A 2. A
15 1. D 2. B　16 1. D 2. B　17 1. A 2. B 3. C　18 1. A 2. C 3. D
19 1. B 2. A 3. A 4. A 5. B　20 1. D 2. C 3. A 4. B 5. A

Test

1. B　2. B　3. A　4. A, B　5. A　6. C　7. A　8. D　9. D　10. B, C, F
11. B　12. C　13. B　14. A　15. C　16. B　17. A　18. B　19. C　20. A, B, E

Practice

본서 I P. 90

01 2004년도 인도양 지진으로 촉발된 엄청난 쓰나미는 동남아시아 많은 지역을 황폐화시킨 대참사였고, 역사상 가장 파괴적인 자연 재해 중 하나로 기록되었다.

지문의 단어 'devastated(황폐화시킨)'와 의미상 가장 가까운 것은

Ⓐ 과장한　　Ⓑ 파괴한　　Ⓒ 노출한　　Ⓓ 지배한

어휘 tremendous adj 엄청난, 굉장한 I trigger v 유발하다 I catastrophe n 대참사, 비극 I record v 기록하다 I destructive adj 파괴적인

---

02 인간 활동에 기인한 세계적인 온도 증가로 인해 지구의 빙하와 만년설은 불가피하게 녹기 시작했고 이는 전 세계적인 해수면 상승에 일조했다.

지문의 단어 'inevitably(불가피하게)'와 의미상 가장 가까운 것은

Ⓐ 마지못해　　Ⓑ 무분별하게　　Ⓒ 공평하게　　Ⓓ 피할 수 없이

어휘 attribute *A* to *B* A를 B의 탓으로 돌리다 I icecap n 만년설, 빙원 I sea level 해수면 I worldwide adj 전 세계적인

---

03 현대 새들의 뼈 구조는 폐의 기능을 돕는 공기 주머니를 포함한 빈 뼈를 가지고 있다는 점에서 일부 공룡의 그것과 비슷하다.

지문의 단어 'akin(비슷한)'과 의미상 가장 가까운 것은

Ⓐ 관련이 있는　　Ⓑ 비슷한　　Ⓒ 뚜렷한　　Ⓓ 별개의

어휘 akin adj 유사한, 동족의 I hollow adj 속이 빈 I sac n 주머니, 낭 I functioning n 기능, 작용

---

04 비록 상업주의 때문에 다다이즘 화가들에게 비판을 받기는 했지만, 가장 유명한 입체파 화가 중 한 명인 피카소는 대상의 내면적 특성을 감정적으로 유의미하고 추상적인 형태로 묘사하는 타고난 능력을 보였다.

지문의 단어 'demonstrated(보였다)'와 의미상 가장 가까운 것은

Ⓐ 무시했다　　Ⓑ 보였다　　Ⓒ 위장했다　　Ⓓ 구분했다

어휘 commercialism n 상업주의, 영리주의 I cubist n 입체파 예술가 I demonstrate v 보여주다, 증명하다 I innate adj 타고난 I depict v 묘사하다

---

05 그 섬 화산은 두 세기 동안 휴면 상태에 있었다. 그러나 최근 지각 변형과 화산의 온도 변화와 같은 자연 신호 측정이 화산의 임박한 폭발 가능성을 입증했다.

지문의 단어 'impending(임박한)'과 의미상 가장 가까운 것은

Ⓐ 최근의　　Ⓑ 활동하지 않는　　Ⓒ 임박한　　Ⓓ 필수적인

어휘 dormant adj 휴면 중인 I deformation n 변형 I gradient n 변화, 기울기 I confirm v 확인하다, 입증하다 I impending adj 임박한

---

06 오늘날 유기농 식품은 건강을 유지하는 데 도움을 줄 수 있고 전통적으로 재배된 식품에 비해 더 나은 영양을 제공할 수 있다고 여겨진다.

지문의 단어 'maintain(유지하다)'과 의미상 가장 가까운 것은

Ⓐ 유지하다　　Ⓑ 증가하다　　Ⓒ 회복시키다　　Ⓓ 제공하다

어휘 maintain v 유지하다, 지속하다 I nutrition n 영양(물) I conventionally adv 전통적으로, 관례적으로 I counterpart n 상응하는 것, 상대물

---

07 연구원들은 일반적인 선충의 수명을 결정하는 한 유전자 집합을 발견했다. 이 발견은 노화 과정에 관한 실마리를 던졌고, 피할 수 없는 노화 과정을 과학자들이 결과적으로 늦추는 것을 가능하게 할 수도 있다.

지문의 구 'sheds light on(실마리를 던지다)'과 의미상 가장 가까운 것은

Ⓐ 알려진 것을 반박하다 Ⓑ 중요성을 강조하다 Ⓒ 더 많은 정보를 주다 Ⓓ 더 많은 주의를 환기하다

어휘 gene n 유전자 | lifespan n 수명 | nematode n 선충 | shed light on ~을 명백히 하다, 실마리를 던지다 | aging n 노화 | inexorable adj 피할 수 없는, 멈출 수 없는

08 아치는 초기 수메르 문명에서 사용되었지만 주로 지하 배수 시스템에 사용되었다. 아치를 처음 개발하고 광범위하게 다양한 기능으로 활용한 이들은 로마인들이었다.

지문의 단어 'exploited(활용했다)'와 의미상 가장 가까운 것은

Ⓐ 사용했다 Ⓑ 얻었다 Ⓒ 개선했다 Ⓓ 찾아냈다

어휘 arch n 활 모양, 아치 | Sumerian adj 수메르의, 수메르 사람의 | chiefly adv 주로 | underground adj 지하의 | drainage system 배수 시스템 | exploit v ~을 이용하다, 개발하다

09

부당한 차별

부당한 차별은 합리적 근거 없이 사람들을 불평등한 대우, 권리, 의무가 적용되는 집단으로 공식적 또는 비공식적으로 분류하는 것이다. 만약 불공평한 지위에 대한 실질적인 합리적 명분이 있다면 차별은 부당하지 않다. 차별의 경계를 정당화하기 위해 흔히 사용되는 기준에는 성별, 인종, 지위, 종교, 나이와 국적이 있다. 그러나 그러한 요소들은 흔히 개인의 업무 수행 능력이나 사회 일원으로서의 능력과는 관련이 없다. 차별하는 사람들은 일반적으로 진실된 명분 없이 권리를 빼앗긴 집단이 열등하다는 믿음을 갖고 있다. 이 용어는 차별이 기반한 요소가 본질적으로 관련이 있지 않다는 것을 암시한다.

1. 지문의 단어 'status(지위)'와 의미상 가장 가까운 것은

Ⓐ 지위 Ⓑ 구조 Ⓒ 관례 Ⓓ 전략

2. 지문의 단어 'relevant(관련이 있는)'와 의미상 가장 가까운 것은

Ⓐ 결과의 Ⓑ 관계가 있는 Ⓒ 주의 깊은 Ⓓ 강제적인

어휘 invidious adj 불공평한, 불쾌한 | classification n 분류 | justification n 근거, 명분 | status n 지위 | criteria n (criterion의 복수형) 기준, 표준 | nationality n 국적, 국민 | bearing n 관련, 영향 | aggrieve v 침해하다, 괴롭히다 | genuine adj 진짜의, 진실한 | relevant adj 관련 있는, 적절한

10

생물 다양성

과학자들은 생물의 다양성이라는 용어를 식물, 동물, 균류, 그리고 미생물과 같은 지구에 서식하는 많은 다양한 종류의 생물들을 묘사할 때 사용한다. 대부분의 과학자들이 현재 최소한 천만 가지의 서로 다른 생물종이 있다는 데 동의하는 반면에, 일부 과학자들은 아직 발견되지 않았거나 분류되지 않은 개별적 생물종의 총합이 사실상 최대 1억 가지나 될 것이라고 믿는다. 이러한 생물종들은 높은 산 정상에서부터 해저면에 이르기까지 각각 독특한 환경에 적응해 왔다. 생물 다양성이라는 용어는 또한 이러한 종들이 사는 서로 다른 서식 환경들을 가리키는 데 사용된다. 각각의 서식지는 여타 환경이 아닌, 그 환경에 적응할 수 있는 적응 형태를 가진 생물종의 집이다. 예를 들어, 어떤 동물은 부작용에 시달리거나 생소한 환경을 훼손하지 않고는 북극 지역에서 열대 우림 지역으로 옮겨질 수 없다.

1. 지문의 단어 'copious(많은)'와 의미상 가장 가까운 것은

Ⓐ 중요한 Ⓑ 풍부한 Ⓒ 뒤이은 Ⓓ 강렬한

2. 지문의 단어 'While(반면에)'과 의미상 가장 가까운 것은

Ⓐ 전에 Ⓑ 반면에 Ⓒ ~때문에 Ⓓ ~을 고려했을 때

어휘 copious adj 많은, 풍부한 | vegetation n 식물, 초목 | fungi n (fungus의 복수형) 균, 진균 | species n 종, 종류 | discrete adj 분리된, 별개의 | classify v 분류하다 | peak n 정상 | ocean floor 해저면 | habitat n 서식지 | enable v 가능하게 하다

11 **여성 참정권 운동가**

제1차 세계대전 전에 영국과 미국의 여성들은 참정권을 위해 싸웠다. '여성 참정권 운동가'라는 용어는 이런 여성들 중 더 급진적인 이들을 가리키기 위해 만들어졌으나, 흔히 투표를 원했던 모든 여성을 지칭했다. 여성 참정권 운동가들은 폭력적인 항의와 극단적 자기 희생으로 정평이 나 있었다. 그렇지만 그들이 실제로 범한 죄는 상대적으로 사소한 것들이었다. 많은 역사학자들은 법의 울타리 안에서 희망했던 헌법 개정을 이루기 위해 일했던 소위 '헌법상의 여성 참정권 운동가들'이 세간의 이목을 끌었던 동지들보다 동등한 투표권을 얻기 위한 더 안정되고 의미 있는 발전을 이루어냈다고 주장한다. 몇몇은 심지어 여성 참정권 운동가들의 충격 요법이 비난을 유발함으로써 사실상 그 운동을 방해했다고 주장한다.

1. 지문의 구 'prior to(~전에)'와 의미상 가장 가까운 것은

Ⓐ ~이래 Ⓑ ~하는 동안에 Ⓒ 뒤에 Ⓓ 이전의

2. 지문의 단어 'provoking(유발함)'과 의미상 가장 가까운 것은

Ⓐ 금지함 Ⓑ 자극함 Ⓒ 보호함 Ⓓ 모음

어휘 right n 권리 I coin v (용어를) 만들다 I radical adj 급진적인 I suffragette n 여성 참정권 운동가 I protest n 항의, 시위 I commit v 저지르다, 범하다 I offense n 범죄, 위반 I constitutional adj 헌법의, 입헌의 I steady adj 꾸준한, 변함 없는 I meaningful adj 유의미한 I progress n 발전, 진전 I claim v 주장하다 I tactic n 전략, 전술 I provoke v 유발하다, 일으키다 I criticism n 비판, 비난

---

12 **툰드라**

세계의 모든 생물군계들 중에서 툰드라는 가장 춥고 혹독한 환경으로 알려져 있다. 툰드라는 길고 추운 겨울과 매우 짧은 여름을 지닌다. 강수량이 거의 없고, 토지가 척박하며 성장 시기가 짧아서 생물종이 적고 인간 정착지가 거의 없다. 게다가 툰드라는 약 20피트 깊이로 뻗어 있는 영구 동토층이라 불리는 영구적으로 얼어붙은 토양 지층을 가지고 있다. 이러한 환경을 견디기 위해 툰드라의 동식물상은 특별한 적응력을 가지고 있다. 툰드라에 사는 식물들은 여름에는 녹는 표토에 얕은 뿌리를 내림으로써 살아 남을 수 있고, 동물들은 새끼를 짧은 여름 동안 빨리 낳고 길러내는 식으로 적응해왔다. 툰드라는 서로 다른 두 가지 종류가 있는데, 북극 지방에서 찾을 수 있는 북극 툰드라와 히말라야나 알프스의 가장 높은 봉우리 같은 높고 추운 산의 정상에 위치한 알파인 툰드라다.

1. 지문의 단어 'frigid(추운)'와 의미상 가장 가까운 것은

Ⓐ 추운 Ⓑ 휴면 중인 Ⓒ 존재하는 Ⓓ 끈질긴

2. 지문의 단어 'dwelling(사는)'과 의미상 가장 가까운 것은

Ⓐ 지지하는 Ⓑ 대량 살육하는 Ⓒ 거주하는 Ⓓ 인접하는

어휘 biome n 생물군계 I devoid adj 결여된, ~가 없는 I precipitation n 강수량 I endure v 견디다, 참다 I fauna n 동물군계 I settlement n 정착 I barren adj 불모의, 황폐한 I thaw v 녹다

---

13 **동물의 주기**

특정 중요 주기는 일반적으로 동물의 행동을 규제한다. 이러한 순환 주기가 가장 분명하게 드러난 형태 중 하나는 일주율이라고 불리는데, 이것은 24시간을 바탕으로 한 행동 유형을 일컫는다. 이 체내 시계는 배고픔, 수면, 배설 같은 동물의 기초적인 욕구에 영향을 미친다. 일상적 순환과 더불어 동물들은 또한 연 단위로 작용하는 일 년 주기의 리듬으로부터 영향을 받는다. 주로 계절적 변화에 의해 결정되는 동물의 연주율은 동면, 번식, 이주 같은 활동을 하게 만든다. 예를 들면, 겨울의 시작 무렵 얼룩다람쥐들은 그 계절 동안 몹시 추운 온도에 대처하는 가장 좋은 방법으로 동면을 택한다. 몸무게를 두 배로 늘리는 것이 길고 추운 겨울의 전제 조건이므로 동면에 들어가기 전 그들은 평소보다 더 많은 음식을 먹는다.

1. 지문의 단어 'onset(시작)'과 의미상 가장 가까운 것은

Ⓐ 통합 Ⓑ 시작 Ⓒ 업적 Ⓓ 풍부함

2. 지문의 구 'cope with(대처하다)'와 의미상 가장 가까운 것은

Ⓐ 고려하다 Ⓑ 다루다 Ⓒ 지지하다 Ⓓ 지연시키다

어휘 manifestation n 명시, 표명, 징후 I circadian adj 24시간 주기의 I behavioral adj 행동의, 행동에 관한 I drive n 충동, 욕구 I excretion n 배설 I circannian adj 1년 주기의 I operate v 작용하다 I annual adj 연간의, 매년의 I hibernation n 동면, 겨울잠 I onset n 시작, 개시 I frigid adj 몹시 추운, 냉담한 I double v 두 배로 되다, 두 배로 만들다 I dormancy n 휴면, 동면 I consume v 먹다, 소모하다 I prerequisite n 전제 조건, 필수 조건

14 **생물 사이의 관계**

꽃이 없는 경우에도 많은 식물들이 화외밀선이라는 잎사귀나 줄기에 발달된 구조를 통해 꿀을 분비한다. 이러한 식물은 주로 개미가 많은 열대나 온대 지역에서 발견된다. 그들 중 몇몇 종류는 아미노산을 가지고 있지만, 꿀은 주로 수분과 용해된 당으로 이루어져 있다. 이러한 식물들은 개미를 유인하여 공생하는 방법을 발달시켰다. 개미들은 끈질긴 방어자로, 꽃을 먹는 곤충과 다른 초식동물과 같은 침략자로부터 이 식물을 보호한다. 이러한 종의 식물과 개미는 서로가 없으면 살아갈 수 없다. 매우 활동적인 일개미들은 바쁜 생활 방식을 지원해줄 만한 많은 에너지원을 필요로 한다. 따라서 이 식물들은 화외밀을 제공함으로써 개미들에게 충분한 에너지원을 주면서 그들을 이용한다. 이 호의의 대가로 개미는 귀중한 자원에 대해서 그들과 경쟁을 벌이는 다른 곤충으로부터 그 식물을 보호해주고, 또한 이 식물들의 잎을 먹는 초식동물을 내쫓아 준다.

1. 지문의 단어 'persistent(끈질긴)'와 의미상 가장 가까운 것은

Ⓐ 지속적인 Ⓑ 뒤따르는 Ⓒ 확고한 Ⓓ 배타적인

2. 지문의 단어 'Therefore(따라서)'와 의미상 가장 가까운 것은

Ⓐ 그래서 Ⓑ 그럼에도 불구하고 Ⓒ 게다가 Ⓓ 그 동안

어휘 extrafloral adj 꽃 밖의 I nectary n 꿀샘 I stem n 줄기 I temperate adj 기후가 온화한 I amino acid 아미노산 I compete v 경쟁하다 I exploit v 이용하다 I ward off 물리치다, 피하다

15 **직접 새기기**

전통적으로 조각품은 미술가에 의해 진흙으로 빚어진 예비 모형에서 시작되었다. 그 다음 그것들은 돌, 회반죽 또는 청동으로 된 완성품을 최종으로 만들어내는 스튜디오 조수들에게 넘겨졌다. 사실상 조수들이 대체로 원래 작가들보다 조각에 훨씬 능숙했기 때문에 신고전주의 조각가가 나무 망치와 끌을 사용하는 일은 매우 드물었다. 그러나 20세기에 직접 새기기가 중간의 점토 모형을 사용하지 않고도 조각을 만들어내는 새로운 방식으로 출현했다. 기억으로부터 또는 대상 그 자체를 두고 작업을 하면서 한 명의 예술가가 단독으로 조각 작업을 했다. 직접 새기기는 형태를 구성하는 접근법으로서 근대 미술의 돌파구 그리고 원시 예술에서 유래한 기법의 부활로 여겨진다. 직접 새기기 기술의 중요한 측면은 표현 수단의 본질을 보여주려는 예술가의 판단력으로, 작가는 그것이 지닌 매력적인 미적, 조직적인 특성을 드러내기 위해 작업한다. 직접 새기기의 재료와 최종 형태는 종종 모양, 짜임새 혹은 사용된 매개체의 결에서 진화한다.

1. 지문의 단어 'adept(능숙한)'와 의미상 가장 가까운 것은

Ⓐ 빠른 Ⓑ 갑작스러운 Ⓒ 튼튼한 Ⓓ 유능한

2. 지문의 단어 'employed(사용된)'와 의미상 가장 가까운 것은

Ⓐ 모인 Ⓑ 이용된 Ⓒ 고려된 Ⓓ 고용된

어휘 preliminary adj 예비의, 최초의 I finalize v 마무리하다, 완결하다 I plaster n 석고, 회반죽 I mallet n 나무 망치 I chisel v 조각하다, 끌로 새기다 I medium n 수단, 재료, 매개체

16 **사파 잉카**

서기 12세기로 거슬러 올라가면 잉카인들은 쿠스코 지역에서 부족으로 시작했다. 그곳에서 그들은 작은 도시국가를 형성했는데 그것은 이후 그들이 융성해지면서 형성한 제국의 행정적, 정치적, 군사적 중심지로 기능했다. 서기 1438년에 사파 잉카의 통솔과 지시 하에 쿠스코 사람들은 현재의 남쪽 페루 지역 대부분을 정복했다. 확장이 만들어낸 거대한 부를 가지고 사파 잉카는 쿠스코 왕국을 강건한 제국의 수도 역할을 하는 큰 도시로 재건했다. 그의 정치적 지배 하에 중앙 정부는 쿠스코의 관할 하에 놓이게 되었고, 사파 잉카에 충성하는 지도자들이 지배하는 네 개의 지방 정부도 있었다. 사파 잉카는 현재 유명한 관광 명소인 마추픽추의 건설에도 관여한 것으로 여겨지며 이는 아마 그의 가족들이 사는 집이나 귀족의 휴양지 역할을 했을 것이다.

1. 지문의 단어 'generated(만들어낸)'와 의미상 가장 가까운 것은

Ⓐ 개발한 Ⓑ 대체한 Ⓒ 쇄도한 Ⓓ 생산한

2. **지문의 단어 'robust(강건한)'와 의미상 가장 가까운 것은**

Ⓐ 전형적인 Ⓑ 튼튼한 Ⓒ 단호한 Ⓓ 부차적인

어휘 date back 거슬러 올라가다 | tribe n 부족, 집단 | city-state n 도시국가 | administrative adj 행정의 | direction n 지시, 명령 | conquer v 정복하다 | expansion n 확장, 팽창 | transform v 변형시키다 | capital n 수도 | robust adj 튼튼한, 강건한 | fall under ~의 책임(관할)이다 | jurisdiction n 사법권 | provincial adj 주의, 지방의 | destination n 목적지, 행선지

17

도시 열섬

1 ➡ 도시 중심에 있는 사람이라면 누구든 그곳의 온도가 그곳을 둘러싼 시골 지역의 온도보다 항상 더 높다는 것을 알아차릴 것이다. '도시 열섬'이라는 용어는 이 현상을 설명하기 위해 연구원들에 의해 만들어졌다. 도시 열섬은 인간의 활동에서 기인한 것으로, 도시 성장과 더불어 인구 밀집 지역에서 흔히 발달한다. 난방과 냉방 시스템, 발전소, 공장, 그리고 도로와 철도 교통 모두 도시 지역의 평균 온도를 높이는 과도한 열을 유발한다. 연구원들은 대도시에서 사람이 만들어낸 열의 규모가 태양의 복사열의 규모와 비슷하다는 것을 발견했다. 사실 일부 도시들은 실제로 겨울 동안 태양으로부터 제공되는 것보다 더 많은 양의 열을 발생시킨다. 흥미롭게도 도시의 높은 여름 밤 온도는 인간 활동으로 발생되는 열의 양에 직접적으로 비례했다. 다시 말하면 더 많은 에너지가 빌딩을 식히는 데 사용될수록 더 많은 열이 발생되고 대기를 훨씬 더 뜨겁게 하는 것이다.

2 ➡ 도시 지역이 더 따뜻한 또 다른 이유는 사람들이 높은 빌딩, 아스팔트 도로, 콘크리트 인도가 주된 표면인 도시의 건축물에 사용한 재료 때문이다. 특히 건물과 도로의 어두운 색으로 인해 이러한 재료들은 태양의 복사열을 식물이나 토양보다 더 많이 흡수하고 저장한다. 비록 해가 진 후에는 도시 지역과 시골 지역 모두 서늘해지지만, 도시의 콘크리트와 아스팔트 표면은 저장해 놓았던 열을 더욱 서서히 발산하고 이것이 도시 지역을 더 덥게 유지한다.

1. **1단락의 단어 'attributed(기인했다)'와 의미상 가장 가까운 것은**

Ⓐ ~의 탓으로 돌렸다 Ⓑ 풍부했다 Ⓒ 수용했다 Ⓓ 옹호했다

2. **1단락의 구 'together with(더불어)'와 의미상 가장 가까운 것은**

Ⓐ ~의 점에서 Ⓑ 협력하여 Ⓒ ~에 고유한 Ⓓ ~전에

3. **2단락의 단어 'prevailing(주된)'과 의미상 가장 가까운 것은**

Ⓐ 최초의 Ⓑ 강력한 Ⓒ 널리 퍼진 Ⓓ 심오한

어휘 rural adj 지방의, 시골의 | coin v (용어를) 만들다 | phenomenon n 현상 | together with ~을 포함하여, ~와 함께 | metropolis n 주요 도시 | magnitude n 정도, 규모 | radiation n 복사열, 방사능 | nighttime n 밤, 야간 | proportionate adj 비례한 | sidewalk n 보도, 인도 | prevailing adj 만연한, 널리 퍼진, 주된 | radiate v 발산하다

18

미국 문학

1 ➡ 미국 남북전쟁의 끝이 가까워지면서 이성 철학과 과학적 방법론, 그리고 체계화된 역사 연구에 대한 관심이 낭만주의에서 사실주의와 자연주의로 지배적인 문학 형식의 전환을 가져왔다. 그 당시에 미국은 경제 위기로 애를 먹고 있었고 이는 서로 다른 맥락 속에서 미국의 삶에 대한 보다 현실적인 묘사를 위해 낭만주의에 대한 격심한 거부를 낳았다. 게다가 이민자 인구의 급속한 증가와 산업화, 도시화, 그리고 읽고 쓸 줄 아는 능력은 더 많은 독자들이 미국이 경험하고 있던 문화적 변화에 호기심을 갖게 했다. 따라서 미국의 사실주의와 자연주의를 대변하는 작품은 그 당시의 폭넓은 사회적 추세를 반영했다.

2 ➡ 미국의 사실주의자들은 있는 그대로의 삶을 반영하기로 마음먹었기 때문에 그들의 주제는 다양했다. 남부의 삶은 조엘 챈들러 해리스와 엘런 글래스고에 의해 주목받았다. 또 다른 저명한 작가 햄린 갈런드는 대초원지대 미국인들의 삶을 묘사했다. 아마도 미국의 사실주의 작가 중 가장 유명했을 새뮤얼 클레먼스는 마크 트웨인이라는 필명으로 활동했는데, 자신 주변의 삶을 유머러스하고 회의적인 시선으로 관찰했다. 그는 자신이 경험한 미국식 삶에 대해 글을 썼는데, 대화에서 표준어 대신 사실적인 방언들로 인물들을 기록했다. 실제로 미국 산문 스타일에 가장 중요한 변화를 가져온 주된 이는 트웨인으로, 미국식 주제와 언어에 기반한 독창적인 미국 문학을 만들어냈다.

3 ➡ 과장된 형태의 사실주의인 자연주의는 인간의 의지가 본성에 휘둘리는 어둠의 세계를 나타냈다. 자연주의 작가들은 개인의 유전적 특질과 사회적 환경이 인물의 성격을 형성하는 결정적 요인이라는 발상을 합리화하기 위해 찰스 다윈의 진화 이론을 이용했다. 시어도어 드라이저는 가장 중요한 자연주의 작가로 여겨지는데, 자신들이 이해하지 못하는 힘에 대해서 무력한 사람들이 사는 어둡고 음침한 세상을 묘사했다. 그는 자연주의 작가는 낭만을 꾸며내기보다 인간의 삶에 관한 진실을 이야기해야 한다고 믿었다.

1. 1단락의 단어 'proliferation(증가)'과 의미상 가장 가까운 것은

Ⓐ 증가 Ⓑ 발전 Ⓒ 특성 Ⓓ 대립

2. 2단락의 단어 'skeptical(회의적인)'과 의미상 가장 가까운 것은

Ⓐ 지속적인 Ⓑ 상당한 Ⓒ 의심스러운 Ⓓ 가능한

3. 3단락의 단어 'fabricating(꾸며내는)'과 의미상 가장 가까운 것은

Ⓐ 만드는 Ⓑ 제한하는 Ⓒ 방해하는 Ⓓ 고안하는

어휘 rational adj 이성/합리적인 I systematized adj 체계화된 I transition n 이행, 변화 I realism n 사실주의 I naturalism n 자연주의 I predominant adj 지배적인 I plague v 시달리다, 전염되다 I rejection n 거절, 배제, 폐기 I proliferation n 급증, 증식, 만연 I spotlight n 주목, 스포트라이트 I pen name 필명 I prose n 산문 I mercy n 자비 I heredity n 유전, 성질, 세습 I fabricate v 꾸며내다, 위조하다

19

무성 생식

1 ➡ 무성 생식은 오로지 하나의 유기체만이 필요한 생식 방법이다. 이러한 종류의 생식은 핵이 없는 단세포 생물에서 흔히 찾아볼 수 있다. 대부분의 식물들도 무성 생식을 할 수 있다고 일컬어진다. 무성 생식은 두 개의 성(性)을 필요로 하지 않는다는 사실 때문에 생식의 진척이 빠를 뿐만 아니라 유성 생식에 비해 적은 에너지를 필요로 한다. 뿐만 아니라 유전적 재조합이 없기 때문에 무성 생식은 모체의 온전한 복제품을 생산할 수 있다. 무성 생식은 진화론적 기준으로 볼 때 열등한 생식 수단으로 간주될 수 있는데 그 이유는 상당히 적은 변화 가능성 때문이다. 그럼에도 불구하고 무성 생식은 양쪽 부모의 유전자를 조합할 때 발생할 수 있는 돌연변이나 다른 문제점을 감소하게 하는 경향이 있으므로 유리할 수도 있다. 무성 생식에는 세 가지 기본 종류가 있는데 이분법, 출아법, 포자법이다.

2 ➡ 이분법은 대체로 박테리아와 단세포 생물에 의해 이용된다. 이분법에서는 살아 있는 세포가 두 개의 동일한 또는 거의 동일한 분절로 나뉘는 과정을 통해 생식이 이뤄진다. 이분법 과정은 DNA 복제에서 시작된다. 다양한 단세포 생물들이 이런 생식 방법을 이용한다. 이분법을 통해 무성 생식하는 박테리아의 좋은 예는 리케차로, 이것은 로키산 홍반열과 같은 질병을 유발한다.

3 ➡ 출아법은 완전히 자란 안정된 생물의 일부에서 새로운 생물이 돌출되는 무성 생식 형태다. 이러한 형태의 무성 생식은 식물계에서 매우 흔하지만 히드라와 같은 동물에서도 찾아볼 수 있다. 히드라의 자손은 모체에서 떨어져 나가기 전 당분간 모체에 붙은 채로 있다. 하나의 모체에서 유래했기 때문에 새로운 발아체는 유전적으로 부모와 동일하다. 해면의 경우 새로운 해면이 모체에서 떨어져 나온 부분에서 자라기 시작할 것이다.

4 ➡ 세 번째 유형은 포자법 또는 포자 형성법이다. 이 방법은 포자라 불리는 생식 세포의 다량 생산을 수반하며, 이 포자는 동일한 DNA를 포함하고 있고 흩어진 후에는 새롭고 독립적인 종으로 성장한다. 이러한 생식 방법은 고사리 같은 여러 복합 식물체에서 찾아볼 수 있다. 그러나 이 방법은 바람, 물, 움직이는 생물에 의해 포자가 퍼져야만 성공할 수 있다. 확산 수단이 없다면 포자는 번성할 수 없다.

5 ➡ 단세포 생물과 식물에게 무성 생식은 몇 가지 장점을 제공한다. 예를 들어 식물과 이동 능력이 없거나 짝을 찾으러 돌아다닐 수 없는 동물은 주로 무성 생식을 한다. 그뿐 아니라 무성 생식을 통해 유기체는 유성 생식의 경우처럼 여분의 에너지를 들이지 않고서도 수많은 자손들을 생산할 수 있다. 식물과 단세포 생물은 사망률이 높기 때문에 다수의 자손을 만들어내는 것은 그들의 생존에 매우 중요하다. 해양 환경과 같이 변화를 거의 겪지 않는 정적인 환경에서는 무성 생식을 하는 생물을 흔히 찾아볼 수 있다.

1. 1단락의 단어 'means(수단)'와 의미상 가장 가까운 것은

Ⓐ 다양성 Ⓑ 방법 Ⓒ 계획 Ⓓ 활기

2. 1단락의 단어 'considerably(상당히)'와 의미상 가장 가까운 것은

Ⓐ 상당히 Ⓑ 결과적으로 Ⓒ 처음에 Ⓓ 무의식 중에

3. 4단락의 단어 'dispersed(퍼진)'와 의미상 가장 가까운 것은

Ⓐ 분산된 Ⓑ 구별된 Ⓒ 양보한 Ⓓ 번성한

4. 4단락의 단어 'flourish(번성하다)'와 의미상 가장 가까운 것은

Ⓐ 번영하다 Ⓑ 우세하다 Ⓒ 먹이를 찾아 다니다 Ⓓ 도피하다

5. 5단락의 단어 'static(정적인)'과 의미상 가장 가까운 것은

Ⓐ 분명한 Ⓑ 불변의 Ⓒ 현저한 Ⓓ 오로지

어휘 asexual adj 무성의 | reproduction n 생식 | sexual reproduction 유성 생식 | inferior adj 열등한 | considerably adv 상당히 | mutation n 돌연변이 | binary adj 두 부분으로 이루어진 | fission n 분열 | sporulation n 포자법 | replication n 복제 | sponge n 해면동물 | abundant adj 풍부한 | disperse v 흩어지다 | flourish v 번성하다 | essential adj 필수적인 | single-celled organism 단세포 생물 | recombination n 재조합 | evolutionary adj 진화론적인 | reduce v 감소시키다 | primary adj 주요한 | budding n 출아법 | segment n 분절 | protrusion n 돌출 | identical adj 동일한 | spore n 포자 | fern n 양치류 | dispersal n 분산

20

로이 풀러

1 ➡ 로이 풀러는 19세기 후반과 20세기 초반에 활동한 미국의 무용수였다. 그녀는 1800년대 말 미국의 시골을 순회하면서 가수와 무용수 및 버라이어티 쇼 배우가 등장하는 서커스와 보드빌 쇼를 할 때만 해도 이렇다 할 성공을 거두지 못했으나, 유럽 순회 공연을 위해 대서양을 건넌 뒤 결국 명성을 얻었다. 파리에서 그녀는 무용수로서 자신만의 자연스럽고 즉흥적인 테크닉을 개발할 수 있었다. 그녀의 업적은 연기에만 국한되지 않았고 안무 및 무대 공연의 기술 조명 분야에까지 확대되었다.

2 ➡ 로이 풀러는 일리노이주 시카고 교외의 풀러스버그에서 본명 마리 루이즈 풀러로 태어났다. 그녀는 네 살에 미국 연예계에서 아동 배우로 경력을 쌓기 시작했다. 시간이 흐르면서 무용과 안무 쪽으로 전향했고, 25년 동안 버라이어티 쇼를 하며 북미 지역을 순회했는데 그 쇼 중 다수는 무용단에 집중된 것이었다. 무용과 안무 일을 시작한 초창기에 그녀는 이미 배우로 알려져 있었고, 약간의 무용 교육밖에 받은 적이 없었기 때문에 대중은 그녀를 대수롭지 않게 여겼다. 그러나 다른 연기자들의 무용 기법에 대한 예리한 관찰력 덕분에 그녀는 실험을 통해 자신만의 기법을 개발할 수 있었다. 그녀는 뉴욕과 런던의 유명 연예인들과 함께 연기하고 춤췄으며 로이 풀러라는 예명을 제안한 것도 바로 그들이었다.

3 ➡ 로이 풀러의 명성과 악명은 무대 의상 및 조명을 다루는 그녀의 기술적 혁신에서 비롯되었다. 그녀는 무대 조명과 상호 작용하는 의상을 디자인하여 그 둘을 성공적으로 결합했다. 그녀는 의상을 디자인할 때 반사되는 소재를 사용했고, 무대 조명을 가리기 위해 색 있는 비단을 썼으며, 색 조명이 무대나 연기자에게 비치도록 거울을 이용했다. 풀러는 자신의 혁신이 얼마나 획기적인 것인지 인식하고, 화학 물질을 이용해 색깔 있는 젤을 만든다거나 화학 소금을 이용해 반짝이고 빛나는 조명과 의상을 만드는 등 자신의 발명품에 관해 여러 개의 특허를 냈다. 풀러는 심지어 저명한 과학자였던 자신의 친구 마리 퀴리에게 연극에서 방사성 원소 라듐을 이용할 수 있게 해달라고 힘쓰기도 했다. 그러나 마리 퀴리는 그 물질을 사용하는 것과 관련된 위험성 때문에 그 부탁을 거절했다.

4 ➡ 풀러는 전위적인 조명 및 의상에서의 이렇게 전례 없는 획기적인 방법들을 자유로운 무용 스타일 및 안무와 결합했다. 과학과 무용의 이러한 결합은 그녀가 '뱀 춤'이라고 이름 붙인 공연을 통해 갈채를 받게 되었으며 이 작품은 1892년 2월 뉴욕시의 엉클 셀러스틴 풍자극에서 초연되었다. 그녀가 유럽을 순회하고 전 세계적으로 명성을 얻게 된 것은 그 유명한 공연 이후였다. 그녀는 몇몇 쇼에 주연 배우로 출연하면서 유럽에서 공연한 최초의 현대 무용수였다. 유럽 공연 중 가장 눈에 띄는 작품은 아래쪽에서 조명이 비춰지는 유리 표면 위에서 춤을 춘 '불 춤'이었다.

5 ➡ 그 당시에는 아르누보 운동이 인기였으며 로이 풀러는 그것의 살아 있는, 춤추는 화신으로 여겨졌다. 그녀의 안무와 기술적 혁신적 방법들은 그녀를 무용계를 뛰어 넘어 그림과 조각 같은 다른 예술 영역으로 이끌었다. 미술계에서 그녀의 명성과 영향력은 앙리 드 툴루즈 로트레크의 그림과 오귀스트 로댕의 조각으로도 남아 있다. 그녀는 1928년에 사망했으나 그녀의 작품에 대한 관심은 여전히 남아 있다. 특히 안무 분야는 그녀의 창조력에 강한 영향을 받았다.

1. 1단락의 단어 'feats(업적)'와 의미상 가장 가까운 것은

Ⓐ 교리 Ⓑ 설명 Ⓒ 원동력 Ⓓ 업적

2. 3단락의 단어 'merged(결합했다)'와 의미상 가장 가까운 것은

Ⓐ 바꿨다 Ⓑ 방해했다 Ⓒ 섞었다 Ⓓ 고갈시켰다

3. 4단락의 단어 'unprecedented(전례 없는)'와 의미상 가장 가까운 것은

Ⓐ 비할 데 없는 Ⓑ 흐릿한 Ⓒ 우아한 Ⓓ 일치하는

4. 4단락의 단어 'notable(눈에 띄는)'과 의미상 가장 가까운 것은

Ⓐ 설득력 있는 Ⓑ 뛰어난 Ⓒ 풍부한 Ⓓ 효험 있는

5. 5단락의 단어 'embodiment(화신)'과 의미상 가장 가까운 것은

Ⓐ 구체적인 예 Ⓑ 진화 Ⓒ 대조 Ⓓ 물리적인 확장

어휘 modest adj 크지 않은, 겸소한 | hone v (기술을) 연마하다 | improvisational adj 즉흥적인 | choreography n 안무(법) | observance n 관찰, 준수 | notoriety n 악명 | innovation n 혁신, 혁신적인 방법 | merge v 통합하다 | reflective adj 반사하는 | take out 취득하다 | luminescent adj 빛을 내는 | garment n 의상 | renowned adj 유명한, 명성 있는 | hazard n 위험 | proposition n 제의 | serpentine

adj 뱀 모양의 | **vaudeville** **n** 보드빌(희극 배우·가수·곡예사 등이 출연하는 쇼, 다양한 볼거리로 꾸며지는 공연) | **ultimately** **adv** 궁극적으로 | **solely** **adv** 단지 | **transition** **n** 변화, 전환 | **alongside** **prep** ~와 함께 | **spring** **v** ~에서 나오다 | **costume** **n** 무대 의상 | **interact** **v** 상호 작용하다 | **shade** **v** 가리다 | **patent** **n** 특허 | **manipulate** **v** 조작하다 | **strive** **v** 분투하다 | **radioactive** **adj** 방사성의 | **turn down** 거절하다 | **combine** **v** 결합하다 | **embodiment** **n** 구현, 화신

Test

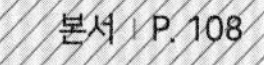
본서 | P. 108

글쓰기의 기원

1 ➡ 성문화된 문자 체계는 문명의 주요 특징으로 간주된다. 글쓰기의 발달은 한 문화가 그 민족이 그들의 과거를 기록하는 데 시간을 투자할 수 있을 정도의 안정기에 도달했다는 것을 보여준다. 그들은 단순한 생존을 고려하는 것에서 벗어나 사회적 정체성이 있는 정착된 공동체를 형성한 것이다. 이것이 언제 어디서 처음 발생했는지를 절대적으로 확신하기는 힘들지만 대부분의 사학자들은 가장 오래된 문어가 메소포타미아의 수메르인들의 것이라는 데 동의한다. 다른 문어들이 수메르어보다 앞섰을 수 있고 이집트어와 같은 많은 사례들이 제안되었지만 그런 주장을 뒷받침하는 증거는 거의 없다.

2 ➡ 수메르인들의 문자 체계는 라틴어로 '쐐기 모양'이라는 뜻을 지닌 쐐기문자로 불리는데, 이것은 뭉툭한 갈대를 사용해 점토판에 모양을 찍어내는 방식으로 만들어졌다. 다른 고대 문자 체계처럼 쐐기문자는 상형 언어로 시작했는데, 그것은 그림들이 그것들이 가리키는 것들을 직접 나타낸다는 의미이다. 약 9천 년 전에 원형 필기의 첫 증거는 물표라는 형태로 메소포타미아에 등장했다. 이런 물표들은 점토로 만들어졌고 각각 다른 물품과 양을 나타내는 다른 표시들이 새겨졌다. 시간이 흐르면서 이것이 수백 개의 문자로 발달되었는데, 이는 단지 엄선된 몇 사람만이 온전히 글을 읽고 쓸 수 있었고 그들은 흔히 문서를 만드는 직업을 가진 서기관들이었다는 것을 뜻했다. 수 세기에 걸쳐 이런 기호들은 점차 형태와 의미에 있어서 더 추상적으로 바뀌었고 개념 대신 발음하는 대로의 말을 직접 나타내기에 이르렀다.

3 ➡ 그들이 선호한 자재는 많은 장점을 지녔다. 많은 언어의 최고(最古)의 샘플들은 돌, 뼈와 나무로 만들어졌다. 돌과 달리 점토는 글쓰기가 쉽고 나무나 뼈보다 훨씬 오래간다. 둘 다 불에 훼손될 수 있으나 점토는 구워지며 도자기로 바뀌면서 내구성이 높아진다. 이것은 글쓰기가 단지 기록하는 용도가 아니라 일상에서 쉽게 사용될 수 있다는 것을 뜻했다. [■A] 이집트인들도 그들만의 표음 문자를 발전시켰으나, 쉽게 생산되지만 쉽게 물에 손상되고 불에 소멸될 수 있는 파피루스 갈대로 만들어진 두루마리에 기록했다. [■B] 점토판은 대량으로 생산될 수 있고 내구성이 매우 높기 때문에 고고학자들은 그것들을 흔히 수천 개가 담겨있는 저장고에서 발견한다. [■C] 고고학자들은 이런 저장고를 기록 보관소라고 부르며 그것들은 미래의 세대들을 위해 정보를 보관하기 위한 도서관으로 시작된 것처럼 보인다. [■D] 이런 기록 보관소에 있는 많은 점토판은 그것들을 보관하고 있던 건물들이 파괴될 때 도자기로 바뀌었다.

4 ➡ 쐐기문자 기록 보관소의 내용물을 분석함으로써 메소포타미아에서의 글쓰기의 성장을 추적할 수 있다. 이 언어의 가장 초기의 사용은 부기, 특별히 세금 징수를 돕기 위함이었다. 나중에 이것은 재고 물품과 사업 기록과 결혼과 이혼을 위한 다양한 법률 문서를 기

1. 1단락의 단어 'key(주요한)'와 의미상 가장 가까운 것은
Ⓐ 기본적인
Ⓑ 가장 중요한
Ⓒ 근본적인
Ⓓ 상당한

2. 1단락에 근거하여 수메르어가 가장 오래된 문어라는 것을 어떻게 알 수 있는가?
Ⓐ 대부분의 사학자들이 그렇다고 주장한다.
Ⓑ 수메르어보다 더 오래된 문자 체계의 증거가 없다.
Ⓒ 다른 문어가 수메르어를 앞섰을 가능성이 거의 없다.
Ⓓ 메소포타미아는 가장 오래된 문화가 발견된 곳이다.

3. 다음 중 2단락에서 쐐기문자에 대해 추론 가능한 것은 무엇인가?
Ⓐ 그것은 사물과 숫자에 각각 다른 상징을 갖고 있었다.
Ⓑ 수메르어와 유사한 상형문자들은 수메르어가 발달한 비슷한 시기에 발달했다.
Ⓒ 생각을 표현하는 것에서 소리를 표현하는 것으로의 변화는 더 많은 사람들로 하여금 글을 쓰고 읽을 수 있게 했다.
Ⓓ 원형 필기의 발달은 매우 긴 기간에 걸쳐 일어났다.

4. 3단락에 따르면, 다른 재료에 비해 점토판의 장점은 무엇인가? 2개를 고르시오.
Ⓐ 대량 생산될 수 있다.
Ⓑ 일상의 기록을 가능케 했다.
Ⓒ 기록 보관소에 쉽게 쌓을 수 있었다.
Ⓓ 물이나 불에 손상을 입지 않는다.

5. 4단락의 단어 'documenting(기록하는)'과 의미상 가장 가까운 것은
Ⓐ 기록하는
Ⓑ 정리하는
Ⓒ 착수시키는
Ⓓ 구성하는

6. 다음 중 5단락에서 언급된 것은 무엇인가?
Ⓐ 수메르 쐐기문자가 아람어에게 추월당한 시기
Ⓑ 수메르와 고대 페르시아 쐐기문자 간의 차이
Ⓒ 수메르 쐐기문자를 계속 활용한 정복자들
Ⓓ 다리우스 대왕이 수메르 쐐기문자를 확장시키는 데 한 역할

록하는 것을 포함하는 것으로 확장되었다. 이런 사실적 정보는 역사, 신화와 종교 서적, 궁극적으로 시와 문학을 포함하기까지 성장했다. 소설의 발달은 한 문화가 과거를 기록할 뿐만 아니라 미래를 상상하기 시작했다는 것을 뜻하기 때문에 특별히 중요하다. 글의 사용이 급증하자 기호 언어에서 음성 언어로의 이행은 계속 진전을 이루었다. 문자의 숫자는 천 개를 넘는 것에서 600개로 감소해 문자 체계를 더 간소화시켰고 글을 읽고 쓸 수 있는 사람들의 숫자가 증가할 수 있도록 했다.

5 ➡ 그 지역이 아카디아 제국에 의해 정복된 후 현지 문화와 언어는 점차 사라졌지만 그들의 문자 체계는 살아남았다. 아카디아 사람들은 쐐기문자를 채택했고 그들 자신의 언어로 그 문자들에 새로운 소리와 단어를 붙였다. 이런 패턴은 수세기에 걸쳐 이어졌고, 바빌론과 차후의 다른 왕국들이 이따금 그 지역의 통제권을 취했을 때 쐐기문자는 계속 사용되며 개선되었다. 수메르 문학은 수메르어를 그들의 언어로 제대로 번역하기 위해 그것을 필요로 하는 문화의 서기관들에 의해 유지되고 읽혔다. 결국 쐐기문자는 아람어로 대체되었지만 그 전에 페르시아의 다리우스 대왕이 고대 페르시아 쐐기문자를 발달시키게끔 영감을 주었다. 그것은 파르티아 제국이 로마 제국의 지배권에 들기 전까지 문학과 과학적 용도로 계속 사용되었다.

6 ➡ 오늘날 수메르어는 그 어느 문화 집단의 모국어로도 사용되지 않기 때문에 사어로 간주된다. 하지만 수메르 문자 체계의 탄력성은 그것을 라틴어처럼 사어 중에서도 특별한 부류로 분류되게 만든다. 비록 이 두 개의 언어는 다른 방법으로 확산되었지만(쐐기문자는 패배한 수메르인들에게서 차용된 반면 로마자는 정복자인 로마인들에 의해 확산되었다) 둘 다 세계의 넓은 지역에서 다양한 문화권에 의해 사용되었고 그들의 문자가 구어 사용보다 더 오래 살아남았다는 사실에서 많은 유사점을 공유한다. 둘 다 그것을 처음 만들었던 사람들이 역사 속으로 사라진 훨씬 후에도 문학적, 과학적, 종교적 목적으로 계속 사용되었다. 하지만 오늘날 쐐기문자를 해독할 수 있는 자격을 갖춘 전문가는 몇 명밖에 되지 않는 반면에 유럽 대부분의 언어는 여전히 로마자를 사용한다.

7. 6단락에 따르면, 다음 중 수메르어와 라틴어의 공통점이 아닌 것은

Ⓐ 그것들의 흔적이 현대 언어에서 여전히 발견된다
Ⓑ 그것들을 처음 개발한 문명들은 더 이상 존재하지 않는다
Ⓒ 문자 체계는 구어보다 더 오래 지속되었다
Ⓓ 현재 그 어떠한 문명 집단도 그것들을 모국어로 채택하지 않고 있다

8. 다음 중 지문에 음영 표시된 문장의 핵심 정보를 가장 잘 표현한 문장은 무엇인가? 오답은 의미를 크게 왜곡하거나 핵심 정보를 누락하고 있다.

Ⓐ 쐐기문자와 로마자는 오늘날에도 세계 많은 지역에서 사용된다는 점에서 유사하지만 전자는 수메르인들에게서 비롯되었고 후자는 로마인들에게서 비롯되었다는 점에서 다르다.
Ⓑ 쐐기문자는 피정복민의 언어이기 때문에 라틴어와 다르지만, 이러한 점이 더 이상 구어로 사용되지 않게 된 이후에도 오랫동안 다른 문화들 속에서 살아남는 것을 막지는 못했다.
Ⓒ 비록 다른 문명에서 유래되었지만, 수메르어와 라틴어 모두 더 이상 구어로 사용되지 않더라도 문자 체계가 많은 문화들로 퍼져서 여전히 사용되고 있다.
Ⓓ 수메르 쐐기문자와 로마자는 다르게 확산되었지만, 더 이상 구어로 사용되지 않게 된 이후에도 문자 형태가 오랫동안 존재했다는 점과 그들의 문화 밖에서 널리 사용되었다는 점에서 비슷하다.

9. 지문에 다음 문장이 들어갈 수 있는 위치를 나타내는 네 개의 사각형 [■]을 확인하시오.

이런 기록 보관소에 있는 많은 점토판은 그것들을 보관하고 있던 건물들이 파괴될 때 도자기로 바뀌었다.

이 문장이 들어가기에 가장 적합한 곳은? [■D]

10. 지시문: 지문을 간략하게 요약한 글의 첫 문장이 아래 제시되어 있다. 지문의 가장 중요한 내용을 표현하는 세 개의 선택지를 골라 요약문을 완성하시오. 일부 문장들은 지문에 제시되지 않았거나 지문의 지엽적인 내용을 나타내기 때문에 요약문에 포함되지 않는다. ***이 문제의 배점은 2점이다.***

우리에게 알려진 가장 오래된 문자 체계는 수메르 쐐기문자다.

Ⓑ 초기에 사업 기록과 법률 문서를 기록하는 방법으로 시작된 것이 결국 시, 문학과 종교 서적의 번성을 가능하게 했다.
Ⓒ 문자들은 원래 특정 사물이나 개념을 상징했지만 쐐기문자가 개념보다 소리를 직접적으로 나타내는 것으로 발달하자 문자의 개수는 감소했다.
Ⓕ 수메르 문화가 사라진 지 오랜 후에도 주변 왕국들은 그들 고유의 용도를 위해 쐐기문자를 채택하고 개선하여 계속 사용했다.

Ⓐ 쐐기문자가 수 세기에 걸쳐 살아남은 이유는 다른 문화권의 서기관들이 수메르어를 그들의 모국어로 번역하기 위해 그 문자가 필요했기 때문이다.

Ⓓ 라틴어처럼 수메르어는 그 어떠한 문화 집단에서도 모국어로서 구어로 사용되고 있지 않지만 여전히 오늘날까지 문자 체계가 살아남아 있는 언어다.

Ⓔ 점토판이 불에 소멸되지 않기 때문에 수메르 서기관들은 그것을 나무, 뼈나 파피루스 두루마리와 같은 재질보다 선호했다.

어휘 codified adj 성문화된 I writing system 문자 체계 I key adj 가장 중요한, 필수적인 I sedentary adj 한 곳에 머물러 사는, 정주(定住)하는 I ascertain v 알아내다, 확인하다 I precede v ~에 앞서다, 선행하다 I cuneiform n 쐐기문자 I blunt adj 뭉툭한, 무딘 I reed n 갈대 I pictographic adj 그림 문자의 I proto-writing n 원형 필기 I incise v 새기다 I literate adj 글을 읽고 쓸 줄 아는 I scribe n 서기관 I abstract adj 추상적인 I phonetic adj 음성/발음을 나타내는 I virtue n 덕목, 장점 I durable adj 내구성이 있는 I ceramic n 도자기 I obliterate v 없애다 I archaeologist n 고고학자 I cache n 은닉처, 저장소 I bookkeeping n 부기 I facilitate v 가능하게 하다, 용이하게 하다 I document v 기록하다 I inventory n 물품 목록 I literature n 문학 I signify v 의미하다, 뜻하다 I proliferate v 급증하다, 확산되다 I now and then 때때로, 가끔 I refine v 정제하다, 개선하다 I supersede v 대체하다 I inspire v 영감을 주다 I subjugate v 정복하다 I dead language 사어(死語) I native tongue 모국어 I resilience n 회복력 I originator n 창시자, 시조 I decipher v 판독하다, 해독하다

Lesson 03 Identifying Details

열적 성층

1 ➡ 수생 환경에서 생물체의 분포는 온도, 빛, 염도와 압력을 포함하는 많은 요소들에 의해 결정되지만 그 중 가장 중요한 것은 온도와 열적 성층 현상이다. 햇빛이 수역 표면을 비출 때 작은 양은 반사되지만 대부분의 태양 복사는 물을 투과하고 서서히 약해져서 결국 흡수된다. 물은 무색이고 투명하지만 공기보다 훨씬 밀도가 높고 태양 에너지를 빠르게 흡수한다. [■A] 매우 투명한 물에서는 표면으로부터 100미터 아래까지 햇빛의 99퍼센트가 흡수된다. [■B] 물에 침전물이나 생물체가 있다면 빛이 도달할 수 있는 깊이는 줄어든다. **[■C] 매우 탁한 물에서 태양 복사는 불과 몇 센티미터만 투과할 수 있다.** 가시광선은 여러 파장을 포함하는데 적외선처럼 가장 긴 파장은 먼저 흡수되는 반면에 자외선처럼 짧은 것들은 물 속 더 깊이 다다라서 깊은 물이 파란색으로 보이게 한다. [■D]

2 ➡ 물이 태양 복사를 흡수하는 정도는 두 가지 중요한 영향을 미친다. 첫째, 이것은 광합성이 수면 30미터까지 제한된다는 것을 뜻하는데, 이것은 광합성에 필요한 양의 빛이 수면 30미터 아래로는 닿지 않기 때문이다. 그러므로 대양과 호수에 있는 거의 모든 제1차 생산자가 그 지역에 존재한다. 얕은 수역과 해안가에는 켈프 같은 식물 종이 크게 자라서 바닥에 뿌리를 내리고 번성할 수 있으며, 거기에서 그것들은 식량과 안식처를 둘 다 제공함으로써 다양한 생물체를 지원하는 수중 숲을 형성할 수 있다. 하지만 이들은 연안에 인접하지 않은 깊은 물에서 생존할 수 없기 때문에 먹이 사슬의 기반에는 해표면 근처에 떠서 서식하고 흔히 단세포인 식물성 플랑크톤이라고 불리는 미생물이 있다. 이들은 동물성 플랑크톤이라고 불리는 생물들에 의해 먹히는데, 그것들은 밤엔 수면에 돌아다니고 낮에는 시각적으로 먹이를 감지하는 작은 물고기를 피해 깊은 물 속으로 물러가며 주야 이동의 수직 순환을 형성하는 매우 작은 갑각류와 무척추동물이다.

3 ➡ 물이 태양 복사를 흡수하는 정도가 낳는 중요한 결과 두 번째는 물의 첫 몇 미터만 뜨거워진다는 것이다. 이것은 열대 바다에서도 깊은 물은 차갑다는 것을 뜻하고 열이 더 깊은 곳까지 미치기 위해서는 열이 물을 수직으로 순환시키는 해류를 통해서 교환되어야 한다는 것이다. 물은 섭씨 4도에서 제일 밀도가 높으며 그 지점에서 온도가 올라가거나 내려가면 밀도가 떨어진다. 수면의 물이 더 따뜻하기 때

11. 1단락의 단어 'ultimately(결국)'와 의미상 가장 가까운 것은

Ⓐ 완전히
Ⓑ 결국
Ⓒ 효과적으로
Ⓓ 손쉽게

12. 1단락에 따르면, 다음 중 빛의 흡수에 대해 사실인 것은 무엇인가?

Ⓐ 밀도가 높은 수역은 낮은 밀도의 수역보다 빛을 더 빠르게 흡수한다.
Ⓑ 물 속 높은 수준의 침전물은 대부분의 태양 에너지를 반사한다.
Ⓒ 빛 대부분은 수면 근처에서 흡수된다.
Ⓓ 더 긴 파장은 물 속 더 깊이 침투한다.

13. 2단락에 따르면, 다음 중 켈프에 대해 사실이 아닌 것은

Ⓐ 거대한 크기로 성장한다
Ⓑ 유기 탄소 복합물을 생산한다
Ⓒ 얕은 물에서 자란다
Ⓓ 다른 생물들에게 먹이가 된다

14. 다음 중 지문에 음영 표시된 문장의 핵심 정보를 가장 잘 표현한 문장은 무엇인가? 오답은 의미를 크게 왜곡하거나 핵심 정보를 누락하고 있다.

Ⓐ 동물성 플랑크톤은 식물성 플랑크톤을 먹기 위해 밤에 수면의 물로 이동하고 낮에는 포식자들을 피해 깊은 물에 머무른다.
Ⓑ 식물성 플랑크톤은 낮에는 포식자들로부터 숨어 있고 밤에는 미생물인 동물성 플랑크톤을 먹기 위해 수직으로 이동하며 생존한다.
Ⓒ 동물성 플랑크톤은 수면의 물과 심층수에서 모두 생존하는 미생물인데 이것은 그들이 수직 이동 순환을 통해 식물성 플랑크톤을 먹을 수 있게 도와준다.

문에 밀도도 더 낮은데 이것은 그 물이 계속 수면에 남아서 더 뜨거워져서 더 깊고 더 차갑고 밀도가 더 높은 물과 섞이지 않게 된다는 것을 뜻한다. 여름에 열대 혹은 온대 지방의 깊은 수역에는 수면 아래 훨씬 더 차가운 물이 있고 수면 근처에는 따뜻한 물이 뚜렷한 층으로 존재한다. 온도 차이로 인해 물이 층으로 나뉘는 것은 수온 약층이라고 불리며 이것의 깊이는 수면의 파 활동의 양에 따라 다르다.

4 ➡ 열대 지방의 호수에는 수면의 물이 일년 내내 따뜻하게 유지되기 때문에 수온 약층은 물리적 성질의 중요한 구분을 하는 영구적인 특징이다. 수면 근처의 물은 밝고 따뜻하며 다량의 산소가 부유하고 있는 반면에 깊은 곳은 어둡고 춥고 거의 완전히 산소가 없다. 산소를 생산하는 광합성 생물들은 수온 약층 위의 지역으로 제한되고 극심한 성층은 물이 순환되는 것을 막기 때문에 깊은 곳에서는 산소가 보충될 수 없다. 심층수의 극한 조건들은 대부분의 생물에게 가혹하지만 죽은 생물의 사체와 살아 있는 생물의 배설물은 바닥에 가라앉는다. 이는 곧 맨 위층의 환경이 우호적일지는 몰라도, 깊은 물과의 교환이 없다는 것은 위쪽에 사는 생물들이 이용할 수 있는 영양소가 거의 없다는 의미이다.

5 ➡ 온대 지방과 극지방의 수역은 계절이 변하면서 극적인 변화를 견디기 때문에 상황이 꽤 다르다. 수면의 물이 따뜻해지기 때문에 여름에는 수온 약층이 발생하지만 겨울 긴 기간 동안 기온이 영하로 떨어지면서 수면이 얼어붙는다. 봄과 가을에 이런 극치 간의 변화는 호수 전체가 1년에 두 번 동일한 온도와 밀도를 갖게 된다는 것을 뜻한다. 열적 성층이 제거됐을 때 수면에 부는 바람은 호수 전역에 물을 순환시키는 파 활동을 생성한다. 이런 역전은 위에 있는 산소화된 물이 아래에 인 같은 영양소가 풍부한 물과 교환될 수 있게 한다. 이 과정 때문에 온대 지방의 호수들은 열대 지방 호수들보다 훨씬 더 생산적이며 심지어 극지방 것들이 더 균일하다.

Ⓓ 동물성 플랑크톤은 주야 이동해서 낮에는 포식자들을 피하고 밤에 먹이를 먹는 미생물인 식물성 플랑크톤을 주로 먹는다.

15. **3단락에 따르면, 다음 중 수온 약층의 정의는 무엇인가?**

Ⓐ 파 활동의 효과가 가장 많이 느껴지는 깊이
Ⓑ 밀도로 구분이 되는 물의 여러 개의 층
Ⓒ 수온이 변화하는 지점
Ⓓ 계절 변화로 인한 물 밀도의 변화

16. **4단락의 단어 'replenished(보충되다)'와 의미상 가장 가까운 것은**

Ⓐ 공급되다
Ⓑ 다시 채워지다
Ⓒ 얻어지다
Ⓓ 복제되다

17. **5단락에 따르면, 다음 중 역전에 대해 사실인 것은 무엇인가?**

Ⓐ 온대 지방 수역이 열대 지방 수역보다 더 생산적이도록 만들어 준다.
Ⓑ 물 순환을 야기하는 파 활동을 통해 성층을 제거한다.
Ⓒ 영양소를 아래로 보내고 산소화된 물을 수면으로 올려 보낸다.
Ⓓ 호수 전체가 동일한 온도와 밀도를 이룰 수 있게 한다.

18. **5단락에 따르면, 다음 중 온대지방 수역에서 봄과 가을마다 아래로 이동되는 것은 무엇인가?**

Ⓐ 식물성 플랑크톤
Ⓑ 산소
Ⓒ 인
Ⓓ 따뜻한 수면의 물

19. 지문에 다음 문장이 들어갈 수 있는 위치를 나타내는 네 개의 사각형 [■]을 확인하시오.

매우 탁한 물에서 태양 복사는 불과 몇 센티미터만 투과할 수 있다.

이 문장이 들어가기에 가장 적합한 곳은? [■C]

20. **지시문:** 지문을 간략하게 요약한 글의 첫 문장이 아래 제시되어 있다. 지문의 가장 중요한 내용을 표현하는 세 개의 선택지를 골라 요약문을 완성하시오. 일부 문장들은 지문에 제시되지 않았거나 지문의 지엽적인 내용을 나타내기 때문에 요약문에 포함되지 않는다. ***이 문제의 배점은 2점이다.***

열적 성층은 수중 생물의 분포를 결정하는 데 중요한 역할을 한다.

Ⓐ 수온 약층은 열대 지방 수역처럼 수면의 물이 지속적으로 가열되는 반면에 깊은 물은 그렇지 않은 곳에서 더 두드러진다.
Ⓑ 태양 복사 흡수의 정도는 광합성이 수면의 물에서만으로 제한되고 수온 약층이 생성되는 것을 야기한다.
Ⓔ 온대 수역과 극지 수역에서 일 년에 두 번 물이 섞이는 것은 영양소와 산소가 교환되도록 한다.

Ⓒ 빛이 물의 맨 위층에만 닿기 때문에 플랑크톤 같은 제1차 생산자는 오직 수면의 물에서만 생존할 수 있다.

Ⓓ 물이 섭씨 4도에서 최대 밀도를 이룬다는 것은 수온 약층이 형성되는 깊이에서 알 수 있다.

Ⓕ 태양 복사가 물을 투과하는 깊이는 물의 투명도에 크게 좌우된다.

어휘 aquatic adj 수생의 I salinity n 염도 I thermal stratification 열적 성층 I solar radiation 태양 복사 I penetrate v 관통하다, 침투하다 I ultimately adv 궁극적으로, 결국 I dense adj 밀집한 I sediment n 침전물 I visible light 가시광선 I infrared n 적외선 I ultraviolet n 자외선 I repercussion n 영향, 파급 효과 I virtually adv 거의, 사실상 I primary producer 제1차 생산자 I thrive v 번창하다 I anchored adj 고정된, 닻을 내린 I open water 연안에 인접하지 않은 넓고 깊은 수역; 개빙 구역, 부동해(겨울에도 얼어붙지 않는 바다) I suspended adj 떠 있는 I miniscule adj 대단히 작은 I crustacean n 갑각류 동물 I invertebrate n 무척추동물 I retreat v 후퇴하다 I detect v 감지하다 I vertical adj 수직의 I daily migration 주야이동 I tropical adj 열대의 I current n 해류, 기류 I circulate v 순환하다 I density n 밀도 I temperate adj 온대의 I distinct adj 뚜렷한 I thermocline n 수온 약층 I wave action 파 활동 I suspension n 부유(浮遊) I frigid adj 몹시 추운/찬 I thoroughly adv 대단히, 완전히 I generate v 발생시키다 I stark adj 냉혹한, 극명한 I replenish v 다시 채우다, 보충하다 I corpse n 사체 I feces n 배설물 I dramatic adj 극적인 I transition n 이행, 과도 I extreme n 극도, 극단 I overturn n (온도차에 의한 물의) 역전 I oxygenated adj 산소화된 I phosphorus n 인(비금속 원소) I uniform adj 균일한

Lesson 04 Reference

본서 I P. 116

Practice

01 D **02** A **03** A **04** D **05** C **06** D **07** D **08** C **09** A **10** B

11 1. A 2. A **12** 1. D 2. A **13** 1. D 2. C **14** 1. A 2. D **15** 1. B 2. D

16 1. C 2. B **17** 1. C 2. C **18** 1. D 2. D 3. C **19** 1. A 2. B 3. A **20** 1. D 2. D 3. B

Test

1. B 2. A 3. C 4. C 5. C 6. C 7. A 8. D 9. B 10. A, C, D

11. A 12. D 13. D 14. B 15. A 16. B 17. A 18. A 19. B 20. A, B, E

Practice

본서 I P. 118

01 우리의 두뇌는 좌반구와 우반구 두 부분으로 나뉘어 있다. 전자는 언어 능력과 관련 있고 후자는 지각과 꿈에 영향을 끼친다.

지문의 구 'The former(전자)'가 가리키는 것은

Ⓐ 우리의 뇌 Ⓑ 두 개의 반구들 Ⓒ 우반구 Ⓓ 좌반구

어휘 half n 절반, 반 I former n 전자 I affect v 영향을 끼치다

02 비록 원형은 아시아에서 고안되었지만 1439년에 만들어진 구텐베르크의 인쇄기는 잘 팔리는 기술로 성장했다. 그것은 궁극적으로 다른 종류의 인쇄기들을 대체했다. 그러나 그것은 결국 더 정교한 인쇄기로 대체되었다.

지문의 단어 'It(그것)'이 가리키는 것은

Ⓐ 구텐베르크의 인쇄기 Ⓑ 원형 Ⓒ 다른 종류의 인쇄기 Ⓓ 더 정교한 인쇄기

어휘 printing press 인쇄기 I sophisticated adj 정교한 I prototype n 원형 I supplant v 대체하다

03 대다수의 과학자들이 모든 종은 오랜 시간 동안 자연 선택설이라고 일컫는 과정을 통해 같은 조상들로부터 유래했다는 다윈의 진화론을 받아들이고 있지만, 일부는 우주와 지구, 그리고 인류가 초자연적 존재 혹은 신에 의해 창조되었다고 끊임없이 주장하고 있다.

지문의 단어 'some(일부)'이 가리키는 것은

Ⓐ 과학자들 Ⓑ 조상들 Ⓒ 종들 Ⓓ 인류

어휘 majority n 대부분 I indicate v 나타내다, 보여 주다 I natural selection 자연 선택 I insistent adj 주장하는

---

04 구석기 시대에 그려졌다고 믿어지는 동굴 벽화는 전 세계적으로 발견되지만, 인도네시아에서 발견된 고대 동굴 벽화는 사람이 한 손은 벽에 두고 다른 쪽으로 그림을 그림으로써 사람 손 윤곽을 나타냈다는 점에서 독특하다.

지문의 구 'the other(다른 쪽)'이 가리키는 것은

Ⓐ 윤곽 Ⓑ 인간 Ⓒ 그림 Ⓓ 손

어휘 cave painting 동굴 벽화 I Paleolithic adj 구석기의 I ancient adj 고대의 I spot v 발견하다 I peculiar adj 특이한, 독특한 I depict v 묘사하다, 그리다 I place v 두다 I apply v (페인트를) 바르다, 적용하다

---

05 20세기 전반에 다다이즘과 초현실주의가 생겨났고, 이는 19세기의 사실주의 운동에 영향을 받은 것이었다. 전자는 제1차 세계대전 동안 스위스 취리히에서 시작되었던 반면, 후자는 1920년대 초기 다다 운동을 거친 이후 파리에서 생겨났다.

지문의 구 'the latter(후자)'가 가리키는 것은

Ⓐ 20세기 Ⓑ 다다이즘 Ⓒ 초현실주의 Ⓓ 사실주의

어휘 give rise to 일으키다, ~이 생기게 하다 I during prep ~동안, ~중에 I Surrealism n 초현실주의

---

06 지구 내부의 열은 지열에너지 형태로 에너지 자원으로 이용되는데, 지열에너지의 환경적 영향은 다른 에너지원의 그것만큼 광범위하지 않을 수도 있다. 현재 지구의 많은 인구는 화석이나 핵연료 같은 다른 에너지원의 비용과 비슷한 비용으로 지하에 있는 지열정(井)에서 나오는 증기로 전기를 사용할 수 있다.

지문의 단어 'that(그것)'이 가리키는 것은

Ⓐ 열 Ⓑ 에너지 Ⓒ 원천 Ⓓ 영향

어휘 harness v 이용하다, 활용하다 I geothermal adj 지열의 I extensive adj 아주 넓은, 대규모의 I electricity n 전기, 전류 I well n 우물, (유전 등의) 정

---

07 호흡할 때 동물들은 먹은 음식을 태우기 위해 산소를 들이마시고 그 부산물로 이산화탄소(CO2)가 생산된다. 과거 바다에 살던 초기 어류들은 공기로 숨을 쉬는 능력을 발달시켰을 수도 있다. 이것은 이러한 생물들이 물보다 공기에서 산소를 얻는 것이 훨씬 더 효율적이고 유리했기 때문인데, 왜냐하면 그것이 수백 배 더 밀도가 높고 점성이 있으며 더 적은 양의 공기를 포함하고 있기 때문이다.

지문의 단어 'it(그것)'이 가리키는 것은

Ⓐ 호흡 Ⓑ 바다 Ⓒ 공기 Ⓓ 물

어휘 respiration n 호흡 I byproduct n 부산물 I extract v 추출하다 I viscous adj 끈적거리는

08

동물 사육

신석기 사람들이 특정 종의 생물학적 과정을 조작함으로써 야생 동물을 사육했다는 증거가 세계 도처에서 고고학자들에 의해 발견되었다. 이러한 가설을 지지하는 증거에는 많은 신석기 유적에서 발견된 동물 뼈들이 포함된다. 그것들 중 염소의 뼈가 가장 흔하며 다른 종에 비해 그 수가 훨씬 많다. 이것은 식량 생산 목적으로 선택적 사육을 했거나 적어도 번식 주기의 조작을 통해 동물 종을 의도적으로 이용했음을 시사한다.

지문의 단어 'them(그것들)'이 가리키는 것은

Ⓐ 고고학자들 Ⓑ 유적지들 Ⓒ 뼈들 Ⓓ 종들

어휘 Neolithic adj 신석기 시대의 I supportive adj 도와주는, 지지하는 I hypothesis n 가정, 가설 I breeding cycle 번식 주기 I outnumber v ~보다 수가 많다 I indicative adj 나타내는, 보여주는 I exploitation n 이용 I manipulation n 교묘한 처리, 조작

---

09 짧은꼬리푸른어치와 피뇬 소나무

공진화의 좋은 예 중 하나는 까마귀과의 중간 크기 새인 짧은꼬리푸른어치와 피뇬 소나무 사이의 관계로, 피뇬 소나무는 미국 남서부와 멕시코에서 피뇬 열매를 생산한다. 피뇬 소나무의 씨앗은 짧은꼬리푸른어치의 주된 먹이여서 이 새들은 이 소나무에 둥지를 트는 경향이 있다. 또한 짧은꼬리푸른어치는 피뇬 소나무를 재생시키는 데 중요한 역할을 하는데, 이는 그것이 나중에 먹기 위해 많은 양의 피뇬 소나무 씨앗을 땅에 보존하고, 그 여분의 씨앗들은 적절한 위치에서 싹을 틔워 새로운 나무로 성장하기 때문이다.

지문의 단어 'it(그것)'이 가리키는 것은

Ⓐ 짧은꼬리푸른어치 Ⓑ 씨앗 Ⓒ 피뇬 소나무 Ⓓ 주된 먹이

어휘 coevolution n 공진화 | crow n 까마귀 | yield v 생산하다, 내다 | staple adj 주된, 주요한 | regenerate v 재건하다, 재생시키다 | germinate v 싹트다 | mature v 다 자라다, 성숙하다

10 침팬지 대 인간

유명한 인류학자 제인 구달이 연구한, 데이비드 그레이비어드로 알려진 침팬지에 대한 연구는 침팬지에 대한 수많은 놀라운 발견들을 보여주었다. 오늘날 우리는 침팬지의 유전적 정보가 인간의 그것과 단 1퍼센트밖에 다르지 않다는 것을 알고 있다. 게다가 침팬지의 혈액 구성요소와 면역체계 또한 놀랍게도 인간의 그것과 유사하다. 둘의 뇌와 중추신경계도 거의 동일하다. 무엇보다 인간과 비슷하게 침팬지도 추론하고, 다른 이들과 협력하고, 결정을 내리며, 심지어 도구를 이용하는 능력을 증명했다. 데이비드를 관찰함으로써 그녀는 침팬지들이 흰개미를 사냥할 때 도구를 이용한다는 것과 상황을 미리 계획한다는 것, 그리고 다음 세대에게 지식을 전한다는 것을 발견했다.

지문의 단어 'that(그것)'이 가리키는 것은

Ⓐ 침팬지 Ⓑ 유전적 정보 Ⓒ 혈액 구성요소 Ⓓ 인간

어휘 renowned adj 유명한, 명성 있는 | anthropologist n 인류학자 | astonishing adj 정말 놀라운 | differ v 다르다, 의견이 같지 않다 | immune system 면역체계 | identical adj 동일한, 똑같은 | premeditate v 미리 계획하다 | impart v (정보, 지식 등을) 전하다

11 무성 영화 시대

20세기 초 '무성 영화 시대'라는 이름이 보여주듯 영화 산업은 음향을 가진 활동 사진을 녹화해서 상영하는 데 큰 기술적 제약이 있었다. 에디슨의 키네토스코프 출현으로 사람들은 움직이는 영상을 볼 수 있게 되었지만 그것은 영화를 화면 위에 비춰주지는 않았다. 키네토스코프는 순차적인 이미지가 담긴 필름 한 줄을 돌리며 대화가 없는 움직임의 환영을 만들어내는 기초적인 방법을 도입했다. 그러므로 배우들은 마임이나 제스처를 통해 말을 하지 않고도 생각을 전달할 수 있는 그들의 기술을 연마하기를 요구 받았다. 게다가 영화관 사장들은 관객들을 위해 자막 카드, 즉 삽입 자막을 사용하여 이야기의 요점을 묘사하고 중요한 대화를 보여주고 종종 행동에 관해 언급했다. 자막 작가의 역할은 무성 영화 산업에서 중요하게 여겨졌으며 종종 원래의 시나리오 작가의 역할과 분리되었다.

1. 지문의 단어 'it(그것)'이 가리키는 것은

Ⓐ 키네토스코프 Ⓑ 녹화 Ⓒ 영화 Ⓓ 스크린

2. 지문의 단어 'their(그들의)'가 가리키는 것은

Ⓐ 배우들의 Ⓑ 기술의 Ⓒ 말들의 Ⓓ 제스처의

어휘 advent n 출현, 도래 | kinetoscope n 활동 사진 영사기 | allow v ~을 가능하게 하다, 허락하다 | rudimentary adj 가장 기본적인 | illusion n 환영, 오해 | sequential adj 순차적인 | hone v 연마하다, 닦다 | convey v 전달하다 | inter-title n 삽입 자막 | narrate v 이야기를 들려주다 | separate v 분리하다

12 동물들의 멸종

몸집이 큰 대부분의 동물종이 홍적세가 끝날 무렵 멸종했다. 가정된 많은 원인들 중 가장 주요한 것은 자연적 기후 변화로 인한 빙하 작용과 인간의 이주다. 후자의 경우, 북미와 남미 대륙에 걸친 인간의 수렵 채집 사회 확산은 마지막 빙하기가 끝날 무렵인 12,000년 전에 시작되었다. 이것은 많은 동물 종의 감소와 때를 같이 하였고, 약 10,000년 전까지 매머드, 마스토돈과 같은 대형 포유류의 대다수, 그리고 다른 많은 동물들이 사라졌다. 멸종 또한 자연적 진화 과정의 일부이지만, 이 지역에서 멸종하게 된 동물종의 수와 인간이 도착하고 난 후 그들의 명백히 빠른 멸종 속도는 몇몇 과학자들로 하여금 인간 사냥꾼이 많은 포유류 동물을 멸종에 이르도록 했다는 결론에 도달하게 했다.

1. 지문의 구 'the latter instance(후자의 경우)'가 가리키는 것은

Ⓐ 홍적세　　Ⓑ 빙하 작용　　Ⓒ 기후 변화　　Ⓓ 인간 이주

2. 지문의 단어 'their(그들의)'가 가리키는 것은

Ⓐ 동물종들　　Ⓑ 장소들　　Ⓒ 과학자들　　Ⓓ 사냥꾼들

어휘 predominately adv 대개, 대부분 I Pleistocene adj 홍적세의 I hypothesize v 가설을 세우다 I prominent adj 중요한, 주요한 I glaciation n 빙하 작용 I coincide v 동시에 일어나다 I mammalian n 포유류 I mammoth n 매머드(멸종한 코끼리과 동물) I mastodon n 마스토돈(코끼리와 유사한 멸종한 동물) I evolutionary adj 진화의 I extinct adj 멸종된

13

눈 화장

고대 이집트인들은 남자와 여자 모두 눈 화장을 하는 일이 흔했는데, 이는 높은 지위를 지닌 이집트인들의 가장 눈에 띄는 특징 중 하나였다. 오늘날에는 화장이 단지 더 매력적으로 보이기 위해 사용되는 것과 달리 고대 이집트인들의 화장은 아름다움에서 보호에 이르기까지 다른 특정한 목적들이 있었다. 이집트인들은 눈꺼풀을 어둡게 하기 위해 '콜'이라는 다양한 재료로 만들어진 고대의 눈 화장품을 사용했다. 그것은 원래 눈 질병 발병을 예방하기 위해 사용되었으며 또한 눈 주위 표면을 어둡게 하면 혹독한 태양 광선으로부터 눈을 보호할 수 있다는 믿음이 있었다. 더욱이 엄마들은 신생아가 태어나면 곧바로 콜을 눈에 발랐다. 일부는 그것이 아이의 눈을 튼튼하게 하리라고 생각했기 때문에 그렇게 했다. 다른 이들은 이렇게 하면 많은 고대 문화에서 질투심 많은 사람의 공격 목표가 된 사람에게 피해나 불운을 초래한다고 믿어지는 '사악한 눈'으로부터 아이가 저주를 받지 않으리라 믿었다.

1. 지문의 단어 'It(그것)'이 가리키는 것은

Ⓐ 신분　　Ⓑ 화장　　Ⓒ 보호　　Ⓓ 콜

2. 지문의 단어 'Some(일부)'이 가리키는 것은

Ⓐ 표면들　　Ⓑ 눈들　　Ⓒ 엄마들　　Ⓓ 아이들

어휘 wear makeup 화장하다 I notable adj 주목할 만한, 눈에 띄는 I feature n 특징, 특성 I ingredient n 재료, 구성요소 I ailment n 질병 I curse v 저주를 내리다

14

퀼팅

퀼팅은 두 겹이나 그 이상의 직물을 함께 바느질하는 과정이며 때때로 그 천들 사이에는 속심이 들어간다. 그것은 처음에는 착용자를 추운 날씨에서 보호하기 위한 옷을 만드는 데 사용되었고, 얼마 동안은 갑옷 패딩(갑옷 속에 입는 누빈 옷)으로 사용되었다. 그러나 화기가 등장하면서 그것은 더 이상 충격을 완화하는 기능을 하지 못했다. 따라서 그 이후 그것은 주로 추운 공기를 피하기 위한 단열 덮개로만 사용되어 왔다. 18세기와 19세기에 퀼팅은 흔히 가족 내 또는 더 큰 지역 사회의 여성과 소녀들을 참여시키는 공동 작업이었다. '퀼트 만드는 모임'은 한 팀이 하나의 퀼트를 공동 작업하는 형태로써 여러 지역 사회에서 중요한 사회적 행사였고, 일반적으로 농업 노동력이 많이 요구되는 시기들의 사이인 농한기에 개최되었다. 퀼트는 주로 결혼식 같은 중요한 일생의 사건을 기념하기 위해 만들어졌다. 이 기간에 여성들은 퀼트를 이용해 사회적 이슈에 대한 그들의 의견을 표현하거나 그들 사이의 사회적 유대감을 강화했다.

1. 지문의 단어 'it(그것)'이 가리키는 것은

Ⓐ 퀼트　　Ⓑ 옷　　Ⓒ 착용자　　Ⓓ 날씨

2. 지문의 단어 'their(그들의)'가 가리키는 것은

Ⓐ 행사들　　Ⓑ 지역 사회들　　Ⓒ 의식들　　Ⓓ 여성들

어휘 sew v 바느질하다, 깁다 I layer n 층, 겹 I pad n 패드, 보호대, 완충대 I armor n 갑옷 I firearm n 화기 I insulating adj 단열을 위한 I communal adj 공동의, 공용의 I quilting bee 퀼트를 만드는 여자들의 모임 I agricultural off-season 농한기 I commemorate v 기념하다 I articulate v 분명히 표현하다, 설명하다 I fortify v 강화하다

15

반향 위치 측정

1 ➡ 많은 동물들은 주위의 길을 찾거나 중요한 매일의 일을 수행하기 위해 시각에 의지한다. 그러나 일부 동물은 그들의 시력을 거의 쓸모 없게 하는 빛이 희미하거나 어두운 환경에서 사는 한편, 다른 것들은 좋지 않은 시력을 가지고 있어 장애물을 피하고 먹이를 찾는 데 다른 감각

에 의존해야 한다. 고래, 돌고래, 박쥐, 뾰족뒤쥐 같은 이러한 많은 동물이 반향 위치 측정이라 불리는 기술에 의존한다.

2 ➡ 이런 기술을 사용하는 동물은 짧고 높은 음조의 소리를 낸 뒤 다시 튕겨 오는 소리의 반향을 듣는다. 그런 다음 물체의 크기, 움직임의 방향, 그리고 자신들로부터의 거리를 알아내기 위해 반향을 신중히 해석한다. 소리를 발성하는 순간과 울림이 돌아오는 순간의 시간차는 물체와의 거리를 나타낸다. 그 간격이 길면 길수록 그것도 더 멀리 있다. 반향의 음량은 물체의 크기와 질감을 나타낸다. 실제로 반향 위치 측정은 대단히 효과적이어서, 연구원들은 박쥐가 엄청난 속도로 날면서 얇은 전선을 찾고 피하는 데 그것을 사용하는 것을 관찰했다.

1. **1단락의 단어 'others(다른 것들)'가 가리키는 것은**

Ⓐ 일들 Ⓑ 동물들 Ⓒ 환경들 Ⓓ 감각들

2. **2단락의 단어 'it(그것)'이 가리키는 것은**

Ⓐ 기법 Ⓑ 방향 Ⓒ 거리 Ⓓ 물체

어휘 echolocation n 반향 위치 측정 | dimly adv 어둑하게 | shrew n 뾰족뒤쥐 | emit v 내뿜다 | high-pitched adj (소리가) 아주 높은 | echo n 메아리 | bounce v 튀다, 산란하다 | locate v 찾다 | render v (어떤 상태가 되게) 만들다 | interval n 간격

16 **화산**

1 ➡ 화산은 지각 아래서부터 표면 위로 마그마(매우 뜨거운 용해된 암석)를 분출하기 때문에 어떤 사람들은 화산을 지구의 배관 시스템으로 생각한다. 열점 화산으로 알려진 것들이 대륙 판의 표면 아래에 있는 대단히 활동적인 지점에 위치해 있기는 하지만, 화산 폭발은 대부분 대륙 판이나 지질 구조판의 가장자리 근처에서 일어난다. 대개 오래 가지 않는 화산들은 육지에서 이전 화산 분화로부터 비롯된 물질의 축적 결과로 나온 넓고 평평한 화산추 또는 굴뚝과 매우 닮은 분석구를 형성한다. 수면 아래의 화산은 때때로 가파른 기둥을 형성하는데 결국 이것은 해수면을 뚫고 올라와 새로운 섬을 형성하게 된다.

2 ➡ 활화산은 현재 계속 증기 및 여러 종류의 용암과 이산화탄소 같은 가스를 내뿜고 있는 화산이다. 또한 화쇄류(화산암 조각으로 만들어진 흐름)를 만들어 내는데 이는 액화된 뜨거운 가스, 재와 암석이 빠르게 이동하는 강이다. 또한 화산재 이류가 될 수도 있는데 이것은 콘크리트의 농도를 지닌 돌, 진흙, 물의 혼합물로 화산에서 빠른 속도로 강 유역까지 흘러 내린다. 활화산이 있는 지역은 종종 인기 있는 관광 지역이 되는데 이는 그것들이 온천, 간헐천, 머드 포트(진흙이 열 때문에 부글부글 끓는 지점)와 같은 자연의 기적을 포함하고 있기 때문이다. 그러나 불행히도 그곳에는 종종 지진도 일어난다.

3 ➡ 어떤 화산이 활동적인 상태인지 아닌지 말하기는 쉽지 않을 수 있다. 일정 기간 활동을 보여주지 않은 화산들은 휴화산으로 분류되지만 그것들은 경고 없이 다시 분화할 잠재적 가능성이 있다. 영구적으로 멈춘 것으로 여겨지는 다른 것들은 사화산으로 분류된다. 사람들은 사화산이 다시는 폭발하지 않을 것이라고 확신한 나머지 이러한 화산의 분화구 몇 군데에 휴양지를 세우기도 했다.

1. **1단락의 단어 'which(이것)'가 가리키는 것은**

Ⓐ 분석구들 Ⓑ 화산들 Ⓒ 기둥들 Ⓓ 섬들

2. **2단락의 단어 'they(그것들)'가 가리키는 것은**

Ⓐ 강 유역들 Ⓑ 활화산이 있는 지역들 Ⓒ 관광 명소들 Ⓓ 지진들

어휘 plumbing system 배관 시스템 | continental adj 대륙의 | tectonic plate 지각판 | hot spot 열점 (뜨거운 마그마를 분출하는 지역) | cinder n 나무나 석탄이 다 타고 남은 재 | cone n 원뿔 | pillar n 기둥 | lava n 용암 | consistency n 농도, 밀도 | pyroclastic adj 화쇄암의 | fluidize v 유동화하다 | hot spring 온천 | geyser n 간헐 온천 | dormant adj 휴면기의 | deem v ~로 여기다 | resort n 리조트, 휴양지 | crater n 분화구

17 **맨틀**

1 ➡ 지구형 행성의 진화 단계 중 첫 번째는 '분화'이며 이것은 밀도에 따라 구성 요소가 분리되는 것이다. 이 단계에서 더 무거운 물질은 지속적으로 중심부를 향해 가라앉아 단단하고 금속성을 지닌 핵을 형성하며 마침내 상대적으로 얇은 지각으로 둘러싸이게 된다. 현재 지구는 세 개의 주요 층으로 구성되어 있다. 우리가 살고 있는 단단하지만 얇은 층은 일반적으로 지각으로 알려져 있다. 용해된 철로 된 중앙의 구는 핵이다. 그리고 맨틀은 둘 사이에 있는 영역으로 사실상 지구 성분의 2/3를 차지한다. 단단한 지각과 달리 맨틀의 본질은 꽤 유동적이며 밀도가 높은 액체와 비슷하다.

2 ➡ 맨틀은 균일하지 않지만 세 가지 다른 구조적 영역을 지니고 있다. 지각과 맨틀이 만나는 지점에는 다양한 종류의 암석이 마구잡이로 뒤섞여 있다. 맨틀 깊이 들어갈수록 암석은 점차 부드러워지면서 연약권을 만들어낸다. 지각의 지질 구조판을 움직일 수 있게 하는 것이 바로 이

지대이다. 이 연약권 아래는 중간권으로 더 연한 광물질이 결정체로 변하는 곳이며 지표면의 암석 판이 침강하고 중심 핵으로부터 슬래그(액체 상태의 광재)가 맨틀로 융기되는 부분이다. 이 지대는 끊임없이 움직이는 지대이기 때문에 열에너지가 중심 핵에서 상승하거나 가끔 지표면까지 전달되는 두껍고 얇은 지점이 형성된다.

3 ➡ 직접적으로 조사될 수 없기 때문에 맨틀의 나머지 부분에 관해서는 많은 것이 알려져 있지 않다. 오히려 지표면 아래 중간권처럼 깊은 곳에서, 하지만 그보다 더 깊은 곳에서는 일어나지 않는 지진의 지진 측정을 통해 연구된다.

1. 1단락의 구 'the two(둘)'가 가리키는 것은

Ⓐ 행성 진화와 분화　Ⓑ 물질과 밀도　Ⓒ 지각과 핵　Ⓓ 핵과 맨틀

2. 2단락의 구 'this zone(이 지대)'이 가리키는 것은

Ⓐ 지각　Ⓑ 맨틀　Ⓒ 연약권　Ⓓ 중간권

어휘 terrestrial adj 지구의 | density n 밀도 | metallic adj 금속성의 | core n 핵, 중심 | relatively adv 상대적으로 | crust n 지각 | flexible adj 유동적인 | uniform adj 획일적인, 통일된 | malleable adj (금속이) 가단성이 있는 | tectonic adj 지질 구조의 | slab n 판 | slag n 슬래그, 광재, 화산암재 | constant adj 불변의, 일정한 | seismic adj 지진의, 지진에 의한

18

문화 전파 방법

1 ➡ 문화 전파는 어떤 사회의 문화적인 요소가 다른 사회에 의해 선택될 때 일어나는 것으로, 종종 이 문화 요소들을 다른 먼 지역으로 확장시키기도 한다. 문화 전파는 독자적인 발견과 혁신을 보완하면서 일부 인류학자들에게는 역사 전반에 걸친 문화 교환의 주요 과정으로 여겨지기도 한다. 문화 전파는 직접 전파, 간접 전파, 자극 전파라는 세 가지 뚜렷한 유형으로 일어난다.

2 ➡ 어떤 문화 요소가 지역적으로 가까운 사회에 차용되었을 때 그 문화적 요소는 종종 다른 문화로 계속 전파된다. 이런 현상을 직접 전파라고 하며 그 예로 종이의 전파를 들 수 있다. 중국 군대는 기원전 8세기에 종이를 사용하기 시작했다. 그러나 그것이 나중에 다른 동아시아 문화로 전파되었을 때, 그들은 그것을 어떻게 생산하는지 알아내지 못했다. 중국인들은 중국에서 종이가 발명된 지 한참 후인 서기 604년에 이 기술을 전수받은 첫 번째 나라인 한국에 기술을 가르칠 사람들을 보냈다. 몇 년 후에 종이와 제지 기술은 불교 승려에 의해 일본으로 소개되었고, 나중에는 중동까지 소개되었다. 종이는 11세기가 되어서야 스페인의 이슬람 지역을 통해 유럽으로 전달되었다. 광범위한 아이디어 확산을 통해 종이는 도입 뒤 한 왕조 시기의 중국, 중동 전 지역에의 이슬람 전파, 르네상스를 겪고 있던 유럽 등 여러 문화에서 큰 발전을 촉발했다.

3 ➡ 제3자가 문화 요소를 새로운 사회에 소개하는 것은 간접 전파라고 알려져 있다. 역사적으로 상인들은 다른 지역으로 새로운 물건을 가져갔을 뿐 아니라 그곳의 사람들에게 새로운 생각을 소개하기도 했었다. 이 과정의 예로는 북미의 원주민 부족에게 말이 도입된 것을 들 수 있다. 사실상 그들은 스페인에서 온 탐험가들을 통해 말을 알게 되었다. 곧 평원 원주민들의 문화는 말이 필수적인 요소가 되면서 대변혁을 겪게 되었다.

4 ➡ 자극 전파는 한 문화의 인기 있는 특징이 다른 문화에 의해 처음에 받아들여지는 것이 아니라 수용 문화권으로 전파된 어떤 자극이 실험을 거쳐 독특한 지역 특색을 지닌 발명이나 발전을 낳는 것이다. 예를 들어 산업 혁명은 18세기 후반 영국에서 시작되었으나 다른 나라에서는 바로 받아들여지지 않았다. 그러나 그것이 지역 제조업들을 기계화하는 데 자극을 준 후 결국 산업 혁명은 유럽 나머지 영역과 미국에서 19세기에 뿌리를 내리게 되었다.

1. 2단락의 단어 'it(그것)'이 가리키는 것은

Ⓐ 현상　Ⓑ 직접 전파　Ⓒ 중국 군대　Ⓓ 종이

2. 3단락의 단어 'they(그들)'가 가리키는 것은

Ⓐ 제3자　Ⓑ 무역상들　Ⓒ 말들　Ⓓ 원주민 부족들

3. 4단락의 단어 'it(그것)'이 가리키는 것은

Ⓐ 자극 전파　Ⓑ 실험　Ⓒ 산업 혁명　Ⓓ 영국

어휘 diffusion n 전파, 보급 | distant adj 먼 | anthropologist n 인류학자 | geographical adj 지리상의, 지리적인 | proximity n 근접, 접근 | explorer n 탐험가 | stimulate v 자극하다 | Industrial Revolution 산업 혁명 | manufacturing n 제조업 | extend v 퍼지다, 뻗다 | complement v 보충하다, 보완하다 | stimulus n 자극제, 자극 | extensive adj 아주 넓은, 광범위한 | prompt v 자극하다, 고무하다 | spawn v 결과를 낳다 | mechanize v 기계화하다

19 공생 관계

1 ➡ 공생, 즉 종이 다른 둘 이상의 생물 사이에 맺어지는 긴밀하고 상호 의존적인 관계는 모든 생태계에서 자연스럽게 찾아볼 수 있다. 이러한 관계로 얻을 수 있는 이익은 다양하며, 따라서 공생 관계는 기생, 편리공생과 상리공생, 이 세 가지로 분류된다. 그것들 중 특히 기생과 상리공생은 공생 관계가 종에게 어떻게 이로운지 보여준다.

2 ➡ 기생은 한 종이 피해를 보는 가운데 다른 한 종이 번성하는 공생 관계다. 그러나 다윈의 진화론에서 나타난 바와 같이 형세는 세대가 지나면서 바뀔 수 있다. 자연 선택의 과정을 통해, 손해를 입는 종은 수세를 취해 회복할 수 있다. 이것의 좋은 사례는 호주 토끼와 점액종 바이러스의 기생 관계에서 찾아볼 수 있다. 토끼는 유럽의 호주 대륙 식민 지배를 통해 호주에 유입되었다. 토끼는 골칫거리가 될 정도로 그 수가 급방 증가했다. 점액종 바이러스는 토끼 개체수를 억제하기 위해 과학자들이 유입했다. 처음 보기에는 성공적인 시도처럼 보였고 토끼의 개체 수는 줄어들었다. 그 뒤 토끼의 면역 체계가 방어적으로 바뀌었다. 3년 만에 토끼들은 그것에 대한 면역력을 가지고 태어나기 시작했다. 이는 바이러스가 토끼 개체수의 희생으로 번성했으므로 기생 관계를 입증하는 동시에, 토끼 같은 생물이 생존을 위해 적응하는 능력을 입증하기도 한다.

3 ➡ 한 종이 번성하고 다른 종은 아무런 영향을 받지 않는 공생 관계인 편리공생은 자연에서 찾아보기가 훨씬 더 어렵다. 생물학자들에 의하면 이것은 두 생물의 긴밀한 상호 작용이 양측에 중립적인 결과를 미칠 가능성이 적기 때문이라고 한다. 편리공생은 대개 한 종이 포식자에게 공격을 당하기 쉽거나 이동이 비효율적인 상황에서 발생한다. 예를 들어 쥐들은 하늘에서 사냥감을 노리는 매의 날카로운 눈으로부터 스스로를 보호하기 위해 프레리독의 굴을 이용할 수 있다. 프레리독의 노동은 쥐에게 도움을 주었지만 프레리독은 그 관계에서 아무것도 얻지 못한다. 해양 서식지에서 일부 작은 생물체들은 더 큰 생물의 몸에 자신들을 붙여서 이득을 보는데, 이는 그들이 음식이나 새로운 살 곳을 찾기 위해 먼 거리를 이동하게 해주지만 그 대가로 돌려주는 것은 아무것도 없다.

4 ➡ 세 번째 공생 형태는 상리공생이다. 이런 형태의 공생 관계에 개입하는 생물은 각각 모두 이익을 얻는다. 이것은 평생에 걸친 관계가 될 수 있고 심지어 여러 세대에 걸쳐 이어질 수도 있다. 멕시코, 중앙아메리카와 남아메리카에서 발견되는 아카시아 나무와 다양한 종의 개미들은 이러한 공생 형태의 좋은 예를 제공한다. 아카시아 나무는 풀을 먹는 초식 동물을 쫓기 위해 커다란 가시가 있지만 2차 방어선도 가지고 있다. 가시는 속이 비어 있어 깨무는 개미떼의 집이 된다. 개미 집단은 나무에 해를 끼칠 수 있는 다른 곤충들의 습격을 막을 뿐 아니라 포유류가 나무를 먹는 것을 저지함으로써 아카시아 나무의 수호자 역할을 한다. 그 대가로 아카시아 나무는 나뭇잎 끝에 개미에게 영양분을 제공하는 (단백질-지질이 함유된) 특별한 즙을 만들어 낸다.

5 ➡ 이렇게 다양한 종류의 공생이 고정적이지 않다는 사실을 기억하는 것이 중요하다. 실제로 편리공생으로 시작한 관계가 상리공생 또는 기생으로 발전할 수 있다. 예를 들어 소등쪼기새와 아프리카의 덩치 큰 포유류들 사이의 관계는 오랫동안 상리공생의 완벽한 예로 여겨졌다. 소등쪼기새는 버팔로, 코끼리 및 다른 포유동물의 등에 있는 곤충을 잡아 먹었다. 소등쪼기새는 먹이를 얻고 포유 동물들은 기생 곤충의 피해로부터 안심할 수 있었다. 그러나 나중에 발견된 바로는 그들은 숙주 동물의 등에 상처를 내고 심지어 거기서 스며 나오는 피를 먹으며 더욱 기생적이 되는 경향이 있는 것으로 알려졌다. 따라서 공생적 상호 관계는 관계가 이루어지는 환경의 변화뿐 아니라 발달상의 변화 때문에 생물의 일생 중에 변하기도 한다.

1. 2단락의 단어 'it(그것)'이 가리키는 것은

Ⓐ 바이러스 Ⓑ 토끼 Ⓒ 면역 체계 Ⓓ 능력

2. 3단락의 단어 'themselves(자신들)'가 가리키는 것은

Ⓐ 큰 생물들 Ⓑ 작은 생물들 Ⓒ 쥐들 Ⓓ 매들

3. 5단락의 단어 'they(그들)'이 가리키는 것은

Ⓐ 소등쪼기새들 Ⓑ 포유류들 Ⓒ 곤충들 Ⓓ 숙주들

어휘 symbiosis n 공생 | interdependent adj 상호 의존적인 | ecological adj 생태계의 | parasitism n 기생 관계 | commensalism n 편리공생 | mutualism n 상리공생 | colonization n 식민지화 | multiply v 급증하다 | pest n 해충, 유해 동물 | curb v 억제하다 | immune adj 면역의 | immunity n 면역력 | forage v 식량을 찾아 다니다 | neutral adj 중립적인 | locomotion n 이동 | lifelong adj 평생의 | herbivore n 초식동물 | sting v 찌르다 | invasion n 침입 | lipid n 지질, 지방질 | leaflet n 나뭇잎 | sustenance n 영양물, 음식물 | oxpecker n 소등쪼기새 | relief n 안심, 위안, 구제

---

20 인지 발달 단계

1 ➡ 발달 심리학의 역사상 가장 영향력 있는 이론은 피아제의 인지 발달 이론, 즉 생각하고 이해하는 능력의 발달에 관한 이론이다. 스위스의 심리학자 장 피아제는 지능 발달에 이론의 초점을 맞추었다. 그의 이론은 스키마타, 즉 인간이 세계를 보는 방식의 발현 및 습득에 대해 다룬다. 피아제에 따르면 어린이는 정보의 지적 표현 방법을 새로이 습득하며 뚜렷이 구분되는 네 단계를 거친다. 그는 아동 발달의 네 단계를 상정하고 각 단계에서 아동이 보여주는 외부 세계 인지 수준을 묘사했다.

2 ➡ 감각 운동기는 피아제가 설명한 4단계 중 첫 번째이고 출생부터 대략 2세까지 지속된다. 그의 이론에 따르면 이 시기는 아이들이 주변에 대한 포괄적인 이해력을 발달시키는 시기다. 우선 아이는 기본적인 반사 행동을 발달시키며 이것은 첫 6주에 걸쳐 서서히 자발적인 행동이 되고, 그런 다음 아이는 행동의 반복을 통해 습관을 발달시킨다. 이 시기에 유아들은 의도적으로 물체를 잡으려고 노력할 것이다. 또 12개월에서 18개월 사이 아이들은 간단한 실험을 통해 도전 과제를 극복하기 위한 새로운 방법을 찾는다.

3 ➡ 전조작기는 피아제의 인지 발달 4단계 중 두 번째이고 대략 2세에서 7세까지 지속된다. 피아제는 놀고 있는 아이들을 관찰하여 새로운 사고 과정이 이루어지는 몇 가지 사건들을 확인할 수 있었다. 이 단계에서 아이들은 상징 기능을 보이는데, 이것은 물리적으로 존재하지 않는 무언가를 표현하기 위해 아이들이 상징, 단어, 또는 그림을 사용하는 현상이 특징이다. 피아제는 원래의 형태가 바뀌어도 양, 부피, 수가 유지된다는 개념이 이 단계의 아이들에게 부족하다는 사실을 발견했다. 게다가 아이는 자극이나 상황의 한 가지 측면에만 집중하거나 주의를 기울일 수 있다. 예를 들어, 긴 유리잔에 든 우유를 납작한 그릇에 부으면 아이는 그것이 '더 낮아졌기' 때문에 양이 줄었다고 생각할 것이다. 아이들은 직관적으로 사고할 수 있는데, 즉 이유를 납득하지 않고도 어떤 것을 믿을 수 있는 빠른 직관 능력이 있다.

4 ➡ 7세에서 11세에 해당하는 구체적 조작기는 피아제 이론의 세 번째 단계다. 논리를 적절히 이용하는 것이 특징이며 몇 가지 뚜렷한 과정이 나타난다. 첫째, 아이들은 문제를 해결할 때 여러 측면을 고려한다. 둘째, 그들은 상황이나 환경에 따라 물체가 변할 수 있고 그들의 원래 형태로 돌아갈 수 있다는 것을 인지한다. 마지막으로 자기 중심성이 사라지는 것이 이 단계이며 아이들은 대상을 다른 시각에서 이해할 수 있게 된다.

5 ➡ 피아제 이론의 마지막 단계는 형식적 조작기다. 이 단계는 약 11세에서 15세 사이에 시작되어 성인기까지 지속된다. 이 단계는 추상적으로 사고하고 이용 가능한 정보에서 결론을 도출하는 능력이 특징이다. 생각을 보다 추상적으로 함으로써 청소년들은 이상적인 자아상과 상황을 가정할 수 있게 된다. 그들은 자신의 미래와 목표에 대해서도 심사숙고하게 된다. 아울러 문제를 보다 체계적으로 해결하고 결과에 대해서도 가정할 수 있다. 연역적 추론은 그들의 문제 해결 능력을 훨씬 더 향상할 수 있도록 보완해준다.

1. 3단락의 단어 'it(그것)'이 가리키는 것은

Ⓐ 유리 Ⓑ 그릇 Ⓒ 아이 Ⓓ 우유

2. 4단락의 단어 'their(그들의)'가 가리키는 것은

Ⓐ 과정들의 Ⓑ 아이들의 Ⓒ 측면들의 Ⓓ 물체들의

3. 5단락의 단어 'They(그들)'이 가리키는 것은

Ⓐ 결론들 Ⓑ 청소년들 Ⓒ 상황들 Ⓓ 결과들

어휘 influential adj 영향력 있는 I developmental psychology 발달 심리학 I cognitive development 인지 발달 I intelligence n 지능 I emergence n 출현 I acquisition n 습득 I distinct adj 분명한 I sensorimotor stage 감각 운동기 I reflex n 반사 I voluntary adj 자발적인 I infant n 유아 I intentionally adv 의도적으로 I grab v 움켜쥐다 I preoperational stage 전조작기 I conservation n 보존 I mass n 양 I volume n 부피 I stimulus n 자극 I insight n 통찰 I concrete operational stage 구체적 조작기 I aptly adv 적절하게 I egocentrism n 자기 중심성 I formal operational stage 형식적 조작기 I systematic adj 체계적인 I hypothesize v 가설/가정을 세우다 I outcome n 결과 I decrease v 감소하다 I quantity n 양 I deductive adj 연역적인 I complement v 보충하다

Test

본서 I P. 136

조류 군집

1 ➡ 많은 조류종들은 특정 지역에 함께 모여 둥지를 틀거나 휴식을 위해 큰 집단을 이룬다. 이런 집단들은 조류 군집이라 불리며 만일 그들이 모이는 목적이 번식하고 새끼를 키우는 것이라면 그들의 집단은 번식 군집이라고 한다. 군집 번식 조류들 대다수는 신천옹과 바다쇠오리 같은 바닷새 종들이지만 왜가리 같은 많은 습지 종들과 제비 같은 연작류 새들 또한 군집을 형성한다. 쉬어가는 새들은 번식의 목적으로 모인 것이 아니라 이주를 위해 모였으며 그곳에 단지 잠시 머물러 있을 것이기 때문에 둥지를 트지 않는다. 쉬어가는 새 무리들은 보통 나무나 들판에서 밤을 보내고 그 다음날 이동한다. 어느 경우에나 조류 군집들은 수천에서 수십만의 개체들을 포함할 수 있다. 번식 군집과 집단 휴식은 이런 습성이 있는 새들에게 많은 장점들을 제공하지만 거기에는 또한 몇 가지 심각한 단점들이 있다.

1. 1단락에 따르면, 다음 중 조류 군집에 대해 사실인 것은 무엇인가?

Ⓐ 둥지를 트는 새들은 대부분 더 따뜻한 나라로의 이동을 위해 모인다.

Ⓑ 군집 유형들은 모인 목적 면에서 차이가 있다.

Ⓒ 쉬어가는 새들은 보통 다른 새들의 둥지를 빌려 하룻밤을 지낸다.

Ⓓ 고작 몇 십여 마리의 개체들로 이루어진 조류 군집들이 많다.

2 ➡ 군집을 이루어 둥지를 트는 것의 주요 장점은 그것이 제공할 수 있는 안전이다. 군집 번식은 모든 조류종들의 약 13퍼센트에 의해 실행되며 바닷새는 95퍼센트에 가깝게 바다 절벽과 섬들에 군집을 이루며 둥지를 튼다. 군집을 이루며 둥지를 트는 것은 여러 면에서 생존 가능성을 높여준다. 많은 새들은 대양에 위치한 바위섬처럼 그들의 천적이 없는 지역에 둥지를 튼다. 함께 둥지를 트는 큰 무리는 추가적인 보호를 제공하는데 이것은 포식자들에 맞서는 방어 태세를 갖출 수 있는 새들이 많다는 것이다. 또한 군집으로 둥지를 트는 많은 새들은 동기화된 번식을 하는데 이것은 그들이 짝짓기와 부화를 함께 한다는 것이다. 이것은 포식자들이 먹을 수 있는 것보다 더 많은 새끼들이 있다는 것을 뜻하며 그들이 일단 만족하고 나면 나머지 새끼들을 그냥 놔둘 거라는 뜻이다. 다른 새들은 훨씬 더 정교한 전략들을 사용하여 포식으로부터 그들의 새끼를 보호한다.

3 ➡ 새끼를 보호하기 위해 많은 노력을 하는 한 가지 종은 남미 북쪽 지역에 서식하는 옐로럼프카시케다. 이 식충성 조류들은 매우 사회적이며 숲 지붕에서 그들의 생존을 보장하기 위해 여러 단계의 방어 체계를 구축한다. 가능한 경우 그들은 뱀 같은 육상 포식자를 감소시키기 위해 섬의 나무에 둥지를 트는 것으로 효과적으로 해자를 형성한다. 이것은 숲 지붕을 지나다닐 수 있는 영장류들을 막지 못하기 때문에 카시케들은 보통 사용 중인 말벌 둥지들이 있는 나무들에 둥지를 짓는다. 말벌들이 위협을 느끼면 그들까지 공격할 수 있기 때문에 신중한 거리를 유지해야 하지만 말벌들은 새들의 둥지를 공격하려는 원숭이들을 내쫓는 것으로 관찰되었다. 그들은 사용하지 않는 오래된 둥지들과 새로운 둥지들을 섞어서 유인용 둥지들을 놔두기도 하는데 이것은 포식자들의 시간을 낭비하며 조기 발견의 가능성을 높인다. 다른 새 종들이 그들의 지역을 침범하면 수컷 카시케들은 떼를 지어 그들을 쫓아내려 공격한다. 이런 기술은 무리 공격이라 불리며 수컷들은 오래된 카시케 둥지들을 사용하는 다른 새들도 보호하는 것으로 관찰되었다. 이런 전략들을 가장 효과적으로 통합하는 번식 군집들은 포식자들로부터 피해를 제일 적게 입는 경향이 있다.

4 ➡ 다른 종들에게 안전보다 더 시급한 문제는 적절한 먹이 공급원의 할당이다. 이름에서 알 수 있듯이 삼색제비는 절벽의 전면과 다리들과 건물들을 포함하는 여러 수직 구조물에 진흙 둥지를 만드는데, 이것은 대부분의 포식자들이 접근하는 것을 불가능하게 한다. 비록 단독으로 둥지를 틀더라도 삼색제비들은 보통 수천 마리에 달하는 군집들을 형성한다. 그들의 둥지들은 보호가 매우 잘되어 있기 때문에 그들의 군집은 먹이를 위해 형성된다. 삼색제비는 공중 사냥꾼인데 큰 무리를 형성한 그들이 효과적으로 먹어 치울 수 있는 밀집된 곤충 떼를 불러일으키는 기류를 활용한다. 하지만 먹이가 부족할 때 사냥감을 찾는 데 어려움을 겪은 새들은 그들의 이웃을 관찰한다. 한 마리가 먹이를 찾아서 돌아오는 것을 보면 그들은 그 새를 따라서 먹이를 얻은 곳으로 간다. 또한 불리한 기후 조건 속에서 사냥감을 발견한 개체들은 소리를 내서 집단에게 그들을 따라오라고 신호를 보낸다. 사냥 무리의 크기를 키움으로써 먹이 떼를 발견한 새는 그 떼의 경로를 추적하는 데 다른 새들의 도움을 받을 수 있다.

5 ➡ 하지만 군집을 형성하는 것은 특히 안전과 관련해서 해로운 효과도 있다. 번식 군집들은 육상 동물에 맞서서 더 많은 보호를 제공하는 것 같지만 그들은 종종 덩치가 더 큰 맹금류들을 끌어들인다. 수리부엉이들은 밤에 제비갈매기 군집의 중심을 계속적으로 공격하

2. 다음 중 음영 표시된 문장의 핵심 정보를 가장 잘 표현한 문장은 무엇인가? 오답은 의미를 크게 왜곡하거나 핵심 정보를 누락하고 있다.

Ⓐ 조류 새끼들의 개체수가 너무 많아서 현실적으로 한꺼번에 그 새끼들을 전부 잡아먹을 수 있는 숫자의 포식자는 없을 것이기 때문에, 새끼들 중 몇몇은 생존할 것이다.
Ⓑ 포식자들이 완전히 만족하면 그들은 다른 조류 새끼들을 풀어주고 날아갈 것이다.
Ⓒ 조류 새끼들 대다수는 포식자들의 맹렬한 공격 후에도 살아남을 수 있다.
Ⓓ 둥지를 트는 새들은 새끼를 함께 키워서 여러 면에서 생존 가능성을 높인다.

3. 다음 중 3단락에서 옐로럼프카시케들에 관해 언급되지 않은 것은

Ⓐ 그들은 남미 북쪽 지역에서 왔다
Ⓑ 그들은 무리 공격을 방어기제로 활용한다
Ⓒ 그들은 말벌들과 상호간에 이익이 되는 관계를 형성한다
Ⓓ 그들은 뱀들과 영장류들로부터 그들의 둥지를 보호한다

4. 3단락에 따르면, 카시케들은 버려진 둥지들 주변에 둥지를 짓는데 그 이유는

Ⓐ 말벌의 도움을 얻을 수 있는 효과적인 방법이기 때문에
Ⓑ 육생 포식자들을 피하길 원하기 때문에
Ⓒ 포식자들을 빈 둥지들로 유인하려고 하기 때문에
Ⓓ 수컷 카시케들이 버려진 둥지를 사용하는 다른 새들을 보호할 수 있게 하기 때문에

5. 4단락에 따르면, 다음 중 삼색제비에 대해 사실이 아닌 것은 무엇인가?

Ⓐ 기류를 타는 곤충 떼들을 사냥한다.
Ⓑ 그들의 둥지는 대체적으로 포식자들에게 노출되지 않는다.
Ⓒ 그들의 둥지는 보통 먹이 공급원 근처에 위치한다.
Ⓓ 무리를 지을 때 더 효과적으로 먹이를 잡는다.

6. 4단락에서 글쓴이는 군집 번식에 대해 어떻게 설명하는가?

Ⓐ 삼색제비들을 위험에 빠뜨리는 식량 부족을 강조함으로써
Ⓑ 삼색제비들을 둥지를 트는 것에 더 집중하는 다른 새들과 비교함으로써
Ⓒ 둥지 트기와 사냥 같은 삼색제비들의 습성들을 묘사함으로써
Ⓓ 모든 바닷새들이 그들의 새끼를 보호하기 위해 모인다는 주장을 반박함으로써

7. 4단락의 단어 'them(그들)'이 가리키는 것은

Ⓐ 개체들
Ⓑ 먹이
Ⓒ 조건들
Ⓓ 다른 새들

지만 저항을 거의 받지 않거나 전혀 받지 않는 것으로 관찰되었다. [■A] 신천옹도 작은 사냥 무리로 펭귄 군집을 공격하며 공격 능력이 부족한 불행한 부모에게서 새끼들을 빼앗아간다. [■B] 하지만 군집을 이루어 둥지를 트는 것의 가장 큰 단점은 인간의 영향으로부터 비롯된다. 섬에 서식하는 많은 종들과 바닷새들은 그들을 먹이로 활용하는 선원들에게 발견되었으며 큰바다오리 같은 몇몇 종들은 완전히 전멸되었다. [■C] 게다가 인간은 부주의하고 고의적으로 쥐와 여우 같이 큰 피해를 입히는 외래종들을 도입했다. [■D] 휴식하는 군집들도 나그네비둘기처럼 인간의 희생물이 되었다. 이 새들은 과거에 만 마리 이상 떼를 지어 이동했지만 인간은 의도적으로 그물을 사용해서 사냥했고 그들을 멸종에 이르게 했다.

8. 5단락에서 추론할 수 있는 것은

Ⓐ 신천옹들은 바닷새들에게 가장 큰 위협이다
Ⓑ 제비갈매기는 수리부엉이의 주요 먹이다
Ⓒ 군집들을 형성하는 것은 혼자 사는 것보다 더 안전한 것으로 밝혀졌다
Ⓓ 인간은 조류 개체수를 통제하기 위한 고의적인 시도들을 한다

9. 지문에 다음 문장이 들어갈 수 있는 위치를 나타내는 네 개의 사각형 [■]을 확인하시오.

하지만 군집을 이루어 둥지를 트는 것의 가장 큰 단점은 인간의 영향으로부터 비롯된다.

이 문장이 들어가기에 가장 적합한 곳은? [■B]

10. **지시문:** 지문을 간략하게 요약한 글의 첫 문장이 아래 제시되어 있다. 지문의 가장 중요한 내용을 표현하는 세 개의 선택지를 골라 요약문을 완성하시오. 일부 문장들은 지문에 제시되지 않았거나 지문의 지엽적인 내용을 나타내기 때문에 요약문에 포함되지 않는다. ***이 문제의 배점은 2점이다.***

조류 군집이 함께 둥지를 틀고 휴식하는 데에는 장점과 단점이 있다.

Ⓐ 조류 군집의 주요 장점은 안전인데 이것은 그들의 둥지를 포식자들로부터 더 효과적으로 보호할 수 있기 때문이다.
Ⓒ 안전한 장소에 둥지를 트는 삼색제비들과 같은 몇몇 조류 군집들은 먹이 공급원의 할당에 더 집중한다.
Ⓓ 큰 무리는 맹금류와 인간의 눈에 더 띄기 때문에 군집 번식은 종종 위험할 수 있다.

Ⓑ 어떤 종들은 어린 새들을 위협하는 원숭이들을 쫓아내기 위해 의도적으로 그들의 둥지를 사용 중인 말벌 둥지 주변에 짓는다.
Ⓔ 조류 종들 대부분은 군집 번식을 하는 것으로 관찰되며 이들 중 대다수는 바닷새 종들이다.
Ⓕ 외래종들의 도입은 섬에 서식하는 많은 바닷새 종들의 멸종과 군집 번식 습성의 감소로 이어졌다.

어휘 roost v 쉬다, 유숙하다, 하룻밤을 보내다 I rear v 기르다, 양육하다 I breeding n 번식 I wetland n 습지 I mating n (동물의) 짝짓기, 교미 I migration n 이주 I communal adj 공동의, 공용의 I predator n 포식자 I security n 보안, 안보 I mount v ~을 조직하여 시작하다 I synchronized adj 동시에 발생하는, 동기화된 I hatch v 부화하다 I satiate v 충분히 만족시키다 I tactic n 전략, 작전 I insectivorous adj 식충성의, 곤충을 먹는 I multi-tiered adj 여러 단계의 I canopy n 숲 지붕 I terrestrial adj 육생의, 지생의 I moat n 해자(성 주위에 둘러 판 못) I deter v 단념시키다, 그만두게 하다 I primate n 영장류 I negotiate v 넘다(지나다), 협상하다 I wasp n 말벌 I intent adj 꾀하는, 작정한 I raid v 침입하다, 공격하다 I mingle v 섞다, 어우르다 I decoy n 유인용, 바람잡이 I detection n 발견, 탐지 I invade v 난입하다, 침범하다 I integrate v 통합시키다 I allocation n 할당 I immediate adj 당면한, 즉각적인 I inaccessible adj 접근하기 어려운 I solitarily adv 혼자서, 고립되어 I aerial adj 공중의 I air current 기류 I dense adj 밀집한, 빽빽한 I scarce adj 부족한, 드문 I unfavorable adj 불리한, 순조롭지 않은 I utter v (입으로) 소리를 내다 I hunting party 사냥 무리 I detrimental adj 해로운 I predatory bird 맹금류, 육식조 I resistance n 저항 I hapless adj 불운한, 불행한 I offensive adj 공격(용)의, 공격적인 I exploit v (부당하게) 이용하다 I annihilate v 전멸시키다 I inadvertently adv 무심코, 부주의하게 I knowingly adv 다 알고도, 고의로 I invasive species 외래종 I deliberately adv 고의로, 의도적으로

또 다른 황진을 예방하는 방법

1 ➡ 1930년대에 일련의 파괴적인 모래 폭풍이 북미 평원 지대를 황폐하게 만들었는데 이것은 지역 생태계를 훼손하고 농업을 마비시켰다. 황진이라 불리는 이 재앙은 수십 년 전에 시작된 사건들의 정점이었으며 이것은 막을 수도 있었을 일이었다. 1850년대 이전에 고지

11. 2단락에 따르면, 다음 중 황진의 발생에 영향을 미치지 않는 것은 무엇인가?

Ⓐ 잡초들과 관목들
Ⓑ 기후 조건들
Ⓒ 과방목
Ⓓ 가뭄들

대초원의 대부분은 지표수와 나무의 부족으로 인해 정착민들에게 '미국의 거대한 사막'이라고 불리었고 그들은 그런 이유로 그곳에 정착하는 것을 피했다. 그 평원은 평균적인 해에 고작 25센티미터의 강우량을 보였는데, 엄밀히 따지면 그 지역이 실제로 사막이 아니더라도 매우 건조한 것이기에 이 명칭은 실제로 꽤 정확했다. 하지만 그 다음 10년 동안 그 지역에 정착하는 것이 장려되었고 그 지역에서 농업에 사용된 기술은 토지에 점차적으로 해가 되었다.

2 ➡ 평원은 기후 조건과 상관없이 표토를 고정시키는 뿌리가 깊은 토종 잡초로 덮여 있었다. 처음에 사람들은 거기에서 가축을 기르기 시작하면서 동물들을 방목시켜서 잡초를 활용했다. 하지만 가혹한 겨울과 가뭄과 전반적인 과방목이 곧 피해로 이어지자 농업이 목축을 대체했다. 그 후 수십 년 동안 곡물과 목화와 같은 환금 작물을 재배하는 농부들에게 점점 더 넓은 부지가 주어지거나 팔렸다. 강수량이 많아진 기간에 힘입어 농업은 확장을 계속했고 더 기계화되었다. 깊은 쟁기질은 얇은 표토를 흩트려놓았고 농부들은 갈수록 겨울 동안 밭들을 메마른 상태로 놔두었다. 극심한 가뭄과 강한 폭풍이 몰아치자 흙을 고정시킬 수 있는 것이 아무것도 없었고 검은 먼지 구름이 대륙을 휩쓸었다.

3 ➡ 재앙 후에 많은 지역들은 그들의 비옥한 표토 중 17퍼센트에서 28퍼센트를 손실했고 이것은 토지의 가치를 떨어뜨렸다. 이것은 많은 농부들을 파산하게 만들었고 남은 농부들은 그들의 토지를 생육 가능하게 유지하기 위해 화학 비료에 점차 의존했다. 하지만 피해를 덜 입은 지역의 많은 농부들은 그들의 농장을 보호하기 위해 예방책을 받아들이기 시작했다. 흥미롭게도 가장 효과적이었던 기법들은 최근에 발명된 것들이 아니었다. 그들의 토지를 생산적으로 유지하기 위해 많은 농부들은 윤작을 재개했다. 그들은 밭의 일부분을 1년 혹은 2년 동안 자생하도록 놀리는데 이것은 토종 식물들이 자라는 것을 장려함으로써 침식을 감소시키고 자연적으로 토양을 비옥하게 한다. 다른 농부들은 그들의 밭을 나누어 여러 작물들을 돌려가며 재배하는데 이것은 식물들이 번갈아 서로에게 비료를 제공하는 역할을 하게 한다.

4 ➡ 그 지역에 영향을 미치는 끊임없는 바람에 맞서기 위하여 농부들은 방풍림을 심기 시작했다. 이것은 기류를 방해해 기류 방향을 위로 돌려놓기 위한, 밭 주변에 심어진 여러 줄로 정렬된 나무들과 관목들이다. 이것은 바람과 물로 인한 침식으로부터 토양을 보호할 뿐만 아니라 작물을 더 따뜻하게 보호해서 식물들로 하여금 더 높이 건강하게 자랄 수 있게 한다. 이것은 또한 과일을 생산하는 나무나 목재로 사용되는 나무를 심음으로써 땅의 수익성을 증가시킨다. 하지만 이 두 가지 방법은 대기업들이 점차 농업을 장악하기 시작하면서 인기를 잃었다. 그들의 높은 이윤폭 때문에 기업들은 화학 비료를 사용하는 것을 선호하며 침식에 대해 무관심하다. 결과적으로 근래 가뭄들은 더 많은 피해를 입히며 오염이 증가했다.

5 ➡ 도시와 교외 지역의 지속적 성장으로 인해 산업화된 농업의 확장은 억제하기 힘들다. 증가하는 인구를 먹이기 위해서는 더 많은 식량을 제공할 수 있어야 하며 이는 더 많은 토지가 사용되어야 한다는 뜻이다. 하지만 도시들 자체가 해답을 제공할 수 있다. 일본에서는 놀랍도록 넓은 지역의 도심 토지가 소규모 농사에 사용된다. 이런 농장들은 대체적으로 주택가에 위치하며 거기에서는 보통 채소와 다른

12. 3단락의 단어 'viable(생육 가능한)'과 의미상 가장 가까운 것은

Ⓐ 바람직한
Ⓑ 귀중한
Ⓒ 일회용의
Ⓓ 사용 가능한

13. 3단락에 따르면, 농부들이 윤작으로 돌아선 이유는

Ⓐ 토종 식물들로 하여금 더 빠르게 자라게 하고 유해한 식물을 내쫓는다
Ⓑ 그 환경에서 곤충들이 번성하는 것을 방지하고 곤충들을 박멸한다
Ⓒ 환경적 위협으로부터 토양을 보호하고 습한 상태를 유지하게 한다
Ⓓ 침식을 감소시키고 토양을 자연적으로 비옥하게 한다

14. 다음 중 4단락에서 가뭄과 오염에 기여한 요인으로 언급되지 않은 것은

Ⓐ 화학 비료의 빈번한 사용
Ⓑ 토지의 증가된 수익성
Ⓒ 환경에 대한 관심 부재
Ⓓ 밭 주변에 심겨진 더 적은 숫자의 방풍림

15. 5단락에서 추론 가능한 바에 따르면 도심 농장은

Ⓐ 경제적 혜택을 제공할 뿐만 아니라 생활 조건을 향상시킨다
Ⓑ 상승한 평균 기온을 제공함으로써 편안한 도심 분위기를 형성한다
Ⓒ 사람들이 과일과 채소를 직접 재배함으로써 지속 가능한 생활을 할 수 있게 도와준다
Ⓓ 도시 내의 토양 침식과 유수를 방지하여 토지에 가해지는 피해를 줄인다

16. 5단락의 단어 'they(거기)'가 가리키는 것은

Ⓐ 도시들
Ⓑ 농장들
Ⓒ 지역들
Ⓓ 채소

17. 6단락에 따르면, 황진과 유사한 또 다른 재앙을 방지하는 데 사용될 수 있는 방법은 무엇인가?

Ⓐ 윤작
Ⓑ 시골에서의 농사
Ⓒ 방목
Ⓓ 관목 제거

농작물을 키운다. 도시 환경은 그들을 바람으로부터 보호하며 유수로 충분한 물 공급을 제공한다. 이런 농사의 경제적 이득은 분명하게 드러나는데 나라 전체 농업 생산량의 약 3분의 1이 도심 농장에서 비롯되며 그들은 농가의 25퍼센트를 차지한다. 이 농장들은 다른 장점들도 갖고 있다. 그들은 평균 기온을 떨어뜨리고 산소 수준을 증가시키고 사람들에게 더 편안한 분위기를 제공하는 녹지 공간을 도시 안에 만든다.

6 ➡ 만일 미국에서 대규모 농사의 추세를 뒤집기 위한 그 무엇도 행해지지 않는다면 이것은 황진과 같은 또 다른 재앙을 야기할지도 모른다. [■A] 예를 들면 지난 몇 년 간 심각한 가뭄이 평원의 농업 생산량을 매우 심하게 떨어뜨렸기 때문에 미국 국내 및 미국의 수출에 의존하는 다른 국가들에 동물성 사료가 부족하게 되었다. [■B] 하지만 이런 어려움을 다시 겪을 필요는 없다. 만일 기업형 농장들이 1930년대 이후 농부들이 받아들인 기법들을 채택한다면 대부분의 피해를 역전시킬 수 있다. [■C] 일본의 통계가 증명하듯이 도시 농업 또한 이런 농장들이 억지로 지던 부담을 줄이는 역할을 할 수 있다. [■D] 하지만 도시 농업이 몇몇 미국 도시에서 유행이 된 반면에 이것은 여전히 매우 제한적이다.

18. 다음 중 지문에 음영 표시된 문장의 핵심 정보를 가장 잘 표현한 문장은 무엇인가? 오답은 의미를 크게 왜곡하거나 핵심 정보를 누락하고 있다.

Ⓐ 가뭄에 의한 미국의 농업 생산량 감소는 많은 국가들에게 영향을 미쳤다.

Ⓑ 동물성 사료의 부족은 농업 생산량의 상당한 감소를 야기했다.

Ⓒ 많은 국가들은 가뭄으로 인해 지난 몇 년간 미국 수출에 의존하고 있다.

Ⓓ 극심한 가뭄은 평원을 파괴했고 이것은 많은 국가들이 의존하고 있는 가축의 부족을 야기했다.

19. 지문에 다음 문장이 들어갈 수 있는 위치를 나타내는 네 개의 사각형 [■]을 확인하시오.

하지만 이런 어려움을 다시 겪을 필요는 없다.

이 문장이 들어가기에 가장 적합한 곳은? [■B]

20. 지시문: 지문을 간략하게 요약한 글의 첫 문장이 아래 제시되어 있다. 지문의 가장 중요한 내용을 표현하는 세 개의 선택지를 골라 요약문을 완성하시오. 일부 문장들은 지문에 제시되지 않았거나 지문의 지엽적인 내용을 나타내기 때문에 요약문에 포함되지 않는다. ***이 문제의 배점은 2점이다.***

일련의 파괴적인 먼지 폭풍들인 황진은 1930년대에 북미 평원에 심각한 피해를 입혔다.

Ⓐ 과방목, 깊은 쟁기질, 극심한 가뭄과 폭풍은 전부 황진 발생의 원인이 되었다.
Ⓑ 그 재앙 후에 농부들은 윤작으로 돌아갔고 또 다른 재앙이 발생하는 것을 방지하기 위해 방풍림을 심었다.
Ⓔ 꽤 최근의 기법인 도시 농업은 도시와 주변 환경에 제공하는 혜택으로 인기를 얻고 있다.

Ⓒ 윤작은 미국 몇몇 지역에서 성공적인 것으로 드러난 반면에 다른 지역에서는 나무들과 관목들을 심는 것이 더 효과적인 것으로 나타났다.

Ⓓ 대기업들은 화학 비료들과 다른 유해한 방법을 사용함으로써 다시 토지에 피해를 입히기 시작했다.

Ⓕ 일본에서처럼 도시 농업은 다른 동아시아 국가들에서도 서서히 유행이 되고 있다.

어휘 dust storm 모래 폭풍, 황사 I ravage v 황폐/피폐하게 만들다 I plain n 평원, 평지 I ecology n 생태(계), 생태학 I cripple v 제대로 기능을 못 하게 만들다 I culmination n 정점 I prairie n 대초원 I settler n 정착민 I accordingly adv 그에 맞춰, 부응해서 I arid adj 매우 건조한 I detrimental adj 해로운 I topsoil n 겉흙 I graze v 풀을 뜯다, 방목하다 I cash crop 환금 작물 I plowing n 쟁기질, 밭갈이 I barren adj 척박한 I viable adj 실행 가능한, 성공할 수 있는 I preventative adj 예방/방지를 위한 I fertilize v (토지에) 비료를 주다 I combat v ~에 맞서 다, 싸우다 I windbreak n 방풍림 I disrupt v 방해하다 I deflect v 방향을 바꾸다/바꾸게 하다 I profitability n 수익성 I suburb n 교외 I residential area 주택가 I produce n 농산물 I ample adj 충분한 I runoff n 유수 I green space 녹지 공간 I feed n (동물의) 먹이

Lesson 01 Rhetorical Purpose

본서 I P. 146

Practice

01 D 02 C 03 B 04 D 05 B 06 C 07 B 08 A 09 C 10 D

11 1. D 2. C 3. B 12 1. B 2. C 3. D 13 1. B 2. C 3. D 14 1. A 2. B 3. D 15 1. B 2. B 3. A

Test

1. B 2. B 3. C 4. C, D 5. C 6. C 7. B 8. A 9. D 10. A, B, F

11. B 12. D 13. C 14. D 15. A 16. B 17. C 18. A 19. B 20. A, E, F

Practice

본서 I P. 148

01 사막 환경에 적응한 가장 좋은 사례 중 하나는 캥거루쥐와 같은 작은 포유동물인데 이들은 극심한 열을 피하기 위해 지하에 굴을 파는 능력이 있다.

글쓴이가 '캥거루쥐'를 언급하는 이유는 무엇인가?

Ⓐ 어려운 개념을 독자가 더 쉽게 이해하도록 하기 위해서
Ⓑ 그 동물의 가장 중요한 적응 형태를 소개하기 위해서
Ⓒ 모든 사막 포유동물들이 가지고 있는 적응 능력을 언급하기 위해서
Ⓓ 사막 기후에 잘 적응한 생물의 예를 제공하기 위해서

어휘 mammal n 포유동물 I burrow v 굴을 파다 I extreme adj 극도의, 극심한

02 동물들이 과거의 사건을 회상하며 미래를 예측하고, 선택하며 계획할 수 있다는 의견을 지지하는 동물 행동심리학자들이 많다. 그러나 10,000분의 4온스 되는 두뇌를 가진 꿀벌이 자리를 옮긴 먹이를 어떻게 찾을 수 있는지에 관한 설명은 여전히 없다.

글쓴이가 '10,000분의 4온스 되는 두뇌를 가진'을 언급하는 이유는 무엇인가?

Ⓐ 꿀벌의 영리함을 설명하기 위해
Ⓑ 뇌의 작은 크기를 묘사하기 위해
Ⓒ 꿀벌의 지적 능력의 신비함을 강조하기 위해
Ⓓ 꿀벌의 지적 능력에 대해 반박하기 위해

어휘 behaviorist n 행동주의 심리학자 I recall v 기억해 내다, 상기하다 I weigh v 무게가 나가다

03 몇몇 과학자들은 몸의 움직임을 통해 의사소통할 수 있는 꿀벌의 능력이 특별한 지적 능력을 보여 주는 것은 아니라고 추정했다. 그러나 꿀벌의 능력에 관한 재미있는 실험이 최근 행해졌다. 한 조사에서 연구원들은 각 실험이 행해질 때마다 벌들이 찾아야 하는 먹이의 위치를 25% 더 멀리 이동시켰다. 먹이를 찾는 꿀벌은 먹이의 다음 위치를 예측하기 시작했다. 연구자들은 벌들이 도착했을 때 그 위치에서 맴돌며 먹이를 기다리고 있는 것을 발견하곤 했다.

글쓴이가 '꿀벌의 능력에 관한 재미있는 실험'을 언급하는 이유는 무엇인가?

Ⓐ 서로 다른 과학자들의 능력을 비교하려고
Ⓑ 일부 과학자들이 가정했던 내용이 틀렸을 수도 있음을 주장하려고
Ⓒ 꿀벌의 의사소통의 복잡함을 보여주려고
Ⓓ 꿀벌의 의사소통의 서로 다른 종류들을 보여주려고

어휘 assume v 추정하다, 가정하다 I conduct v 실행하다, 조사하다 I successive adj 연속적인, 뒤따르는

04 동물의 인지를 나타내는 한 가지 행동은 선택이다. 한 실험에서 침팬지는 안에 초콜릿 칩이 든 두 쌍의 통들을 비교했다. 예를 들어 한 쌍에는 4개와 2개의 칩이, 다른 하나에는 3개와 1개의 칩이 있었다. 원하는 것을 고르도록 허락했을 때 침팬지는 거의 항상 가장 많은 칩이 들어 있는 쌍을 선택했다.

글쓴이가 '침팬지'를 언급하는 이유는 무엇인가?

Ⓐ 왜 침팬지가 인지 능력을 가지고 있는지를 설명하기 위해
Ⓑ 인간과 침팬지의 행동을 구별하기 위해
Ⓒ 침팬지가 훈련되는 방법을 설명하기 위해
Ⓓ 동물이 의식적 선택을 할 수 있다는 증거를 보여주기 위해

어휘 indicate v 나타내다, 가리키다 I compare v 비교하다

---

05 북미 남서부의 아메리카 원주민은 사막 지형에 적응해야 했다. 건조한 남서 지역에서는 물이 귀했기 때문에, 호피족과 주니족 인디언들은 농경지에 물을 대기 위해 관개 도랑을 사용했다. 물은 그들에게 매우 중요해서 비는 종교 의식의 중요한 주제였다. 우테족과 쇼쇼니족 같은 더 작은 부족들은 로키 산맥과 태평양 사이의 건조한 산악 지대를 돌아다녔다. 그들의 유랑하는 생활양식은 더 단순했고 자연에 더 많은 영향을 받았다. 그들은 생계를 위해 씨앗을 채집했고 토끼와 뱀 같은 작은 동물을 사냥했다.

글쓴이가 '우테족과 쇼쇼니족'을 언급하는 이유는 무엇인가?

Ⓐ 왜 아메리카 원주민들이 유랑했는지 설명하기 위해서
Ⓑ 남서부의 서로 다른 부족들의 생활 방식을 비교하기 위해서
Ⓒ 남서부 지역 부족들의 정착의 증거를 제공하기 위해서
Ⓓ 아메리카 원주민들이 사막에서 생계를 유지한 방법에 대해 반박하기 위해서

어휘 irrigation n 관개 I ditch n 배수로 I scarce adj 부족한, 드문 I roam v 돌아다니다, 배회하다

06

제조업 지역

제조업 지역은 이전에 중공업과 제조업을 경제의 기반으로 했던 미국의 북동부와 중북부 지역을 말한다. 안타깝게도 1960년대 국제 자유무역 협정의 확대는 강철 같은 중공업 제품을 미국에서 생산하기보다 제3세계 국가들에서 생산한 후 미국으로 수입하는 것이 더 저렴하도록 만들었다. 이는 제조업 지역 전체에 걸친 공장 폐쇄로 이어졌고 그 지역 경제의 몰락을 초래했다. 1969년에 시작된 연이은 불황기에 제조업 일자리는 사라지고 저임금 서비스 일자리로 대체되었다. 그 지역의 새 이름인 녹슨 지역은 산업 시기에 남겨져 녹슬어가는 기계를 일컫는 것이자 그 지역의 전반적인 쇠퇴를 비유적으로 일컫는 말이다.

글쓴이가 제조업 지역 논의에서 '제3세계 국가들'을 언급하는 이유는 무엇인가?

Ⓐ 그 지역의 경제가 취약하다는 것을 보여주기 위해서
Ⓑ 그 지역이 그 영향으로부터 회복될 것임을 보여주기 위해서
Ⓒ 그 지역의 경제가 어떻게 퇴보했는지 설명하기 위해서
Ⓓ 경제에 끼친 영향의 심각함을 나타내기 위해서

어휘 recession n 경기 불황 I rust n 녹 I figurative adj 비유적인 I reference n 언급, 언급 대상

07

시조새

시조새는 일반적으로 새라고 여겨지는 가장 오래된 동물 화석인데 그 이유는 이 새의 깃털이 오늘날의 새의 깃털과 구조와 형태 면에서 매우 흡사하기 때문이다. 사실, 발견된 최초로 알려진 시조새 화석은 이 동물이 가졌던 깃털의 흔적을 확실히 보여준다. 그러나 다른 과학자들은 시조새가 공룡에 더 가까웠다고 믿는데, 왜냐하면 새가 가지고 있지 않은 많은 공룡의 특징을 가지고 있기 때문이었다. 오늘날의 새들과 달리 시조새는 뼈가 있는 긴 꼬리는 물론 작은 이빨을 가지고 있었다. 그들의 세 개의 발가락은 발톱을 가지고 있었고 현존하는 새들의 합쳐진 발가락과 달리 개별적으로 움직였다. 또한 비행과 연관 있는 골격 구조는 불완전하게 발달한 듯 보이고, 이것은 시조새가 아주 먼 거리를 비행하지는 못했을 것이라는 점을 시사한다. 그래서 이러한 구조들은 비행 목적을 위해 진화한 것이 아닐 수도 있는데, 왜냐하면 새나 비행 능력이 진화하기 전에 이미 공룡에서 그러한 것들이 나타났기 때문이다.

글쓴이가 지문에서 '뼈가 있는 긴 꼬리는 물론 작은 이빨'을 언급하는 이유는 무엇인가?

Ⓐ 시조새가 과학자들의 흥미를 끄는 이유를 설명하기 위해
Ⓑ 공룡과 더 비슷한 특징들의 예시를 제시하기 위해
Ⓒ 시조새가 새였다는 사실을 확증하기 위해
Ⓓ 시조새가 사냥감을 사냥했던 방법을 보여주기 위해

어휘 Archaeopteryx n 시조새 | plumage n 깃털 | bony adj 뼈의, 뼈를 가지고 있는 | bear v 갖다, 지니다 | claw n 발톱

---

08 **유럽의 연료**

영국은 18세기에 심각한 에너지 부족 문제를 경험했다. 그 전에는 나무가 연료의 주요한 공급원이자 필수 건축 재료였다. 그러나 대도시의 인구 증가로 나무의 소비가 상승했고 그 결과 영국뿐만 아니라 유럽 대륙 전반에 걸쳐 빠른 산림 벌채 현상이 나타났다. 산림 벌채의 결과로 공급이 제한되었지만 수요는 지속적으로 상승하여 중요한 주택과 산업을 위한 충분한 목재가 없는 지경까지 이르게 되었다. 게다가 석탄 같은 다른 대체 연료는 기반 시설과 알려져 있던 생산 방법이 제한적이었기 때문에 당시로서는 이용할 수가 없었다. 그래서 정제되지 않은 철을 생산하기 위해 용광로에서 철광석을 태우는 데 목재를 필요로 했던 영국의 제철업은 부족한 나무 공급으로 1790년대에 약화되었다. 당시 오스트리아의 거대한 숲은 이 나라로 하여금 영국이 이미 전에 경험했던 것과 같은 문제에 봉착하기 전까지 수십 년 동안 세계에서 가장 큰 철 생산국이 되는 것을 가능하게 했다.

글쓴이가 지문에서 '오스트리아'를 언급하는 이유는

Ⓐ 패턴이 유럽에서 어떻게 반복되었는지 보여주기 위해서
Ⓑ 나무가 에너지원으로 사용하기에 제일 좋은 재료가 아님을 보여주기 위해서
Ⓒ 그 당시 영국이 얼마나 더 진보했는지를 보여주기 위해서
Ⓓ 당시 왜 제철업이 그렇게 중요했는지를 보여주기 위해서

어휘 deforestation n 산림 벌채 | lumber n 목재 | housing n 주택 | coal n 석탄 | infrastructure n 기반 시설, 기초 시설 | iron industry 제철업 | iron ore 철광석 | decade n 10년

---

09 **화석**

화석은 수천 혹은 수백만 년 전 지구에 살았던 많은 식물과 동물이 남긴 흔적 또는 유해이다. 어떤 화석은 식물과 동물이 죽은 후 보존된 조개껍데기나 뼈처럼 생물체의 단단한 부분이 될 수도 있고, 다른 것은 동물들이 이동하며 남겨놓은 자국이나 흔적이 될 수 있다. 화석의 대부분은 퇴적암에서 발견된다. 그러한 화석은 강, 호수, 늪, 바다의 바닥에 모인 진흙과 모래 아래 빠르게 매립된 식물이나 동물의 유해에서 형성된다. 수천 년이 지나면서 압력이 퇴적물을 바위로 바꾸었다. 동시에 광물이 유해에 스며 유기물을 대체했다. 이것은 결과적으로 그 생물의 돌 복제품을 형성했다. 다른 화석들은 얼음, 타르, 단단한 수액에 통째로 보존된 식물과 동물이다. 예를 들어 작은 벌레나 무척추동물이 나무의 수액 안에 갇히고 시간이 흐르면서 그 수액이 호박으로 변화하면 그것들은 화석화된다. 생물체를 분해하는 박테리아나 곰팡이 같은 분해자가 적은 장소가 화석화에 이상적이다.

지문에서 글쓴이가 '조개껍데기나 뼈'를 언급하는 이유는

Ⓐ 분해자의 존재가 중요함을 강조하기 위해서
Ⓑ 자국이나 흔적 화석과 생물체의 단단한 부분 화석을 대조하기 위해서
Ⓒ 생물의 어떤 부분이 화석이 되는 경향이 있는지를 보여주기 위해서
Ⓓ 굳은 수액 안에서 발견되는 화석의 사례를 보이기 위해서

어휘 myriad n 무수히 많음 | flora n 식물군 | fauna n 동물군 | seashell n 조개껍데기 | sedimentary adj 퇴적물의 | swamp n 늪, 습지대 | tar n 타르 | sap n 수액 | invertebrate n 무척추동물 | scavenger n 죽은 동물을 먹는 동물 | fungi n (fungus의 복수형) 곰팡이 | fossilization n 화석화

---

10 **꽃가루 매개자의 감소**

식물이 번식하기 위해서는 수정되어야 한다. 이것은 대개 타화 수분을 통해 일어나며 이 과정은 꽃가루가 나비, 벌, 나방 같은 수분 매개자의 도움으로 하나의 식물에서 또 다른 식물로 이동하는 과정을 일컫는다. 불행히도 20세기 후반 전세계의 여러 생태계에서 수많은 요인이 이로운 수분 매개자의 수를 감소시켰다. 식물들은 동물들의 일차적 먹이가 되기 때문에 주요한 매개자 감소 혹은 심지어 소멸에 가까운 상황이 우려를

낳았다. 그래서 매개자 보호가 생물 종의 다양성을 보존하는 노력의 일환이 되었다. 주요 매개자인 야생벌에 대한 모든 위협 중에서도 현대 사회에서 증가한 국제 교역이 새로운 지역에 몇 가지 심각한 생물학적 위협들을 불러왔다. 미국 부저병과 백묵병 같은 질병들, 바로아 응애와 같은 기생충은 처치되지 않는 경우, 야생벌들이 이러한 해충에 대한 내성이 없는 지역에서는 대개 벌 군단의 죽음을 초래한다. 게다가 작은 아프리카 딱정벌레는 많은 벌의 죽음을 초래하고 있으며, 외국 불개미가 미국 남부 지역의 야생에서 땅에 집을 짓고 사는 벌들을 대량으로 죽였다.

글쓴이가 지문에서 '미국 부저병과 백묵병'을 언급하는 이유는 무엇인가?

Ⓐ 이주하는 생물이 옮긴 질병들을 묘사하기 위해
Ⓑ 나비들에게 해를 입할 수 있는 주요 기생충들의 예시를 들기 위해
Ⓒ 다른 종들 사이에 전염되는 질병의 사례를 보여주기 위해
Ⓓ 국제 교역을 통해 전해질 수 있는 질병들을 가리키기 위해

어휘 cross-pollination n 타화 수분 | pollen n 꽃가루, 화분 | pollinator n 꽃가루 매개자 | moth n 나방 | agent n 중요하게 작용하는 것, 요인 | resistance n 저항, 저항력, 내성 | exotic adj 외국의, 이국적인 | decimate v 대량으로 죽이다

---

11 **미국의 도시화**

1 ➡ 미국에서 도시화는 미국의 급속한 산업화로 촉진되었으며, 이는 많은 이주민이 미국의 광산과 공장에서 일하게 이끌었다. 그러나 19세기 후반과 20세기 초반에는 미국 내에 체계적인 도시 계획이 아직 이루어지지 않았다. 도시 계획자들은 도시 지역을 임의로 건설했고 사람들은 과밀 거주와 상업 구역과 거주 구역의 구별이 거의 없는 것이 특징인 무계획적인 도시에 살았다. 게다가 길과 건물은 필요할 때마다 생겨났고 도시 자체뿐 아니라 그곳에 거주하는 사람들에게도 수많은 부정적 영향을 끼쳤다.

2 ➡ 예를 들어 뉴욕시에 제대로 된 도시 계획이 없었던 것은 빠르게 증가하는 인구에 심각한 건강 문제를 초래했다. 그 문제는 뉴욕에서 일어난 대규모 이주에 관한 계획을 세운 사람이 없었다는 점과 대부분의 건물이 단순히 개인 또는 기업체가 개인적인 용도로 지은 것이라는 데서 유래했다. 따라서 이 도시는 사람들이 만들어내는 엄청난 양의 폐기물을 처리할 적절한 시설이 없는 방식으로 발달했다. 이는 말라리아와 콜레라 같은 전염병의 확산에 이상적인 장소를 만들어냈으며, 이로 인해 20세기 초반 수천 명이 사망했다.

3 ➡ 게다가 시카고에서는 도시의 많은 부분이 빽빽하게 밀집된 목재 건축물로 이루어져 있어서 시카고 대화재로 알려진 큰 화재가 도시의 3평방 마일 이상을 초토화시켰다. 거의 10만 명의 사람들이 집을 잃었고 300명 가량이 목숨을 잃었다. 그 당시 개별 건축가들은 목재 건물들을 그렇게 가깝게 붙여서 건축하는 것에 대한 위험성을 인지하지 못했다.

1. 2단락에서 글쓴이가 '말라리아와 콜레라'를 언급하는 이유는 무엇인가?

Ⓐ 초기 뉴욕시의 사람 대부분을 죽인 질병들의 이름을 대려고
Ⓑ 형편없는 위생 때문에 확산된 질병들의 예시를 제공하려고
Ⓒ 도시 지역에서 사람들에게 자주 영향을 미친 질병들을 가리키려고
Ⓓ 제대로 조직되지 않은 도시들을 덮친 전염병들을 묘사하려고

2. 3단락에서 글쓴이가 '시카고'를 언급하는 이유는 무엇인가?

Ⓐ 왜 항구 도시들이 초기 미국에서 발전했는지에 대한 이유를 밝히기 위해서
Ⓑ 미국의 초기 도시들이 위생상 문제가 있었다고 주장하기 위해서
Ⓒ 체계적이지 않은 도시 계획 때문에 어려움을 겪은 도시들의 예를 들기 위해서
Ⓓ 도시화가 어떻게 제대로 진행되어야 하는지 설명하기 위해서

3. 다음 중 지문의 구성을 가장 잘 설명하는 것은 무엇인가?

Ⓐ 두 미국 도시들 사이의 차이점들을 개요로 나타냈다.
Ⓑ 잘못된 도시 계획의 파급 효과를 보여주는 예시 두 개가 묘사되었다.
Ⓒ 미국의 도시 계획 발달이 세부적으로 나타났다.
Ⓓ 두 도시를 대조하여 도시화의 결과를 보여주었다.

어휘 utilize v 활용하다 | haphazard adj 무계획적인 | severe adj 심각한 | massive adj 거대한, 대규모의 | malaria n 말라리아 | cholera n 콜레라 | densely adv 빽빽하게 | conflagration n 큰 불, 대화재

---

12 오케스트라

1 ➡ 오늘날 우리에게 친숙한 현대 오케스트라의 역사는 고대 이집트 시대까지 거슬러 올라간다. 최초의 오케스트라는 축제나 경축일, 장례식을 위해 모이는 소규모의 음악가 그룹으로 구성되었다. 로마 제국 시대에는 정부가 비정부 음악가들을 억압했고 비공식적 합주가 금지되었지만 이들은 제국이 멸망한 이후 다시 등장했다. 같은 그룹의 악기들이 서로 다른 음색과 옥타브를 가지고 등장하기 시작한 것은 11세기 이후의 일이었다.

2 ➡ 진정한 의미의 현대 오케스트라는 작곡가들이 악기 그룹을 위한 음악을 작곡하기 시작한 16세기 후반에 시작되었다. 그러나 당시에 사용된 악기들은 오늘날 볼 수 있는 악기들은 아니었다. 17세기에는 바이올린, 첼로, 비올라 같은 현악기 시대가 막을 열었고 이들은 현대 오케스트라의 중심으로 진화했다. 이 시점에서 악기 구성 및 작곡, 연주 기술 부문의 혁신이 일어났다.

3 ➡ 오케스트라에서 그 다음으로 주요한 발전은 18세기 리하르트 바그너가 자신의 음악극 반주에 쓸 음악을 필요로 했기에 일어났다. 그의 무대 작업에는 전례 없는 복잡함과 폭넓은 기악 편성이 요구되었고 오보에에서 클라리넷까지 이 악기들 대부분은 지금까지 사용되고 있다. 더욱이 그는 음악가들을 지휘하는 지휘자에게 더 비중 있는 역할을 고안해냈다. 바그너의 음악 이론은 박자의 중요성, 강약법, 현악기의 활 켜기 및 오케스트라에서 수석 연주자들의 역할을 새로운 시각으로 조명했다. 이러한 혁신은 오케스트라 작곡에 혁명을 불러일으켰고 이는 이후 80년간의 오케스트라 연주 형식을 정립했다.

4 ➡ 오늘날 오케스트라는 대부분의 대도시와 문화 생활에서 중요한 중심적 위치를 차지하고 있다. 현대 오케스트라는 광범위한 악기 편성을 선택해서 쓸 수 있는 수준까지 이르렀으며, 기회가 닿는 대로 발전이 이루어지고 있다. 오케스트라가 어떻게 진보했는지 고찰함으로써 우리는 여러 시대에 걸친 음악의 발전에 관한 가치 있는 통찰을 할 수 있다.

1. 1단락에서 글쓴이가 '로마 제국'을 언급하는 이유는

Ⓐ 음악에 끼친 로마 제국의 영향력을 보여주기 위해서
Ⓑ 음악 발달이 직면했던 문제점의 예시를 제공하기 위해서
Ⓒ 오케스트라 발달의 주요한 시기를 알아보기 위해서
Ⓓ 서방 세계에서의 음악의 중요성을 주장하기 위해서

2. 3단락에서 글쓴이가 '오보에에서 클라리넷까지'를 언급하는 이유는

Ⓐ 오케스트라 악기가 관악기임을 보여주기 위해서
Ⓑ 오늘날까지도 사용되는 악기 몇 개의 이름을 대기 위해서
Ⓒ 바그너에 의해서 적용된 오케스트라 악기의 예를 보여주기 위해서
Ⓓ 바그너의 복잡한 악보를 연주할 수 있는 유일한 악기들의 사례를 보여주기 위해서

3. 오케스트라에 관한 전반적인 논의에서 4단락의 목적은 무엇인가?

Ⓐ 앞 단락들에서 설명한 진화의 이면에 있는 요인들을 보여준다.
Ⓑ 여러 시대에 걸친 음악의 발전에 관해 질문을 던진다.
Ⓒ 오케스트라가 연주를 더 향상하는 법을 강조한다.
Ⓓ 현대 사회에서의 오케스트라의 양상을 보여준다.

어휘 suppress v 억압하다 | ensemble n 합주, 앙상블 | tone n 음색 | octave n 옥타브 | stringed adj 현이 있는 | composition n 작곡 | unprecedented adj 전례 없는 | conductor n 지휘자 | bowing n 활 켜기, 보잉 | instrumentation n 기악 편성

13 할렘 르네상스

1 ➡ 뉴욕시의 흑인 동네인 할렘은 1920년대와 1930년대 할렘 르네상스의 등장과 더불어 전국적으로, 그리고 세계적으로 명성을 얻었다. 이는 하나의 문화 운동이었으며 그 이름이 암시하는 것처럼 문예 부흥이나 재건은 아니었다. 그보다 이는 흑인 문화가 주목 받게 했으며, 많은 이들이 이를 흑인 예술의 탄생으로 여기게 했다. 흑인 문학과 예술이 전국적인 관심을 끌게 되면서 주류 출판사와 비평가들이 흑인들에게 진지하게 관심을 기울인 것은 실제로 이때가 처음이었다.

2 ➡ 그것은 비록 주로 문예 활동이기는 했으나 다른 흑인 예술과 정치 분야 발달에도 직접적인 영향을 주기도 했다. 여러 다양한 요소가 이 예술 활동의 기반을 제공했다. 세기가 바뀌면서 더 많은 교육과 취업 기회에 힘입어 흑인 중산층이 성장했다. 수천 명의 흑인이 직업을 구하기 위해 남부에서 북부 도시들로 이주했다. 대규모 이주라고 불린 이 이동은 제1차 세계대전으로 생겨난 직업들로 인해 일어났다. 점점 더 많은 흑인들이 할렘을 거처로 정하면서 할렘은 흑인들의 문화적, 정치적 중심지로 변모했다. 동등한 권리를 요구하는 정치적 사안이 여기서 시작되었다. 이 새로 찾은 인종적 자부심은 문학, 예술, 음악의 지속적인 발전으로 이어졌다. 제임스 웰던 존슨의 소설과 클로드 맥케이의 시는 제1차 세계대전이 끝날 무렵 인지도를 얻었고 이 작품들은 다음에 곧 이어진 맥케이의 시집 〈할렘의 그림자〉와 진 투머의 〈사탕수수〉 같은 많은 문학 작

품들에 영감을 주었다.

3 ➡ 할렘 르네상스는 흑인들이 스스로를 새로운 시각으로 바라보게 된 시점에 나타났다. 이러한 사실은 민족주의 경향에 발맞추어 사실주의와 민족 의식에 강조를 두었다. 그들의 예술, 특히 문학 분야에 이러한 새롭고 심오한 가치들을 불어넣은 뒤 흑인들 역시 주류 미국 대중들에게 다른 방식으로 인지되었다.

4 ➡ 할렘 르네상스는 한 가지 스타일이나 정치적 이데올로기로 정의되지 않았다. 참여자들을 하나로 결속한 것은 공동 목표의 일부가 되고자 하는 소속감과 흑인의 경험을 예술적으로 표현하려는 결심이었다. 흑인들 경험의 근본을 보여주는 공통적인 주제가 있었는데 이는 인종적 자부심과 평등을 향한 염원이었다. 이 예술 사조의 가장 두드러진 양상은 표현의 다양성이었다. 1920년대 중반부터 1930년대 중반까지 16명이나 되는 흑인 작가들이 50권이 넘는 시와 소설을 출간했다.

1. 2단락에서 글쓴이가 '대규모 이주'를 언급하는 이유는 무엇인가?

Ⓐ 미국 역사상 가장 유명한 이주의 하나를 세부적으로 설명하기 위해서
Ⓑ 북부 도시들로 이주한 흑인들의 숫자를 강조하기 위해서
Ⓒ 제1차 세계대전은 소수민족들의 지원 없이는 싸울 수 없었다는 점을 증명하기 위해서
Ⓓ 흑인들의 뉴욕으로의 이주에 이름을 붙이기 위해서

2. 2단락에서 글쓴이가 '제1차 세계대전'을 언급하는 이유는 무엇인가?

Ⓐ 흑인 작가들이 가장 활발하게 활동했던 시점을 알려주기 위해서
Ⓑ 왜 흑인들이 평등한 권리를 위한 캠페인을 시작했는지 설명하기 위해서
Ⓒ 흑인들에게 취업 기회를 만들어준 것이 무엇인지 강조하기 위해서
Ⓓ 전쟁과 흑인 공동체 사이의 관계를 보여주기 위해서

3. 이 지문의 목적은 무엇인가?

Ⓐ 예술 운동의 원인들에 대한 구체적 사례를 제공하는 것
Ⓑ 할렘 르네상스를 또 다른 유명한 미국 스타일과 연관짓는 것
Ⓒ 할렘 르네상스가 발달한 과정을 보여주는 것
Ⓓ 할렘 르네상스와 관련 있는 다양한 주제를 보여주는 것

어휘 attain v 이루다, 획득하다 I critic n 비평가, 평론가 I pursuit n 추구 I agenda n 사안, 의제 I newfound adj 새로 발견된 I inspire v 영감을 주다 I revelation n 뜻밖의 사실/발견, 폭로(된 사실) I ethnic adj 민족의 I nationalistic adj 민족주의의, 국수주의적인 I infuse v 불어넣다, 주입하다 I profound adj 심오한 I perceive v 인지하다 I determination n 결심, 결의 I showcase v 보여주다 I equality n 평등

---

14 **행위의 귀인**

1 ➡ 사람들은 세상과 세상에서 벌어지는 일을 볼 때 대부분 그것을 일련의 무작위적인 사건으로 간주하지 않는다. 그와 반대로, 사람들은 벌어지는 일에 의미를 부여하여 인지하고 평가하려는 경향을 갖고 있다. 결론을 내리고자 하는 이런 성향은 보통 개인 본위적 동기를 바탕으로 하고 있고, 대체로 정확하게 해석해 낸다. 그러나 이것은 또한 개인적이고 편향된 요인에 영향을 받기도 한다. 때로는 이용 가능한 정보의 양이 제한적이어서 다른 사람의 행동에 관한 명확한 통찰을 부여하지 못할 수도 있다. 다른 경우, 개인이 숨겨진 동기나 목적을 추구해서 시각이 왜곡되기도 하고 또는 모든 자원을 이용하지 못해 정확한 인지적 지각이 결핍될 수도 있다. 이것은 귀인 이론이라고 알려진 사회심리학 이론의 관심사로, 사람들이 본인과 타인들의 행동을 판단하는 방식을 설명하고자 한다.

2 ➡ 귀인이란 세상에 관한 우리의 경험에서 정보를 수집하고 그 정보에 의미를 부여하는 과정이다. 의미는 사건에 대한 이유의 형태로 나타나며, 개인의 지각적 성향, 나아가 세계관을 설명하는 데 일관성 있게 도움을 준다. 더구나 자각은 개인에 따라 상대적이므로 특정 사건이나 행동이 다르게 해석되기 마련이다. 비행기 탑승 시간에 늦은 한 남자의 행동을 생각해보면 좋은 예가 될 것이다. 남자는 비행기를 놓칠까 봐 너무 걱정이 되어서 터미널을 질주해서 통과하고, 가방을 들고 뛰면서 다른 사람들과 부딪친다. 당신은 이 남자의 행동을 어떻게 인식하겠는가? 남자는 이기적이고 공격적인 사람인가, 아니면 비행기 탑승 시간에 늦었으니 그런 행동이 정당화되는가? 물론 그의 행동에 대한 다양한 주장이 있을 것이고 그것은 이 상황에 부여되는 의미에 영향을 미칠 뿐만 아니라 관찰자의 신념 체계와 성격을 특정짓게 된다.

3 ➡ 인간 행동에 의미를 부여하는 데 있어 우리는 그 행동이 성격이라는 내적 인과 요인 때문인지 아니면 다른 사람들도 동일한 상황에 직면했다면 똑같이 행동했을지, 즉 외적 인과 요인 때문인지 선택해야 한다. 귀인 이론의 토대를 이루는 데 기여한 사회심리학자 해럴드 켈리는 사람들이 행동을 해석하는 방식이 대체로 논리적이고 정확하다고 가정했다. 이러한 가정을 가지고 그는 사람들이 행동을 설명할 수 있게 하는 간단한 질문 몇 가지를 파악했다. 첫째, 이 사람은 이런 상황에 직면했을 때 항상 이런 식으로 반응하는가? 또한 다른 사람들도 같은 상황에 처해 있었다면 똑같이 행동할 것인가? 그리고 마지막으로, 이 사람은 다른 상황에서도 똑같은 행동을 보이는가? 이런 질문을 통해 개인은 어떤 행

동의 원인이 내적인 것인지 아니면 상황적 요인에 따른 것인지 결정할 수 있다. 이 질문에 답함으로써 관찰자는 행위자를 평가하고 그의 성격을 이론상 정확하게 판단할 수 있다.

4 ➡ 그러나 귀인에는 관찰자의 편향이 상당한 역할을 한다. 개인이 특정 행동을 한 이유에 대한 설명이 행동과 함께 제시되지 않는다고 받아들일 때 관찰자가 행동 귀인에 사용할 수 있는 정보는 제한적이다. 관찰자들은 100% 정확한 판단을 내리기 위해 필요한 모든 자원을 늘 가지고 있지는 않으므로 편향에 의존해 추론한다. 편향의 종류 중 하나로 기본적 귀인 오류라고 알려진 것이 있는데, 이는 관찰자가 어떤 행동을 외적 인과 요인 대신 개인의 성격 때문으로 돌릴 때 일어난다. 이런 유형의 편향을 사용하는 사람이 가령 대중 연설 중 말을 더듬는 여자를 관찰한다고 치자. 그는 그녀가 연설 준비를 하지 않았거나, 이런 일에는 천부적인 재능이 없다고 추론할 수도 있다. 하지만 관찰자는 그녀가 자기 어머니가 생명을 위협하는 질병으로 방금 병원에 입원한 데 정신이 팔려 있을 뿐이라는 사실을 모르고 있다. 그런가 하면 관찰자가 누군가의 단순한 실수를 설명하는 데에 있어 기본적 귀인 오류를 범하며 시작할 수도 있는데, 자기가 똑같은 실수를 저지른 사람 쪽이었다면 자기 본위적 외적 원인을 제시했을 것이다.

5 ➡ 시간이 지나면서 귀인은 편향을 강화하고 신념과 열망에 영향을 주면서 인간의 인지적 자각을 형성한다. 분명히 사람들은 자기 본위적 판단을 내리는 성향이 있고, 행동의 완벽한 이해에 필요한 모든 세부 사항을 알고 있는 경우는 거의 없으므로 남을 판단할 때는 극도의 주의를 기울여야 한다.

1. 2단락에서 글쓴이가 '비행기 탑승 시간에 늦은 한 남자의 행동'을 언급하는 이유는

Ⓐ 실제로 볼 수 있는 이론의 흔한 예시를 독자에게 제공하려고
Ⓑ 비행기 여행이 사람들의 행동에 미칠 수 있는 영향을 관찰하려고
Ⓒ 인기 있는 심리학 이론에 영감을 준 것을 인용하려고
Ⓓ 어떤 이론에 관한 연구가 어떻게 진행되었는지 보이려고

2. 3단락에서 글쓴이가 '성격'을 언급하는 이유는 무엇인가?

Ⓐ 모든 사람이 특정 상황에서 비슷하게 반응하듯 성격 외의 요인들이 얼마나 중요한지 보이려고
Ⓑ 사람들이 똑같은 상황에서도 다르게 행동하는 경우와 같이 외적으로 또는 내적으로 촉발되는 행동을 대조하기 위해서
Ⓒ 사람들이 그들의 편향된 성격에 근거해 다른 사람의 행동을 어떻게 잘못 이해하는지 보여주기 위해서
Ⓓ 시간이 지남에 따라 성격과 귀인의 방식을 우리가 어떻게 의식적으로 바꾸는지 보여주기 위해서

3. 다음 중 어느 것이 지문의 나머지 내용과 5단락의 관계를 가장 잘 설명하는가?

Ⓐ 최근의 심리학 연구에 기반한 새로운 이론을 제시한다.
Ⓑ 지배적인 이론에 관한 논란이 되는 아이디어를 소개한다.
Ⓒ 틀렸다고 증명된 심리학 이론의 평론을 제공한다.
Ⓓ 지문에서 자세히 설명한 행동에 대해 주의를 준다.

어휘 arbitrary adj 임의적인 | evaluate v 평가하다 | motive n 동기 | interpretation n 해석 | biased adj 편향된 | distort v 왜곡하다 | cognitive adj 인식의, 자각의 | attribution n 귀인, 귀속 | perceptional adj 지각의 | bound adj ~할 것 같은 | rush v 서두르다 | bump v ~에 부딪치다 | assign v 맡기다, 배정하다 | causative adj 원인이 되는 | presupposition n 가정, 추정 | assess v 평가하다, 가늠하다 | stammer v 말을 더듬다 | deduce v 추론하다 | bolster v 강화하다 | aspiration n 열망

15

잉카 제국

1 ➡ 잉카 제국은 13세기부터 16세기까지 페루의 고지대에 존재했다. 유럽인들이 남미 대륙에 도착하기 전 잉카 제국은 북남미를 통틀어 앞서 존재했던 여러 문명 가운데 가장 규모가 큰 나라였다. 지리적으로 잉카 제국은 현재의 에콰도르, 볼리비아, 칠레, 아르헨티나, 그리고 물론 페루에 이르는 방대한 영토를 포함했다. 쿠스코에 위치한 수도는 평화적인 합병부터 강제적인 통제에 이르기까지 다양한 방법을 이용해 여러 독립적인 다민족 사회를 하나의 통치 체계로 통합했다.

2 ➡ 잉카인들은 건축과 토목 기술로 유명하며 두 가지 모두 기술적인 진보가 아니라 대규모의 노동에서 도출된 것이었다. 잉카인들은 회반죽을 사용하지 않고 정확하게 자른 돌로 거대한 구조물을 만들 수 있었다. 실제로 그 돌들은 세밀하게 조각되어 틈에 칼날 하나도 집어넣을 수 없을 정도였으며 바위를 다른 바위 위에 반복적으로 내려놓으면서 그 사이에 공간이 없어질 때까지 모난 돌을 깎아냈다는 말이 전해지고 있다. 인상적이긴 하지만 석조물에 관한 잉카의 명성에는 약간 오해의 소지가 있다. 사실 잉카인들의 잘 알려진 건축 기술은 대개 공공 기관의 건물로 사용되었던 유명한 구조물에 국한되었기 때문이다. 다른 구조물은 그 정도로 세심하게 작업되지 않았으며 따라서 수명도 그렇게 길지 않았다. 일반적인 잉카인들이 생활하기 위해 지어진 더 작은 건축물이 발견되는 것은 예외적인 경우이다.

3 ➡ 현대적인 기준에서 봐도 인상적인 건물을 지을 수 있었던 능력 외에도 잉카인들은 거대한 도로망을 확충하고 유지할 수 있었다. 이는 개

발 작업에 엄청난 양의 노동력을 투입하는 그들의 철학 때문에 가능한 일이었다. 그 결과 그들은 14,000마일의 도로를 건설할 수 있었고 바퀴를 사용하지 않고도 사람, 물품, 정보의 흐름이 상대적으로 빠르게 이루어졌다. 사실 모든 물품과 재료는 손으로 운반되었다. 이 도로망을 이용해, 잉카인들은 차스끼라는 파발꾼을 두었는데 이들은 잉카의 상류층을 위해 제국 전체에 걸쳐 정보와 왕족의 물건을 신속히 전달하던 사람들이었다. 그리고 무거운 물건의 경우, 잉카인들은 가장 귀하게 여기던 동물인 라마를 이용했는데 라마는 그 모습과 지구력에 있어서 낙타와 닮은 동물이다. 그러나 아마 가장 주목할 만한 일은 이 복잡한 운송망 덕분에 잉카 군대의 이동이 쉬워졌고, 잉카 문화와 세력이 더 먼 지역까지 전파될 수 있게 도왔다는 점이다.

4 ➡ 잉카 제국은 앞서 로마 제국과 접촉한 일이 없음에도 불구하고, 방대한 영역에 걸쳐 엄청난 세력과 영향력을 떨칠 수 있게 한 몇 가지 공통점을 가지고 있었다. 첫째, 고도로 발달한 잉카의 운송망은 아메리카 대륙에서 그것의 종류로서는 최초였고, 마치 로마의 시스템처럼 넓은 영토를 아울렀다. 또한 잉카 제국은 한 명의 왕과 자문을 제공하는 조언자들이 있었다는 점에서 로마 제국과 유사한 방식으로 조직되어 있었다. 이 그룹이 잉카의 권력을 체계적으로 통합할 수 있었기에 잉카인들은 자원의 효율적인 할당을 통해 번성할 수 있었다. 이 두 제국 사이에서 또 한 가지 눈에 띄는 유사점은 군대의 운용에서 찾아볼 수 있다. 두 제국은 어떤 전쟁에서든 가급적 최소한의 군사력을 사용해야 한다고 생각했다. 이는 병사들이 싸움터에 나가 적을 이기도록 의욕을 고취했을 뿐 아니라 군비를 최소한으로 유지해주었다.

5 ➡ 잉카인들은 천연 자원과 인적 자원에 높은 가치를 두었기에 다른 문화를 자신들의 문화로 통합하기 위해 정복보다는 다른 방법을 취했다. 한 가지 방법은 부족들에게서 현지 추장을 면직시키고 잉카의 수도 쿠스코에 데려오는 것이었다. 거기서 추장과 추장의 가족들은 부를 누리고 잉카 방식에 대해 교육을 받았다. 그 뒤 모든 사람들을 위한 여러 가지 선물과 함께 추장을 자기 백성들에게 돌려보냈다. 이 방법은 말할 것도 없이 보다 많은 문화를 거대한 잉카 제국에 통합하는 데 매우 효과적이었고, 이로 인해 잉카인들은 다른 군대를 무력으로 제압하기 위한 대규모의 군대를 육성할 필요가 없었다. 이처럼 효율적인 통합 방식은 잉카인들이 우리가 오늘날까지 볼 수 있는 기념비적인 석조 건물을 만드는 데 힘을 쏟도록 해주었다.

1. 2단락에서 글쓴이가 '칼날'을 언급하는 이유는 무엇인가?

Ⓐ 잉카 강철의 품질을 보여주기 위해
Ⓑ 잉카인들의 정밀한 수공예를 보여주기 위해
Ⓒ 보통의 잉카 조각 기술을 보여주기 위해
Ⓓ 어떻게 잉카의 건축가들이 그런 큰 구조물을 건축할 수 있었는지 보여주기 위해

2. 4단락에서 글쓴이가 '로마 제국'을 언급하는 이유는 무엇인가?

Ⓐ 잉카 군대가 얼마나 성공적이었는지 보여주려고
Ⓑ 잉카 제국을 더 익숙한 예시와 비교하려고
Ⓒ 잉카 제국이 왜 그렇게 수명이 짧았는지 설명하려고
Ⓓ 잉카인들이 도로망을 어떻게 건설했는지 설명하려고

3. 잉카 제국에 관한 전반적인 논의와 관련해 5단락의 목적은 무엇인가?

Ⓐ 제국을 확장하기 위해 잉카인들이 사용한 또 다른 방법을 소개한다.
Ⓑ 잉카 제국의 궁극적 최후를 야기한 요인들을 살펴본다.
Ⓒ 그 지역에서 이뤄진 새로운 발견에 기반한 새 이론을 제시한다.
Ⓓ 잉카 문화에 관한 흔한 오해를 지적한다.

어휘 ethnic adj 민족의 | annexation n 통합 | derive v ~에서 나오다, 비롯되다 | mortar n 회반죽 | impressiveness n 인상적임, 장엄함 | reputation n 명성 | longevity n 수명 | imposing adj 인상적인 | pour v 들이붓다 | prized adj 소중한 | comprehensive adj 포괄적인 | encompass v 아우르다, 망라하다 | council n 의회, 자문 위원회 | conduct v (특정 활동을) 하다 | consolidation n 통합 | allocation n 할당 | expense n 비용 | undertake v 착수하다 | integrate v 통합하다 | bathed adj 휩싸인, 범벅이 된

Test

본서 | P. 162

중세 성기

1 ➡ 중세 성기(中世盛期)는 11세기 말에서 14세기 초기까지 이어지는 유럽의 역사적 시기이다. 그것은 그 시대를 앞선 정치적, 심리적, 농업의 변화에 기인하는 변화와 확장의 시기였다. 이 시기 전에 유럽은 흔히 서로 전쟁을 치르는 작은 왕국들과 공국들의 분열로 분단되

1. 글쓴이가 1단락에서 여러 침략자들을 열거하는 이유는 무엇인가?

Ⓐ 어느 침략자들이 평화를 맺고 유럽 사회에 흡수되었는지 알아보기 위해

어 있었는데, 사방에서 밀려오는 잦은 침략으로 상황은 더 악화될 뿐이었다. 동쪽으로는 아시아 대초원 지대의 여러 야만족들이 괴롭혔고, 북쪽에서는 바이킹들이 침략했으며, 남쪽으로는 이슬람 점령지가 지중해 지역 대부분을 차지했었다. 하지만 몇몇 침략자들에게 치명적인 패배를 안기고 또 다른 이들과는 화친을 맺은 강한 지도자들이 결국 등장했으며 이들은 유럽 국경 지역을 강한 왕국들로 단결시키고 문화적 정체성의 개념이 발달하게끔 했다. 심리적으로 유럽 사람들은 예언들로 인해 지구가 1000년 즈음 멸망할 것이라 생각했고 만연한 전쟁과 갈등은 종말이 정말 임박한 것처럼 보이게 했지만 세상의 종말은 닥치지 않았고 그들은 낙관과 증가된 자유의 시대에 들어섰다. 경제적으로는 농부들이 이포제에서 삼포제로 체계를 바꾸면서 농업이 호황을 맞았다. 이런 요소들이 함께 하면서 엄청난 인구 증가, 무역 길드와 국제 무역의 발달, 그리고 사회 질서의 재편성으로 이어졌다.

2 ➡ 중세 성기에 유럽의 인구는 극적으로 증가했다. 이것은 부분적으로는 과거에 그 지역을 괴롭힌 외국 침략군의 침입이 중단되었기 때문이기도 했지만 죽는 사람들의 숫자가 줄어서만은 아니었다. 그 위협의 제거는 사람들로 하여금 한 번도 사람들이 정착하지 않았던 지역뿐만 아니라 방치되어 자연으로 되돌아간 지역으로 확장할 수 있게 했다. 여기에는 북쪽으로는 발트 해에서부터 남쪽으로는 발칸 지역까지의 동유럽과 스페인과 이탈리아의 일부 지역까지 포함되었다. 그들은 이런 땅을 숲과 습지로 이루어진 황무지에서 생산적인 농지로 전환시켰고 이것은 '대규모 삼림 벌채'라고 불린다. 증가된 경작지는 자연스럽게 잉여 식량을 제공했고 이것은 인구 증가로 나타났다. 정확한 수치는 존재하지 않지만 유럽 인구는 약 1억에서 1억 2천만 명에 달했다고 추측되며, 많은 지역이 19세기가 되어서야 다시 그 수를 넘어설 수 있었을 만큼 많은 수의 인구를 보유했다.

3 ➡ 농업과 인구가 번성하자 무역 또한 크게 증가했다. 다양한 산업들이 확장되자 공급이 지역 수요를 초과했고, 그들은 생산품을 대륙의 다른 지역으로 수출하기 시작했다. 집단의 이익을 보호하고 그들의 제품에 대한 엄격한 기준을 유지하기 위해 이런 전문적인 기술을 보유한 장인들과 상인들은 길드라고 알려진 집단을 형성했다. [■A] 이런 집단은 매우 부유해졌으며 무역뿐만 아니라 지역 정치도 좌우하기 시작했다. [■B] 이것은 중심이 되는 위치에 있었으며 많은 항만 도시를 보유한 이탈리아에서 특히 두드러졌는데 하나의 주가 실제로 분리된 독립국이 되었다. [■C] 피렌체 공화국은 1115년에 사람들이 공작에 대항해 반란을 일으키고 피렌체의 길드 일원들이 선발한 지도자에 의해 선택된 의회가 이끄는 지방 자치제를 형성하면서 세워졌다. [■D] 이런 길드 중 가장 강력한 것의 하나는 아르테 디 칼리말라였다. 그것은 오늘날 벨기에 북부 지방인 플랑드르에서부터 직물을 수입하는 직물 마무리 숙련공들과 직물 무역상들로 구성되었다. 플랑드르의 방직공들은 그들이 천으로 만드는 양모를 영국에서부터 수입했다. 이 길드의 일원들은 또한 은행가들이 되었고 교황과 영국 헨리3세 간의 중개자 역할을 했는데, 이것은 그들의 영향력이 얼마나 멀리 미쳤는지 보여준다.

4 ➡ 상인 계급이 등장하자 사회의 기반도 극적인 변화를 겪었다. 중세 성기 이전에 유럽은 봉건 제도라고 불리는 체제에 의해 지탱되었는데, 거기에서는 농부들이 왕의 토지를 관리하는 귀족들 아래서 소작농으로 일했었다. 각 농민 가정에는 농사를 짓거나 가축을 사육

Ⓑ 중세 유럽의 정치적 불안정을 야기한 것이 무엇인지 언급하기 위해
Ⓒ 영역을 유럽까지 확장한 다양한 침략자들의 예를 들기 위해
Ⓓ 유럽 내의 분열이 침략의 결과였다는 것을 암시하기 위해

2. 다음 중 1단락에서 유럽이 겪은 변화에 대해 추론 가능한 것은 무엇인가?
Ⓐ 유럽의 작은 왕국들 중 몇몇은 더 큰 국가로 합쳐졌다.
Ⓑ 삼포제 농업이 더 효과적이었다.
Ⓒ 사회적 혼란은 11세기의 시작과 함께 끝났다.
Ⓓ 사람들은 세계 종말이 실제로 일어나지 않자 더 이상 예언을 믿지 않게 되었다.

3. 2단락의 단어 'reflected(나타났다)'와 의미상 가장 가까운 것은
Ⓐ 보장되었다
Ⓑ 장려되었다
Ⓒ 보여졌다
Ⓓ 가능하게 되었다

4. 2단락에 따르면, 인구 증가를 야기한 것은 무엇인가? 2개를 고르시오.
Ⓐ 외국 이민자의 급증
Ⓑ 발칸 지역의 복구
Ⓒ 사람이 살지 않는 지역의 개척
Ⓓ 전쟁과 갈등으로 인한 죽음의 감소

5. 다음 중 지문에 음영 표시된 문장의 핵심 정보를 가장 잘 표현한 문장은 무엇인가? 오답은 의미를 크게 왜곡하거나 핵심 정보를 누락하고 있다.
Ⓐ 유럽에는 약 1억에서 1억 2천만 명의 사람들이 살았고, 19세기까지 다른 지역에는 심지어 더 많은 사람들이 살고 있었다.
Ⓑ 비록 유럽에 1억에서 1억 2천만 명의 사람들이 살았다고 명시하는 역사적 기록은 없지만 우리는 이 수치가 19세기 유럽의 것을 초과하지 않는다는 것을 알고 있다.
Ⓒ 확실한 기록의 부재로 인해 우리는 유럽에 약 1억에서 1억 2천만 명의 사람들이 살았다고 추측할 뿐이고 이 수치는 19세기까지 독보적이었다.
Ⓓ 유럽에 대략 1억에서 1억 2천만 명의 사람들이 살았다고 추측되며 많은 다른 지역들은 19세기까지 그 수치에 미치지 못했다.

6. 3단락에 따르면, 다음 중 길드가 얼마나 성공적이었는지 보여주는 것은 무엇인가?
Ⓐ 피렌체 공화국을 다스리는 지방 자치제를 형성했다.
Ⓑ 그들의 무역을 다른 대륙으로 확장했다.
Ⓒ 국가 원수들 간의 중개자 역할을 했다.
Ⓓ 수입하는 물품에 대해 엄격한 지침을 시행했다.

할 수 있는 약간의 토지가 할당되었다. 수확기가 되면 그들이 생산한 것들을 귀족이 가져갔고, 귀족은 일부를 교회와 농민들에게 나누어 주고 나머지는 자기가 가졌다. 노동력의 대가로 귀족은 농민들을 보호해주었다. 농민들은 귀족의 노예가 아니었지만 그 땅에 얽매여서 귀족의 허락 없이는 거기를 떠날 수 없었다. 하지만 이 관계는 귀족들이 완전히 땅을 소유하게 되면서 변했다. 몇몇 귀족들은 왕에게서 직접 땅을 구입한 반면, 대부분은 그 토지를 수 세대 동안 관리해 온 가문 사람들이어서 왕은 세금의 대가로 그들이 그 땅을 계속 소유할 수 있게 했다. 그들은 세금을 낼 돈을 마련하기 위해 먼저 그들에게 할당된 몫의 수확물 중 일부를 팔았다. 나중에 그들은 농부들이 일하는 토지에 대한 소작료를 청구하기 시작했다. 이는 농민들이 수확물 대부분을 소유할 수 있었지만 소작료를 내기 위해 시장에 그것을 내다 팔아야 했다는 것을 의미했다. 농민들은 보다 많은 자치권을 누렸지만 그들은 더 이상 일하거나 거주할 수 있는 땅을 보장받지 못했기 때문에 서로 경쟁해야 했다.

7. 4단락에 따르면, 다음 중 봉건 제도에 대해 사실이 아닌 것은

Ⓐ 농민들의 수확물 중 일부는 농민들에게 주어졌다
Ⓑ 농민들은 작물을 재배하거나 가축을 사육하는 것 중 하나를 택할 수 있었다
Ⓒ 많은 귀족들은 수 세대에 걸쳐 같은 토지를 관리했다
Ⓓ 왕들은 토지를 전부 소유했다

8. 다음 중 4단락에서 언급된 것은 무엇인가?

Ⓐ 농민들과 귀족들 간의 관계의 변화
Ⓑ 세금을 모은 방식
Ⓒ 토지 소유권의 변화에 대한 이유
Ⓓ 봉건 제도가 유지된 기간

9. 지문에 다음 문장이 들어갈 수 있는 위치를 나타내는 네 개의 사각형 [■]을 확인하시오.

이런 길드 중 가장 강력한 것의 하나는 아르테 디 칼리말라였다.

이 문장이 들어가기에 가장 적합한 곳은? [■D]

10. 지시문: 지문을 간략하게 요약한 글의 첫 문장이 아래 제시되어 있다. 지문의 가장 중요한 내용을 표현하는 세 개의 선택지를 골라 요약문을 완성하시오. 일부 문장들은 지문에 제시되지 않았거나 지문의 지엽적인 내용을 나타내기 때문에 요약문에 포함되지 않는다. ***이 문제의 배점은 2점이다.***

서유럽의 중세 성기는 낙관과 확장의 시대였다.

Ⓐ 봉건 제도에서 벗어나는 것은 농부들이 귀족들에게 소작료를 내는 대가로 수확물을 갖고 있을 수 있다는 것을 뜻했다.
Ⓑ 개간지는 식량 생산량 증가로 이어졌고 이것은 유럽 인구가 증가할 수 있게 해 주었다.
Ⓕ 길드들은 상인들이 그들의 이익을 보호하면서 더 효과적으로 거래할 수 있는 방법을 찾으며 형성된 집단들이다.

Ⓒ 중세 성기 이전에 유럽 사람들은 미래에 대한 끊임없는 갈등과 불안 속에 살았다.
Ⓓ 정치에 미친 길드의 영향력은 교황과 헨리3세 간의 중개자 역할에서 볼 수 있다.
Ⓔ 미지의 땅에 정착하는 과정은 발칸 지역 전체를 가로질러 행해졌고 남유럽까지 확장되었다.

어휘 transition n 과도, 변화 | expansion n 확장 | attribute v ~의 결과로 보다 | precede v 앞서다, 선행하다 | fragment v 해체되다, 부서지다 | principality n 공국 | invasion n 침략 | barbarian n 야만인 | steppe n 스텝 지대(강, 호수와 멀리 떨어져 있고 나무가 없으며 짧은 풀들이 자라 있는 평야) | raid v 습격하다, 급습하다 | conquest n 정복, 점령지 | emerge v 나오다, 드러나다 | crushing adj 참담한 | solidify v 굳어지다, 확고해지다 | pervasive adj 만연하는 | apocalypse n 파멸, 세계의 종말 | optimism n 낙관, 낙관론 | boom v 호황을 맞다, 번창하다 | guild n 길드(중세시대 기능인들의 조합) | commerce n 무역 | halt n 멈춤, 중단 | incursion n 급습 | plague v 괴롭히다 | revert v 되돌아가다 | settled adj 정착한, 자리를 잡은 | wilderness n 황야, 황무지 | arable adj 곡식을 경작하는 | surplus n 과잉 | reflect v 보여주다, 비추다 | flourish v 번창하다 | boost n 증가, 격려 | outgrow v ~보다 더 커지다, 많아지다 | collective adj 집단의, 단체의 | tradesman n 상인, 장인, 숙련공 | merchant n 상인, 무역상 | association n 협회, 연계 | dominate v 지배하다, 군림하다 | port n 항구 | entity n 독립체 | revolt v 반란을 일으키다 | commune n 지방 자치제 | council n 의회 | textile n 직물 | weaver n 방직공 | go-between n 중개자 | feudalism n 봉건 제도 | peasant n 소농, 농민 | tenant farmer 소작인, 소작농 | lord n 귀족 | allot v 할당하다, 배당하다 | outright adv 완전히, 명백히 | autonomy n 자치권

토양 비옥화

1 ➡ 높은 수준의 생산량을 유지하기 위해 농부들은 토양을 더 비옥하게 만드는 물질을 사용해야 한다. 이런 비료들은 토양 표면에 뿌려지거나 토양 안으로 투입되어야 하며 그것은 식물이 제대로 성장하기 위해 필요로 하는 질소, 인, 칼륨과 같은 영양소를 제공한다. 현대 농부들은 구비(廏肥), 녹비, 퇴비와 같은 유기농 비료 혹은 무기물 화학 화합물로 된 비료와 같은 다양한 종류의 비료를 선택할 수 있다.

2 ➡ 비료를 처음 의도적으로 사용한 것은 동물 배설물과 동물 잠자리에 까는 짚과 같은 식물성 재료의 혼합인 거름의 사용이었다. 작물과 함께 가축을 사육하기 시작하면서 사람들은 동물 배설물이 식물 성장을 촉진시킨다는 것을 곧 알게 되었다. 그래서 그들은 동물 배설물을 가축 우리와 그들을 방목하는 들판에서 모아서 토양 위에 뿌렸다. 말, 당나귀와 황소가 주요 이동 수단이 되자 도로는 무분별하게 흩어져 있는 배설물로 덮였고 이것은 수거되어 농장으로 옮겨졌다. 이런 비료의 풍부한 공급은 농부들이 농장에서 특정 농작물에 보다 집중할 수 있게 했고 가축 사육은 작물 재배와 분리되었다. 자동차의 발명이 동물을 이동 수단에서 제외시키자, 동물 배설물을 구해서 옮기는 것은 더욱 어려워졌는데 이는 보통 동물 배설물을 계속 배출하는 목장이 그것을 비료로 사용하는 데 의존하는 농장들로부터 먼 곳에 자리잡고 있었기 때문이었다.

3 ➡ 천연 비료는 녹비와 퇴비의 경우처럼 거의 전적으로 식물성 재료로 만들 수 있다. 이 두 가지 비료는 토양을 비옥하게 만드는 데 사용되는 죽은 식물성 재료로 대부분 구성되지만 중요한 점에서 차이를 보인다. 녹비는 다 자랄 때까지 들판에 자라도록 놔두었다가 그 후에 토양에 직접적으로 갈아 넣는 식물들이다. 이런 식물은 흔히 토양에 질소를 잘 고정시키는 콩과 클로버 같은 것들이다. 이 식물들은 꽃을 피우고 추수할 식량을 생산할 때까지 놔두거나 그렇게 하지 않을 수도 있지만 어쨌든 식물이 녹색일 때 토양에 섞어넣게 된다. 반면에 퇴비는 땅에서 거두어서 다른 장소에 모아둔 식물들로 만들어진다. 거기서 그것은 지면에서 썩어 영양소가 풍부한 부엽토로 분해되기까지 방치된다. 이 물질은 그 후 들판으로 옮겨져서 토양에 투입된다.

4 ➡ 땅을 비옥하게 만드는 다른 천연 수단들은 살아 있는 유기체의 적용을 필요로 한다. 연구 자료에 따르면 모든 식물 종의 약 95%는 여러 가지 균류와 공생 관계를 맺고 있다. [■A] 이런 균류는 식물의 뿌리계 안쪽과 주변에 자라나서 뿌리의 표면적을 증가시켜 식물이 영양소, 특히 인을 흡수하는 것을 도와준다. [■B] 대신 그 균류는 식물이 광합성으로 생성하는 당을 받는다. 농부들은 균류가 부족한 토양에 균류를 투입함으로써 작물 생산량을 증가시킬 수 있다. [■C] 많은 종류는 그들이 수확할 수 있는 송로버섯과 같은 식용 부분을 생산한다. [■D]

5 ➡ 농부들은 윤작이라고 불리는 체계를 통해 수 년 혹은 수 계절에 걸쳐 다른 종류의 작물을 순차적으로 재배하여 토양을 보충할 수 있다. 농부들은 동일한 부지에 동일한 작물을 계속 재배하는 것은 그 토양에서 식물이 요구하는 영양소를 불가피하게 고갈시킨다는 것을 빠르게 깨달았다. 그것에 대응해 그들은 토지를 반쪽으로 나누어 한 쪽에 작물을 재배하는 동안 그 반대쪽엔 토지의 토종 식물군이 자라게 방치하고 그 이듬해에 그것들을 전환했다. 묵힌 들판은 휴경지로

11. 다음 중 1단락에서 언급되지 않은 것은

Ⓐ 비료를 사용하는 목적
Ⓑ 비료를 선택하는 것의 이점
Ⓒ 이용 가능한 비료의 종류
Ⓓ 비료가 활용되는 방식

12. 2단락의 단어 'relied(의존하는)'와 의미상 가장 가까운 것은

Ⓐ 수확하는
Ⓑ 소유하는
Ⓒ 들러붙는
Ⓓ 의존하는

13. 2단락과의 관계에 비추어 3단락의 목적은 무엇인가?

Ⓐ 2단락에서 설명된 구비 공급의 감소를 야기시켰을 수 있는 사건을 설명하기 위해
Ⓑ 구비와 녹비 간의 차이가 어떻게 존재하게 됐는지에 대한 설명을 제공하기 위해
Ⓒ 2단락에서 시작된 다양한 종류의 유기물 비료의 설명을 이어가기 위해
Ⓓ 특정 제품을 생산하는 방향으로의 농업의 변화가 어떻게 퇴비 공급량에 영향을 끼쳤는지에 대해 추가적으로 설명하기 위해

14. 3단락에 따르면, 녹비와 퇴비 간의 주요 차이점은 무엇인가?

Ⓐ 분해가 일어나는 데 필요한 시간
Ⓑ 농업에 활용되는 방식
Ⓒ 그것들을 형성하는 물질의 종류
Ⓓ 생산되는 방식

15. 4단락에서 글쓴이가 제시하는 것은

Ⓐ 토양에 균류를 투입하는 것은 식물이 영양소를 흡수하게 도와주는 것 외에 다른 혜택을 제공한다
Ⓑ 균류는 일반적으로 식물과 영양소 간에 쌍방에 유익한 관계를 조성한다
Ⓒ 식물은 균류의 도움 없이는 인과 같은 영양소를 흡수할 수 없었을 것이다
Ⓓ 균류가 없는 지역에서는 많은 작물 성장을 이루기가 힘들다

16. 5단락에 따르면, 윤작의 이점은 무엇인가?

Ⓐ 동일 작물의 규칙적인 수확
Ⓑ 지속적인 영양소의 회복
Ⓒ 토종 식물군 성장의 장려
Ⓓ 다른 것보다 더 유용한 작물의 재배

17. 6단락에서 글쓴이가 '현대 식량 생산량은 그것들 없이는 현재 양의 3분의 1에 그칠 것'이라고 말하는 이유는 무엇인가?

Ⓐ 현대에 식량 생산량이 얼마나 많이 증가했는지 강조하기 위해

불렸고 자연적 성장은 토질을 향상시켰다. 나중에 사람들은 특정 식물이 다른 것보다 더 많은 유익한 효과를 지녔다는 것과 그 중 많은 종류는 또한 식량을 제공한다는 것을 깨닫게 되었고, 이것은 사람들로 하여금 특정 작물을 연속으로 심게 만들었다. 이것은 토양에 영양소가 보충될 뿐만 아니라 토양이 항상 생산성을 지닐 수 있도록 보장해 주었다.

6 ➡ 이러한 모든 천연 비옥화 방식은 무기물 비료의 발명 후 대량 농업에서 대부분 쓰이지 않게 되었다. 정확히 어느 영양소가 작물에 가장 유익한지 확인한 후 과학자들은 그것들을 토양에 직접적으로 뿌릴 수 있는 화학 화합물로 생산할 수 있는 방법을 창안했다. 이것들은 식물 성장을 극적으로 증가시켰고 그들의 사용은 특히 1950년대 이후 전세계적으로 빠르게 성장했다. 현대 식량 생산량은 그것들 없이는 현재 양의 3분의 1에 그칠 것이라 여겨진다.

7 ➡ 무기물 비료의 명백한 장점에도 불구하고, 비료 사용은 많은 부작용으로 인해 1990년대 이후 감소하기 시작했다. 첫째, 너무 많은 양의 비료를 사용하는 것은 그것이 도와야 할 식물을 해한다. 둘째, 과도한 비료는 불가피하게 상수도에 유입되어 그 오염 물질이 물을 마시는 생물들을 직접적으로 해칠 수 있다. 그것은 또한 특정 종류의 박테리아 성장을 촉진시키는데 이것은 담수나 소금물에서 기하급수적으로 성장한다. 이렇게 대량으로 발생한 박테리아가 죽을 때 그들은 물 속의 산소를 먹어치워 아무것도 생존할 수 없는 구역들을 남긴다. 비료가 성장을 촉진시키는 다른 종류의 박테리아는 물을 독성으로 만드는 화학물질을 방출한다. 비료는 또한 다양한 방식으로 토양 그 자체에 해를 끼칠 수 있다. 질소 비료는 토양의 산도를 높이는데, 이것은 균류에 해를 입히고 알루미늄의 공급량을 늘려서 토양을 황폐하게 만든다. 인 복합물 또한 카드뮴과 같은 중금속을 흔히 포함하고 있는데 이것은 토양에 누적되어 거기서 생산된 작물을 섭취하는 가축이나 사람들에게 유해할 수 있다.

Ⓑ 세계 식량 공급을 증가시키는 데 기여한 유기물 비료의 역할을 강조하기 위해
Ⓒ 무기물 비료가 유기물 비료보다 더 효과적이라는 것을 시사하기 위해
Ⓓ 미래 식량 생산량은 지속적인 비료 공급에 의존한다는 것을 암시하기 위해

18. 다음 중 7단락에서 무기물 비료의 부작용으로 언급되지 않은 것은 무엇인가?

Ⓐ 전염성 박테리아 성장을 촉진시키는 것
Ⓑ 토양을 산성화하고 황폐화하는 것
Ⓒ 작물과 가축을 위한 물을 오염시키는 것
Ⓓ 토양에 중금속을 누적시키는 것

19. 지문에 다음 문장이 들어갈 수 있는 위치를 나타내는 네 개의 사각형 [■]을 확인하시오.

대신 그 균류는 식물이 광합성으로 생성하는 당을 받는다.

이 문장이 들어가기에 가장 적합한 곳은? [■B]

20. 지시문: 지문을 간략하게 요약한 글의 첫 문장이 아래 제시되어 있다. 지문의 가장 중요한 내용을 표현하는 세 개의 선택지를 골라 요약문을 완성하시오. 일부 문장들은 지문에 제시되지 않았거나 지문의 지엽적인 내용을 나타내기 때문에 요약문에 포함되지 않는다. ***이 문제의 배점은 2점이다.***

작물 성장을 촉진하는 것이 목적인 토양 비옥화는 다양한 종류의 비료를 통해 이루어질 수 있다.

Ⓐ 동물 배설물로 구성된 구비와 달리, 녹비와 퇴비는 대부분 죽은 식물성 재료로부터 비롯된다.
Ⓔ 세계 식량 생산에 기여함에도 불구하고 무기물 비료는 부작용이 없지 않았으며 이로 인해 1990년대에 들어 사용이 감소하게 되었다.
Ⓕ 윤작과 같은 자연 비옥화 방식은 직접적으로 영양소를 공급하지는 않지만, 식물이 더 많은 영양소를 얻을 수 있는 환경을 조성한다.

Ⓑ 윤작 방식에 있어서 사람들은 특정 식물이 다른 것보다 더 유익하다는 것을 발견했고, 연속적인 순환에 사용된 것들은 바로 그런 식물들이었다.
Ⓒ 1950년대에 과학자들에 의해 만들어진 화학 비료는 극적으로 식량 생산량을 증가시켰으며 높은 인기를 누렸다.
Ⓓ 목축업과 농업이 다른 길로 나가게 되자 농장에서 충분한 구비를 확보하는 것이 더 어려워졌다.

어휘 fertilizer n 비료 | nitrogen n 질소 | phosphorus n 인 | potassium n 칼륨 | organic adj 유기물의 | animal manure 구비(동물 배설물로 만든 거름) | green manure 녹비(생풀이나 생나뭇잎으로 만든 충분히 썩지 않은 거름) | compost n 퇴비 | excreta n 배설물 | livestock n 가축 | waste n 배설물 | pen n (가축의) 우리 | graze v 방목하다 | indiscriminate adj 무분별한 | leavings n 잔여물, 찌꺼기 | select adj 엄선된 | rearing n 사육 | ranch n 목장 | typically adv 일반적으로 | rely v 의존하다 | enrich v 풍요롭게 하다, 강화하다 | till v 갈다, 경작하다 | decompose v 분해되다, 부패되다 | humus n 부엽토 | or so ~ 가량 | symbiotic adj 공생하는 | surface area 표면적 | edible adj 식용의 | replenish v 다시 채우다, 보충하다 | sequentially adv 연속적으로 | crop rotation 윤작 | inevitably adv 필연적으로 | deplete v 고갈시키다 | fallow n 휴경지 | succession n 연속 | fall out of use 쓰이지 않게 되다 | beneficial adj 유익한, 이로운 | devise v 창안하다, 고안하다 | dramatically adv 극적으로 | side effect 부작용 | unavoidably adv 불가피하게 | pollutant n 오염 물질 | exponentially adv 기하급수적으로 | devour v 먹어 치우다 | promote v 촉진하다 | toxic adj 유독성의 | acidity n 산성 | heavy metal 중금속

Lesson 02 Inference

본서 | P. 170

Practice

01 A　02 B　03 C　04 A　05 C　06 D　07 A　08 C　09 C　10 D

11 C　12 1. B 2. A　13 1. C 2. D　14 1. B 2. B　15 1. B 2. B　16 1. B 2. A

Test

1. A　2. B　3. D　4. A　5. B　6. C　7. C　8. C　9. C　10. A, E, F

11. B　12. D　13. B　14. A　15. B　16. B　17. B　18. A　19. C　20. B, E, F

Practice

본서 | P. 172

01 지구가 45억 년 동안 존재해 온 대부분의 기간에 진화는 고작 단순한 박테리아나 조류 정도의 것을 만들어냈다. 그러나 5억 4천 2백만 년 전, 캄브리아기로 고생대가 시작되면서 수많은 동물군의 계보가 만들어졌다. 캄브리아기라는 이름은 캄브리아기의 첫 번째 화석화된 유해가 발견된 웨일스의 옛 이름 캄브리아에서 유래했다.

지문을 바탕으로 다음 중 캄브리아라는 이름에 관해 추론 가능한 것은 무엇인가?

Ⓐ 더 이상 웨일스를 가리키기 위해 널리 사용되지 않는다.
Ⓑ 과학자들이 원래 이름으로 이 지역을 언급하는 것이 일반적이다.
Ⓒ 웨일스에서 발견된 동물의 몇 가지 종류들을 가리키기 위해 사용된다.
Ⓓ 웨일스의 화석과 관련하여 보게 될 가능성이 없는 용어이다.

어휘 evolution n 진화, 발전 | algae n 말, 조류 | lineage n 혈통 | fauna n 동물군, 동물상 | materialize v 구체화되다, 실현되다

02 불면증은 사람들이 잠드는 데 어려움을 겪거나 밤에 종종 잠에서 깨어 다시 잠을 이루기 힘든 것, 혹은 너무 이른 아침에 잠에서 깨거나 전날 밤만큼 피곤함을 느끼면서 잠에서 깨어나게 만드는 수면 장애이다. 불면증 환자들은 낮 동안 졸음, 피로, 집중 곤란, 신경질 등과 같은 문제점을 갖기도 한다. 일반적으로 알려진 것과 반대로 불면증은 개인의 수면 시간과 관련이 없다. 어떤 사람들은 다른 사람들보다 그저 좀 더 길거나 좀 더 짧은 수면을 필요로 한다.

다음 중 지문에서 불면증에 관해 추론 가능한 것은 무엇인가?

Ⓐ 불면증이 있는 사람들은 불면증이 없는 사람들보다 더 적게 잠을 잔다.
Ⓑ 불면증은 낮 동안 환자들에게 부정적 영향을 끼친다.
Ⓒ 불면증의 주간 증상은 밤에 발생하는 증상보다 인간의 삶에 더 많은 악영향을 미칠 수 있다.
Ⓓ 불면증이 있는 사람들은 심리적 문제로 고통을 받는다.

어휘 fatigue n 피로 | concentrate v 집중하다 | irritability n 신경질, 화 냄, 신경 과민 | perception n 인식

03 뮤지컬은 대중적인 노래를 이용한 연극, TV, 또는 영화 작품으로 길고 다양한 역사를 지녔다. 뮤지컬은 일찍이 기원전 5세기에 고대 그리스인들이 음악과 춤을 연극에 포함시켰던 때부터 공연되었다. 노래는 보통 합창단이 주연들의 행동에 대해 해설할 수 있도록 하는 데 사용되었다.

로마인들은 그리스인들이 연극에 음악을 사용하는 것을 따라했고 확장했는데, 춤추는 사람들의 신발 밑창에 금속 조각을 붙였다. 이것이 탭 댄스의 최초 형태였다. 중세 시대에는 방랑 음유시인과 유랑극단이 여흥을 위해 유명한 노래와 슬랩스틱 코미디를 상연했다. 결국 이는 오페라와 다른 뮤지컬 연극의 형태로 공식화되었다.

지문에 따르면, 뮤지컬에 관해 추론 가능한 것은 무엇인가?

Ⓐ 일반적으로 전통 음악을 포함한다.
Ⓑ 유랑 극단에 의해 로마인들에게 소개되었다.
Ⓒ 2000년 이상 존재해 왔다.
Ⓓ 인형극에서 사용되었다.

어휘 tap dancing 탭 댄스 I nomadic adj 유목의, 방랑의 I troupe n 공연단, 극단 I slapstick n 익살

---

04 서기 900년에 서예와 장식 그림을 포함하는 이슬람 책들은 예술가들이 자신들의 예술적 표현을 전달하는 주요 수단이 되었다. 그 당시에 이러한 책을 생산하는 것이 가능하게 된 이유는 두 가지 발달 덕분이다. 이런 방향의 진전 중 하나는 종이의 등장이었다. 그 전에 사람들은 양피지를 사용했는데, 이것은 필기 재료로 사용할 수 있게 준비된 양이나 염소 같은 동물 가죽이었다. 양피지와 달리 종이는 비싸지도 않았고 생산이 어렵지도 않았으며 대규모로 만들어질 수도 있었다. 또 다른 기여 요인은 둥근 서체로 알려진 좀 더 간단한 쓰기 형태의 발명이었다. 이 문자는 문자의 고르지 못한 높이와 글쓰기 방식의 불규칙성 때문에 쓰기도 어렵고 고도의 전문성이 요구되었던 각진 서체를 효율적으로 대체했다.

지문을 바탕으로 유추할 수 있는 것은

Ⓐ 서기 900년에는 양피지를 생산하는 것이 쉽지 않았다
Ⓑ 서기 900년에 이슬람인들은 각진 서체만 사용했다
Ⓒ 서기 900년 이전에 이슬람인들은 양피지를 구입할 수 없었다
Ⓓ 서기 900년 이전에 역사가들은 단순한 필기 방법을 개발하기 위해 분투했다

어휘 calligraphy n 서예 I render v (어떤 상태가 되게) 하다 I feasible adj 실현 가능한 I stride n 진전 I advent n 도래, 출현 I angular adj 각이 진, 모난 I expertise n 전문 기술

---

05 화학이나 다른 과학 분야를 연구하는 데 가장 중요한 것은 과학적 이론이 단지 많은 실험 결과의 논리적 해석에 불과하다는 것을 기억하는 것이다. 이런 이론들은 난데없이 혹은 우연히 나오는 것이 아니다. 오히려 시행 착오를 거쳐, 특히 수 년에 걸친 과정 동안 수천 명의 사람들이 행한 고된 작업에서 나오는 것이다. 이전에 채택된 이론들이 설명할 수 없었던 결과를 추가 실험이 밝혀낸다면, 시간이 지나면서 이론들이 더 나은 이론들로 수정되거나 교체되는 것은 드문 일이 아니다. 기본적으로 지금 이 순간 확립된 이론으로 간주되는 것은 완전히 확정된 것이 아니라 지금까지 과학자들이 알아낸 것을 대변하는 것일 뿐이다.

지문에 따르면 이론에 관해 추론 가능한 것은 무엇인가?

Ⓐ 일단 타당한 이론이 확립되면 절대로 의문이 제기되어서는 안 된다.
Ⓑ 훌륭한 이론들은 추가 실험으로 결코 대체되거나 수정될 필요가 없다.
Ⓒ 연구를 수행하는 최신 방법들은 더 나은 이론을 낳는 데 기여했다.
Ⓓ 아주 많은 이론들이 만들어지기 때문에 화학은 독특한 과학 분야이다.

어휘 utmost adj 최고의, 극도의 I interpretation n 해석, 이해 I modify v 수정하다, 바꾸다

06

올림픽의 여성들

그리스 신화에 따르면, 올림픽 경기는 언제나 헤라이아라 불리는 여성들의 축제를 포함했다. 그것은 4년마다 남성들의 축제 직전에 개최되었고 그리스 전역에서 온 소녀들에게 개방되어 있었을 것이다. 세 종류의 도보 경주가 있었는데, 세 가지 연령대별로 각각 하나씩 있었다. 이런 구분은 고대 자료에 정확히 인용되어 있지는 않지만 학자들은 그 범위가 6세부터 18세까지에 달했을 것으로 추측한다. 헤라이아의 우승자들은 남성 경기의 우승자들과 마찬가지로 경기의 모든 참가자들을 대표해 올리브 월계관과 수호신을 위해 도살된 한 마리의 황소 중 일부를 받았다. 헤라이아의 우승자들은 올림픽 성전에 있는 헤라 사원에 자신들의 초상화를 붙였다. 그 초상화들은 오래 전에 사라졌지만 사원 기둥에 그 초상화들이 설치되어 있던 벽면의 움푹 들어간 자리는 여전히 선명하다.

다음 중 지문에서 헤라이아의 우승자들에 관해 추론 가능한 것은 무엇인가?

Ⓐ 일부는 후에 올림픽 우승자들과 결혼했다.
Ⓑ 일부는 후에 종교 교단의 일원이 되었다.
Ⓒ 후세의 소녀들에게 신화적인 여신이 되었다.
Ⓓ 그들의 업적에 대해 높은 존경을 받았다.

어휘 footrace n 도보 경주 | slaughter v 도살하다, 도축하다 | sanctuary n 성소, 성역 | niche n 벽감(벽의 움푹 들어간 곳), 틈새

---

07 **바이킹**

바이킹은 유럽의 많은 지역을 공격하고 침입한 공격적인 야만인으로 오랫동안 묘사되어 왔다. 그러나 그것은 바이킹 문화의 한 국면에 불과하다. 그들은 로마 군대와 싸워서 자신들의 영역을 성공적으로 지킨 사나운 전사들이었으며, 이로 인해서 '야만인'이라는 꼬리표를 얻게 되었는데, 이는 로마인들이 자신들이 무찌르지 못한 모든 집단을 그렇게 불렀기 때문이다. 그러나 바이킹은 현대의 스칸디나비아에서 여전히 찾아볼 수 있는 인권 수호 전통을 갖춘 뛰어난 뱃사람들이자 상인, 농부, 기능공이었으며 탐험가이기도 했다. 3백 년 간의 바이킹 시대 동안에 그들은 모피, 철 제품, 노예를 비단, 향료, 은과 거래했다. 바이킹 사회는 백작, 자유민, 노예의 세 신분 계층으로 나뉘어 있었다. 한 사람의 계층을 정하는 가장 큰 요인이 그 사람의 출신이기는 했지만, 한 개인이 스스로의 지위를 높이고 낮추는 것이 가능했다.

다음 중 지문에서 바이킹에 관해 추론 가능한 것은 무엇인가?

Ⓐ 바이킹은 이웃 나라들로부터 두려움을 샀다.
Ⓑ 바이킹은 사람의 계급을 태어날 때 고정된 것이라 여겼다.
Ⓒ 바이킹 사회는 대체로 농업 사회였다.
Ⓓ 바이킹은 로마 제국에 필적할 만한 그들만의 제국을 갖는 것을 목표로 삼았다.

어휘 raid v 급습하다, 습격하다 | ferocious adj 흉포한, 맹렬한 | warrior n 전사 | barbarian n 야만인 | craftsman n 기능공 | earl n 백작 | status n 지위 | hierarchy n 계층

---

08 **고릴라**

영장류 동물학자들은 얼마나 많은 종이 존재하는지 규명하기 위해 다양한 고릴라 개체군 사이의 관계를 지속적으로 연구하고 있다. 최근까지는 마운틴고릴라, 웨스턴로랜드고릴라, 이스턴로랜드고릴라의 세 종이 있다는 데 의견이 일치했었다. 그러나 현재 합의된 바로는 두 종의 고릴라만 존재하며 각각의 종에 두 개의 아종이 있다고 한다. 두 종 중 첫 번째는 웨스턴고릴라인데, 웨스턴로랜드고릴라와 크로스리버고릴라라는 두 아종을 가지고 있다. 두 번째 종은 이스턴고릴라인데, 마운틴고릴라와 이스턴로랜드고릴라라는 두 아종을 가지고 있다. 때때로 브윈디고릴라라고 불리는 또 다른 아종이 이스턴고릴라의 세 번째 추가 아종으로 제안되기도 했지만 이 제안은 영장류 학자들 사이에서 완전히 받아들여지지는 않고 있다.

지문에 따르면 다음 중 동물 종에 관해 추론 가능한 것은 무엇인가?

Ⓐ 한 가지 종에는 항상 두 가지 아종이 있다.
Ⓑ 고릴라 종에 대한 과학적 분류는 결코 바뀐 적이 없다.
Ⓒ 과학자들이 동물 종을 분류하기 위해 이용하는 기준은 시간이 지나면서 바뀔 수 있다.
Ⓓ 영장류 학자들은 최근에 고릴라 종의 분류를 완성했다.

어휘 primatologist n 영장류 동물학자 | subspecies n 아종, 변종 | proposal n 제안, 제의

---

09 **최초의 문명**

방랑하던 수렵 채집인들이 언제, 어디서 처음으로 문명 창조를 시작했는지 아무도 정확하게 알아내지 못했다. 명백한 증거는 없지만 일반적으로 문명은 대략 일만 년 전 시작되었고, 그때 사람들이 씨앗을 보존하기 위한 방법으로 우연히 땅에 씨앗을 심었던 것으로 여겨진다. 전에 씨앗을 묻었던 땅 표면을 뚫고 나오는 어린 묘목을 보고 농부들은 놀랐을 것이다. 이것이 농사법 발달에 최초의 박차를 가했고, 이는 결국 작은 지역에 많은 사람들을 살게 할 만큼 충분한 식량 생산을 가능하게 했다. 이런 사실은 역사 기록에서 쉽게 볼 수 있고, 이것은 농사와 최초의 대규모 문명이 거의 동시에 발생했다는 것을 분명하게 보여준다.

지문에 따르면 최초의 농부들에 관해 추론 가능한 것은 무엇인가?

Ⓐ 씨앗을 심기 적절한 땅을 선택하는 방법에 대한 지식이 있었다.
Ⓑ 땅에 모든 씨앗을 저장할 수 있었다.
Ⓒ 최초의 사람들은 우연히 농사짓는 법을 발견했을 가능성이 높다.
Ⓓ 최초의 농부들이 씨앗을 보존하기 시작한 시점이 언제였는지 확실히 알 수 있다.

어휘 embark on ~에 착수하다, 시작하다 | nomadic adj 유목의, 방랑의 | inadvertently adv 무심코, 우연히 | momentum n (일 진행의) 가속도 | contemporaneous adj 동시에 발생하는

---

10 **미어캣**

미어캣은 남서 앙골라 지역과 남아프리카 지역에 20~50마리에 달하는 집단으로 서식하는 작은 포유류 동물이다. 최근 과학자들은 미어캣이 복잡한 사회적 행동을 보인다는 것을 알게 되었다. 예를 들어 조사를 통해 미어캣은 꽤 엄격한 사회적 계층을 가지고 있으며, 집단 내에서 권력을 얻기 위해 경쟁하기도 한다는 사실이 드러났다. 게다가 다른 많은 동물들과 반대로 미어캣은 집단 내에서 많은 이타적 행위를 보인다. 예를 들면 다른 미어캣들이 음식을 찾거나 놀고 있는 동안 그들에게 다가오는 위험을 알리기 위해 한 마리 이상의 미어캣이 보초를 선다. 포식자가 목격되면 보초를 서고 있던 미어캣은 경고 소리를 내고 집단의 다른 구성원들은 도망가서 자신들의 굴에 있는 구멍으로 숨는다. 미어캣은 또한 집단 내의 어린 새끼들을 돌보기도 한다. 아이를 돌보는 미어캣은 위협으로부터 어린 새끼를 보호하다가 때로는 자신의 목숨까지 위험에 처하기도 한다.

지문에 따르면, 미어캣 이외의 동물 종에 관해 추론 가능한 것은 무엇인가?

Ⓐ 개체가 집단 작업에 참여하게 만든다.
Ⓑ 새끼를 돌볼 필요가 없다.
Ⓒ 적이 다가올 때 보통 도망가서 숨는다.
Ⓓ 다른 이들을 위해 스스로를 희생할 가능성이 적다.

어휘 mammalian adj 포유류의 | number v (합한 수가) 총 ~이 되다 | hierarchy n 계층, 위계 질서 | compete v 경쟁하다 | altruistic adj 이타적인 | forage v 먹이를 찾다 | spot v 발견하다, 찾다 | bark n 짖음 | babysit v 아이를 돌보다 | endanger v 위험에 빠뜨리다

---

11 **나방**

나방은 크기가 엄청나게 다양해서 날개 폭이 4mm에서 거의 300mm에 이른다. 굉장히 종류가 다양해서 극지방의 서식지를 제외하고 모든 지역에서 거주한다. 이들은 나비와 밀접한 관련이 있는 곤충이다. 나비와 마찬가지로 나방의 날개, 몸, 다리는 건드리면 떨어지는 먼지 같은 얇은 비늘로 덮여 있다. 그러나 나비와 나방 사이에는 몇 가지 차이점이 있다. 일부 나방종은 주행성이지만 대부분의 나방은 야행성이다. 나비와 비교했을 때, 그것들은 더 두터운 몸통과 상대적으로 더 작은 날개를 가졌다. 나비는 밝은 색의 날개로 알려진 반면 나방은 주로 숨는 것을 용이하게 해주는 지그재그 무늬가 있는 검은색, 회색, 갈색, 흰색 등의 탁색이다. 또 다른 차이는 더듬이이다. 골프채 모양의 얇은 더듬이를 가지고 있는 나비와 달리 나방은 솜털 같은 더듬이를 가지고 있다. 여기에 더해, 나방은 휴식을 취할 때 날개를 접거나, 몸 주변을 감싸거나 양쪽 측면으로 펼친 채로 있는다.

지문에서 나방에 대해 추론할 수 있는 것은

Ⓐ 보통 매우 넓은 날개 폭을 갖고 있다
Ⓑ 다른 곤충보다 더 연약한 몸을 갖고 있다
Ⓒ 다양한 서식지에서 살 수 있다
Ⓓ 나비와 마찬가지로 보통 주행성이다

어휘 range v ~에서 …에 이르다 | polar adj 북극의, 극지의 | nocturnal adj 야행성의 | stout adj 튼튼한, 통통한 | proportionately adv 비례해서 | antennae n 더듬이 | feathery adj 솜털 같은 | wrap v 싸다

---

12 **빙하 감소**

1 ➡ 미국 몬태나주에 있는 글래시어 국립공원은 마지막 빙하기의 커다란 빙하에 의해 지금의 모습으로 형성된 산맥으로 주로 이루어져 있다. 하지만 이 공원 대부분의 빙하는 지난 12,000년에 걸쳐 대체로 사라졌다. 글래시어 국립공원 지역이 1800년대 중반 기후학자에 의해 처음 조사되었을 때는 150개가 넘는 빙하가 있었다. 그러나 현재 공원에는 약 25개의 빙하만 남아 있고, 그것마저 처음 보고되었던 크기보다 훨씬 더

적은 양이다. 이 엄청난 빙하가 사라지는 현상의 주 원인은 지구 온난화로 여겨지며, 지금의 온난화 상황이 계속된다면 2030년에는 산악 빙하가 존재하지 않게 될 것이다.

2 ➡ 빙하가 사라지는 것이 공원의 환경에 끼치는 영향은 눈이 녹으면서 생기는 물에 의존하는 식물군과 동물군의 서식지 부족이다. 빙하가 없어지는 것은 농업에도 불리한 영향을 끼친다. 여름철의 물 대부분은 로키 산맥의 대수층에서 물을 끌어오는 시스템뿐 아니라 산에 남아 있는 얼음이 녹아서 공급된다. 이는 그 지역 거주민 절반 이상을 위한 식수원이었고 이 지역의 초기 정착을 가능하게 했지만 그 양은 엄청나게 감소했다.

1. 1단락의 글래시어 국립공원에 관해 추론할 수 있는 것은

Ⓐ 공원에 빙하가 남지 않는 것은 불가피하다
Ⓑ 산들은 빙하기 전에 아주 다른 모습이었다
Ⓒ 글래시어 국립공원은 1800년대 중반에 세워졌다
Ⓓ 공원에는 오늘날 약 150개의 빙하만 있다

2. 다음 중 기온이 계속 오르면 발생할 수 있는 일은 무엇인가?

Ⓐ 경작지에 관개할 물이 충분하지 않을 것이다.
Ⓑ 빙하가 예상된 시일 내에 더욱 커질 것이다.
Ⓒ 더 빠르게 녹는 얼음 때문에 식수 공급이 늘어날 것이다.
Ⓓ 동물들이 충분한 물을 찾아 다른 주로 이동할 것이다.

어휘 climatologist **n** 기후학자 | retreat **n** 후퇴, 퇴각 | flora **n** 식물군 | fauna **n** 동물군

---

13 **생체막**

1 ➡ 생체막은 진핵세포 내의 각 세포 기관뿐 아니라 모든 세포들을 감싸는 얇은 막 같은 구조물이다. 이 막은 생화학 과정을 독립된 부분으로 나눌 뿐 아니라 이런 여러 반응에 활발히 참여한다. 예를 들어 세포막은 세포에 영양분을 전달하고 독성 찌꺼기를 세포에서 제거하는 특별한 운송 체계를 가지고 있고, 엽록체 막은 햇빛을 필수 화학 에너지로 바꾸어 준다. 게다가 세포막은 물에 녹지 않는 분자를 포함하는 생화학 반응을 위해 소수성(疏水性) 환경을 조성해 준다.

2 ➡ 전문화된 생리학적 기능에도 불구하고, 모든 세포막은 지방질과 단백질이라는 두 종류의 화학 성분으로 주로 구성된다. 단백질은 일련의 아미노산인 반면 지방질은 유기 용액에서는 녹지만 물에서는 잘 녹지 않는 생체 분자이다. 지방질의 정의는 단백질, 탄수화물, 핵산의 정의와 다르며 그 이유는 정의가 구조가 아닌 가용성을 바탕으로 한 것이기 때문이다. 하나의 세포 내 지방질 분자군은 물에 녹는 분자군처럼 구조적으로, 기능적으로 다양하다. 생체막의 각 형태에는 특정 생물학적 기능에 특히 적합한 특유의 단백질이 있다.

1. 1단락에서 세포의 생화학 작용에 관해 추론 가능한 것은 무엇인가?

Ⓐ 모든 작용에는 진핵세포 내의 소기관에 의해 형성된 독특한 환경이 필요하다.
Ⓑ 햇빛을 화학 에너지로 전환하는 것은 엽록체 막에만 있는 작용이다.
Ⓒ 일부 생화학 반응은 생체막의 참여를 필요로 하지 않을 수 있다.
Ⓓ 같은 운송체계를 통해 찌꺼기 배출과 양분 흡수를 동시에 할 수 있다.

2. 다음 중 지문에서 추론할 수 있는 것은

Ⓐ 생체막의 주요 기능은 형태에 상관 없이 거의 동일하다
Ⓑ 탄수화물은 지방질에서 용해되는 지용성 요소이다
Ⓒ 모든 생체막은 특징에 따라 각각 한 가지 기능만 가지고 있다
Ⓓ 단백질의 정의는 가용성이 아니라 구조에 근거한다

어휘 biological membrane 생체막 | encase **v** 감싸다 | organelle **n** 세포 기관 | eukaryotic cell 진핵 세포 | compartment **n** 독립된 부분, 칸 | chloroplast **n** 엽록체 | hydrophobic **adj** 소수성(물과의 친화력이 적은 성질)의 | physiological **adj** 생리학적인 | lipid **n** 지방질 | solvent **n** 용액 | nucleic acid 핵산

---

14 **DDT**

1 ➡ DDT는 최초의 현대식 살충제로, 물에 녹지 않지만 유기 용매, 지방, 기름에서 잘 녹는 무색의 고체이다. 제2차 세계대전 초기 발명된 이후 DDT는 모기와 다른 질병을 퍼트리는 곤충을 없애는 데 효과적으로 사용되었다. 사실 DDT는 유럽과 북아메리카에서 말라리아를 근절했다.

DDT를 발명한 스위스 화학자는 1948년에 노벨 생리의학상을 수상했다.

2 ➡ 그러나 1960년대에 미국의 한 운동가가 DDT가 암을 유발하고 알의 껍질을 얇게 하여 조류의 번식에 해를 끼친다고 주장한 책을 출간하여 동요를 일으켰다. 그 항의는 결국 살충제 사용 금지라는 결과를 가져왔다. DDT는 가재, 새우, 그리고 많은 물고기 종과 같은 해양 동물에 몹시 독성이 강하다고 입증되었다. 게다가 많은 환경론자들은 미국 대머리독수리의 멸종 위기를 DDT의 탓으로 돌리고 있다. DDT는 잔류성 유기 오염 물질인데, 이는 대머리독수리 같은 최상위 포식동물이 같은 지역의 다른 동물들보다 화학 물질을 더욱 고농도로 체내에 축적하게 될 것이라는 의미다.

3 ➡ DDT가 인간에게 해롭거나 암을 유발한다는 것이 아직 입증되지 않았기 때문에 DDT의 해악을 둘러싼 논쟁은 계속되고 있다. 따라서 말라리아와 곤충으로 인한 기타 질병들과 싸우는 많은 국가는 잠재적 위험보다 이득이 더 크기 때문에 DDT 사용을 계속하고 있다.

1. 다음 중 DDT의 영향에 관해 추론 가능한 것은 무엇인가?

Ⓐ DDT는 장기적인 유전자 변이를 유발할 수 있다.
Ⓑ DDT는 아마도 대머리독수리의 알 껍질을 얇게 해서 그 종을 거의 멸종시킬 뻔했다.
Ⓒ DDT는 모기 수를 증가시키는 데 지대한 역할을 했다.
Ⓓ DDT는 다른 살충제에 비해 인간에게 더 안전하다.

2. DDT가 잔류성 유기 오염 물질이라는 사실로부터 추론 가능한 것은 무엇인가?

Ⓐ DDT는 인간에게 암을 유발할 수 있다.
Ⓑ DDT는 동물의 피와 신체 조직에 남을 수 있다.
Ⓒ DDT는 전 세계적으로 곤충이 옮기는 병을 근절할 수 있다.
Ⓓ DDT는 대머리독수리와 수중 동물들을 죽일 수 있다.

어휘 pesticide n 살충제 I outcry n 항의 I apex n 꼭대기, 정점 I ongoing adj 계속 진행 중인 I outweigh v ~보다 더 크다

---

15 곤충의 길 찾기

1 ➡ 일 년 내내 많은 종의 동물이 계절에 따라 이동하지만 이들은 적당한 장소를 찾아 무작정 떠도는 것이 아니다. 오히려 찾아가야 하는 특정한 목적지가 있으며 고도의 방향 판단과 길 찾기 기술이 이 과제를 성공적으로 완수하는 데 필요하다. 효율적으로 이동하고 더 짧은 여행을 하기 위해 이 종들은 여러 가지 다른 시스템을 진화시켰다. 그러한 길 찾기 기술은 종종 경험이나 교육을 통해 학습되는 것이 아니라 유전적으로 전달된다. 특히 곤충은 그들이 길을 찾는 것을 가능하게 해주는 놀라운 내재 시스템을 발달시켰다.

2 ➡ 곤충은 먹이를 찾아야 할 때 집을 떠나 보금자리로 가져갈 영양분을 찾으며 돌아다녀야 한다. 분명히, 곤충은 집으로 돌아갈 수 있게 해주는 시스템을 보유하고 있는 것이 틀림없기에 길 찾기 시스템을 이루는 다양한 메커니즘을 일반적으로 가지고 있다. 예를 들어 기어 다니는 곤충들은 먹이의 위치를 찾는 것뿐 아니라 집으로 되돌아가는 길을 표시하는 데 화학적 신호를 사용한다. 일례로 개미들은 지나온 길과 먹이가 있는 곳을 표시하는 등 보금자리에서 하는 일들을 표시하기 위해 페로몬(상대방의 행동에 영향을 주는 호르몬)을 많이 사용한다. 지나온 길을 표시하기 위해 페로몬을 사용해서 개미는 자신의 위치를 파악하고 먹이가 있는 곳의 위치나 다른 장소의 위치를 제공할 수 있다.

3 ➡ 길 찾기 수단으로 화학적 신호를 쓰는 대신 어떤 곤충들은 길 찾기에 태양을 이용한다. 즉 집을 나서면서 자신의 위치를 분석하고 경로를 표시하기 위한 기준점으로 태양을 이용하는 것이다. 사하라 사막 개미는 태양을 길 찾기에 이용하는 곤충의 예시다. 이 개미는 먹이를 찾으러 보금자리를 떠날 때 집과 비례하여 자신의 위치를 알아내기 위해 태양을 보고 규칙적으로 계산을 한다. 따라서 모래 속에 있어 눈에 띄지 않는 보금자리로 되돌아가는 길을 재빨리 찾을 수 있다. 이 개미의 숨겨진 보금자리는 사하라 사막 개미의 생존 가능성을 높여 주는데, 이는 포식자가 개미들이 많은 곳을 찾을 수 없기 때문이다.

4 ➡ 그러나 태양 자체가 가려지면 이 곤충들은 어떻게 길을 찾을까? 때때로 언덕이나 식물 등의 장애물에 가려지면 태양은 보이지 않기 때문에 이러한 곤충들 대부분은 일주율과 연결된 시스템을 발달시켜 왔으며, 이 생물학적 일일 활동 주기 덕분에 그들은 시간에 따른 태양의 위치를 가늠할 수 있다. 지구와 태양의 위치가 연중 변화한다는 점을 고려할 때 이는 다소 버거운 방법처럼 느껴질 수 있다. 그러나 곤충들은 태양의 일정한 편차와 생물학적 과정이 일치하도록 일주율을 조정하여 이러한 변화에 적응할 수 있다.

5 ➡ 악천후 또한 해를 가릴 수 있다. 일부 비가 많은 지역에서는 잔뜩 낀 구름 때문에 연달아 몇 주 동안 태양이 보이지 않는 경우도 있다. 이런 상황에서 태양의 위치를 추측하기란 가능하지 않다. 이러한 어려움을 해결하기 위해 곤충들은 더 직접적인 길 찾기 방법을 이용한다. 성공적인 여행을 위해 필요한 귀소 정보를 경계표에서 찾는 것이다. 그러한 시각적 확인은 다른 종류의 길 찾기에도 도움이 될 수 있다. 그뿐 아니라 곤충들은 거리 계산을 이용하기도 하는데, 이는 기본적으로 출발점에서 떠나온 후 몇 걸음을 걸었고 몇 번을 돌았는지 세는 방법이다. 이 두 가지 행동을 궤도 적분이라는 과정에 통합하여 많은 곤충이 자신의 위치를 정확히 계산할 수 있다. 확실히, 만약 동물이 원래 출발점과 비교해 자신의 위치를 판단할 수 없다면 길을 잃고 포식자나 기타 환경적 위험에 노출될 것이다. 생존은 길 찾기 능력에 달려있음이 분명하다. 그러므로 이렇게 다양한 방법을 발달시킴으로써 곤충들은 환경의 난제를 극복하고 종의 생존을 보장할 수 있다.

1. 지문에서 개미의 행동에 관해 추론 가능한 것은 무엇인가?

Ⓐ 포식자에게서 보금자리를 보호하기 위해 페로몬을 사용한다.
Ⓑ 각각의 종이 길 찾기를 위해 몇 가지의 수단을 가질 수 있다.
Ⓒ 사막 환경에서는 페로몬이 쓸모 없다.
Ⓓ 개미들은 시력이 좋지 않아서 다른 감각에 의존해야 한다.

2. 다음 중 5단락에서 동물의 길 찾기에 관해 추론 가능한 것은 무엇인가?

Ⓐ 동물의 사회적 행동은 새로운 길 찾기 방식의 발달에 아주 중요하다.
Ⓑ 새로운 길 찾기 방식은 환경에 따라 발달할 것이다.
Ⓒ 동물의 유전자 연구가 인간의 길 찾기에 도움이 될 것이다.
Ⓓ 동물들이 길 찾기에 성공하는 것은 오로지 진화된 계산 능력에서만 기인한 것이다.

어휘 aimlessly adv 목적 없이 I destination n 목적지 I complete v 완수하다 I capacity n 능력, 용량 I predominantly adv 대개, 대부분 I instruction n 교육 I comprise v ~로 구성되다 I cue n 신호 I extensively adv 널리, 광범위하게 I reference n 참고, 참조 I plot v 표시하다, 도표를 만들다 I periodically adv 주기적으로 I circadian adj 24시간 주기의, 생물학적 주기의 I procedure n 절차 I synchronize v 동시에 발생하게 하다 I deviation n 일탈, 탈선 I obscure v 보기 어렵게 하다 I confirmation n 확인 I footstep n 발소리, 발자국 I integration n 통합 I compute v 계산하다, 산출하다 I hazard n 위험 (요소)

16

유럽의 에너지 전환

1 ➡ 역사를 통틀어 발전에 있어 변화는 새롭고 더 효율적인 에너지원의 이용과 함께 이루어지는 경우가 많았다. 산업 혁명이 시작되기 전, 다른 유럽 국가들은 물론이고 영국은 나무에서 석탄으로 에너지원을 대체하게 되었고 석탄은 영국의 지배적인 연료 자원으로 자리잡게 되었다. 이러한 중대한 변화가 일어나기까지는 서로 연관된 몇 가지 요인이 함께 작용했다. 첫째는 유럽에 대대적인 산림 벌목이 있었다. 이것은 그 자체만으로도 문제였지만 나무를 대체하기 위해 작물을 심으면서 문제점은 더욱 증폭되었다. 식량 공급 증가는 급속한 인구 증가와 맞물렸다. 인구 과밀은 환경을 악화시킬 뿐이었고 에너지원인 나무의 수요 증가로 이어졌다. 이러한 문제점을 해결하기 위해 정부는 앞장서서 나무 사용을 제한하고 일차적인 에너지원으로 나무를 대체할 방법을 찾기 시작했다.

2 ➡ 산업 혁명이 시작되기 전, 영국의 목재 가격이 국내 공급량의 고갈로 인해 치솟았다. 영국의 숲은 집을 데우고 산업에 연료를 공급하는 에너지를 나무에 의존하는 작은 마을과 혼잡한 도시들에 연료가 될 나무를 충분히 제공하기 위해 거의 파괴된 상태였다. 국내의 장기적인 개벌(皆伐)로 인한 경제적, 환경적 영향에 대응해 영국 정부는 산림을 보호하기 위한 조치를 취했다. 14세기에 벌써 영국 왕은 딘 숲과 같은 지역을 광범위한 벌목에서 보호하려는 노력을 기울였다. 그러나 여전히 왕이 개인적인 용도로 사용할 만큼의 벌목은 허용했다. 부족한 공급량을 메우기 위해 영국은 값비싼 방법이지만 스칸디나비아와 동부 유럽에서 목재를 수입하거나 대체 에너지원을 찾아야 했다.

3 ➡ 석탄은 중세 시대부터 사용되었으며 처음에는 용광로를 가열하려는 대장장이들만 사용했다. 석탄은 풍부한 에너지원이지만 몇 가지 단점도 있었다. 석탄의 가장 큰 문제점은 연소 시 황 불순물과 이산화탄소가 다량 방출된다는 사실이었다. 가정용 난방원으로 석탄을 사용하면 옷이 더러워지고 음식에서 나쁜 맛이 나며 참을 수 없을 정도로 많은 연기가 집안에 가득 차곤 했다. 산업 현장에서조차 석탄은 대부분의 공정에 부적합했다. 양조장은 맥주를 만드는 공정에 석탄을 사용하려고 시도했지만 석탄에서 방출되는 황이 맥주 맛을 바꿔서 마실 수 없는 상태로 만든다는 것을 알게 되었다. 그뿐 아니라 당시의 낡은 용광로에서 석탄을 제련에 사용할 경우 많은 양의 황 불순물이 금속에 들어가 금속을 못 쓰게 만들었다.

4 ➡ 반면 대체 에너지원으로서 석탄 사용의 장점 또한 여러 가지 있었다. 석탄은 동일한 양의 생산 투입량으로 나무보다 더 많은 에너지를 공급했다. 또한 석탄은 나무보다 풍부한 데다 공급 가격도 더 저렴했다. 산업 혁명이 시작되면서 산업에 필요한 철을 생산하기 위해 많은 양의 에너지원이 필요했다. 이러한 수요 증가에 따라 과학자들은 석탄을 편리한 에너지원으로 만드는 데 보다 많은 관심을 쏟기 시작했고 석탄 사용을 개선하기 위해 새로운 발명품 개발에 착수했다. 1709년 영국인 에이브러햄 다비는 코킹법, 즉 정제를 통해 석탄에서 연기를 발생시키는 물질을 없애는 방법을 발명했다. 이 혁신적인 기술의 또 다른 장점은 석탄을 더 강하게 만들어 자체 무게에 의해 석탄이 부서지지 않게 해준다는 점이었다. 이 기술로 석탄은 화로와 용광로를 가열하는 편리한 자원이 되었을 뿐 아니라 더 크고 더 효과적인 용광로 개발에 박차가 가해지면서 가정과 산업에서 보편적인 열원으로 사용되기 시작했다.

5 ➡ 석탄이 실용적인 대체 연료가 되기 위해서는 아직 새로운 기술이 발명되고 실용화되어야 했지만 영국을 주축으로 한 세계는 머지 않아 석탄이 주요 에너지원으로 출현하는 상황을 목격하게 되었다. 한때 변변찮은 에너지원으로 여겨졌던 석탄은 세계적으로 손꼽히는 에너지원 중 하나가 되었다. 실제로 이는 요즘에도 유효한 사실로, 미국은 전기 에너지의 90%를 석탄에서 얻고 있다. 석탄은 여전히 세계에서 가장 빠른 속도의 사용량 증가를 보이는 에너지원으로 2001년에서 2004년 사이 사용량이 25% 증가하기도 했다. 또한 석탄 연소 기술이 여전히 향상되고 있으므로 석탄의 잠재 에너지 가운데 지금보다 40% 높은 85% 이상을 활용할 수 있는 날이 곧 다가올 것이다. 사실 산업 혁명 이전의 영국이 직면했던 문제점들은 석탄이 지금까지 가정과 세계 곳곳에서 에너지원으로 널리 이용되는 계기가 되었다고 볼 수 있다.

1. **2단락에서 추론할 수 있는 것은**

Ⓐ 영국은 수세기동안 값비싼 목재 수입에 의존할 수 밖에 없었다
Ⓑ 삼림 벌채는 산업혁명 이전부터 영국의 주된 문제였다
Ⓒ 영국 왕은 직접 벌목에 참여하기 위해 일부 숲을 보존했다
Ⓓ 영국은 산업혁명으로 인해 자원부족을 겪었다

2. **다음 중 4단락에서 석탄에 관해 추론 가능한 것은 무엇인가?**

Ⓐ 산업 혁명 이전에는 보편적 열원이 아니었다.
Ⓑ 산업 혁명 이전에 과학자들은 석탄의 유용성을 개선하는 것에 실패했다.
Ⓒ 에이브러햄 다비는 석탄을 더 강하고 더 깨끗한 연료로 만들고 싶어했다.
Ⓓ 가용성과 가격 때문에 석탄을 구입하는 것이 더 어려웠다.

어휘 shift n 변화 | utilization n 이용 | interrelated adj 밀접한 | magnified adj 증폭된 | lumber n 목재, 나무 | deplete v 격감시키다 | logging n 벌목 | timber n 수목, 산림 | medieval adj 중세의 | blacksmith n 대장장이 | furnace n 용광로 | copious adj 방대한 | impurity n 불순물 | combustion n 연소 | unbearably adv 참을 수 없을 정도로 | brew n 양조 맥주 | archaic adj 낡은 | pursue v 추구하다 | bountiful adj 많은, 풍부한

Test

본서 | P. 186

아즈텍의 예술과 공예

1 ➡ 어디서 유래했는지는 알려지지 않았지만 아즈텍인들은 15세기 중반 무렵에 멕시코 계곡의 지배적인 문화 집단이 되었다. [■A] 그들의 문화의 많은 부분들은 이웃 부족들에게서 빌려온 것으로 보이며, 이것은 그들을 독자적인 사회로 정의하는 것을 꽤 어렵게 만든다. [■B] 그들의 문자 체계, 언어, 건축 기술과 예술과 공예는 전부 그 부근에 거주하던 다른 북미 원주민 집단들과 유사성을 갖고 있지만 그 중 많은 것들은 그들 아래서 표현의 정점에 달했다. [■C] 이것은 최고 수준의 정교함과 아름다움에 달했던 그들의 예술에 있어서 특히 그렇다. 아즈텍 사회의 예술가들은 두 부류, 즉 실용품 예술가와 사치품 예술가로 나뉘었다. [■D] 실용품 예술가들은 기본적인 옷가지와 샌들, 엮은 바구니들과 부엌 도구들과 같은 일상에 사용되는 제품들을 만들었다. 사치품 예술가들은 귀금속과 보석과 깃털을 사용하여 사회의 가장 높은 계급을 차지했던 귀족들과 사제들을 위한 제품들을 만들었다.

2 ➡ 두 집단의 예술가들은 둘 다 그들의 예술 형식에 알맞은 기법에 있어서 수년간의 훈련이 요구되는 전문가들이었다. 그들 간의 주된 차이점들은 그들이 어디에 거주했는지와 그들이 얼마나 공예에 집중했는지에 있다. 실용품 예술가들은 주요 도시 밖의 시골 지역에 거주했으며 집에서 제품들을 생산했다. 그들은 보통 부업으로 예술가 활동을 했으며 나머지 시간을 농업에 투자하며 보냈다. 이 비율은 밭에서의 노동과 실용품에 대한 계절적인 수요에 따라 바뀌었다. 그들이 생산했던 주요 제품들 중 하나는 옷을 만드는 데 사용되었지만 일종의 통화(通貨)로도 사용되던 면포였다. 그들은 또한 나무로 된 기구들, 도자기와 칼과 같은 부엌 용품들을 제작했다. 그들의 칼날은 흑요석으로 만들어졌는데, 이것은 어렵고 정교한 작업을 필요로 했다. 이 칼날들은 역사상 알려진 가장 날카로운 날을 갖고 있었으며 무기를 포함하여 가정에서와 일터에서의 많은 다양한 작업에 사용되었다.

3 ➡ 그 반대로 사치품 예술가들은 도시 내에 거주했으며 그들의 공예품은 대부분 제작 의뢰를 통해 만들어졌다. 이것은 작업에 들어가

1. **1단락에서 아즈텍인들에 대해 추론 가능한 것은 무엇인가?**

Ⓐ 아즈텍인들이 멕시코 계곡에 언제 정착했는지에 대한 기록이 없다.
Ⓑ 아즈텍인들은 그들의 신념 체계를 멕시코 계곡에 있는 다른 부족들에게 강요했다.
Ⓒ 아즈텍 예술가들은 사회에서 가장 높은 계급을 차지하는 것으로 여겨졌다.
Ⓓ 오늘날 남아 있는 다양한 형태의 북미 원주민 예술은 아즈텍 사회에서 유래했다.

2. **2단락에 근거하여 실용품 예술가들에 대해 추론 가능한 것은 무엇인가?**

Ⓐ 사회를 위해 제품을 만드는 데 효율적이지 않았다.
Ⓑ 농업은 그들에게 다른 수입원이었다.
Ⓒ 주로 무기 제작자들이었다.
Ⓓ 사치품 예술가들과의 경쟁은 그들로 하여금 전업 농부가 되는 것을 막았다.

3. **2와 3단락에 따르면, 두 부류의 예술가들 간의 차이점이 아닌 것은**

Ⓐ 그들이 만든 제품의 종류
Ⓑ 그들이 거주한 곳
Ⓒ 그들이 예술에 투자한 시간
Ⓓ 그들이 받은 훈련의 양

4. **다음 중 음영 표시된 문장의 핵심 정보를 가장 잘 표현한 문장은 무엇인가? 오답은 의미를 크게 왜곡하거나 핵심 정보를 누락하고 있다.**

Ⓐ 그들이 재료를 위해 얼마나 멀리까지 교역했는지에 대한 한 가지 예는 옷을 위해 남미에서 수입한 화려한 색깔의 깃털이다.

는 재료들이 매우 귀했고 그들의 의뢰인들은 상류층이었기 때문이다. 사치품 예술가들은 예술 활동을 전임으로 했고 다른 의무들이 없었다. 그들은 신들과 중요한 역사적 인물들을 상징하는 장신구와 조각품들을 금, 은, 동 같은 금속과 보석으로 제작했다. 그들은 또한 조개 껍질, 목재와 깃털 같은 천연 재료들을 사용했다. 그들이 머리 장식, 망토를 만들고 심지어 갑옷을 장식하는 데에도 사용한 화려한 색깔의 깃털들 중 대부분은 남미에서 수입되었는데, 이것은 그들이 필요로 하는 재료를 위해 얼마나 광범위하게 교역했는지 보여준다. 그들이 다룬 원석들은 보석과 준보석이었으며 그것들에는 루비, 옥, 자수정, 오팔, 터키석과 월장석이 포함되었다. 이 원석들을 빛나는 상태로 광을 내기 위해 현대 예술가들이 사포를 사용하는 것처럼 그들은 다양한 결의 모래를 사용했다.

4 ➡ 사치품을 구매하던 상류층 시민들은 아즈텍 사회의 10퍼센트밖에 차지하지 않았지만 새 장신구와 옷에 대한 욕구는 무한한 것 같았다. 실제로 전설에 의하면 아즈텍 통치자는 같은 옷을 한 번 이상 입지 않았다고 한다. 또한 귀족들이 사회적 정치적 연줄을 맺고 강화하기 위해 장신구를 사서 다른 귀족들에게 주는 것이 관례적이었다. 사제들 또한 호화로운 제복을 입고 장신구를 찼으며 많은 신전들과 궁전들은 귀금속과 보석들로 장식되었다. 몇몇 방들의 벽은 바닥에서 천장까지 금으로 덮여 있었고 이것은 하루 중 정확한 때에 눈부시게 빛나곤 했다. 이런 부에 대한 과시는 궁극적으로 아즈텍의 멸망을 야기했을 수 있다.

5 ➡ 스페인 정복자들이 중미에 도착했을 때 그들은 스페인 왕을 위해서는 영토와 종들을, 교회를 위해서는 영혼들을, 자신들을 포함한 모두를 위해서는 금을 얻으려는 의욕이 높았다. 해안가 인근에서 상당수가 아즈텍인들의 적이었던 보다 작은 규모의 부족들을 만났을 때, 그들은 멕시코 계곡 거주민들의 엄청난 부에 대해 듣게 되었다. 에르난도 코르테스와 그의 군사가 수도인 테노치티틀란에 도달했을 때 그들이 발견한 것은 그들의 부푼 기대를 훨씬 넘어서는 것이었다. 스페인인들의 도착에 앞서 있었던 징조들과 코르테스가 자신을 강한 왕의 특사라고 소개한 것 때문에 스페인인들은 환영받았다. 아즈텍 관습에 따라 그들에게는 호화로운 선물들이 주어졌는데 이것은 더 많은 재물에 대한 그들의 욕구를 돋우었다. 결국 그들은 그들을 대접한 사람들을 공격했으며 전쟁과 천연두 유행이 아즈텍인들을 피폐하게 만든 후에 아즈텍 제국은 무너졌다.

Ⓑ 화려한 색깔의 깃털로 만들어진 머리 장식들은 널리 거래되었다.
Ⓒ 그들이 만든 머리 장식, 망토와 갑옷은 남미로 수출되었는데, 이것은 그것들이 얼마나 인기가 높았는지 보여준다.
Ⓓ 머리 장식과 망토에 필요한 화려한 색깔의 깃털을 얻기 위해 남미까지 교역한 것으로 인해 이 제품들은 값이 비싸졌다.

5. 4단락의 단어 'reinforce(강화하다)'와 의미상 가장 가까운 것은

Ⓐ 과장하다
Ⓑ 강화하다
Ⓒ 약화시키다
Ⓓ 모여들다

6. 4단락에 따르면, 사치품 예술가들이 생산한 제품들은 어떻게 사용되었는가?

Ⓐ 다른 예술가들과의 무역에 사용
Ⓑ 아즈텍 통치자들에게 세금을 납부하는 데 사용
Ⓒ 신전들을 장식하는 데 사용
Ⓓ 사제들이 거행한 종교 의식들에 사용

7. 5단락에서 글쓴이가 '스페인 정복자들'을 언급하는 이유는 무엇인가?

Ⓐ 아즈텍인들의 장신구가 얼마나 유명했는지에 대한 사례를 제공하기 위해
Ⓑ 실용품 예술가들과 사치품 예술가들을 어떻게 구분할 수 있게 됐는지 설명하기 위해
Ⓒ 아즈텍인들의 몰락의 시작을 암시하기 위해
Ⓓ 아즈텍인들에게 새로운 기술을 소개한 사람들이 누구인지 확인시키기 위해

8. 5단락에 따르면, 스페인인들이 아즈텍인들에게 환영받은 이유는 무엇인가?

Ⓐ 스페인인들은 아즈텍인들에게 호화로운 선물들을 주었다.
Ⓑ 아즈텍인들은 새로 온 사람들에 대해 긍정적인 조짐을 받았다.
Ⓒ 스페인인들은 강한 왕이 자기들을 보냈다고 주장했다.
Ⓓ 스페인인들은 교회를 위해 영혼을 구하기 위해 왔다.

9. 지문에 다음 문장이 들어갈 수 있는 위치를 나타내는 네 개의 사각형 [■]을 확인하시오.

이것은 최고 수준의 정교함과 아름다움에 달했던 그들의 예술에 있어서 특히 그렇다.

이 문장이 들어가기에 가장 적합한 곳은? [■C]

10. 지시문: 지문을 간략하게 요약한 글의 첫 문장이 아래 제시되어 있다. 지문의 가장 중요한 내용을 표현하는 세 개의 선택지를 골라 요약문을 완성하시오. 일부 문장들은 지문에 제시되지 않았거나 지문의 지엽적인 내용을 나타내기 때문에 요약문에 포함되지 않는다. ***이 문제의 배점은 2점이다.***

아즈텍 사회의 예술가들은 두 집단, 즉 실용품 예술가들과 사치품 예술가들로 나뉘었다.

Ⓐ 실용품 예술가들은 일상 용품들을 만들었으며 자신들의 시간을 공예품과 농업에 분배했다.
Ⓔ 사치품 예술가들은 상류층을 위한 제품들을 만드는 데 많은 희귀한 재료들을 사용했으며 몇몇 비싼 제품들은 남미에서 수입되었다.
Ⓕ 아즈텍인들의 어마어마한 부와 정교한 공예품들은 그들의 몰락에 기여했다.

Ⓑ 스페인인들의 도착과 함께 대부분의 아즈텍 예술가들과 그들의 놀라운 공예품들이 유럽으로 실려갔다.
Ⓒ 몇몇 신전 벽들은 바닥에서 천장까지 금으로 덮여 있었는데 이것은 정확한 각도에 햇빛이 비추면 빛났다.
Ⓓ 아즈텍 칼날들을 만드는 데 사용된 화산 유리인 흑요석은 멕시코 계곡에서 흔한 재료였다.

어휘 originate v 유래하다 | dominate v 지배하다 | define v 정의하다 | craft n 공예 | vicinity n 부근 | peak n 절정, 정점 | precious metal 귀금속 | gemstone n 보석의 원석 | aristocrat n 귀족 | rural adj 시골의, 지방의 | currency n 통화 | blade n (칼의) 날 | conversely adv 정반대로 | commission n (설계, 그림 등의 제작) 의뢰, 주문 | sculpture n 조각품 | adorn v 장식하다, 꾸미다 | gleam n 반짝거림 | grit n 모래 | fineness n 촘촘함, 입도 | appetite n 욕구 | customary adj 관례적인 | reinforce v 강화하다 | ostentatious adj 호사스러운, 과시하는 | downfall n 몰락 | conquistador n (스페인어로) 정복자 | coast n 해안 | exceed v 초과하다 | inflate v 부풀리다, 부풀다 | omen n 징조, 조짐 | precede v ~에 앞서다 | envoy n 사절, 특사 | whet v 돋우다 | turn on ~를 공격하다 | host n (손님을 초대한) 주인 | epidemic n 유행병 | smallpox n 천연두 | ravage v 황폐/피폐하게 만들다

인류의 사냥 진화

1 ➡ 농업의 등장 이전에 인간은 생존하기 위해 수렵 채집인 생활 방식에 의존했다. 이것은 집단의 몇몇 구성원은 과일, 채소, 견과류와 씨앗을 찾는 데 시간을 보냈다는 것을 뜻한다. 집단의 다른 구성원들 중 흔히 남성들은 뭐든지 구할 수 있는 사냥감을 사냥하는 데 시간을 보냈다. 이것은 그들이 따뜻한 계절에는 꽤 다양한 잡식성 식사를 했지만 겨울, 그리고 빙하기 중에는 거의 일년 내내 고기에 크게 의존했다는 것을 뜻한다. 하지만 과거와 현재 대다수의 영장류는 과일, 잎사귀, 뿌리와 종종 곤충 섭취를 선호해 온 초식동물이다. 호모 속(屬)의 영장류들이 수천 년간 사냥에 의존해 온 것은 명백하지만 그렇게 하는 것에 대한 그들의 동기는 여전히 잘 알려져 있지 않다. 이런 식습관의 변화에 관한 지배적인 이론들 중 하나는 기후 변화, 진화와 확장의 조합으로써 인간이 왜 고기를 먹게 됐으며 그것이 그들에게 어떻게 이익이 됐는지에 초점을 맞춘다.

2 ➡ 영장류들은 원래 아프리카 열대와 아열대 지역에서 초식동물로 진화했고 약 1,500만 년 전까지 많은 유인원 종들로 분화되었다. 그들이 서식하던 적도 우림은 섭취에 적합한 수많은 식물군을 제공했고 그들은 다른 먹이 공급원에 의지할 필요가 없었다. 하지만 동아프리카 지구대가 생성되면서 그 배후에 있는 구조력이 기후를 훨씬 더 건조해지게 했다. 초원이 그 지역을 뒤덮으면서 숲은 줄어들었다. 약 600만년 전 호모 속이 아닌 인류의 마지막 선조 오스트랄로피테쿠스는 변화하는 생태계에 적응하기 위해 진화했다. 그들은 두 다리로 걷는 것이 가능했고 직립 자세와 증가한 뇌 용량을 갖추었다. 이런 적응은 그 종이 환경의 자원을 더 효과적으로 활용할 수 있게 했다. 직립 자세는 땅 위에서 대초원의 나무들 사이를 누비며 더 멀리 바라볼 수 있게 했다. 이런 적응은 인간이 유인원으로부터 분화한 시기인 냉각기 동안 살아남을 수 있게 도왔다.

3 ➡ 많은 과학자들은 호모 하빌리스가 오스트랄로피테쿠스와 매우 유사하긴 하지만 그것을 호모 속의 첫 구성원으로 분류한다. 그러나 그것은 현세 인류 뇌 용량의 반 정도 되는 큰 뇌 용량을 지녔고 이름

11. 1단락에서 추론할 수 있는 것은
Ⓐ 인간은 고기를 먹기 시작한 이후로 훨씬 더 건강해졌다
Ⓑ 겨울에 섭취할 야생 식물을 충분히 채집하기가 꽤 어려웠다
Ⓒ 인간은 토양이 농사 짓기에 너무 척박해서 사냥을 시작했다
Ⓓ 채식과 육식 식단의 균형을 유지하는 것이 중요했다

12. 2단락에 따르면, 다음 중 오스트랄로피테쿠스에 관해 사실이 아닌 것은 무엇인가?
Ⓐ 그들은 환경 변화에 효과적으로 적응했다.
Ⓑ 그들은 직립 보행할 수 있었고, 그것은 그들이 더 멀리 바라볼 수 있게 해주었다.
Ⓒ 그들의 뇌 용량은 그들의 선조들의 것보다 더 컸다.
Ⓓ 그들은 인간이라 분류된 최초의 선조였다.

13. 2단락의 단어 'dwindled(줄어들었다)'와 의미상 가장 가까운 것은
Ⓐ 확장했다
Ⓑ 감소했다
Ⓒ 섞였다
Ⓓ 번성했다

14. 3단락에 따르면, 다음 중 호모 에르가스테르에 관해 사실인 것은 무엇인가?
Ⓐ 그들의 치아는 새로운 식습관에 더 알맞게 진화했다.
Ⓑ 그들은 과일, 견과류와 장작을 쪼개기 위해 석기를 처음 만들었다.
Ⓒ 그들의 뇌 용량은 현세 인류 뇌 용량의 절반밖에 되지 않았다.
Ⓓ 그들은 더 따뜻한 지역을 찾기 위해 장거리 이동을 해야 했다.

이 암시하듯이 도구를 만들었다. 이 도구들은 다른 약한 사물을 부수거나 쪼개는데 사용될 수 있는 다듬어진 돌로 되어 있었다. 하지만 진화 단계의 다음 대표자는 인류 계통의 뚜렷한 특징을 지닌다. 여행자라는 뜻을 지닌 호모 에르가스테르는 유라시아 대륙에 성공적으로 진입한 첫 종이다. [■A] 그것은 긴 몸통과 사지와 가는 골반을 지녔는데 이는 장거리 이동을 위한 적응이다. [■B] 에르가스테르는 또한 더 증가한 뇌 용량과 작아진 치아를 가졌는데 이것은 식습관이 변했다는 것을 뜻한다. [■C] 그들의 치아는 더 이상 거친 채소를 섭취하는 데 적절하지 않았기 때문에 새로운 식량원을 찾은 것이 분명했다. 호모 하빌리스, 호모 에르가스테르와 그의 후손인 호모 에렉투스의 유해와 함께 발견된 석기와 동물 뼈 모음은 그 새로운 형태의 영양소, 즉 골수를 가리키고 있다. [■D]

4 ➡ 이런 유적지에서 발견된 대다수의 뼈는 영양들의 하퇴부인데, 이것은 고기가 적었고 덩치가 더 큰 포식자들이 버려둔 것이었을 것이다. 인간들은 이 뼈들을 모았고 석기로 그것을 부수어 열어 그 안에 있는 고단백 골수를 드러냈다. 이것은 초목이 사라짐에 따라 그들을 지탱하는 보충 식품을 제공했을 뿐만 아니라 빠른 뇌 발달을 돕는데 필요한 영양을 제공했다. 모든 포유류는 새끼일 때 어미 젖을 섭취하여 신체적으로 그리고 정신적으로 빠르게 발달할 수 있게 한다. 동물성 단백질 섭취는 인간들에게 유사한 효과를 미친 것으로 보인다. 고기 섭취에 맛을 들이자 그들은 그것을 더 손쉽게 얻을 수 있는 방법을 찾았을 것이다. 이것은 의심의 여지 없이 첫 사냥 시도로 이어졌다. 그 당시 그들의 무기인 뾰족한 막대와 다듬어진 돌도끼는 사냥감을 공격하기 위해선 꽤 가까이 다가가야만 했기 때문에 이상적인 사냥 도구가 아니었다. 그들의 사냥감은 보통 싸울 태세를 더 잘 갖추고 있었기 때문에 그들은 다른 능력에 의존해야 했다. 그들에게 가장 적합한 것은 장거리를 이동할 수 있는 능력이었다.

5 ➡ 전문가들 대부분은 사냥의 초기 형태가 아마 지구력 사냥이라 불리는 것일 거라는 데에 동의한다. 이런 사냥 형태가 인간에게 효과적인 이유는 직립 보행이 가능하고 뛰어난 체온 조절 능력이 있기 때문이다. 사냥꾼들은 짐승을 목격하면 그것이 시야에서 사라질 때까지 추적했다. 직립 보행할 수 있었기 때문에 시각적으로 사냥감을 쉽게 추적할 수 있었고 사냥감이 쉬려고 멈췄을 때 놀래킬 수 있었다. 이 과정은 인간만큼 효율적으로 땀을 흘리지 못하고, 인간은 갖고 있지 않은 털 외피로 덮여있는 동물이 일사병으로 쓰러질 때까지 반복되었다. 그러면 인간은 그 동물을 위험 부담이 거의 또는 전혀 없이 죽일 수 있었다. 이런 사냥 기법은 인간이 유라시아 전역으로 확장할 수 있게 했고 당면한 빙하기에 살아남을 열쇠를 제공했다. 호모 네안데르탈렌시스와 호모 사피엔스는 더 정교한 도구와 사냥 전략을 발달시켰고 진정한 수렵 채집자로 간주되지만 그들은 먼저 동물 사체를 먹고 사냥을 했던 선조들에게 빚을 지고 있다.

15. 4단락에 따르면, 인간이 처음으로 골수를 얻게 된 방법은

Ⓐ 쉽게 포획되는 약한 동물들을 사냥해서
Ⓑ 동물 사체를 모아 석기로 뼈를 쪼개어서
Ⓒ 포식자들의 추격을 받는 지친 동물들이 가까이 오길 기다려서
Ⓓ 사냥감에 다가가서 사냥 무기로 공격해서

16. 다음 중 지문에 음영 표시된 문장의 핵심 정보를 가장 잘 표현한 문장은 무엇인가? 오답은 의미를 크게 왜곡하거나 핵심 정보를 누락하고 있다.

Ⓐ 그들은 큰 동물들을 사냥하기 위해 뾰족한 막대와 돌도끼를 만들었는데 이 무기들은 실제로 실용적이지 않았다.
Ⓑ 그들의 사냥용 막대와 도끼들은 정교하지 않았기 때문에 근거리에서 사냥감을 포획할 때만 사용될 수 있었다.
Ⓒ 그들은 멀리 떨어져 있는 동물들을 포획하기 위해 손잡이가 긴 도끼 같은 적절한 사냥 무기를 만들려고 노력했다.
Ⓓ 그들의 무기는 너무 구식이었기 때문에 이런 막대와 도끼로 사냥감을 공격할 때마다 위험에 처했다.

17. 5단락에서 글쓴이가 '지구력 사냥'에 대해 설명한 방법은

Ⓐ 사냥은 꽤 위험한 것이라는 주장을 반박함으로써
Ⓑ 동물을 추적하는 과정을 묘사함으로써
Ⓒ 그것을 호모 사피엔스의 사냥 전략과 비교함으로써
Ⓓ 빙하기 중 두꺼운 털 외피의 장점을 열거함으로써

18. 5단락에 따르면, 다음 중 체온 조절 능력에 대해 사실인 것은 무엇인가?

Ⓐ 인간의 몸은 과도한 열을 분산시키기 위해 효과적으로 땀을 분출한다.
Ⓑ 동물들은 두꺼운 털 외피가 없어서 체온을 일정하게 유지할 수 있다.
Ⓒ 인간과 동물은 비슷한 방법으로 체온을 조절한다.
Ⓓ 동물들은 몸을 식히기 위해 숨을 헐떡이고 땀을 많이 흘린다.

Lesson 02 Making Inference

19. 지문에 다음 문장이 들어갈 수 있는 위치를 나타내는 네 개의 사각형 [■]을 확인하시오.

그들의 치아는 더 이상 거친 채소를 섭취하는 데 적절하지 않았기 때문에 새로운 식량원을 찾은 것이 분명했다.

이 문장이 들어가기에 가장 적합한 곳은? [■C]

20. 지시문: 지문을 간략하게 요약한 글의 첫 문장이 아래 제시되어 있다. 지문의 가장 중요한 내용을 표현하는 세 개의 선택지를 골라 요약문을 완성하시오. 일부 문장들은 지문에 제시되지 않았거나 지문의 지엽적인 내용을 나타내기 때문에 요약문에 포함되지 않는다. ***이 문제의 배점은 2점이다.***

오직 채식 식단에만 의존했던 인류의 조상은 환경 변화와 인류 진화를 통해 사냥을 하기 시작했다.

Ⓑ 초기 인간은 그들의 신체적 모습에 변화를 겪었고 도구를 만들었는데, 이것은 그들로 하여금 새로운 식량원을 성공적으로 확보할 수 있게 했다.
Ⓔ 기후가 건조해지고 거대한 숲들이 서서히 줄어들자 인간의 선조들은 이런 변화에 적응하기 위해 진화했다.
Ⓕ 인간의 직립 보행과 체온 조절 능력은 사냥의 원시적 형태인 지구력 사냥을 야기했다.

Ⓐ 암컷 영장류들은 식용 식물을 채집하는 데 집중한 반면 수컷들은 야생 동물을 사냥하는 데 대부분의 시간을 사용했다.
Ⓒ 인간은 약 1,500만 년 전 열대 지방에서 진화했기 때문에 식량원에 대해 걱정하지 않았다.
Ⓓ 영장류들은 호모 하빌리스, 호모 에렉투스와 현세 인류인 호모 사피엔스와 같은 다양한 호모 종으로 분화했다.

어휘 advent n 등장, 도래, 출현 I game n 사냥감 I omnivorous adj 잡식성의 I primate n 영장류 I millennium n 천년 I indisputable adj 반론의 여지가 없는, 명백한 I prevailing adj 우세한, 지배적인 I differentiate v 분화하다, 구별하다 I equatorial adj 적도의 I resort to ~에 기대다, 의지하다 I tectonic adj 구조상의 I dwindle v 줄어들다 I erect adj 똑바로 선 I upright adj (자세가) 똑바른, 꼿꼿한 I savannah n 대초원 I diverge v 갈라지다, 분기하다 I cleave v 쪼개다 I lineage n 혈통, 계통 I infiltrate v 잠입하다, 침투하다 I torso n 몸통 I limb n 사지 I remains n 유적 I nutrition n 영양, 영양분 I bone marrow 골수 I antelope n 영양 I supplement n 보충물 I vegetation n 초목 I cerebral adj 뇌의 I procure v 구하다, 입수하다 I persistence n 지속됨, 집요함 I thermoregulation n 체온 조절 I track v 추적하다, 뒤쫓다 I exhaustion n 탈진, 기진맥진 I coming adj 다가오는 I scavenge v (직접 사냥한 것이 아닌) 죽은 고기를 먹다

III. Recognizing Organization

Lesson 01 Insertion

본서 I P. 196

Practice

01 C-B-A **02** B-A-D-C **03** D-B-A-C **04** C-A-D-B **05** B-A-C-D
06 B **07** C **08** C **09** B **10** B **11** B **12** C **13** A **14** D **15** A
16 C **17** A **18** D **19** 1. D 2. A **20** 1. D 2. C **21** 1. D 2. C
22 1. B 2. B

Test

1. A 2. D 3. D 4. C 5. D 6. A 7. B 8. C 9. B 10. B, D, F
11. C 12. D 13. B 14. A 15. D 16. B 17. D 18. B 19. A 20. B, C, D

Practice

본서 I P. 198

[01-05] 문장을 읽고 순서대로 나열하시오.

01 Ⓒ In architecture and structural engineering, a vertical architectural support that transmits the weight of the structure downward is called a column. Ⓑ They are used primarily to support beams or arches that hold the upper parts of walls or ceilings. Ⓐ Having such a simple and central use, the form that columns take has changed very little over the millennia.

Ⓒ 건축학과 구조공학에서 아래로 구조물의 하중을 전달하는 수직으로 된 건축 지지대를 기둥이라고 한다. Ⓑ 이것들은 주로 벽의 상층부나 천장을 받치는 들보나 아치를 지탱하는 데 쓰인다. Ⓐ 간단하면서도 중추적인 이러한 쓰임 때문에 기둥의 형태는 수천 년간 거의 변하지 않았다.

어휘 millennia n (millennium의 복수형) 수천 년 | vertical adj 수직의 | transmit v 전달하다, 옮기다

---

02 Ⓑ Historically, terracotta was used to make sculptures and pottery, as well as bricks and roof tiles. Ⓐ In ancient times, people baked clay sculptures in the sun after forming them. Ⓓ Later, potters put terracotta sculptures in the ashes of open hearths to harden. Ⓒ The resulting products were similar to the pottery of today.

Ⓑ 역사적으로 테라코타는 벽돌과 지붕 기와는 물론 조각품과 도기를 만드는 데 사용되었다. Ⓐ 고대에 사람들은 점토 조각품을 만든 후 햇볕에 말렸다. Ⓓ 이후에, 도공들은 그것들을 굳히기 위해 평가마의 재 위에 놓아두었다. Ⓒ 그 결과물은 오늘날의 도기와 유사했다.

어휘 form v 빚다, 만들어내다 | open hearth 평가마 | harden v 굳히다

---

03 Ⓓ Prehistory is the period of human history before written records. Ⓑ Although there is still much debate about when prehistory started and ended, it is generally agreed that it began about 100,000 to 200,000 years ago when the first modern Homo sapiens appeared. Ⓐ However, some insist that prehistory started when the first tools were invented, about 2.5 million years ago. Ⓒ Others would say it began around 40,000 BCE with the appearance of Cro-Magnons.

Ⓓ 선사 시대는 문자 기록 이전의 인류 역사 시대를 가리킨다. Ⓑ 선사 시대가 언제 시작되었고 언제 끝났는지에 대한 논쟁이 계속되고 있기는 하지만 최초의 현생 호모 사피엔스가 출현한 10만 년에서 20만 년 전 즈음에 시작되었다는 설이 일반적으로 받아들여지고 있다. Ⓐ 하지만 일부는 선사 시대가 최초의 연장이 발명된 250만 년 전에 시작되었다고 주장한다. Ⓒ 다른 사람들은 선사 시대가 크로마뇽인의 출현과 함께 기원전 4만년 경 시작되었다고 말하기도 한다.

어휘 prehistory n 선사 시대 | record n 기록 | modern adj 근대의, 현대의

---

04 Ⓒ Wilson's disease is a hereditary disease that causes copper to accumulate in the body. Ⓐ This disease, if untreated, can eventually result in damage to the brain and liver. Ⓓ Similarly, research shows that people with some mental illnesses, such as schizophrenia, had high concentrations of copper in their systems. Ⓑ Therefore, copper, although necessary, should be considered toxic to the human body in large quantities.

Ⓒ 윌슨병은 체내에 구리가 축적되는 것을 초래하는 유전성 질환이다. Ⓐ 이 질병은 치료되지 않으면 결국엔 뇌와 간에 손상을 초래한다. Ⓓ 마찬가지로 정신분열증과 같은 정신 질환을 앓고 있는 사람들의 몸에는 많은 양의 구리가 축적되어 있다는 것이 조사 결과 드러났다. Ⓑ 그러므로 비록 구리는 필요한 것이기는 하지만 많은 양이 인체에 축적되었을 경우 독성 물질로 여겨져야 한다.

어휘 hereditary adj 유전적인 | accumulate v 축적되다, 쌓이다 | liver n 간 | schizophrenia n 정신분열증 | quantity n 양, 수량

---

05 Ⓑ The Italian Renaissance began in the 14th century during the initial phase of the Renaissance movement in Europe. Ⓐ The word renaissance literally means 'rebirth', and refers to the widespread intellectual and cultural changes brought about after European culture emerged from the Dark Ages. Ⓒ While these changes were significant for the Italian elite, life remained almost unchanged during the Middle Ages for the majority of the population. Ⓓ However, the ideas of the Italian Renaissance influenced the rest of Europe, thus embellishing the Northern Renaissance and English Renaissance.

Ⓑ 이탈리아 르네상스는 14세기 유럽의 르네상스 운동 초반기에 시작되었다. Ⓐ 르네상스라는 단어는 문자 그대로 '재생, 부활'을 뜻하며 유럽 문화가 암흑 시대에서 벗어난 이후 널리 퍼진 지적, 문화적 변화를 가리킨다. Ⓒ 이런 변화들은 이탈리아 상류층에게는 중대한 의미를 갖는 반면 대다수 사람들의 삶은 중세 시대의 삶과 거의 변한 것이 없었다. Ⓓ 하지만 이탈리아 르네상스의 사상은 유럽의 나머지 지역에 영향을 주었고 북부 르네상스와 영국 르네상스가 발전하게 되었다.

어휘 initial adj 초기의 I intellectual adj 지적인, 지능의 I emerge v 모습을 드러내다 I embellish v 꾸미다, 장식하다

06 **모나크 나비**

[■A] 비록 과학에서 기념비적인 발전이 있기는 했지만 많은 자연 현상은 여전히 이유가 밝혀지지 않은 채 남아 있다. [■B] 이것들 중 가장 영문 모를 것은 매우 아름다운 모나크 나비의 삶이다. 매년 모나크 나비는 미국과 캐나다에서 수천 마일에 걸친 두 번의 대규모 이동을 한다. [■C] 본능적으로 보이는 이 행동이 다른 동물들, 특히 새들 사이에서도 흔하기는 하지만 왜 모나크 나비가 이런 행동을 진화시켰으며 어떻게 이런 굉장한 일을 완수하는지에 관해서는 여전히 의문이 많다. [■D]

지문에 다음 문장이 들어갈 수 있는 위치를 나타내는 네 개의 사각형[■]을 확인하시오.

이것들 중 가장 영문 모를 것은 매우 아름다운 모나크 나비의 삶이다.

이 문장이 들어가기에 가장 적합한 곳은? [■B]

어휘 monumental adj 기념비적인 I stride n 큰 걸음, 발전 I puzzling adj 수수께끼의 I exquisite adj 매우 아름다운 I massive adj 커다란, 거대한 I migration n 이주 I instinctive adj 본능적인 I particularly adv 특별히

07 **알래스카**

1867년에 러시아 정부는 알래스카의 모든 영토를 팔기로 결정했다. 미국 의회는 1867년에 알래스카의 매입을 승인했고 같은 해 말에 공식적으로 지역의 지배권을 얻었다. [■A] 1877년까지 미 육군성이 알래스카를 통치했다. 의회는 1884년에 알래스카를 사법지구로 정하고 연방법원, 관청, 그리고 학교를 세웠다. [■B] 막대한 양의 금과 구리가 매장된 것이 발견되었을 때, 정부는 그 지역의 엄청난 가치를 알게 되었다. [■C] 이 사실이 발견되기 전까지 대부분의 미국인은 알래스카가 전혀 가치 없는 땅이라고 여겼다. 20세기 초반부터 시작해 정부는 그 지역에 광산, 철도, 농장과 그 지역의 경제적 발전에 도움이 될 다른 대규모 사업의 개발을 장려했다. [■D] 석유와 천연 가스의 발견과 함께 알래스카의 인구는 더욱 성장했고, 알래스카는 1959년에 공식 주가 되었다.

지문에 다음 문장이 들어갈 수 있는 위치를 나타내는 네 개의 사각형[■]을 확인하시오.

이 사실이 발견되기 전까지 대부분의 미국인은 알래스카가 전혀 가치 없는 땅이라고 여겼다.

이 문장이 들어가기에 가장 적합한 곳은? [■C]

어휘 territory n 영토 I congress n 의회 I approve v 승인하다 I purchase n 매입 I judicial adj 사법의, 재판의 I federal adj 연방의 I copper n 구리 I mine n 광산 I enterprise n 대규모 사업, 기업 I accompany v 동반하다

08 **아즈텍 제국의 식량 생산**

지금의 멕시코 지역은 한때 아즈텍 제국에 점령당했었는데, 아즈텍 제국은 오늘날의 중앙아메리카에 존재했던 가장 융성한 문화권 중 하나였다. [■A] 정복 이전의 아즈텍 사회는 거친 기후와 메마른 토양 등 농업에 가장 불리한 환경을 갖고 있었다. [■B] 그러나 이러한 곤경은 아즈텍 사람들이 발전시킨 놀라운 농사와 관개 체제를 통해 효과적으로 해결되었다. [■C] 아즈텍인들은 이 방법을 활용하여 더 많은 곡물 수확량을 얻을 수 있었다. 아즈텍인들이 기른 많은 곡물들 중 특히 옥수수가 아즈텍의 주요 작물이었고 온 제국에 걸쳐 고원지대의 계단식 밭이나 골짜기의 농장에서 경작되었다. [■D] 제분 도구는 아즈텍 여성들이 토르티야 같은 것을 만들기 위한 굵은 가루를 준비하기 위해 옥수수를 빻는 데 필수적이었다. 아즈텍인들이 의지했던 다른 여러 작물은 아보카도, 콩, 호박, 고구마, 토마토와 칠리였다.

지문에 다음 문장이 들어갈 수 있는 위치를 나타내는 네 개의 사각형[■]을 확인하시오.

아즈텍인들은 이 방법을 활용하여 더 많은 곡물 수확량을 얻을 수 있었다.

이 문장이 들어가기에 가장 적합한 곳은? [■C]

어휘 occupy v 차지하다, 사용하다 I civilized adj 문명화된, 개화된 I along with ~에 덧붙여, ~에 따라 I conquest n 정복 I conducive adj ~에 좋은 I predicament n 곤경, 궁지 I irrigation n 관개 I staple adj 주된, 주요한 I cultivate v 경작하다, 일구다 I terrace n 계단식 논밭 I grind v 갈다, 빻다 I coarse adj 거친, 굵은 I pulverize v 가루로 만들다 I assorted adj 여러 가지의, 갖가지의

09 **비단 생산**

역사적 기록에 따르면 주나라는 비단 생산을 위한 체계적인 공정을 가지고 있었다고 한다. 그 문서는 비단 장인, 염색하는 사람, 그리고 베 짜는 사람의 존재를 들며 다양한 직업을 분류함으로써 비단 생산을 설명한다. [■A] 중국에서의 이 고된 비단 생산 과정은 처음부터 굉장히 대규

모로 고안되었다. [■B] 많은 수의 노동자들은 무리로 나뉘어 비단 제조 과정에서 하나의 특정 업무를 맡도록 훈련받았다. 예를 들면 뽕잎 채집자들은 누에를 위한 식량을 제공했고, 어떤 사람들은 고치에서 실을 뽑아내는 일을 훈련 받았으며 다른 이들은 옷감을 짜는 법을 배웠을 것이다. [■C] 노동자들은 거의 여성으로 구성되었고 궁 안의 여성 구역에서 거주했다. 18세기와 19세기에 이 공정 과정에 매료된 서양 사람들은 다양한 공정 단계를 보여주는 문헌을 얻으려고 했다. [■D]

지문에 다음 문장이 들어갈 수 있는 위치를 나타내는 네 개의 사각형[■]을 확인하시오.

많은 수의 노동자들은 무리로 나뉘어 비단 제조 과정에서 하나의 특정 업무를 맡도록 훈련받았다.

이 문장이 들어가기에 가장 적합한 곳은? [■B]

어휘 text n 글, 문서 I elaborate v 자세히 말하다, 설명하다 I categorize v 분류하다 I dye v 염색하다 I laborious adj 힘든, 어려운 I conceive v 생각하다, 상상하다 I mulberry n 뽕나무, 오디 I reel v (실을) 고치에서 뽑아내다 I weave v 베를 짜다, 만들다 I reside v 거주하다 I procure v 얻다, 획득하다 I reference n 참고 문헌

10

멕시코의 정복

16세기까지 멕시코 정복 이야기는 스페인의 군대 기량 측면에서 거론되었다. [■A] 더 잘 무장된 병사와 더 나은 전술만이 스페인인들이 해당 지역을 지배한 이유로 여겨졌다. [■B] 그러나 나중에 밝혀진 바로는 이들의 성공에 영향을 미친 중대한 요소가 된 것은 유럽인들과 그들의 아프리카인 노예들이 들여온 질병이었다. 토착 주민들은 이러한 새로운 질병에 익숙하지 않은 사람들이었고 병은 파국을 초래하는 전염병이 되었다. [■C] 이는 마을을 방어할 수 있는 사람들의 수를 감소시켰고 선진화된 스페인 군대는 침략에 거의 힘을 들이지 않아도 됐다. [■D] 다른 요인은 새로운 외래종이 지역의 동식물을 대체하면서 지역 생태계가 급격한 변화를 겪었다는 것이다. 유럽인들의 군사 작전 성공에 질병이 주요한 역할을 했지만, 군대의 승리를 굳히고 수많은 사람과 땅을 차지한 정복 패턴이 지속되도록 한 것은 이러한 생태계 변화였던 것으로 여겨진다.

지문에 다음 문장이 들어갈 수 있는 위치를 나타내는 네 개의 사각형[■]을 확인하시오.

그러나 나중에 밝혀진 바로는 그들의 성공에 영향을 미친 중대한 요소가 된 것은 유럽인들과 그들의 아프리카 노예들이 들여온 질병이었다.

이 문장이 들어가기에 가장 적합한 곳은? [■B]

어휘 prowess n 기량 I equip v 장비를 갖추다 I tactic n 전략, 전술 I Spaniard n 스페인 사람 I indigenous adj 토착의, 원산의 I catastrophic adj 대재앙의 I epidemic adj 유행병 I undergo v 겪다, 경험하다 I campaign n 캠페인, 운동, 군사 작전 I ecological adj 생태계의 I consolidation n 합병, 통합, 강화

11

농법

지금까지도 많은 국가들은 식량 생산량을 늘리거나 농장의 환경을 향상시키기 위해 기계 기술이나 합성 화학 물질을 포함한 많은 방법을 사용한다. 그러나 세상에는 관개 시설이나 비료 이용이 비합리적인 다른 장소들도 있다. [■A] 대신 이러한 지역에서는 현지에 맞게 적용된 기술들이 생산성을 증가시키는 데 매우 긍정적인 결과를 보여주었다. [■B] 기후가 뜨겁고 건조한 아프리카는 땅을 관개하고 비료를 운송하는 비용이 지나치게 높은 바로 그런 장소이다. 아프리카 농부들은 밀과 콩과의 나무를 동시에 심었을 때 생산성이 증가하는 것을 목격하기 시작했다. [■C] 나무들은 천천히 자라기 시작하면서 밀의 바람막이가 되어 주었고 밀이 다 자라고 수확될 때까지 충분한 시간을 주었다. [■D] 이후에 나무들은 수 피트에 달할 정도로 급격히 자랐다. 잎은 결국 땅에 떨어져서 땅을 비옥하게 하고 땅에 필요한 많은 유기물을 제공했다. 나무들은 나중에 잘려나가고 목재는 연료로 쓰인다. 이러한 기술을 통해 아프리카의 농부들은 그들이 경작하는 땅이 더 비옥해지면서 곡물 생산량에서 매년 생산성이 증가하는 것을 계속 보게 될 것이다.

지문에 다음 문장이 들어갈 수 있는 위치를 나타내는 네 개의 사각형[■]을 확인하시오.

기후가 뜨겁고 건조한 아프리카는 땅을 관개하고 비료를 운송하는 비용이 지나치게 높은 바로 그런 장소이다.

이 문장이 들어가기에 가장 적합한 곳은? [■B]

어휘 synthetic adj 합성의, 인조의 I reasonable adj 합리적인, 합당한 I productivity n 생산성 I simultaneously adv 동시에 I leguminous adj 콩과의 I shoot up 급속히 자라다 I lumber n 재목, 목재 I output n 생산량, 산출량 I cultivate v 경작하다, 일구다

12

미국의 철도 건설

1855년까지 일리노이주 시카고와 루이지애나주 뉴올리언스, 그리고 앨라배마주를 잇는 주요 노선을 가진 일리노이 중앙 철도는 자국 내 어떤 다른 단일 철도 회사보다 더 많은 선로를 깔았다. 이 철도 회사는 철도 산업 분야에서 자신의 강점을 깨닫기 시작했고 추가적인 부수입을 모색

했다. [■A] 사람들이 전국적으로 여행을 할 때 철도를 점점 더 많이 이용하게 되면서 철도 회사는 기차 운행을 통해 돈을 벌어들였을 뿐 아니라 부동산 투기로도 돈을 벌었다. [■B] 예를 들어 철도 회사는 정류장을 만들려고 계획한 장소의 값싼 부지를 사들이기 시작했다. [■C] 정류장에 근접한 이러한 지역들을 개발하여 시장 가치를 올리는 것이 가능했고, 부동산은 상당한 이익을 남기고 되팔 수 있었다. 일리노이주 만테노가 좋은 예로, 일리노이 중앙 철도의 정류장 역할을 한 곳들 중 하나였다. [■D] 1854년에 일리노이 중앙 철도는 그 지역이 집 한 채 없이 황량한 교차로 하나밖에 없는 곳이었을 때 그 땅의 전체 소유권을 사들였다. 1860년에 이르자 그 황량한 땅은 호텔과 목재 저장소, 그리고 창고로 가득한 북적거리는 도시로 성장했다.

지문에 다음 문장이 들어갈 수 있는 위치를 나타내는 네 개의 사각형[■]을 확인하시오.

정류장에 근접한 이러한 지역들을 개발하여 시장 가치를 올리는 것이 가능했고, 부동산은 상당한 이익을 남기고 되팔 수 있었다.

이 문장이 들어가기에 가장 적합한 곳은? [■C]

어휘 seek v 찾다, 모색하다 I revenue n 수익, 세입 I real estate 부동산 I speculation n 투기, 추측 I right n 권리, 소유권 I barren adj 황량한 I crossroad n 교차로 I desolate adj 황량한, 사람이 없는

---

13 사막의 침식 요인

사막의 불리한 기후와 척박한 토양에서도 여전히 지질학적 변화를 불러오는 몇 가지 요인이 있다. [■A] 물은 그러한 지역에 극적인 변화를 야기하는 주된 요소 중 하나이다. 물은 강 골짜기나 호수에서 침식으로 사막을 공공연히 변화시키는데, 더 중요한 것은 낮과 밤 사이에 큰 기온차가 발생하는 동안 사막 환경에 보이지 않게 영향을 준다. [■B] 밤 동안 바위 위에 남아 있는 이슬이나 안개는 돌의 미네랄과 소금기에 흡수된다. [■C] 낮이 가까워지면 그것은 공기 중으로 증발하고, 이러한 물의 소규모 순환은 반복된다. [■D] 바위가 물을 흡수함에 따라 바위는 약간 팽창했다가 낮 동안에는 다시 축소되고, 이는 바위에 작지만 상당한 손상을 입힌다. 비록 대수롭지 않게 보이겠지만 이런 미묘한 변화는 긴 시간에 걸쳐 바위의 생김새에 극적인 변화를 가져온다. 고대의 유적에 있는 틈이나 흔적은 이러한 유형의 침식을 보여주며, 극심한 경우에는 이것이 심지어 큰 바위를 깨기도 한다.

지문에 다음 문장이 들어갈 수 있는 위치를 나타내는 네 개의 사각형[■]을 확인하시오.

물은 그러한 지역에 극적인 변화를 야기하는 주된 요소 중 하나이다.

이 문장이 들어가기에 가장 적합한 곳은? [■A]

어휘 adverse adj 부정적인, 불리한 I agent n 중요한 역할을 하는 것, 물질 I openly adv 터놓고, 드러내 놓고 I erosion n 침식, 부식 I secretly adv 몰래, 숨어서 I dew n 이슬 I hydrologic cycle 물 순환 I slightly adv 약간, 조금 I insignificant adj 대수롭지 않은, 사소한 I subtle adj 미묘한 I gradually adv 서서히, 점차 I crack n 균열, 금 I relic n 유물 I boulder n 바위

---

14 식민지 정원

정원의 식목과 설계는 시대, 부, 그리고 그것들의 용도에 따라 상당히 달라졌기 때문에 미국이 영국의 지배를 받던 식민지 기간의 주택 정원을 쉽게 정의할 수는 없다. 그러나 식민지 시대의 미국에 끼친 영국의 막대한 영향 때문에 '식민지 정원'은 일반적으로 13개의 영국 식민지에서 가장 널리 찾아볼 수 있었던 형태의 정원을 일컫는다. 식민지 정원은 크기가 작고 집과 가까운 경향이 있었다. [■A] 곧은 인도가 일반적으로 집의 입구에서 정원 중앙을 가로질러 일렬로 이어졌다. [■B] 정원 안의 길은 대체로 평평하고 단단한 소재인 벽돌, 자갈 그리고 돌 같은 것으로 이루어져 있었다. [■C] 식민지 정원의 식목은 일반적으로 식물의 종류에 따라 나뉘지는 않았다. [■D] 과일, 허브, 장식용 꽃, 그리고 채소가 대개 섞여서 같은 화단에 심어졌다. 그러한 식물들은 집 가까이에서 길러진 반면 자랄 공간이 필요한 채소(옥수수나 호박처럼)는 종종 집에서 멀리 떨어진 곳에서 길러지곤 했다.

지문에 다음 문장이 들어갈 수 있는 위치를 나타내는 네 개의 사각형[■]을 확인하시오.

과일, 허브, 장식용 꽃, 그리고 채소는 대개 섞여서 같은 화단에 심어졌다.

이 문장이 들어가기에 가장 적합한 곳은? [■D]

어휘 planting n (나무) 심기 I considerably adv 많이, 상당히 I overwhelmingly adv 압도적으로 I refer to ~을 나타내다, 관련이 있다 I on a line 일렬로 I path n 길 I brick n 벽돌 I gravel n 자갈 I botanical adj 식물(학)의 I ornamental adj 장식용의

---

15 증기 기관

석탄 광산 침수는 18세기에 영국 광부들이 직면한 가장 파괴적인 위험 요소였다. 이 곤경을 마침내 해결한 것은 제임스 와트의 증기기관이었다. 와트의 초기 증기기관은 깊은 광산에서 물을 효과적으로 끌어올렸다. [■A] 그러나 와트는 공장에서 사용할 수 있는 증기기관을 개발하는

데 관심이 있었다. 그의 첫 번째 증기기관은 1776년에 설치되었으며 전 세계적으로 공장 생산 라인의 패러다임에 변화를 가져왔다. [■B] 우선 공장형 증기기관의 출현은 더 많은 생산과 생산 시간 단축을 가능하게 했다. [■C] 게다가 공장의 전력 공급원으로 수력을 필요로 하지 않았기 때문에 공장 건설을 위한 부지가 제한을 덜 받게 되었고, 이는 공장이 어디에나 지어질 수 있게 만들었다. [■D] 마지막으로 증기기관을 가진 공장은 많은 수작업 노동자를 필요로 했으므로 시골에서 확장되고 있는 도심으로 대규모 인구 이동이 있었다. 이 대규모 이동의 영향은 50년 만에 영국을 가내 공업 및 농업 사회에서 공장을 기반으로 한 도시 거주 산업 강국으로 바꾸었다.

지문에 다음 문장이 들어갈 수 있는 위치를 나타내는 네 개의 사각형[■]을 확인하시오.

그러나 와트는 공장에서 사용할 수 있는 증기기관을 개발하는 데 관심이 있었다.

이 문장이 들어가기에 가장 적합한 곳은? [■A]

어휘 devastating adj 대단히 파괴적인 I hazard n 위험 I confront v 맞서다, 정면으로 부딪히다 I address v 다루다 I effectively adv 효과적으로 I predicament n 곤경, 궁지, 어려움 I paradigm n 전형적인 예, 양식 I manual adj 손으로 하는, 육체 노동의 I cottage industry 가내 공업 I agrarian adj 농업의 I powerhouse n 유력 집단

16

오리온 성운

젊은 별과 먼지, 기체 더미가 있는 오리온 성운을 바라볼 때 우리가 무질서 가운데서 볼 수 있는 것은 별 공장과 우리 태양계가 초창기에 지녔을 법한 모습이다. [■A] 성운을 구성하는 별들의 나이는 대략 30만 살에서 200만 살이며 별들의 나이치고 매우 젊은 편이다. 비교해 보자면, 우리 태양의 나이는 45억 살이다. [■B] 이런 젊은 별들 중 가장 작은 것은 주로 색이 붉으며 질량이 작다. 이런 작은 별들에 더해 트라페지움을 이루는 네 개의 거대하고 뜨거운 별들이 있다. 트라페지움은 성운에 있는 별 공장의 중심부로 볼 수 있다. 이 네 개의 별 중 가장 큰 오리온자리 세타1C는 우리 태양보다 약 20배쯤 더 크고 약 10만 배쯤 더 밝다. 실은 이 별은 매우 밝아서 성운 전체를 혼자 환하게 비출 수 있다. [■C] 트라페지움의 별들은 자외선을 방출하여 주위에 있는 성운의 먼지와 가스를 밝게 빛나게 한다. 트라페지움 주위 인접 지역에는 성운의 기본 물질이 풍부하기 때문에 수백 개의 더 작은 별로 가득하다. [■D] 별을 형성하는 이런 모든 원료는 이 지역을 우리 은하에서 알려진 그 어느 곳보다도 별들이 가장 빽빽하게 들어찬 무리 중 하나로 만든다.

지문에 다음 문장이 들어갈 수 있는 위치를 나타내는 네 개의 사각형[■]을 확인하시오.

트라페지움의 별들은 자외선을 방출하여 주위에 있는 성운의 먼지와 가스를 밝게 빛나게 한다.

이 문장이 들어가기에 가장 적합한 곳은? [■C]

어휘 nebula n 성운 I amidst prep ~사이에 I infancy n 초기, 유아기 I roughly adv 대략 I reddish adj 불그스름한 I mass n 질량 I trapezium n 사각형 성단 I light up 환하게 만들다 I immediate adj 인접한, 가까이에 있는 I raw adj 날것의, 가공하지 않은 I congest v 혼잡하게 하다, 정체시키다 I cluster n 무리 I galaxy n 은하계

17

화학의 목적과 연구

1 ➡ 인류의 삶은 이전에 기록된 인류의 모든 역사에서보다 지난 두 세기 동안 더 많이 바뀌었다. 세계 인구는 1800년 이후 5배 이상 크게 증가했으며 인간의 기대 수명은 질병의 확산을 제어하고, 의약품을 합성하고, 식량 작물의 수확량을 늘릴 수 있는 인류의 능력으로 인해 거의 두 배가 되었다. 인간의 운송 방식은 말타기에서 자동차와 비행기로 바뀌었는데, 이는 석유에서 이용 가능한 에너지를 활용하는 인류의 능력 덕분이다. 우리가 현재 제조하는 많은 제품들은 나무와 금속 대신 세라믹과 중합체로 만들어지며, 이는 자연계에서 발견되는 것과는 다른 특성을 지닌 물질을 만들어낼 수 있는 인류의 능력 덕분이다.

2 ➡ 삶을 변화시키는 이런 각각의 발전은 어떤 식으로라도 직접적으로든 간접적으로든 화학, 즉 물질의 구성, 특성, 변형에 관한 연구를 포함하고 있다. [■A] 화학은 자연계에서 발생하는 변화들의 원인이다. 마찬가지로 화학은 매우 여러 면에서 지난 2백 년 동안 일어난 엄청난 사회적 변화의 원인이기도 하다. [■B] 게다가 화학은 생물체가 어떻게 유전적으로 조절되는지에 관한 세부 내용을 탐구하는 분자 생물학에서 최근 혁명의 핵심에 놓여 있다. [■C] 사실상 오늘날 학식이 있는 사람이라 해도 화학에 관한 최소한의 기본 지식 없이는 우리 주변의 세계를 진정으로 이해할 수 없다. [■D]

지문에 다음 문장이 들어갈 수 있는 위치를 나타내는 네 개의 사각형[■]을 확인하시오.

화학은 자연계에서 발생하는 변화들의 원인이다.

이 문장이 들어가기에 가장 적합한 곳은? [■A]

어휘 previously adv 이전에 I fivefold adj 5배의 I life expectancy 기대 수명 I synthesize v 합성하다 I yield n 산출량 I transportation n 운송 I horseback adj 말을 타고 하는 I harness v 활용하다 I petroleum n 석유 I manufacture v 제조하다 I ceramic n 도자기 I polymer n 중합체 I property n 고유의 성질 I composition n 구성 I transformation n 변형 I profound adj 엄청난, 깊은 I core n 핵심 I revolution n 혁명 | molecular biology 분자 생물학 | ins and outs 자세한 내용 | genetically adv 유전적으로

18

미국의 혁명주의자들과 그들의 정부 체제

1 ➡ 영향력 있는 모든 문서와 마찬가지로, 미합중국 헌법의 근본적인 목적은 헌법 구성과 그 후 사람들이 이를 채택하는 과정으로 이어지는 상황과 사건의 연구를 통해서만 밝혀질 수 있다. 먼저 미 헌법이 채택된 시기에 두 개의 큰 당파가 있었음을 기억해야 한다. 한 정당은 정부의 힘과 효율성을 강조했고 다른 정당은 정부의 대중적인 측면을 강조했다.

2 ➡ 물론 영국의 지배적인 존재에 대항하는 반란을 선동하고 혁명가들의 전투적 기질을 높은 수준으로 유지하도록 이끌었던 사람들은 토머스 제퍼슨, 새뮤얼 애덤스, 토머스 페인, 패트릭 헨리와 같은 가장 대담하고 급진적인 사상가들이었다. [■A] 일반적으로 이들은 막대한 자산을 보유한 것도, 풍부한 사업 경험을 가진 것도 아니었다. 그러나 혼돈의 시대에 이들은 사회적 통제보다 개인의 자유를 지속적으로 더 강조했다. [■B] 이들은 귀족 권력에 대항하는 소지주들과 상업 계층들의 시련과 고난의 시기 동안 영국에서 발전했던 인권주의를 극단적으로 밀고 나갔다. [■C] 이러한 상황은 18세기 말 미국의 우세한 경제 상황에 상응하는 것이었다. [■D] **그들은 강한 정부를 군주제와 연관지었기 때문에 최고의 정부는 최소한으로 통치하는 정부라고 믿게 되었다.** 이런 다수의 급진주의자들은 모든 정부를, 특히 매우 중앙 집권화된 유형의 정부를 악마의 산물로 보았다. 정부는 단지 약간의 질서 유지에 대한 필요성 때문에 용인되긴 했지만 동시에 지속적인 경계를 통해 최소 수준으로 유지되어야 했다.

지문에 다음 문장이 들어갈 수 있는 위치를 나타내는 네 개의 사각형[■]을 확인하시오.

그들은 강한 정부를 군주제와 연관지었기 때문에 최고의 정부는 최소한으로 통치하는 정부라고 믿게 되었다.

이 문장이 들어가기에 가장 적합한 곳은? [■D]

어휘 influential adj 영향력 있는 | underlying adj 근본적인 | constitution n 헌법 | subsequent adj 그 이후의 | adoption n 채택 | faction n 당파 | stir up 고무하다, 불러 일으키다 | revolt n 반란 | temper n 성질 | dominating adj 지배하는 | radical adj 급진적인 | revolutionist n 혁명론자 | disorder n 혼란 | property n 자산 | to the extreme 극단까지 | consistently adv 지속적으로 | evolve v 발달하다 | doctrine n 원칙 | tribulation n 고난 | trial n 시련 | correspond to ~와 일치하다, ~에 상응하다 | centralized adj 중앙 집권화된 | aristocracy n 귀족 계층 | tolerate v 용인하다 | prevailing adj 우세한 | vigilance n 경계, 조심 | spawn n 산물 | keep ~ to minimum ~를 최소한으로 하다

19

원소

1 ➡ 우리가 주위에서 볼 수 있는 모든 것은 현재 알려진 118개의 원소 중 하나 또는 그 이상으로 구성되어 있다. [■A] 원소들은 화학적으로 변하거나 더 간단한 형태로 분해될 수 없는 기본 물질이다. [■B] 예를 들면 은은 하나의 원소이다. [■C] 다른 원소들이 은에 첨가되어 새로운 물질을 만들 수는 있지만, 은 자체는 더 이상 분해될 수 없다. [■D] **우리가 알고 있는 118개의 원소 중 94개는 자연적으로 존재한다.** 나머지 원소들은 핵화학자들이 고에너지 입자 가속기를 사용하여 인위적으로 만든 것들이다.

2 ➡ [■A] **우리가 알고 있는 자연적으로 존재하는 94개의 원소들은 각기 존재하는 양이 크게 다르다.** 예를 들어 수소 원소는 우주의 질량에서 약 75퍼센트를 차지하고, 산소와 규소 원소는 지구 표면의 약 77퍼센트를 차지한다. [■B] 마찬가지로 산소, 탄소, 수소는 인체의 90퍼센트 이상을 구성한다. [■C] 이와 대조적으로, 지구라는 행성 전체에 흩어져 있는 방사성의 불안정한 원소인 프란슘은 아마 언제나 총 20그램 이하일 것으로 추측된다. [■D]

1. 단락 1에서 다음 문장이 들어갈 수 있는 위치를 나타내는 네 개의 사각형[■]을 확인하시오.

   우리가 알고 있는 118개의 원소 중 94개는 자연적으로 존재한다.

   이 문장이 들어가기에 가장 적합한 곳은? [■D]

2. 단락 2에서 다음 문장이 들어갈 수 있는 위치를 나타내는 네 개의 사각형[■]을 확인하시오.

   우리가 알고 있는 자연적으로 존재하는 94개의 원소들은 각기 존재하는 양이 크게 다르다.

   이 문장이 들어가기에 가장 적합한 곳은? [■A]

어휘 fundamental adj 근본적인 | substance n 물질 | artificially adv 인위적으로 | mass n 질량 | radioactive adv 방사성의

20

식(蝕)

1 ➡ [■A] 식(蝕) 현상은 천체상의 한 물체가 다른 물체의 그림자 속으로 이동하여 가려질 때 일어난다. [■B] 달이 지표면으로부터 태양을 막

을 때 일어나는 일식과, 달이 지구 그림자에 가려졌을 때 나타나는 월식이 우주에서 일어나는 유일한 식 현상은 아니다. [■C] 태양계 밖에서도 한 행성이나 위성이 다른 위성이나 행성의 그림자 속으로 이동하게 되면 언제든지 식 현상이 발생할 수 있다. [■D] 그러나 지구에 있는 우리의 관점으로는 월식과 일식 모두 목격하기에 극적인 사건이 될 수 있다.

2 ➡ 지구의 본영(本影), 즉 그림자는 지구가 태양과 달 사이에 위치할 때 월식을 일으킨다. 이 현상은 적어도 일 년에 두 번 발생하며 약 두 시간 가량 지속된다. [■A] 더욱이 달이 지구의 본영을 지나갈 때 완전히 어두워지는 것은 아니다. [■B] 이것은 여전히 지구의 대기에서 굴절된 태양 광선을 받아 당시 대기 중에 존재하는 구름이나 먼지의 양에 따라 황색, 적색, 심지어 청색 색조를 띠게 된다. [■C] 이렇게 다채로운 색 때문에 월식을 보는 것은 잊지 못할 경험이 될 수 있다. 그러나 월식이 좀 더 일반적으로 일어나고 일식에 비해 덜 두드러지기 때문에 월식은 덜 주목할 만하다고 여겨진다. [■D]

1. 단락 1에서 다음 문장이 들어갈 수 있는 위치를 나타내는 네 개의 사각형[■]을 확인하시오.

그러나 지구에 있는 우리의 관점으로는 월식과 일식 모두 목격하기에 극적인 사건이 될 수 있다.

이 문장이 들어가기에 가장 적합한 곳은? [■D]

2. 단락 2에서 다음 문장이 들어갈 수 있는 위치를 나타내는 네 개의 사각형[■]을 확인하시오.

이렇게 다채로운 색 때문에 월식을 보는 것은 잊지 못할 경험이 될 수 있다.

이 문장이 들어가기에 가장 적합한 곳은? [■C]

어휘 eclipse n 식 | celestial adj 천체의, 하늘의 | obscure v 잘 안 보이게 하다, 가리다 | solar eclipse 일식 | block v 가로막다 | lunar eclipse 월식 | solar system 태양계 | umbra n 본영 (태양 빛이 차단되어 지구나 달에 생기는 그림자) | approximately adv 대략 | hue n 색조 | refract v 굴절시키다 | prevalent adj 널리 퍼진

21 무중력 상태와 인체

1 ➡ [■A] 수백만 년의 진화는 인체가 지구상에서 살 수 있는 조건을 갖추게 했지만 우주 여행에 대비하도록 하지는 않았다. [■B] 우주 여행을 하기 위해 우주 비행사들은 기체(우주선)를 지구 대기 바깥으로 밀어내 궤도상으로 진입시킬 수 있을 만큼 강한 추진력으로 움직이는 우주선 내에 탑승해야 한다. [■C] 궤도를 여행하는 것은 이들의 신체에 대체로 무중력 상태의 생활 환경을 만들어낸다. [■D] 그러므로 그들은 짧은 시간 내에 상당한 위축과 쇠퇴를 경험할 수 있다.

2 ➡ 인체는 신체적 활동, 또는 근육이나 뼈에 가해지는 하중을 필요로 한다. 그러나 우주 여행 중에는 보통 지구에서 중력의 형태로 존재하는 이 하중이 존재하지 않는다. [■A] 그리고 뼈에 가해지는 압력이 없기 때문에 뼈는 분해되고 약해진다. [■B] 마찬가지로 근육 역시 아무런 힘을 일으키지 않기 때문에 부피와 강도가 줄어들고 힘있게 수축하는 능력이 떨어진다. [■C] 또한 순환계 반응이 상황을 더욱 복잡하게 만든다. 말단 혈관은 수축하여 더 많은 체액을 흉강과 머리로 밀어내고 이는 적혈구 수치를 낮춘다. [■D] 그 결과 신체는 혈액의 순환량을 줄여 상체의 높아진 체액 농도에 적응한다. 이것은 신체가 겪는 근골격의 퇴화와 더불어 치명적인 문제를 일으킬 수 있다.

1. 단락 1에서 다음 문장이 들어갈 수 있는 위치를 나타내는 네 개의 사각형[■]을 확인하시오.

그러므로 그들은 짧은 시간 내에 상당한 위축과 쇠퇴를 경험할 수 있다.

이 문장이 들어가기에 가장 적합한 곳은? [■D]

2. 단락 2에서 다음 문장이 들어갈 수 있는 위치를 나타내는 네 개의 사각형[■]을 확인하시오.

또한 순환계 반응이 상황을 더욱 복잡하게 만든다.

이 문장이 들어가기에 가장 적합한 곳은? [■C]

어휘 evolution n 진화 | prepare v 준비하다 | astronaut n 우주 비행사 | spacecraft n 우주선 | thrust n 추진력 | orbit n 궤도 | musculoskeletal adj 근골격의 | exertion n 노력, 분발 | skeleton n 골격 | extremity n 말단 | constrict v 수축하다 | thoracic cavity 흉강 | atrophy n 퇴화 | devastating adj 치명적인

22 살충제의 효과

1 ➡ 살충제를 사용하기 전 농부들은 해충으로부터 작물을 보호하기 위해 윤작, 혼작, 포획작물 이용 등 다양한 방법들을 사용했다. 그러나 20세기에 과학의 발전은 합성 살충제의 발달로 이어졌고, 이것은 천적 형태의 생물학적 방법을 대신하며 표적 해충 개체수를 관리하는 수단으로 이용되었다. 이러한 합성 살충제 발달은 농업에 커다란 도움을 주는 것처럼 보일 수도 있지만 그것의 이용으로 인해 생태학적 문제점들이 발생하기도 한다.

2 ➡ 살충제는 해충을 죽이는 데 대단히 효과적이다. [■A] 그러나 의도적인 것은 아니지만 표적 곤충 집단뿐 아니라 그 경쟁 상대와 천적까지 죽이곤 한다. 하지만 표적종들이 죽고 나면 천적들은 먹이가 없어 마찬가지로 죽기 시작한다. [■B] 이런 상황에서는 필연적으로 표적 해충의 개체수를 억제할 적이 없어지게 된다. 그 결과 표적 해충 개체수가 다시 증가하여 그 숫자가 예전보다 더 커진다. [■C] 천적들은 살충제의 약효가 사라지고 먹이사슬이 회복될 때까지 기다려야 하기 때문에 이런 일이 가능하게 된다. [■D] 표적 해충 부활이라고 알려져 있는 이 현상으로 천적들은 개체의 재증식 속도가 더뎌지기 때문에 극도로 불리한 상황에 처하게 된다.

3 ➡ 살충제 이용의 또 다른 생태학적 반응으로 알려져 있는 것은 2차 해충 발생이다. 해충 관리 전술을 이용해 주요 해충을 지속적으로 공격하면 이전에 그 지역에서 적은 수였던 또 다른 해충이 주요 해충을 대체한다. 이제는 이 2차 해충 개체를 통제할 천적이 없기 때문에 이 종의 수가 증가하고 새로운 주요 해충이 된다. 그 결과 해당 지역의 전체적인 해충 개체수는 실제로는 줄어드는 게 아니라 다른 종의 곤충으로 대체될 뿐이다. 실제로 캐나다의 뉴브런즈윅에서는 1940년 이후 20년 동안 생물학적 제어 방법으로 유럽 가문비나무 잎벌레를 성공적으로 관리해 왔다. 그러나 1960년에서 1962년 사이에 그 지역에 살던 또 다른 절지동물인 가문비나무 눈벌레에 효과적인 합성 살충제가 사용되었다. 확실히 두 곤충의 개체수는 극적으로 감소했다. 그러다 1964년에 잎벌레수가 급증해 그 지역의 전체 곤충 개체수를 압도하게 되었다. 이 사건은 살충제 이용의 또 다른 부작용을 보여주었고 이는 유전자 내성과 관련이 있다.

4 ➡ 자연 선택은 종족의 생존을 보장하는 과정이며 표적 곤충의 살충제 내성 증가로 이어진다. [■A] 살충제를 사용하면 그것이 효과가 있다 하더라도 그 약효에 내성을 보이는 일부 개체가 있고 그 내성이 이후의 더 튼튼한 세대로 전달된다. [■B] 이러한 특성의 유전은 살충제에 면역이 생긴 해충의 수를 대량으로 증가시킨다. 따라서 이 경우 지속적인 살충제 이용으로 얻을 수 있는 유일한 '결과'는 살충제의 약효에 면역력을 지닌 곤충을 만들어 내는 것뿐이다. [■C] 게다가 내성이 있는 종이 나타나기까지는 오랜 시간이 걸리지도 않는다. [■D] 효과적인 합성 살충제 DDT를 널리 사용하기 시작한 지 불과 7년 뒤인 1946년에 집파리에서 살충제 내성이 관찰되었다. 놀랍게도 1990년까지 500종 이상의 절지동물들이 살충제에 내성을 보이는 것으로 파악되었다. 물론 농부들은 살충제의 양을 늘리거나 다른 형태의 살충제를 사용하여 이 문제를 해결하려 했다. 그러나 이런 방법을 써도 한 살충제에 내성이 생긴 곤충들은 다른 살충제에도 내성을 보였다.

5 ➡ 살충제 이용과 관련된 딜레마를 일컬어 '살충제 쳇바퀴'라는 용어가 생겨났다. 살충제 사용 때문에 발생할 수 있는 상황이 너무나 많아 승산 없는 싸움처럼 느껴질 수도 있지만, 작물의 해충 피해를 줄이기 위한 대안이 몇 가지 존재한다. 포식자와 천적 형태의 생물 방제 수단은 사람의 노력 없이 해충을 통제하는 데 효과적이다. 말할 것도 없이 이런 수단은 식물을 먹고 사는 곤충들로 인한 경제적 피해를 방지하는 데 중요한 역할을 한다. 살충제를 사용할 때는 천적에 영향을 주지 않도록 선별성을 유지해야 한다.

1. 단락 2에서 다음 문장이 들어갈 수 있는 위치를 나타내는 네 개의 사각형[■]을 확인하시오.

   이런 상황에서는 필연적으로 표적 해충의 개체수를 억제할 적이 없어지게 된다.

   이 문장이 들어가기에 가장 적합한 곳은? [■B]

2. 단락 4에서 다음 문장이 들어갈 수 있는 위치를 나타내는 네 개의 사각형[■]을 확인하시오.

   이러한 특성의 유전은 살충제에 면역이 생긴 해충의 수를 대량으로 증가시킨다.

   이 문장이 들어가기에 가장 적합한 곳은? [■B]

어휘 pesticide n 살충제 | rotate crop 윤작하다 | trap crop 포획작물 | pest n 해충 | synthetic adj 합성의 | natural enemy 천적 | agricultural adj 농업의 | ecological adj 생태계의 | complication n 문제 | extremely adv 극도로 | competitor n 경쟁자 | intentional adj 의도적인 | inevitably adv 필연적으로 | suppress v 진압하다, 억제하다 | resurge n 부활, 재기 | fade v 사라지다 | repopulate v 재증식하다 | outbreak n 발생 | tactic n 전략, 전술 | reduce v 감소하다 | sawfly n 잎벌레 | arthropod n 절지동물 | budworm n 눈을 갉아먹는 벌레 | decline v 감소하다 | drastically adv 급격히 | overwhelm v 제압하다 | resistance n 내성 | transmit v 전달하다 | robust adj 튼튼한 | coin v 만들다 | treadmill n 쳇바퀴 | alternative n 대안 | regulate v 조절하다 | nuisance n 골칫거리, 불편 | selectivity n 선별성

Test

본서 | P. 212

8세기 일본의 변화

1 ➡ 8세기 동안에 일본은 사회 전반에 영향을 끼친 극적인 변화의 시기를 경험했다. 이 시대는 나라 시대라고 불리는데, 일본의 수도가 나라로 이전했기 때문이며, 이곳은 이후 수 세대 동안 권좌를 유지했다. 이전에도 천황과 그의 전 수행원들은 종종 장소를 옮기고 새로운 왕실을 짓도록 했다. 전 통치자가 세상을 떠난 후 새로운 통치자가 궁전을 사용하는 것은 금기시되었고 철저하게 피해졌다. 이 시대에

1. 1단락의 단어 'fostering(발전)'과 의미상 가장 가까운 것은

   Ⓐ 장려
   Ⓑ 억압
   Ⓒ 유지
   Ⓓ 적응

일어났던 변화들에는 도시화, 정치적 재조정, 종교적 개종, 건축 양식의 변화가 포함된다. 이러한 포괄적인 변화의 주요 이유는 거대한 왕국과 불교 발전을 통제하는 새로운 일본 정부가 설립되었던 데에 있다. 이 변화들은 중국으로부터 종교와 문화를 의도적으로 수입함으로써 가능해졌다.

2 ➡ 나라 시대는 710년에 시작되었고, 이는 겐메이 천황이 나라에 최초의 영구적인 수도를 설립한 때였다. 일본 통치자들은 6세기 후반부터 정치를 운용하기 위해 궁전을 사용해 왔지만, 권력이 점차 중앙 집권화되면서, 왕실의 권리와 특권도 빠른 속도로 커져갔다. 이로 인해 정부를 지원하기 위한 엄청난 규모의 수도를 건설할 필요성이 생겼다. 새로운 왕도는 궁전을 짓는 것보다 훨씬 더 많은 비용이 들었기에, 정부가 다른 곳으로 이전할 수 없게 되었고, 그로 인해 사람들은 전보다 더 한 곳에 머물러 살게 되었다. 나라와 왕궁은 중국 당나라의 수도인 장안을 충실하게 모방하였다. 도시 건설을 위한 부지는 중국의 지리학적 조화 원칙을 참고해 선정했고, 길 또한 중국 사람들이 사용한 것과 동일한 정확한 격자형으로 배치하였다. 인구는 빠르게 급증하여 200,000명에 이르렀으며, 이는 국가 전체 인구의 약 7퍼센트에 해당하는 것이었다.

3 ➡ 나라가 영구적인 수도가 되고 난 후, 정부는 경제 및 행정적 활동에 대한 통제에 더욱 힘쓰기 시작했다. 나라와 지방 수도를 연결하기 위한 도로가 지어졌으며, 이로 인해 무역이 번성했다. 동전이 공식적인 통화로써 주조되었으나, 일반적인 상업에까지 널리 쓰이진 않았다. 조세 제도 또한 재정비되었고 세금 징수가 더욱 규칙적이고 효율적으로 이루어졌다. 이 시대의 가장 중요한 황제는 724년부터 749년까지 통치했던 독실한 불교도, 쇼무 천황이다. 그는 정치적 불안과 천연두와 같은 전염병을 해결해야 했는데, 불교를 그 문제들을 극복하기 위한 수단으로 여겼다. 그러나 많은 다른 당파들이 그의 불교 진흥에 반대하였고, 그의 통치에 저항하였다. 결과적으로 쇼무 천황은 그에게 반대하는 신도(神道)를 믿는 사람들로부터 승리를 거두었고, 비록 불교를 공식적인 국교로 만드는 것은 실패로 끝났지만, 종교를 후원하고 서민들을 통합하기 위해 국가 전역에 사원 건립 프로그램을 시작하였다.

4 ➡ 나라 시대의 가장 중요한 문화적 발전 중 하나는 일본에서의 영구적인 불교의 확립이다. 불교는 6세기에 한국을 통해 일본으로 도입되었으나, 토착 신앙인 신도를 옹호하는 전통주의자들의 거센 저항에 직면하였다. 신도는 샤머니즘과 산악 숭배의 혼합이다. 이 종교는 완전한 구성을 갖추지 않았고, 관습도 장소에 따라 다양했기에, 그것을 불교와 구별하기 위해 신도라고 불렀다. 쇼무 천황은 자신을 불교의 '삼보(三寶): 불보(佛寶), 법보(法寶), 승보(僧寶)의 종'이라 칭하였다. 그 이후 그는 나라에 거대한 청동 부처상이 있는 큰 사원을 짓도록 명령했다. [■A] 그는 사람들을 불교로 귀의시키도록 승려들을 파견하였으나 이들은 사람들에게 세속적인 문제에 관해서도 조언을 해주었다. [■B] 그들은 사람들에게 기근에서 살아남기, 저수지 짓기, 도로와 논 수리하기, 집 짓기, 의료적 행위에 관한 가르침을 주었다. 일본은 점차적으로 축제와 의식과 같은 신도의 많은 측면을 포함한 고유한 형태의 불교를 발달시켜 나갔다. [■C] 이것은 이 종교가 새로운 신도들을 개종시키고 지속되는 인기를 보장하는 데 도움이 되었다. [■D]

2. 1단락에 따르면, 다음 중 8세기 일본에서 일어난 일이 아닌 것은

Ⓐ 도시 성장
Ⓑ 정부 변화
Ⓒ 종교적 변화
Ⓓ 경기 침체

3. 2단락에 따르면, 다음 중 나라라는 도시에 대해 추론 가능한 것은 무엇인가?

Ⓐ 겐메이 천황이 자신의 권력을 과시하기 위해 설립했다.
Ⓑ 정부가 다른 곳으로 이동하는 것을 막기 위해 거대한 규모로 건설되었다.
Ⓒ 그것이 건설된 가장 주된 동기는 당나라 문화의 유입이었다.
Ⓓ 도시의 큰 규모와 안정성이 도시 인구 증가에 기여했다.

4. 3단락에 따르면, 다음 중 영구적 수도의 설립으로 인해 일어난 변화가 아닌 것은

Ⓐ 사람들에 대한 정부의 통제가 더욱 강화되었다
Ⓑ 이동 수단의 발전으로 국내 무역이 번성하였다
Ⓒ 공식 화폐의 등장이 시장 경제에 혁명을 일으켰다
Ⓓ 조세 제도가 개정되어 세금이 효율적으로 징수될 수 있었다

5. 다음 중 지문에 음영 표시된 문장의 핵심 정보를 가장 잘 표현한 문장은 무엇인가? 오답은 의미를 크게 왜곡하거나 핵심 정보를 누락하고 있다.

Ⓐ 쇼무 천황의 반대자들은 불교를 공식 국교로 만들려는 그의 시도를 비난했고 그래서 그는 사원 건축 프로그램을 끝내게 되었다.
Ⓑ 반대에도 불구하고 쇼무 천황은 성공적으로 불교를 공식 국교로 확립하였다.
Ⓒ 쇼무 천황은 가까스로 그의 반대자들을 상대로 승리했지만, 불교를 공식 국교로 지정하는 데 실패하였다.
Ⓓ 비록 불교를 공식 국교로 지정하려는 시도는 실패로 끝났지만, 쇼무 천황은 사원 건축을 통해 종교를 전파하고 사회를 통합하였다.

6. 4단락에 따르면, 다음 중 신도의 가장 구별되는 특징은 무엇인가?

Ⓐ 체계가 느슨하며 여러 지역적, 국지적 전통의 다양한 종교적인 관습들을 통합하였다.
Ⓑ 성전의 가르침보다는 종교의 실용적인 측면을 더 강조하였다.
Ⓒ 자연과 동물의 영혼에 대한 숭배를 기반으로 하였다.
Ⓓ 타종교에 개방적이었고 그것의 발전은 한국과 중국의 영향을 받았다.

Lesson 01 Recognizing Organization

5 ➡ 불교가 퍼져나감에 따라 이는 건축에도 영향을 주었다. 사원의 디자인은 중국 사원의 디자인과 유사하게 바뀌어갔으며, 결과적으로 모든 일반 건물에도 영향을 끼쳤다. 이러한 새로운 영구적인 건물들에는 돌로 된 토대와, 거대한 수직 · 수평의 지지 구조물, 그리고 기와를 올린 큰 지붕이 있었다. 건물 내부는 상황에 따라 재배열할 수 있는 장지(粧紙)문으로 이루어져 있었다. 그러나, 대륙 스타일은 일본과는 상당히 다른 기후에 맞추어진 것이었고, 특정 요소들은 꽤 초기에 조정되었다. 건물의 지붕은 훨씬 더 넓었고, 처마 쪽으로 약간 기울어져 있어서 훨씬 많은 강우량을 이겨낼 수 있도록 하였다. 중국식 건물의 무거운 외벽은 이 기후에는 적합하지 않았다. 외벽이 건물의 무게를 지탱할 필요가 없었기 때문에, 얇은 나무판과 종이로 대체되었다. 많은 불교 사원들이 오래된 신도 사원 안에 지어졌고, 신도 사원이 종종 불교 사원에 붙어 있다는 점에서, 이러한 양식과 (건축) 자재들의 통합 방식은 불교와 신도 사원들을 흉내낸 것이었다.

7. 다음 중 5단락에서 중국의 건축 양식을 일본이 수정한 것으로 언급된 것은 무엇인가?

Ⓐ 장식용 조각품이 있는 거대 석상 구조물
Ⓑ 곡선 처마가 있는 넓은 지붕
Ⓒ 합성 물질로 만들어진 견고한 내벽
Ⓓ 건물의 무게를 지탱하기 위한 무거운 외벽

8. 5단락의 단어 'feasible(적합한)'과 의미상 가장 가까운 것은

Ⓐ 알맞은 가격의
Ⓑ 내부의
Ⓒ 실용적인
Ⓓ 연속된

9. 지문에 다음 문장이 들어갈 수 있는 위치를 나타내는 네 개의 사각형 [■]을 확인하시오.

그들은 사람들에게 기근에서 살아남기, 저수지 짓기, 도로와 논 수리하기, 집 짓기, 의료적 행위에 대한 가르침을 주었다.

이 문장이 들어가기에 가장 적합한 곳은? [■B]

10. 지시문: 지문을 간략하게 요약한 글의 첫 문장이 아래 제시되어 있다. 지문의 가장 중요한 내용을 표현하는 세 개의 선택지를 골라 요약문을 완성하시오. 일부 문장들은 지문에 제시되지 않았거나 지문의 지엽적인 내용을 나타내기 때문에 요약문에 포함되지 않는다. ***이 문제의 배점은 2점이다.***

일본의 나라 시대는 불교가 일본의 정치, 문화, 건축에 지대한 영향을 끼쳤던 주목할 만한 시대였다.

Ⓑ 영구적인 수도의 건설로 인해 제국 정부가 전국적인 통제를 가하는 것이 더 쉬워졌다.
Ⓓ 불교는 6세기에 도입되었으나, 쇼무 천황에 의해 수용되었던 나라 시대 전까지는 오직 부분적으로만 받아들여졌다.
Ⓕ 일본 내에서 증가한 불교의 영향력의 결과로, 전통적인 일본의 건축 양식이 불교식 사원 건축의 영향에 사로잡혔다.

Ⓐ 8세기 초에 겐메이 천황이 즉위했을 때, 그녀는 빈번한 전염병의 발생 후에 새로운 왕도를 건설해야 했다.
Ⓒ 중국 수도를 본뜬 나라의 건설은 일반 서민들로부터 일본 귀족을 극적으로 분리시키는 결과를 초래했다.
Ⓔ 자연신과 조상신을 숭배하는 신도는 쇼무 천황의 지속적인 노력으로 인해 일본의 토착 신앙으로 발전했다.

어휘 dramatic adj 극적인 | entourage n 수행단 | urbanization n 도시화 | conversion n 개종, 전향 | comprehensive adj 포괄적인, 종합적인 | facilitate v 가능하게 하다, 용이하게 하다 | centralize v 중앙 집권화하다 | necessitate v ~을 필요하게 만들다 | sedentary adj 한 곳에 머물러 사는, 정주하는 | grid pattern 격자형, 정방형 | administrative adj 관리상의, 행정상의 | provincial adj 지방의 | mint v (화폐를) 주조하다 | currency n 통화 | commerce n 상업, 무역 | reign v 다스리다, 통치하다 | unrest n 불안, 불만 | epidemic n 유행병, 전염병 | means n 수단, 방법 | rebel v 반란을 일으키다, 저항하다 | indigenous adj 토착의, 토종의 | definitive adj 최종적인, 확정적인 | secular adj 세속적인 | incorporate v 포함하다 | ensure v 보장하다 | continental adj 대륙의, 대륙풍의 | adapt v 맞추다, 조정하다 | eave n (가옥의) 처마, 차양 | synthesis n 합성, 종합

태양계의 기원

1 ➡ 지구가 우주의 중심이 아니며, 우리가 알고 있는 행성들이 태양을 돌고 있다는 것이 확실히 자리잡게 되자 과학자들은 태양계가 어떻게 형성됐을지 이론을 세우기 시작했다. 이 과정을 설명하는 가장 널리 인정받는 이론은 성운설인데, 이 이론은 태양계가 중력 때문에 안쪽으로 붕괴한 성운으로부터 형성됐다고 주장한다. 물질이 응축되

11. 다음 중 1단락에서 언급된 성운설과 관련해서 사실인 것은 무엇인가?

Ⓐ 과학자들로 하여금 행성들이 주위에 원판이 있는 별들을 중심으로 돈다고 정확하게 추측할 수 있게 했다.
Ⓑ 과학자들로 하여금 지구가 우주의 중심이라는 지배적인 믿음으로부터 돌아서게 만들었다.

면서 그것의 회전은 물질 대부분이 중심에 위치한 디스크 모양을 형성하게 만들었다. 중심이 젊은 별이 된 후 디스크의 나머지 부분은 행성을 형성했다. 다른 별을 도는 행성들과 주변에 디스크가 있는 것이 감지되고 확인된 별들은 이 이론의 가장 강력한 근거가 된다.

2 ➡ 우리 태양계는 약 46억년 전 거대한 별이 일생의 말미에 다다라서 폭발하며 생긴 성운으로부터 형성되기 시작했으며, 이 폭발은 거의 전적으로 수소와 헬륨으로 구성된 광범위한 구름을 만들었다. 성운 속 기체 물질은 중력의 끌림으로 인해 안쪽으로 붕괴되기 시작했다. [■A] **작은 기체 분자조차 질량을 갖고 있고 그 질량은 중력의 힘으로 인해 다른 질량에게 끌린다.** 이런 수소 분자들이 합체하여* 점점 더 밀집된 중핵을 형성했다. [■B] 중력의 힘은 사방으로 동일하기 때문에 물질은 완벽하게 균일한 모양인 구를 형성했다. [■C] 에너지는 파괴될 수 없기 때문에 분자들이 충돌하고 핵이 더 밀집되면서 그들의 운동 에너지는 보존되었지만 핵 중심을 도는 회전 움직임으로 바뀌었다. [■D] 이 현상은 각운동량의 보존이라고 불리며 이는 핵이 수축되면서 돌게 만들었다. 아이스 스케이트 선수가 팔을 안쪽으로 끌어당길 때 더 빨리 도는 것처럼 핵은 밀집될수록 더 빨리 회전했다. 이 회전은 구름에 남아 있던 물질도 회전하게 만들면서 적도 지점에서 납작하게 펼쳐져서 핵을 둘러싼 원판 모양으로 퍼지게 만들었다.

3 ➡ 분자들의 운동 에너지는 그들이 충돌하면서 열로 전환되었고 핵 중심의 압력이 증가하면서 온도가 올라가자 밝게 빛나기 시작했다. 성운 속의 밀집된 뜨거운 핵은 원시성이라고 불린다. 중심에 있는 수소 원자들이 융합하기 시작할 때까지 압력과 열은 계속 증가했으며, 이것은 결국 중력 수축에 대응할 만큼 강해진 내부의 에너지 원천을 만들었고 젊은 별은 평형 상태에 도달했다. 우리 태양이 안정된 젊은 별이 되었을 때 성운은 대부분 사라졌으며 남겨진 기체와 먼지 원판은 태양계의 다른 천체들로 뭉쳐서 커지기 시작했다.

4 ➡ 오늘날 8개의 행성과 많은 왜소행성, 소행성과 혜성을 포함한 많은 천체들이 태양을 돌고 있다. 행성은 원시성 주변의 원판에 들어있는 먼지 알갱이로부터 시작해, 부착을 통해 더 커졌다. 먼지 알갱이는 다른 알갱이와 서로 충돌하며 엉겨붙었고 지름 10킬로미터 정도의 원시행성이라고 불리는 행성의 시초가 될 때까지 그 과정을 반복했다. 이런 원시행성이 수천 개가 있었고 현재 크기에 달할 때까지 서로와 충돌하며 크기를 키워나갔다. 4개의 내행성인 수성, 금성, 지구와 화성은 태양과 매우 가까운 곳에 형성되었기 때문에 그들의 물질은 철, 니켈, 알루미늄 같은 금속과 규소를 기반으로 한 암석 물질처럼 고융점을 갖고 있는 원소들로 대부분 구성되었다. 이런 원소들은 성운의 물질 중 단지 작은 부분에 해당하고, 이것은 바위로 구성된 행성이 왜 그렇게 크지 않은지를 설명해준다.

5 ➡ 몹시 추운 외행성은 내행성들처럼 암석과 금속 재질 주변에 형성되었을 수 있지만 그들의 물질 대부분은 기체다. 그들이 형성된 지역은 태양에서 너무 멀리 있어서 기체가 흔히 얼음으로 얼어 있다. 이 물질은 내행성을 구성하는 물질보다 훨씬 더 풍부했기 때문에 목성, 토성, 천왕성과 해왕성은 모두 거대한 얼음 핵으로 시작했다. 목성은 토성이 생기기 수백만 년 전에 형성되었지만 둘은 모두 핵 주변으로 거대한 양의 수소와 다른 기체를 모았다. 천왕성과 해왕성은 이 두 거인 사이에서 형성되기 시작해, 나중에 바깥으로 내던져져서 현

Ⓒ 우리 태양계가 어떻게 형성되었는지에 대해 현재 우리가 이해하고 있는 바를 나타낸다.
Ⓓ 그것은 다른 천체를 도는 행성들의 증거로 인해 사실이 아닌 것으로 증명되었다.

12. 2단락에 따르면, 성운 물질이 어떻게 핵과 그 주위의 원판을 형성했는가?
Ⓐ 수소 분자들 간의 끌어당기는 힘이 사방으로 동일하기 때문에 그것은 물질을 구와 원판으로 형성했다.
Ⓑ 추가 에너지가 수소 분자들이 서로 충돌하게끔 만들었다.
Ⓒ 각운동량은 밀집한 핵이 더 빠르게 돌게 만들었고 구의 바깥 층이 떨어져나가 원판을 형성하게 했다.
Ⓓ 중력이 물질로 하여금 회전하는 핵을 형성하게 만들었고, 그 움직임은 나머지 물질이 원판을 형성하게 만들었다.

13. 3단락에 따르면, 핵 중심의 온도가 증가한 이유는 무엇인가?
Ⓐ 분자의 충돌은 핵 중심의 압력을 증가시켰다.
Ⓑ 운동 에너지에서 열 에너지로의 전환이 있었다.
Ⓒ 수소 원자의 융합은 더 많은 에너지를 만들어냈다.
Ⓓ 분자들의 운동 에너지는 핵의 중심이 빛나게 만들었다.

14. 다음 중 지문에 음영 표시된 문장의 핵심 정보를 가장 잘 표현한 문장은 무엇인가? 오답은 의미를 크게 왜곡하거나 핵심 정보를 누락하고 있다.
Ⓐ 수소 원자의 융합으로 생성된 에너지는 수축하는 힘을 상쇄하기에 충분했고 별로 하여금 평형 상태에 도달하게 했다.
Ⓑ 중력 수축의 힘은 수소 원자가 서로 융합하여 별이 평형 상태에 도달하는 것을 도울 수 있게 만들 정도로 강해졌다.
Ⓒ 중력 수축의 힘은 강했지만 수소 원자가 융합하여 평형 상태에 도달할 수 있도록 충분한 압력과 열을 핵에 가할 정도로 강력하지 않았다.
Ⓓ 증가하는 압력과 열은 핵 중심에 있는 수소 원자의 융합을 야기했으며 이것은 별이 결국 중력을 이겨내게 만들었다.

15. 다음 중 4단락에서 행성의 형성에 대해서 추론 가능한 것은 무엇인가?
Ⓐ 원시행성은 원시성이 안정된 별로 바뀐 후에 형성되었다.
Ⓑ 우리 태양계의 소행성과 혜성은 구성 물질을 먼지 알갱이로부터 얻지 않는다.
Ⓒ 모든 원시행성들은 뭉쳐져서 결국 오늘날 태양을 도는 8개의 행성들을 형성했다.
Ⓓ 내행성들과 태양 간의 거리는 기체 물질들이 행성들의 주된 구성 성분이 되는 것을 막았다.

16. 4단락의 구 'accounts for(설명하다)'와 의미상 가장 가까운 것은
Ⓐ 지배하다
Ⓑ 설명하다
Ⓒ 보상하다
Ⓓ 회복하다

재 궤도에 위치하게 된 것으로 간주된다. 그들의 발달은 목성과 토성이 이용 가능한 수소 대부분을 이미 흡수했기 때문에 얼음 핵 단계에서 멈춘 것처럼 보인다.

6 ➡ 행성의 내부 온도와 외부 온도는 3개의 주된 요소에 의해 결정되는데, 태양과의 거리, 행성의 크기, 행성의 밀도가 바로 그것이다. 내행성들의 표면은 태양과 얼마나 가까운지, 그리고 대기가 얼마나 두꺼운지에 따라 뜨거운 상태에서부터 따뜻한 상태에까지 분포해 있다. 응축된 물질로 구성되어 있기 때문에 그들의 핵 온도는 매우 높다. 반면에 외행성은 태양에서 멀리 있기 때문에 전부 표면이 매우 차갑다. 하지만 그들의 물질은 응축되어 있지 않더라도 행성의 거대한 크기로 인해 극심한 압력을 받고 있기 때문에 핵은 뜨겁다.

***합체하다:** 한데 모여서 더 큰 무리를 형성하다

17. 5단락에 따르면, 다음 중 외행성에 관해 사실인 것은 무엇인가?

Ⓐ 다른 원시행성과의 충돌로 인해 부분적으로 크기가 커졌다.

Ⓑ 그들의 핵은 주로 금속 원소들로 만들어졌다.

Ⓒ 토성은 목성보다 형성되는 데 더 오랜 시간이 걸렸다.

Ⓓ 대부분 가스로 구성되어 있다.

18. 6단락에 따르면, 다음 중 외행성과 내행성 간의 차이가 아닌 것은

Ⓐ 구성하는 원소

Ⓑ 핵의 온도

Ⓒ 태양과의 거리

Ⓓ 표면 온도

19. 지문에 다음 문장이 들어갈 수 있는 위치를 나타내는 네 개의 사각형 [■]을 확인하시오.

작은 기체 분자조차 질량을 갖고 있고 그 질량은 중력의 힘으로 인해 다른 질량에게 끌린다.

이 문장이 들어가기에 가장 적합한 곳은? [■A]

20. 지시문: 지문을 간략하게 요약한 글의 첫 문장이 아래 제시되어 있다. 지문의 가장 중요한 내용을 표현하는 세 개의 선택지를 골라 요약문을 완성하시오. 일부 문장들은 지문에 제시되지 않았거나 지문의 지엽적인 내용을 나타내기 때문에 요약문에 포함되지 않는다. ***이 문제의 배점은 2점이다.***

우리 태양계는 약 46억 년 전에 형성되었다.

Ⓑ 수소 분자들이 함께 융합해 응집된 핵을 형성했고, 그들의 에너지가 핵을 돌게 하고 원판을 형성하게 만들자 원시성이 생겼다. Ⓒ 젊은 태양 주변 성운의 원판은 가스와 먼지를 포함하고 있었는데 이는 응집되어서 결국 원시행성을 형성했다. Ⓓ 내행성이 외행성보다 더 작은 이유는 언 상태의 가스가 금속보다 훨씬 더 흔했기 때문이다.

Ⓐ 외행성은 내행성이 형성된 후에 남은 물질로 형성되었는데, 이것은 대부분 수소였다.

Ⓔ 우주에 퍼져 있는 성운 물질이 중력의 힘으로 인해 안쪽으로 수축하면서 새로운 천체가 형성된다.

Ⓕ 수소 원자의 융합 중 운동 에너지에서 열 에너지로의 전환은 원시성을 밝게 타오르게 만들었다.

어휘 establish v 설립하다 | revolve v 돌다, 회전하다 | theorize v 이론을 세우다 | nebula n 성운 | condense v 응결되다, 응결시키다 | rotation n 회전 | remainder n 나머지 | orbit v 궤도를 돌다 | detect v 감지하다 | extensive adj 아주 넓은 | gaseous adj 기체의, 가스의 | collapse v 붕괴되다, 무너지다 | coalesce v 합치다 | dense adj 밀집한 | core n 중심부, 핵 | collide v 충돌하다, 부딪치다 | phenomenon n 현상 | spin v 돌다, 회전하다 | contract v 수축하다 | flatten v 납작하게 만들다 | equator n 적도 | convert v 변환시키다 | protostar n 원시성 | fuse v 융합시키다 | counteract v 대응하다, (반작용으로) 중화하다 | equilibrium n 평형(상태) | accrete v (부착하여) 커지다 | celestial body 천체 | dwarf planet 왜소행성 | asteroid n 소행성 | comet n 혜성 | protoplanet n 원시행성 | impact v 충돌하다 | inner planet 내행성 | fraction n 부분, 일부 | account for ~을 설명하다, ~의 이유가 되다 | frigid adj 몹시 추운 | outer planet 외행성 | massive adj 거대한 | fling v 내던지다, 내팽개치다 | density n 밀도 | immense adj 엄청난

Lesson 02 Summary

본서 | P. 220

Practice

01 D **02** D **03** B **04** C **05** B, E, F **06** A, C, E **07** B, D, E
08 A, C, E **09** C, D, F **10** A, D, F **11** A, C, F **12** B, C, F

Test

1. B	2. B	3. C	4. B	5. B	6. A	7. D	8. C	9. C	10. A, C, D
11. C	12. B	13. D	14. B	15. C	16. A	17. A	18. C	19. B	20. A, D, F

Practice

본서 I P. 223

[01-04] 각 글을 가장 잘 요약한 것을 고르시오.

01

인쇄 산업

19세기 초에 인쇄 산업계가 증기력을 사용하기 시작했을 때 이는 광범위한 사회 변화로 이어졌다. 신문과 대중적인 책의 출판은 급속도로 확대되었고 식자율을 높이는 데 일조했다. 결과적으로 이것은 대중의 좀 더 폭넓은 정치 참여를 야기했는데, 사람들이 매일의 쟁점은 물론 그들을 대표하는 후보자들에 관한 정보를 읽을 수 있게 되었기 때문이다. 정당들은 선거에서의 대중의 참여에 적응하기 시작했다. 미국에서 백인 남성의 보통 선거권이 채택되었을 때 그 결과로 1828년에 앤드류 잭슨 장군이 당선되었으며, 그는 일반 투표로 선출된 최초의 미국 대통령이었다.

Ⓐ 신문과 책 출판이 확대된 뒤 식자율이 빠르게 상승했다.
Ⓑ 신문 제작 증가는 사람들이 정치 입후보자에 대해 더 잘 알게 해주었다.
Ⓒ 인쇄 산업계는 19세기 초에 증기력을 사용하기 시작했다.
Ⓓ 증기력 인쇄기의 도입은 사회에 깊은 영향을 미쳤다.

어휘 printing industry 인쇄 산업계 I steam power 증기력 I expand v 확대/확장되다 I rapidly adv 빠르게 I literacy n 글을 읽고 쓸 줄 아는 능력 I political adj 정치의 I participation n 참여 I public n 대중 I candidate n 후보 I represent v 대표하다 I election n 선거 I universal adj 보편적인 I suffrage n 투표권 I popular vote 일반 투표

02

카나리아 제도

1 ➡ 7개의 섬과 6개의 작은 섬으로 이루어진 스페인령 군도인 카나리아 제도는 아프리카의 서쪽 해안에 자리잡고 있다. 이 군도는 두 지역으로 나뉘어 있다. 그란 카나리아, 푸에르테벤투라, 란사로테 및 작은 섬 6개 모두를 포함하는 지역인 라스 팔마스 데 그란 카나리아와, 테네리페, 라 팔마, 라 고메라, 엘 이에로로 구성된 산타 크루스 데 테네리페이다. 섬들이 스페인에 속해 있으므로 이들은 유럽 연합의 일부이며 유럽에서 최고로 손꼽히는 해변과 가장 인상적인 풍경을 갖고 있다고 여겨진다. 이 점이 섬들을 아주 유명한 관광지로 만들었다.

2 ➡ 섬들은 사실 수중 화산 산맥의 끝부분으로, 스페인 영토 내에서 가장 높은 지점이자 세계에서 3번째로 높은 화산을 갖고 있다. 카나리아 제도의 각기 다른 해발 고도는 화산 고원부터 구름 낀 산림, 폭풍우에 마모된 절벽에서부터 푸른 들판과 포도와 올리브가 자라나는 농업 지역에 이르기까지 다채로운 풍경을 갖게 하는 미기후(상대적으로 좁은 지역의 기후)를 만들어냈다. 카나리아 제도는 또한 섬의 자연 식물과 토종 야생 생물을 보호하기 위한 수많은 국립 공원을 자랑하고 있다. 물론 명금의 이름을 지닌 섬답게 카나리아 새들이 있지만, 노란빛의 관상종과 달리 카나리아 제도의 토종 카나리아들은 칙칙한 갈색을 띠고 있다.

Ⓐ 제도는 화산 활동을 통해 형성되었다.
Ⓑ 제도는 높은 고도 때문에 다양한 지형을 지니고 있다.
Ⓒ 제도에는 섬의 이름과 동일한 밝은 노란빛의 명금이 가득하다.
Ⓓ 제도의 독특한 지형적 특색은 이곳을 유명한 관광지로 만들었다.

어휘 archipelago n 군도 I islet n 작은 섬 I destination n 목적지 I tip n 끝부분 I submerged adj 수중의 I volcanic adj 화산의 I altitude n 고도 I microclimate n 미기후 I spawn v 생기게 하다 I plateau n 고원 I indigenous adj 토종의 I songbird n 명금 I dull adj 흐린, 탁한

03

화석 연대 측정

1 ➡ 19세기 지질학자들은 화석의 연대를 측정할 때 상대적인 지질 연대만 알아낼 수 있었다. 상대 연대 측정법은 다양한 암석층을 관찰하여 지질학적 시간을 측정한다. 화석이 표면 가까이에서 발견된 것부터 암석의 더 깊은 층에 박혀서 발견된 것 순서로 놓이게 될 때, 발견된 화석들에는 일반적인 순서가 정해져 있다. 위쪽의 층은 좀더 최근에 생긴 것인 반면 더 깊은 층들은 그것들보다 이전에 생긴 것들이다. 게다가 화석은 시간이 흐를수록 더 복잡해지며 시간에 따른 다양한 종의 발달 단계를 보여준다. 그러므로 암석층에 박힌 화석을 발견할 때, 지질학자들은 그 층을 둘러싸고 있는 층들과 비교하면서 그에 상응하는 화석의 연대를 결정할 수 있다.

2 ➡ 그러나 암석의 연대를 측정할 수 있는 완벽하게 정확한 방법은 없었기 때문에 이 연대 측정법은 어떤 층이 더 오래되고 덜 오래되었는지

결정하기 위해 단지 화석 내용물만을 사용할 수밖에 없었다. 그러므로 이 방법은 어떤 사건이 일어난 실제 시기를 보여 주지 못하고 암석을 연대순으로만 분류했다.

3 ➡ 이러한 상대 연대 측정법이 화석의 연대 측정에 실수를 초래하는 경향이 있기 때문에 방사성 연대 측정법 같은 절대 연대 측정법이 1940년대 말에 개발되었다. 우라늄과 납 같은 일련의 동위 원소를 분석하는 방사성 연대 측정법은 두 화합물의 상대적인 구성비를 알아내는 방식으로 작용한다. 이 원소들은 백만 년에서 5천만 년까지 오랜 기간 동안 남아 있으며 과학자들이 상대 연대 측정법을 사용해서는 측정할 수 없는 화석의 연대를 가늠할 수 있게 해준다. 절대 연대 측정법과 상대 연대 측정법 모두 오늘날 사용되고 있고, 더 높은 정확도를 위해 서로를 보완한다.

Ⓐ 화석은 생물체가 시간이 흐르면서 진화하고 더 복잡해진다는 것을 보이며 진화 이론을 뒷받침한다.
Ⓑ 화석 연대법은 전통적으로는 상대적인 추정치에 의해서 이루어졌고, 현대에는 절대 연대 측정법을 통해 보완되었다.
Ⓒ 암석층들은 지구의 가장 초기 시기부터의 화석을 가지고 있는 바위층이고, 그 내용물로 분석될 수 있다.
Ⓓ 19세기 과학자들은 자연적으로 발생한 원소들을 분석하여 화석의 나이를 결정할 수 있는 절대적인 방식을 고안했다.

어휘 geologist n 지질학자 I relative adj 상대적인 I stratum n 층 I embed v 속에 묻다 I predate v 앞서다 I chronological adj 연대순의 I erroneous adj 실수의 I radiometric adj 방사 측정(분석)의 I isotope n 동위 원소 I compound n 화합물

---

04 조경

1 ➡ 건축에 대해 생각할 때 사람들은 좀처럼 식물, 공원, 정원을 상상하지 않지만, 조원 혹은 조경이라고 알려진 건축 분야는 건물을 짓는 것과는 전혀 상관이 없다. 그보다 조경 건축가들은 언덕과 계곡, 강, 연못, 나무, 풀, 그리고 꽃을 포함하는 자연 요소와 재배된 토지 요소 양쪽 모두를 정리하고 배열한다.

2 ➡ 다양한 형태의 조경은 기원전 3천 년 혹은 그 이전부터 존재했다. 고대 이집트인들은 안뜰과 담으로 둘러싸인 공간에 정원을 가꾸었고, 시간이 흐르면서 그러한 정원들은 점차 인공 연못이나 과수원 같은 특징을 강조하도록 설계된 일정한 양식을 갖춘 정원이 되었다. 바빌로니아, 아시리아, 페르시아, 그리고 그리스를 포함한 다른 주요 문명 사회도 조경 설계자들의 도움으로 이러한 일정한 양식을 갖춘 정원을 설계하고 만들었다.

3 ➡ 유럽에서 15~16세기 동안 조경은 진정한 예술 형태로 떠오르기 시작했다. 왕과 귀족들은 자신과 가족을 위해 거대한 궁전을 지을 때 자주 일정한 양식을 갖춘 거대한 정원을 설계하기 위해 건축 전문가들을 고용했다. 이 시기에 수많은 정원들은 대칭적이고 잘 정돈되어 있었다. 관목 숲과 관상 나무들은 세심하게 손질되어 일렬로 심어졌고, 화단, 연못, 그리고 조각품은 모두 엄격하게 조직화된 계획에 꼭 들어맞았다. 17세기 동안 일정한 양식을 갖춘 정원들은 더욱 정교하고 복잡해졌다.

4 ➡ 조경은 20세기에 또 다른 변화를 겪었다. 20세기 초반에 유명한 건축가들은 구조물이 주위 환경과 조화를 이루어야 한다고 믿었다. 20세기 후반 동안에는 조경의 초점이 개인의 정원이 아닌 대규모의 공공사업으로 바뀌었다. 현재 수많은 조경 건축가들은 도시 내의 녹지 공간 설계를 위해 시, 주, 중앙 정부와 함께 일하고 있다. 미국에서는 도시 지역이 성장하면서 조경 건축가들은 그들의 예술을 행할 새로운 기회를 얻게 되었고, 점점 더 많은 사람들이 거주하고, 일하고, 휴식하는 환경을 만들고 있다.

Ⓐ 15세기에서 17세기 사이에 유럽 귀족들은 더욱 정교한 조경술을 발전시켰다.
Ⓑ 현대 조경 건축가들은 도시 거주민들에게 거주하고, 근무하고, 휴식을 취할 수 있는 아름다운 건물을 제공한다.
Ⓒ 조경은 인간 환경의 자연적인 요소와 인위적 요소들을 다루는 오랫동안 지속되어 온 전통이다.
Ⓓ 대부분의 고대 문명은 안뜰의 정원을 만들기 위해 조경술을 적용했다.

어휘 landscape architecture 조경 I envision v 상상하다 I courtyard n 안뜰 I enclosure n (갇힌) 공간 I orchard n 과수원 I civilization n 문명 I emerge v 나타나다 I noble n 귀족 I immense adj 거대한 I symmetrical adj 대칭적인 I shrubbery n 관목 I ornamental adj 장식용의, 관상의 I trim v 다듬다, 손질하다 I regimented adj 대오를 엄격하게 맞춘 I elaborate adj 정교한 I prominent adj 저명한 I blend v 섞다, 혼합하다

---

05 동물의 의사소통

1 ➡ 동물은 지극히 기본적인 청각 의사소통 기술이 있거나 아예 없기 때문에 많은 동물이 시각적 의사소통 방법에 의존한다. 특히 곤충과 새는 매우 정교한 시각적 의사소통 체계를 갖고 있다. 이 시각 체계는 주로 두 개의 다른 범주인 수동적 신호와 능동적 신호에 속하며, 따로 사용되거나 혹은 두 개가 같이 사용될 수도 있다.

2 ➡ 수동적 신호는 동물의 입장에서 아무런 에너지 소비도 필요로 하지 않는다. 이는 수동적 신호가 신체적인 모양의 일부라는 사실에 기인한다. 예를 들어 나비는 다양한 색과 무늬가 있다. 밝은 색의 안점, 줄무늬와 단색으로 나비들은 성과 나이, 종이 무엇인지 알릴 수 있다. 이러한 수동적 신호는 또한 다른 종의 생물들에게 나비가 먹을 수 없다거나 독이 있다는 것을 알려준다. 마찬가지로 나비와 같은 이유로 여러 종류의 새들은 특히 성을 구별하고 번식 활동을 개시하기 위해 여러 색의 무늬를 선보인다.

3 ➡ 능동적 신호 사용은 더 신체적이며, 사용하는 생물체의 에너지를 필요로 한다. 구애와 짝짓기 의식은 능동적 신호가 활기차게 드러나는 영역이다. 몇몇 곤충들은 짝을 유혹하기 위해 복잡한 공중 춤을 춘다. 밤에 개똥벌레들은 생식할 준비가 되어 있거나 이미 생식을 마쳤다는 것을 나타내기 위해 특정한 불빛을 발산한다. 또한 어떤 종의 새는 짝짓기 춤을 춘다. 수컷 초원뇌조는 암컷에게 자기와 짝짓기하도록 확신을 주기 위해 그 주변을 원형으로 뽐내며 걷거나 폴짝폴짝 뛰며 시간을 보낼 것이다. 새들은 또한 침입자의 접근 같은 위험을 무리에 경고하기 위해 날개를 치거나 갑자기 하늘로 날아 오름으로써 능동적인 신호를 사용한다. 이러한 시각적 경고는 빠르게 무리로 퍼지며, 다른 구성원들이 차례로 따라 하게 된다.

지시문: 지문을 간략하게 요약한 글의 첫 문장이 아래에 제시되어 있다. 지문의 가장 중요한 내용을 표현하는 세 개의 선택지를 골라 요약문을 완성하시오. 일부 문장은 지문에 제시되지 않았거나 지문의 지엽적인 내용을 나타내기 때문에 요약문에 포함되지 않는다. ***이 문제의 배점은 2점이다.***

새들과 곤충들은 의사소통을 위해 시각적 수단을 활용한다.

Ⓑ 능동적 신호는 다른 개체에 위험을 경고할 수 있을뿐 아니라 짝짓기하려는 의지와 능력을 보여줄 수 있다.
Ⓔ 수동적 신호는 전달자의 신체적 특징으로 전달된다.
Ⓕ 동물의 의사소통에는 두 개의 시각적 체계가 있다.

Ⓐ 의사소통의 시각적 형태는 매우 명백하다.
Ⓒ 새들은 같은 종에게 수동적 신호를 보내기 위해 매우 정교한 장식을 사용한다.
Ⓓ 개똥벌레는 언어를 표현하는 연속적인 빛의 번쩍임을 이용한다.

어휘 auditory adj 청각의 | sophisticated adj 정교한 | expenditure n 소비 | stripe n 줄무늬 | inedible adj 먹을 수 없는 | mating n 짝짓기 | ritual n 의식 | vigor n 활기, 힘 | intricate adj 복잡한 | airborne adj 공중의 | flock n 무리

Lesson 02 Recognizing Organization

---

06 동물 인지

1 ➡ 20세기 초반에 동물 심리학은 기본적인 사고 과정을 밝혀내 이후 인간의 발달된 지능을 설명하는 데 사용하고자 하는 실험으로 가득 차 있었다. 행동주의라고 알려진 심리학적 운동에서 유래된 이러한 실험들은 자극과 반응 사이의 관계를 알아내어 특정 행동을 분류하고자 했다. 이러한 실험들의 자료는 동물이 느끼지 않는다고 전제한 정신적, 감정적 상태의 영향은 무시한 채 행동을 과학적으로 설명하기 위해 사용되었다.

2 ➡ 그 후 1950년대 후반에 인지 심리학의 발전은 그것을 인간과 동물 모두의 행동을 설명하기 위한 지배적인 형태로 만들어 주었다. 인지 심리학은 행동주의와는 반대로 행동을 설명했는데 자극과 반응보다는 오히려 내부 상태와 그것의 결과에 대한 영향을 고려했기 때문이었다. 게다가 동물 행동은 인간의 지적인 과정에 대해 알려진 것과 비교하여 분석되었다. 이전에 행동주의자의 실험에 사용된 일반적인 동물은 새, 개, 그리고 쥐였다. 그러나 인지 심리학자들은 원숭이나 유인원 같은 영장류에 연구 초점을 두기로 선택했는데, 이는 이 동물들이 인간과 같이 발달한 변연계를 갖고 있으며 인간과 유전학적으로도 비슷했기 때문이었다. 이 공유된 신경학적 특징은 감정과 동기, 기억에 관련된 감정과 연관되어 있는데 가설적으로 연구자들에게 자신들의 이론을 인간 행동에 적용하는 데 더 합리적인 이유를 제공했다.

3 ➡ 인지 심리학이 동물 인지를 분석하는 표준이 된 이후로 인간 행동과 동물 행동 사이에 많은 유사점이 발견되었다. 동물 인지에 관한 연구는 언어와 기억, 문제 해결 영역에 초점이 맞춰져 왔다. 원숭이들은 인간과 비슷한 단기 기억 현상을 갖고 있다고 밝혀졌지만, 연구가 가장 많이 진척된 부분은 공간 기억과 관련된 연구이다. 동물은 특히 공간적으로 어디에 물체가 위치했는지 기억하는 능력이 있다. 이 현상이 일어나는 가장 대표적인 예는 다람쥐인데, 다람쥐는 먹이를 넓은 범위에 걸친 비밀 장소에 저장한다. 환경의 급격한 변화에도 불구하고 다람쥐는 공간 기억을 사용하여 먹이를 저장한 장소를 능숙하게 기억할 수 있다.

지시문: 지문을 간략하게 요약한 글의 첫 문장이 아래에 제시되어 있다. 지문의 가장 중요한 내용을 표현하는 세 개의 선택지를 골라 요약문을 완성하시오. 일부 문장은 지문에 제시되지 않았거나 지문의 지엽적인 내용을 나타내기 때문에 요약문에 포함되지 않는다. ***이 문제의 배점은 2점이다.***

동물의 사고 과정에 대한 발견은 인간의 인지 작용에 관한 과학적인 통찰력을 제공했다.

Ⓐ 인간의 사고 과정을 이해하려는 초기 시도들은 동물이 행동하는 방식을 분석함으로써 이루어졌다.
Ⓒ 인지 심리학은 심리학자들이 행동을 보고 설명한 방식을 뒤집었고, 실험에서 사용된 동물들마저 변경했다.
Ⓔ 인지 심리학은 주로 기억, 문제 해결, 언어에 주목하여 동물의 행동을 연구하는 데 선호되는 방법이다.

Ⓑ 행동 과학과 연구 기술의 모든 진보에도, 모든 행동을 완벽히 설명하는 것은 여전히 불가능하다.
Ⓓ 원숭이와 유인원은 인간과 대부분 똑같은 유전자 형질과 행동 양식을 공유한다.
Ⓕ 풍경의 커다란 변화는 정확한 공간 기억력을 갖지 않은 동물을 혼란에 빠뜨리고 장소를 인지하지 못하게 할 수 있다.

어휘 cognition n 인지 | be derived from ~에서 파생되다, 유래하다 | stimulus n 자극 | disregard v 경시하다, 무시하다 | predominant adj 우월한, 주된 | primate n 영장류 | ape n 원숭이, 유인원 | limbic adj 대뇌 변연계의 | neurological adj 신경학의 | trait n 특징 | hypothetically adv 가설적으로 | spatial adj 공간의 | radical adj 급격한

07

콜럼버스의 교역

1 ➡ 크리스토퍼 콜럼버스의 원정대가 카리브해에 도착한 이후 정복자들과 식민지 개척자들의 물결이 아메리카 대륙으로 밀려들었다. 유럽인들은 북미 원주민들과 교류하며 의도적이었든 우연이었든 많은 것을 교환했다. 이런 교환의 상당수는 실물 거래의 형태로 이루어졌다. 긍정적이든 부정적이든 이런 교환은 신세계와 구세계 모두에 극적인 영향을 주었다.

2 ➡ 콜럼버스는 자신의 스페인 후원자들을 위해 카리브해에서 많은 기념품을 가지고 돌아왔다. 그의 본래 임무는 아시아의 향신료 및 다른 풍부한 자원을 위한 새로운 무역 항로를 개척하는 것이었다. 기본적으로 그 임무 완수에는 실패했으나 스페인의 왕과 여왕은 그가 발견한 것에 관심을 보였다. 그 중에는 옥수수, 토마토, 감자, 호박, 초콜릿 등의 새로운 작물이 있었으며, 일부는 후에 유럽인들의 주식이 되었다. 그러나 아메리카 대륙에 대해서 스페인 사람들의 관심을 가장 많이 끌었던 것은 금전적 가치와 희소성을 지닌 금이었다. 스페인 정복자들은 소규모의 군대를 보내어 자신들이 소유권을 주장했던 땅을 탐사하고 그곳의 모든 금을 가져오게 했다. 반면에 유럽인들 또한 많은 농작물을 아메리카에 전해주었는데 가장 중요한 것은 사탕수수와 커피였다. 그들은 또한 닭, 돼지, 소를 포함한 많은 동물들을 가져왔으며 그중 아메리카 원주민들에게 가장 중요한 존재가 된 동물은 말이었다.

3 ➡ 하지만 이러한 교역에는 부정적인 면도 있었다. 유럽인들은 전쟁과 탄압을 가져왔으나 당시 자신들도 모르는 사이 검이나 총보다 훨씬 더 해로운 것을 전했으니, 바로 신종 질병이었다. 유럽은 때때로 마을 전체를 초토화한 여러 전염병 때문에 수 세기 동안 고통을 받았다. 시간이 흐르며 이러한 전염병 생존자들에게는 이 유행병들에 대한 면역력이 생겼다. 천연두, 인플루엔자, 콜레라, 티푸스, 페스트 등의 질병은 유럽에서도 여전히 심각한 문제였지만 이 질병들이 신세계로 퍼져 나가자 아메리카 원주민들은 초토화되었다. 사망률을 정확히 측정하는 것은 불가능하지만, 외국에서 들어온 질병이 130년 만에 캐나다에서 아르헨티나에 이르기까지 원주민들의 80~90퍼센트를 사망에 이르게 한 것으로 추정된다. 이런 질병들은 정복, 식민지화, 심지어 교역을 위한 짧은 만남을 통해서도 확산되었다. 이후 영국인들이 북아메리카를 식민지화하기 위해 왔을 때에는 아주 적은 수의 지역 주민들만 남아 있었다.

지시문: 지문을 간략하게 요약한 글의 첫 문장이 아래에 제시되어 있다. 지문의 가장 중요한 내용을 표현하는 세 개의 선택지를 골라 요약문을 완성하시오. 일부 문장은 지문에 제시되지 않았거나 지문의 지엽적인 내용을 나타내기 때문에 요약문에 포함되지 않는다. ***이 문제의 배점은 2점이다.***

크리스토퍼 콜럼버스는 신세계를 발견했을 때 유럽과 아메리카 대륙 간 교역의 장을 열었다.

Ⓑ 당시의 가장 중요한 교역품에는 아메리카 대륙에서 나온 금과 유럽에서 온 가축이 포함되어 있었다.
Ⓓ 이런 교환은 양 대륙에 긍정적, 부정적 방식으로 지속적인 영향을 주었다.
Ⓔ 그들의 의도와는 다르게 유럽인들은 원주민 인구의 대부분을 거의 몰살한 질병을 가져왔다.

Ⓐ 원정대의 주 목적은 아시아의 중요한 무역항을 군사력으로 장악하는 것이었으나 그 대륙에 도달하지 못했다.
Ⓒ 스페인 사람들은 중남미 전역에 군대를 보내 금을 찾아오게 했으며 많은 부족들을 정복했다.
Ⓕ 외국산 농작물, 가축, 기술과 재물들이 모두 북미 원주민들과의 사이에 교환되었다.

어휘 expedition n 원정대 | wave n 물결, 집단적 이동 | conqueror n 정복자 | colonist n 식민지 개척자 | interact with ~와 교류하다 | exchange v 교환하다 | intentionally adv 의도적으로 | dramatic adj 극적인 | souvenir n 기념품 | sponsor n 후원자 | trade route 무역로, 항로 | spice n 향신료 | essentially adv 본질적으로 | maize n 옥수수 | staple n 주식 | interest v 관심을 끌다 | sugar cane 사탕수수 | warfare n 전쟁 | oppression n 압제 | plague n 전염병 | immunity n 면역 | devastate v 완전히 파괴하다 | estimate v 추정하다 | conquest n 정복 | colonization n 식민지화 | fraction n 부분, 일부 | inhabitant n 거주자 | military takeover 군부 집권, 군사 쿠데타 | intent n 의도 | wipe out 말살하다, 파괴하다 | livestock n 가축

08

잉카 도로

1 ➡ 13세기에 잉카인들은 페루의 산악 지대에 문명을 처음 세웠다. 잉카 제국은 스페인 사람들이 그 지역을 정복하기 전까지 남미에서 가장 큰 제국이었다. 이 거대한 제국을 연결하여 더 수월하게 통치하기 위해 잉카인들은 당시 아메리카 대륙에서 가장 대규모 교통 체계를 이루었던 도로망을 형성했다. 수도인 쿠스코에서부터 잉카인들은 인접한 여러 문화를 통합했다. 일부는 평화롭게 합류했지만 군사력을 동원해 납득시켜야 했던 경우도 있었다. 잉카인들은 알렉산더 대왕이 자국에서 그랬던 것과 거의 비슷하게 제국 도처에서 잉카 고유의 문화를 강요했다. 잉카인들은 사람들에게 자기들의 언어인 퀘찬을 쓰도록 했으며 무엇보다 잉카의 태양신 인티를 숭배해야 했다. 이와 같이 그들은 체계적인 도로망이 고유의 문화를 유지하고 전파하는 데 도움이 된다고 생각했다.

2 ➡ 잉카의 도로망은 남북으로 이어지는 두 개의 주요 도로로 구성되어 있었으며 이 두 개의 도로는 서로 이어졌고 많은 작은 간선 도로를 통해 외부 지역과도 연결되어 있었다. 서부 도로는 주로 해안 평야를 따라 나 있었지만 사막 지역 근처에 있는 안데스 산맥의 작은 언덕 가까이로 곡선을 이루고 있었다. 동부 도로는 석재로 포장되어 있었으며 폭은 보통 1~3미터 정도로, 안데스 산맥의 높은 산골짜기와 초원을 통과해 나 있었다. 걸어서 하루 거리 간격만큼 떨어져 있는 탐보스라는 휴게소들이 도로를 따라 있었고, 그보다 큰 휴게소는 5~6일 정도의 간격마다 있었다. 여행객들은 그 석조 건물에서 휴식을 취하고 그곳에 보관되어 있는 음식으로 물자를 보충할 수 있었다.

3 ➡ 잉카인들은 바퀴를 개발한 적이 없었으며 말은 이후에 스페인인들에 의해 도입되었는데, 따라서 도로 위의 운송 수단은 사람과 라마였다. 그리하여 도로가 가파른 경사면을 가로지르는 경우 더 편하게 걸을 수 있도록 해주는 긴 층계가 있었다. 모래로 뒤덮인 지역에서는 낮은 벽을 세워 모래가 도로 위로 불어오는 것을 막았다. 그리고 도로가 가파른 지역을 지나가는 곳에는 더 높은 벽을 세워서 사람들이 추락하지 않도록 했다. 전성기 때 도로는 총 4만 킬로미터까지 뻗어나갔다. 하지만 1533년에 스페인이 침입한 이후 이 도로들은 더 이상 유지되지 않았다. 스페인 사람들은 도로의 일부 구간을 뜯어냈고 다른 구간은 그들이 타는 말의 금속 편자 때문에 상태가 악화되었다. 대부분의 도로 체계는 결국 자연적으로 매립되었지만 오늘날 그 도로의 가능한 한 많은 부분을 복구하기 위한 노력이 이루어지고 있다.

지시문: 지문을 간략하게 요약한 글의 첫 문장이 아래에 제시되어 있다. 지문의 가장 중요한 내용을 표현하는 세 개의 선택지를 골라 요약문을 완성하시오. 일부 문장은 지문에 제시되지 않았거나 지문의 지엽적인 내용을 나타내기 때문에 요약문에 포함되지 않는다. ***이 문제의 배점은 2점이다.***

잉카인들은 아메리카 대륙에서 제일 큰 제국을 연결하기 위해 대규모 도로망을 형성했다.

Ⓐ 이 도로 체계에는 제국을 북에서 남으로 가로지르는 두 개의 주요 도로가 있었다.
Ⓒ 잉카인들은 이 광범위한 도로망으로 언어와 종교를 전파해 제국을 통합하려고 했다.
Ⓔ 잉카인들은 도로를 건설하는 데 큰 정성을 들였으나 그것들은 이후에 유지되지 않았다.

Ⓑ 잉카인들은 알렉산더 대왕의 군사 작전을 본떠 인근의 부족을 정복했다.
Ⓓ 이 도로에는 특별한 휴게소가 있어 여행객들은 그곳에서 식량을 보충하고 밤에 잠을 잘 수 있었다
Ⓕ 오늘날에는 도로를 이전의 상태로 복구하기 위한 보존 활동이 계속 진행되고 있다.

어휘 civilization n 문명 | highland n 산악 지대 | empire n 제국 | vast adj 어마어마한, 방대한 | network of roads 도로망 | transportation system 교통 체계 | incorporate v 통합하다 | neighboring adj 인근의, 인접한 | join v 합류하다 | convince v 설득하다 | military force 군사력 | impose v 강요하다, 부과하다 | worship v 숭배하다 | systematic adj 체계적인 | outlying area 외곽 지역 | connect v 잇다, 연결하다 | make up ~을 이루다 | extensive adj 광범위한 | consist of ~로 구성되다 | curve v 곡선을 이루다 | foothill n 작은 언덕 | grassland n 초원 | pave v (길을) 포장하다 | space v 간격을 두다 | replenish v 보충하다 | steep adj 가파른 | campaign n 군사 작전 | restock v 다시 채우다, 보충하다 | foodstuff n 식량 | underway adj 진행 중인 | restore v 복구하다 | former adj 이전의

---

09 **박물관의 역사**

1 ➡ 17세기에 영국에서 처음으로 사용된 '박물관'이란 단어는 '뮤즈신의 자리'라는 뜻의 그리스 단어 'mouseion'에서 유래한 것이다. 박물관의 설립은 여러 가지 이유에서 시작되었는데, 문화를 보존하고 사회적, 정치적, 경제적 지위를 구축하려는 소망과 지식 추구의 소망 등이었다. 박물관의 기원은 다분히 서구의 것이지만 박물관이라는 아이디어가 아프리카나 아시아 등의 세계 다른 지역에서 없었던 것은 아니다.

2 ➡ 최초의 박물관은 오늘날 우리가 아는 것과 달랐으며 대신 도서관이나 학문적인 노력의 중심지에 더 가까웠다. 박물관은 본래 영감과 지적인 계몽의 원천이 되도록 지어졌다. 이집트에서 파라오 아크나톤은 동맹국과 그의 통치하에 있던 많은 피지배자들에게 받은 진상품과 선물을 보관하기 위해 거대한 도서관을 건축하게 했다. 이집트의 또 다른 통치자였던 프톨레마이오스왕은 기원전 3세기에 mouseion이라는 용어를 최초로 사용했다. 프톨레마이오스는 과학 분야의 연구를 진척시키기 위해 알렉산드리아 박물관을 세웠다. 전 세계에서 온 학자들은 몇 가지 과목의 예를 들자면 과학과 철학, 문학 같은 영역의 배움을 더 진척시키기 위해 알렉산드리아에 모였다.

3 ➡ 오늘날 우리에게 친숙한 유럽 유명 박물관들의 설립은 부유한 상인이나 귀족, 교회 고위 성직자의 개인적인 수집품에서 유래를 찾을 수 있다. 이는 상대보다 더 많이 수집하고자 다투는 영국, 프랑스, 스페인 왕족들 간의 경쟁 같은 형태가 되었다. 이런 수집품들은 결국 양이 엄청나게 늘어 그것들을 보관하기 위해 여러 동으로 구성된 건물 전체를 필요로 했다. 사실상 프랑스의 루브르처럼 왕궁 전체가 박물관 수집품 저장소로 완전히 양도되기도 했다. 17세기에 세계 무역이 시작되고 해외에서 온 물건이 관심의 대상이 되면서 부자들은 사람이 만든 것과 자연에서 얻은 물건을 보다 광범위한 규모로 전시하기 위한 개인 박물관을 건설하게 되었다.

4 ➡ 르네상스와 17세기 부자들의 수집품이 대중의 영역으로 옮겨온 것은 18세기가 되어서였다. 최초의 공공 박물관은 유럽에서 산업 혁명으로 급부상한 부유한 중산 계급과 함께 시작되었다. 이것은 일반 대중들에게 과학에 대한 궁금증과 예술에 관한 흥미를 불러일으켰다. 신세계에서 미국인들은 유럽을 따라잡기를 갈망했고, 그래서 1750년부터 박물관을 짓기 시작했다. 그러나 1814년이 되어서야 특별히 박물관 역할을 하기 위해 지어진 최초의 건축물인 필 박물관이 볼티모어에서 개관했다. 이곳의 예술과 자연 표본, 다양한 진기한 물건들은 오늘날 우리에게 친

숙한 현대 박물관에 영감을 주었다.

지시문: 지문을 간략하게 요약한 글의 첫 문장이 아래에 제시되어 있다. 지문의 가장 중요한 내용을 표현하는 세 개의 선택지를 골라 요약문을 완성하시오. 일부 문장은 지문에 제시되지 않았거나 지문의 지엽적인 내용을 나타내기 때문에 요약문에 포함되지 않는다. ***이 문제의 배점은 2점이다.***

고대부터 박물관은 경제적, 사회적, 지적 발전을 나타내 보였다.

Ⓒ 가장 초기의 박물관은 학술적 연구의 중심으로서의 기능 때문에 현대 박물관과는 사뭇 달랐다.
Ⓓ 유럽의 지배 계층은 그들의 개인 소장품을 전시했다.
Ⓕ 많은 수의 개인 소장품이 결국 공공 박물관의 일부가 되었다.

Ⓐ 최초의 박물관은 아시아에 건설되었고 서양에 그 개념이 전해졌다.
Ⓑ 초기에 박물관을 짓는 것은 설립자에게 경제적 지위를 부여할 수 있었다.
Ⓔ 르네상스는 대부분의 박물관이 사적인 영역에서 공적인 영역으로 옮겨 가게 했다.

어휘 evolve from ~로부터 발달하다 I come about 생기다, 일어나다 I dominantly adv 지배적으로 I inspiration n 영감 I intellectual adj 지적인 I enlightenment n 계몽 I tribute n 선물, 진상품 I ally n 동맹, 동맹국 I congregate v 모이다, 집합하다 I dignitary n 고위 인사 I house v 저장하다, 보관하다 I achievement n 성취, 성과 I promote v 촉진하다

10

초신성

1 ➡ 초신성은 어떤 별이 에너지를 다 소진하고 나서 자신의 무게를 이기지 못하고 붕괴된 후 일어나는 거대한 폭발로, 우주의 은하계 전반에 걸쳐 발생한다. 이 폭발로부터 초래되는 충격파는 폭발의 중심으로부터 별의 대기에 있는 물질을 함께 운반하며 퍼진다. 이 물질은 별의 생존 기간 동안 생성된 화학 원소가 풍부하고, 잔해는 우주 공간을 떠돌면서 새로운 별이나 행성의 근원 물질이 된다. 초신성은 드물지만 일부는 심지어 낮에도 발견될 수 있으며 오랜 기간 동안 빛이 날 수도 있다.

2 ➡ 별의 질량은 초신성이 폭발하게 될 것인지 아닌지의 여부를 결정한다. 모든 별은 중심부에서 열핵융합 반응의 형태로 수소를 헬륨으로 전환시키는 과정을 거친다. 이 반응은 강력한 열과 별의 중력이 수소 원자를 함께 끌어당겨 그것들을 헬륨 원자로 융합하면서 일어나게 되며, 엄청난 양의 에너지를 방출하게 된다. 일단 별들의 수소가 고갈되면 별은 헬륨이 탄소로 변환되는 탄소 생성 국면에 들어가게 된다. 헬륨이 다 없어지면 대부분의 별은 더 이상 열을 발하지 않는 점까지 천천히 식게 될 것이다. 그러나 별이 특히 클 때에는 헬륨이 모두 소모되어도 연소 주기가 끝나지 않는다. 더 큰 별들의 경우, 이들의 중량은 탄소로 된 중심이 줄어들게 만드는데, 탄소가 산소, 네온, 규소, 황, 그리고 궁극적으로 철로 변화할 수 있을 정도로 온도를 상승시킨다. 철은 별에서 찾을 수 있는 가장 안정된 원소 가운데 하나이며, 원자는 더 이상 융합하지 못한다. 별이 이 지점에 다다랐을 때 핵반응에 의해 생성된 압력은 원자 간의 인력 균형을 유지할 수 없으며, 이는 핵의 붕괴, 즉 내부 파열을 초래한다. 이 파열은 운동 에너지를 꾸준히 상승시켜 별이 초신성이 되어 외부를 향해 폭발하게 만든다.

3 ➡ 초신성에는 유형 1과 유형 2로 불리는 두 가지 주요 유형이 있다. 이 분류 기준은 초신성이 자기 빛의 스펙트럼 안으로 흡수하는 원소와 관련되어 있다. 간단히 말해 유형 2 초신성은 대기에 수소를 다량 포함하고 있으나 유형 1 초신성은 그렇지 않다. 각각의 유형에는 차이가 있다. 일반적으로 유형 1 초신성은 더 오래된 별에서 생기는 반면, 유형 2 초신성은 더 어린 별에서 생긴다. 유형 2 초신성은 비록 중심부에서 사라지기는 하지만 대기에 많은 양의 수소를 포함하고 있다.

4 ➡ 초신성은 거대한 별의 최종 진화 단계에 대한 연구에 중요한 정보를 제공하기 때문에 끊임없이 탐구되고 있다. 게다가 과학자들은 별부터 생명체까지 우주의 모든 것을 구성하고 있는 화학 원소들의 기원에 대한 실마리를 찾고 있다. 더불어 이 현상들은 별의 대기권에 의해 생성된 방사선 조사와 측정을 통해 우주의 지점들 간의 거리를 측정하는 데 도움을 준다.

지시문: 지문을 간략하게 요약한 글의 첫 문장이 아래에 제시되어 있다. 지문의 가장 중요한 내용을 표현하는 세 개의 선택지를 골라 요약문을 완성하시오. 일부 문장은 지문에 제시되지 않았거나 지문의 지엽적인 내용을 나타내기 때문에 요약문에 포함되지 않는다. ***이 문제의 배점은 2점이다.***

별들은 때로 폭발하여 초신성을 형성할 수 있고, 이것은 우주에 새로운 행성을 형성하는 물질을 확산시킨다.

Ⓐ 초신성은 별이 필요한 요소들을 갖춘 경우 발생할 수 있다.
Ⓓ 초신성의 두 가지 형태는 그들이 가지고 있는 수소의 양으로 분류될 수 있다.
Ⓕ 초신성은 우주의 기원과 별의 발달에 대한 이해를 도울 수 있다.

Ⓑ 초신성은 식물체에 비료가 되는 화학 원소들을 지니고 있다.
Ⓒ 별들은 폭발하여 초신성으로 변하고 나면 오랜 기간 동안 변화하지 않는다.
Ⓔ 모든 화학 원소는 별과 초신성의 폭발에서 비롯된다.

어휘 supernova **n** 초신성 | massive **adj** 대규모의, 거대한 | explosion **n** 폭발 | deplete **v** 써버리다, 고갈시키다 | debris **n** 파편, 잔해 | thermonuclear **adj** 열핵 반응의 | fusion **n** 융합 | gravitational **adj** 중력의, 인력의 | carbon **n** 탄소 | radiation **n** 복사, 방사, 발산 | exhaustion **n** 배출, 고갈 | ultimately **adv** 궁극적으로 | iron **n** 철 | stable **adj** 안정된, 견고한 | implode **v** 내파하다, 폭파하여 안쪽으로 붕괴하다 | kinetic **adj** 운동의 | plentiful **adj** 풍부한 | diminish **v** 축소하다, 줄이다 | evolutionary **adj** 진화의, 발달의

11

지진 공학

1 ➡ 보통 이상 규모의 지진을 견디도록 공학적으로 설계된 구조물이 반드시 극히 튼튼하거나 비용이 많이 들 필요는 없다. 과거에 사람들은 지진이 특히 자주 일어나는 지역에서 강한 지진에 견디려면 건물이 더 튼튼해야 하고, 자재 비용이 더 많이 들 것이라고 여겼다. 그러나 지진 공학에 종사하는 이들은 아주 다른 의견을 제시한다. 구조 공학과 토목 공학의 뚜렷한 하위 분류로서 지진 공학은 지진 하중을 받았을 때의 건축과 구조 성능에 관한 연구이다.

2 ➡ 지진 공학자들은 건물이나 다른 구조물을 설계할 때 근본적으로 두 가지 주요 목표를 가지고 있다. 첫째로 그들은 기반 시설(건물, 교각 등)과 지반 사이의 상호작용을 이해하려 노력함으로써 강력한 지진이 도시 지역에 미치는 잠재적 결과를 예측하려고 한다. 두 번째로 그들은 자신들의 이해와 예측을 바탕으로 상당한 지진 활동을 견뎌내고도 사람과 차량 등이 여전히 이용할 수 있는 구조물을 설계하고 건축하며 관리한다.

3 ➡ 지진 하중은 지진으로 발생한 흔들림이 구조물에 미치는 영향이다. 이러한 흔들림은 구조물의 접촉면이 땅과 닿는 곳이나 인접한 구조물과의 접촉면, 혹은 쓰나미 중력파와의 접촉면에서 일어난다. 다시 말해 흔들림이 구조물이 있는 곳에 영향을 미친다면, 그리고 그것이 근처 구조물과 어떤 식으로든 이어져 있다면, 그 근처 구조물 또한 그 흔들림에 영향을 받을 것이다. 지진에서 오는 지진 하중 강도는 여러 요인에 달려 있다. 즉 흔들림이 일어난 지점에서 예상 지진의 변수, 그 지점의 지질공학적인 변수, 구조물의 변수에 달려 있다. 이러한 요인 분석은 건축가들과 공학자들이 훨씬 더 안전하고 더 높은 건물을 건설할 수 있게 했다.

4 ➡ 고대 건축가들은 지진에 관해 운명론적인 시각을 가지고 있었다. 예를 들어 그리스인들은 지진이 바다의 신이자 그리스 신전의 가장 악명 높은 '땅을 뒤흔드는 신'인 포세이돈 같은 신들의 분노에서 온 직접적인 결과라고 믿었다. 그래서 이런 고대인들은 지진의 영향을 인간이 저지할 수 있다고 생각하지 않았다. 그러나 이제 지진에 대한 태도는 급격히 변했다. 지금은 지진 하중을 보완함으로써 구조물이 다양한 정도로 지진에 저항하는 능력을 갖추어 지어질 수 있다는 점이 알려져 있다.

5 ➡ 이제 주요 도시에 있는 대부분의 구조물은 지진 또는 내진 성능을 염두에 두고 건축된다. 지진 또는 내진 성능은 지진 활동이 일어나는 동안 혹은 그 이후에 구조물이 안전과 유용성을 유지하는 능력이다. 일부 혹은 전체가 붕괴되어 구조물 안팎의 사람들의 생명과 안전을 위험하게 하지 않는다면 구조물은 보통 '안전'하다고 여겨진다. 구조물이 지진 활동 이후에도 설계 목적에 맞게 운영 기능을 수행할 수 있다면 '유용하다'고 여겨진다. 예를 들어 지진이 일어난 이후 교각이 지어진 목적에 걸맞은 교통량을 지탱할 수 있다면 유용하다고 여겨질 것이다. 전 세계적으로 주요 건축법에서 시행되고 있는 현대 지진 공학의 기본 개념에 따르면 제대로 설계된 구조물은 '큰 지진'에도 끄떡 없을 것이다. 이 용어는 샌안드레아스 단층 가까이 위치한 캘리포니아주의 베이에어리어처럼 특히 취약한 지역에 대규모 지진이 일어날 가능성을 나타낸다.

6 ➡ 주요 지진 활동에도 견딜 수 있는 구조물을 가장 잘 지으려면 공학자들은 지진의 영향을 받는 개별 구조물에 관한 직접적인 피해와 관련해 실질적인 혹은 예상되는 지진 활동의 수량화된 수치를 알아야 한다. 이렇게 할 수 있는 가장 좋은 방법은 문제의 구조물의 상세 모델을 진동판에 올려보는 것이다. 진동판은 그 이름이 의미하는 그대로다. 지진의 흔들림을 그대로 모방할 수 있는 판이나 단 또는 대이며 기술자들은 이 흔들림을 보고 실제 상황의 가능성을 관찰하고 측정할 수 있다. 이 방법은 100년 이상 사용되었으며 더 안전한 건물 건설에 크게 도움이 되어 왔다.

7 ➡ 진동판의 활용은 내진 성능 분석 혹은 지진 분석의 작은 일부일 뿐이다. 지진 분석은 지진 공학의 중요한 지능적 도구이다. 그것은 구조물의 내진 성능을 더 잘 이해할 수 있도록 복잡한 주제들을 다루기 쉬운 더 작은 부분으로 분할한다. 공식적인 공학 개념의 지진 분석은 학문 분야에서 상대적으로 최근에 생겨난 개념이다. 일반적으로 지진 분석은 구조 역학이라는 체계에 근거하며 이는 지진 하중에 노출된 구조물의 작용을 말한다.

지시문: 지문을 간략하게 요약한 글의 첫 문장이 아래에 제시되어 있다. 지문의 가장 중요한 내용을 표현하는 세 개의 선택지를 골라 요약문을 완성하시오. 일부 문장은 지문에 제시되지 않았거나 지문의 지엽적인 내용을 나타내기 때문에 요약문에 포함되지 않는다. ***이 문제의 배점은 2점이다.***

지진 공학은 지진 하중에 영향을 받는 구조물에 관한 연구이다.

Ⓐ 지진 하중은 다양한 요인에 의해 결정되는 구조물에 미치는 지진의 영향이다.
Ⓒ 내진 성능은 건물들이 지진 후에 안전성과 유용성을 얼마나 잘 유지할 수 있는지를 말한다.
Ⓕ 공학자들은 실제 지진이 초래할 수 있는 결과를 예측하기 위해 진동판을 사용한다.

Ⓑ 지진으로 인한 흔들림은 구조물과 땅을 연결하는 표면에서 발생한다.
Ⓓ 고대인들은 지진이 포세이돈 같은 포악한 신이 내리는 치명적인 형벌이라고 생각했다.
Ⓔ 공학자들은 지진에 영향을 받는 구조물의 역학을 분석하기 위해 가상 현실을 이용한다.

어휘 engineering n 공학(기술) | withstand v 견뎌내다 | magnitude n 지진 규모 | sturdy adj 튼튼한 | distinct adj 뚜렷한, 분명한 | subset n 부분 집합 | civil engineering 토목 공학 | infrastructure n 사회 기반 시설 | seismic loading 지진 하중 | agitation n 불안, 동요, 뒤흔들림 | adjacent adj 인접한 | tsunami n 쓰나미 | severity n 강도, 격렬함, 혹독함 | parameter n 한도, 변수 | fatalistic adj 운명론적인 | wrath n 격노 | notorious adj 악명 높은 | serviceable adj 쓸 만한 | collapse v 무너지다 | implement v 시행하다 | likelihood n 가능성 | vulnerable adj 취약한 | quantify v 수량화하다 | gauge v 측정하다 | seismic analysis 지진 분석

---

12 **기후 변화와 농업의 관계**

1 ➡ 기후 변화와 인간의 농업 활동은 서로 밀접히 관련된 두 가지 과정인데, 이 과정들은 사실상 분리가 불가능하고 전 세계적 규모로 일어난다. 이 밀접한 관계는 많은 사람들을 불안하게 했는데, 이는 지구 온난화가 농업에 영향을 미치는 조건들에 큰 영향을 미칠 것이라고 현재 예상되기 때문이다. 이런 조건들에는 기온, 빙하 감소, 강수량, 이산화탄소 수치 및 이러한 다양한 요인들 사이에 알려진 혹은 알려지지 않은 상호작용들이 포함된다. 이런 모든 조건들은 가축뿐만 아니라 인류를 위해 충분한 식량을 생산하기 위한 지구의 능력을 결정하기 때문에 중요하다. 기후 변화가 농업 활동에 미치는 전반적인 영향은 이러한 영향들의 조화에 크게 의존할 것이다. 그래서 기후 변화가 농업 활동에 미치는 영향에 대한 평가는 농업 생산을 극대화하기 위한 농업 기술을 예측하고 조정하는 데 도움을 줄 수 있다.

2 ➡ 동시에 농업 활동은 기후 변화에 중요한 영향을 초래하는 것으로 나타났다. 이는 이산화탄소뿐 아니라 아산화질소와 메탄 같은 다른 온실가스의 생산과 배출을 통해 주로 발생한다. 게다가 농업은 지구의 토양 피층을 바꾼다. 이것은 태양으로부터 열기와 빛을 흡수하거나 반사하는 지구의 능력을 바꿀 수 있다. 사막화와 산림 벌채와 같은 피층의 변화는 석탄, 석유, 천연가스 같은 화석 연료의 사용과 함께 이산화탄소 수치에 영향을 미치는 주요 원인들이다. 그리고 가축 사육, 벼 경작 등의 농업 활동 또한 지구 대기에 아산화질소와 메탄의 수치를 증가시킨다.

3 ➡ 유전자 변형 생물체, 관개 시스템과 개량된 다양한 작물 같은 기술 발전에도 불구하고 날씨는 식량이 재배되는 토양의 특성과 더불어 농업 생산에 여전히 중요한 역할을 한다. 농업에 대한 기후 조건의 영향은 지구 기후 패턴보다는 지역 기후의 변수에 더욱 직접적으로 관계가 있다. 지구의 평균 표면 온도는 지난 100년간 화씨 1도만큼 상승했다. 이것이 큰 상승처럼 들리지 않을지라도 그 영향은 상당하며 체감되고 있다. 따라서 농학자들, 즉 인류가 사용할 식물의 이용을 전문으로 연구하는 과학자들은 어떤 평가이든 지역마다 개별적으로 고려되어야 한다고 생각한다.

4 ➡ 반면 기후 변화의 위협에도 불구하고 농산물 무역은 최근 실제로 증가했다. 무역은 현재 국내 수준뿐 아니라 다른 국가에의 수출에 있어서도 상당한 양의 식량을 제공한다. 무역과 안보의 국제적 측면을 식량 문제에 적용해서 보면 전 세계적으로 기후 변화가 농업에 미치는 영향 또한 고려할 필요성을 암시한다.

5 ➡ '사이언스'지에 게재된 연구에 따르면 기후 변화 때문에 아프리카 남부는 2030년경 주요 작물인 옥수수에서 30퍼센트 이상의 피해를 볼 수 있고 쌀, 기장, 옥수수 같은 남아시아 지역 주요 산물의 손실은 10퍼센트 이상 될 수 있다고 한다. 이런 대형 사건은 수백만 명에게 영향을 미칠 것이다. 2001 기후 변화에 관한 정부 간 패널의 제3차 평가보고서는 최빈국들이 기후 변화의 영향에 가장 심한 타격을 입게 될 것이라고 했다. 그들은 대부분의 열대 및 아열대 지역에서 작물 수확량이 감소한 것은 물의 이용이 점차 용이하지 않은 점과 새로운 혹은 변화된 해충 종들의 출현 때문일 것이라고 결론 내린다. 현재 아프리카와 라틴 아메리카에서 강수에 의존하는 작물은 최대 온도 저항력에 거의 달해 있어서 심지어 작은 기후 변화에도 생산량은 급격히 감소할 것으로 보인다. 생산성 손실에 대한 예상치는 21세기 동안 대략 30퍼센트 정도가 될 것이다. 이 손실은 의심할 여지 없이 지구상에 있는 모든 국가들이 느끼게 될 것이다.

6 ➡ 장기적으로 볼 때 기후 변화는 수많은 방식으로 농업 활동에 영향을 미친다. 명백히 기후 변화는 양적, 질적 두 가지 측면 모두에서 생산성 감소를 의미할 수 있다. 또한 기후 변화는 농업 방식에 영향을 미칠 수 있는데 특히 물(관개 시스템)과 제초제, 살충제와 비료 사용의 경우이다. 토양 배수, 토양 침식 및 작물의 다양성 감소 등이 일어나는 빈도와 강도 같은 환경적 영향은 매우 분명해질 것이다. 예상되는 다른 변화들로는 인간과 다소 경쟁 관계에 접어들게 되면서 발생하는 다른 유기체들의 환경 적응이 있다. 게다가 인류는 홍수에 견디는 쌀이나 염분에 강한 밀과 같이 더욱 경쟁력 있는 작물을 개발하는 것이 시급함을 알게 될 것이다.

지시문: 지문을 간략하게 요약한 글의 첫 문장이 아래에 제시되어 있다. 지문의 가장 중요한 내용을 표현하는 세 개의 선택지를 골라 요약문을 완성하시오. 일부 문장은 지문에 제시되지 않았거나 지문의 지엽적인 내용을 나타내기 때문에 요약문에 포함되지 않는다. ***이 문제의 배점은 2점이다.***

지구 온난화가 농업에 미치는 영향에 대한 우려는 기후 변화와 인간의 농업 활동이 밀접하게 연관된 두 가지 과정임을 깨닫게 해 주었다.

Ⓑ 농업은 토양 피층의 변화 및 이산화탄소, 아산화질소, 메탄 같은 온실가스 생산과 배출을 통해 기후에 영향을 미친다.
Ⓒ 기온, 강수량, 이산화탄소 수치의 변화 및 상호작용과 함께 지구 온난화가 농업에 크게 영향을 미칠 것으로 예상된다.
Ⓕ 장기적으로 볼 때 농업 생산성의 양적 및 질적인 감소, 농업 방식의 변화, 다른 환경적 영향들은 기후 변화 때문일 것이다.

Ⓐ 나무들이 기온을 낮출 뿐만 아니라 이산화탄소 수치를 줄일 수 있기 때문에 산림 벌채는 사막화보다 기후 변화에 더 큰 부정적 영향을 미친다.

Ⓓ 기후 변화로 아프리카 남부는 2030년경 주요 작물의 30퍼센트 이상을 잃게 되고 남아시아는 지역 주요 산물의 10퍼센트를 잃게 될 것으로 예상된다.

Ⓔ 2001 기후 변화에 관한 정부 간 패널의 제3차 평가보고서에 의하면 최빈국들이 기후 변화에 가장 크게 영향을 받을 것이다.

어휘 agricultural adj 농업의 I interrelated adj 서로 관계가 있는 I virtually adv 사실상 I be projected to ~할 것으로 예상된다 I impact n 영향 I glacial adj 빙하의 I runoff n 감소, 유출 I precipitation n 강수(량) I carbon dioxide 이산화탄소 I factor n 요인 I domesticated animal 가축 I overall adj 전반적인 I assessment n 평가 I anticipate v 예상하다 I maximize v 최대화하다 I primarily adv 주로 I alter v 바꾸다 I absorb v 흡수하다 I desertification n 사막화 I deforestation n 산림 벌채 I fossil fuel 화석 연료 I coal n 석탄 I petroleum n 석유 I natural gas 천연가스 I livestock n 가축 I irrigation n 관개 I property n 특성 I variable n 변수 I sizeable adj 상당한, 꽤 큰 I agronomist n 농경학자 I specialize in ~을 전문으로 하다 I utilization n 이용 I export n 수출 I security n 안보 I maize n 옥수수 I staple n 주요 산물 I incidence n 발생률 I pest n 해충 I herbicide n 제초제 I insecticide n 살충제 I fertilizer n 비료 I frequency n 빈도 I intensity n 세기 I soil drainage 토양 배수 I soil erosion 토양 침식

Test

본서 I P. 242

이집트 왕조 설립

1 ➡ 나일강 계곡은 태곳적부터 이집트 사회의 핵심에 주거지를 제공했다. 하지만 그곳의 주변 지역이 오늘날 그러한 것처럼 항상 황량해 보였던 것은 아니었다. 그 지역은 훨씬 덜 건조했으며 많은 부분은 완만하게 경사진 모래 언덕이 아니라 나무가 흩어져 있는 초원이었다. 그 지역의 초기 정착민들은 약 12만년 전 그 지역을 돌아다니던 수렵 채집인이었다. 하지만 기후가 변하면서 끊임없는 더위와 부족한 강수량이 초기 이집트인들을 강변을 따라 모이게 만들었다. 이 집단들이 정착하기 시작하자 그들은 강을 따라 최초의 문화들을 형성하며 생존을 위해 농업에 의존하기 시작했다. 이런 초기 사회 중 가장 중요한 것은 나일강 서쪽 둑의 사막에서 기원한 바다리였다. 그들은 도자기와 석기의 생산과 구리를 사용하는 데 뛰어났다.

2 ➡ 바다리 이후에 나카다 문화가 등장했는데, 그것은 그 계곡의 모든 사람과 자원에 통제력을 행사하는 최초의 문명으로 성장했다. 그들의 첫 수도는 히에라콘폴리스에 세워졌고 그들은 자신들의 세력을 강 북쪽으로 확장했다. 이것은 그들을 중동에서 발달하고 있는 다른 사회와 접하게 했다. 그들은 남쪽으로 훗날 그들과 널리 무역한 누비아와 에티오피아 사람들도 접했다. 천 년 넘게 그들은 그들의 증가하는 세력과 상류층을 반영하는 다양한 제품들을 생산하는 사회로 발달했다. 그들은 또한 상형문자로 발달할 표어문자 체계를 발전시키기 시작했고 흰색 왕관과 매를 왕권의 상징으로 정했다.

3 ➡ 이집트의 제1왕조는 파라오 나르메르가 약 기원전 3150년에 상이집트와 하이집트를 통일하면서 설립되었다. 그는 멤피스를 수도로 삼았는데 이것은 나일 삼각주의 농업 노동 인구와 중동으로 향하는 귀중한 무역로를 둘 다 통제할 수 있게 했다. 뒤를 이은 통치자들의 증가하는 부와 권력은 파라오들의 죽음 후에 그들을 기념하기 위해 세워진 구조물들에서 볼 수 있다. 이것들은 아비도스에 건설된 마스타바 분묘로 알려진 거대한 계단 피라미드들을 포함했다. 그만큼 많은 시간, 자원과 노동력을 묘지 준비에 투자했다는 것은 그들의 사회가 얼마나 안정적으로 바뀌었는지를 보여주지만 그것들은 이집트인들의 가장 놀라운 업적은 아니었다. 이집트인들이 지은 가장 거대한 구조물들은 그 다음 시대에 등장했다.

1. 1단락에 따르면, 다음 중 나일강 계곡에 대해 사실이 아닌 것은 무엇인가?

Ⓐ 계곡 근처 삼림 지대는 황량한 지역으로 바뀌었다.
Ⓑ 거주민들은 기후 변화로 인해 그 지역을 떠날 수 밖에 없었다.
Ⓒ 농업은 사람들이 강가에 모이면서 발달했다.
Ⓓ 그 지역의 가장 초기 정착민들은 사냥과 채집을 하면서 살았다.

2. 2단락에 따르면, 다음 중 나카다 문화에 관해 사실인 것은 무엇인가?

Ⓐ 숲에 둘러싸인 외진 지역에 정착했다.
Ⓑ 왕실 문장은 흰색 왕관과 매였다.
Ⓒ 수도를 다시 히에라콘폴리스로 옮겼다.
Ⓓ 언어는 중동에서 빌려온 것이었다.

3. 2단락의 단어 'encountered(접했다)'와 의미상 가장 가까운 것은

Ⓐ 통제했다
Ⓑ 지배했다
Ⓒ 만났다
Ⓓ 이해시켰다

4. 3단락에 따르면, 이집트의 첫 번째 왕조에 대해 추론 가능한 것은 무엇인가?

Ⓐ 상이집트와 하이집트 간의 지역 갈등으로 끝났다.
Ⓑ 백성들은 이 시기에 건축 기술을 발달시켰다.
Ⓒ 중동과의 무역이 가장 큰 수입원이었다.
Ⓓ 나르메르는 이 왕조의 마지막 파라오였다.

4 ➡ 고왕국 시대에 기술, 건축과 예술에 중요한 진보가 있었는데, 그것은 갈수록 증가하는 농업 생산량과 그에 동일하게 증가하는 인구로 인해 가능했다. 기자의 피라미드들과 스핑크스도 그때 건축되었고 그것들은 신왕(神王)의 영광과 권력의 중앙 집권을 표현했다. 파라오의 대변인인 재상의 지시 하에 법과 질서를 확고하게 하기 위해 사법 제도가 세워졌고, 국가의 재정을 충원하기 위해 세금을 징수했고 농업을 개선할 관개 계획들이 착수되었고, 농민들은 다양한 작업에 일하기 위해 동원되었다. 이 당시에 교육도 번성했고 서기관과 관료의 새로운 계급이 커져서 파라오를 섬겼다.

5 ➡ 파라오는 이런 상류층과 자신의 추종자들에게 증가하는 양의 토지를 내어주었고 죽음 후에도 자신의 숭배를 확실히 하기 위해 묘지를 내어주었다. [■A] 이런 후함은 경제를 악화시켰고 수 세기 후에 중앙 집권은 다른 지역 지도자들이 군주에 저항하는 지점까지 약화되었다. [■B] 이것은 기원전 2200년에 시작된 일련의 극심한 가뭄과 함께 왕국을 불안정하게 만들었고 왕국은 중간기라고 불리는 140년 동안 지속된 갈등과 기근의 시기로 빠져들었다. [■C] 왕국은 이 시기에 분열되었는데 그것은 지역 지도자들과 그들의 개별적인 왕국이 번성할 수 있도록 해주었다. 그리고 중앙 권력에 대한 존중이 완전히 결여되어 있어서 대다수의 묘지와 피라미드들이 이때 약탈당했다. [■D]

6 ➡ 결국 이 분열된 조각들은 멘투호테프 2세의 통치 하에 재결합되어 중왕국이 세워졌다. 그와 그의 계승자들은 누비아에서 잃은 영토를 되찾았고, 팔레스타인을 공격했고 리비아를 제압해 이집트의 국경을 지켰다. 이 시기에는 고왕국 시대의 실용적이고 종교적인 목적의 글쓰기 대신에 오락을 위한 문학을 생산하기 위한 글쓰기와 새로운 양식의 조각상을 포함하는 문화적 발달도 있었다. 후자의 다수는 여성을 위해 의뢰되었기 때문에 이것은 개인 재산 뿐만 아니라 어느 정도의 성평등이 형성됐다는 것을 나타낸다. 하지만 인구는 농업 생산량을 추월하기 시작했고 기근과 외부 압력은 왕국의 붕괴로 이어졌다. 이것은 이집트에 일종의 무너졌다가 회복하는 패턴을 형성했고 마지막 왕조가 끝내 로마인들에게 정복될 때까지 계속되었다.

5. 3단락의 단어 'These(이것들)'가 가리키는 것은

Ⓐ 통치자들
Ⓑ 구조물들
Ⓒ 죽음들
Ⓓ 피라미드들

6. **4단락에 따르면, 다음 중 고왕국에 관해 사실인 것은 무엇인가?**

Ⓐ 농업을 발달시키기 위해 관개 시설들이 지어졌거나 확장되었다.
Ⓑ 삼림 파괴의 속도는 농지를 확장하기 위해 가속화되었다.
Ⓒ 파라오들은 지역 정부들에게 그들의 권력을 양도했다.
Ⓓ 농민들은 보호를 받는 대신 그들의 귀족에게 공물을 바쳤다.

7. **다음 중 지문에 음영 표시된 문장의 핵심 정보를 가장 잘 표현한 문장은 무엇인가? 오답은 의미를 크게 왜곡하거나 핵심 정보를 누락하고 있다.**

Ⓐ 왕국이 내부 갈등과 극심한 기근으로 와해된 후에 중간기라는 새로운 시기가 기원전 약 2200년에 시작되었다.
Ⓑ 고왕국이 가난과 굶주림 때문에 기원전 약 2200년에 멸망했기 때문에 중간기는 심각한 가뭄을 해결하려고 노력했다.
Ⓒ 비록 가뭄과 같은 자연재해가 기원전 약 2200년에 왕국을 휩쓸었지만 중간기는 그 후로부터 140년 동안 건재했다.
Ⓓ 기원전 약 2200년에 발생한 심각한 가뭄에 더하여 지역 지도자들의 파라오에 대한 불복종은 왕국 몰락의 결과를 낳았고, 이는 불화와 굶주림의 중간기로 이어졌다.

8. **다음 중 6단락에서 언급되지 않은 것은**

Ⓐ 분열된 왕국들은 멘투호테프 2세에 의해 하나로 통일되었다
Ⓑ 중왕국은 국방을 강화하는 데 집중했다
Ⓒ 이집트의 마지막 왕조는 반복되는 내전으로 인해 몰락했다
Ⓓ 중왕국 때에는 성평등이 달성되었다

9. 지문에 다음 문장이 들어갈 수 있는 위치를 나타내는 네 개의 사각형 [■]을 확인하시오.

왕국은 이 시기에 분열되었는데 그것은 지역 지도자들과 그들의 개별적인 왕국이 번성할 수 있도록 해주었다.

이 문장이 들어가기에 가장 적합한 곳은? [■C]

10. **지시문:** 지문을 간략하게 요약한 글의 첫 문장이 아래 제시되어 있다. 지문의 가장 중요한 내용을 표현하는 세 개의 선택지를 골라 요약문을 완성하시오. 일부 문장들은 지문에 제시되지 않았거나 지문의 지엽적인 내용을 나타내기 때문에 요약문에 포함되지 않는다. ***이 문제의 배점은 2점이다.***

고대 이집트 문명은 마지막 왕조가 멸망할 때까지 나일강 계곡 지역에서 번성했다.

Ⓐ 상이집트와 하이집트를 통일시킨 첫 번째 왕조는 농업과 무역을 통제한 나르메르에 의해 설립되었다.
Ⓒ 고왕국은 중앙 집권화된 왕권을 기반으로 기술, 건축과 예술에 있어서 놀라운 발전을 이루어냈다.
Ⓓ 불안정해졌던 왕국 영토의 조각들은 중왕국으로 통일되었지만 마지막 왕조는 로마 점령 하에 끝났다.

Ⓑ 고대 사람들이 사후 세계를 강력하게 믿었기 때문에 기자의 피라미드들은 이집트의 파라오들을 위한 왕릉으로 건설되었다.
Ⓔ 바다리 문화는 나일강 서쪽에서 발달했고 도자기와 석기로 유명하다.
Ⓕ 멘투호테프 2세는 자신의 왕권을 회복하고 중앙 집권화된 정부를 세우기 위해 강한 군사적 힘을 키웠다.

어휘 shelter n 피신처, 보호소 I immemorial adj 태곳적부터의 I surroundings n 환경 I desolate adj 황량한, 적막한 I arid adj 매우 건조한 I dot v 여기저기 흩어져 있다, 산재하다 I grassland n 풀밭, 초원 I rolling adj 완만하게 경사진 I sand dune 사구 I inhabitant n 주민 I roam v 돌아다니다, 방랑하다 I climate n 기후 I shift v 이동하다, 바꾸다 I relentless adj 끈질긴, 수그러들지 않는 I rainfall n 강우 I cluster v 무리를 이루다, 모이다 I bank n 둑, 제방 I sedentary adj 한 곳에 머물러 사는 I rely v 의존하다 I agriculture n 농업 I survival n 생존 I originate v 기원하다 I desert n 사막 I ceramic n 도자기 I stone tool 석기 I copper n 구리 I civilization n 문명 I wield v 행사하다, 휘두르다 I entire adj 전체의 I resource n 자원 I capital n 수도 I extend v 확장하다 I contact n 접촉 I encounter v 맞닥뜨리다 I trade v 교역하다 I extensively adv 널리, 광범위하게 I manufacture v 생산하다, 만들어 내다 I reflect v 반영하다 I logographic adj 어표(語標; 한 단어나 구를 나타내는 기호 또는 상징)의 I evolve v 진화하다, 발달하다 I hieroglyphics n 상형문자로 된 글 I establish v 설립하다, 정하다 I falcon n 매 I royal adj 국왕의 I dynasty n 왕조 I unite v 통합하다, 통일하다 I valuable adj 가치 있는 I trade route 교역로 I subsequent adj 그 다음의, 차후의 I ruler n 지도자 I erect v 세우다 I memorialize v 기념하다, 추모하다 I tomb n 무덤 I construct v 건설하다 I devote v 바치다, 헌신하다 I mortuary n 시체 안치소 I arrangement n 준비, 마련 I stable adj 안정적인 I remarkable adj 놀라운, 굉장한 I achievement n 업적 I colossal adj 거대한, 엄청난 I appear v 나타나다 I era n 시대 I significant adj 중요한, 큰 I architecture n 건축 I equally adv 똑같이, 동일하게 I population n 인구 I express v 표현하다 I centralization n 중앙 집권 I spokesperson n 대변인 I vizier n 고관, 재상 I justice system 사법 제도 I secure v 획득하다, 확보하다 I tax n 세금 I collect v 징수하다 I finance v 자금을 대다 I irrigation n 관개 I undertake v 착수하다 I improve v 향상하다 I peasant n 소작농 I mobilize v 동원하다 I various adj 다양한 I flourish v 번창하다, 잘 자라다 I scribe n 필경사 I official n 관료 I serve v 시중을 들다 I grant v 승인하다, 허락하다 I cult n 숭배 I burial site 매장지 I ensure v 반드시 ~하게 하다, 보장하다 I worship n 숭배, 예배 I deteriorate v 악화되다, 더 나빠지다 I powerbase n 세력 기반 I erode v 약화하다, 무너지다 I defy v 반항하다, 저항하다 I monarch n 군주 I combine v 합치다 I severe adj 심각한 I drought n 가뭄 I destabilize v 불안정하게 만들다 I plummet v 급락하다, 곤두박질하다 I conflict n 갈등 I famine n 기근 I last v 지속되다 I Intermediate Period 중간기 I fragment v 부서지다, 해체되다 I thrive v 번성하다 I respect n 존중, 존경 I authority n 지휘권, 권위 I tomb complex 무덤 단지, 고분 I loot v 훔치다, 약탈하다 I recombine v 다시 결합하다 I rule n 통치 I successor n 후임자, 계승자 I regain v 되찾다 I territory n 영토 I attack v 공격하다 I subdue v 진압하다, 억누르다 I border n 국경 I practical adj 현실적인 I religious adj 종교의 I statue n 조각상 I commission v 의뢰하다, 주문하다 I gender equality 성평등 I private adj 개인의, 개인적인 I outstrip v 앞지르다, 앞서다 I pressure n 압박 I downfall n 몰락 I kingdom n 제국 I collapse v 무너지다 I recover v 회복하다 I repeat v 반복하다 I conquer v 정복하다

심해에서의 생존 적응

1 ➡ 외해에 대해서 이야기할 때, 물의 한 구획을 표면부터 바닥에 있는 퇴적층에 이르는 수직의 기둥으로 생각하면 편리하다. 이 '물 기둥'이라는 개념이 물을 화학적, 물리적, 혹은 생물학적으로 구분하는 것을 용이하게 해주며, 심해의 물기둥은 보통 5개의 기본 층으로 나뉘는데, 그 중 위의 두 층은 물이 오염이나 침전물이 없을 때 태양빛이 그 물 속으로 얼마나 멀리 투과할 수 있는지에 따라 결정된다. 맨 위층은 표해수대(表海水帶)라고 불리며, 해심 200미터까지 이어진다. 그곳에는 식물이 존재할 수 있을 정도의 충분한 빛이 있으며 산소가 풍부하다. 두 번째 층은 중층표영대(中層漂泳帶)라고 불리며, 해심 1000미터까지 이어진다. 이곳은 약광층이라고도 불리는데, 이는 이용할 수 있는 빛은 존재하지만 희미할 뿐 아니라 깊이가 깊어질수록 아무것도 보이지 않을 정도로 점점 더 어두워지기 때문이다. 존재하는 산소의 양 역시 그 바로 위의 층보다 훨씬 더 적다.

2 ➡ 중층표영대에 사는 종들은 그들의 섭식 행동에 따라 세 범주로 구분된다. 잔사식 동물로 분류되는 종들은 시체나 배설물, 벗겨진 허물, 외골격 등과 같이 표해수대에서 떠내려온 잔여 유기물을 먹고 산다. 다른 종들은 초식 동물로 낮 동안에는 비교적 안전한 중층표영대에 숨어 지내다가 밤에 되면 먹이를 구하기 위해 표면 가까이 이동한

11. 다음 중 지문에 음영 표시된 문장의 핵심 정보를 가장 잘 표현한 문장은 무엇인가? 오답은 의미를 크게 왜곡하거나 핵심 정보를 누락하고 있다.

Ⓐ 여러 수층의 깊이는 빛이 얼마나 깊이 투과될 수 있는지를 결정하는 물의 투명도에 따라 달라진다.
Ⓑ 물 기둥은 각 수층이 띠는 물리적 속성에 따라 해양을 수직으로 구분하여 설명하기 위해 만들어진 용어이다.
Ⓒ 물 기둥은 보통 5개의 층으로 구성되며, 그 중 위의 두 층은 태양빛이 물에 도달하는 깊이에 의해 결정된다.
Ⓓ 수층은 화학적, 물리적, 생물학적 특성에 따라 다르게 배열되며, 해양은 보통 5개의 층으로 나뉘어져 있다.

12. 다음 중 2단락에서 추론 가능한 것은 무엇인가?

Ⓐ 중층표영대에 사는 대부분의 종들은 잔여 유기물을 먹기 위해 수직으로 이동한다.
Ⓑ 중층표영대는 먹을 것이 더 풍부하지는 않지만, 그 위의 표해수대보다는 살기가 더 안전하다.
Ⓒ 중층표영대는 제한된 양의 빛으로 인해 식물이 살지 않는다.
Ⓓ 표해수대에서 만들어지는 먹이 중 많은 양이 밑의 중층표영대로 내려온다.

다. 육식을 하며 다른 두 종을 먹고 사는 종도 있는데 이들은 대부분 중층표영대에서 지내며, 밤에는 위로 올라오기도 한다. 브리슬마우스, 오징어, 갑오징어, 울프일, 황새치 및 기타 반심해 생물들이 여기에 포함된다.

3 ➡ 중층표영대에서의 삶은 힘들고, 이 구역에 사는 생물들은 그들의 환경에 적응해야만 했다. 이 적응 중 대부분은 먹이를 잡는 것이나 다른 생물의 먹이가 되는 것을 피하는 것과 연관이 있다. 흔한 신체적 적응에는 매우 크고 민감한 눈을 지니는 것이나, 위장술, 생체 발광 등이 있다. 크고 민감한 눈은 이용할 수 있는 최대한의 빛을 모아서 생명체가 위협을 감지하고 피할 수 있게 해주며, 먹이를 발견할 수 있도록 해준다. 중층표영대의 생물들이 사용하는 위장술은 세 가지 유형 내에서 다양하다. 일부 동물들은 주변의 어두운 물 색깔과 잘 섞일 수 있도록 균일하게 어두운 몸체를 갖고 있다. 어떤 동물들은 완전히 색채를 띠지 않는 대신에 반투명한 몸체를 갖고 있다. 이것은 그들이 내부 장기를 제외하고는 보이지 않는다는 것인데, 이는 포식자들이 그것들이 무엇인지 알아보기가 힘들다는 것을 의미한다. 마지막 유형의 위장술은 생물의 윤곽을 모호하게 만드는 얼룩덜룩한 겉모습을 갖는 것이다.

4 ➡ 중층표영대에 사는 모든 범주의 생물들에게 공통적으로 발견되는 적응 형태는 생체 발광, 즉 몸 안에서 빛을 발생시키는 것이다. 빛은 발광기라고 불리는 특별한 기관에서 발생되는데, 이 발광기는 자극을 받으면 화학적인 반응을 통해 빛을 생산해 내는 박테리아를 가지고 있다. 다른 동물들은 빛을 만들어내는 세포인 발광포를 기관 내에 가지고 있다. 두 경우 모두, 열을 발생시키지 않으면서 빛을 만들어내며, 이로 인해 일종의 냉광(무열광)이 된다. 심해어들은 보통 먹이를 유인하거나 자신들을 먹으려고 하는 포식자를 혼란스럽게 하기 위해 생체 발광을 사용한다. 샛비늘치는 먹이를 찾는 것과 방어적인 목적 둘 다를 위해 생체 발광을 이용한다. 이들은 발광기를 사용하여 자기 몸 위의 빛의 밝기와 일치하는 빛을 만들어냄으로써 자신의 윤곽을 흐리게 한다. 이렇게 함으로써 그들 아래에 있는 포식자들이 그들의 윤곽을 알아보는 것이 어려워진다. 어떤 종류의 오징어 또한 자신들의 정교한 발광포를 사용하여 복잡한 빛을 연출하는데, 이는 아마 의사소통 수단일 것으로 추측된다.

5 ➡ 해양의 어느 곳에서든 그곳에 살고 있는 생물들은 활동 시에 물에 포함되어 있는 산소 공급을 고갈시킨다. 중층표영대는 표해수대보다도 산소의 양이 상당히 적기 때문에, 그 층에 사는 생물들은 활동성이 훨씬 덜한 경향이 있다. [■A] 먹이를 잡기 위해 사냥을 하는 대신 이 동물들은 그저 자신들이 좋아하는 먹이가 옆을 지나가기만을 기다리며 해수대 전체에 걸쳐 드문드문 떠다닐 뿐이다. [■B] 이들 중 상당수는 먹이를 자신들에게 유인하기 위해 생체 발광을 사용한다. 이 동물들은 느릿느릿 움직이는 것처럼 보이지만, 공격할 수 있을 정도로 먹이가 가까이 오거나 다른 포식자에게 위협을 받으면 재빠르게 속도를 낼 수 있다. [■C] 성공적으로 먹이를 잡거나 공격을 피하게 되면, 다시 비활동적인 상태로 돌아간다. [■D] 가시가 많은 물고기의 경우 이런 식으로 떠다닐 수 있는데 이는 부레라고 불리는 가스로 가득 찬 기관 덕분이다. 부레는 상반신 위쪽에, 무게 중심 아래 쪽에 달려 있다. 이것은 물고기를 안정적으로 유지해주며, 헤엄치는 데 에너지를 소모하지 않고 특정 깊이에서 머물러 있을 수 있도록 도와준다.

13. 3단락에서 중층표영대 동물들이 크고 민감한 눈을 가짐으로써 갖게 되는 이점으로 언급되지 않은 것은

Ⓐ 동물들이 자기 자신을 위험으로부터 보호하고 먹이를 발견하는데 도움을 준다
Ⓑ 중층표영대의 희미한 빛을 모을 수 있도록 진화되었다
Ⓒ 포식자와 먹이를 구별하는 것에 도움을 준다
Ⓓ 위에 있는 먹이의 윤곽을 감지할 수 있도록 위를 향해 있다

14. 3단락의 단어 'perceive(감지하다)'와 의미상 가장 가까운 것은

Ⓐ 따르다
Ⓑ 보다
Ⓒ 평가하다
Ⓓ ~에 반응하다

15. 4단락에 따르면, 생체 발광에 대해 사실이 아닌 것은 무엇인가?

Ⓐ 살아 있는 생물에 의해 빛이 생산되고 방출되는 것을 말한다.
Ⓑ 주요 기능은 포식자를 피하고 먹이를 유인하고 잡는 것이다.
Ⓒ 어떤 종들은 그것을 사용하여 다른 개체에게 신호를 보냄으로써 이성을 유인한다.
Ⓓ 발광기와 발광포가 그것을 담당하는 특별한 기관이다.

16. 4단락에서 글쓴이가 '샛비늘치'를 언급하는 이유는 무엇인가?

Ⓐ 위장술의 수단으로써 윤곽을 흐리게 하는 종의 예를 들기 위해
Ⓑ 먹이를 잡는 데 있어서 발광포의 역할을 설명하기 위해
Ⓒ 체내에서 빛을 발생시키는 독특한 방법을 보여주기 위해
Ⓓ 더 흔한 위장술을 갖고 있는 다른 종과 비교하기 위해

17. 5단락에 따르면, 다음 중 중층표영대에 사는 생물들이 부족한 산소 공급을 보충하기 위해 취하는 행동은 무엇인가?

Ⓐ 먹이를 쫓지 않고 먹이가 자신들 쪽으로 오기를 기다린다.
Ⓑ 부레라고 불리는 특별한 기관을 사용하여 높은 수압을 견딘다.
Ⓒ 더 많은 산소를 마시기 위해 밤에 표면으로 올라온다.
Ⓓ 산소를 최대한으로 흡수할 수 있는 잘 발달된 아가미를 가지고 있다.

18. 5단락의 단어 'scattered(드문드문 있는)'와 의미상 가장 가까운 것은

Ⓐ 외부의
Ⓑ 전문화된
Ⓒ 뿔뿔이 흩어진
Ⓓ 아주 작은

19. 지문에 다음 문장이 들어갈 수 있는 위치를 나타내는 네 개의 사각형 [■]을 확인하시오.

이들 중 상당수는 먹이를 자신들에게 유인하기 위해 생체 발광을 사용한다.

이 문장이 들어가기에 가장 적합한 곳은? [■B]

20. 지시문: 지문을 간략하게 요약한 글의 첫 문장이 아래 제시되어 있다. 지문의 가장 중요한 내용을 표현하는 세 개의 선택지를 골라 요약문을 완성하시오. 일부 문장들은 지문에 제시되지 않았거나 지문의 지엽적인 내용을 나타내기 때문에 요약문에 포함되지 않는다. ***이 문제의 배점은 2점이다.***

심해에 사는 해양 동물들은 해심이 깊어질수록 빛과 산소가 희박해지는 환경에 적응해 왔다.

Ⓐ 물기둥은 각 층마다 다른 종류의 생물들이 살고 있는 해양 수층의 계층화를 설명하는 개념으로 존재하는 물의 기둥이다.
Ⓓ 중층표영대에 사는 동물들은 혹독한 환경에 적응하며 크고 민감한 눈, 위장술, 생체 발광과 같은 자신들만의 생존 방식을 발달시켜 왔다.
Ⓕ 산소가 부족한 수층에 사는 생물들은 산소를 아끼기 위해 먹이를 사냥하러 다니기보다 느릿느릿 움직이는 것을 택한다.

Ⓑ 표해수대에는 먹이에 따라 세 종류의 종이 사는데, 잔사식 동물, 초식 동물, 육식 동물이 그것이다.
Ⓒ 중층표영대에 사는 대부분의 생물들은 밤에 먹이를 얻기 위해 표해수대로 이동하는 수직 이동을 한다.
Ⓔ 일부 심해동물들은 박테리아를 이용해서 빛을 방출하는 기관에서 화학 반응을 통해 빛을 만들어 내는 능력을 가지고 있다.

어휘 vertical adj 수직의, 세로의 | column n 기둥 | layer n 막, 층 | penetrate v 뚫고 들어가다, 침투하다 | sediment n 침전물, 앙금 | be referred to as ~로 불리다 | twilight n 황혼, 땅거미 | classify v 분류하다, 구분하다 | detritivore n 잔사식 동물(배설물을 먹고 사는 동물) | corpse n 시체 | feces n 똥, 배설물 | exoskeleton n 외골격 | herbivore n 초식 동물 | migrate v 이동하다, 이주하다 | carnivorous adj 육식성의 | inhabit v 살다, 거주하다 | be forced to 어쩔 수 없이 ~하다 | adapt v 적응하다, 맞추다 | camouflage n (보호색이나 형태 등을 통한 동물들의) 위장 | bioluminescence n 생체 발광 | uniformly adv 균일하게 | lack v ~이 없다, 부족하다 | coloration n 천연색, 색채 | translucent adj 반투명한 | generate v 발생시키다, 만들어내다 | stimulate v 자극하다 | attract v 유인하다, 끌어들이다 | confuse v 혼란시키다 | predator n 포식동물, 포식자 | defensive adj 방어의 | make out ~을 알아보다, 알아듣다 | sophisticated adj 정교한, 복잡한 | complicated adj 복잡한 | deplete v 격감시키다, 고갈시키다 | significantly adv 상당히, 크게 | sluggish adj 느릿느릿 움직이는 | be capable of ~할 수 있다 | inactive adj 활동하지 않는 | stable adj 안정된

Lesson 03 Category Chart

본서 | P. 250

Practice

01 The North: B, G / The South: C, D, F
02 Tornadoes: A, C, H / Hurricanes: D, E, G, I
03 Fungi: A, D, E / Plants: B, F
04 Left: A, G / Right: B, D, E
05 Education: A, D, F / Schooling: B, C
06 Hardwoods: A, D, E / Softwoods: C, G
07 Census of 1790: B, C, F / Modern Census: D, G
08 Type 1: A, C, E, G / Type 2: B, D, H
09 Paleolithic People: A, B, D, E / Neolithic People: C, H, I
10 Behavioral Psychology: B, E, G / Cognitive Psychology: C, D
11 Tribes: A, C, G / Chiefdoms: B, E
12 Archaic Period: A, F, G / Hellenistic Period: B, D

Test

1. C 2. B 3. D 4. A 5. A 6. C 7. B 8. A 9. C
10. Direct Current: C, G / Alternating Current: B, D, F
11. B 12. D 13. B 14. D 15. A 16. B 17. C 18. A 19. B
20. Sumerian cuneiform: A, D / Mayan hieroglyphs: C, E, G

01

남북 전쟁

미국 남북 전쟁의 마지막 총성이 울린 지 150년이 지난 후에도 북부인들과 남부인들은 여전히 갈등의 진짜 원인에 대해 논쟁하고 있다. 보통 생각나는 원인으로는 인간을 노예의 형태로 소유했던 문제가 있다. 미국 북부 연합을 형성했던 북부 여러 주의 사람들은 진정으로 유의미한 수의 노예를 소유한 적이 없었으며 그들의 경제는 이미 노예 제도에 대한 의존을 넘어설 만큼 성장해 있었다. 북부는 유럽에서 넘어온 엄청난 수의 이민자를 노동력으로 하는 산업화된 경제로 대부분 전환된 상태였다. 하지만 남부는 농장과 대농장에서 노예 노동력에 계속 의존했고 남부인들은 북부의 노예 폐지 또는 반 노예제 활동이 남부의 자신들의 삶과 생계를 위협한다고 생각했다. 그러나 모든 남부인이 노예를 소유하고 있었고 그들에 대한 소유권을 지키려고 싸웠다고 생각한다면 오산일 것이다. 남부인 대부분은 사실 대농장 지주에게 분개했던 가난한 백인 농부들이었다. 그들은 이런 상류층들의 권리를 지키기 위해 싸웠던 것이 아니라, 강압적으로 보였던 정부로부터 주권을 지키기 위해 싸웠다.

지시문: 아래 문장들을 알맞게 넣어 다음 표를 완성하시오. 선택지 중 적절한 문장들을 골라 관계된 개념과 연결하시오. 선택지 두 개는 정답이 될 수 없다. ***이 문제의 배점은 3점이다.***

선택지	북부	남부
Ⓐ 급격한 산업화 때문에 많은 수의 노예를 소유했다.	Ⓑ	Ⓒ
Ⓑ 주로 공장의 이민 노동자들로 구성된 노동력에 의존했다.	Ⓖ	Ⓓ
Ⓒ 농업 경제 때문에 노예들에게 의존해야 했다.		Ⓕ
Ⓓ 주민들은 노예 제도가 폐지되면 심각한 상황에 직면할 거라고 생각했다.		
Ⓔ 여전히 노예 제도를 유지하는 주가 몇 군데 있다.		
Ⓕ 주민들은 대부분 자신의 권리를 지키기 위해 싸웠던 영세농들이었다.		
Ⓖ 노예 제도에 반대하고 그것을 폐지하려 했던 사람들로 이루어져 있었다.		

어휘 shot Ⓝ 총성 | conflict Ⓝ 갈등, 충돌, 투쟁 | come to mind 생각나다 | Union Ⓝ (남북 전쟁 당시의) 미국 북부 | outgrow Ⓥ ~보다 커지다 | shift over to ~로 전환하다 | plantation Ⓝ 대농장 | abolitionist Ⓝ 폐지론자 | anti-slavery 노예 제도 반대 | livelihood Ⓝ 생계 | resent Ⓥ 원망하다, 분개하다

02

토네이도와 허리케인

북미 대륙은 여름철 동안 허리케인과 토네이도라는 뚜렷이 다른 두 가지 형태의 사나운 날씨에 시달린다. 허리케인과 토네이도는 둘 다 원운동을 하며 회전하고, 지구가 자전하는 방향과 동일한 방향으로 회전한다. 둘 다 저기압 지역에서 발생하며 이 저기압 세력의 중심에는 태풍의 눈이라고 알려진 태풍의 일부분이 있다. 태풍의 눈은 주위의 강렬한 소용돌이에 의해 만들어지는 거의 완벽하게 고요한 지역이다. 하지만 허리케인은 탁 트인 바다에서 형성되는 반면 토네이도는 거의 항상 육상에서 형성된다. 두 가지 현상 모두 극도의 강풍을 특징으로 하고 있으나 토네이도가 동반하는 바람이 훨씬 더 강력하다. 토네이도는 허리케인보다 훨씬 자주 발생하고, 단지 몇 분만에도 형성될 수 있지만 허리케인은 몇 주에 걸쳐 형성된다. 이는 토네이도가 이미 존재하는 뇌우에서 만들어지는 반면 허리케인은 그 자체가 태풍이기 때문이다. 하지만 허리케인은 인명과 재산에 더 큰 위험을 불러일으킬 수 있는데 왜냐하면 폭풍 해일이라 불리는 파도를 동반하기 때문이다. 이 파도는 쓰나미와 매우 비슷한 작용을 하여 태풍이 해안 지대를 덮칠 때 내륙으로 밀려온다.

지시문: 아래 구절들을 알맞게 넣어 다음 표를 완성하시오. 선택지 중 적절한 구절들을 골라 관계된 개념과 연결하시오. 선택지 두 개는 정답이 될 수 없다. ***이 문제의 배점은 3점이다.***

선택지	토네이도	허리케인
Ⓐ 육지에서 생긴다	Ⓐ	Ⓓ
Ⓑ 지구의 자전과 반대 방향으로 회전한다	Ⓒ	Ⓔ
Ⓒ 더 자주 발생하고 형성 기간이 더 짧다	Ⓗ	Ⓖ
Ⓓ 사람들을 위협하는 위험한 파도를 동반한다		Ⓘ
Ⓔ 처음에는 물 위에서 발달하여 내륙으로 이동할 수 있다		
Ⓕ 대륙성 고기압에 기인한다		
Ⓖ 발생하는 데 상대적으로 더 오랜 시간이 걸린다		
Ⓗ 다른 하나보다 더 강력한 바람을 만들어낸다		
Ⓘ 다른 요인 없이 자체적으로 발생한다		

어휘 distinct adj 별개의, (전혀) 다른 | circular motion 원운동 | low atmospheric pressure 저기압 | eye of the storm 태풍의 눈 | cyclonic adj 강렬한 | vortex n 소용돌이 | spawn v (어떤 결과, 상황을) 낳다 | thunderstorm n 뇌우 | storm surge 폭풍 해일 | tsunami n 쓰나미, 지진해일 | reverse adj 반대 방향의 | formative adj 형성에 중요한 | autonomously adv 자체적으로

---

03 **균류 대 식물**

1 ➡ 생명체는 연구를 위해 계(界)라는 광범위하고 기본적인 그룹으로 체계화된다. 균류는 오랫동안 식물계로 분류되었다. 그러다가 과학자들은 균류가 동물과 더 밀접한 관련성이 있긴 하지만 독특한 별도의 생명체라는 사실을 알게 되었다. 이제 균류는 자체 계로 분류되고 있다. 주된 이유는 어떤 균류에게도 엽록소가 없어서 식물과 달리 자체적으로 탄수화물을 합성할 수 없기 때문이다. 균류는 죽은 유기체 찌꺼기나 다른 생명체에서 양분을 얻는다.

2 ➡ 게다가 균류의 세포벽은 식물의 세포벽처럼 섬유소로 구성된 것이 아니라 키틴질이라는 복합당과 같은 중합체로 이루어져 있는데, 이것은 새우, 거미, 곤충의 딱딱한 외골격을 이루고 있는 재질이다. 균류의 세포벽과 식물 세포벽의 화학적 구성의 차이점은 매우 중요한데 그 이유는 자라나는 균사, 즉 균류의 실처럼 생긴 세포 끝에서 균류 자체에는 영향을 미치지 않고 식물의 세포벽을 분해하는 효소를 분비할 수 있기 때문이다.

지시문: 아래 문장들을 알맞게 넣어 다음 표를 완성하시오. 선택지 중 적절한 문장들을 골라 관계된 개념과 연결하시오. 선택지 두 개는 정답이 될 수 없다. ***이 문제의 배점은 3점이다.***

선택지	균류	식물
Ⓐ 엽록소가 없다. Ⓑ 자체적으로 탄수화물을 합성한다. Ⓒ 오직 죽은 유기물에서만 탄수화물을 얻는다. Ⓓ 세포벽이 새우와 곤충의 껍질과 같은 소재를 포함하고 있다. Ⓔ 탄수화물을 합성할 수 없다. Ⓕ 양분을 얻기 위해 엽록소를 이용한다. Ⓖ 식물 세포에 영향을 미치지 않는 효소를 분비하는 균사를 가지고 있다.	Ⓐ Ⓓ Ⓔ	Ⓑ Ⓕ

어휘 kingdom n (생물 분류의) 계 | principal adj 주요한, 주된 | chlorophyll n 엽록소 | synthesize v 합성하다 | cellulose n 섬유소 | polymer n 중합체, 고분자 | enormous adj 막대한, 거대한 | enzyme n 효소

---

04 **뇌의 좌반구와 우반구**

1 ➡ 인간의 두뇌는 한 기관이지만 두 개의 반쪽, 즉 반구로 나뉘어 있다. 각각의 반구는 다른 기능을 가졌고 각기 다른 방법으로 정보를 처리한다. 실행되는 일에 따라 한쪽 혹은 다른 한쪽의 반구가 더 지배적이다.

2 ➡ 왼쪽 반구는 세부적인 것에 집중한다. 논리적이고 분석적인 사고를 더 잘 처리한다. 다양한 여러 단계를 거쳐야 하는 조직적 업무를 수행하거나 주변 환경의 특정 부분에 집중하는 것이 필요할 때는 두뇌의 왼쪽 부분이 사용된다. 특징적 기능 중 하나가 상징적 사고인 두뇌의 왼쪽 부분은 사람들이 언어를 해독하여 문자 그대로의, 또는 표면상의 의미를 찾도록 해준다. 그러나 세부적인 것에 집중하는 왼쪽 반구는 보이는 물체들 사이의 관계를 식별하는 능력인 공간 인지에는 적절하지 못하다. 이 일은 세부적인 것에 대한 집중을 덜 요구한다.

3 ➡ 반면 오른쪽 반구는 정보를 더 총체적인 수준에서 처리한다. 이는 장소, 사물, 상황에 관한 총체적 관점을 제공하는 두뇌 부분이다. 오른쪽 반구는 인간 상상력의 중심부이기 때문에 사람들은 창조적 접근을 요구하는, 제한을 두지 않은 업무를 수행할 때 이 반구에 의존한다. 언어를 처리할 때 사람들이 유머나 감정, 은유를 이해하게 하여 함축적 또는 문맥상의 의미를 제공하는 것이 바로 이 오른쪽 반구이다. 더욱이 오른쪽 반구는 공간 지각의 원천으로, 우리가 환경을 3차원적으로 분석하고 거리를 판단할 수 있게 해준다.

지시문: 아래 구절들을 알맞게 넣어 다음 표를 완성하시오. 선택지 중 적절한 구절들을 골라 관계된 개념과 연결하시오. 선택지 두 개는 정답이 될 수 없다. ***이 문제의 배점은 3점이다.***

선택지	좌반구	우반구
Ⓐ 주변 환경의 세부 사항을 알아차리게 해준다	Ⓐ	Ⓑ
Ⓑ 거리를 판단할 수 있게 해준다	Ⓖ	Ⓓ
Ⓒ 꿈을 꾸게 해준다		Ⓔ
Ⓓ 문제를 창조적으로 해결하게 해준다		
Ⓔ 문맥을 파악할 수 있게 해준다		
Ⓕ 해결되어야 하는 문제를 구조화하게 해준다		
Ⓖ 언어를 문자 그대로 이해하게 해준다		

어휘 hemisphere n 반구 I dominant adj 지배적인 I logical adj 논리적인 I analytical adj 분석적인 I concentration n 집중 I decode v 해독하다, 번역하다 I superficial adj 표면상의 I spatial adj 공간의 I discern v 인지하다, 구별하다 I connotative adj 암시적인, 내포하는 I contextual adj 전후 관계상의, 문맥상의 I metaphorical adj 은유적인

05

교육과 학교 교육

1 ➡ 미국에서는 학교가 사람이 교육을 위해 반드시 다녀야 하는 곳이라는 믿음이 흔하다. 그러나 어떤 사람들은 학교에 다니는 것이 아이의 교육을 방해한다고 생각한다. 여기서 제시되는 학교 교육과 교육의 차이점은 중요하다.

2 ➡ 교육은 학교 교육보다 더 광범위하고 포괄적이다. 교육에는 제약이 없다. 교육은 공식적인 학교 교육과 모든 종류의 비공식적 학습을 다 포함한다. 교육 행위자는 훌륭한 조부모, 라디오 대담 프로그램에서 토론을 벌이는 사람들, 다른 아이, 혹은 유명한 학자 등이 될 수 있다. 학교 교육은 여러 가지 면에서 예측 가능한 반면 교육은 자연스럽게 이루어지는 경우가 많다. 예를 들어 낯선 사람과 우연히 나눈 대화를 통해 전에는 잘 알지 못했던 새로운 주제를 접할 수 있다. 사람들은 유아기 때부터 교육을 시작해 죽을 때까지 멈추지 않는다. 이것은 개인이 학교에 가기 전부터 시작되는 평생에 걸친 과정이며, 개인의 일생에서 계속 필수적인 부분이어야 한다.

3 ➡ 반면 학교 교육은 좀 더 형식을 갖춘 구체적인 과정이다. 학교 교육의 일반적 양상은 한 가지 상황이나 다른 것에 따라 거의 달라지지 않는다. 아이들은 똑같은 시간에 등교해 지정된 좌석에 앉으며 성인들에게 교육을 받고, 숙제를 하고 시험을 본다. 알파벳이든 간단한 계산이든, 가르침을 받는 현실의 단편은 대개 교육 과목의 경계에 제약을 받는다. 예를 들어 고등학생들은 지역 사회의 정치적 문제점과 관련한 진실이나 영화 제작자들이 어떤 신기술을 탐색 중인지 등에 관해 배울 가능성은 낮다는 점을 알고 있다. 제도화된 학교 교육에는 명백한 경계가 존재한다.

지시문: 아래 문장들을 알맞게 넣어 다음 표를 완성하시오. 선택지 중 적절한 문장들을 골라 관계된 개념과 연결하시오. 선택지 두 개는 정답이 될 수 없다. ***이 문제의 배점은 3점이다.***

선택지	교육	학교 교육
Ⓐ 태어날 때부터 죽을 때까지 계속된다.	Ⓐ	Ⓑ
Ⓑ 보통 어디에서든 내용이 같다.	Ⓓ	Ⓒ
Ⓒ 결과물을 대부분 예측할 수 있다.	Ⓕ	
Ⓓ 제약이 없다.		
Ⓔ 학업의 연속성을 방해한다.		
Ⓕ 예상하기 어렵고 계획되지 않은 것이다.		
Ⓖ 인간의 발달에 유용하다는 생각은 완전히 무시되어야 한다.		

어휘 interrupt v 방해하다, 중단시키다 I all-inclusive adj 모두를 포함한 I spontaneous adj 자연스러운, 마음에서 우러난 I infancy n 유아기 I integral adj 필수적인, 필요 불가결한 I segment n 부분

06

경재 대 연재

1 ➡ 목공과 건축에서 사용되는 나무의 종류는 보통 경재와 연재 두 종류로 나뉜다. 이렇게 분류한 이유는 꽤 명백해 보인다. 일반적으로 경재는 연재보다 더 단단한 경향이 있다. 하지만 항상 그런 것은 아니다. 경재는 확실히 연재보다 밀도가 높지만 모든 경재가 더 단단하지는 않다. 예를 들어 발사나무의 목재는 지구상에서 가장 부드러운 종류의 목재 중 하나이지만 사실 경재로 지정되어 있다. 그래서 이 두 종류의 나무를 제대로 구별하는 것은 더 복잡하다.

2 ➡ 경재와 연재 사이의 진짜 차이점은 목재를 얻은 나무의 종류와 관련이 있다. 경재는 낙엽수로, 매년 가을에 잎을 떨어뜨리고 대체로 껍질이 단단한 씨앗을 맺는 활엽수이다. 이런 나무에는 단풍나무, 오크나무, 벚나무, 마호가니 등이 있다. 연재는 대개 상록수로, 계절에 따라 잎이

지지 않으며 잎이 가늘고 바늘처럼 생겼다. 씨앗은 보통 원뿔형 열매 안에 들어 있으며(이것이 종종 구과 식물이라 불리는 이유이다) 단단한 보호 껍질이 없다. 이 종류에는 특히 소나무, 전나무, 가문비나무, 삼나무 등이 있다.

3 ➡ 이런 두 집단 간의 차이는 모두 외부에서 식별 가능한 것들이지만 가장 중요한 차이점은 안에 있다. 미세한 수준에서 보면 나무들의 구조가 다르다. 연재는 길쭉하고 수직으로 자라는 세포를 가지고 있으며 이 세포들은 힘을 공급하고 수분과 영양분을 나무 전체에 전달한다. 이들은 세포벽을 통해 물질을 전달하는데, 이는 세포벽 내에 물을 함유할 수 있다는 뜻이다. 이 나무들이 일년 내내 초록색을 유지할 수 있는 이유이다. 경재에는 동물의 혈관과 아주 비슷하게 이런 성분을 운반하는 물관이라는 조직이 있다. 이 물관은 나무에 있는 구멍처럼 생겼으며 벽은 도관 요소라는 튼튼한 세포로 만들어져 있다. 벽은 나무에 힘을 추가적으로 공급하고, 벽을 둘러싼 다른 세포는 서로 빽빽하게 모여 나무의 밀도를 더 높여준다. 하지만 겨울에는 기능이 조금 떨어지며 그 때문에 매년 나무의 잎이 지게 된다.

지시문: 아래 구절들을 알맞게 넣어 다음 표를 완성하시오. 선택지 중 적절한 구절들을 골라 관계된 개념과 연결하시오. 선택지 두 개는 정답이 될 수 없다. ***이 문제의 배점은 3점이다.***

선택지	경재	연재
Ⓐ 물과 영양분을 나르는 관 같은 구조를 갖고 있다 Ⓑ 보통 고도가 높은 빽빽한 숲에서 자란다 Ⓒ 항상 푸른 잎을 지닌 비낙엽성 나무이다 Ⓓ 일반적으로 고밀도의 더 단단한 세포를 갖고 있다 Ⓔ 연 단위로 잎을 떨어뜨린다 Ⓕ 원뿔형 열매 안에 들어 있는 딱딱한 껍질을 가진 씨앗을 생산한다 Ⓖ 세포 조직 내에 수분을 저장할 수 있다	Ⓐ Ⓓ Ⓔ	Ⓒ Ⓖ

어휘 hardwood n 경재 | softwood n 연재 | woodworking n 목공 | reasoning n 이유, 추론 | grouping n 분류, 그룹으로 나누기 | indeed adv 확실히 | dense adj 고밀도의 | designate v 지정하다 | distinction n 구별 | elaborate adj 복잡한 | discrepancy n 차이, 불일치 | deciduous adj 낙엽성의 | broad-leafed tree 활엽수 | maple n 단풍나무 | oak n 오크나무 | cherry n 벚나무 | mahogany n 마호가니(적색을 띤 목질을 지닌 열대산 활엽수) | seasonally adv 계절에 따라 | foliage n 잎사귀 | cone n 원뿔형 열매 | conifer n 구과 식물, 침엽수 | pine n 소나무 | fir n 전나무 | spruce n 가문비나무 | cedar n 삼나무 | microscopic adj 미세한 | vertically adv 수직으로 | retain v 보유하다 | vessel n (식물의) 물관 | blood vessel 혈관 | pore n 작은 구멍 | vessel element 도관 요소 | tube-like 관 같은 | shed v (잎을) 떨어지게 하다, 떨어뜨리다

07 미국 인구 조사

1 ➡ 미국 헌법은 인구 조사를 매 10년마다 시행하는 것을 의무화하고 있다. 초기에 미국 정부는 공정하게 세금을 징수하고 자원을 골고루 배분하는 데 많은 어려움을 겪었다. 인구 조사는 각 주나 지방의 인구에 대한 정확한 기록을 제공하여 이러한 문제점을 많이 해결했다. 의회 의원들은 이 정보를 이용하여 각 주에서 거둬들일 세금의 양을 결정할 수 있게 되었다. 과세뿐만 아니라 인구 조사는 또한 의회에서 각 행정구를 대표하는 선출 임원의 수를 결정했다.

2 ➡ 미국의 공식적인 첫 인구 조사는 1790년에 행해졌다. 당시 국무 장관이었던 토머스 제퍼슨이 인구 조사를 감독했다. 그는 미국 연방 보안 보좌관들을 임명하여 전국을 돌아다니며 미국의 모든 세대 거주자 수를 조사하게 했다. 그러나 이러한 방법을 통한 정보 수집은 연방 보안 보좌관들에게 어려움을 주었다. 미국은 상대적으로 신생 국가였기 때문에 나라 전체에 대한 정확한 지도가 거의 없었고 특히 외딴 지역의 지도는 더 없는 상태였다. 게다가 많은 시민들은 연방 보안 보좌관들을 믿지 못해 그들의 질문에 대답하기를 꺼렸다. 이러한 어려움에도 불구하고 18개월 후에 첫 번째 인구 조사가 끝났고 미국의 인구 수는 390만 명으로 판정되었다.

3 ➡ 1790년에 실시한 인구 조사는 오늘날 시행되는 인구 조사와 많이 달랐다. 현 인구 조사도 여전히 입법 대표자 수를 결정하기는 하지만 현대의 컴퓨터는 현재 인구 조사 자료 수집을 맡은 기관인 미국 인구 조사국이 1790년에 비해 훨씬 더 빠른 속도로 정보를 분류하고 목록을 작성하는 것을 가능하게 해준다. 1940년부터 인구 조사국은 인구의 일부로부터 자료를 수집하는 것을 가능하게 하는 표본 통계 기술을 사용하기 시작했다. 그 후에 이 자료는 국가 전체의 정보를 예측하는 데 사용되었다. 표본 통계 사용은 인구 조사를 하는 데 필요한 시간을 엄청나게 줄였다. 1960년대에 인구 조사국은 컴퓨터화된 주소 파일을 개발했고, 1970년에는 거의 우편에만 의존하여 인구 조사를 수행했다. 사실상 현재 미국인들의 90퍼센트 이상이 우편으로 인구 조사 서식을 받고 있다. 소수의 가정만이 방문 인구 조사원의 질문에 직접 응답하고 있다.

지시문: 아래 구절들을 알맞게 넣어 다음 표를 완성하시오. 선택지 중 적절한 구절들을 골라 관계된 개념과 연결하시오. 선택지 두 개는 정답이 될 수 없다. ***이 문제의 배점은 3점이다.***

선택지	1790년의 인구 조사	현대의 인구 조사
Ⓐ 2년마다 완수되었다	Ⓑ	Ⓓ
Ⓑ 인구 조사관들은 때때로 의심을 받았다	Ⓒ	Ⓖ
Ⓒ 완전히 인구 조사관들에 의해서만 시행되었다	Ⓕ	
Ⓓ 모든 외딴 지역을 방문할 필요가 없다		
Ⓔ 현장 인원 없이 실시되었다		
Ⓕ 부분적으로는 의회 대표자들을 결정하기 위해 고안되었다		
Ⓖ 미국의 우편 배달부가 이 과정에 포함되었다		

어휘 census n 인구 조사 I mandate v 요구하다, 위임하다 I fairly adv 공정하게 I allocate v 배치하다, 배분하다 I appoint v 임명하다, 지명하다 I marshal n 연방 보안관 I reluctant adj 꺼리는, 내키지 않는 I legislative adj 입법의 I compile v 집계하다, 자료를 모으다 I statistical adj 통계의 I enumerator n 조사원

08

당뇨병

1 ➡ 본질적으로 당뇨병은 신체가 인슐린을 제대로 생성하거나 사용하지 못하는 것이다. 소화를 통해 음식물은 세포가 에너지로 사용하는 당분의 한 유형인 포도당으로 변한다. 인슐린은 건강한 신체에서 자연스럽게 생성되는 호르몬으로, 체내 세포의 포도당 대사를 돕는다. 만약 인슐린이 없으면 세포는 포도당을 흡수할 수 없다. 제1형 당뇨병 환자는 섭취한 음식을 세포가 사용하도록 하는 데 충분한 인슐린을 생성하지 못한다. 제1형 당뇨병은 소아 당뇨병이라고 알려져 있긴 하지만 어떤 연령의 사람이라도 제1형 당뇨병에 걸릴 수 있다. 제2형 당뇨병은 신체가 충분한 인슐린을 생성한다 하더라도 신체 세포가 인슐린을 사용할 수 없을 때 발생한다. 제2형 당뇨병은 종종 성인 발병 당뇨병이라 불리고 일반적으로 40세 이상의 사람에게 발병한다. 사실 이 둘은 다소 다른 별개의 병이지만 둘 다 인슐린과 연관되어 있고 모두 당뇨병이라고 알려져 있다.

2 ➡ 병의 경로가 완전하게 알려져 있는 것은 아니지만 사람들은 다양한 경로로 당뇨병에 걸린다. 알려진 것은 당뇨병이 전염되지 않는다는 정도이다. 다른 사람과 접촉한다거나 같은 컵으로 음료를 마신다고 해서 병에 걸리지는 않는다. 하지만 당뇨병은 유전될 수 있다. 제2형 당뇨병은 유전되므로 조상 중에 병에 걸렸던 사람들이 있는 경우에는 제2형 당뇨병에 걸릴 확률이 더 높다. 어떤 사람들은 과식과 비만이 당뇨병의 원인이라고 생각하며 의사들은 집안 내력이라 할지라도 당뇨병에 걸릴 위험을 줄이기 위해 균형 잡힌 식사와 규칙적인 운동을 할 것을 권장한다. 흑인과 라틴아메리카계 사람들은 백인들보다 약 두 배 이상 이 병에 많이 걸리지만 유전이나 생활 습관이 이 현상에 얼마나 영향을 미치는지는 확실하지 않다. 제1형 당뇨병에 어떻게 걸리는지 정확히 알아내는 것은 어렵다. 제2형 당뇨병과 달리 제1형 당뇨병은 가족에 유전되어 나타나지 않으므로 아마 유전적인 연결고리는 없을 것이다. 연구자들이 당뇨병에서의 바이러스의 역할에 대하여 연구하고 있기는 하지만 어떻게 제1형 당뇨병에 걸리는지 전문가들도 모르는 것이 사실이다. 하지만 그들은 여러 요인이 당뇨병 발병의 원인이 된다는 것과, 건강한 생활 습관이 병을 예방하는 데 도움이 될 것이라는 점은 알고 있다.

지시문: 아래 구절들을 알맞게 넣어 다음 표를 완성하시오. 선택지 중 적절한 구절들을 골라 관계된 개념과 연결하시오. 선택지 두 개는 정답이 될 수 없다. ***이 문제의 배점은 3점이다.***

선택지	제1형 당뇨병	제2형 당뇨병
Ⓐ 바이러스의 영향이 의심된다	Ⓐ	Ⓑ
Ⓑ 유전적 발생 패턴을 보여준다	Ⓒ	Ⓓ
Ⓒ 나이 어린 사람들이 앓는 병으로 알려져 있다	Ⓔ	Ⓗ
Ⓓ 포도당 대사를 위해 인슐린을 사용하지 못하는 것과 관련이 있다	Ⓖ	
Ⓔ 원인이 밝혀지지 않았다		
Ⓕ 직접 접촉으로 전염될 수 있다		
Ⓖ 유전적 연결 고리는 아마 없을 것이다		
Ⓗ 충분한 인슐린 공급과 더불어 발생한다		
Ⓘ 포도당 생성과 연계된 기능 장애 때문에 발생한다		

어휘 diabetes n 당뇨병 I insulin n 인슐린 I glucose n 포도당 I involve v 포함하다, 필요로 하다 I contract v (병에) 걸리다 I obesity n 비만 I recommend v 추천하다 I heredity n 유전 I contribute v ~의 원인이 되다, 기여하다 I onset n 시작, 개시

09

구석기 문화와 신석기 문화

1 ➡ 약 2백만 년 전 시작된 석기 시대는 구석기와 신석기라는 두 개의 구분되는 시대로 특징지어진다. 이 두 시대의 두드러진 특징들은 식량 생산의 주된 수단이었다. 구석기 시기에는 사냥이, 신석기 시기에는 농사가 행해졌다. 사실 구석기 시대에 원시적인 사냥 무기의 발달을 초래한 석기라는 기술 혁신과 신석기 시대에 농업 사회의 출현을 자극한 농업 기술은 이 두 시대의 발전과 차이점을 가져왔다. 결과적으로 둘 사이에는 중대한 문화와 생활 방식의 차이가 있었다.

2 ➡ 사냥은 구석기 시대를 정의하며, 선사시대 초기 인류 사냥꾼들이 식량원을 따라다녀야 했기 때문에 유목 생활을 하도록 만들었다. 구석기인들은 너무 자주 이동했기 때문에 영구적인 거주지를 만들지 못했고, 동굴에서 거처를 찾거나 일시적으로 머물기 위해 나뭇가지로 임시 거처를 만들기도 했다. 흥미롭게도 동굴 벽화는 구석기 시대의 생활 양식에 대한 가장 가치 있는 이해를 제공한다. 이 작품들은 석기 시대 초기의 사냥 생활 방식에 대한 추상적인 이미지를 보여주었다. 아울러 성공적인 사냥을 확실히 가르쳐주는 지침서 역할을 했으며 이는 구석기 사람들이 독립적이었으나 동족의 곤경에 대한 동정심이 있었음을 보여준다. 구석기 사람들은 그들이 잡은 사냥감과 곡물과 과일을 먹었다. 시간이 흘러 이러한 것들을 경작하고 꾸준한 식량 공급을 보장하기 위한 방법이 나타나게 되었다.

3 ➡ 농업의 발달은 인간이 살아가는 방식에 중대한 변화를 가져왔다. 1만년 전, 현 인류의 인종인 호모 사피엔스는 가축을 키우고 제한된 수의 식물을 키우는 기술을 발견하게 되면서 신석기 시대에 진입했다. 가장 중요한 것은 사냥이 덜 필요해지면서 신석기 사람들이 정착하게 되었다는 사실이다. 이것은 이들이 영구적인 거주지를 짓고 살 수 있었다는 것뿐 아니라 정착지를 형성할 수 있었음을 의미한다. 이 정착된 생활 방식과 함께 실용적인 보관 용기이자 지배적인 예술 형태로서의 도자기의 발달이 이루어졌다. 구석기 시대에는 그런 물건을 갖고 다니는 것이 불필요했지만 이제 잉여 식량을 보관하고 신석기 시대의 삶을 보여주는 이미지를 기록하는 데 쓰였을 것이다. 흥미로운 것은 영적 세계를 나타내려는 원형적인 시도를 보여주는 순전히 장식적인 예술 형태의 등장이었다.

지시문: 아래 구절들을 알맞게 넣어 다음 표를 완성하시오. 선택지 중 적절한 구절들을 골라 관계된 개념과 연결하시오. 선택지 두 개는 정답이 될 수 없다. ***이 문제의 배점은 3점이다.***

선택지	구석기 인류	신석기 인류
Ⓐ 생활 방식을 기록한 예술로 집을 장식했다	Ⓐ	Ⓒ
Ⓑ 유랑하는 생활 방식을 취하여 사냥에 적응했다	Ⓑ	Ⓗ
Ⓒ 식량 생산을 위한 농업 기술을 처음으로 만들어냈다	Ⓓ	Ⓘ
Ⓓ 영구적 거주지 대신 임시 거처를 선택했다	Ⓔ	
Ⓔ 석기 도구의 출현으로부터 나타났다		
Ⓕ 자신들의 정착지를 위해 정부를 발전시켰다		
Ⓖ 동굴 벽화로 영적 세계에 관한 힌트를 주었다		
Ⓗ 다른 이들과 가깝게 영구적 거처를 지었다		
Ⓘ 도자기의 형태로 운반 가능한 예술을 발달시켰다		

어휘 Stone Age 석기 시대 | distinct adj 구분된 | epoch n 시대 | Paleolithic adj 구석기 시대의 | Neolithic adj 신석기 시대의 | innovation n 혁신, 쇄신 | primitive adj 원시적인 | stimulate v 자극하다 | divergence n 나뉨, 다름 | necessitate v ~을 필요로 하다, 수반하다 | nomadic adj 유목민의 | permanent adj 영구적인 | makeshift adj 임시의 | abstract adj 추상적인 | prosperous adj 번창하는 | domesticate v 길들이다, 가축화하다 | predominant adj 우월한, 현저한

10

행동 심리학과 인지 심리학

1 ➡ 인간 행동에 관한 과학적인 연구, 즉 심리학이 도입된 지 5세기가 넘었다. 그동안 일상 생활에 영향을 미치는 정신 질환과 문제를 포함하여 인간 행동을 평가하고 관리하기 위해 많은 이론과 학파가 개발되었다. 20세기에 주목할 만한 두 가지 과학적 접근법이 행동을 설명하고 다루기 위해 개발되었다. 행동 심리학과 인지 심리학 둘 다 같은 결과를 얻는 데 목적이 있지만 철학은 서로 반대이다.

2 ➡ 행동 심리학은 정신적, 감정적 상태의 영향 없이 모든 행동이 과학적으로 연구되고 설명될 수 있다는 견해에서 기능한다. 심리 분석의 발전과 나란히 발생한 행동주의는 피실험자를 조건화하는 연구를 수행한 B. F. 스키너의 행동 조건화, 그리고 개를 이용한 유명한 실험을 통해 자극-반응 이론을 발전시키고 또한 이를 입증한 이반 파블로프의 발견을 따라 발달했다. 행동 심리학은 실증적 데이터를 기본으로 한 이론에서 발전했다. 행동 심리학의 기본 전제는 모든 행동이 설명될 수 있다는 것이기 때문에 실험은 피실험자가 실험에 참여하며 겪게 되는 어떠한 내부적인 과정보다는 결과에 초점을 맞추었다.

3 ➡ 인지 심리학은 내부의 지적 처리 과정의 상호 작용을 관찰함으로써 인간 활동을 설명하는 것을 목표로 하고 있다. 그것의 관점은 기억, 문제 해결, 언어 처리, 그리고 인지 같은 과정을 평가하는 것에 기반하고 있으며 그것들이 어떻게 자극과 반응 사이에서 상호 작용하는지에 중점을 둔다. 인지 심리학에서는 감각적으로 입력된 정보와 개인의 경험보다는 한 개인의 필요와 야망, 충동을 기반으로 개인의 행동을 분석하는

것이 가능하다고 여겨진다. 이것은 아마 인지 심리학과 행동 심리학 사이에서 가장 중요한 차이일 것이다.

4 ➡ 이 상반된 심리학 학파를 교육 환경에 적용하는 것은 이 둘의 서로 다른 견해를 가장 잘 보여준다. 행동 심리학의 원칙은 교수 중심의 교실에서 우세하다. 자극과 반응이 중요한 요소로 간주되기 때문에 교사는 외부적인 결과 때문에 학습에 동기 부여를 받은 것으로 가정되는 학생들에게 지식을 제공한다. 실제의 경우 이 지식은 학생들이 수동적으로 기억하는 형태로 나타난다. 반면 인지 심리학은 개인의 내부 상태가 가장 중요하다고 가정하기 때문에 학습자를 정보를 적극적으로 처리하는 사람으로 묘사한다. 따라서 인지 심리학은 학생들이 스스로 지식을 발견하고 구성하여 결과적으로 학습 경험을 최대화하는 학습 전략을 발달시키는 현대의 학습자 중심의 교실에서 중요하다.

지시문: 아래 구절들을 알맞게 넣어 다음 표를 완성하시오. 선택지 중 적절한 구절들을 골라 관계된 개념과 연결하시오. 선택지 두 개는 정답이 될 수 없다. ***이 문제의 배점은 3점이다.***

선택지	행동 심리학	인지 심리학
Ⓐ 교사가 없을 때만 학생들이 배운다고 가정한다	Ⓑ	Ⓒ
Ⓑ 사람의 행동은 기분과 독립적인 것이라고 믿는다	Ⓔ	Ⓓ
Ⓒ 정보를 처리하는 개인의 능력을 고려한다	Ⓖ	
Ⓓ 학생들이 적극적으로 활동하는 교실에서 우세하다		
Ⓔ 모든 행동을 설명 가능한 것으로 간주한다		
Ⓕ 실험 자극을 기반으로 이론을 만들었다		
Ⓖ 결과가 학생들이 학습하는 것에 영향을 끼친다고 생각한다		

어휘 evaluate **v** 평가하다 | notable **adj** 주목할 만한, 중요한 | behavioral psychology 행동 심리학 | cognitive psychology 인지 심리학 | psychoanalysis **n** 정신 분석 | behaviorism **n** 행동주의 | assert **v** 단언하다, 주장하다 | empirical **adj** 실험에 근거를 둔, 경험적인 | premise **n** 전제 | outcome **n** 결과 | interplay **n** 상호 작용 | impulse **n** 충동, 자극 | postulate **v** 가정하다

11

국가의 발달

1 ➡ 인류학자들은 인간 사회가 어떻게 발달했는지에 관해 의견의 일치를 보이지 못하고 있다. 상충하는 이론들은 문명이 단순한 조직 형태에서 복잡한 조직 형태로 변화했을 거라는 데 초점을 맞추고 있다. 가장 주목하게 만드는 가설 중 하나는 이 위계적인 변환 양상이 실제로 존재한다는 것이다. 이 진화의 순차적인 양상은 각각 군집 사회, 부족 사회, 군장 사회, 국가로 구분된다. 한 정치 구조에서 다음 구조로 변하는 데 영향을 줄 수 있는 상황은 거의 무제한이지만 각 체계는 필요에 의해 등장한다.

2 ➡ 수렵 채집인들로 구성된 군집 사회는 가장 기본적인 형태의 인간 사회로 간주된다. 종종 혈연이나 가족 관계를 바탕으로 하며 하나의 군집 사회는 보통 구성원 수 100명 이하로 확대 가족 규모 이상을 벗어나지 않는다. 비공식적 조직 체계인 군집 사회는 성문화된 법이 없기 때문에 지침이 될 만한 기록이 없다. 따라서 군집 사회는 나이 든 가족 구성원들이 지배하며, 이들은 조언과 지침으로 다른 사람들의 존경을 받는다. 지도층이 거의 없기 때문에 군집 사회 구성원들은 의사 결정권과 세력을 공평하게 나누어 갖는다. 일반적으로 유목 군집 사회는 잉여 생산물을 만들어내지 않으며 이는 생계만 이으면 된다는 사고 방식으로 이어진다. 마지막으로 군집 사회에는 차등적인 지위 계층이 없기 때문에 부족 구성원들이 계층, 배타적 계급, 또는 사회적 신분으로 나뉘지 않는다.

3 ➡ 부족 사회는 서로 연관된 여러 가족과 공동체로 구성되기 때문에 규모가 상당히 더 크다. 따라서 가족 관계가 부족 구성원의 사회적 지위에 중요한 영향을 미친다는 점에서 국가와 다르다. 부족 제도는 동식물을 길들여 얻은 자원이 풍족하지만 예측이 불가능한 시기에 형성되며 이 체제의 효율성과 유연성은 부족 구성원들에게 자원의 잉여 시기 동안 자유를 허용하고, 부족한 시기에는 비축 식량을 제공해 준다. 그러나 부족 안팎의 구성원이 많이 뒤섞여 있기 때문에 부족 내에 사상적 차이와 관련한 갈등이 존재하는 경우가 많다. 또한 여러 다른 언어가 사용될 가능성도 있으므로 정체성이나 사상적 혼란 및 문화적 분열이 발생할 수 있다. 이러한 여러 가지 어려움 때문에 부족들은 한 명의 공동 지도자를 두고 뭉치는 경우가 많으며 이렇게 국가 발생 직전 단계로 넘어가게 된다.

4 ➡ 수천 명 가량으로 이루어진 군장 사회는 부족 사회보다 규모가 상당히 더 크다. 군장 사회는 사회적 신분이 존재하고 중앙 집권화되어 있다는 점에서 부족 사회나 군집 사회와는 다르다. 종종 군장 사회는 몇 개의 부족이 모여 일시적으로 형성되었다가 붕괴 및 분열되고, 이들이 또 다시 다른 군장 사회를 형성한다. 군장 사회는 몇 개의 공동체에 지배력을 발휘하는 하나의 군장을 두는 것이 특징이다. 단순한 군장 사회는 그들에게 재화와 서비스를 제공하는 몇몇 노동 계층, 하위 공동체들이 둘러싼 하나의 중심 공동체에 의해 형성된다. 군장 사회는 조세와 공물 제도에 따라 평민층이 지배층에게 식량 및 노동력 등의 자원을 제공한다. 따라서 이 두 군장 사회 계급 사이에는 보편화된 불평등이 일반적으로 존재한다. 뛰어난 업적을 세우거나 사회적 지위가 더 높은 사람과 결혼하거나 계급을 높인 사람과 친인척 관계인 경우 신분이 상승할 수도 있지만 계급은 승계된다. 군장은 단순히 힘 있는 부모에게서 태어났다는 이유로 여러 가지 특권을 부여받으며 이러한 권리는 그의 권력을 정당화하는 여러 신화로 뒷받침되기도 한다. 그 중요성을 더욱 뒷받침하기 위해 이 신화들은 사람들에게 쉽게 받아들여지도록 종종 종교적인 어조로 만들어진다. 불만으로 군장 사회가 위협받게 되는 경우에 군장과 지배 계급 사람들은 이 반란을 막기 위해 무력을 행사한다. 이는 일시적으로

지배 계급이 세력을 유지하게 해줄 수 있지만, 또한 두 계급 사이에 지속적인 갈등을 만든다. 결국 군장 사회는 불안정한데, 왜냐하면 군장 사회가 낮은 계급의 사람들이 자신들의 상황을 개선할 수 있는 여지가 거의 없는 사회를 만들기 때문이다.

5 ➡ 인간의 모든 조직적 구조 중 가장 안정된 발전 단계는 국가인데, 국가는 사회 계층 체계와 중앙 집권화라는 점에서 군장 사회와 비슷하다. 그럼에도 국가의 사회 계층 모델은 가상의 하층부와 최고점 사이에 여러 사회적 단계가 있는 피라미드형이다. 게다가 국가의 규모가 훨씬 크고 혁신적으로 발전해 있기 때문에 국가는 방대한 영토에 통치권을 행사할 수 있다. 이것은 군대, 공무원, 법원, 경찰 등의 기관이 있어 가능한 일이며 이 모든 기관은 국가의 높은 생산성 때문에 유지된다. 또한 통치자와 시민 사이에 혈연 관계에 기반하지 않은 관계가 형성되기 때문에 국가는 이전의 발전 단계와 크게 다르다. 국가 조직하의 사회는 자치적인 정치 단위이기 때문에 국민들에게 영향을 미치는 위기에 관한 대응 능력이 더 뛰어나다. 만약 갈등이 대중 여론을 국가와 대치하게 만드는 상황이 오더라도, 국가는 와해되지 않고 대중이 수용하는 지배 세력으로 교체될 가능성이 높다.

지시문: 아래 문장들을 알맞게 넣어 다음 표를 완성하시오. 선택지 중 적절한 문장들을 골라 관계된 개념과 연결하시오. 선택지 두 개는 정답이 될 수 없다. ***이 문제의 배점은 3점이다.***

선택지	부족 사회	군장 사회
Ⓐ 다수의 언어를 갖고 있을 수 있다.	Ⓐ	Ⓑ
Ⓑ 억압적인 것이 특징이다.	Ⓒ	Ⓔ
Ⓒ 가족 기반인 경향이 있다.	Ⓖ	
Ⓓ 일반적으로 존경받는 가족의 연장자에 의해 이끌린다.		
Ⓔ 뚜렷한 계급 체계가 있다.		
Ⓕ 자치 단체가 있다.		
Ⓖ 구성원들은 무리 안팎의 사람들과 쉽게 어울릴 수 있다.		

어휘 anthropology n 인류학 | civilization n 문명 | hierarchical adj 계급 제도의 | chronological adj 연대순의 | kinship n 혈족 관계, 친척 관계 | nomadic adj 유목민의, 유목의 | surplus n 잉여물 | subsistence n 생존, 생계 | markedly adv 현저하게, 크게 | tribal adj 부족의 | domestication n 사육 | plentiful adj 다량의, 풍부한 | fragmentation n 분열, 붕괴 | temporarily adv 일시적으로 | auxiliary adj 보조의, 예비의 | taxation n 징세, 과세 | tribute n 공물 | commoner n 서민, 평민 | inequality n 불평등 | entitlement n 권리, 자격 부여 | suppress v 억압하다, 금지하다 | upheaval n 격변 | ultimately adv 궁극적으로 | sovereignty n 주권, 통치권

12

고대 그리스 조각

1 ➡ 고대 그리스인들이 많은 형태의 예술 작품을 만들어냈다는 증거는 존재하지만 오랜 세월이 흐르는 동안 그 중 몇 가지만 살아남았으며 대부분은 조각품이다. 이 얼마 안 되는 표본만 보더라도 고대 그리스인들이 아주 단순한 기술을 갖고서도 놀라울 만큼 아름다운 조각품을 만들 수 있었음이 확실하다. 사실 고대 그리스인들의 조각은 예술과 미에 관한 서구적 개념의 발달에 깊은 영향을 끼쳤다. 고대 그리스 예술은 로마 예술의 기반이 되었다. 수 세기 후 고대 그리스 조각은 이탈리아 르네상스 예술가들에게 영감을 불어 넣었고 19세기까지의 서양 미술에 영향을 주었으며 모더니즘의 등장을 이끌었다. 영향력 있는 고대 그리스 조각의 정교함과 표현력은 기원전 8세기에서 기원전 1세기 사이에 세 가지 뚜렷한 시기로 나뉘어 발전했다.

2 ➡ 지금까지 남아 있는 고대 그리스 조각 중 가장 초기 작품은 기원전 8세기 것이다. 이때가 상고 시대의 시작으로, 이 시기에 조각들은 부유한 귀족들의 무덤을 장식하기 위해 만들어졌으며 가장 유명한 예는 크로이소스라는 아테네 군인의 무덤에서 발견된 것이다. 코우로스(복수형: kouroi)라고 알려진 이 조각들은 원시적인 철기를 이용해 돌, 보통 대리석을 깎아 만들었다. 이 단순한 기술은 조각가가 묘사할 수 있는 자세에 한계를 주었고, 따라서 코우로스는 두 발을 모으고 똑바로 서서 매우 경직되고 부자연스러운 모습을 하고 있다. 모든 코우로스의 얼굴은 똑같이 무표정하다. 또한 크로이소스처럼 나이 많은 사람의 무덤을 위해 만들어진 경우라 해도 조각상들은 한결같이 건장한 젊은 남자를 표현하고 있다. 이는 이러한 상들이 특정 개인의 초상이 아니라 대신 아름다움, 애국심, 영예와 희생 같은 이상을 상징한 것임을 증명한다. 사회적 계급이 더 높은 사람은 무덤을 표시하는 코우로스의 크기가 더 컸기에 조각상을 구분하는 유일한 차이점은 크기였다.

3 ➡ 기원전 5세기 초 그리스의 사회 정치적 변화는 귀족 계급 지배의 종말을 불러왔고 그에 따라 그들만이 가질 수 있었던 코우로스도 구식이 되었다. 이는 고전 시대의 시작을 특징 짓는 그리스 조각 스타일과 기능의 변화로 이어졌다. 이 시기는 몇 가지 중요한 요인들로 차별화된다. 조각가들은 금속으로 돌을 강화하는 방법을 터득했고 청동 같은 금속으로 조각상을 주조하는 방법도 배우기 시작했다. 기술적인 숙련도가 높아짐에 따라 예술가들은 더 다양한 자세와 표정을 묘사할 수 있었으며 따라서 조각상이 더 자연스럽고 사실적으로 바뀌었다. 미론의 조각 '원반 던지는 사람'은 원반을 던지고 있는 사람의 중간 동작을 표현한 작품으로, 고전 시대의 이러한 경향을 잘 나타내고 있다. 조각의 역동적인 자세는 수축된 근육 및 집중하는 표정과 함께 활기 있고 설득력 있는 움직임을 포착하고 있다. 조각은 무덤을 장식하는 용도로 계속 사용되면서 더 다양하고 풍부한 자세의 실제 인물을 묘사하기 시작했다. 고전 시대 동안에는 조각이 아테네의 파르테논처럼 신전 장식을 비롯한 다른 목적으로도 사용되기 시작했다.

4 ➡ 4세기 후반, 알렉산더 대왕의 군사 정복이 유라시아 대륙 전역으로 확산되며 그리스 미술이 동쪽으로 멀리는 파키스탄까지 퍼지게 되었다. 이와 동시에 그리스 예술가들이 갑자기 흘러 들어온 문화적 영향을 흡수했다. 미술사학자들이 헬레니즘 시대라고 지칭하는 이 시기에 고대 그리스 조각 스타일은 다시 한 번 급격한 변화를 겪었다. 자연주의, 역동적인 자세, 움직임에 치우치는 고전 시대의 성향이 계속 정교함을 더하기 시작했지만 예술가들은 조각에 옷 주름과 질감도 도입했다. 이러한 요소들은 자세의 역동성과 움직임을 강조하기 위해 사용되었다. 고대 그리스 조각 중 가장 유명한 작품 중 하나인 '사모트라케의 니케 여신상'에서도 자세를 강조하기 위해 옷 주름이 사용되었으며 뛰어난 효과를 연출했다. 조각상의 머리와 팔은 현재 소실되었지만 우리는 바람에 옷을 나부끼며 날개를 활짝 펴고 곧 날아갈 준비가 되어 있는 아름다운 날개를 단 여신을 지금도 상상할 수 있다. 또한 이 시기에는 조각의 주제도 더 사실적으로 변모했다. 일상 생활 장면도 용납 가능해졌고, 예술가들은 이상적인 미나 신체적 완벽함을 묘사해야 한다는 의무감을 더 이상 느끼지 않게 되었으며, 따라서 모든 연령대의 남녀에 관한 더 사실적인 묘사가 등장하기 시작했다.

지시문: 아래 문장들을 알맞게 넣어 다음 표를 완성하시오. 선택지 중 적절한 문장들을 골라 관계된 개념과 연결하시오. 선택지 두 개는 정답이 될 수 없다. ***이 문제의 배점은 3점이다.***

선택지	상고 시대	헬레니즘 시대
Ⓐ 조각들은 보통 부유한 후원자들로부터 의뢰를 받아 만들어졌다. Ⓑ 다른 문화의 영향 때문에 발생했다. Ⓒ 조각들은 다양한 장식적 목적을 갖기 시작했다. Ⓓ 주제들은 이상적 환상 대신 생기 있는 사실주의로 묘사되었다. Ⓔ 조각들은 경직되었지만 매우 자연스러웠다. Ⓕ 조각들은 하나의 주된 장식적 목적을 갖고 있었다. Ⓖ 조각들은 사회적 지위를 상징했다.	Ⓐ Ⓕ Ⓖ	Ⓑ Ⓓ

어휘 profound adj 엄청난, 깊은 | foundation n 기반 | inspire v 영감을 주다 | advent n 등장, 도래 | subtlety n 정교함 | influential adj 영향력 있는 | aristocrat n 귀족 | rudimentary adj 기본적인, 원시적인 | rigid adj 경직된 | invariably adv 한결같이, 변함없이 | depict v 묘사하다 | commission n 임무를 주다 | attest v 입증하다 | statue n 조각상 | piety n (종교적인) 경건함 | supremacy n 지배 | reinforce v 강화하다 | proficiency n 숙련도 | exemplify v 예시가 되다 | discus n 원반 | vigorous adj 활기 있는 | convincing adj 설득력 있는 | flexed adj 수축된 | influx n 유입 | absorb v 흡수하다 | sophistication n 정교함 | drapery n 옷주름, 휘장 | texture n 질감 | accentuate v 강조하다 | enhance v 강화하다 | extraordinary adj 뛰어난 | outspread n 확산 | obligate v 의무화하다 | emerge v 출현하다

Test

본서 P. 272

미국 전기 시스템의 도입

1 ➡ 현대 미국 사회에서 전기는 너무 흔해서 많은 사람들이 그것을 매우 당연시한다. 우리가 들이마시는 공기처럼 사람들은 전기가 없을 때까지 그것의 중요성을 깨닫지 못한다. 우리 집과 사무실의 생명선에 대해 매달 날아오는 청구서에도 불구하고, 우리는 정전이 발생해서 무슨 이유 때문인지 불이 켜지지 않을 때까지 그것이 항상 존재할 거라고 단순히 기대한다. 필수적인 자원에 대한 이런 안일한 태도는 사실 꽤 최근의 현상이다. 비록 과학자들은 전기의 특성을 이미 알고 있었지만 19세기 후반까지 실용적인 용도로 전기를 활용할 수 없었다. 그들이 그런 업적을 달성하자 개발은 빠르게 진전되었고 그것은 미국 사회와 세계 전반에 어마어마한 영향을 미쳤다.

2 ➡ 최초의 사용 가능한 전기 시스템이 언제 만들어졌는지에 대해서는 확실하게 말할 수 없다. 하지만 가장 초기의 시스템들은 전하가 한 방향으로만 흐르는 직류로 가동되었다. 전기 배급이 미국에 도입되었을 때 그것은 토머스 에디슨이 지지하는 직류 시스템에 기반을 두었다. 직류 시스템은 그 당시의 전기 주요 용도인 백열등과 전동기에 적합했다. 그것은 축전지를 충전하는 데도 사용될 수 있었는데,

1. 1단락에서 글쓴이가 '생명선'을 언급하는 이유는 무엇인가?
Ⓐ 전기와 운동의 중요성을 비교하기 위해
Ⓑ 현대인들이 고액의 의료비를 지출한다는 것을 보여주기 위해
Ⓒ 우리 삶에서 전기의 중요성을 강조하기 위해
Ⓓ 우리가 쉽게 당연시하는 것의 사례를 제공하기 위해

2. 다음 중 2단락에서 언급되지 않은 것은
Ⓐ 직류는 오직 한 방향으로만 흐르는 전류다
Ⓑ 토머스 에디슨은 직류를 발명하고 대중화했다
Ⓒ 첫 전기 시스템이 언제 설치되었는지는 불확실하다
Ⓓ 인공광은 전기가 처음으로 사용된 경우 중 하나였다

3. 2단락에서 전기에 대해 추론 가능한 것은 무엇인가?
Ⓐ 발전소들은 급등하는 수요를 충족시키기 위해 출력을 증가시키려고 했다.
Ⓑ 정확한 청구서 발부를 가능케 한 미터기의 발명은 환영받지 못했다.

이는 중요한 전기 부하 조정을 가능하게 했고 발전기의 출력이 중단되었을 때 비상 공급을 제공할 수 있었다. 발전기들은 또한 손쉽게 차례대로 연결될 수 있었는데, 이것은 발전소로 하여금 수요가 낮을 때는 출력을 쉽게 낮추고 더 안정적으로 전력을 공급할 수 있게 했다. 에디슨은 고객들의 실제 사용량에 따른 정확한 청구를 가능케 하는 미터기를 발명했는데, 그의 많은 발명품처럼 그것은 오직 직류에서만 작동했다.

3 ➡ 에디슨이 보유한 많은 특허권으로 인해 그는 직류가 표준으로 남기를 강하게 바라고 있었지만, 웨스팅하우스 전력 및 제조사가 교류라는 형태로 도전장을 내밀었다. 교류는 유럽에서 개발되었는데, 간츠 제작소가 1886년에 로마시에 전력을 공급한 후에 신뢰성으로 명성을 얻었다. 교류에서는 전하의 방향이 주기적으로 뒤바뀌어 반대 방향으로 움직인다. 그것을 사용하게 될 장치들과 동일한 전압 수준에서 전력이 생산되어야 하는 직류와는 달리, 교류는 변압기라고 불리는 발명품을 통해 조절될 수 있었다. 이것은 전력이 발전소에서 매우 높은 전압으로 생산되어 더 적은 수의, 상대적으로 더 얇은 전선을 통해서 공급될 수 있으며, 그런 다음 변압기에 의해 고객들이 사용 가능한 수준으로 전압을 낮출 수 있다는 것을 의미했다. 따라서 교류 발전소는 훨씬 더 커지고 전기를 공급받는 사람들에게서 더 멀리 위치할 수 있었다.4 ➡ 이런 장점들을 고려하여 조지 웨스팅하우스는 니콜라 테슬라의 교류 기술 특허에 대한 사용권을 얻기로 결정했다. 이것은 '전류 전쟁'이라 불리는 에디슨과 웨스팅하우스의 충돌로 이어졌고, 여기에는 자신들의 선택이 우세하게 되기를 기대하며 두 전류 시스템 중 하나에 막대한 투자를 한 미국과 유럽의 많은 회사들이 포함되었다. [■A] 에디슨은 대다수의 소비자들이 사용하게 될 낮은 전압 상태에서 교류가 치명적일 수 있는 가능성이 크다는 사실을 포착했다. [■B] 교류 전류의 교차하는 특성은 바로잡지 않으면 곧 치명적으로 변할 수 있는 리듬을 유발해, 심장이 조정력을 잃게 만들 수 있다. [■C] 이 결점에 집중해서 에디슨은 교류 시스템의 채택을 막기 위해 의도된 선전 활동을 시작했다. 그는 주 입법부에서 교류 사용을 반대하는 로비를 적극적으로 했고, 잘못된 정보를 배포했으며, 교류 전류를 사용해 동물들을 공개적으로 죽였고 심지어는 그 자신이 사형 제도에 반대함에도 불구하고 전기 의자 발명가를 후원했다. [■D]

5 ➡ 에디슨의 노력에도 불구하고, 교류 전류는 결국 산업 표준이 되었다. 미국에서 직류 전기의 첫 성공적인 장거리 전송은 1889년에 오리건주 오리건시에 위치한 윌래밋 폭포 발전소에서 이루어졌다. 불행히도 그 발전소는 이듬해 홍수로 파괴되었다. 윌래밋 폭포 전력회사가 시설을 재건할 때 그들은 웨스팅하우스에서 생산된 실험적인 교류 전류 발전기를 도입하기로 결정했다. 같은 해에 나이아가라 폭포의 동력을 사용해 전기를 생산하는 것이 결정되었고 어떤 종류의 전류를 사용할지를 결정할 전문가 특별 위원회가 구성되었다. 그들은 결국 나이아가라 폭포 프로젝트를 위한 발전기에 대한 계약을 웨스팅하우스와 했지만, 협력을 위해 에디슨의 제너럴 일렉트릭사와 뉴욕의 버팔로까지 송전선을 건설하는 계약을 맺었다. 그 후에 제너럴 일렉트릭은 에디슨을 몰아내고 교류 동력에 빠르고 철저하게 투자하는 방향으로 나아갔다. 오늘날 직류는 제3궤조 전철과 같은 극히 일부의 특정 용도를 위해서만 지속되고 있다.

Ⓒ 에디슨의 발명품 대부분은 미국 전기 회사들에게 팔렸다.
Ⓓ 전기 사용량은 하루 중 시간대별로 달랐다.

4. 2단락의 단어 'which(그것)'가 가리키는 것은
Ⓐ 미터기
Ⓑ 청구서 발부
Ⓒ 사용량
Ⓓ 직류

5. 다음 중 지문에 음영 표시된 문장의 핵심 정보를 가장 잘 표현한 문장은 무엇인가? 오답은 의미를 크게 왜곡하거나 핵심 정보를 누락하고 있다.
Ⓐ 교류는 사용 가능한 수준으로 변압될 수 있는 반면에 직류는 기기가 요구하는 전압으로 생산되어야만 했다.
Ⓑ 동일한 전압 수준을 유지하는 직류와는 대조적으로 교류는 변압기를 사용해 고전압 수준으로 변압될 수 있었다.
Ⓒ 매우 고전압의 교류 전기를 생산할 수 있도록 변압기가 발명되기 이전에 직류는 전기 기기에 널리 사용되었다.
Ⓓ 어느 전압으로든 변압될 수 있는 직류와는 달리 교류는 기기들을 위해 표준 전압으로 생산되어야 한다.

6. 4단락에 따르면, 다음 중 교류 시스템이 채택되는 것을 막으려는 에디슨의 노력으로 언급되지 않은 것은 무엇인가?
Ⓐ 교류 시스템에 대한 허구 소문을 퍼트렸다.
Ⓑ 전기 충격으로 죽은 짐승들을 보여주었다.
Ⓒ 사형 제도의 폐지를 제안했다.
Ⓓ 전기 의자 사업에 투자했다.

7. 4단락의 단어 'predominant(우세한)'와 의미상 가장 가까운 것은
Ⓐ 수익성이 좋은
Ⓑ 우월한
Ⓒ 필수적인
Ⓓ 선행하는

8. 5단락에 따르면, 다음 중 윌래밋 폭포 발전소에 대해 사실인 것은 무엇인가?
Ⓐ 재건될 때 교류 시스템을 채택하기로 결정했다.
Ⓑ 발전기들이 1890년에 지진으로 파손되었다.
Ⓒ 미국에서 최초로 교류 전류를 전송하는 데 성공했다.
Ⓓ 그것의 원래 시설은 교류에 적합하게 설계되어 있었다.

9. 지문에 다음 문장이 들어갈 수 있는 위치를 나타내는 네 개의 사각형 [■]을 확인하시오.

이 결점에 집중해서 에디슨은 교류 시스템의 채택을 막기 위해 의도된 선전 활동을 시작했다.

이 문장이 들어가기에 가장 적합한 곳은? [■C]

10. 지시문: 아래 문장들을 알맞게 넣어 다음 표를 완성하시오. 선택지 중 적절한 문장들을 골라 관계된 개념과 연결하시오. 선택지 두 개는 정답이 될 수 없다. ***이 문제의 배점은 3점이다.***

선택지	직류	교류
Ⓐ 고전압 때문에 과거에 제3궤조 전철에 흔히 사용되었다.	Ⓒ	Ⓑ
Ⓑ 유럽에서 만들어졌고 로마의 전기 시스템으로 사용된 후 인기가 높아졌다.	Ⓖ	Ⓓ
Ⓒ 미국에서 처음으로 윌래밋 폭포 전력회사에서 장거리 송전이 시행되었다.		Ⓕ
Ⓓ 낮은 전압에서 생명을 위협하는 잠재적 위험으로 반대자들의 비판을 받았다.		
Ⓔ 에디슨의 협력으로 '전류 전쟁'의 최종 승자가 되었다.		
Ⓕ 나이아가라 폭포 프로젝트를 실행하는 데 최종 채택되었다.		
Ⓖ 그것의 지지자들은 다른 시스템이 널리 사용되는 것을 막는 운동을 펼쳤다.		

어휘 commonplace adj 아주 흔한 n 흔히 있는 일, 다반사 I take for granted 당연한 일로 여기다, 대수롭지 않게 여기다 I deprive v 빼앗다, 박탈하다 I lifeblood n 생명선, 혈액 I inexplicably adv 불가해하게, 알 수 없이 I property n 속성, 특성 I harness v 이용/활용하다 I operational adj 사용/가동할 준비가 갖춰진 I direct current (전기의) 직류 I champion v ~을 위해 싸우다, ~을 옹호하다 I incandescent adj 백열성의, 눈부시게 밝은 I generator n 발전기 I power plant 발전/동력 장치, 발전소 I billing n 청구서 발부 I patent n 특허권 I vested interest (개인적 또는 경제적으로) 편파적인 관심/흥미, 기득권 I alternating current (전기의) 교류 I reputation n 평판, 명성 I reliability n 신뢰도, 확실성 I periodically adv 정기/주기적으로 I reverse v 뒤바꾸다, 뒤집다, 역전시키다 I voltage n 전압 I modulate v 조절하다, 바꾸다 I transformer n 변압기 I emit v (빛, 열 등을) 내다, 내뿜다 I recipient n 받는 사람, 수령인 I predominant adj 뚜렷한, 우세한, 지배적인 I seize upon ~에 달려들다, ~를 붙잡다 I lethal adj 치명적인 I instigate v 유발시키다, 일으키다, 부추기다 I legislature n 입법 기관(의 사람들), 입법부 I disinformation n 허위 정보 I execute v 처형하다 I incorporate v 포함하다 I experimental adj 실험적인, 실험의 I conciliation n 조정, 화해, 협력 관계

역사 기록과 언어 번역

1 ➡ 한 문화의 기록된 역사는 문헌 기록과 다양한 문서로 기록된 형태의 소통에 근거한 서술이다. 많은 문화권에서 기술된 역사는 청동기 시대로 거슬러 올라가지만 다른 문화권들은 문자 체계를 꽤 최근에 구축했기 때문에 그들의 기록된 역사는 그에 따라 짧다. 선사 시대라는 용어는 기록된 역사 이전 시기를 가리키기 때문에 한 문화의 문자 체계의 창조와 함께 끝난다. 물론 문자 체계는 갑자기 완전한 상태로 생겨나지 않기 때문에 선사 시대와 역사 시대 사이의 과도기를 원사(原史) 시대라고 부른다. 이 시기에는 식자율이 증가하고 역사 기록을 만드는 데 사용될 수 있는 문서들이 있지만, 그 문화 내 사람들은 아직 그들의 역사를 기록하는 것을 시작하지 않은 때다.

2 ➡ 기록된 역사의 최초 사례는 최초의 해독 가능한 문자 체계와 함께 중동과 이집트에서 온 것이다. 이것들은 고대 수메르 설형문자와 이집트 상형문자로써 약 기원전 3500년에 독립적으로 만들어진 서로 매우 다른 문자 체계다. 수메르어 기록은 상거래와 정부에 납세한 세금을 기록하기 위해 생겨났고 그것은 점토판에 기록되었다. 최초 이집트 기록은 파라오의 상속자들과 그들의 통치 중 주요 사건들을 기록한 연대기였다. 그들의 후손이 그 문자를 읽는 방법을 잊은 지 오래됐기 때문에 현대 고고학자들은 그것을 해독해야 했다. 이 많은 역사 기록들은 고고학자들이 고대 유적지에서 열쇠를 발견하기까지

11. 1단락에서 추론 가능한 것은

Ⓐ 원사 시대의 사람들 대부분은 글을 읽고 쓸 줄 알고 고등교육을 받았다

Ⓑ 문자 언어가 발달하는 과정은 흔히 점진적으로 이루어진다

Ⓒ 문자의 초기 형태는 모두 그림과 비슷했다

Ⓓ 최초의 기록된 역사는 신석기 시대로 거슬러 올라간다

12. 2단락에 따르면, 다음 중 이집트 상형문자에 관해 사실인 것은 무엇인가?

Ⓐ 대부분의 이집트 후손들은 그들의 고대어를 이해했다.

Ⓑ 이 문자들은 사적지의 동굴 벽에 새겨졌다.

Ⓒ 모든 문서는 군사 기밀을 보호하기 위해 부호화되었다.

Ⓓ 그것들은 파라오들과 관련된 역사적 사건들을 기록하는 데 사용되었다.

13. 2단락의 단어 'they(그것들)'가 가리키는 것은

Ⓐ 고고학자들

Ⓑ 비문들

Ⓒ 암호들

Ⓓ 문자들

수 세기 동안 잃어버린 상태로 남아 있었다. 그들이 발견한 비문들은 암호로 사용되도록 의도된 것이 아니었지만 세 가지 다른 문자로 기록되었기 때문에 그것들은 그 목적을 잘 수행했다.

3 ➡ 수메르어는 이란 북서부의 베히스툰 비문의 발견으로 번역되었다. 그 비문은 페르시아 왕인 다리우스 1세의 짧은 전기와 키루스 대왕의 죽음 후 이어진 격변 속에서 그가 왕좌에 앉을 수 있게 해 준 많은 군사적 승리에 대해 말하고 있다. 그의 통치 중 만들어진 그 비문은 세 가지 다른 설형문자 언어, 즉 고대 페르시아어, 엘람어, 바빌로니아어로 기록되었다. 이 언어들은 그의 왕국과 그가 정복한 지역에서 사용되는 것이었으며 온 백성과 후손이 그의 영광을 알 수 있게 했다. 고대 페르시아어는 문자 구조를 공유하는 중세와 현대 페르시아어의 도움으로 번역되었고 그 후 다른 문자도 서서히 해독되었다.

4 ➡ 이집트 상형문자는 로제타석이라 불리는 유물의 도움으로 번역되었다. 베히스툰 비문처럼 이 바위도 원래 신전 같은 공공 건물에 전시되었을 것으로 생각되지만, 재활용되어 나일 삼각주에 있는 라시드(로제타) 지역의 요새 건축에 사용되었다가, 훗날 그곳에서 프랑스 군인에게 발견되었다. 맨 위에서 맨 아래까지 그 비문은 고대 이집트 상형문자와, 문서 기록에 사용된 고대 이집트 문자인 민중 문자, 그리고 고대 그리스어로 기록되어 있다. 그 바위의 기록은 프톨레마이오스 5세가 자신을 이집트의 새로운 신성한 통치자로 선포한 칙령이다. 비록 윗부분은 명백하게 불완전했지만 그들은 함께 모여 중요한 해석의 열쇠를 제공했다. 다른 유사한 비문들이 그 후에도 발견되었지만 로제타석의 영향으로 인해 새로운 지식을 밝히는 데 중요한 단서는 흔히 로제타석이라 불린다.

5 ➡ 대개의 경우 고대 문서를 해독하는 것은 여러 세대에 걸쳐 많은 언어학자의 작업을 수반하는 매우 길고 어려운 과정이다. 순전한 끈기로 인해 성공적으로 분석된 한 언어는 고대 마야어다. [■A] 마야 상형문자는 중미 전역에서 발견되었으며 기원전 약 300년까지 거슬러 올라가는데, 이로 인해 아메리카 대륙을 통틀어서 그 수준의 복잡성과 완성도를 지닌 가장 오래된 언어가 된다. [■B] 그것은 원래 그림들이 사물과 사건을 직접적으로 상징하는 완전한 상형문자라고 생각되었다. 1900년까지 숫자 체계 외에 해석된 것이 거의 없었지만, 과학자들은 어떤 그림들이 실제 단어를 상징할 뿐만 아니라 음절을 형성하는 소리 모음도 된다는 것을 서서히 깨닫게 되었다. [■C] 1950년대와 70년대의 중대한 발견에 따라 해석은 빠르게 진전되었다. [■D] 오늘날 과학자들은 우리가 갖고 있는 문서들의 대부분을 읽을 수 있으며 마야인들도 그들의 고대 문자 체계를 다시 배우기 시작했다.

6 ➡ 불행히도 로마인들 이전의 사회에서 비롯된 조어(祖語)인 에트루리아어와 같은 언어들은 여전히 해석 시도를 허용치 않고 있다. 에트루리아어 문자는 그리스어 문자에서 비롯되었고 가장 오래된 기록들은 기원전 약 500년까지 거슬러 올라간다. 수천 개의 기록이 비석, 동상, 꽃병, 묘석, 심지어 보석과 같은 개인 물건에서도 발견되었고 언어학자들은 그 단어들을 소리나는 대로 읽을 수 있다. 하지만 그들은 라틴어로 차용되었다가 나중에 영어로 차용된 단어들을 포함해 몇 백 단어의 뜻만 확신할 수 있다.

14. 다음 중 3단락에서 언급되지 않은 것은

Ⓐ 베히스툰 비문은 고대 수메르 문자를 해독하는 데 도움이 되었다

Ⓑ 현대 페르시아어는 고대의 것과 동일한 알파벳 구조를 사용한다

Ⓒ 베히스툰 비문은 페르시아 다리우스 왕의 일생 이야기에 관한 것이다

Ⓓ 다리우스는 선왕인 키루스를 암살한 후 왕이 되었다

15. 다음 중 지문에 음영 표시된 문장의 핵심 정보를 가장 잘 표현한 문장은 무엇인가? 오답은 의미를 크게 왜곡하거나 핵심 정보를 누락하고 있다.

Ⓐ 그 언어들은 그의 영토에서 사용되는 것들이었기 때문에 그의 명성을 백성과 후손에게 전달할 수 있었다.

Ⓑ 그들이 모두 이해할 수 있는 언어로 기록되었기 때문에 그의 백성은 그의 영광스러운 이야기를 읽을 수 있었다.

Ⓒ 그 언어들은 그의 왕국에서 널리 사용되었기 때문에 그의 백성과 후손이 그것을 읽는 데 어려움이 없었다.

Ⓓ 그의 백성과 후손은 그의 영광스러운 이야기들이 구전으로 전해졌기 때문에 익히 알고 있었다.

16. 4단락에서 글쓴이가 '로제타석'을 언급하는 이유는 무엇인가?

Ⓐ 나일 삼각주 근처 역사 기념물의 사례를 제공하기 위해

Ⓑ 고대 이집트어를 해독하는 데 도움을 준 유명한 비문을 소개하기 위해

Ⓒ 그것이 현존하는 돌로 된 가장 오래된 유물인 것을 보여주기 위해

Ⓓ 프톨레마이오스 5세가 공표한 칙령의 중요성을 강조하기 위해

17. 5단락에 따르면, 다음 중 마야 상형문자에 관해 사실인 것은 무엇인가?

Ⓐ 세계에서 가장 복잡한 언어로 알려져 있다.

Ⓑ 마야 사람들은 이 문자를 번역하는 데 중요한 단서들을 제공했다.

Ⓒ 해독 작업은 1950년대와 70년대에 빠른 진척을 보였다.

Ⓓ 과학자들은 숫자 체계가 소리도 나타낸다고 밝혔다.

18. 6단락에 따르면, 다음 중 에트루리아어에 대해 사실이 아닌 것은 무엇인가?

Ⓐ 언어학자들은 갖고 있는 문서들 대부분을 이해할 수 있다.

Ⓑ 라틴어와 영어가 거기서 몇몇 단어들을 차용했다.

Ⓒ 그리스어 문자는 에트루리아어 문자의 근원이었다.

Ⓓ 가장 오래된 기록은 기원전 약 500년의 것이다.

19. 지문에 다음 문장이 들어갈 위치를 나타내는 네 개의 사각형 [■]을 확인하시오.

그것은 원래 그림들이 사물과 사건을 직접적으로 상징하는 완전한 상형문자라고 생각되었다.

이 문장이 들어가기에 가장 적합한 곳은? [■B]

20. 지시문: 아래 문장들을 알맞게 넣어 다음 표를 완성하시오. 선택지 중 적절한 문장들을 골라 관계된 개념과 연결하시오. 선택지 두 개는 정답이 될 수 없다. ***이 문제의 배점은 3점이다.***

선택지	수메르 설형문자	마야 상형문자
Ⓐ 그것들을 해독할 수 있게 도와준 비문은 세 개의 다른 언어로 기록되었다. Ⓑ 언어학자들은 여전히 대다수의 단어의 뜻에 대해 확신이 없다. Ⓒ 복잡성과 완성도로 유명하다. Ⓓ 정부에 상거래와 납세 기록을 제출하기 위해 처음 발달했다. Ⓔ 몇몇 그림은 소리와 단어를 둘 다 나타내는 것으로 밝혀졌다. Ⓕ 그것의 중요한 해독 열쇠는 나일 삼각주의 라시드 지역 근처에 위치했다. Ⓖ 그것은 약 기원전 300년까지 거슬러 올라가는 것으로 중미 전역에서 발견되었다.	Ⓐ Ⓓ	Ⓒ Ⓔ Ⓖ

어휘 recorded history 기록된 역사 I narrative n 서술, 진술 I written account 문헌 기록 I writing system 문자 체계 I accordingly adv 그에 맞춰 I prehistory n 선사 시대 I transition n 과도기 I protohistory n 원사 시대 I literacy n 식자율(識者率) I comprehensible adj 이해할 수 있는 I archaic adj 구식의 I cuneiform n 설형문자 I script n 문자, 기록 I hieroglyph n 상형문자 I emerge v 드러나다, 나오다 I chronology n 연대기 I succession n 승계 I archaeologist n 고고학자 I decipher v 해독하다 I ruin n 유적 I inscription n 비문 I biography n 전기 I upheaval n 격변 I commission v (작품을) 의뢰하다 I realm n 영역, 왕국 I subject n 국민, 신하 I artifact n 유물 I decree n 칙령, 법령 I divine adj 신성한 I lengthy adj 너무 긴 I linguist n 언어학자 I parse v 분석하다 I sheer adj 순전한 I complexity n 복잡함 I pictographic adj 상형문자의 I number system 진법 I syllable n 음절 I breakthrough n 돌파구 I proto-language n 조어(祖語) I defy v 저항하다, 무시하다, 허용하지 않다 I derive v 끌어내다, 얻다 I phonetically adv 발음대로

Actual Test

Actual Test 1

본서 I P. 282

1. B **2.** C **3.** C **4.** D **5.** A **6.** B **7.** C **8.** A **9.** B

10. Terrestrial Planets: B, D, E / Jovian Planets: A, F

11. A **12.** D **13.** C **14.** B **15.** B **16.** C **17.** B **18.** D **19.** C **20.** C, E, F

본서 I P. 283

행성의 두 종류

1 ➡ 지구를 포함해 태양계의 모든 행성은 태양 주변에 타원형에 가까운 궤도를 형성하며, 거의 같은 평면에 정렬되어 있다. 태양계 안의 행성이 오직 여덟 개라는 사실을 고려할 때 이들 사이에 얼마나 큰 다양성이 존재하는지 생각해 보면 상당히 놀랍다. 그러나 지난 두 세기에 걸쳐 이웃 행성들에 관해 점점 더 많은 사실들이 밝혀지며 행성들이 크게 두 범주로 분류될 수 있다는 점이 서서히 명확해졌다. 지구형 행성은 고밀도의 암석 물질로 구성된 작은 행성들이고 목성형 행성은 수소 및 헬륨같이 대부분 기체로 이루어진 저밀도의 거대

1. **1단락에 따르면, 행성 분류에 대해 추론 가능한 것은 무엇인가?**

Ⓐ 태양계 내의 행성들을 더 분류하기 위해 더 많은 조사를 할 필요가 없다.
Ⓑ 행성의 밀도와 물질은 그것을 분류하는 데 중요한 역할을 한다.
Ⓒ 우리 태양계는 여덟 개 이상의 집단으로 분류될 수 있다.
Ⓓ 행성 분류는 다른 천체가 어떻게 시작되었는지 설명할 수 있게 해주었다.

한 행성들이다. 이러한 범주는 행성 분류의 편리한 기준이기도 하지만 태양계가 어떻게 탄생하게 되었는지를 이해하는 데에도 많은 도움을 주는 것으로 증명되었다.

2 ➡ 수성, 금성, 지구, 화성은 지구형 행성이다. '지구형(terrestrial)'이라는 용어는 지구를 의미하는 라틴어 'terra'에서 유래했다. 따라서 이 용어는 이 행성들이 모두 중요한 면에서 지구와 유사하다는 점을 가리키며 실제로도 이들은 몇 가지 공통된 특징을 가지고 있다. 첫째, 이 행성들은 모두 크기가 비슷하고, 더욱 중요한 점은 목성형 행성들보다 훨씬 더 작다는 것이다. 목성형 행성 중 가장 작은 해왕성은 지구형 행성 중에서 가장 큰 지구보다 50배 이상 크다. 또한 지구형 행성은 모두 다른 행성들에 비해 태양에 가깝게 공전한다. 행성 궤도 사이의 거리는 태양에서 멀수록 증가한다. 결과적으로 네 개의 지구형 행성의 궤도는 태양 가까이 몰려 있는 반면 네 개의 외행성은 궤도 사이의 거리가 광대하다. 태양에 더 가까이 있기 때문에 지구형 행성은 태양의 열 에너지로 데워져 있다. 또한 모든 지구형 행성에는 대기가 있는데, 이는 태양열을 보유하는 데 도움이 되고 지구형 행성들의 평균 기온이 더 먼 외행성들에 비해 훨씬 높은 이유를 설명해 준다. 그러나 지구형 행성의 가장 현저한 특징은 그 조밀한 구성이다. 이들의 표면은 주로 규산염암으로 이루어져 있으며 이는 그들이 겪은 험난한 역사를 기록하면서 혜성 충돌로 인한 분화구, 협곡, 산맥, 화산 등이 특징인 이들 행성의 극적인 풍경을 설명해 준다.

3 ➡ 목성, 토성, 천왕성, 해왕성은 목성형(Jovian) 행성이라고 불린다. 이 용어는 주피터라고도 하는 로마신 조브(Jove)의 이름에서 유래한 것으로 따라서 이들 행성과 목성 사이의 유사함을 나타낸다. 네 개의 목성형 행성은 태양계의 거대 행성들로, 지구형 행성들을 작아 보이게 한다. 또한 태양의 온기에서 너무 멀리 떨어진 궤도로 인해 그것들은 모든 행성들 중에서 가장 추운데, 가장 바깥쪽 행성들의 온도는 섭씨 영하 200도까지 내려간다. 목성형 행성의 또 한 가지 뚜렷한 특징은 표면이다. 겉으로 보기에는 단단해 보이지만 이들 행성은 대부분 기체로 이루어져 있어 바위투성이인 지구형 행성들과 달리 표면의 윤곽이 뚜렷하지 않다. [■A] 대신 대부분 수소와 헬륨인 대기가 중앙으로 갈수록 더 조밀해져 매우 높은 압력 아래 액체 상태인 내부와 뒤섞여 있다. [■B] 따라서 외부 대기와 내부 표면 사이에 명확한 구분이 없다. 또한 기체 상태인 이 네 개의 거대 행성들을 둘러싼 화려한 고리와 위성이 장관을 이루는 것도 특징이다. [■C] 최대 두 개의 위성을 가지고 있는 지구형 행성과 눈에 띄게 대조적으로 목성은 63개의 위성을 가지고 있다. [■D] 이들 사이의 극적인 차이점을 고려할 때 지구형 행성들이 목성형 행성들과 극단적으로 다른 특징을 가지고 있음은 분명하다.

4 ➡ 목성형 행성과 지구형 행성의 두드러진 차이점은 태양계 탄생 시 그것들이 형성된 방식의 차이점으로 설명된다. 현재의 이론은 태양계가 원래 태양 성운이라는 거대한 회전 구름이었다는 입장을 취하고 있다. 이 구름은 주로 헬륨 및 수소 같은 기체, 그리고 그보다 훨씬 더 적은 양의 고밀도 물질로 이루어져 있었다. 이 구름은 회전하면서 서서히 고밀도 부위가 중심에 모인 원반 형태를 갖추게 되었다. 우리 태양계는 기체가 응축 및 융합되면서 이 구름에서 형성되었다. 기체는 저온과 고압 상태에서 응축한다. 그러나 성운 중심 근처의 조건은 너무 혹독해서 이것이 일어나지 않았다. 그래서 그곳에서

2. 2단락의 단어 'retain(보유하다)'과 의미상 가장 가까운 것은

Ⓐ 생산하다
Ⓑ 반영하다
Ⓒ 보유하다
Ⓓ 증가하다

3. 2단락에서 글쓴이가 '해왕성'을 언급하는 이유는 무엇인가?

Ⓐ 지구형 행성들과 목성형 행성들의 구성 성분 차이를 보여주기 위해서
Ⓑ 목성형 행성들은 지구형 행성들보다 더 적절한 곳에 위치해 있다는 증거를 보여주기 위해서
Ⓒ 지구형 행성들이 목성형 행성들에 비해 얼마나 작은지 강조하기 위해서
Ⓓ 지구형 행성들이 목성형 행성들에 비해 태양에 더 가까이 있는 이유를 설명하기 위해서

4. 다음 중 지문에 음영 표시된 문장의 핵심 정보를 가장 잘 표현한 문장은 무엇인가? 오답은 문장의 의미를 크게 왜곡하거나 핵심 정보를 누락하고 있다.

Ⓐ 분화구, 협곡, 산맥, 화산은 바위로 된 표면을 가지고 있는 지구형 행성의 극적인 풍경을 설명해 준다.
Ⓑ 험난한 역사를 가지고 있어서 이 행성들에는 분화구가 있다.
Ⓒ 그래서 분화구, 협곡, 산맥, 화산으로 뒤덮인 이들의 표면은 대부분 규산염암이다.
Ⓓ 바위와 규산염으로 된 표면 때문에 지구형 행성들은 다양한 지형적 특징들로 증명되는 역사적 트라우마의 흔적을 보여준다.

5. 3단락에서 'they(그것들)'가 가리키는 것은

Ⓐ 목성형 행성들
Ⓑ 지구형 행성들
Ⓒ 궤도들
Ⓓ 표면들

6. 3단락에 따르면, 목성형 행성들은 지구형 행성들에 비해서 무엇이 독특한가?

Ⓐ 지구형 행성들이 발달하기 전에 형성되었다.
Ⓑ 주로 가스로 이루어져 있다.
Ⓒ 대기는 주로 수소로 이루어져 있다.
Ⓓ 핵은 상대적으로 단단하다.

7. 4단락에 따르면, 다음 중 우리 태양계에 대해 사실인 것은 무엇인가?

Ⓐ 가스가 압축되면서 만들어졌다.
Ⓑ 융합되기 전에 가스가 압축되어 응축되었다.
Ⓒ 온도가 떨어지고 기압이 올라갈 때 가스는 압축된다.
Ⓓ 중력은 목성형 행성들의 형성에만 역할을 했다.

형성된 행성들은 대부분 규소와 금속처럼 녹는점이 높은 혼합물로 이루어졌고, 이 혼합물들의 양이 많지 않았기 때문에 크기가 더 작았다. 이것이 지구형 행성이 되었다. 성운 내의 멀리 떨어진 곳은 조건이 이보다 유리해서 기체가 응축될 수 있었고 중력에 의해 한 곳에 모여 목성형 행성들을 형성할 수 있었다. 이것은 태양계에 존재하는 두 범주의 행성들이 가진 구성 요소, 크기, 밀도 차이를 설명해 준다.

8. 4단락의 단어 'coalesced(융합되다)'와 의미상 가장 가까운 것은

Ⓐ 결합되다
Ⓑ 정렬되다
Ⓒ 퍼뜨려지다
Ⓓ 팽창되다

9. 지문에 다음 문장이 들어갈 수 있는 위치를 나타내는 네 개의 사각형 [■]을 확인하시오.

따라서 외부 대기와 내부 표면 사이에 명확한 구분이 없다.

이 문장이 들어가기에 가장 적합한 곳은? [■B]

10. 지시문: 다음 문장들을 알맞게 넣어 다음 표를 완성하시오. 선택지 중 적절한 문장들을 골라 관계된 개념과 연결하시오. 선택지 두 개는 정답이 될 수 없다. 이 문제의 배점은 3점이다.

선택지	지구형 행성들	목성형 행성들
Ⓐ 크기 면에서 이들은 다른 분류에 속한 행성들을 작아 보이게 한다. Ⓑ 다른 분류에 속한 행성들에 비해 작다. Ⓒ 태양의 열에너지에 더 가까이 다가가면서 따뜻해진다. Ⓓ 이 그룹의 행성들은 서로 크기가 비슷하다. Ⓔ 암석이 많은 표면을 갖고 있다. Ⓕ 위성이 많은 것이 특징이다. Ⓖ 이 행성들에서는 가스 공급이 불충분하다.	Ⓑ Ⓓ Ⓔ	Ⓐ Ⓕ

어휘 planet n 행성 I solar system 태양계 I terrestrial adj 지구의 I density n 밀도 I Jovian adj 목성의 I helium n 헬륨 I classification n 분류 I revealing adj 흥미로운 사실을 보여주는 I Mercury n 수성 I Venus n 금성 I Mars n 화성 I indicate v 암시하다 I Neptune n 해왕성 I orbit n 궤도 v 궤도를 돌다 I immense adj 광대한 I retain v 보유하다 I primarily adv 주로 I silicate n 규산염 I crater n 분화구 I canyon n 협곡 I Jupiter n 목성 I Saturn n 토성 I Uranus n 천왕성 I designate v 명시하다 I outermost adj 가장 바깥의 I conspicuous adj 눈에 띄는 I seemingly adv 겉으로 보기에 I prominent adj 두드러진 I spectacular adj 화려한 I encircle v 에워싸다 I phenomenal adj 비범한, 놀라운 I nebula n 성운 I spin v 돌다 I flatten v 평평하게 하다 I disk n 원반 I condense v 압축/응축하다 I coalesce v 응결하다 I melting point 녹는점 I gravity n 중력

본서 I P. 287

구텐베르크와 금속활자 인쇄

1 ➡ [■A] 활자란 각 기호와 글자를 표현하기 위해 이동 가능한 주조된 금속 조각을 사용하는 인쇄 및 활판 체계를 말한다. [■B] 활자의 발전은 고대 이집트의 목판 인쇄에서 시작되었다. [■C] 8세기 무렵에 중국인들은 문서와 그림으로 가득한 책 전체를 인쇄하는 데 이 기술을 사용했다. 15세기 독일의 인쇄공이자 금세공인이었던 요하네스 구텐베르크는 이후 이것을 더욱 발전시켜 금속활자를 부속물로 이용한 새로운 인쇄 시스템을 도입하여 명성을 얻게 되었다. [■D] 인쇄 기술이 유럽에 도달하기 전에는 책은 수도사들이 손으로 세심하게 따라 써야 했다. 목판 인쇄는 손으로 따라 쓰는 것보다 더 쉽고 더 믿을 만했기 때문에 유럽에 도착했을 때 빠르게 도입되었지만, 속도가 훨씬 더 빠르지는 않았다.

11. 다른 단락들과의 관계에 비추어 1단락의 역할은 무엇인가?

Ⓐ 주제와 그것의 발달에 기여한 사람에 대한 역사적 배경을 소개한다.
Ⓑ 종이 인쇄술 영역에 혁신을 일으켰던 사람의 배경을 제공한다.
Ⓒ 인쇄술에서의 주요 기술적 변화와 활자를 만드는 데 이용된 방법을 설명한다.
Ⓓ 주제와 종이가 인쇄되는 방식에 혁신을 일으켰던 발명품의 결과를 밝혀준다.

12. 2단락에 따르면, 다음 중 인쇄에 사용된 목재의 한계가 아닌 것은 무엇인가?

2 ➡ 금속활자가 나오기 전에는 상대적으로 속도가 느린 목판 인쇄로 인쇄가 이루어졌다. 이 고된 작업에서는 인쇄면 각각에 하나의 목판을 이용해 표면에 글자와 그림을 새겨 넣는 과정이 필수적이었다. 그러다 13세기 후반 중국에서 이것이 목판활자로 대체되었다. 덕분에 인쇄공들은 각각의 조각을 끼워 맞춰 단어를 만들 수 있었고, 새로운 면을 인쇄할 때마다 완전히 새로운 이미지를 조각해 넣을 필요가 없어졌다. 생산 시간은 크게 줄어들었으나 나무를 인쇄 도구로 이용하는 데는 여전히 한계가 있었다. 나무는 내구성 있는 재질이었지만 반복적인 인쇄로 압력을 받으면 닳아 없어져서 꽤 자주 교체해야 했다. 게다가 나무에는 자연적인 결과 줄무늬가 있어 글자를 조심스럽게 새겨야 했기 때문에 이것이 글자의 명확성에 영향을 주었고, 생산하는 데 더 많은 시간을 필요로 했다.

3 ➡ 이러한 한계를 극복하기 위해 금속을 이용해 활자를 만들려는 시도가 이루어졌다. 이를 위해 글씨를 새긴 나무 조각을 모래에 눌러 각 글씨나 기호의 음각을 얻었다. 그런 다음 활자를 만들기 위해 청동, 구리, 철, 주석 같은 용융된 금속을 형틀, 즉 주형 안에 부어 넣었다. 이와 같은 금속활자는 요하네스 구텐베르크가 실용적이고 효율적인 인쇄 시스템을 만들기 몇 세기 이전부터 아시아에서 발전해 오고 있었다. 인쇄에 사용되는 각각의 기계적인 부분에 관심을 보였던 발명가들과 달리 구텐베르크는 인쇄와 관련이 있는 모든 부분을 하나로 간주함으로써 그 공정을 다루었다. 그는 금속활자를 제작하기 위한 공정을 개발할 수 있었고 이것은 전에 만들어진 것보다 더 뚜렷한 상을 제작하기 위해 구리 주형을 사용했으므로 이전의 시도들과 차이가 있었다. 게다가 구텐베르크는 인쇄용으로 특별히 제작된 유성 잉크를 새로 개발했다. 이 잉크는 테레빈유, 숯, 호두 기름을 사용해 만들어졌으며 인쇄기에 사용하기 아주 적합한 기름기가 함유된 농도를 갖고 있었다. 마지막으로 그는 올리브 오일과 와인 생산에 사용하는 스크류식 기계와 구조적으로 비슷한 목판 인쇄기를 사용하는 인쇄 기술을 발명했고, 이는 인쇄된 면의 모든 부분에 동일한 압력이 작용하게끔 했다. 그 결과 이미지 전체에 잉크가 고르게 분포된 일관된 인쇄물을 얻을 수 있었다.

4 ➡ 구텐베르크의 가장 유명한 도서 인쇄물은 180부가 제작된 구텐베르크 성경이었다. 이 책이 그의 활자 공정으로 인쇄된 첫 번째 책은 아니었지만, 그것은 구텐베르크의 상징일 뿐만 아니라 인쇄서 시대의 시작 역할을 하는 책이다. 이 발명으로 구텐베르크는 여러 세기 동안 지속된 인쇄 시대의 도래를 알렸고, 금속활자의 제작 공정은 오랫동안 바뀌지 않았으며 세계의 거의 모든 사회에 엄청난 영향을 가져왔다. 이것은 주로 금속활자의 높은 내구성 때문이었다. 덕분에 인쇄는 정보를 기록하는 경제적인 방법이 될 수 있었고 인쇄물의 보급을 촉진했다. 실제로 지식층뿐만 아니라 대중도 인쇄물을 접할 수 있게 되면서 금속활자의 효율성은 사회 전반에 영향을 끼쳤다. 확실히 이는 금속활자 사용 초창기에 상류 계층에 대한 위협으로 비추어졌고, 몇몇 사회에서는 정부가 금속활자 인쇄를 정부용으로만 제한하는 법을 만들기도 했다.

5 ➡ 구텐베르크는 글과 이미지를 대량으로 재생산할 수 있는 신뢰할 만하고 효율적인 방법을 만들어냄으로써 르네상스의 정착을 도운 것으로 평가되고 있다. 금속활자 인쇄는 책의 대량 생산을 최초로 가능하게 했고, 뉴스와 정보가 그 어느 때보다 빠르게 유럽 전역으로 퍼졌다. 이는 또한 책을 훨씬 더 싸게 만들어 글을 읽고 쓰는 능력이

Ⓐ 비교적 빠르게 마모된다.
Ⓑ 새기는 데 오래 걸린다.
Ⓒ 글자의 가독성에 영향을 끼치는 재질을 갖고 있다.
Ⓓ 어떤 지역에서는 쉽게 구할 수 없다.

13. 3단락에 따르면, 다음 중 구텐베르크의 인쇄술에 대해 사실이 아닌 것은 무엇인가?

Ⓐ 그의 기계에서 나온 인쇄물은 다른 인쇄 기술에 비해 더 선명하고 더 골랐다.
Ⓑ 구텐베르크는 인쇄 전용 잉크를 개발했다.
Ⓒ 구텐베르크는 올리브 오일과 와인 생산에 자신의 기계를 사용했다.
Ⓓ 인쇄물을 만들기 위한 믿을 만한 공정이었다.

14. 4단락에서 'it(그것)'이 가리키는 것은

Ⓐ 인쇄술
Ⓑ 구텐베르크 성경
Ⓒ 활자 공정
Ⓓ 상징

15. 다음 중 지문에 음영 표시된 문장의 핵심 정보를 가장 잘 표현한 문장은 무엇인가? 오답은 문장의 의미를 크게 왜곡하거나 핵심 정보를 누락하고 있다.

Ⓐ 금속활자가 전 세계적으로 많은 사회에 영향을 끼쳤다는 사실은 알려져 있다.
Ⓑ 구텐베르크의 인쇄술은 수백 년간 지속되었고, 전 세계적 문화에 영향을 끼쳤다.
Ⓒ 구텐베르크는 여러 차례 그의 기계를 다시 설계했고, 그 내구성 있는 기계장치가 수 세기에 걸쳐 사용될 수 있게 했다.
Ⓓ 구텐베르크가 금속활자를 개발할 때 세계 여러 사회에서 그에게 이를 위한 정보를 제공해 주었다.

16. 4단락에 따르면, 다음 중 구텐베르크 성경에 대해 사실인 것은 무엇인가?

Ⓐ 구텐베르크가 새롭게 만들어낸 인쇄 공정을 이용한 첫 번째 인쇄물이었다.
Ⓑ 인쇄 기계를 사용해서 만든 첫 번째 책이었다.
Ⓒ 금속활자와 유성 잉크로 인쇄되었다.
Ⓓ 대부분의 유럽 사회에서 일어난 엄청난 변화의 결과였다

17. 4단락에 따르면, 초기의 금속활자가 상류층 사람들에게 위협으로 여겨진 이유는

Ⓐ 인쇄술이 과거에 그랬던 것보다 훨씬 더 효율적이었기 때문에
Ⓑ 책이 사회의 하층 계급에게도 이용 가능한 것이 되었기 때문에
Ⓒ 책을 출간하는 사람을 규제하는 법안을 만들어야만 했기 때문에
Ⓓ 대중들이 금속활자를 사용하여 책을 인쇄했기 때문에

빠르게 증가하도록 했다. 사람들은 과거에는 공부할 수 없었을 새로운 아이디어와 주제들에 노출되었다. 실제로 아이디어의 교환이 빠르게 가속화되어 과학 혁명의 시작에 불을 당겼다.

18. 5단락의 단어 'reliable(신뢰할 만한)'과 의미상 가장 가까운 것은

Ⓐ 평판이 좋은
Ⓑ 괜찮은
Ⓒ 복잡한
Ⓓ 믿을 만한

19. 지문에 다음 문장이 들어갈 수 있는 위치를 나타내는 네 개의 사각형 [■]을 확인하시오.

8세기 무렵에 중국인들은 문서와 그림으로 가득한 책 전체를 인쇄하는 데 이 기술을 사용했다.

이 문장이 들어가기에 가장 적합한 곳은? [■C]

20. 지시문: 지문을 간략하게 요약한 글의 첫 문장이 아래 제시되어 있다. 지문의 가장 중요한 내용을 표현하는 세 개의 선택지를 골라 요약문을 완성하시오. 일부 문장들은 지문에 제시되지 않았거나 지문의 지엽적인 내용을 나타내기 때문에 요약문에 포함되지 않는다. ***이 문제의 배점은 2점이다.***

활자는 역사적 중요성이 매우 큰 인쇄 과정이다.

Ⓒ 인쇄술은 원래 조각된 나무의 전체 판을 사용해서 행했지만 이것이 나중에는 목판활자로 바뀌었다.
Ⓔ 구텐베르크는 금속활자를 부속물로 사용하는 인쇄술을 만들어서 인쇄술의 혁신을 가져왔다.
Ⓕ 구텐베르크의 업적은 정보가 교류되는 속도를 높였으며 영향력이 있는 새로운 움직임들의 도화선이 되었다.

Ⓐ 종이 인쇄는 1400년대 이후로 존재했고 그 기간에 구텐베르크가 잘 알려진 인쇄술을 발달시키기 시작했다.
Ⓑ 목판 활자는 새겨 넣어야 했고 오랜 시간이 걸렸으므로 기능공의 세심한 주의를 필요로 했다.
Ⓓ 금속은 아주 오래가는 재료이기 때문에 인쇄 과정에서 사용되는 자형들을 만드는 데 상당히 유용하다.

어휘 movable adj 움직일 수 있는 I typography n 활판술, 인쇄술 I woodblock n 목판 I goldsmith n 금세공사 I fame n 명성 I implement v 이행하다, 수행하다 I component n 구성 요소 I accomplish v 이룩하다, 성취하다 I arduous adj 힘든 I necessitate v 필요로 하다 I profoundly adv 깊이, 완전히 I durable adj 내구성 있는, 오래가는 I chisel v 조각하다, 끌로 파다 I bronze n 청동 I copper n 구리 I iron n 철 I tin n 주석 I matrices n (matrix의 복수형) 주형, 형틀 I mold n 거푸집, 주형 I place one's attention on ~에 주의를 기울이다 I turpentine n 테레빈유 I soot n 검댕, 그을음 I uniform adj 동일한 I evenly adv 고르게 I reliable adj 믿을 수 있는 I accelerate v 촉진하다

Actual Test 2

본서 I P. 291

1. C	**2.** B	**3.** A	**4.** C	**5.** D	**6.** A	**7.** C	**8.** B	**9.** B	**10.** A, D, E
11. A	**12.** C	**13.** B	**14.** B	**15.** B	**16.** C	**17.** A	**18.** D	**19.** A	**20.** B, C, D

본서 I P. 292

지진 예측

1 ➡ 지진은 지구에 영향을 미치는 가장 파괴적인 자연 재해 중 하나이고 그것의 예측 불가능한 특성은 그것을 더 심각하게 만든다. 그런 광범위한 파괴에 흔히 동반되는 심각한 인명 손실을 방지하는 데 도움이 될 수 있는 지진 움직임에 대한 정확한 예측은 오랫동안 과학자들의 목표였다. 불행히도 믿을 만한 지진 예측 방법은 아직 알려지지 않았지만 과학자들은 유망한 많은 지진 예측 방법을 계속 연구하

1. 다음 중 지문에 음영 표시된 문장의 핵심 정보를 가장 잘 표현한 문장은 무엇인가? 오답은 의미를 크게 왜곡하거나 핵심 정보를 누락하고 있다.

Ⓐ 감사하게도 과학자들은 지진이 언제 일어날지 예측할 믿을 만한 방법들을 개발해냈으며 이것들은 두 개의 기본 범주로 나뉜다.

고 있으며, 이 방법들은 장기 예측과 단기 예측이라는 두 개의 커다란 범주로 분류된다.

2 ➡ 지진의 장기 예측은 단층대의 특정 분절에 발생한 지진 활동의 역사적 기록을 연구함으로써 이루어진다. 과거 지진이 언제 발생했는지 연대표를 그리고 각 지진의 규모를 기록함으로써 과학자들은 활동 패턴을 만들고 특정 규모의 지진들 사이의 평균 간격을 알아낼 수 있다. 지진 활동 간의 간격을 연구함으로써 그들은 상당한 규모의 지진 사이에 흐른 평균 시간을 알아낼 수 있다. 특정 규모의 지진이 언제 마지막으로 발생했는지에 따라서 그들은 그 다음 것이 언제 발생할지에 대해 어느 정도 알고 추측할 수 있다. 이 방식은 평균치로 이루어지기 때문에 언제 지진이 일어날 가능성이 있는지 예측하는 데에만 사용될 수 있다. 이것은 몇 년에서 몇 십 년이라는 명시된 시간 간격보다 더 정확할 수 없다는 것을 뜻한다.

3 ➡ 단기 예측은 다음 지진이 언제 일어날지 충분히 정확하게 알아내어 인근 지역 사람들을 대피시킬 수 있게 하는 것에 초점을 둔다. 그러기 위해 과학자들은 전조라고 불리는 지난 지진들 직전에 발생한 현상을 연구하는 데 시간을 투자한다. 역사를 통틀어 그 사건들 전에 그 지역에 있었던 생존자들과 과학자들은 다양한 물리적, 화학적 현상을 관찰했다. 쉽게 관찰되는 현상에는 지반 변형과 물의 화학적 성분 변화와 우물과 호수의 수위 변화가 포함된다. 감지하기 위해 정교한 장치를 요구하는 다른 것들은 달라진 지진 활동과 더 직접적으로 관련이 있다. 단층대는 절대로 완전히 안정적이지 않기 때문에 잦은 미진과 지진파가 발생하지만 지진이 임박했을 때 지진파의 속도, 전진이라고 불리는 강한 진동의 빈도와 암석의 전기 저항은 전부 바뀐다.

4 ➡ 이런 많은 전조들을 설명하는 한 가지 이론은 체적팽창 이론이라고 불린다. 단층선에 위치한 암석이 압력 아래서 한계점에 근접하면 체적이 상당히 증가할 수 있다. [■A] 이런 부풀어 오름 또는 팽창이라고 불리는 이것은 암석의 결정체로 된 층 사이의 미세한 균열로 인해 생긴다. [■B] 암석의 약한 알갱이가 분리되면 그 틈으로 지하수가 흘러 들어가 그 틈이 벌어져 있게 만든다. 이것은 암석의 밀도를 바꿔 바위가 지진 에너지를 전달하는 방법을 바꾸고 물 또한 그것의 전기 전도성을 바꾼다. [■C] 팽창이 커다란 바위 층 전역에 발생하면 불가피한 지진 파열이 임박했을 때 지형이 극적으로 변할 수 있다. [■D] 과학자들의 우려를 사고 있는 이런 땅의 융기된 부분 중 한 곳은 샌안드레아스 단층을 따라 로스앤젤레스 근처에 발생했다. 장기 예측이 이 지역에 대규모 지진이 곧 일어날 가능성이 있다고 보여주기 때문에 과학자들은 팜데일 융기라고 불리는 이 특징적인 부분을 앞으로 있을 전조를 감지하기 위해 면밀히 감시하고 있다. 팽창은 지하수 움직임과 우물 또는 호수의 수질에 영향을 미치기도 한다. 물이 암석 균열을 채우면 우물과 호수에 있는 수량이 감소할 수 있다. 암석이 쪼개져서 벌어질 때 가스와 광물이 암석으로부터 방출되면 물의 화학적 성분 또한 바뀔 수 있다. 특히 단층에 압력이 증가할 때 라돈 가스 수치가 물 속에서 증가하는 것으로 보여진다. 진동의 빈도와 강도 또한 증가하는 경향을 보이다가 실제 지진이 일어나기 바로 직전에 급작스럽게 감소한다. 이런 폭풍전야는 물이 암석을 채우기 전에 일시적인 암석 강도의 증가로 야기된다고 여겨진다.

5 ➡ 체적팽창 이론의 현상은 전형적인 일련의 사건들로 정리될 수

Ⓑ 안타깝게도 과학자들은 지진을 장기적으로 정확히 예측하는 어떠한 방법도 발견하지 못할지 모르지만, 단기적 방법은 가능성을 보인다.
Ⓒ 과학자들은 실패할 염려가 없는 지진 예측 방법을 아직 발견하지 못했지만 장기적 예측과 단기적 예측에 맞는 많은 가능성 있는 방법들을 연구하고 있다.
Ⓓ 과학자들은 지진을 예측할 많은 방법들을 개발했지만 이들은 범위가 넓은 장기적 예측에만 쓸모가 있다.

2. 2단락에 따르면, 지진의 장기 예측은 어떻게 이루어지는가?
Ⓐ 한 단층 분절과 그 근처 단층들에서 발생한 비슷한 규모의 지진을 비교함으로써
Ⓑ 지진 활동 패턴에서 확인된 지진 간격을 분석함으로써
Ⓒ 한 단층의 여러 분절에서 발생한 지진의 역사적 연대를 비교함으로써
Ⓓ 모든 지진 사이의 평균적인 시간 간격을 계산함으로써

3. 2단락의 단어 'specified(명시된)'와 의미상 가장 가까운 것은
Ⓐ 정해진
Ⓑ 관찰된
Ⓒ 전형적인
Ⓓ 확고한

4. 3단락에 따르면, 다음 중 지진의 전조 현상이 아닌 것은
Ⓐ 지질의 변화
Ⓑ 암석의 저항력
Ⓒ 단층대의 불안정함
Ⓓ 증가된 지진 활동

5. 3단락의 단어 'imminent(임박한)'와 의미상 가장 가까운 것은
Ⓐ 매우 중요한
Ⓑ 강한 강도의
Ⓒ 짧은 간격으로 발생하는
Ⓓ 곧 일어나려고 하는

6. 글쓴이가 4단락에서 '샌안드레아스 단층'을 언급하는 이유는 무엇인가?
Ⓐ 지형을 변화시키는 전조 현상의 예를 제공하기 위해
Ⓑ 그 지역이 왜 팜데일 융기라고 불리는지 설명하기 위해
Ⓒ 체적팽창 이론의 반례가 되는 지역을 소개하기 위해
Ⓓ 고위험 지역을 파악하는 데에 있어 장기 예측의 효과를 강조하기 위해

7. 4단락에 따르면, 다음 중 물과 관련된 전조 현상에 대해 사실인 것은 무엇인가?
Ⓐ 바위 균열을 채우는 물 속의 라돈 농도는 감소한다.
Ⓑ 지하수 수위의 변화는 전진의 빈도를 증가시킨다.

Actual Test 2

있다. 1단계에서는 단층대 한 지역에 압력이 증가한다. 2, 3단계에서는 암석이 팽창하고 미세균열에 물이 차오르면서 팽창의 효과가 느껴진다. 4단계는 대규모 지진이고 5단계는 여진이라고 불리는 추가적인 강진을 흔히 포함하는 큰 지진 후의 여파다. 불행히도 이런 단계들은 모든 지진마다 그 길이가 일정하지는 않으며 전조 현상들은 큰 지진이 일어날 것을 보장하지 않는다. 모든 지진 사건은 제각각 다르기 때문에 전조 현상을 사용해 지진이 언제 일어날지 정확하게 예측하는 것은 매우 힘들다. 예를 들면 1989년에 로마프리타 지진이 발생했을 때 두 번의 규모 5.0의 전진이 15개월과 2개월 전에 앞서 있었고 매번 과학자들은 며칠 이내에 더 강한 지진이 발생할 것이라고 예측했다. 하지만 지진은 일어나지 않았고, 규모 6.9의 지진이 결국 발생했을 때 사람들은 준비되어 있지 않았다. 과학자들은 더 많은 연구와 분석을 통해 체적팽창 이론의 개선이 가능하다고 믿으며 또는 더 나은 새로운 방법이 개발될 수 있다고 생각한다.

Ⓒ 바위에서 방출된 광물은 물의 화학적 성분에 변화를 일으킨다.
Ⓓ 수역은 수량의 증가를 보인다.

8. 5단락은 어떻게 조직되어 있는가?

Ⓐ 체적팽창 이론의 개요를 설명하고 지진 예측의 새로운 방법이 왜 발달될 필요가 있는지 이유를 제공한다.
Ⓑ 체적팽창 이론이 어떻게 다섯 단계로 나뉘어져 있는지와 실생활 적용에서의 한계를 설명한다.
Ⓒ 대규모 지진의 진행과 지진 예측이 왜 어려운지 이유를 보여준다.
Ⓓ 전조 현상을 다섯 개의 분명한 범주로 나누고 그들이 어떻게 나타나는지 실제 사례를 제공한다.

9. 지문에 다음 문장이 들어갈 수 있는 위치를 나타내는 네 개의 사각형 [■]을 확인하시오.

암석의 약한 알갱이가 분리되면 그 틈으로 지하수가 흘러 들어가 그 틈이 벌어져 있게 만든다.

이 문장이 들어가기에 가장 적합한 곳은? [■B]

10. 지시문: 지문을 간략하게 요약한 글의 첫 문장이 아래 제시되어 있다. 지문의 가장 중요한 내용을 표현하는 세 개의 선택지를 골라 요약문을 완성하시오. 일부 문장들은 지문에 제시되지 않았거나 지문의 지엽적인 내용을 나타내기 때문에 요약문에 포함되지 않는다. ***이 문제의 배점은 2점이다.***

정확한 지진 예측은 수년 동안 과학적인 목표였지만 완전히 신뢰할 만한 방법은 아직 발견되지 않았다.

Ⓐ 큰 지진의 단계 순서는 알려졌지만 각 단계의 지속 기간은 동일하지 않아서 예측을 어렵게 만든다.
Ⓓ 땅의 팽창, 증가하는 전진과 수위의 변화와 같은 사건들은 임박한 지진의 지표들이다.
Ⓔ 지진 활동의 연대표를 만듦으로써 과학자들은 비슷한 규모의 지진이 언제 발생할지 예측하는 것을 도와주는 패턴을 찾는다.

Ⓑ 지각 변동의 예 중 하나는 대규모 지진이 곧 발생할 가능성이 있는 샌안드레아스 단층의 팜데일 융기다.
Ⓒ 체적 팽창 이론에서 1단계에서 3단계까지는 각각 4, 5단계로 분류된 큰 지진과 여진을 앞서는 전조 현상들이다.
Ⓕ 로마프리타 지진의 예측은 과학자들이 앞선 전진 후 얼마나 더 있어야 지진이 발생할지를 정확하게 예측하지 못했기 때문에 실패했다.

어휘 devastating adj 대단히 파괴적인 | natural disaster 자연 재해 | unpredictable adj 예측할 수 없는 | seismic event 지진 움직임 | accompany v 동반하다 | destruction n 파괴 | promising adj 유망한, 촉망되는 | seismic activity 지진 활동 | segment n 부분, 한쪽 | fault zone 단층대 | timeline n 연대표 | interval n 간격 | gap n 틈, 공백 | significant adj 중요한, 상당한 | magnitude n 규모 | educated guess 경험에서 우러난 추측 | potential n 가능성 | specified adj 명시된 | focused adj 집중한 | determine v 알아내다, 밝히다 | evacuate v 대피하다 | devote v 전념하다, 바치다 | precursor n 전조 | phenomenon n 현상 | deformation n 변형, 기형 | sophisticated adj 세련된, 정교한 | altered adj 바뀐 | imminent adj 임박한 | seismic wave 지진파 | tremor n 미진, 떨림 | foreshock n 전진 | electrical resistance 전기 저항 | dilatancy model 체적팽창 이론 | fault line 단층선 | breaking point 한계점 | dilation n 팽창 | microcrack n 미세균열 | crystalline adj 결정(질)의, 결정체로 된 | conductivity n 전도성 | inevitable adj 불가피한 | rupture n 파열, 터짐 | uplift n (땅의) 융기 | groundwater n 지하수 | fissure n (암석의) 길게 갈라진 틈 | abruptly adv 갑자기 | impregnate v 스며들게 하다, 포화시키다 | aftermath n 여파 | aftershock n 여진 | precede v 앞서다 | refinement n 개선, 개량

영화의 발달

1 ➡ 영화의 발달은 19세기 중반에 활동 요지경의 발명으로 시작되었다. 화가들은 움직임의 다양한 단계를 보여주는 일련의 그림들, 예를 들자면 커플이 춤추는 그림 같은 것을 그렸다. 이런 그림들은 한 사람이 들여다 볼 수 있는 입구가 있는 원통 안에 넣어졌다. 원통이 적절한 속도로 회전하면 관찰자에게는 원통이 움직이는 대신 실제로 춤추는 사람들이 움직이는 것처럼 보였다. 이런 착시 현상은 파이 현상이라 불리고 이것은 인간이 빠르게 연속으로 일련의 영상을 보면 우리의 눈이 연속 동작을 인지하기 때문에 발생한다. 춤추는 사람들의 그림은 변하지 않지만 우리의 머리는 그것을 움직이는 한 개의 영상으로 보는 방식으로 정보를 처리한다. 1870년대까지 카메라 기술은 예술가인 에드워드 마이브리지가 이 현상을 일련의 카메라를 사용해 모사할 수 있을 정도로 진보했다.

2 ➡ 에드워드 마이브리지는 자연 풍경 사진과 미국 서부의 연구로 유명한 전문 사진가였다. 1872년에 그는 릴런드 스탠퍼드에게서 말의 움직임에 대한 질문을 해결해 달라는 요청을 받았다. 많은 사람들은 말이 빠른 걸음이나 전속력으로 움직일 때 균형을 위해 최소한 한 발굽은 땅에 두고 있다고 믿었다. [■A] 다른 사람들은 말이 특정 시점에서는 네 발굽 모두 공중에 떠 있을 거라고 주장했다. 카메라의 셔터 속도는 마이브리지가 24개를 한 줄로 정렬시켜 말의 움직임을 담아낼 수 있을 정도로 충분히 빨라졌다. [■B] 기수가 말을 타고 시속 36마일 속도로 카메라를 지날 때 그것은 카메라를 작동시키는 트립 와이어를 작동시켰다. [■C] 그 결과로 찍힌 사진들 중 몇몇은 말이 때로는 네 발굽 전부 실제로 공중에 떠 있는 것을 보여줬다. [■D] 마이브리지는 그 사진들을 실루엣으로 변환했고 자신의 설계로 만든 장치에 함께 넣어서 청중이 볼 수 있게끔 스크린에 비추어 첫 영화 전시회를 열었다.

3 ➡ 영화에 있어 다음으로 큰 혁신은 1880년대 후반에 셀룰로이드 사진 필름과 단일 렌즈로 사진을 연속으로 찍을 수 있는 카메라의 탄생으로 이루어졌다. 유연한 셀룰로이드는 필름 스트립이 카메라에 넣어지는 릴로 감아지는 것을 가능하게 했는데 이것은 몇 초가 아닌 몇 분의 움직임이 촬영되는 것을 가능하게 했다. 마이브리지를 만난 후 토머스 에디슨은 자신만의 영사기와 전시 기구를 개발하기로 결심했다. 그 최종 결과는 필름 스트립을 전구와 렌즈 사이에 통과시키는 키네토스코프였다. 불행히도 키네토스코프는 한번에 한 사람만 사용할 수 있었기 때문에 1894년 뉴욕시에 첫 상업 영화관이 열렸을 때 주인은 기계를 10개 구입해야 했다. 이것이 요구하는 상당한 투자액에도 불구하고 키네토스코프 영화관들은 전국의 주요 도시에 생겨났고 에디슨의 회사는 큰 수익을 거둬들였다.

4 ➡ 키네토스코프가 벌어들이는 수익액 때문에 에디슨은 투사 시스템을 개발해야 할 필요성을 느끼지 않았다. 하지만 다른 회사에 있는 그의 경쟁 상대들은 기계 대 관객 비율 때문에 영화를 더 많은 관객에게 보여주는 것이 훨씬 더 수익성이 있을 거란 것을 인지했다. 많은 기술 혁신이 다른 회사들에서 있었지만 결국 에디슨은 그 결과물인 바이터스코프를 대량생산할 것을 제안받았다. 이 기기는 고휘도 전구를 사용해 영화를 벽이나 천막에 투사했고 그 기술은 수십 년 동

11. 1단락에서 글쓴이가 '파이 현상'을 언급하는 이유는 무엇인가?
Ⓐ 영화를 가능케 한 개념을 설명하기 위해
Ⓑ 인간의 시각적 능력의 다재다능함을 강조하기 위해
Ⓒ 활동 요지경이 왜 원통 형태로 나왔는지를 설명하기 위해
Ⓓ 활동 요지경을 만든 화가들은 분명히 과학자들이었을 거라고 암시하기 위해

12. 2단락의 단어 'converted(변환했다)'와 의미상 가장 가까운 것은
Ⓐ 재현했다
Ⓑ 이동했다
Ⓒ 바꾸었다
Ⓓ 적용했다

13. 2단락에서 마이브리지의 작업에 대해 추론 가능한 것은 무엇인가?
Ⓐ 그는 기수가 말을 특정 속도로 몰 것을 특별히 요청했다.
Ⓑ 카메라들은 단일 렌즈로 여러 장의 사진을 촬영할 만큼 진보하지 않았다.
Ⓒ 그가 움직이는 동물과 작업을 한 것은 처음이었다.
Ⓓ 그는 의도치 않게 동물학 분야에 돌파구를 제공했다.

14. 3단락의 단어 'flexible(유연한)'과 의미상 가장 가까운 것은
Ⓐ 손상되기 쉬운
Ⓑ 구부릴 수 있는
Ⓒ 적응할 수 있는
Ⓓ 뻣뻣한

15. 다음 중 3단락에서 키네토스코프에 대해 언급되지 않은 것은 무엇인가?
Ⓐ 셀룰로이드 필름을 활용했다.
Ⓑ 렌즈를 통해 몇 분 길이의 필름 스트립을 투사했다.
Ⓒ 한 번에 한 관람자만 허용했다.
Ⓓ 사용을 위해 상당한 재정적 투자를 필요로 했다.

16. 4단락에 따르면, 에디슨이 투사 시스템을 향한 움직임에 늦게 합류한 이유는 무엇인가?
Ⓐ 그의 키네토스코프 장사가 증가된 기기 대 관객 비율로 어려워질 것이었다.
Ⓑ 그는 그의 키네토스코프를 넘어설 더 이상의 혁신이 있을 수 없다고 믿었다.
Ⓒ 그는 더 많은 관객이 더 수익성이 있을 거라는 것을 깨닫는 선견지명이 없었다.
Ⓓ 그의 회사는 투사 시스템을 대량 생산하는 것에 대해 마지막으로 요청을 받은 회사였다.

안 근본적으로 동일하게 유지되었다. 제작된 가장 초창기의 영화들은 오늘날 기준으로는 단순해 보이지만 그것들은 관중에게 엄청난 영향을 미쳤다. 그것들은 한 시점에서 촬영되었고 아무 수정 없이 한 가지 행위나 사건을 묘사했다. 그것들은 춤, 체육 행사, 자연 풍경, 그리고 유명한 것으로는 기차역에 도착하는 기차를 보여주었다. 기차 영화가 촬영된 각도는 기차가 마치 관객에게 다가오는 것처럼 보이게 했고 스크린과 가깝던 사람들은 두려움으로 좌석에서 달아났다.

5 ➡ 영화의 두 번째 단계는 이야기를 전하기 시작했고 여러 거리와 각도에서 촬영한 다른 장면과 샷을 도입했다. 이런 영화들은 고작 5분에서 10분 길이였는데 이것은 필름 릴이 그만큼의 필름만 수용할 수 있었기 때문이었다. 음향은 기술이 상업적으로 사용 가능해진 1920년대 후반에야 가능해졌다. 그래서 등장인물 간의 대화나 이야기에 대한 설명은 타이틀 카드라고 불리는 글씨가 담긴 빈 스크린을 사용하는 것으로 이루어졌다. 이런 이유로 이 시대의 영화들은 '무성 영화'라고 불리지만 영화관 주인들은 피아노나 오르간 연주자를 고용해 장면들에 보탤 음악을 반주하게 했다. 영화들은 연주되는 음악이 적절하도록 보장하기 위해 보통 준비된 악보와 함께 유통되었고 어떤 영화들은 오케스트라를 고용하는 큰 영화관들을 위해 악보 전부를 갖추었다. 음향 기술이 말소리와 음악과 음향 효과와 함께 사운드 트랙을 포함하기에 적합해지자 영화 스튜디오들은 겉으로 보기에 하룻밤 사이에 '발성 영화'를 제작하는 것으로 변천했다.

17. 다음 중 지문에 음영 표시된 문장의 핵심 정보를 가장 잘 표현한 문장은 무엇인가? 오답은 의미를 크게 왜곡하거나 핵심 정보를 누락하고 있다.

Ⓐ 기차 영화는 기차가 충돌할 거라고 관객이 생각하게 만드는 방식으로 촬영되어 관객들은 도망갔다.
Ⓑ 기차 영화는 역으로 다가서는 기차가 잘못된 방향으로 와서 사람들을 치는 모습을 보여주었고 이는 관객이 두려움에 질리게 했다.
Ⓒ 한 영화에 나오는 기차는 엄청나게 빠른 속도로 카메라에 다가오는 모습이 보였고, 이는 관객들의 일부가 겁을 먹게 했다.
Ⓓ 기차 영화는 카메라 앵글이 관객들을 칠 것처럼 보이게 했기 때문에 인기가 아주 많았다.

18. 다음 중 5단락에서 언급되지 않은 것은

Ⓐ 영화가 어떻게 이야기를 전달하는 매체로 등장했는지
Ⓑ 초기 영화에서 상대적으로 정교한 영화 제작 기술의 진보
Ⓒ 발성 영화로의 이행이 일어난 시기
Ⓓ 영화관 주인들이 오케스트라를 위해 악보를 준비한 이유

19. 지문에 다음 문장이 들어갈 수 있는 위치를 나타내는 네 개의 사각형 [■]을 확인하시오.

다른 사람들은 말이 특정 시점에서는 네 발굽 모두 공중에 떠 있을 거라고 주장했다.

이 문장이 들어가기에 가장 적합한 곳은? [■A]

20. 지시문: 지문을 간략하게 요약한 글의 첫 문장이 아래 제시되어 있다. 지문의 가장 중요한 내용을 표현하는 세 개의 선택지를 골라 요약문을 완성하시오. 일부 문장들은 지문에 제시되지 않았거나 지문의 지엽적인 내용을 나타내기 때문에 요약문에 포함되지 않는다. ***이 문제의 배점은 2점이다.***

영화는 19세기 후반과 20세기 초반에 과학적 혁신품에서 주류 오락거리의 형태로 빠르게 발전했다.

Ⓑ 에디슨의 키네토스코프는 그 자체로도 혁신이었지만 또한 처음으로 대중이 짧은 영화들을 오락거리로 소비할 수 있게 해준 것이었다.
Ⓒ 더 많은 관객이 들 경우의 큰 수익성을 감지하고 많은 사람들이 투사 시스템을 개발하는 데 뛰어들었고 바이터스코프를 만들어냈다.
Ⓓ 초기 '무성 영화'들은 '발성 영화'로의 이행이 일어날 때까지 음향의 부재를 타이틀 카드와 라이브 음악 반주를 포함하는 것으로 보충했다.

Ⓐ 마이브리지의 기발한 카메라 설치는 말들이 달릴 때 정말로 네 발굽 모두 공중에 떠 있다는 결론을 제공하도록 해주었다.
Ⓔ 초기 키네토스코프 영화관들은 선불로 상당한 투자를 해야 했지만 그것들에 대한 높은 수요는 그 비용을 상쇄했다.
Ⓕ 움직이지 않는 일련의 그림들을 움직이는 것으로 인지하게끔 하는 파이 현상은 영화 산업에 동력을 제공하는 과학적 돌파구다.

어휘 motion picture 영화 | zoetrope n 활동 요지경(통 안의 그림이 움직이는 것처럼 보이는 회전 장치) | cylinder n 원통 | optical illusion 착시 현상 | succession n 연속, 잇따름 | perceive v 감지하다, 인지하다 | advance v 전진하다 | replicate v 모사하다, 복제하다 | trot n 속보 | gallop n 질주 | jockey n 기수 | trigger v 촉발시키다 | activate v 작동시키다, 활성화하다 | convert v 전환시키다 | project v 투사하다, 투영하다 | exhibition n 전시 | innovation n 혁신 | flexible adj 유연한 | apparatus n 기구, 장치 | commercial adj 상업의 | investment n 투자 | launch v 개시하다 | reap v 거두다, 수확하다 | generate v 발생시키다, 만들어 내다 | compel v 강요하다, ~하게 만들다 | counterpart n (동일한 지위나 기능을 갖는) 상대 | profitable adj 수익성이 있는 | mass produce 대량생산하다 | profound adj 엄청난,

깊은 I perspective n 관점, 시각 I depict v 그리다, 묘사하다 I alteration n 변화, 개조 I incorporate v 포함하다 I character n 등장인물 I sheet music 악보 I score n 악보 I transition v 변천하다, 이행하다 I seemingly adv 외견상으로, 겉보기에는

Actual Test 3

본서 I P. 300

1. C	**2.** B	**3.** D	**4.** D	**5.** D	**6.** C	**7.** B	**8.** A	**9.** B	**10.** C, E, F
11. D	**12.** A	**13.** B	**14.** D	**15.** A	**16.** B	**17.** C	**18.** B	**19.** D	**20.** C, D, F

본서 I P. 301

티라노사우루스 렉스

1 ➡ 아마도 모든 공룡 중 가장 쉽게 알아볼 수 있는 것이 '티라노사우루스 렉스' 혹은 흔히 줄여서 T. 렉스라고 하는 공룡일 것이다. 이 유명한 수각아목(육식성 이족 보행) 공룡은 엄청나게 사나운 외모와 뛰어난 사냥 기술로 그런 어울리는 이름을 얻었으며 그 의미는 그리스어로 '폭군 도마뱀 왕'이라는 뜻이다. T. 렉스는 오늘날의 북미 서부 전역에 분포했고 그 시대의 다른 포식 공룡보다 훨씬 더 넓은 사냥 범위를 가지고 있었다. 북미의 여러 암석층에서 발견된 T. 렉스의 화석 증거에 근거해 보면 이 무시무시한 사냥꾼은 대략 6천 5백만 년 전인 백악기의 마지막 3백만 년 동안 활동했다. 그 공룡들이 살았던 시대 때문에 T. 렉스는 공룡들을 이후 멸종으로 몰고 간 엄청난 사건이 무엇이었든 그 사건 전에 지구라는 행성을 돌아다닌 마지막 공룡 중 하나가 되었다.

2 ➡ 티라노사우루스 렉스는 의심할 여지 없이 인상적인 피조물이었다. 발견된 온전한 화석 표본 중 가장 큰 것으로는 표본 FMNH PR2081이 있고, 이는 애칭으로 '수'라고 불린다. 수는 사우스다코타 주 페이스 근방의 헬크리크 지층에서 아마추어 고생물학자 수 헨드릭슨에 의해 발견되었다. 이 화석은 과학자들에게 T. 렉스의 예상 크기에 관해 많은 아이디어를 제공했다. 수는 길이가 대략 42피트였고 엉덩이에서 키가 13피트였다. 화석에는 뼈 외의 다른 부드러운 조직이 전혀 남아 있지 않으므로 수의 정확한 무게를 알아내는 것은 불가능하다. 따라서 추정치만 나올 수 있었고 이는 다양했다. 그러나 가장 최근의 추정치는 6톤에서 7.5톤 사이이다. 분명히 거대했던 것은 사실이지만 T. 렉스는 이족 보행(두 발로 걷기)을 한 두 종의 다른 백악기 육식 공룡 스피노사우루스와 기가노토사우루스보다는 약간 더 작았다.

3 ➡ T. 렉스의 중요한 특징은 목이었다. T. 렉스의 목은 다른 수각아목 공룡과 마찬가지로 자연스러운 S모양의 곡선을 형성했지만 거대한 머리의 무게를 지탱하기 위해 목은 짧고 근육질이었다. T. 렉스의 앞발은 오랫동안 손가락이 두 개뿐이라고 생각되었지만 최소 한 개의 표본에서 세 번째 손가락의 증거가 나타났다. 이에 비해 T. 렉스의 튼튼한 뒷다리는 몸 크기에 비례해서 볼 때 다른 어떤 수각아목 공룡보다도 가장 길었다. 모든 T. 렉스 종의 꼬리는 길고 무거웠고 40개 이상의 척추를 가질 수 있었다. 엄청나게 큰 꼬리는 거대한 머리와 상반신의 균형을 잡아야 했으므로 절대적으로 필요한 것이었다. 게다가 이런 무거운 몸집을 보완하기 위해 T. 렉스 골격 대부분의 뼈는 안이 비어 있었다. 이렇게 비어 있는 뼈들은 실제 힘의 손실이 없

1. 1단락에 따르면, 'T. 렉스'라는 이름은 어디서 유래했는가?
- Ⓐ 그들은 육식 공룡들이었다.
- Ⓑ 그들은 다른 종의 공룡들을 지배했다.
- Ⓒ 그들은 먹이를 사냥하는 데 뛰어났다.
- Ⓓ 그들은 넓은 지역에 걸쳐 분포했다.

2. 1단락에서 공룡들에 대해 추론 가능한 것은 무엇인가?
- Ⓐ 멸종의 원인을 밝히기 위한 연구에 남겨진 화석이 더 이상 없다.
- Ⓑ 그들이 소멸된 정확한 원인은 아직도 불분명하다.
- Ⓒ 백악기는 그들을 멸종시킨 극한의 기후를 가졌다.
- Ⓓ 공룡의 이름은 그들의 서식지와 관계가 있다.

3. 2단락과 3단락에서 티라노사우루스 렉스에 대해 사실이 아닌 것은 무엇인가?
- Ⓐ 화석 골격으로부터 대략의 무게를 측정할 수 있다.
- Ⓑ 대부분 두 개의 손가락을 가졌지만, 때로는 세 개일 때도 있었다.
- Ⓒ 최소 두 종의 다른 유사한 공룡들이 T. 렉스보다 덩치가 더 컸다.
- Ⓓ '수'는 유일하게 완벽한 화석 표본이다.

4. 2단락의 단어 'imposing(인상적인)'과 의미상 가장 가까운 것은
- Ⓐ 영웅적인
- Ⓑ 우월한
- Ⓒ 평범한
- Ⓓ 인상적인

5. 3단락에 의하면, T. 렉스의 신체에 대해 사실인 것은 무엇인가?
- Ⓐ 꼬리가 몸에 비해 불균형적으로 길었다.
- Ⓑ 다른 수각아목 공룡과 비슷하게 목이 짧고 근육질이었다.
- Ⓒ 힘의 대부분은 속이 빈 골격 구조에서 나왔다.
- Ⓓ 거대한 머리와 육중한 꼬리가 몸의 균형을 유지했다.

6. 4단락에서 글쓴이가 'V자 모양의 위턱'을 언급하는 이유는 무엇인가?
- Ⓐ T. 렉스가 다른 육식동물과 공유했던 특징을 나타내기 위해

Actual Test 3

이도 그 무게를 줄이는 데 도움을 주었다.

4 ➡ 발견된 가장 큰 T. 렉스 두개골은 길이가 5피트까지 측정된다. 다른 수각아목 공룡들의 경우처럼 이들의 두개골에는 천공이라는 큰 구멍이 있었으며, 그것은 속이 빈 뼈처럼 포식자 T. 렉스의 전반적인 몸무게를 줄여주는 역할을 했다. 게다가 천공은 근육이 붙을 수 있는 부분을 제공하기도 했다. 천공을 제외하고 T. 렉스의 두개골은 당시 존재했던 다른 큰 수각아목 공룡들의 두개골과 대단히 달랐다. [■A] 두개골의 뒷면은 대단히 넓지만 앞면에는 아주 좁은 코가 있는데, 이는 보기 드물게 뛰어난 양안시가 가능하게 해 주었다. [■B] 두개골의 뼈는 아주 컸고 코뼈 같은 일부 더 작은 뼈들이 결합되어 두개골을 더 단단하게 만들었다. 그러나 많은 뼈들이 공기로 채워져 있었는데, 이는 요컨대 뼈들이 외관상 벌집과 비슷한 작은 공기 공간을 갖고 있었다는 의미다. [■C] 이 벌집 형태는 이들의 유별나게 거대한 몸집에도 불구하고 뼈를 더 가볍고 더 유연하게 해주었을 것이다. [■D] 이런 특징과 두개골을 강화하는 다른 중요한 특징들은 T. 렉스가 그 전설적인 무는 힘을 갖게 된 방법이었으며, 이는 그 시대의 다른 어떤 포식자들보다 훨씬 위력적이었다. 위턱의 끝은 U자 모양으로 되어 있었는데, 반면 다른 대부분의 육식동물들은 V자 모양의 위턱을 가지고 있었다. 이 U자 모양은 T. 렉스가 한 번 물어뜯어 먹이에서 찢을 수 있는 조직과 뼈의 양을 늘릴 수 있게 해 주었다. 그러나 이는 또한 앞니에 가해지는 압박의 정도를 증가시켰다.

5 ➡ T. 렉스의 가장 유명한 특징 중 하나는 이빨인데, 이치성이 분명히 나타난다는 것이다. 이치성이라는 단어는 이빨의 모양에 차이가 있다는 것을 나타낸다. 위턱 앞쪽에 있는 전상악골 이빨은 D자 모양의 단면을 이루어 조밀하게 모여 있다. 그것들은 뒤쪽 표면에 경사가 져 있고 끝에 끌 같은 날이 있으며 뒤로 구부러져 있다. 전상악골 치아의 이러한 특징은 T. 렉스가 먹이를 물고 잡아당길 때 이빨이 갑자기 부러질 위험을 줄이는 데 효과가 있었다. T. 렉스 두개골의 다른 치아들은 크고 두꺼워서 단검이라기보다는 바나나 모양의 치명적인 끝부분을 가지고 있었다.

Ⓑ 대부분의 육식동물이 특정한 모양의 턱을 가진 이유를 설명하기 위해
Ⓒ U자 모양의 위턱이 V자 모양의 위턱보다 더욱 효과적임을 보여주기 위해
Ⓓ 육식동물의 신체 부위 진화 과정을 설명하기 위해

7. 4단락에서 다음 중 T. 렉스에 관한 특징으로 언급되지 않은 것은

Ⓐ 두개골에는 근육이 붙었던 큰 구멍들이 있었다
Ⓑ 두개골의 앞부분은 매우 넓었다
Ⓒ 좁은 코는 선명한 시력을 부여했다
Ⓓ 뼈의 내부가 벌집 모양과 유사했다

8. 다음 중 지문에 음영 표시된 문장의 핵심 정보를 가장 잘 표현한 문장은 무엇인가? 오답은 문장의 의미를 크게 왜곡하거나 핵심 정보를 누락하고 있다.

Ⓐ 전상악골 치아의 특징들은 T. 렉스가 먹잇감을 사냥하는 동안 치아가 부러지는 것을 막는 데 도움이 되었다.
Ⓑ 전상악골 치아는 죽은 먹잇감을 당기는 갈고리로 쓰일 때 부러질 가능성이 높다.
Ⓒ 전상악골 치아의 특별한 모양은 T. 렉스가 잃어버린 치아를 대신할 또 다른 치아를 빨리 자라게 해 주었다.
Ⓓ T. 렉스는 그것의 독특한 특징 때문에 전상악골 치아를 다른 종들보다 더 오래 유지할 수 있었다.

9. 지문에 다음 문장이 들어갈 수 있는 위치를 나타내는 네 개의 사각형 [■]을 확인하시오.

두개골의 뼈는 아주 컸고 코뼈 같은 일부 더 작은 뼈들이 결합되어 두개골을 더 단단하게 만들었다.

이 문장이 들어가기에 가장 적합한 곳은? [■B]

10. 지시문: 지문을 간략하게 요약한 글의 첫 문장이 아래 제시되어 있다. 지문의 가장 중요한 내용을 표현하는 세 개의 선택지를 골라 요약문을 완성하시오. 일부 문장들은 지문에 제시되지 않았거나 지문의 지엽적인 내용을 나타내기 때문에 요약문에 포함되지 않는다. ***이 문제의 배점은 2점이다.***

티라노사우루스 렉스는 백악기 시대에 살았던 공룡 종이었다.

Ⓒ 두개골에 있는 큰 구멍과 다른 속이 빈 뼈들은 전반적인 무게를 줄이는 데 도움을 주었다.
Ⓔ 이 종의 크기에 관한 자료의 대부분은 지금까지 발견된 예시들 중 가장 완전한 예시인 수라는 이름의 표본에서 왔다.
Ⓕ 치아의 모양이 다른 것은 T. 렉스가 먹이를 물어서 당길 때 부러질 가능성을 줄여주었다.

Ⓐ 수라고 불리는 화석 표본을 통해 T. 렉스의 평균 몸무게는 6톤에서 7.5톤 사이로 추정된다.
Ⓑ 대부분의 T. 렉스는 두 개의 손가락을 가진 것으로 여겨졌고 세 손가락의 돌연변이 사례가 적은 비율로 있다.
Ⓓ T. 렉스가 다른 수각아목 공룡과 공유한 유일한 특징은 천공이라고 불리는 두개골에 난 큰 구멍이었다.

어휘 recognizable adj 쉽게 알아볼 수 있는 | abbreviate v 줄여 쓰다, 축약하다 | incredibly adv 엄청나게 | theropod n 수각아목의 공룡 | carnivorous adj 육식성의 | superior adj 우수한, 뛰어난 | befitting adj 어울리는, 걸맞은 | predatory adj 포식성의 | Cretaceous adj 백악기의 | roam v 돌아다니다 | cataclysmic adj 격변하는 | subsequent adj 그 다음의 | imposing adj 인상적인 | paleontologist n 고생물학자 | probable adj 개연성 있는, 사실일 것 같은 | tissue n 조직 | bipedal adj 이족 보행의 | carnivore n 육식 동물 | muscular adj 근육질의 | forearm n 팔뚝 | hind leg 뒷다리 | digit n 숫자, 손가락, 발가락 | sturdy adj 튼튼한 | vertebrae n 척추골 | massive adj 거대한, 엄청나게 큰 | skeleton n 뼈대, 골격 | hollow adj 속이 빈 | skull n 두개골 | extraordinarily adv 비상하게, 유별나게 | measure up 측정하다, 재다 | opening n 구멍, 틈 | fenestra n 천공 | snout n 코, 주둥이 | binocular adj 두 눈으로 보는 | pneumatized adj 공기로 채워진 | honeycomb n 벌집 | legendary adj 전설적인 | jaw n 턱 | heterodonty n 이치성 | cross section 횡단면, 단면도 | ridge n 산등성이 | chisel n 끌 | blade n 칼날 | snap off 부러지다, 부러뜨리다 | prey n 먹이 | dagger n 단검 | fossilized adj 화석화 된 | specimen n 견본, 샘플 | mutation n 돌연변이, 변화 | disproportionately adv 불균형적으로 | flimsy adj 조잡한 | nasal bone 코뼈

본서 | P. 305

라이브 공연

1 ➡ 무대와 스크린에서 전부 성공한 배우들에게 어느 매체에서 작업하는 것을 선호하는지 물어보면 그들은 압도적으로 전자를 선택한다. 영화 계약이 보통 더 높은 수입을 수반한다는 사실에도 불구하고 그들은 연극에서 연기하는 것을 더 보람 있다고 느낀다. 그 이유는 연극은 연기자와 관객이 같은 시공간을 차지하며 서로 소통할 수 있는 라이브 무대이기 때문이다. 연극은 영화가 제공하지 못하는 3가지를 제공하기 때문에 라이브 공연과 녹화된 공연의 차이는 매우 중요하다. 연기자들은 관객과 역동적인 관계를 맺으며, 관객들은 모두 하나가 되며, 각 공연은 유일무이하다.

2 ➡ 라이브 공연은 배우들이 연극을 공연할 때 관객과 일종의 관계를 형성하기 때문에 배우들에게 매력적이다. 동시에 같은 공간을 차지하면서, 같은 공기를 마시며 연극이 펼치는 이야기의 세계에 몰입하게 된다. 영화 세트에서 연기를 지켜볼 수 있는 유일한 사람들은 그것을 촬영하기 위해 거리를 두어야 하는 제작진과 테이크 사이에 지시와 비판을 하는 감독밖에 없다. 라이브 공연에서 관객은 배우들만큼 관여하며 그들이 보고 있는 장면에 대한 반응은 배우들에게 영향을 미친다. 물론 박수, 환호와 침묵을 통한 의도적인 소통은 배우들에게 영향을 미친다. 하지만 고의적으로 웃긴 장면에서 참지 못하는 웃음이나 충격적인 반전에 집단적으로 놀라서 숨이 막히거나 긴장감이 도는 장면에서 술렁거리는 무의식적인 반응은 배우에게 영향을 미쳐 비할 데 없는 공연을 펼치도록 자극한다.

3 ➡ 연극을 볼 때 관객들 또한 배우들이 주는 신호에 반응하는 일종의 집합의식에 빠져든다. 그들은 각자의 성격과 선입관을 가진 개인으로서 극장에 입장하지만 그 경험을 공유하면서 빠르게 단일체로 변한다. 등장인물들과 공감하고 동일한 농담에 웃고 동일한 깨달음에 놀란다. 이것은 그들이 함께 온 몇몇 친구들을 제외하곤 전혀 모르는 사람들로 가득 찬 공간에 있다는 사실에도 불구하고 일어난다. [■A] 이런 종류의 반응은 영화관에서는 찾을 수 없는데, 거기에서는 시청자가 오직 화면의 등장인물에 집중하는 개인으로 남는다. [■B] 그 환경은 암흑과 크게 울리는 음향 장치로 그들을 대체로 고립시키고 그들이 집단적으로 반응하는 경우는 드물다. [■C] 텔레비전 프로그램도 광고로 인한 잦은 중단 때문에 시청자를 완전히 몰입하게 만드는 데 실패한다. [■D] 반대로 극장은 사교에 매우 도움이 되는 환경을 조성한다. 관객은 중간 휴식 시간에 어울리고 지난 막에 대해서 얘기를 할 수 있고 연극 중에도 다른 사람들이 연극으로부터

11. 다음 중 1단락에서 답변이 된 질문은 어느 것인가?

Ⓐ 무대와 스크린에서의 배우의 성공을 평가할 때 어느 기준이 사용되는가?
Ⓑ 녹화된 공연만의 고유 특징은 무엇인가?
Ⓒ 배우들이 다른 매체보다 영화 계약에서 보수를 더 많이 받는 것에 기여하는 것은 무엇인가?
Ⓓ 배우가 연극에서 연기하는 것을 보람 있다고 느끼는 이유들은 무엇인가?

12. 2단락에 따르면, 다음 중 라이브 공연에 관해 사실인 것은 무엇인가?

Ⓐ 라이브 공연은 배우와 관객 상호간의 소통이다.
Ⓑ 관객의 무의식적인 반응은 의도적인 소통보다 훨씬 강력하다.
Ⓒ 성공적인 라이브 공연을 위해 배우들은 관객의 반응에 반응해야 한다.
Ⓓ 배우들은 감독의 간섭 없이 연기할 수 있기 때문에 라이브 공연을 선호한다.

13. 다음 중 2단락에서 영화 제작에 대해 추론 가능한 것은 무엇인가?

Ⓐ 연극과 달리 고립된 공간에서 연기하는 것은 영화 세트에서 효과적인 기법이다.
Ⓑ 영화 촬영 중 배우들에게 피드백을 제공할 수 있는 유일한 사람은 영화 감독이다.
Ⓒ 영화에서 연기하는 배우들은 영화 전개와 그들의 배역과 동질감을 갖는 것에서부터 거리를 둔다.
Ⓓ 영화에서 연기하는 배우들은 지난 작품을 능가하도록 동기 부여되기 더 힘들다.

14. 3단락에 따르면, 연극은 다른 매체와 어떻게 다른가?

Ⓐ 공연은 매우 어두운 환경에서 진행된다.
Ⓑ 관객 대부분은 서로를 거의 잘 모른다.
Ⓒ 공연은 휴식 시간으로 중단된다.
Ⓓ 관객은 공연 끝에 기립 박수를 보낼 수 있다.

받는 감명을 공유한다는 것을 깨닫게 될 때 더욱 강렬해지는 웃음소리와 박수가 전염되면서 서로 소통할 수 있다. 관객이 특별히 감동받은 경우 그들은 자리에서 일어나 열광적으로 박수갈채를 보낸다. 이는 기립 박수라고 불리는데 관객은 연기자를 축하하는 것뿐만 아니라 함께 공유한 공연의 탁월함을 알아본 자기 자신과 서로를 축하하는 것이기도 하다. 이런 집단 의식의 극단적인 예를 끌어낸 하나의 연극은 1935년도 작 〈레프티를 기다리며〉이다. 이 연극은 명백하게 정치적인 메시지를 갖고 있었으며 관객이 노조원 집단의 역할을 맡게 되는 식으로 연출되었다. 관객은 연극에 매우 감동해서 일제히 소리치며 가상의 정치 집회에 대한 지지를 보여줬다.

4 ➡ 배우들에게 강력하게 매력을 발산하는 라이브 공연의 마지막 측면은 매 공연이 다른 공연들과 다르다는 것이다. 비록 연기자들이 연극 대본에 최대한 충실히 따라야 하지만 각 공연 간에는 오직 전문가만이 감지할 수 있을 만한 미묘한 차이가 있는데, 어떤 면에선 출연진과 관객을 포함한 관련된 모든 사람이 이 사실을 인지하고 있다. 새로운 버전으로 편집되지 않는 이상 변하지 않는 영화와 달리 연극은 공연될 때마다 현재에 벌어지고 있는 일이고 그것은 무엇이든 일어날 수 있다는 것을 뜻한다. 실수를 범할 수 있고, 사고가 일어날 수 있고, 갈등이 있을 수 있고, 심지어 무대 공포증의 기미가 보일 수 있기 때문에 이런 깨달음은 극장에 활력의 분위기를 준다. 반면에 배우들이 매 공연이 이전의 것을 능가할 수 있도록 노력할 때 뛰어난 재기의 순간들이 있을 수 있다. 이것이 라이브 공연의 궁극적인 설렘을 가져오는데, 즉 그것이 현실과 동일한 불확실성을 지녔다는 것이다. 배우와 관객은 그 이야기가 펼쳐지는 순간을 살아가고 있고 그것이 어디로 향하는지에 대한 개념은 갖고 있을지라도 현실 속에서의 미래보다 더 예측 가능하지 않다. 연극의 근본적인 목적 중 하나는 인간 생활의 불확실성을 묘사하는 것인데 라이브 공연은 표현할 수 있는 가장 직접적인 방식으로 그 불확실성을 묘사한다.

15. 글쓴이가 3단락에서 '〈레프티를 기다리며〉'를 언급하는 이유는 무엇인가?

Ⓐ 연극이 관객을 어떻게 하나로 만드는지에 대한 예를 제공하기 위해

Ⓑ 정치적인 주제를 공연 예술에 포함시키는 위험을 보여주기 위해

Ⓒ 기립 박수가 관객이 공연에 대한 감사 표시를 하는 유일한 방법이 아니라는 것을 보여주기 위해

Ⓓ 1930년대의 사회 분위기에 대한 배경 지식을 제공하기 위해

16. 다음 중 지문에 음영 표시된 문장의 핵심 정보를 가장 잘 표현한 문장은 무엇인가? 오답은 의미를 크게 왜곡하거나 핵심 정보를 누락하고 있다.

Ⓐ 배우들이 매 공연을 한결같게 유지하려고 최선을 다하지만 전문가들과 관객은 각 공연 간의 차이를 알 수 있다.

Ⓑ 각 공연 간의 차이는 보통 전문가들만이 감지할 수 있을 정도로 작지만 각 공연이 유일무이하다는 것은 모두가 알고 있다.

Ⓒ 전문 배우들이 각 공연 간의 차이를 최소로 두어서 전문가들에게만 보일 수 있게 하는 것이 당연하지만 관객이 가끔 그것을 감지할 수 있다.

Ⓓ 배우들이 모든 공연을 일관되게 유지하려고 노력하지만 연기자들과 관객은 전문가들이 각 공연 간의 변화를 감지할 수 있다는 것을 깨닫는다.

17. 4단락의 단어 'vitality(활력)'와 의미상 가장 가까운 것은

Ⓐ 숙명

Ⓑ 긴장

Ⓒ 활기

Ⓓ 강렬함

18. 4단락에 따르면, 라이브 공연은 현실과 어떻게 유사한가?

Ⓐ 배우들은 연극의 궁극적 목표가 무엇인지 알고 있다.

Ⓑ 배우들은 연극을 공연하면서 그것을 현재에 만들어내고 있다.

Ⓒ 배우들은 연극 대본에 따라서 무대에서 공연한다.

Ⓓ 배우들은 끊임없이 이전 공연을 능가하려고 시도한다.

19. 지문에 다음 문장이 들어갈 수 있는 위치를 나타내는 네 개의 사각형 [■]을 확인하시오.

반대로 극장은 사교에 매우 도움이 되는 환경을 조성한다.

이 문장이 들어가기에 가장 적합한 곳은? [■D]

20. 지시문: 지문을 간략하게 요약한 글의 첫 문장이 아래 제시되어 있다. 지문의 가장 중요한 내용을 표현하는 세 개의 선택지를 골라 요약문을 완성하시오. 일부 문장들은 지문에 제시되지 않았거나 지문의 지엽적인 내용을 나타내기 때문에 요약문에 포함되지 않는다. ***이 문제의 배점은 2점이다.***

라이브 공연은 다른 매체와 비교할 수 없는 매력을 지니고 있다.

Ⓒ 관객은 공동의 경험을 공유하면서 한 몸이 되어 연극에 몰입되어 있는 자기 자신을 발견한다.
Ⓓ 라이브 공연은 매번 똑같을 수 없고 그것은 삶의 불확실성을 상징한다.
Ⓕ 배우들은 관객의 반응에 영감을 받기 때문에 라이브로 공연하는 것을 즐긴다.

Ⓐ 관객 앞에서 실시간으로 일어난 실수는 되돌릴 수 없기 때문에 연극은 어느 정도의 긴장감을 유지한다.
Ⓑ 〈레프티를 기다리며〉는 관객에게서 강렬한 정치적 반응을 불러일으키는 연극의 힘을 보여주었다.
Ⓔ 텔레비전 연속극 중간의 광고와 달리 연극 중간의 휴식 시간은 그곳에 있는 사람들로 하여금 다른 사람들과 어울릴 수 있게 한다.

어휘 medium n 매체, 수단 I contract n 계약 I paycheck n 급료 I rewarding adj 보람 있는 I distinction n 차이 I entity n 독립체 I appeal v 관심을 끌다 I rapport n 관계 I narrative n 묘사, 기술, 이야기 I crew n 제작진 I distance v 거리를 두다 I criticism n 혹평, 비판 I intentional adj 의도적인 I applause n 박수 I unconscious adj 무의식적인 I stifle v 억누르다, 억제하다 I collective adj 집단의 I twist n 반전 I suspenseful adj 긴장감이 있는 I trigger v 촉발시키다 I unparalleled adj 비할 데 없는 I consciousness n 의식 I preconceived notion 선입관 I empathize v 공감하다 I awed adj 외경심에 휩싸인 I revelation n 뜻밖의 새 사실, 발견 I solely adv 오로지, 단독으로 I isolated adj 외떨어진, 고립된 I engage v 사로잡다, 끌다 I interruption n 중단 I commercial break (TV 프로그램 중간에 나오는) 광고 방송 I conducive to ~에 도움이 되는 I socializing n 사교 I mingle v 어울리다 I intermission n (연극 등의) 중간 휴식 시간 I act n (연극 등의) 막 I contagious adj 전염되는 I enthusiastically adv 열광적으로 I standing ovation 기립 박수 I elicit v 끌어내다 I group mentality 집단 의식 I explicitly adv 명쾌하게, 분명하게 I union n 노조 I rally n 집회 I adhere v 충실하다 I script n 대본 I perceive v 감지하다 I cast n 출연진 I vitality n 활력 I conflict n 갈등, 충돌 I stage fright 무대 공포증 I sheer adj 순수한 I brilliance n 뛰어난 재기 I surpass v 능가하다, 뛰어넘다 I thrill n 설렘, 흥분 I uncertainty n 불확실성 I notion n 개념, 생각 I essential adj 필수적인, 기본적인 I depict v 묘사하다 I portray v 묘사하다 I immediate adj 즉각적인, 직접적인

PAGODA TOEFL 80+ Reading

PAGODA

TOEFL

80+ Reading | 해설서